MySQL:
The Complete Reference

Vikram Vaswani

McGraw-Hill/Osborne

New York   Chicago   San Francisco
Lisbon   London   Madrid   Mexico City
Milan   New Delhi   San Juan
Seoul   Singapore   Sydney   Toronto

The **McGraw·Hill** Companies

McGraw-Hill/Osborne
2100 Powell Street, 10th Floor
Emeryville, California 94608
U.S.A.

To arrange bulk purchase discounts for sales promotions, premiums, or fund-raisers, please contact **McGraw-Hill**/Osborne at the above address. For information on translations or book distributors outside the U.S.A., please see the International Contact Information page immediately following the index of this book.

MySQL: The Complete Reference

1234567890 CUS CUS 019876543

ISBN 0-07-222477-0

Publisher
Brandon A. Nordin

Vice President & Associate Publisher
Scott Rogers

Senior Sponsoring Editor
Chris Johnson

Project Editors
Jenn Tust, Elizabeth Seymour,
Monika Faltiss

Acquisitions Coordinator
Athena Honore

Technical Editor
Alexander Pachev

Copy Editor
Marcia Baker

Proofreader
Paul Medoff

Indexer
Valerie Perry

Computer Designers
Tabitha M. Cagan, John Patrus

Illustrators
Kathleen Edwards, Melinda Lytle,
Michael Mueller

Series Design
Peter F. Hancik, Lyssa Wald

This book was composed with Corel VENTURA™ Publisher.

You see things; and you say "Why?"
But I dream things that never were; and I say "Why not?"

George Bernard Shaw

To the baby, for saying "Why not?"

To the Other One, for the laughs.

About the Author

Vikram Vaswani is the founder and CEO of Melonfire (`http://www.melonfire.com/`), a company specializing in software consultancy, content creation, and content syndication services. He is a passionate proponent of the open-source movement and frequently contributes articles and tutorials on open-source technologies (including Perl, Python, PHP, MySQL, and Linux) to the community at large through his weekly column at `http://www.melonfire.com/community/columns/trog/`. His last book was *XML and PHP* (`http://www.xmlphp.com/`).

Vikram has over eight years of experience in the IT world and has spent six of those years interacting with the MySQL RDBMS as user, administrator, and application developer. He has deployed MySQL in a variety of environments, including corporate intranets, high-traffic Internet web sites and mission-critical thin client applications—experience which came in handy while authoring this book! He continues to be a vocal advocate of MySQL in his role as software consultant.

When not plotting to rule the world from a heavily guarded conference room at Melonfire HQ, Vikram amuses himself by reading, sleeping, watching old movies, playing squash, fiddling with his ever-growing collection of electronic gadgets, and keeping an eye out for unfriendly agents. Read more about him, download sample code, and connect with other MySQL enthusiasts online at `http://www.mysql-tcr.com/`.

About the Technical Editors

Alexander "Sasha" Pachev worked for MySQL., Inc, between 2000 and 2003 with the development, support, and sales teams. He implemented the replication feature in the server, handled numerous support cases, and did a fair amount of consulting. Sasha is currently working as the IT director at SurveyPro.Com.

Brian Kaney, co-founder of Vermonster LLC, graduated from the University of Massachusetts with a bachelor's degree in engineering. While in college, he worked as a consultant for various companies in New England. He later co-founded Askfor.com, piloting a new middleware technology. In 2000 he co-founded Vermonster, a consulting company located in Boston, that focuses on open software and open standards for the enterprise.

Jay Powers is a graduate of the University of Vermont and has been working with open-source technology for over seven years. He is experienced in designing and building web applications and web services. Before starting Vermonster, he worked as a technology director at Askfor.com, an Internet startup company. Prior to that, he worked as a director at AdSmart, a CMGI company. When Jay is not writing code, he enjoys riding around Boston on his fixed-gear Pinarello bicycle.

Arjen Lentz works for MySQL AB as lead technical writer for the MySQL documentation team. He also teaches MySQL training courses, gives talks and tutorials on MySQL at conferences and user group meetings, and maintains contacts with the MySQL and open-source community in Australia.

Contents

Foreword

The author, Vikram Vaswani, is an expert on MySQL® and many other open-source technologies. While writing this reference book, Vikram worked actively with the MySQL development team to ensure that the book is technically correct and that nothing important regarding the covered topics was forgotten.

MySQL: The Complete Reference takes a thorough approach: It covers the key features of MySQL and advanced topics such as replication and various programming APIs. It also provides a solid foundation for understanding the relational model and has thorough coverage of ACID transactions and other concepts that are essential for anyone who is relatively new to relational databases.

The book also covers the essential topics for users and administrators who are familiar with Oracle® or other database systems. People experienced with MySQL may find a new angle on familiar topics that will give them additional insight to the world of MySQL and thus enhance their existing knowledge and experience.

I hope this book will be a valuable resource to you while using MySQL!

Michael "Monty" Widenius
CTO of MySQL AB
Helsingfors, Finland
November 2003

Acknowledgments

This book was written over the course of a (long!) year, under tight deadlines and in unusual environments. Fortunately, I was aided immeasurably in the process by a diverse group of people, all of whom played an important role in getting this book into your hands.

First and foremost, I'd like to thank my family, for providing me with a quiet place to work, and for putting up with my odd work hours (and even odder behavior) while this book was being written. Your forbearance was noted, and much appreciated!

A mega-thank you to Harish Kamath, for bringing his considerable experience and knowledge of SQL to the technical editing process, for his patience with my meandering phone calls and e-mail messages, and for his contributions to Chapter 11. His ideas and opinions were significant in shaping the structure of this book, and in ensuring that it was as "complete" as possible. Thanks also to Claude Seidman and Efren Estevez for their contributions to Chapter 2 and Chapters 15, 16, and 17 respectively.

I must mention here the great team at McGraw-Hill/Osborne—Senior Sponsoring Editor Christopher Johnson, acquisitions coordinator Athena Honore, project editors Jenn Tust, Elizabeth Seymour, and Monika Faltiss—who guided this book through the development process. Thanks go to technical editors Sasha Pachev, Jay Powers, Brian Kaney, and Arjen Lentz for their contributions to the technical edit. Special acknowledgment also to MySQL AB and its team of dedicated volunteers and developers, for building and continuing to enhance a truly cool piece of software.

Finally, for making the entire book-writing process more enjoyable than it usually is, thanks to: Lawrence Block, Bryan Adams, the Stones, MAD Magazine, Scott Adams, Gary Larson, MTV, Kylie Minogue, *Buffy*, Farah Malegam, the MySQL mailing lists, Stephen King, John le Carre, Subway, Barry White, the Kamaths, Apple, Robert Crais, Robert B. Parker, Baz Luhrmann, Anna Kournikova, Swatch, Ling's Pavilion, Tonka, HBO, Ferrari, Mark Twain, Tim Burton, the entire cast of *Friends*, John Sandford, the Tube, Dido, Google.com, *The Matrix*, Alfred Hitchcock, Bruno D'Costa, Woody Allen, Palm, Michael Schumacher, Mambo's and Tito's, Kalindi Mehta, Humphrey Bogart, the Library Bar, Amazon.com, U2, The Three Stooges, Oscar Wilde, Punch, Harry Potter, Scott Turow, Slackware Linux, Calvin and Hobbes, Blizzard Entertainment, Popeye and Olive, Dennis Lehane, Trattoria, Xerxes Antia, Dire Straits, Bruce Springsteen, Santana, David Mitchell, and all my friends, at home and elsewhere.

Introduction

From its beginnings in 1996 as a simple SQL implementation to its current status as "the world's most popular open-source database," MySQL has come a long way. According to information published by MySQL AB (the developers of MySQL), there were over four million MySQL installations worldwide in 2003. MySQL powers Internet web sites, search engines, data warehouses, and mission-critical software applications and systems; and it's actively used by companies like Sony, Xerox, HP, and NASA. In short, it's everywhere, and it's only going to get bigger!

The reasons for this meteoric rise are not hard to find. A fast, robust, and user-friendly database engine; an advanced suite of tools for data management and recovery; a continually improving feature set; compliance with existing SQL standards; and a business-friendly licensing philosophy are all factors that have contributed to make MySQL a viable alternative to more commercial, closed-source systems like Oracle and Microsoft SQL Server. More and more businesses are migrating their systems to MySQL and reaping the benefits of MySQL's open-source roots in terms of lower total cost of ownership and a more stable, secure system.

That's where this book comes in. If you're a business professional charged with the task of migrating your RDBMS infrastructure to MySQL; a developer interested in building MySQL-backed applications; or simply a hobbyist curious about MySQL and what it can do for you, the book you're holding is the only map you'll need to navigate the MySQL world.

Overview

MySQL: The Complete Reference has been designed as a comprehensive reference for MySQL users, developers, and database administrators. It contains extensive information on the MySQL RDBMS (including MySQL 4.*x*), and provides one-stop coverage of all topics related to MySQL deployment, right from software installation and configuration to data backup and replication.

MySQL's particular dialect of Structured Query Language (SQL) is examined in detail. The commands to create and manage databases and tables; insert, update and delete records; create reports matching particular criteria; use joins and subqueries; enforce data integrity through keys; and optimize queries for greater speed and efficiency are dealt with in significant depth.

MySQL developers aren't forgotten, either—the book includes a special section specifically geared towards MySQL-based application development and offers real-world guidelines and tips for developers interested in working on the MySQL architecture.

Audience

MySQL: The Complete Reference is targeted at a number of reader segments, with one thing in common: a desire to learn how to best deploy and use MySQL in their organization. Regardless of whether you're a student looking for a free RDBMS on which to practice your SQL, a developer interested in creating MySQL-backed applications, or a database administrator concerned with lowering cost by migrating your data to MySQL, this book contains the theory and practical examples needed to get you up and running with this powerful open-source application.

Unlike many other books, this one doesn't assume prior knowledge of SQL or database fundamentals. Rather, it teaches by example, using tutorials and real-world examples to explain basic concepts and thus increase your familiarity with the MySQL RDBMS. In the chapters that follow, you're encouraged to try out the various examples on your own MySQL installation; you won't break anything, and you're sure to gain a great deal from the hands-on experience.

This book is structured as both a tutorial and a reference guide, so you can read it in any sequence you like. Here are some ideas:

- If you're new to MySQL, you might find it easier to read the chapters sequentially, so that you learn the basics in a structured manner. This is the recommended approach and one new users should adopt.

- If you've already used MySQL, you might prefer to see this book as a desktop reference, flipping it open on an as-needed basis to read about specific topics. (The extensive index at the back of this book is designed specifically for this sort of quick look-up.)

- If you're a specialist (say, a database administrator or a Web developer), this book contains separate sections on MySQL administration and development designed specifically to address your most frequently asked questions and provide you with information on all the issues and topics relevant to your job description.

Organization

MySQL: The Complete Reference is broadly divided into four parts. Here's what each part contains:

Part I, "Installation," provides an introduction to MySQL and guides you through the process of installing it on both UNIX and Windows.

Chapter 1, "Introduction to Databases," discusses MySQL's history and evolution, looks at its feature set, and explains why it offers such a compelling value proposition.

Chapter 2, "A Technical Tour of MySQL," peeks under the hood to see what makes MySQL tick, explaining the various MySQL subsystems and how they interact with each other.

Chapter 3, "MySQL Installation and Configuration," discusses how to obtain, install, configure, and test the MySQL server on UNIX and Microsoft Windows. It also explains the differences between the different MySQL server versions available, with a view to helping you select the right one for your needs.

Part II, "Usage," discusses practical usage of the MySQL server, explaining how to use the SQL command set to create databases and tables, add and remove records, execute queries, and use advanced MySQL 4.x features like transactions and subqueries.

Chapter 4, "SQL Basics," discusses the history and evolution of SQL and includes a simple tutorial to familiarize new users with the basic SQL commands used to create and enter information into a database.

Chapter 5, "MySQL Data Types," examines the various data types supported by MySQL and explains how they can be used to enforce table consistency and integrity.

Chapter 6, "MySQL Operators," introduces MySQL's arithmetic, logical, comparison and bit operators and demonstrates how they may be used to perform calculations, comparisons, and conversions.

Chapter 7, "MySQL Functions," discusses MySQL's immense array of built-in functions, showing you how they allow MySQL developers to perform operations ranging from date manipulation to password encryption, with minimal time and fuss.

Chapter 8, "Working with Databases and Tables," takes an in-depth look at the database and table structures used by MySQL to store its data, and explains the SQL commands used to create, alter, and delete databases, tables, and indexes. The core of this chapter is a discussion of MySQL's powerful CREATE TABLE command, which offers a fine degree of control over the table creation process, and an examination of foreign keys and full-text indexes, both of which are relatively new to MySQL.

Chapter 9, "Working with Data," continues where the previous chapter left off, explaining how to insert records into an existing MySQL database. The first part of this chapter discusses the INSERT, UPDATE, and DELETE SQL commands, illustrating how they can be used to manipulate database records and throwing light on some MySQL-specific twists to the standard command syntax. The second half examines the SELECT statement in depth, showing how it can be used to create filtered subsets of the records in a database; sort, group and count records; use session variables; and import and export data in a variety of different formats.

Chapter 10, "Joins," discusses multi-table queries, showing how the relationships between tables can be used to combine records in different ways to produce more useful reports. This chapter discusses the various types of joins and demonstrates their usage in a number of different situations.

Chapter 11, "Subqueries," teaches you how to nest queries within one another for more sophisticated query operations, a feature newly introduced in MySQL 4.1.

Chapter 12, "Transactions," examines another new (and extremely powerful) MySQL 4.*x* feature: the ability to group a series of SQL statements into a single unit and execute them atomically, or undo the entire set of changes in the event of an error.

Part III, "Administration," discusses the tasks involved in administering and maintaining a MySQL RDBMS, covering such topics as database backup and repair, security, access control, activity logging, server optimization, and troubleshooting.

Chapter 13, "Administration and Configuration," examines the role of a MySQL database administrator, explaining common tasks like starting and stopping the server, altering the default server configuration, and inspecting the MySQL log files.

Chapter 14, "Security, Access Control, and Privileges," discusses the MySQL security and privilege system, and it explores the management of user accounts and passwords (including what do to if you forget the MySQL superuser password).

Chapter 15, "Maintenance, Backup, and Recovery," provides instructions and information on how to back up and restore a MySQL database, as well as how to use MySQL-supplied utilities to recover data from a damaged database.

Chapter 16, "Performance Optimization," offers tips and tricks to squeeze the maximum performance out of your MySQL server, including information on how to optimize queries for faster execution; alter cache and buffer settings for quicker responses; and use special run-time parameters for more efficient resource usage.

Chapter 17, "MySQL Replication," discusses another of MySQL's more interesting and powerful features: the ability to automatically synchronize databases across different hosts.

Part IV, "Development," is aimed squarely at developers—it discusses the MySQL APIs, a set of full-featured, powerful tools for building custom data-driven MySQL applications. This section includes examples and source code for the C, Perl, and PHP APIs.

Chapter 18, "The MySQL APIs," explains the need and rationale behind exposing MySQL's innards via a series of APIs, and it provides a brief description of the capabilities included in the various APIs. In an attempt to help developers select the API that is best suited to their specific needs, the chapter also includes a discussion of the benefits of the different APIs vis-a-vis each other.

Chapter 19, "MySQL and C," explains how to write MySQL client applications using the C library API that ships with the MySQL distribution. Real-world examples include an interactive command-line SQL client and an interactive expense tracker that supports data entry and simple report generation.

Chapter 20, "MySQL and Perl," discusses the Perl DBI, with specific reference to the MySQL driver and the DBI methods that make it possible to interact with a MySQL database through a Perl script. The real-world application here is a CGI-based threaded comments system, accessible via a standard web browser and suitable for use on any content-rich web site.

Chapter 21, "MySQL and PHP," rounds out the section with a look at PHP, a popular scripting language for database-backed web applications that comes with built-in support for MySQL. In addition to a detailed discussion of the relevant PHP functions, the chapter demonstrates the real-world viability of the MySQL-PHP combination through a database-driven bookmark application suitable for use in any web browser.

Conventions Used in This Book

This book uses several icons to highlight special advice:

TIP   *A handy way to make MySQL work better for you.*

NOTE   *An observation that gives insight into the way that MySQL and other programs work.*

CAUTION   *Something to watch out for, so you don't have to learn the hard way.*

When we refer you to related material, we usually tell you the name of the section that contains the information we think you'll want to read. If the section is in the same chapter you are reading, we don't mention a chapter number.

In the code listings in this book, sentences highlighted in bold are commands that are to be entered at the prompt. For example, in the following listing,

```
mysql> SELECT * FROM articles;
+-----+-----------------------------------+--------+
| aid | aname                             | fk_cid |
+-----+-----------------------------------+--------+
|   1 | Sample article on winter fashions |      2 |
+-----+-----------------------------------+--------+
1 row in set (0.00 sec)
```

the line in bold is the query the user would type in at the MySQL command prompt. You can use this as a guide to try out the various examples in this book.

Sidebars

This is a sidebar. Sidebars are set somewhat apart from the normal text and include information related to the current subject, but that doesn't necessarily fit into the flow of information.

Companion Web Site

The best way to learn MySQL is through hands-on interaction with the application. To this end, you can find the SQL code used to create many of the example databases in this book on the companion web site, at http://www.mysql-tcr.com/, together with the source code for the various applications and scripts demonstrated in Part IV. While you're there, drop by the MySQL discussion forums, connect with other MySQL users, and share your thoughts on MySQL usage and administration with the rest of the community.

PART I

Installation

Introduction to Databases

Whether you love 'em or hate 'em, in today's wired world, it's no longer possible to live without databases. No more the sole province of bespectacled geeks in tiny back-office cubbyholes, databases have hit the mainstream in recent years, finding applications in disciplines ranging from biotechnology to electronic commerce. You'll find them in your bank, your local library, your web browser—heck, even your neighborhood grocery store uses one. They're everywhere, and they keep getting smarter.

As the open-source movement has gathered momentum during the past few years, more and more attention has become focused on a little-known database system called MySQL. This database system is available free of charge over the Internet, provides a wealth of features at minimal performance loss, and has been battle-tested for reliability and speed in a variety of applications and situations. Today, with more than 4 million users, it is rapidly becoming a standard for database administrators and users worldwide.

Throughout the course of this introductory chapter, I'm going to take a closer look at MySQL, explaining what it is, how it came to be, and why its feature set makes it such a compelling alternative to its better-known, better-funded commercial counterparts.

The Big Picture...

Before we get into the nitty-gritty of what MySQL is and isn't, let's take a little time out to answer a basic question: What's a database, anyhow?

A database, fundamentally, is a collection of data organized and classified according to some criteria. The traditional analogy is that of a filing cabinet organized into drawers (see the following illustration), with each drawer holding files related to a particular subject; these files may be further classified according to a particular set of criteria (alphabetically, by color, by numeric code, and so on). This organization of information into drawers and files makes it easy to retrieve specific bits of information quickly—

to lay your hands on a particular piece of information, you pull open the appropriate drawer and select the file(s) matching your criteria.

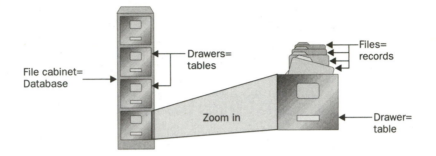

An electronic database helps you organize information and provides the tools necessary to access specific bits of it quickly and efficiently. The drawers that contain the files are referred to in database parlance as *tables*, the files themselves are called *records*, the act of pulling out information is referred to as a *query*, and the resulting data is referred to as a *result set*. The following illustration shows how you query the database (here, a filing cabinet) to retrieve information. You'll be seeing a lot of these terms in this book, and you'll get used to them gradually, so don't worry if they seem a little foreign at the moment.

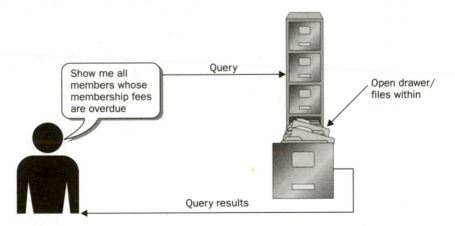

Although you can use a database to organize both small and large amounts of information, its true power becomes apparent when you need to manage a substantial volume of data. If, for example, you have a small amount of data to deal with, you can easily manipulate and search it manually; however, as the volume of information increases, performing a manual search becomes both tedious and costly. Consider a filing cabinet containing 20 files versus one containing 20 million files—locating a single file in the first cabinet takes a matter of minutes, whereas locating a single file in the second cabinet is well nigh impossible (given efficiency constraints).

In such situations, an electronic *database management system* (DBMS) can substantially simplify your work. Not only does such a system take up less physical space than its traditional paper-based counterpart, but it also comes with tools that assist you in organizing your data and simplifying information retrieval and modification. Built-in indexing makes it possible to locate information rapidly and efficiently, while automated processes ensure that data is always stored and cross-referenced in a consistent, error-free manner. A database also offers portability and compatibility (once the data is organized and stored in a database, it can be extracted and displayed in any manner you choose), and it provides a centralized storage location for important information.

A *relational database management system* (RDBMS) takes things one step further by creating relationships among the tables that make up a database. These relationships can then be used to combine data from multiple tables in various ways, allowing a user to view the same data from various perspectives and then use this enhanced vision to make better (read: more efficient and cost-effective) business decisions. By creating links among related pieces of information, an RDBMS thus not only makes it possible to store information more efficiently (by removing redundancies and repetition), but it also brings to the fore hitherto undiscovered relationships among disparate segments of data and permits efficient exploitation of those relationships.

As you might imagine, this kind of information management has important implications—both in business and elsewhere, which is just one of the many reasons why RDBMSs are so popular in today's wired world. Large software companies such as Microsoft and Oracle spend millions annually on researching and developing commercial database systems, well aware that the old adage "knowledge is power" is as true here as it was when Sir Francis Bacon first uttered it.

These commercial RDBMSs are powerful, flexible, feature-rich software systems that are designed specifically for high-volume, transaction-heavy, mission-critical applications; they can (and do) zip through millions of records and perform hundreds of transactions every second without batting an eyelid.

The only problem? They're way beyond the budget of most small- and medium-sized businesses, which typically run smaller, less complex applications that do not require quite so much firepower.

What these users usually need is a fast, reliable alternative that meets their needs in a cost-effective and efficient manner.

That's where MySQL comes in.

Doing Your Homework

Interested in learning more about relational database management systems? Consider adding the following book to your shopping list: *Introduction to Relational Databases and SQL Programming*, by Catherine Creary and Christopher Allen (McGraw-Hill, ISBN 0-07-222924-1, 2003).

...And the Little Database that Could

MySQL is a high-performance, multi-threaded, multi-user RDBMS built around a client-server architecture. Designed specifically for speed and stability, it has, over the last few years, become one of the most popular RDBMS for database-driven software applications, both on and off the web. Today, more than 4 million web sites create, use, and deploy MySQL-based applications; that number rises daily (as stated on the official MySQL web site, at `http://www.mysql.com/`).

The MySQL RDBMS consists of the following two components:

- **Server-side tools**   These include the MySQL database server, which is the core software engine responsible for creating and managing databases, executing queries and returning query results, and maintaining security, together with additional tools to manage multiple MySQL servers, optimize and repair MySQL tables, and create bug reports.

- **Client-side tools**   These include a command-line MySQL client, tools to manage MySQL user permissions, and utilities to import and export MySQL databases. Also included are command-line tools to view and copy MySQL databases and tables, maintain tables, and retrieve server status information.

These components are discussed in detail in subsequent chapters of this book.

History and Evolution

MySQL came into being in 1979, when Michael "Monty" Widenius created a database system named UNIREG for the Swedish company TcX. UNIREG didn't, however, have a Structured Query Language (SQL) interface—something that caused it to fall out of favor with TcX in the mid-1990s. So TcX began looking for alternatives. One of those alternatives was mSQL, a competing DBMS created by David Hughes.

mSQL didn't work for TcX, however, so Widenius decided to create a new database server customized to his specific requirements. That system, completed and released to a small group in May 1996, became the first version of what is today known as MySQL.

A few months later, MySQL 3.11 saw its first public release as a binary distribution for Solaris. Linux source and binaries followed shortly; an enthusiastic developer community and a friendly, General Public License (GPL)-based licensing policy took care of the rest. (For the story from the horse's mouth, look at `http://www.linuxjournal.com/article.php?sid=3609`.) Today, MySQL is available for a wide variety of platforms, including Linux, MacOS, and Windows, in both source and binary form.

A few years later, TcX spun off MySQL AB, a private company that today is the sole owner of the MySQL server source code and trademark and is responsible for maintenance, marketing, and further development of the MySQL database server.

Widenius remains at the helm of the ship, and together with David Axmark and Allan Larsson, they are ably supported in their efforts to improve and enhance MySQL by both a full-time staff and the active support of a worldwide developer community.

> **What's in a Name?**
>
> Wondering where the name MySQL came from? An entry in the MySQL manual (http://www.mysql.com/doc/en/History.html) suggests that even MySQL's developers don't know the origin: "The derivation of the name MySQL is not perfectly clear. Our base directory and a large number of our libraries and tools have had the prefix 'my' for well over 10 years. However, Monty's daughter (some years younger) is also named My. Which of the two gave its name to MySQL is still a mystery, even for us."

Features

MySQL has always been designed around three fundamental principles: performance, reliability, and ease of use. Strict adherence to these principles has resulted in an RDBMS that is inexpensive yet feature-rich, standards-compliant yet easily extensible, and fast yet efficient—making MySQL the perfect tool for developers and administrators looking to build, maintain, and deploy complex software applications.

Following are discussions of MySQL's most compelling features.

Speed

In an RDBMS, *speed*—the time it takes to execute a query and return the results to the caller—is everything. Even MySQL's most ardent critics will admit that MySQL is zippy, sometimes orders of magnitude faster than its competition. Benchmarks available on the MySQL web site show that MySQL outperforms almost every other database currently available, including commercial counterparts like Microsoft SQL Server 2000 and IBM DB2. See "The Need For Speed" sidebar in this chapter for more on how MySQL achieves this high level of performance.

NOTE   *You can read the full results of the benchmark tests at http://www.eweek.com/article2/ 0,3959,293,00.asp.*

> **The Need for Speed**
>
> Part of the reason for MySQL's blazing performance is its fully multi-threaded architecture, which allows multiple concurrent accesses to the database. This multi-threaded architecture is the core of the MySQL engine, allowing multiple clients to read the same database simultaneously and providing a substantial performance gain. The MySQL code tree is also structured in a modular, multi-layered manner, with minimum redundancies and special optimizers for such complex tasks as joins and indexing.
>
> MySQL's designers also initially left out many of the features that cause performance degradation on competing systems, including transactions, referential

integrity, and stored procedures. (These features typically add complexity to the server and result in a performance hit.) User requests for these features, however, have resulted in a creative compromise: versions of MySQL later than 3.23.34a do include support for transactions but allow users to make the choice of whether to enable them (and lose some measure of performance) or exclude them (and continue to operate at peak efficiency). This choice may even be made on a table-by-table basis, making it possible to perform fine-grained optimization for maximum performance.

Finally, MySQL 4.0 also includes a unique new feature, a *query cache*, which can substantially improve performance by caching the results of common queries and returning this cached data to the caller without having to reexecute the query each time. (This is different from competing systems, such as Oracle, in that those systems merely cache the execution plan, not the results. However, they still need to execute the query, including all joins, and re-retrieve the query results on every run.) MySQL benchmarks claim that this feature improves performance by more than 200 percent, with no special programming required on the part of the user.

Reliability

Most of the time, high database performance comes at a price: low reliability. Not true with MySQL, however. The system is designed to offer maximum reliability and uptime, and it has been tested and certified for use in high-volume, mission-critical applications. MySQL's large user base assists in rapidly locating and resolving bugs and in testing the software in a variety of environments; this proactive approach has resulted in software that is virtually bug-free. Further, every new release of MySQL has to pass both MySQL's in-house test suite, which tests each feature and also contains test cases for previously-fixed bugs, and MySQL's *crash-me* tool, whose primary goal is to evaluate the system's capabilities by pushing it up to (and beyond) its limits.

Ease of Use

MySQL is so easy to use that even a novice can pick up the basics in a few hours, and the software is well-supported by a detailed manual, a large number of free online tutorials, a knowledgeable developer community, and a fair number of books (hey, you're reading one right now!). While most interaction with the MySQL server takes place through a command-line interface, a number of graphical tools, both browser-based and otherwise, are also available to simplify the task of managing and administering the MySQL database server. Finally, unlike its proprietary counterparts, which have literally hundreds of adjustable parameters, MySQL is fairly easy to tune and optimize for even the most demanding applications. For commercial environments, MySQL is further supported by MySQL AB, which offers professional training courses, consultancy services. and technical support.

Multi-User Support

MySQL is a full multi-user system, which means that multiple clients can access and use one (or more) MySQL database(s) simultaneously; this is of particular significance during development of web-based applications, which are required to support simultaneous connections by multiple remote clients. MySQL also includes a powerful and flexible privilege system that allows administrators to protect access to sensitive data using a combination of user- and host-based authentication schemes.

Scalability

MySQL can handle extremely large and complex databases without too much of a performance drop. Tables of several gigabytes containing hundreds of thousands of records are not uncommon, and the MySQL web site itself claims to use databases containing 50 million records. In an *eWEEK* magazine benchmark cited on the MySQL web site, MySQL scaled efficiently at loads from 50 to 1000 simultaneous users, with performance dropping only marginally once the 600-user limit had been crossed. Businesses such as as SAP, Yahoo!, NASA, and Texas Instruments; high-volume web sites such as Google (`http://www.google.com/`) and Slashdot (`http://www.slashdot.com/`); and government organizations such as the US Census Bureau and the Rhode Island State Department are all using MySQL to power their systems—and, as `http://www.mysql.com/press/user_stories/` demonstrates, they're all exceedingly pleased with the results.

> **NOTE** *Read the full results of the benchmark tests at* `http://www.eweek.com/article2/` `0,3959,293,00.asp.`

Portability

MySQL is available for both UNIX and non-UNIX operating systems, including Linux, Solaris, FreeBSD, OS/2, MacOS, and Windows 95, 98, Me, 2000, XP, and NT. It runs on a range of architectures, including Intel x86, Alpha, SPARC, PowerPC, and IA64, and it supports many hardware configurations, from low-end 386s to high-end Pentium machines and IBM zSeries mainframes.

Compliance with Existing Standards

MySQL's development team has attempted to make MySQL as standards-compliant as possible. MySQL 4.0 supports most of the important features of the ANSI SQL-99 standard, with support expected to grow in future versions. Additionally, MySQL extends the ANSI standard with custom extensions, functions, and data types designed to improve portability and provide users with enhanced functionality. (See the sidebar entitled "The Right Choice?" for more information on compatibility between MySQL and other SQL-compliant database systems.)

> **The Right Choice?**
> Wondering if MySQL is right for you, or if it's worth switching from your current RDBMS to MySQL? Make an informed decision: take a look at the feature comparison pages on the MySQL web site at http://www.mysql.com/information/crash-me.php and http://www.mysql.com/information/benchmarks.html, which sets MySQL head-to-head with its competition.

Internationalization

As a program that is used by millions in countries across the globe, it would be unusual indeed if MySQL did not include support for various languages and character sets. MySQL 4.0 supports a number of important character sets (including Latin, Chinese, and European character sets), with full Unicode support available from version 4.1.

Wide Application Support

MySQL exposes application programming interfaces (APIs) to many programming languages, thereby making it possible to write database-driven applications in the language of your choice. Currently, MySQL provides hooks to C, C++, ODBC (Open Database Connectivity), Java, PHP, Perl, Python, and Tcl (Tool Command Language). (Chapters 18 through 21 of this book discuss how to use this API to develop applications in C, Perl. and PHP.)

Enthusiastic Developer Community

As with most open-source projects, MySQL is supported by an active developer community, which is at least partly responsible for the software's current popularity. High-volume, well-informed mailing lists and user groups assist in the rapid resolution of questions and problems, and a global network of committed MySQL users and developers provides knowledgeable advice, bug fixes, and third-party utilities.

Open Source Code

MySQL AB, the developer of MySQL, is a firm believer in the open-source movement, and MySQL software is freely available under the GPL (with some caveats—see the sidebar entitled "What Goes Around, Comes Around" for more information). Users are free to download and modify the source code of the application to meet their needs, and they can use it to power their applications free of cost. This open licensing policy has fuelled MySQL's popularity, creating an active and enthusiastic global community of MySQL developers and users. This community plays an active role in keeping MySQL ahead of its competition, both by crash-testing the software for reliability on millions of installations worldwide and by extending the engine to stay abreast of the latest technologies and newest developments.

> ### What Goes Around, Comes Around
>
> It should be noted that the MySQL server and associated drivers are licensed under the GPL and, therefore, you are free to use and redistribute them in your own software applications, provided that your applications are also licensed under the GPL (or any other compatible open-source license approved by MySQL AB). In this case, the MySQL software is offered to you free of charge.
>
> However, if your MySQL-powered application is not licensed under the GPL or an equivalent licensing scheme, and you do intend to redistribute it (whether internally or externally), you are required to purchase a commercial license for the same from MySQL AB.
>
> MySQL AB earns revenue both from the sale of these licenses and by providing support, training, and consultation services for the MySQL database server.

Applications

To quote its official web site, MySQL is "the world's most popular open source database." No small claim, that, but the numbers certainly seem to bear it out: according to recent statistics published on the MySQL web site, MySQL is used in more than 4 million systems worldwide, with more than 25,000 copies of the MySQL database server downloaded every day.

NOTE   *You can visit the official MySQL web site at http://www.mysql.com/.*

As a reliable, feature-rich database server, MySQL has applications in business, education, science, and engineering—a fact amply demonstrated by MySQL AB's customer list, which includes such names as Motorola, Sony, NASA, HP, Xerox, and Silicon Graphics. MySQL software today powers a variety of applications, including Internet web sites, e-commerce applications, search engines, data warehouses, embedded applications, high-volume content portals, and mission-critical software systems.

It's no surprise that MySQL's primary applications today lie in the arena of the web. As web sites and web-based distributed applications grow ever more complex, it becomes more and more important that data be managed efficiently to improve transactional efficiency, reduce response time, and enhance the overall user experience. Consequently, a pressing need exists for a data management solution that is fast, stable, and secure—one can be deployed and used with minimal fuss and that provides solid underpinnings for future development.

MySQL fits the bill for a number of reasons. Its proven track record generates confidence in its reliability and longevity; its open-source roots ensure rapid bug fixes and a continued cycle of enhancements (not to mention a lower overall cost); its portability and support for various programming languages and technologies make it suitable for a wide variety of applications; and its low cost/high performance value

> **Coming Soon...**
>
> While MySQL is one of the most full-featured open-source database servers currently available, it doesn't provide a few things...yet! Here's a quick list:
>
> - **Stored procedures**   Predefined sequences of SQL statements that are compiled and saved within the database itself for more efficient execution.
>
> - **Triggers**   Database actions that are automatically executed when a certain event (such as a change in the data within a table) occurs.
>
> - **Views**   Virtual tables derived from the content of existing tables, which can be manipulated in exactly the same way as regular tables.
>
> The MySQL development roadmap indicates that these features will all be included in subsequent versions of the software.

proposition makes it attractive to everyone from home users to small- and medium-sized businesses and government organizations.

Summary

This chapter provided a gentle introduction into the world of MySQL, setting the stage with a description of how databases work, and then proceeding to an overview of the MySQL relational database management system. It offered insight into MySQL's history and evolution, identified the core features that have made MySQL popular with developers all over the world, and discussed some of MySQL's most common applications.

Now that you know a little bit about MySQL, it's time to drill down to the next level of detail. The next chapter provides a more technical overview of MySQL, discussing the MySQL architecture and the important features of the MySQL database engine.

A Technical Tour of MySQL

The bulk of this book addresses the capabilities of the MySQL engine and illustrates the uses of MySQL through sample applications that manipulate data stored in various types of databases. Before we get into that, though, it's important that you have a sound technical understanding of how MySQL works, so that you can make informed decisions about how best to deploy and optimize the application for your needs.

To that end, this chapter is primarily focused on giving you an overall view of the components and functionality that make up MySQL. Understanding these features will be helpful as you read further through the book and apply your knowledge to the development of MySQL-based applications.

An Overview of MySQL Architecture

MySQL is based on a tiered architecture, consisting of both primary subsystems and support components that interact with each other to read, parse, and execute queries, and to cache and return query results.

Primary Subsystems

The MySQL architecture consists of five primary subsystems that work together to respond to a request made to the MySQL database server:

- The Query Engine
- The Storage Manager
- The Buffer Manager
- The Transaction Manager
- The Recovery Manager

The organization of these features is shown in Figure 2-1. We'll explain each one briefly to help you gain a better understanding of how the parts fit together.

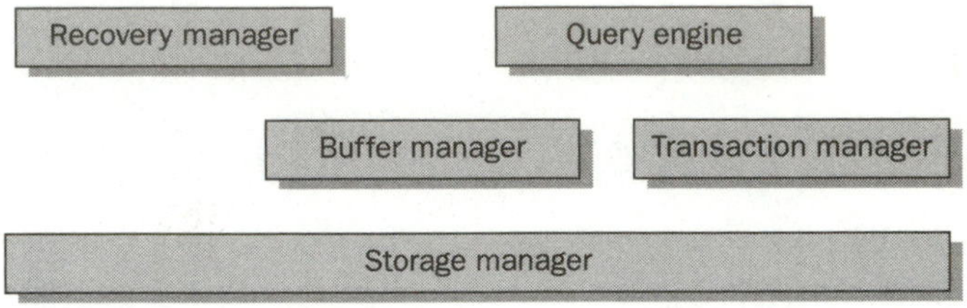

FIGURE 2-1   MySQL subsystems

The Query Engine

This subsystem contains three interrelated components:

- The Syntax Parser
- The Query Optimizer
- The Execution Component

The Syntax Parser decomposes the SQL commands it receives from calling programs into a form that can be understood by the MySQL engine. The objects that will be used are identified, along with the correctness of the syntax. The Syntax Parser also checks the objects being referenced to ensure that the privilege level of the calling program allows it to use them.

The Query Optimizer then streamlines the syntax for use by the Execution Component, which then prepares the most efficient plan of query execution. The Query Optimizer checks to see which index should be used to retrieve the data as quickly and efficiently as possible. It chooses one from among the several ways it has found to execute the query and then creates a plan of execution that can be understood by the Execution Component.

The Query Optimizer uses probability-based induction, so you may want to override it if you think that you already know the ideal way to access your query results; this will prevent the engine from using another, less optimal plan. MySQL provides you the option of giving the engine certain "hints" if you want it to use specific indexes without checking the Optimizer.

The Execution Component then interprets the execution plan and, based on the information it has received, makes requests of the other components to retrieve the records.

The Storage Manager

The Storage Manager interfaces with the operating system (OS) to write data to the disk efficiently. Because the storage functions reside in a separate subsystem, the MySQL engine operates at a level of abstraction away from the operating system. This means that if you port to a different operating system that uses a different storage mechanism, for example, you can rewrite only the storage portion of the code while leaving the rest of the engine as is. With the help of MySQL's Function Libraries (discussed shortly in

---

Adapting to the Environment

MySQL takes advantage of the separation between the Query Engine and the rest of
the components to provide *table handlers* in addition to the native MyISAM handler,
such as handlers for HEAP and MERGE table types. It also provides a new Storage
Manager and a new Transaction Manager for each table handler. Since InnoDB and
BDB table types have transaction features not present in the native MySQL types,
these were modified by their respective third-party creators to adapt to being plugged
into MySQL's existing Query Engine.

You can read more about the various table types supported by MySQL in
Chapter 8.

---

the section "Support Components"), the Storage Manager writes to disk all of the data
in the user tables, indexes, and logs as well as the internal system data.

The Query Cache   If a query returns a given set of records, repeating the same query
should return the same set of records unless the underlying data has somehow changed.
As obvious as this sounds, few of the other major relational database management
system (RDBMS) vendors provide features that take advantage of this principle. Other
database products are efficient in storing optimized access plans that detail the process
by which data is retrieved; such plans allow queries similar to those that have been
issued previously to bypass the process of analyzing indexes yet again to get to the data.

Result set caching takes this principle a step further by storing the result sets
themselves in memory, thus circumventing the need to search the database at all.
The data from a query is simply placed in a cache, and when a similar query is issued,
this data is returned as if in response to the query that created it in the first place.

The MySQL engine uses an extremely efficient result set caching mechanism, known
as the Query Cache, that dramatically enhances response times for queries that are
called upon to retrieve the exact same data as a previous query.

This mechanism is so efficient that a major computing publication declared MySQL
queries to be faster than those of Oracle and SQL Server (which are both known for
their speed). If implemented properly, decision support systems using MySQL with
canned reports or data-driven web pages can provide response speeds far beyond
those that would be expected without the Query Cache.

The Buffer Manager

This subsystem handles all memory management issues between requests for data by
the Query Engine and the Storage Manager. MySQL makes aggressive use of memory
to cache result sets that can be returned as-is rather than making duplicate requests to
the Storage Manager; this cache is maintained in the Buffer Manager.

This is also the area where new records can be cached while waiting for availability
of targeted tables and indexes. If any new data is needed, it's requested from the Storage
Manager and placed in the buffer before then being sent to the Query Engine.

The Transaction Manager

The function of the Transaction Manager is to facilitate concurrency in data access. This subsystem provides a locking facility to ensure that multiple simultaneous users access the data in a consistent way, without corrupting or damaging the data in any way. Transaction control takes place via the Lock Manager subcomponent, which places and releases locks on various objects being used in transactions. Each transactional table handler implements its own Transaction Manager to handle all locking and concurrency needs.

The Recovery Manager

The Recovery Manager's job is to keep copies of data for retrieval later, in case of a loss of data. It also logs commands that modify the data and other significant events inside the database.

So far, only the InnoDB and BDB table handlers provide recovery management. The MyISAM handler doesn't have transactional recovery procedures, but it does provide mechanisms that apply certain recovery features in case of a server outage; these features "fix" any internal inconsistencies that might occur as the result of such a crash. Such inconsistencies are usually related to indexes not being properly updated to reflect the contents of a table or records being incompletely written to a database.

Support Components

In addition to the five primary subsystems, the MySQL architecture contains the following two support components:

- The Process Manager
- Function Libraries

The Process Manager

This component performs two functions in the system. First, it manages user connections, via modules for network connection management with clients. Second, it synchronizes competing tasks and processes, via modules for multi-threading, thread locking, and performing thread-safe operations.

Function Libraries

This component contains general-purpose routines that are used by all the other subsystems. It includes routines for string manipulation, sorting operations, and such operating-system-specific functions as memory management and file I/O.

Subsystem/Component Interaction and Control Flow

The Query Engine requests that data be read from or written to the Buffer Manager to satisfy a user query. It depends on the Transaction Manager to request the locking of data so that concurrency is ensured. To perform table creation and drop operations, the Query Engine accesses the Storage Manager directly, bypassing the Buffer Manager, to create or delete files in the file system.

The Buffer Manager caches data from the Storage Manager for efficient retrieval by the Query Engine. It depends on the Transaction Manager to check the locking status of the data before it performs any modification operations.

The Transaction Manager depends on the Query Cache and the Storage Manager to place locks on data in memory and in the file system, respectively.

The Recovery Manager uses the Storage Manager to store command/event logs and backups of the data in the file system. It depends on the Transaction Manager to obtain locks on the log files being written. The Recovery Manager also needs to use the Buffer Manager during recovery from crashes.

The Storage Manager depends on the operating system file system for persistent storage and retrieval of data. It depends on the Transaction Manager to obtain locking status information.

The MySQL Engine

MySQL supports small, embedded kiosk-style applications as well as the occasional five billion-record data warehouse. This versatility is possible in part because of the MySQL engine, which has been designed for maximum scalability, maximum resource efficiency, and easy portability to various platforms and architectures. This section will discuss the important characteristics of this engine in greater detail.

Connectivity

MySQL is designed on the assumption that the vast majority of its applications will be running on a TCP/IP (Transmission Control Protocol/Internet Protocol) network. This is a fairly good assumption, given that TCP/IP is not only highly robust and secure, but is also common to UNIX, Windows, OS/2, and almost any other serious operating system you'll likely encounter. When the client and the server are on the same UNIX machine, MySQL uses TCP/IP with UNIX sockets, which operate in the UNIX domain; that is, they are generally used between processes on the same UNIX system (as opposed to Internet sockets, which operate between networks).

That being said, MySQL does allow named-pipe connections, which were designed mainly to support network connections in earlier non-TCP/IP networks, such as LAN Manager and Windows NETBEUI. (NETBEUI uses an addressing scheme based on the NETBIOS machine name rather than a routable IP address.)

SQL

The Structured Query Language (SQL) is an open standard that has been maintained by the American National Standards Institute (ANSI) since 1986. Although it's true that the implementation of this standard does differ in varying degrees from vendor to vendor, it's fair to say that SQL is today one of the most widely used cross-vendor languages. As with other implementations, such as SQL Server's T-SQL (Transact-SQL) and Oracle's SQL, MySQL has its own variations of the SQL standard that add power beyond what is available within the standard. Although MySQL's SQL queries will be explored in much greater detail in subsequent chapters, We'll introduce their use in this section to provide a framework for your understanding of the data-retrieval and decision -support capabilities of MySQL.

One thing that can be said about SQL is that it's easy to get started. With a simple statement like this one, you can begin retrieving data:

```
mysql> SELECT year, make, model, price FROM vehiclesales LIMIT 10;
+------+-----------------+----------------------+-------+
| year | make            | model                | price |
+------+-----------------+----------------------+-------+
| 1982 | AMERICAN MOTORS | EAGLE 50-4WD-6 CYL.   |   575 |
| 1983 | BUICK           | CENTURY LIMITED-V6   |  1000 |
| 1983 | BUICK           | REGAL LIMITED        |   525 |
| 1983 | BUICK           | REGAL LIMITED        |  1250 |
| 1983 | BUICK           | REGAL LIMITED        |  2250 |
| 1983 | BUICK           | REGAL LIMITED        |   700 |
| 1983 | BUICK           | SKYLARK LIMITED-V6   |   500 |
| 1983 | BUICK           | LESABRE CUSTOM-V8    |   550 |
| 1983 | BUICK           | ELECTRA LIMITED-V8   |   500 |
| 1984 | BUICK           | CENTURY CUSTOM-V6    |   850 |
+------+-----------------+----------------------+-------+
10 rows in set (0.00 sec)
```

As you can see, the syntax isn't arcane, nor is it difficult to understand—in fact, it looks almost like spoken English (which is great for English speakers). If you wanted to sort the above result set by price, you would simply add the phrase ORDER BY price to the end of the statement and run it.

Compared to C++, Java, and Perl, SQL at first glance seems easy to learn and hard to obfuscate, which often makes newcomers to SQL think that the learning curve will be much shorter than it actually is. In reality, it can take just as long to master SQL as it does other languages—people have written entire books about using SQL for data extraction without even addressing the other data manipulation features that the language offers. Take a look at the following query, which is perhaps more representative of the type you'll be called upon to perform:

```
mysql> SELECT
a.year,
a.make,
a.model,
a.trim,
AVG(a.price) AS s_price,
AVG(b.price) AS a_price
FROM vehiclesales a INNER JOIN vehiclesales b
ON
a.year = (b.year + 1)  and
```

```
a.make = b.make and
a.model = b.model and
a.trim = b.trim
GROUP BY
a.year,
a.make,
a.model,
a.trim,
b.year,
b.make,
b.model,
b.trim
HAVING AVG(a.price) > (AVG(b.price)* 1.25);
```

This query retrieves the names of vehicles that have an average price that has gone over 25 percent of the average price of the same type of vehicle for a previous year.

Data Integrity

MySQL supports engine-level data integrity through the use of primary key and foreign key constraints. Columns can be defined so that explicit NULL values cannot be entered into them. To prevent empty columns, MySQL supports the use of default values, which, when combined with NOT NULL properties, ensure that valid data is entered into a column that would otherwise be left blank.

Transactions

Until recently, MySQL was not known for its transaction-handling capabilities; however, since version 3.23, MySQL has been providing table handlers, such as InnoDB and BDB, that manage transactions in much the same manner as other commercial RDBMS products.

A transaction-safe database system must pass what is known as the ACID test to qualify for compliance. An ACID-compliant database must support the following characteristics:

- Atomicity
- Consistency
- Isolation
- Durability

Let's look at these characteristics in detail.

Coming Soon...

While future releases of MySQL are expected to have foreign keys in all table types, these referential integrity declarations are currently available only with the InnoDB table type.

Atomicity

A *transaction* is defined as an action, or a series of actions, that can access or change the contents of a database. In SQL terminology, a transaction occurs when one or more SQL statements operate as one unit. Each SQL statement in such a unit is dependent on the others; in other words, if one statement does not complete, the entire unit will be rolled back, and all the affected data will be returned to the state it was in before the transaction was started. Grouping the SQL statements as part of a single unit (or transaction) tells MySQL that the entire unit should be executed *atomically*.

Atomic execution is an all-or-nothing proposition. All of the SQL statements must be completed for the database to maintain a state of data integrity; otherwise, none of the statements will be finalized and committed to disk. In MySQL, the beginning of a transaction is marked with a BEGIN statement. The transaction (or unit of work) will not be considered complete until a COMMIT command is issued to tell MySQL to complete the action. When necessary, the ROLLBACK command will initiate a rolling back of all changes to the state before the BEGIN statement.

An everyday real-world example of this can be found in the banking business. By debiting and crediting your bank account, your bank adds and subtracts money from the account within one transaction. These updates usually involve multiple tables. The bank would not be able to maintain data integrity without guaranteeing that the entire transaction will take place, not just part of it.

Transaction management is particularly important to client-server systems that perform data entry or to any application that must be able to count on a high degree of safety from undetected data loss, such as the banking example described here.

Consistency

Consistency exists when every transaction leaves the system in a consistent state, regardless of whether the transaction completes successfully or fails midway.

For example, imagine that your bank uses a transaction that is supposed to transfer money from one bank account to another. If the transaction debits one bank account for the requisite amount but fails to credit the other account with a corresponding amount, the system would no longer be in a consistent state. In this case, the transaction would violate the consistency constraint, and the system would no longer be ACID-compliant.

In MySQL, consistency is primarily handled by MySQL's logging mechanisms, which record all changes to the database and provide an audit trail for transaction recovery. If the system goes down in the middle of a transaction, the MySQL recovery process will use these logs to discover whether or not the transaction was successfully completed and roll it back if required.

In addition to the logging process, MySQL also provides locking mechanisms that ensure that all of the tables, rows, and indexes that make up the transaction are locked by the initiating process long enough to either commit the transaction or roll it back.

Isolation

Isolation implies that every transaction occurs in its own space, isolated from other transactions that may be occurring in the system, and that the results of a transaction are visible only once the entire sequence of events making up the transaction has been fully executed. Even though multiple transactions may be occurring simultaneously in such a system, the isolation principle ensures that the effects of a particular transaction are not visible until the transaction is fully complete.

This is particularly important when the system supports multiple simultaneous users and connections (as MySQL does); systems that do not conform to this fundamental principle can cause massive data corruption, as the integrity of each transaction's individual space will be quickly violated by other competing, often conflicting, transactions.

Interestingly, MySQL offers the use of server-side semaphore variables that act as traffic managers to help programs manage their own isolation mechanisms. These variables are useful in cases for which you prefer not to incur the overhead of the Transaction Managers, or when a recovery plan is possible outside of the confines of log recovery. MySQL InnoDB tables offer isolation in transactions involving multiple queries, while MyISAM tables allow you to simulate isolation via the LOCK TABLES command.

Durability

Durability, which means that changes from a committed transaction persist even if the system crashes, comes into play when a transaction has completed and the logs have been updated in the database. Most RDBMS products ensure data consistency by keeping a log of all activity that alters data in the database in any way. This database log keeps track of any and all updates made to tables, queries, reports, and so on. If you have turned on the database log , you already know that using it will slow down the performance of your database when it comes to writing data. (It will not, however, affect the speed of your queries.)

In MySQL, you can specify whether or not you wish to use transactions by choosing the appropriate table handlers, depending on your application. The InnoDB table handler performs logging a bit differently than BDB does, while MyISAM does not support the type of logs that would permit you to be assured of a durable database. By default, InnoDB tables are 100% durable to the last second prior to a crash. MyISAM tables offer partial durability—all changes committed to the system prior to the last FLUSH TABLES command are guaranteed to be saved to disk.

SQL Server and Oracle, for instance, are able to restore a database to a previous state by restoring a previously backed-up database and, in essence, "replaying" all subsequent transactions up until the point of failure. These database products do not encourage the direct use of—nor do they expose the inner data structures of—the log files, because those files form part of the database engine's recovery mechanism.

MySQL also keeps a binary log of all data manipulation activity in sequential order. However, unlike the logs used in other databases, this log is easy to read, which means that it's a relatively straightforward task to recover lost data by using the last backup in combination with the log.

Extensibility

In most RDBMS products, you can extend the capabilities of the database by using stored procedures. The programmability is usually further extended by enhancements to SQL that contains control-of-flow statements and conditional logic, as SQL Server does with T-SQL and Oracle with PL/SQL.

As of yet, MySQL includes no support for stored procedures, but one of the great benefits of this RDBMS is its *extensibility*. In keeping with its open-source roots, MySQL makes the original source code available as part of the distribution, which permits developers to add new functions and features that are compiled into the engine as part of the core product. MySQL also allows separate C and C++ libraries to be loaded in the same memory space as the engine when MySQL starts up.

Either of these methods will allow users to interact with your functions in the same way as they would with any of the already built-in functions available in MySQL, such as SUM() or AVG(). Because these functions run in the same memory space as MySQL, and because they execute on the server where MySQL is located, using them minimizes network traffic between the calling program and the server, thereby vastly increasing performance.

You can add functions to MySQL through a special user-defined function interface. User-defined functions are created initially as special C/C++ libraries and are then added and removed dynamically by means of the CREATE FUNCTION and DROP FUNCTION statements. User-defined functions come with the added burden of having to install all your libraries with every installation of MySQL; however, this does make deployment faster, since you can load these functions into the binary distribution rather than having to go through the trouble of compiling MySQL all over again to incorporate the new functions. In addition, there's generally a good chance that your libraries will continue to work unchanged as new versions of MySQL are released.

You can also add functions as native (built-in) MySQL functions. Native functions are compiled into the MySQL server engine and become a permanent part of the MySQL installation itself. This makes new installations much easier than using libraries, because once you have defined your distribution, you can be sure that all of your subsequent

Getting Creative

You can simulate the encapsulation and centralization of a stored procedure in MySQL by storing code in a table and then retrieving the text of that code to be executed by the calling program. For example, a Perl program could have a table that includes rows containing nothing but Perl code. The client program would retrieve the needed code block and evaluate the code at run time.

This technique lets you place logic at the server without requiring that client programs be aware of any code changes. Because of the multiple round trips to and from the server, and because this approach works only with interpreted languages, it is not a true replacement for all the capabilities that one gets from stored procedures in other RDBMS implementations...but it's close.

installations will contain the functions that you have added. On the other hand, you must recompile and re-create your distribution for every new release of MySQL.

Symmetric Multiprocessing with MySQL

To take advantage of multiprocessor architecture, MySQL is built using a multi-threaded design, which allows threads to be allocated between processors to achieve a higher degree of parallelism. This is important to know not only for the database administrator, who needs to understand how MySQL takes best advantage of processing power, but also for developers, who can extend MySQL with custom functions. All custom functions must be *thread safe*—that is, that they must not interfere with the workings of other threads in the same process as MySQL.

Threading the Needle

To better understand threads in general, we must look at the relationship between threads and processes. A process contains both an executing program and a collection of resources, such as the file map and address space. All threads associated with a given task share the task's resources. Thus, a thread is essentially a program counter, a stack, and a set of registers; all the other data structures belong to the task. A process effectively starts out as a task with a single thread.

A thread is a miniprocess that has its own stack and that executes a given piece of code. A thread normally shares its memory with other threads, unlike true processes, which will usually have a different memory area for each one. A thread group is a set of threads all executing inside the same process. They all share the same memory and thus can access the same global variables, the same heap memory, the same set of file descriptors, and so on. All the threads in a thread group execute either by using time slices when running on a single processor or in parallel if multiple processors are available.

The advantage of using a thread group over using a process group is that context switching between threads is much faster than context switching between processes; in other words, the system switches from running one thread to running another thread much faster than it can switch from one process to another. Also, communication between two threads is usually faster and easier to implement than communication between two processes, since the threads already share common address space in which to share variables.

The POSIX thread libraries are a standards-based thread API for C and C++. They are most effectively used on multiprocessor systems, where the process flow can be scheduled to run on another processor, thus increasing speed through parallel or distributed processing. Threads require less overhead than forking, or spawning a new process, because the system will not initialize a new virtual memory space and environment for the process. While POSIX is most beneficial on a multiprocessor system, gains are also found on single processor systems, which exploit latency in input/output (I/O) and other system functions that can halt process execution.

MySQL makes use of various thread packages, depending on the platform. POSIX threads are used on most UNIX variants, such as FreeBSD and Solaris. LinuxThreads are used for Linux distributions, while, for efficiency reasons, Windows threads are used on the Windows platform (but the code that handles them is designed to simulate POSIX threads).

Because MySQL is a threaded application, it is able to let the operating system take over the task of coordinating the allocation of threads to balance the workload across multiple processors. MySQL uses these threads to do the following:

- A global connection thread handles all connection requests and creates a new dedicated thread to handle authentication and SQL query processing for each connection. This type of thread works on both TCP/IP and named-pipe connections.

- Internal semaphores and alarm listening functions are handled by a separate thread.

- When requested, a dedicated thread is created to flush all tables at the specified interval.

- Every single table on which a delayed INSERT is being used gets its own thread.

- In replication, master-host synchronization is handled by separate threads.

Of course, another way to take advantage of multiprocessing is to run multiple instances of MySQL on the same machine, thereby spawning a separate process for each instance. This approach is especially practical for hosting companies and even for internal hosting within corporate environments. By running multiple instances of MySQL on the same computer, you can easily accommodate multiple user bases that need different configuration options.

Security

The process of accessing a MySQL database can be broken down into two tasks: connecting to the MySQL server itself, and accessing individual objects, such as tables or columns, in a database. MySQL has built-in security to verify user credentials at both stages.

MySQL manages user authentication through user tables, which check not only that a user has logged on correctly with the proper username and password, but also that the connection is originating from an authorized TCP/IP address.

Once a user is connected, a system administrator can to bestow user-specific privileges on objects and on the actions that can be taken in MySQL. For example, you might allow *fred@thiscompany.com* to perform only SELECT queries against an inventory table, while allowing *anna@thatcompany.net* to run INSERT, UPDATE, and DELETE statements against the same table.

Security is also an issue for connections. Passwords and other important data transmitted across a network are vulnerable to interception by any one of the many network packet analyzers available on the market. By default, older versions of MySQL used a rather simple encryption method for usernames and passwords, which might have discouraged the casual hacker but would not have stopped someone who was willing to spend a little time cracking the encryption algorithms. As of version 4.1, a more secure protocol has been implemented that makes MySQL much more difficult to break into, even if a hacker has the ability to sniff and decode network traffic.

The actual data that travels over a network, such as query results, isn't encrypted and is therefore open to viewing by a hacker. To secure your data, you can use one of the SSH (Secure Shell) protocols; you'll need to install it on both the client applications and the operating system you're using. If you're using MySQL 4.0 or later, you can also use the SSL (Secure Socket Layer) encryption protocol, which can be configured to work from within MySQL, making it safe for use over the Internet or other public network infrastructures.

Replication

Replication is a data distribution mechanism that allows you to place copies of tables and databases in remote locations so that users can more easily access them.

Product databases are typical of such replication mechanisms—for example, a national or global company might have a common product database that is updated centrally but that is used locally by each office. Rather than forcing applications to query this table remotely every time it's needed, it is more cost effective to distribute a copy to everyone, thus incurring the transmission overhead only once for each office.

Prior to release 3.23.15, MySQL had no replication capabilities; subsequent to this release, and continuing to the present day, MySQL supports one-way replication, with one database as the master and one or more databases as the slaves.

The replication mechanism relies on a MySQL log that tracks all changes made to a database. The master ships this log to the slave, which then applies the log to its own data. Nothing about a slave prevents users from updating it outside the context of replication, so great care must be taken to ensure that this doesn't happen, since the relative assurance of synchronization will otherwise be lost and subsequent log playbacks might even fail.

Application Programming Interfaces

For application developers, MySQL provides a client library that is written in the C programming language and a set of APIs that provide an understandable set of rules by which host languages can connect to MySQL and send commands. Using an API protects client programs from any underlying changes in MySQL that could affect connectivity.

Many APIs are available, one or more for almost every programming language. Most of them use the C client library, with the exception of the Java driver, which is written in 100 percent native Java. Currently, MySQL APIs are available for Perl, PHP, C and C++, Java, Visual Basic, Python, Ruby, and .NET.

Add-On Tools

The list of software programs that work in tandem with MySQL is growing. Here's a brief list of the better ones:

- MySQL CC, available from `http://www.mysql.com/products/mysqlcc/index.html`, is an excellent front-end query and database management tool for MySQL. Currently Windows, UNIX, and Linux versions are available, and a version of Mac OS X may be available by the time you read this.

- DBTools Manager Professional, available from `http://www.dbtools.com.br`, is a graphical client used to manage MySQL databases, tables, and indices; import data from other RDBMS; and provide a point-and-click interface to query and report design.

- For web-based MySQL management, you should try phpMyAdmin, available from `http://www.phpmyadmin.org`.

Summary

To help you make the best decisions concerning the installation of the MySQL database sever, database and table design, and eventual optimization efforts, it is of paramount importance that you have a clear understanding of the underlying architecture governing the behavior of tables, rows, indexes, and databases. This knowledge is the basis from which database administrators make their tuning decisions, and from which application designers optimize their code.

In this chapter, we've sought to give you a basic understanding of all the elements of MySQL, both from the standpoint of the database administrator/developer and for those who may eventually create their own libraries or even add to MySQL's source code. The rest of this book will address these concepts in far greater detail.

MySQL Installation and Configuration

One of the nicer things about MySQL is the fact that it's an open-source application licensed under the General Public License (GPL); users are encouraged to download, modify, and use it free of charge. This open licensing policy has played an important role in MySQL's widespread acceptance and popularity in the developer community; according to statistics published on the MySQL web site, MySQL is in use at more than 4 million sites worldwide, with more than 25,000 copies of the MySQL database server downloaded every day!

In this chapter, I'm going to help add to those numbers, by taking you through the process of obtaining, installing, configuring, and testing the MySQL server on your workstation. This chapter covers installation of both binary and source versions on UNIX and Microsoft Windows, and it also explains the differences between the MySQL server versions available, with a view to helping you select the right one for your needs.

Obtaining MySQL

The first order of business is to drop by the official MySQL web site (`http://www.mysql.com/downloads/mysql.html`) and get yourself a copy of the last stable release of the software. This isn't necessarily as easy as it sounds—like ice-cream, MySQL comes in many flavors, and you'll need to select the one that's most appropriate for your needs.

You'll need to make two primary decisions when selecting which MySQL distribution to download and use:

- Choosing which version to install
- Choosing between binary and source distributions

Choosing Which Version to Install

MySQL AB currently makes the following two versions of the MySQL database server available on its web site:

- **MySQL Standard** This is the standard version of the MySQL database server, which includes support for both the regular, non-transactional tables and the newer, transaction-safe tables. It is suited for production environments requiring a stable, flexible, and robust database engine.

- **MySQL Max** This version includes the feature set of the standard version, together with newer, more experimental capabilities. It is not always best suited for production environments, since it usually includes a fair share of not-completely-stable enhancements.

Both these versions of MySQL are licensed under the GPL and may be freely downloaded and used under the terms of that license.

In most cases, MySQL Standard is the version you should use—it's the version used in all the examples in this book, and it's stable, feature-rich, and well-suited for most common applications. You should select MySQL Max only if that version includes new features that you need or are keen to try out—or if you're a geek with a penchant for living life on the bleeding edge all the time.

Choosing Between Binary and Source Distributions

MySQL AB makes both source and binary distributions of the MySQL database server available for download on its web site. As of this writing, binary distributions are available for Linux, Solaris, FreeBSD, Mac OS X, Windows 95/98/2000/XP/NT/ ME, HP-UX, IBM AIX, SCO OpenUNIX, and SGI Irix, and source distributions are available for both Windows and UNIX platforms.

In most cases, it's preferable to use a precompiled binary distribution rather than a source distribution—MySQL AB puts in a lot of time and effort to create binary distributions for various platforms, and using these distributions is generally considered a Good Idea. These precompiled binary distributions are also easier to install than source

---

Pay It Forward

It should be noted that, in addition to the two versions discussed in the section "Choosing Which Version to Install," MySQL AB also offers two other versions of the MySQL database server, MySQL Pro and MySQL Classic, which are licensed commercially and are therefore not freely available for download.

What's the difference between the two? MySQL Pro includes support for transactions (with the exception of the licensing terms, it is identical in every way to MySQL Standard), while MySQL Classic does not.

If you're interested in purchasing a commercial license for these versions of the MySQL database server, drop by http://order.mysql.com and find out more about what your greenbacks buy you.

PART I

distributions, and they are optimized by MySQL's developers to ensure maximum performance on the target systems.

That said, for a number of possible reasons, a source distribution might work better for you than a binary distribution:

- You'd like to recompile MySQL with compile-time options different from the defaults provided by the MySQL team. (For example, you might like to use a different value for the installation path.)

- You'd like to compile a smaller, lighter version of MySQL that doesn't include all the features (and overhead) of the standard binary distribution.

- You'd like to enable support for newer, experimental features that are disabled by default in the standard binaries.

- You'd like to view or make modifications to the source code of the application.

- You have waaaaay too much time on your hands, and you'd like to impress the pretty girl next door with your deep and profound knowledge of MySQL's internals. By the way, according to surveys, only six percent of MySQL users are women.

If you're new to MySQL, I'd recommend that you go with a binary distribution—source distributions are typically used only by experienced developers who either need to tweak MySQL's default values for their own purposes or who are interested in studying the source code to see how it works. Such users usually also have the time, inclination, and expertise to diagnose and troubleshoot compilation and configuration issues that may arise during the installation process.

Once you've figured out which version of MySQL you need, point your browser to `http://www.mysql.com/downloads/mysql.html` and select the appropriate file from the choices available. The MySQL software is also mirrored on a number of other sites around the world, and you can obtain a list of mirrors from `http://www.mysql.com/downloads/mirrors.html`. You can make your download more efficient by selecting the site that is geographically closest to you. Once your download is complete, save it to a directory on your hard drive and skip to the section titled "Installing and Configuring MySQL," a bit later in this chapter.

What's in a Name?

You've probably noticed that MySQL distributions are named using a particular naming scheme—for example, `mysql-4.0.9-gamma.tar.gz`. The numbers in the file name indicate the version number of the software, with the additional suffix indicating the stability level of the software (*alpha*, *beta*, or *gamma*).

Note that we will assume, throughout this chapter, that you are using MySQL version 4.0.15, and that all your downloads are saved in the /tmp (UNIX) or c:\temp (Windows) directory, and I will reference that directory in subsequent instructions.

Installing and Configuring MySQL

Once you've got yourself a copy of MySQL, it's time to install and configure it for your specific platform. This section includes information on how to do just that, for both Windows and UNIX platforms, using both binary and source distributions.

It should be noted at the outset that this section is designed merely to provide an overview and general guide to the process of installing and configuring MySQL. It is *not* intended as a replacement for the installation documentation that ships with MySQL. If you encounter difficulties installing or configuring the various programs described here, drop by the MySQL web site or search the mailing lists for detailed troubleshooting information and advice.

Installing and Configuring MySQL on UNIX

MySQL is available in binary form for almost all versions of UNIX and can even be compiled for those UNIX variants for which no binary distribution exists. This section will discuss installing and configuring MySQL on Linux using both source and binary distributions; the process for other UNIX variants is similar, although you should refer to the documentation included with the MySQL distribution for platform-specific notes.

Installing MySQL from a Binary RPM Distribution

The recommended way to install MySQL on a Linux system is via RPM. MySQL AB makes the following RPMs available for download on its web site:

- **MySQL**   The MySQL database server, which manages databases and tables, controls user access, and processes SQL queries

- **MySQL-client**   MySQL client programs, which makes it possible to connect to, and interact with, the server

---

Needful Things

MySQL software distributions are usually packaged in Zip, tar (tape archive), or RPM (RPM Package Manager) format, and they can range from 7 to 20 MB in size in compressed form, and up to 100 MB in size in uncompressed form. Depending on the format you select, you will need appropriate unpackaging tools to extract the files from the source archive. For Zip and tar files, you will need GNU tar and GNU gunzip, available from http://www.gnu.org.

For RPM files, you will need rpm, available from http://www.rpm.org.

Additionally, if you're planning on compiling and installing MySQL from a source distribution, you will need a C++ compiler like gcc on UNIX or Visual C++ on Windows. The gcc compiler is available from http://www.gnu.org/software/gcc, while Visual C++ is available from http://msdn.microsoft.com/visualc.

- **MySQL-devel** Libraries and header files that come in handy when compiling other programs that use MySQL

- **MySQL-shared** Shared libraries for the MySQL client

- **MySQL-bench** Benchmark and performance testing tools for the MySQL database server

The MySQL RPMs listed here are all built on a SuSE Linux system, but they'll usually work on other Linux variants with no difficulty.

Installing an RPM distribution of MySQL is extremely simple, and it involves running only a single command—the rpm command—for each RPM you wish to install. Here's how you go about doing it:

1. First ensure that you're logged in as *root*:

   ```
   [user@host]# su - root
   ```

2. Switch to the directory containing the RPMs:

   ```
   [root@host]# cd /tmp
   ```

3. Install the MySQL database server by executing the following command (remember to replace the filename in italics with the file name of your RPM):

   ```
   [root@host]# rpm -i MySQL-4.0.9-0.i386.rpm
   ```

   RPM does the following things to get MySQL up and running on your system:

   - Copies the MySQL binaries to appropriate locations on your system (usually, binaries go to /usr/bin and /usr/sbin, while databases and tables are stored in /var/lib/mysql)

   - Adds a mysql user/group to the system to handle all MySQL-related operational and administrative tasks

   - Alters ownership of the MySQL binaries so that they are owned by the mysql user/group

   - Creates and initializes the MySQL grant tables

   - Adds appropriate entries to your system's startup scripts so that the MySQL server starts up automatically at boot time

   - Starts the server so that you can begin using it immediately

   Figure 3-1 shows a snippet of what you might see during the installation process:

4. Now install the remaining RPMs in a similar manner:

   ```
   [root@host]# rpm -i MySQL-client-4.0.9-0.i386.rpm
   [root@host]# rpm -i MySQL-devel-4.0.9-0.i386.rpm
   [root@host]# rpm -i MySQL-shared-4.0.9-0.i386.rpm
   [root@host]# rpm -i MySQL-bench-4.0.9-0.i386.rpm
   ```

Figure 3-2 displays what you should see while performing this task.

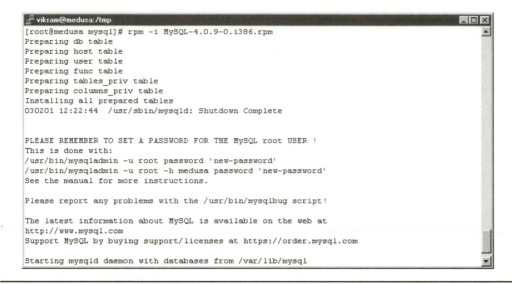

FIGURE 3-1   Installation of the MySQL server via RPM

Note that it's *necessary* to install only the server; however, I would recommend that you install the client as well so that you can interact with the server from the system console. The benchmark utilities should be installed only if you plan to test MySQL performance, while the libraries and header files come in handy when you're compiling other utilities or tools that use MySQL (for example, the PHP scripting language).

Once installation has been successfully completed, you should move later in the chapter to the section titled "Testing MySQL" to verify that everything is working as it should.

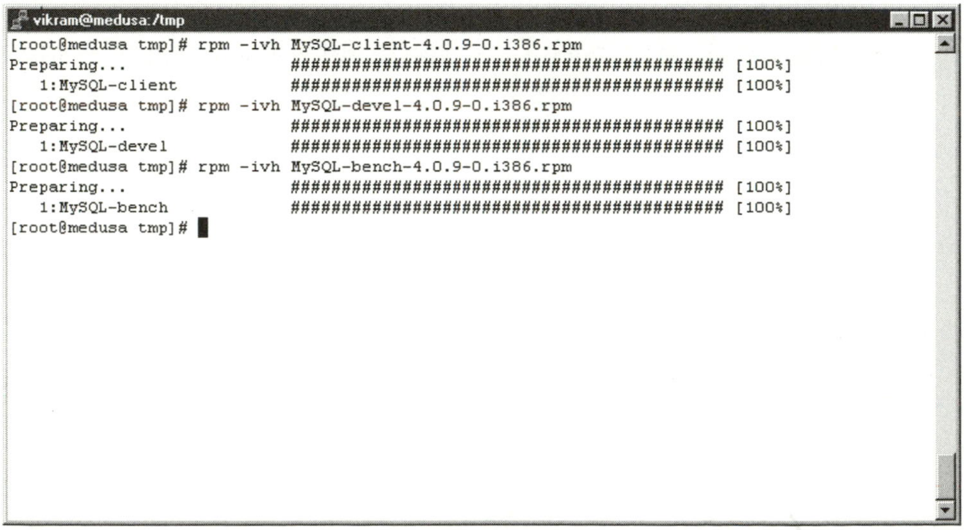

```
vikram@medusa:/tmp                                               _ □ ×
[root@medusa tmp]# rpm -ivh MySQL-client-4.0.9-0.i386.rpm
Preparing...              ######################################### [100%]
    1:MySQL-client        ######################################### [100%]
[root@medusa tmp]# rpm -ivh MySQL-devel-4.0.9-0.i386.rpm
Preparing...              ######################################### [100%]
    1:MySQL-devel         ######################################### [100%]
[root@medusa tmp]# rpm -ivh MySQL-bench-4.0.9-0.i386.rpm
Preparing...              ######################################### [100%]
    1:MySQL-bench         ######################################### [100%]
[root@medusa tmp]# █
```

FIGURE 3-2   Installation of ancillary MySQL tools and utilities via RPM

Installing MySQL from a Binary Tarball Distribution

In case you're using a Linux distribution that doesn't support RPM, you can also install MySQL using a binary tarball from the MySQL web site.

Installing from a binary distribution essentially means that you need to perform the installation steps manually rather than letting RPM automatically take care of it for you. Here's how you go about doing it:

1. Ensure that you're logged in as root:

   ```
   [user@host]# su - root
   ```

2. Extract the content of the tarball to an appropriate directory on your system—I'll assume this location is /usr/local/. Remember to replace the file name in italics with the file name of your tarball.

   ```
   [root@host]# cd /usr/local
   [root@host]# tar -xzvf
   mysql-standard-4.0.9-gamma-pc-linux-i686.tar.gz
   ```

   The MySQL files should get extracted into a directory named according to the format mysql-*version-os-architecture*—for example, mysql-standard-4.0.9-gamma-pc-linux-i686.

3. Now you'll notice that the directory created in the previous step has a somewhat long and cumbersome directory name—something like mysql-standard-4.0.9-gamma-pc-linux-i686. For ease of use, create a soft link to this directory named mysql in the same location.

   ```
   [root@host]# ln -s mysql-standard-4.0.9-gamma-pc-linux-i686 mysql
   ```

4. Change into this directory, and take a look at how the files are arranged. You should see something like Figure 3-3. (Take a look at the sidebar entitled "Up a Tree" for more information on what each directory contains.)

```
 vikram@medusa:/usr/local/mysql                                          _ □ ×
[root@medusa local]# cd mysql
[root@medusa mysql]# ls -l
total 40
drwxr-xr-x    2 root      501             4096 Jan 31 18:16 bin
drwxr-xr-x    3 root      501             4096 Jan 31 18:15 include
drwxr-xr-x    2 root      501             4096 Jan 31 18:15 info
drwxr-xr-x    3 root      501             4096 Jan 31 18:15 lib
drwxr-xr-x    2 root      501             4096 Jan 31 18:16 libexec
drwxr-xr-x    3 root      501             4096 Jan 31 18:16 man
drwxr-xr-x    6 root      501             4096 Jan 31 18:16 mysql-test
drwxr-xr-x    3 root      501             4096 Jan 31 18:16 share
drwxr-xr-x    7 root      501             4096 Jan 31 18:16 sql-bench
drwxr-xr-x    4 501       501             4096 Feb  1 12:09 var
[root@medusa mysql]# █
```

FIGURE 3-3   The directory structure obtained on unpackaging of a MySQL binary tarball on Linux

Up a Tree

If you have the time (and the inclination), you might find it instructive to explore the MySQL directory structure to help you better understand where the important files are located.

For a binary distribution, the directory structure for a typical MySQL installation looks like this:

```
<mysql-install-root>
|-- bin            [client and server binaries]
|-- data           [databases and error log]
|-- include        [header files]
|-- lib            [compiled libraries]
|-- man            [manual pages]
|-- mysql-test     [test suite]
|-- share          [error messages in different languages]
|-- scripts        [startup, shutdown and initialization scripts]
|-- sql-bench      [queries and data files for benchmark tests]
|-- support-files [sample configuration files]
|-- tests          [test cases]
```

For a source distribution, the directory structure for a typical MySQL installation looks like this:

```
<mysql-install-root>
|-- bin            [client binaries]
|-- libexec        [server binaries]
|-- var            [databases and error log]
|-- lib            [compiled libraries]
|-- include        [header files]
|-- info           [info pages]
|-- man            [manual pages]
|-- mysql-test     [test suite]
|-- share          [error messages in different languages]
|-- sql-bench      [queries and data files for benchmark tests]
```

Take a look at the documentation that ships with the MySQL distribution for a more detailed discussion of this directory structure.

5. The MySQL database server can run as either the system root user or any other user on the system. From the security point of view, it's considered a bad idea to run the MySQL database server as root ; hence, it becomes necessary for you to create a special mysql user and group for this purpose.

You can accomplish this using the groupadd and useradd commands:

```
[root@host]# groupadd mysql
[root@host]# useradd -g mysql mysql
```

6. Run the initialization script, `mysql_install_db`, that ships with the program:

   ```
   [root@host]# /usr/local/mysql/scripts/mysql_install_db
   ```

   Figure 3-4 demonstrates what you should see when you do this.:

   As you can see from the output in the figure, this initialization script prepares and installs the various MySQL base tables and also sets up default access permissions for MySQL.

7. Alter the ownership of the MySQL binaries so that they are owned by root:

   ```
   [root@host]# chown -R root /usr/local/mysql
   ```

8. Now ensure that the newly-minted `mysql` user has read/write access to the MySQL data directories:

   ```
   [root@host]# chown -R mysql /usr/local/mysql/data
   [root@host]# chgrp -R mysql /usr/local/mysql
   ```

9. Start the MySQL server by manually running the `mysqld` daemon:

   ```
   [root@host]# /usr/local/mysql/bin/mysqld_safe –user=mysql &
   ```

   MySQL should start up normally, reading the base tables created in `/usr/local/mysql/data`.

```
vikram@medusa: /usr/local/mysql                                    _ □ ✕
[root@medusa mysql]# scripts/mysql_install_db
Preparing db table
Preparing host table
Preparing user table
Preparing func table
Preparing tables_priv table
Preparing columns_priv table
Installing all prepared tables
030201 17:45:38  ./bin/mysqld: Shutdown Complete


To start mysqld at boot time you have to copy support-files/mysql.server
to the right place for your system

PLEASE REMEMBER TO SET A PASSWORD FOR THE MySQL root USER !
This is done with:
./bin/mysqladmin -u root password 'new-password'
./bin/mysqladmin -u root -h medusa password 'new-password'
See the manual for more instructions.

You can start the MySQL daemon with:
cd . ; ./bin/mysqld_safe &

You can test the MySQL daemon with the benchmarks in the 'sql-bench' directory:
cd sql-bench ; perl run-all-tests

Please report any problems with the ./bin/mysqlbug script!

The latest information about MySQL is available on the web at
http://www.mysql.com
Support MySQL by buying support/licenses at https://order.mysql.com
```

FIGURE 3-4   The output of running the MySQL initialization script

Once installation has been successfully completed, you can skip to the section titled "Testing MySQL," later in this chapter, to verify that your server is functioning properly.

Installing MySQL from a Source Distribution

If you're planning to install MySQL from a source distribution, you'll need to untar the source tree and go through the traditional `configure-make-make install` cycle to get MySQL up and running. This is a fairly time-consuming and complex process, and it's one that shouldn't really be attempted by novice users; however, if you're determined to do it, here's how:

1. Ensure that you're logged in as root:

   ```
   [user@host]# su - root
   ```

2. Switch to the directory containing the source tarball, and extract the files within it. (Note that you will need approximately 80 MB of free space for the source tree.)

   ```
   [root@host]# cd /tmp
   [root@host]# tar -xzvf mysql-4.0.9-gamma.tar.gz
   ```

   Remember to replace the file name in italics with the file name of your source tarball.

3. Move into the directory containing the source code,

   ```
   [root@host]# cd mysql-4.0.9-gamma
   ```

   and take a look at the contents with `ls`:

   ```
   [root@host]# ls -l
   ```

   You should see something like Figure 3-5.

```
 vikram@medusa:/tmp/mysql-4.0.9-gamma                                    _ □ ×
[root@medusa mysql-4.0.9-gamma]# ls -l
total 1764
-rw-r--r--    1 root     root        6256 Jan  9 15:05 acconfig.h
-rw-r--r--    1 root     root       38584 Jan  9 15:05 acinclude.m4
-rw-r--r--    1 root     root      170496 Jan  9 15:05 aclocal.m4
drwxrwxrwx   48 root     root        4096 Jan  9 15:31 bdb
drwxrwxrwx    2 root     root        4096 Jan  9 15:31 BUILD
-rw-r--r--    1 root     root       10846 Jan  9 15:05 ChangeLog
drwxrwxrwx    2 root     root        4096 Jan  9 15:31 client
-rwxr-xr-x    1 root     root       38693 Jan  9 15:05 config.guess
-rw-r--r--    1 root     root       21619 Jan  9 15:05 config.h.in
-rwxr-xr-x    1 root     root       28114 Jan  9 15:05 config.sub
-rwxr-xr-x    1 root     root      671343 Jan  9 15:06 configure
-rw-r--r--    1 root     root       73149 Jan  9 15:05 configure.in
-rw-r--r--    1 root     root       19106 Jan  9 15:08 COPYING
-rw-r--r--    1 root     root       28003 Jan  9 15:08 COPYING.LIB
drwxrwxrwx    2 root     root        4096 Jan  9 15:31 dbug
-rwxr-xr-x    1 root     root       12117 Jan  9 15:05 depcomp
drwxrwxrwx    4 root     root        4096 Jan  9 15:31 Docs
drwxrwxrwx    2 root     root        4096 Jan  9 15:31 extra
drwxrwxrwx    2 root     root        4096 Jan  9 15:31 heap
drwxrwxrwx    2 root     root        4096 Jan  9 15:31 include
drwxrwxrwx   34 root     root        4096 Jan  9 15:31 innobase
-rwxr-xr-x    1 root     root        5598 Jan  9 15:05 install-sh
```

FIGURE 3-5   The directory structure obtained on unpackaging of a MySQL source tarball on Linux

```
vikram@medusa:/tmp/mysql-4.0.9-gamma                                        _ □ ×
checking dependency style of g++... gcc3
checking how to run the C preprocessor... gcc -E
checking "C Compiler version"... "gcc gcc (GCC) 3.2 20020903 (Red Hat Linux 8.0 3.2-7)"
checking "C++ compiler version"... "g++ g++ (GCC) 3.2 20020903 (Red Hat Linux 8.0 3.2-7)"
checking for ranlib... ranlib
checking for ld used by GCC... /usr/bin/ld
checking if the linker (/usr/bin/ld) is GNU ld... yes
checking for /usr/bin/ld option to reload object files... -r
checking for BSD-compatible nm... /usr/bin/nm -B
checking whether ln -s works... yes
checking how to recognise dependant libraries... pass_all
checking command to parse /usr/bin/nm -B output... ok
checking for ANSI C header files... yes
checking for sys/types.h... yes
checking for sys/stat.h... yes
checking for stdlib.h... yes
checking for string.h... yes
checking for memory.h... yes
checking for strings.h... yes
checking for inttypes.h... yes
checking for stdint.h... yes
checking for unistd.h... yes
checking dlfcn.h usability... yes
checking dlfcn.h presence... ▌
```

FIGURE 3-6   Configuring the MySQL source tree on Linux

Take a look at the sidebar entitled "Up a Tree" for more information on what each directory contains.

4. Now, set variables for the compile process via the included `configure` script. (Note the use of the `--prefix` argument to `configure`, which sets the default installation path for the compiled binaries.)

```
[root@host]# ./configure --prefix=/usr/local/mysql
```

You should see a few screens of output (Figure 3-6 has a sample) as `configure` configures and sets up the variables needed for the compilation process.

5. Now compile the program using `make`:

```
[root@host]# make
```

Watch as your screen fills up with all manner of strange symbols and characters (see Figure 3-7).

The compilation process takes a fair amount of time (refer to the sidebar titled "Watching the Clock" for my empirical observations on how long you'll be waiting), so this is a good time to get yourself a cup of coffee or check your mail.

Now that you're all done, you can test to ensure that everything is working properly.

6. Run the following command:

```
[root@host]# make tests
```

Handcrafting Your Build

You can pass configure a number of command-line options that affect the build process. Here's a list of the more interesting ones:

- **--prefix**   Sets the prefix for installation paths
- **--without-server**   Disables compilation of the server, and compiles only the MySQL client programs and libraries
- **--localstatedir**   Sets the location in which the MySQL databases will be stored
- **--with-charset**   Sets a default character set
- **--with-debug**   Turns on extended debugging
- **--with-raid**   Enables RAID support
- **--with-embedded-server**   Builds the libmysqld embedded server library
- **--without-query-cache**   Disables the query cache
- **--without-debug**   Disables debugging routines
- **--with-openssl**   Includes OpenSSL support

Use the configure --help command to get a complete list of options.

```
vikram@medusa:/tmp/mysql-4.0.9-gamma                                    _ □ ×
depmode=gcc3 /bin/sh ../depcomp \
gcc -DUNDEF_THREADS_HACK -DHAVE_CONFIG_H -DNO_KILL_INTR -I. -I. -I.. -I./../include -I./.
. -I..    -O3 -DDBUG_OFF   -c `test -f keymaps.c || echo './'`keymaps.c
source='vi_mode.c' object='vi_mode.o' libtool=no \
depfile='.deps/vi_mode.Po' tmpdepfile='.deps/vi_mode.TPo' \
depmode=gcc3 /bin/sh ../depcomp \
gcc -DUNDEF_THREADS_HACK -DHAVE_CONFIG_H -DNO_KILL_INTR -I. -I. -I.. -I./../include -I./.
. -I..    -O3 -DDBUG_OFF   -c `test -f vi_mode.c || echo './'`vi_mode.c
source='parens.c' object='parens.o' libtool=no \
depfile='.deps/parens.Po' tmpdepfile='.deps/parens.TPo' \
depmode=gcc3 /bin/sh ../depcomp \
gcc -DUNDEF_THREADS_HACK -DHAVE_CONFIG_H -DNO_KILL_INTR -I. -I. -I.. -I./../include -I./.
. -I..    -O3 -DDBUG_OFF   -c `test -f parens.c || echo './'`parens.c
source='rltty.c' object='rltty.o' libtool=no \
depfile='.deps/rltty.Po' tmpdepfile='.deps/rltty.TPo' \
depmode=gcc3 /bin/sh ../depcomp \
gcc -DUNDEF_THREADS_HACK -DHAVE_CONFIG_H -DNO_KILL_INTR -I. -I. -I.. -I./../include -I./.
. -I..    -O3 -DDBUG_OFF   -c `test -f rltty.c || echo './'`rltty.c
source='complete.c' object='complete.o' libtool=no \
depfile='.deps/complete.Po' tmpdepfile='.deps/complete.TPo' \
depmode=gcc3 /bin/sh ../depcomp \
gcc -DUNDEF_THREADS_HACK -DHAVE_CONFIG_H -DNO_KILL_INTR -I. -I. -I.. -I./../include -I./.
. -I..    -O3 -DDBUG_OFF   -c `test -f complete.c || echo './'`complete.c
```

FIGURE 3-7   Building MySQL on Linux

Watching the Clock

Compiling MySQL is a fairly time-consuming process, and you should be prepared to spend anywhere between 15 to 60 minutes on the task. The following table contains some empirical observations on the time taken to compile the program on various hardware configurations:

System Configuration	Time Taken to Compile MySQL
Pentium-II@350 MhZ, 64 MB RAM	45 minutes
Pentium-III@700MhZ, 256 MB RAM	30 minutes
AMD Athlon MP 1500+, SuSE Linux 7.3	8 minutes
AMD Opteron@2x1.6 GHz, UnitedLinux 1.0	7 minutes
Apple PowerMac G4@2x1.2 GHz, Mac OS X 10.2.4	14 minutes
Compaq AlphaServer DS20@500 MHz, SuSe Linux 7.0	17 minutes
HP 9000/800/A500-7X, HP-UX 11.11	14 minutes
IBM RS/6000, AIX 4.3.3	35 minutes
Intel Itanium2@900 MHz, Red Hat AS 2.1	14 minutes
MIPS R5000@500 MHz, SGI IRIX 6.5	2 hours 30 minutes

7. Install the MySQL binaries to their new home in `/usr/local/mysql`:

   `[root@host]# `**`make install`**

   Figure 3-8 demonstrates what your screen should look like during the installation process.

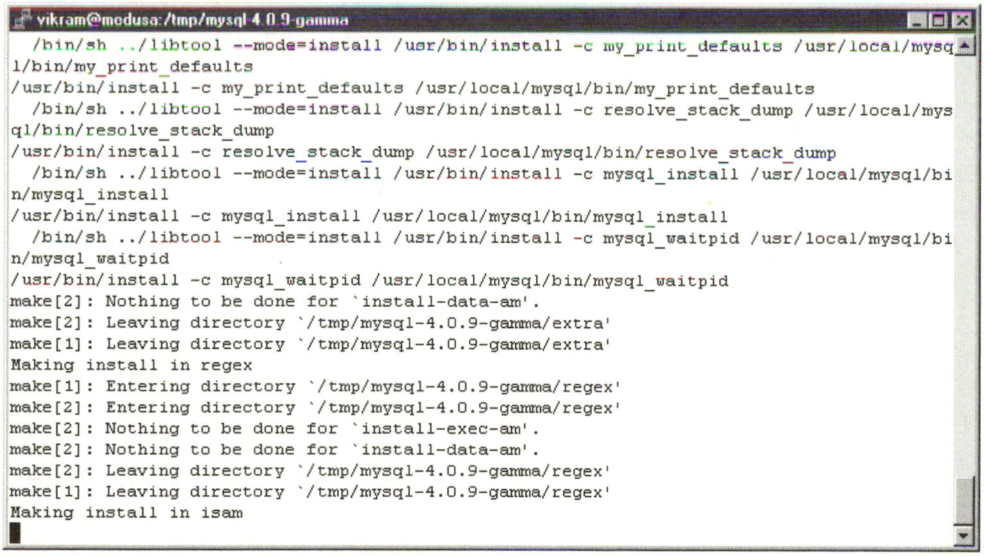

FIGURE 3-8   Installing compiled MySQL binaries on Linux

8. Create the special `mysql` user and group with the `groupadd` and `useradd` commands:

```
[root@host]# groupadd mysql
[root@host]# useradd -g mysql mysql
```

9. Run the initialization script, `mysql_install_db`, which ships with the program, to prepare MySQL for operation:

```
[root@host]# /usr/local/mysql/scripts/mysql_install_db
```

10. Alter the ownership of the MySQL binaries so that they are owned by root:

```
[root@host]# chown -R root /usr/local/mysql
```

Now ensure that the newly minted `mysql` user has read/write access to the MySQL data directories:

```
[root@host]# chown -R mysql /usr/local/mysql/var
[root@host]# chgrp -R mysql /usr/local/mysql
```

11. Start the MySQL server by manually running the `mysqld` daemon:

```
[root@host]# /usr/local/mysql/bin/mysqld_safe --user=mysql &
```

MySQL should start up normally, reading the base tables created in `/usr/local/mysql/var`.

At this point, you can proceed to the section titled "Testing MySQL" to verify that everything is working as it should.

Installing and Configuring MySQL on Windows

MySQL is available in both source and binary form for Windows 95/98/Me/2000/XP/NT. Most often, you will want to use the binary distribution, which comes with an automated installer and allows you to get MySQL up and running on your Windows

---

Version Control

In case you're wondering, all the binaries used when developing this book have been built on Linux using the following software versions:

- mysqld 4.0.15-standard
- mysqld-4.1-alpha
- rpm 4.1
- gcc 3.2
- tar 1.13.25

- gunzip 1.3.3
- unzip 5.50
- make 3.79.1
- autoconf 2.53
- automake 1.6.3

system in just a few minutes. However, if you're the type who likes rolling your own, MySQL AB also makes MySQL source code available for Windows. In this section, I'll be exploring the installation of both source and binary distributions on Windows 98 and Windows NT.

Installing MySQL from a Binary Distribution

Installing a binary distribution of MySQL on Windows is a fairly simple process—all you need to do is point and click your way through the installer provided with the distribution. Here's how:

1. Log in as an administrator (if you're using Windows NT or Windows 2000) and unzip the distribution archive to a temporary directory on your system. After extraction, your directory should look something like Figure 3-9.

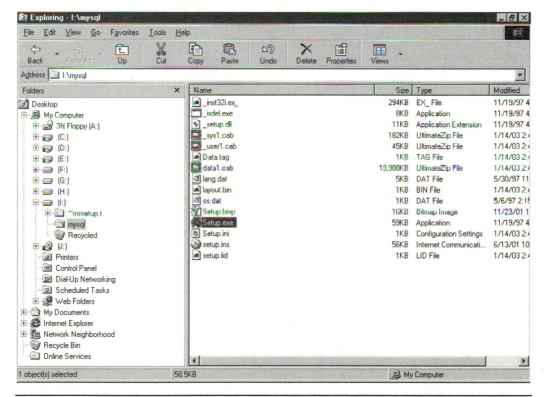

FIGURE 3-9   The directory structure created on unpackaging a MySQL binary distribution for Windows

2. Double-click the `setup.exe` file to begin the installation process. You should see a welcome screen (Figure 3-10). Click Next.

3. Click Browse and select the directory in which MySQL is to be installed—in this example, select `c:\program files\mysql` (Figure 3-11). Click Next.

4. Select the type of installation required (Figure 3-12). Click Next.

   Most often, a Typical Installation will do; however, if you're the kind who likes tweaking default settings, select the Custom Installation option, click Next, and then decide which components of the package should be installed (Figure 3-13).

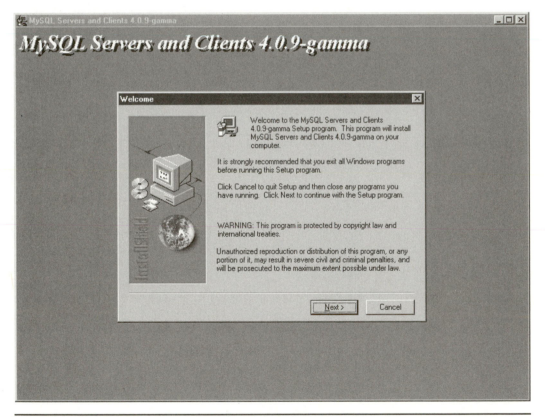

FIGURE 3-10   MySQL installation on Windows

FIGURE 3-11
Selecting
installation
directory on
Windows

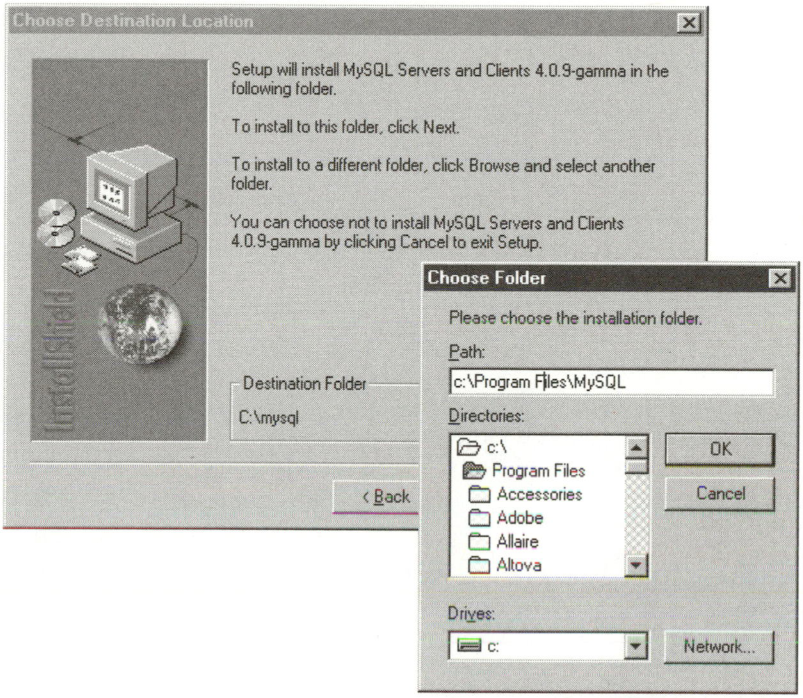

FIGURE 3-12
Selecting
installation type

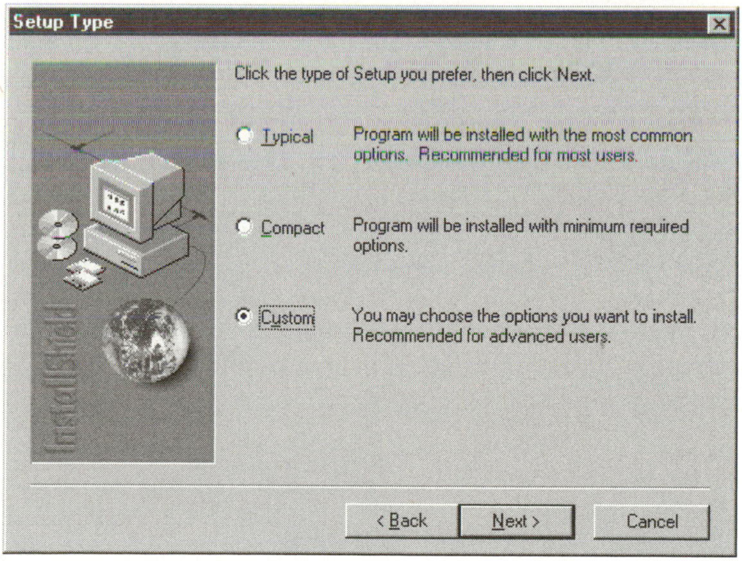

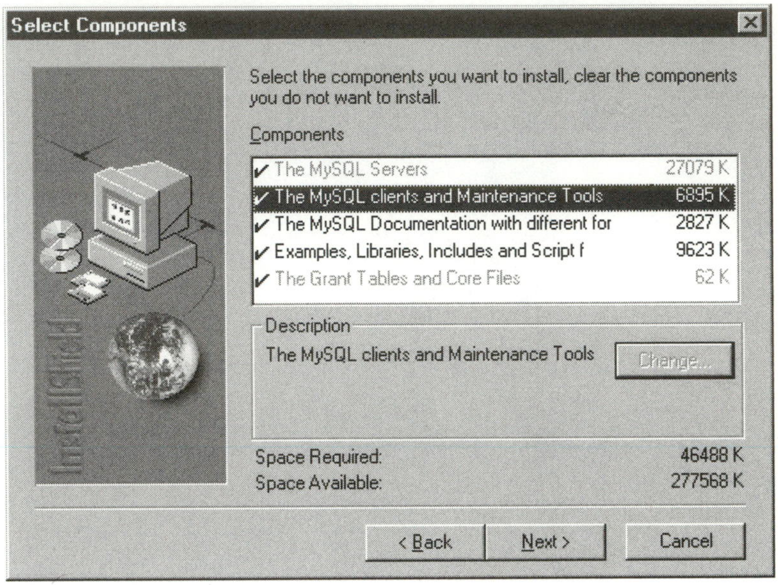

FIGURE 3-13
Selecting
components
for a custom
installation
on Windows

Select Components

Select the components you want to install, clear the components
you do not want to install.

Components

✔ The MySQL Servers	27079 K
✔ The MySQL clients and Maintenance Tools	6895 K
✔ The MySQL Documentation with different for	2827 K
✔ Examples, Libraries, Includes and Script f	9623 K
✔ The Grant Tables and Core Files	62 K

Description

The MySQL clients and Maintenance Tools   Change...

Space Required: 46488 K
Space Available: 277568 K

< Back   Next >   Cancel

5. Click Next, and MySQL should now begin installing to your system (Figure 3-14).

6. After installation is complete, you should see a screen like Figure 3-15.
   Click Finish.

You should now be able to start the MySQL server by diving into the bin\
subdirectory of your MySQL installation and launching the WinMySQLadmin tool
(winmysqladmin.exe). This tool provides a graphical user interface (GUI) to MySQL
configuration, and it is by far the simplest way to configure MySQL on Windows
systems.

The first time you start WinMySQLadmin, you will be asked for the name and
password of the user which the server should run as (Figure 3-16).

After you have entered this information, WinMySQLadmin will automatically
create the MySQL configuration file (named my.ini) and populate it with appropriate
values for your system. You can edit these values at any time through the "my.ini
Setup" tab of the main WinMySQLadmin application window (see Figure 3-17).

FIGURE 3-14
Installation in
progress on
Windows

The MySQL Servers
c:\program files\mysql\bin\mysqld.exe

23 %

Cancel

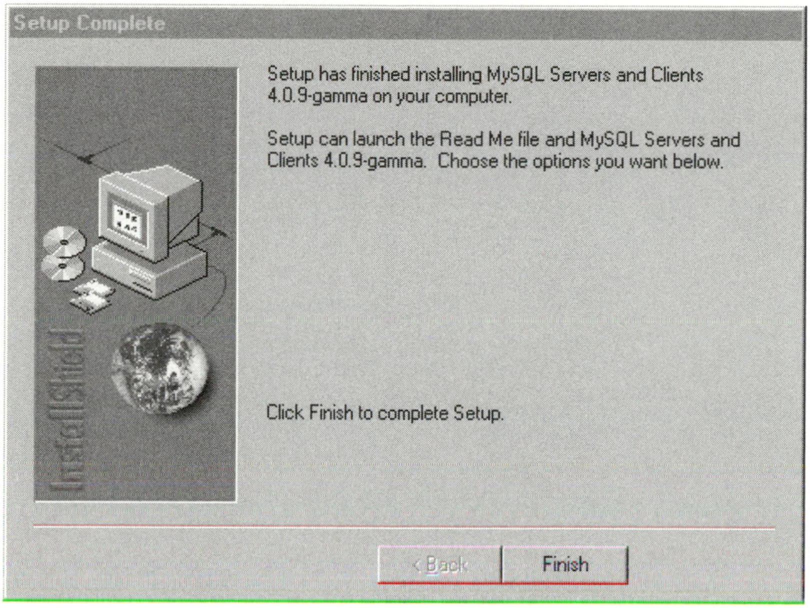

FIGURE 3-15
Installation
successfully
completed on
Windows

NOTE   *You can also start the MySQL server by directly launching the* `mysqld.exe` *or* `mysqld-nt.exe` *binary from the* `bin\` *subdirectory of your MySQL installation.*

Once the server has started, WinMySQLadmin will minimize to a green icon in your Windows taskbar notification area. You can now proceed to test the server as described in the section "Testing MySQL" to ensure that everything is working as it should.

FIGURE 3-16
Configuring the
MySQL user on
Windows via
WinMySQLadmin

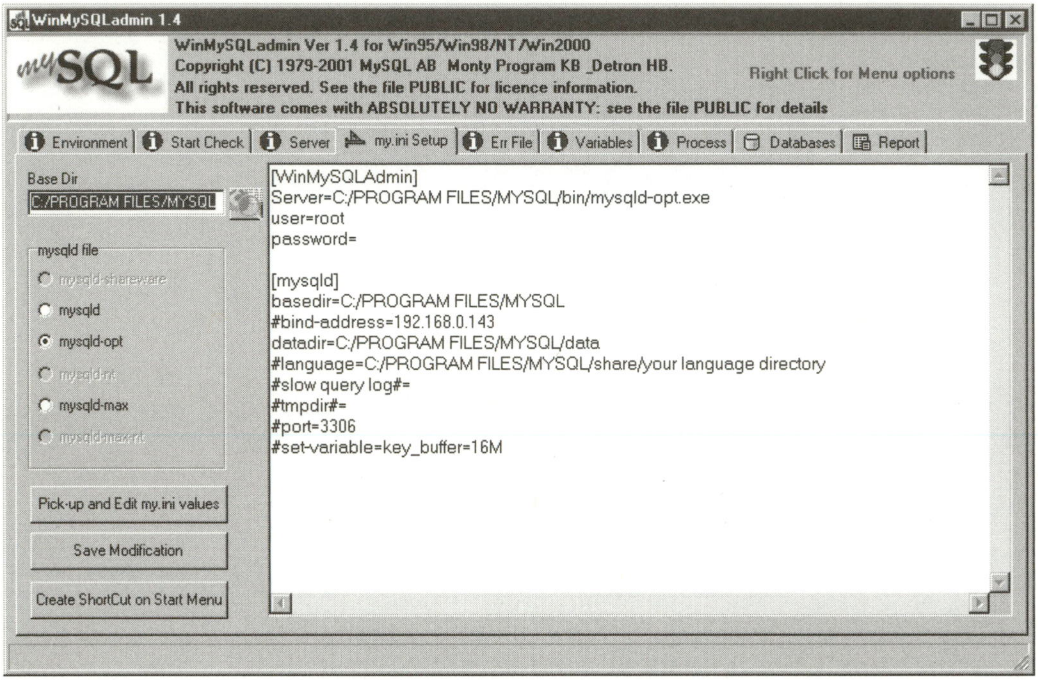

FIGURE 3-17   Editing MySQL configuration on Windows via WinMySQLadmin

Note that you can bring the WinMySQLadmin application back to the foreground at any time by right-clicking the taskbar icon and choosing "Show Me" from the pop-up menu (see Figure 3-18).

Installing MySQL from a Source Distribution

While compiling MySQL for Windows from the source archive is not something that's generally recommended—it's far safer, not to mention easier, to use the provided binaries—it's certainly doable, assuming you have a copy of the Visual C++ 6.0 compiler (with Service Pack 5 and the preprocessor package). Here's how it's done:

1. Unzip the source archive to a working directory on your system.
2. Launch the Visual C++ compiler, and open the mysql.dsw workspace from the working directory. You should see a window like Figure 3-19.

FIGURE 3-18   Using the WinMySQLadmin system tray icon

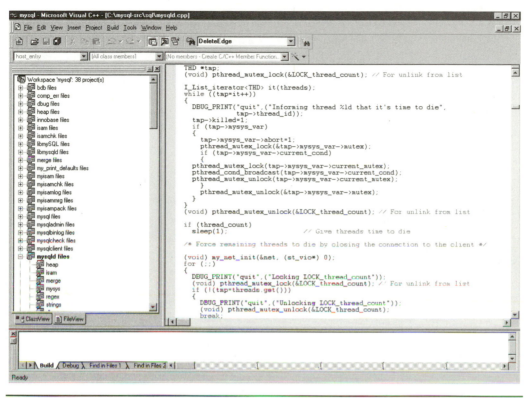

FIGURE 3-19   The MySQL workspace in Visual C++

3. Choose Build | Set Active Configuration to obtain a list of available configurations. Select mysqld – Win32 Release (see Figure 3-20). Click OK.

4. Begin compiling by pressing the F7 key. The various MySQL binaries will be compiled—expect the process to take from 20 minutes to an hour, depending

FIGURE 3-20
Selecting which version of MySQL to build in Visual C++

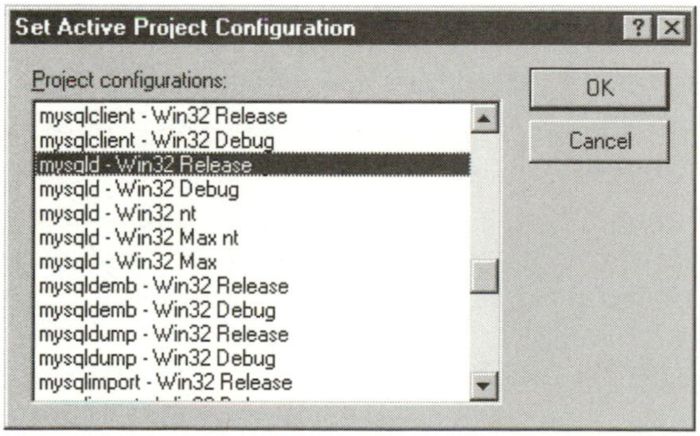

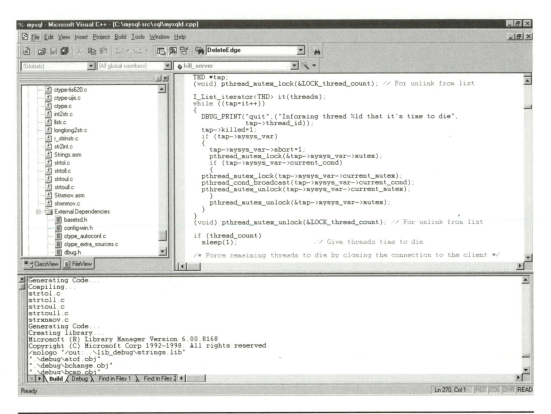

FIGURE 3-21   Compiling MySQL for Windows in Visual C++

on the capabilities of your machine. During the compilation process, the Visual C++ compiler window will display a series of messages, such as those shown in Figure 3-21.

5. After compilation is complete, create a separate installation directory to house the compiled binaries—for example, `c:\program files\mysql`.

6. Create a `bin\` subdirectory under this directory, and move the compiled libraries and executables into this directory. While you're at it, also move the `data\`, `share\`, `docs\`, and `support-files\` directories from the working directory into this directory.

7. You should now be able to start the MySQL server by diving into the `bin\` subdirectory of your MySQL installation and launching the MySQL server daemon directly (`mysqld.exe` or `mysqld-nt.exe`).

Once the server has started, proceed to test it as per the instructions in "Testing MySQL," next.

Testing MySQL

After MySQL has been successfully installed, the base tables have been initialized, and the server has been started, you can verify that all is working as it should via some simple tests.

Note that all these commands should be run from your UNIX or Windows command prompt. I am assuming here that you are running them from your MySQL installation directory (as per the examples in the section "Installing and Configuring MySQL," this will be either `/usr/local/mysql` in UNIX or `c:\program files\ mysql` in Windows).

Use the mysqladmin Utility to Obtain Server Status

The `mysqladmin` utility is usually located in the `bin` subdirectory of your MySQL installation. You can execute it by changing to that directory and executing the following command:

```
[root@host]# mysqladmin version
```

You should see something resembling the output shown in Figure 3-22.

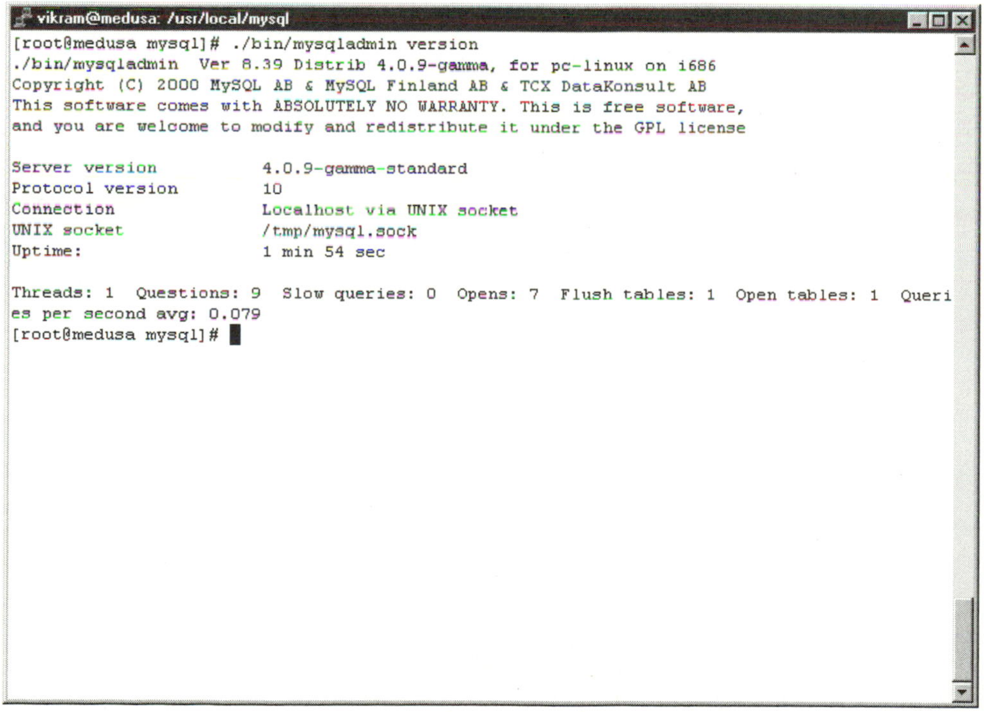

```
 vikram@medusa: /usr/local/mysql
[root@medusa mysql]# ./bin/mysqladmin version
./bin/mysqladmin  Ver 8.39 Distrib 4.0.9-gamma, for pc-linux on i686
Copyright (C) 2000 MySQL AB & MySQL Finland AB & TCX DataKonsult AB
This software comes with ABSOLUTELY NO WARRANTY. This is free software,
and you are welcome to modify and redistribute it under the GPL license

Server version          4.0.9-gamma-standard
Protocol version        10
Connection              Localhost via UNIX socket
UNIX socket             /tmp/mysql.sock
Uptime:                 1 min 54 sec

Threads: 1  Questions: 9  Slow queries: 0  Opens: 7  Flush tables: 1  Open tables: 1  Queri
es per second avg: 0.079
[root@medusa mysql]# █
```

FIGURE 3-22   The output of a call to mysqladmin

Connect to the Server Using the MySQL Client, and Execute Simple SQL Commands

The MySQL client that ships with the MySQL distribution is named, funnily enough, mysql. Fire it up from your command prompt by switching to the bin directory of your MySQL installation and typing

```
[root@host]# mysql
```

You should be rewarded with a mysql> prompt.

At this point, you are connected to the MySQL server and can begin executing SQL commands or queries. Here are a few examples, with their output:

```
mysql> SHOW DATABASES;
+----------+
| Database |
+----------+
| mysql    |
| test     |
+----------+
2 rows in set (0.13 sec)

mysql> USE mysql;
Reading table information for completion of table and column names
You can turn off this feature to get a quicker startup with -A
Database changed

mysql> SHOW TABLES;
+-----------------+
| Tables_in_mysql |
+-----------------+
| columns_priv    |
| db              |
| func            |
| host            |
| tables_priv     |
| user            |
+-----------------+
6 rows in set (0.00 sec)

mysql> SELECT COUNT(*) FROM user;
+----------+
| count(*) |
+----------+
|        4 |
+----------+
1 row in set (0.00 sec)
```

Post-Installation Steps

Once testing is complete, you should perform two more tasks to complete your MySQL installation:

Alter the MySQL root Password

When MySQL is first installed, access to the database server is restricted to the MySQL administrator, aka root. By default, this user is initialized with a null password, which is generally considered a Bad Thing. You should therefore rectify this as soon as possible by setting a password for this user via the included `mysqladmin` utility, using the following syntax in UNIX

```
[root@host]# /usr/local/mysql/bin/mysqladmin -u root
password '<new-password>'
C:\> c:\program files\mysql\bin\mysqladmin -u root
password '<new-password>'
```

This password change goes into effect immediately, with no requirement to restart the server or flush the privilege table.

NOTE   *The MySQL root user is not the same as the system root user on UNIX.*

Configure MySQL to Start Automatically When the System Boots up

On UNIX, MySQL comes with a startup/shutdown script, which is the recommended way of starting and stopping the MySQL database server. This script, named `mysql.server`, is available in the `support-files` subdirectory of your MySQL installation, and it can be invoked as follows:

```
[root@host]# /usr/local/mysql/support-files/mysql.server start
[root@host]# /usr/local/mysql/support-files/mysql.server stop
```

To have MySQL start automatically at boot time, you simply need to copy this script to the `/etc/init.d/*` directory hierarchy of your system, and then you can invoke it with appropriate parameters from your system's bootup and shutdown scripts.

To start MySQL automatically on Windows, you can simply add a link to the `mysqld` server binary to your Startup group. For more information, please refer to Chapter 13.

> **With a Little Help from My Friends...**
>
> In case you have problems starting the MySQL server, you can obtain fairly detailed information on what went wrong by looking at the MySQL error log. Most often, this log can be found in the `var` subdirectory of your MySQL installation, and it is named `hostname.err`. Other common problems, such as a forgotten superuser password or incorrect path settings, can also be discovered and resolved via a close study of this error log. You can also visit the following resources for advice on how to resolve problems you may encounter during the installation process:
>
> - **The MySQL manual** `http://www.mysql.com/documentation`
> - **The MySQL mailing lists** `http://lists.mysql.com`
> - **Google** `http://www.google.com`
> - **Google Groups** `http://groups.google.com`
>
> If you're reporting a problem or a bug, remember to use the supplied `mysqlbug` script to gather necessary system information and include it in your report.

Summary

As a popular open-source application, MySQL is available for a wide variety of platforms and architectures, in both binary and source form. This chapter explained the distinction among the different versions of MySQL, together with recommendations on the most appropriate version for your requirements; it also demonstrated the process of installing MySQL on the two most common platforms, Linux and Windows. It provided installation and configuration instructions for both binary and source distributions and also provided pointers to online resources for other platforms and for detailed troubleshooting advice and assistance.

PART

II

Usage

SQL Basics

If you think about it, you'll realize that you can perform two basic tasks with a
database: you can put data in and pull data out. And most often, your primary
tool to accomplish these two functions is a language known as SQL, or Structured
Query Language.

As a standards-compliant relational database management system (RDBMS),
MySQL understands SQL fairly well, and it even offers up some interesting extensions
to the SQL standard. To use MySQL effectively, you'll need to be able to speak SQL
fluently—it's your primary means of interacting with the database server, and it plays
a very important role in helping you get to the data you need rapidly and efficiently.

Over the course of this chapter, we'll be explaining some of the basic SQL commands
to create and enter information into a database, together with examples that should
make things clearer. In case you've never used a database, or the thought of learning
another language scares you, don't worry, because SQL is considerably simpler than
most programming languages, and you should have no trouble picking it up.

A Brief History of SQL

Before we get into the nitty-gritty of SQL command syntax, let's spend a few moments
understanding how SQL came into existence.

SQL began life as SEQUEL1[1], the Structured English Query Language, a component
of an IBM research project called System/R. System/R was a prototype of the first
relational database system; it was created at IBM's San Jose laboratories in 1974, and
SEQUEL was the first query language to support multiple tables and multiple users.

In the late 1970s, SQL made its first appearance in a commercial role as the query
language used by the Oracle RDBMS. This was quickly followed by the Ingres RDBMS,
which also used SQL, and by the 1980s, SQL had become the de facto standard for the
rapidly growing RDBMS industry. In 1989, SQL became an ANSI standard commonly
referred to as SQL89; this was later updated in 1992 to become SQL92 or SQL2, the
standard in use on most of today's commercial RDBMSs (including MySQL).

---

[1]   The name was later changed to SQL for legal reasons.

> **Breaking the Rules**
>
> Although most of today's commercial RDBMSs do support the SQL92 standard, many of them also take liberties with the specification, extending SQL with proprietary extensions and enhancements. (MySQL is an example of such.) Most often, these enhancements are designed to improve performance or add extra functionality to the system; however, they can cause substantial difficulties when migrating from one DBMS to another.
>
> A complete list of MySQL's deviations from the SQL specification is available at `http://www.mysql.com/doc/en/Compatibility.html`.

An Overview of SQL

As a language, SQL was designed to be "human-friendly"; most of its commands resemble spoken English, making it easy to read, understand, and learn. Commands are formulated as statements, and every statement begins with an "action word." The following examples demonstrate this:

```
CREATE DATABASE toys;
USE toys;
SELECT id FROM toys WHERE targetAge > 3;
DELETE FROM catalog WHERE productionStatus = "Revoked";
```

As you can see, it's pretty easy to understand what each statement does. This simplicity is one of the reasons SQL is so popular, and also so easy to learn.

SQL statements can be divided into three broad categories, each concerned with a different aspect of database management:

- **Statements used to define the structure of a database**   These statements define the relationships among different pieces of data, definitions for database, table and column types, and database indices. In the SQL specification, this component is referred to as Data Definition Language (DDL), and it is discussed in detail in Chapter 8 of this book.

- **Statements used to manipulate data**   These statements control adding and removing records, querying and joining tables, and verifying data integrity. In the SQL specification, this component is referred to as Data Manipulation Language (DML), and it is discussed in detail in Chapter 9 of this book.

- **Statements used to control the permissions and access level to different pieces of data**   These statements define the access levels and security privileges for databases, tables and fields, which may be specified on a per-user and/or per-host basis. In the SQL specification, this component is referred to as Data Control Language (DCL), and it is discussed in detail in Chapter 14.

Typically, every SQL statement ends in a semicolon, and white space, tabs, and carriage returns are ignored by the SQL processor. The following two statements are equivalent, even though the first is on a single line and the second is split over multiple lines.

```
DELETE FROM catalog WHERE productionStatus = "Revoked";

DELETE FROM
        catalog
   WHERE productionStatus =

"Revoked";
```

A (My)SQL Tutorial

With the language basics out of the way, let's run through a quick tutorial to get you up to speed on a few more SQL basics. In the following section, we'll design a set of relational tables, create a database to store them, re-create the table design in MySQL, insert records into the database, and query the system to obtain answers to several burning questions.

At this point, we'll encourage you to try out the examples that follow as you're reading along. This process will not only give you some insight into how MySQL works, but it will also teach you the fundamentals of SQL in preparation for the chapters ahead.

Understanding an RDBMS

Let's start at the beginning. Every database is composed of one or more *tables*. These tables, which structure data into rows and columns, are what lend organization to the data.

Here's an example of what a typical table looks like:

```
+-----------+-------+---------+---------+-------------------------+
| member_id | fname | lname   | tel     | email                   |
+-----------+-------+---------+---------+-------------------------+
|         1 | John  | Doe     | 1234567 | jdoe@somewhere.com      |
|         2 | Jane  | Doe     | 8373728 | jane@site.com           |
|         3 | Steve | Klingon | 7449373 | steve@alien-race.com    |
|         4 | Santa | Claus   | 9999999 | santa@the-north-pole.com |
+-----------+-------+---------+---------+-------------------------+
```

As you can see, a table divides data into rows, with a new entry (or *record*) on every row. If you flip back to my original database-as-filing-cabinet analogy in Chapter 1, you'll see that every file in the cabinet corresponds to one row in the table.

The data in each row is further broken down into cells (or *fields*), each of which contains a value for a particular attribute of the data. For example, if you consider the record for the user Steve Klingon, you'll see that the record is clearly divided into separate fields for member ID, first name, last name, phone number, and e-mail address.

The rows within a table are not arranged in any particular order; they can be sorted alphabetically, by ID, by member name, or by any other criteria you choose to specify. Therefore, it becomes necessary that you have some method of identifying a specific record in a table. In our example, each record is identified by a member ID, which is a number unique to each row or record; this unique field is referred to as the *primary key* for that table.

You should note at this point that MySQL is a *relational database management system*, or RDBMS. A relational database is typically composed of multiple tables that contain interrelated pieces of information. SQL allows you to combine the data from these tables in a variety of ways, thereby allowing you to create and analyze new relationships among your data.

What we have in our first example is a single table. While this is fine by itself, it's when you add more tables and relate the information among them that you truly start to see the power inherent in this system. Consider the following example, which adds two more tables; the second contains a list of movies available for rent, while the third links the movies with the members via their primary keys.

```
+-----------+-------+---------+---------+--------------------------+
| member_id | fname | lname   | tel     | email                    |
+-----------+-------+---------+---------+--------------------------+
|         1 | John  | Doe     | 1234567 | jdoe@somewhere.com       |
|         2 | Jane  | Doe     | 8373728 | jane@site.com            |
|         3 | Steve | Klingon | 7449373 | steve@alien-race.com     |
|         4 | Santa | Claus   | 9999999 | santa@the-north-pole.com |
+-----------+-------+---------+---------+--------------------------+
```

```
+----------+---------------------------+------------------+
| video_id | title                     | director         |
+----------+---------------------------+------------------+
|        1 | Star Wars: The Phantom Menace | George Lucas |
|        2 | ET                        | Steven Spielberg |
|        3 | Charlie's Angels          | McG              |
|        4 | Any Given Sunday          | Oliver Stone     |
|        5 | Hollow Man                | Paul Verhoeven   |
|        6 | Woman On Top              | Fina Torres      |
+----------+---------------------------+------------------+
```

```
+-----------+----------+
| member_id | video_id |
+-----------+----------+
|         2 |        6 |
|         4 |        2 |
|         1 |        1 |
|         1 |        2 |
|         1 |        3 |
+-----------+----------+
```

If you take a close look at the third table, you'll see that it links each member with the video(s) he or she has rented. Thus we see that Jane Doe (member #2) has rented *Woman On Top* (video #6), while John Doe (member #1) has decided to spend the weekend on the couch with *Star Wars* (video #1), *ET* (video #2), and *Charlie's Angels* (video #3).

In other words, the third table has set up a relationship between the first and second table; this is the fundamental concept behind a RDBMS. After one or more relationships are set up, it is possible for you to extract a subset of the data (a *data slice*) to answer specific questions.

Creating a Database

If you've understood the concept so far, it's now time for you to get down to brass tacks. Start up your MySQL client. (Note in the following code listings that anything you type appears in boldface.)

```
[user@host]# mysql -u root -p
Password: ******
```

Assuming everything is set up properly and you entered the correct password, you should see a prompt that looks something like this:

```
Welcome to the MySQL monitor.   Commands end with ; or \g.
Your MySQL connection id is 80 to server version: 4.0.9-gamma-standard
Type 'help;' or '\h' for help.
mysql>
```

This is the MySQL command prompt; you'll be using this to enter all your SQL statements. Note that all MySQL commands end with a semicolon or the \g signal and can be entered in either uppercase or lowercase type.

Since all tables are stored in a database, the first command you need to know is the CREATE DATABASE command, which looks like this:

```
CREATE DATABASE database-name
```

Go on and try it out by creating a database called `library`:

```
mysql> CREATE DATABASE library;
Query OK, 1 row affected (0.05 sec)
```

You can view all available databases with the SHOW DATABASES command:

```
mysql> SHOW DATABASES;
+----------+
| Database |
+----------+
| library  |
| mysql    |
| test     |
+----------+
3 rows in set (0.00 sec)
```

Once you have obtained a list of databases, you can select the database you wish to use with the USE command, which looks like this:

```
USE database-name
```

For the moment, we'll restrict our activities to the database you just created:

```
mysql> USE library;
Database changed
```

After you've selected a database, you can view available tables in it with the SHOW TABLES command.

```
mysql> SHOW TABLES;
Empty set (0.00 sec)
```

Because this is a new database, no tables appear yet. Let's fix that.

You can read more about manipulating databases in Chapter 8.

Adding Tables

The SQL command used to create a new table in a database typically looks like this:

```
CREATE TABLE table-name (field-name-1 field-type-1 modifiers,
field-name-2 field-type-2 modifiers, ... , field-name-n
field-type-n modifiers)
```

The table name cannot contain spaces, slashes, or periods; other than this, any character is fair game. Each table (and the data it contains) is stored as a set of three files in your MySQL data directory.

Here's a sample command to create the members table in the example you saw a couple sections back:

```
mysql> CREATE TABLE members (member_id int(11) NOT NULL auto_increment,
fname varchar(50) NOT NULL, lname varchar(50) NOT NULL, tel varchar(15),
email varchar(50) NOT NULL, PRIMARY KEY (member_id));
Query OK, 0 rows affected (0.05 sec)
```

Note that each field name is followed by a "type," which identifies the type of data that will be allowed in that field, and (sometimes) a length value indicating the maximum length of that field. For example, in the first line, the field named member_id is followed by an int type of maximum length 11. MySQL offers a number of different data types to handle different data requirements. Some of the more important ones are summarized in the sidebar "Not My Type."

Not My Type

Following are some of the important data types you'll find when using MySQL:

- **INT**   A numeric type that can accept values in the range of –2147483648 to 2147483647
- **DECIMAL**   A numeric type with support for floating-point or decimal numbers
- **DOUBLE**   A numeric type for double-precision floating-point numbers
- **DATE**   A date field in the *YYYY-MM-DD* format
- **TIME**   A time field in the *HH:MM:SS* format
- **DATETIME**   A combined date/time type in the *YYYY-MM-DD HH:MM:SS* format
- **YEAR**   A field specifically for year displays in the range 1901 to 2155, in either *YYYY* or *YY* format
- **TIMESTAMP**   A timestamp type, in *YYYYMMDDHHMMSS* format
- **CHAR**   A string type with a maximum size of 255 characters and a fixed length
- **VARCHAR**   A string type with a maximum size of 255 characters and a variable length
- **TEXT**   A string type with a maximum size of 65,535 characters
- **BLOB**   A binary type for variable data
- **ENUM**   A string type that can accept one value from a list of previously defined possible values
- **SET**   A string type that can accept zero or more values from a set of previously defined possible values

You can put a few additional constraints (*modifiers*) on your table, to increase the consistency of the data that will be entered into it:

- You can specify whether the field is allowed to be empty or must necessarily be filled with data by placing the NULL and NOT NULL modifiers after each field definition.

- You can specify a primary key for the table with the PRIMARY KEY modifier, which is followed by the name of the column designated as the primary key.

- You can specify that values entered into a field must be "unique"—that is, not duplicated—with the UNIQUE modifier.

- The AUTO_INCREMENT modifier, which is available only for numeric fields, indicates that MySQL should automatically generate a number for that field (by incrementing the previous value by 1).

Now go ahead and create the other two tables using the following SQL statements:

```
mysql> CREATE TABLE videos (video_id int(11) NOT NULL auto_increment,
title varchar(255) NOT NULL, director varchar(255) NOT NULL,
PRIMARY KEY (video_id));
Query OK, 0 rows affected (0.05 sec)
mysql> CREATE TABLE status (member_id int(11) NOT NULL,
video_id tinyint(11) NOT NULL);
Query OK, 0 rows affected (0.05 sec)
```

In case you make a mistake, note that you can alter a table definition with the ALTER TABLE command, which looks like this:

```
ALTER TABLE table-name ADD new-field-name new-field-type
```

On the other hand, if you simply want to modify an existing column, use this:

```
ALTER TABLE table-name MODIFY old-field-name
new-field-type modifiers
```

Just as you can create a table, you can delete a table with the DROP TABLE command, which looks like this:

```
DROP TABLE table-name
```

Here's an example:

```
mysql> DROP TABLE members;
Query OK, 0 rows affected (0.00 sec)
```

This will immediately wipe out the specified table, together with all the data it contains—so use it with care!

You can read more about manipulating tables in Chapter 8.

Adding Records

Once you've created a table, it's time to begin entering data into it, and the SQL command to accomplish this is the INSERT command. The syntax of the INSERT command is as follows:

```
INSERT into table-name (field-name-1, field-name2, field-name-n)
VALUES (value-1, value-2, value-n)
```

Here's an example:

```
mysql> INSERT INTO members (member_id, fname, lname, tel, email)
VALUES (NULL, 'John', 'Doe', '1234567', 'jdoe@somewhere.com');
Query OK, 1 row affected (0.06 sec)
```

You could also use the abbreviated form of the INSERT statement, in which field names are left unspecified:

```
mysql> INSERT INTO members VALUES (NULL, 'John', 'Doe', '1234567',
'jdoe@somewhere.com');
Query OK, 1 row affected (0.06 sec)
```

Here's the flip side: by specifying field names in the INSERT statement, I have the flexibility of inserting values in any order I please. Because of this, the following statements are equivalent:

```
mysql> INSERT INTO members (member_id, fname, lname, tel, email)
VALUES (NULL, 'John', 'Doe', '1234567', 'jdoe@somewhere.com');
Query OK, 1 row affected (0.06 sec)
mysql> INSERT INTO members (fname, lname, email, tel, member_id)
VALUES ('John', 'Doe', 'jdoe@somewhere.com', '1234567', NULL);
Query OK, 1 row affected (0.00 sec)
```

Fields that are not specified will automatically be set to their default values.

Now that you know how to insert records, try inserting some sample records for the three tables, using the sample data in the section titled "Understanding an RDBMS" as reference. (You can also find the SQL commands to build these tables on this book's accompanying website http://www.mysql-tcr.com/.)

PART II

Removing and Modifying Records

Just as you insert records into a table, you can also delete records with the DELETE command, which looks like this:

```
DELETE FROM table-name
```

For example, the command

```
mysql> DELETE FROM members;
Query OK, 0 rows affected (0.06 sec)
```

would delete all the records from the members table.

You can select a specific subset of rows to be deleted by adding the WHERE clause to the DELETE statement. The following example would delete only those records that had a member ID of 16:

```
mysql> DELETE FROM members WHERE member_id = 16;
Query OK, 1 row affected (0.06 sec)
```

And, finally, there's an UPDATE command designed to help you change existing values in a table; it looks like this:

```
UPDATE table-name SET field-name = new-value
```

This command would act on all values in the field *field-name*, changing them all to <new_value>. If you'd like to alter the value in a single field only, you can use the WHERE clause, as with the DELETE command.

Using this knowledge, I could update John Doe's e-mail address in the table:

```
mysql> UPDATE members SET email = 'john@somewhere.com' WHERE member_id = 1;
Query OK, 1 row affected (0.00 sec)
Rows matched: 1  Changed: 1  Warnings: 0
```

You can also alter multiple fields by separating them with commas:

```
mysql> UPDATE members SET email = 'john@somewhere.com',
lname = 'Doe The First' WHERE member_id = 2;
Query OK, 1 row affected (0.05 sec)
Rows matched: 1  Changed: 1  Warnings: 0
```

Notice how MySQL provides you with feedback on the number of records matching your query and the number of rows changed by it.

Executing Queries

Once the data's in the database, it's time to do something with it. MySQL allows you to extract specific "slices" of data from your database using a variety of SELECT statements.

The simplest form of the SELECT query is the "catch-all" query, which returns all the records in a specific table. It looks like this:

```
mysql> SELECT * FROM members;
+-----------+-------+---------+---------+----------------------------+
| member_id | fname | lname   | tel     | email                      |
+-----------+-------+---------+---------+----------------------------+
|         1 | John  | Doe     | 1234567 | jdoe@somewhere.com         |
|         2 | Jane  | Doe     | 8373728 | jane@site.com              |
|         3 | Steve | Klingon | 7449373 | steve@alien-race.com       |
|         4 | Santa | Claus   | 9999999 | santa@the-north-pole.com   |
+-----------+-------+---------+---------+----------------------------+
4 rows in set (0.00 sec)
```

The asterisk (*) indicates that you'd like to see all the columns present in the table. If, instead, you'd prefer to see only one or two specific columns in the result set, you can specify the column name(s) in the SELECT statement, like this:

```
mysql> SELECT lname FROM members;
+---------+
| lname   |
+---------+
| Doe     |
| Doe     |
| Klingon |
| Claus   |
+---------+
4 rows in set (0.00 sec)
```

In most cases, it is preferable to name the explicit fields that you would like to see in the result set. This allows the application to survive structural changes in its table(s), and it is also usually more efficient because MySQL selects only the fields that it needs.

You can eliminate duplicate entries using the DISTINCT keyword; the following query will not display members with the last name "Doe" more than once.

```
mysql> SELECT DISTINCT lname FROM members;
+---------+
| lname   |
+---------+
| Doe     |
| Klingon |
| Claus   |
+---------+
3 rows in set (0.05 sec)
```

Of course, the whole idea of structuring data into rows and columns is to make it easier to get a focused result set. And a great part of that focus comes from the WHERE clause (you may remember this from the UPDATE and DELETE statements you learned in the preceding sections) to the SELECT statement, which allows you to define specific criteria for the result set. Records that do not meet the specified criteria will not appear in the result set.

For example, let's suppose that you want to see a list of all members with the last name "Doe":

```
mysql> SELECT * FROM members WHERE lname = "Doe";
+-----------+-------+-------+---------+--------------------+
| member_id | fname | lname | tel     | email              |
+-----------+-------+-------+---------+--------------------+
|         1 | John  | Doe   | 1234567 | jdoe@somewhere.com |
|         2 | Jane  | Doe   | 8373728 | jane@site.com      |
+-----------+-------+-------+---------+--------------------+
2 rows in set (0.00 sec)
```

Or let's suppose that you want Santa Claus's e-mail address:

```
mysql> SELECT email FROM members WHERE fname = "Santa";
+----------------------------+
| email                      |
+----------------------------+
| santa@the-north-pole.com | |
+----------------------------+
1 row in set (0.06 sec)
```

Or suppose that you want to see a list of all movies by George Lucas:

```
mysql> SELECT title, director FROM videos WHERE director = "George
Lucas";
+-------------------------------+---------------+
| title                         | director      |
+-------------------------------+---------------+
| Star Wars: The Phantom Menace | George Lucas  |
+-------------------------------+---------------+
1 row in set (0.06 sec)
```

(Yes, I know the collection is incomplete. Maybe I should write to Santa for the rest....)

Using Comparison and Logical Operators

You can also use comparison and logical operators to modify your SQL query further. This comes in handy if your table contains a large amount of numeric data, as illustrated here:

```
+-------+------+---------+------------+
| name  | math | physics | literature |
+-------+------+---------+------------+
| john  |   68 |      37 |         45 |
| jim   |   96 |      89 |         92 |
| bill  |   65 |      12 |         57 |
| harry |   69 |      25 |         82 |
+-------+------+---------+------------+
```

The six comparison operators available to use in MySQL are displayed in Table 4-1.

You can also use the logical operators AND, OR, and NOT to create more complex queries. Table 4-2 explains what each one does.

Now, looking at the table of grades, if you wanted to create a list of all students who scored over 90 on their math papers, you could formulate a query that looked like this:

```
mysql> SELECT * FROM grades WHERE math > 90;
+------+------+---------+------------+
| name | math | physics | literature |
+------+------+---------+------------+
| jim  |   96 |      89 |         92 |
+------+------+---------+------------+
1 row in set (0.00 sec)
```

Suppose you wanted to identify the smartest kid in class (you know this guy—he always sits in the front row, answers every question perfectly, and usually has wires on his teeth).

```
mysql> SELECT name FROM grades WHERE math > 85
AND physics > 85 AND literature > 85;
+------+
| name |
+------+
| jim  |
+------+
1 row in set (0.00 sec)
```

TABLE 4-1
MySQL
Comparison
Operators

Operator	What It Means
=	Is equal to
!=	Is not equal to
>	Is greater than
<	Is less than
>=	Is greater than/equal to
<=	Is less than/equal to

Operator	What It Means
AND	All of the specified conditions must match.
OR	Any of the specified conditions must match.
NOT	Invert the condition.

TABLE 4-2
MySQL Logical
Operators

What if you needed to identify the students who flunked at least one subject?

```
mysql> SELECT * FROM grades WHERE math <= 25
OR physics <= 25 OR literature <= 25;
+--------+------+---------+------------+
| name   | math | physics | literature |
+--------+------+---------+------------+
| bill   |   65 |      12 |         57 |
| harry  |   69 |      25 |         82 |
+--------+------+---------+------------+
2 rows in set (0.00 sec)
```

And finally, you can also perform basic mathematical operations within your query; the next example demonstrates how the three grades can be added together to create a total grade:

```
mysql> SELECT name, math+physics+literature FROM grades;
+--------+-------------------------+
| name   | math+physics+literature |
+--------+-------------------------+
| john   |                     150 |
| jim    |                     277 |
| bill   |                     134 |
| harry  |                     176 |
+--------+-------------------------+
4 rows in set (0.05 sec)
```

Obviously, such an operation should be attempted only on fields of the same type.

Using Built-In Functions

MySQL also offers a bunch of built-in functions that come in handy when you're trying to obtain numeric totals and averages of specific fields. The first of these is the useful COUNT() function, which counts the number of records in the result set and displays this total.

Consider the following example, which displays the total number of records in the videos table:

```
mysql> SELECT COUNT(*) FROM videos;
+----------+
| COUNT(*) |
+----------+
|        6 |
+----------+
1 row in set (0.00 sec)
```

This comes in handy when you quickly need to calculate the total number of records in a table.

The SUM() function calculates the sum of the values in the result set, while the AVG() function calculates the average. For example, if you wanted to calculate the average grade in math, physics, and literature, you could use a query like this:

```
mysql> SELECT AVG(math), AVG(physics), AVG(literature) FROM grades;
+-----------+--------------+-----------------+
| AVG(math) | AVG(physics) | AVG(literature) |
+-----------+--------------+-----------------+
|   74.5000 |      40.7500 |         69.0000 |
+-----------+--------------+-----------------+
1 row in set (0.00 sec)
```

You can identify the smallest and largest value in a specific column with the MIN() and MAX() functions. The following queries display the lowest and highest grade in math, respectively:

```
mysql> SELECT MIN(math) FROM grades;
+-----------+
| MIN(math) |
+-----------+
|        65 |
+-----------+
1 row in set (0.00 sec)
```

```
mysql> SELECT MAX(math) FROM grades;
+-----------+
| MAX(math) |
+-----------+
|        96 |
+-----------+
1 row in set (0.00 sec)
```

You can read more about MySQL's built-in functions in Chapter 7.

Ordering and Limiting Result Sets

If you'd like to see the data from your table ordered by a specific field, MySQL offers the ORDER BY construct. This construct allows you to specify both the column name and the direction (ascending or descending) in which you would like to see data displayed

For example, if you'd like to see data from the members table arranged by ID, you could try this:

```
mysql> SELECT * FROM members ORDER BY member_id;
+-----------+-------+---------+---------+----------------------------+
| member_id | fname | lname   | tel     | email                      |
+-----------+-------+---------+---------+----------------------------+
|         1 | John  | Doe     | 1234567 | jdoe@somewhere.com         |
|         2 | Jane  | Doe     | 8373728 | jane@site.com              |
|         3 | Steve | Klingon | 7449373 | steve@alien-race.com       |
|         4 | Santa | Claus   | 9999999 | santa@the-north-pole.com   |
+-----------+-------+---------+---------+----------------------------+
4 rows in set (0.06 sec)
```

You could reverse the order with the additional DESC modifier:

```
mysql> SELECT * FROM members ORDER BY member_id DESC;
+-----------+-------+---------+---------+----------------------------+
| member_id | fname | lname   | tel     | email                      |
+-----------+-------+---------+---------+----------------------------+
|         4 | Santa | Claus   | 9999999 | santa@the-north-pole.com   |
|         3 | Steve | Klingon | 7449373 | steve@alien-race.com       |
|         2 | Jane  | Doe     | 8373728 | jane@site.com              |
|         1 | John  | Doe     | 1234567 | jdoe@somewhere.com         |
+-----------+-------+---------+---------+----------------------------+
4 rows in set (0.00 sec)
```

You can limit the number of records in the result set with the LIMIT keyword. This keyword takes two parameters, which specify the row to start with and the number of rows to display. So the query

```
SELECT * FROM videos LIMIT 2,2;
```

would return rows 3 and 4 from the result set.

```
mysql> SELECT * FROM videos LIMIT 2,2;
+----------+------------------+--------------+
| video_id | title            | director     |
+----------+------------------+--------------+
|        3 | Charlie's Angels | McG          |
|        4 | Any Given Sunday | Oliver Stone |
+----------+------------------+--------------+
2 rows in set (0.00 sec)
```

You can combine the ORDER BY and LIMIT constructs to get the four newest records in the table quickly, as the following example demonstrates:

```
mysql> SELECT * FROM videos ORDER BY video_id DESC LIMIT 0, 4;
+----------+-----------------+-----------------+
| video_id | title           | director        |
+----------+-----------------+-----------------+
|        6 | Woman On Top    | Fina Torres     |
|        5 | Hollow Man      | Paul Verhoeven  |
|        4 | Any Given Sunday| Oliver Stone    |
|        3 | Charlie's Angels| McG             |
+----------+-----------------+-----------------+
4 rows in set (0.00 sec)
```

Using Wildcards

MySQL also supports the LIKE keyword, which is used to return results from a wildcard search and comes in handy when you're not sure what you're looking for. Two types of wildcards are allowed in a LIKE construct: the % (percent) character, which is used to signify zero or more occurrences of a character, and the _ (underscore) character, which is used to signify exactly one occurrence of a character.

Let's suppose I wanted a list of all members whose first names contained the letter *e*. My query would look like this:

```
mysql> SELECT * FROM members WHERE fname LIKE '%e%';
+-----------+-------+---------+---------+----------------------+
| member_id | fname | lname   | tel     | email                |
+-----------+-------+---------+---------+----------------------+
|         2 | Jane  | Doe     | 8373728 | jane@site.com        |
|         3 | Steve | Klingon | 7449373 | steve@alien-race.com |
+-----------+-------+---------+---------+----------------------+
2 rows in set (0.16 sec)
```

I could also use this technique to search through my videos collection for movies containing the word segment *man* in their title.

```
mysql> SELECT title, director FROM videos WHERE title LIKE '%man%';
+--------------+----------------+
| title        | director       |
+--------------+----------------+
| Hollow Man   | Paul Verhoeven |
| Woman On Top | Fina Torres    |
+--------------+----------------+
2 rows in set (0.05 sec)
```

You can read more about executing queries and manipulating table data in Chapter 9.

> **Like, You Know, Man...**
>
> It should be noted that the ...LIKE %string%... construct is generally considered an inefficient and suboptimal way of performing a full-text search, as MySQL is not able to use keys for lookup in this case. The recommended approach in this case is to use full-text indices and a MATCH AGAINST command instead (see Chapter 8 for more on this).

Joining Tables

So far, all the queries you've seen have been concentrated on a single table. But SQL also allows you to query two or more tables at a time and display a combined result set. This is technically referred to as a *join*, since it involves "joining" different tables at specific points to create new views of the data.

When using a join, it's recommended that you prefix each column name with the name of the table to which it belongs. (I haven't done this in any of the examples you've seen so far because all the columns have been localized to a single table.) For example, you would use members.fname to refer to the column named fname in the table members, and you'd use status.video_id to refer to the video_id column in the status table.

Here's an example of a simple join:

```
mysql> SELECT member_id, video_id, fname FROM status, members WHERE
status.member_id = members.member_id;
+-----------+----------+-------+
| member_id | video_id | fname |
+-----------+----------+-------+
|         1 |        1 | John  |
|         1 |        2 | John  |
|         1 |        3 | John  |
|         2 |        6 | Jane  |
|         4 |        2 | Santa |
+-----------+----------+-------+
5 rows in set (0.00 sec)
```

In this case, the status and members tables have been joined together through the common column member_id.

You can specify the columns you'd like to see from the joined tables, as with any SELECT statement:

```
mysql> SELECT fname, lname, video_id FROM members, status WHERE
members.member_id = status.member_id;
+-------+-------+----------+
| fname | lname | video_id |
+-------+-------+----------+
| Jane  | Doe   |        6 |
| Santa | Claus |        2 |
| John  | Doe   |        1 |
| John  | Doe   |        2 |
| John  | Doe   |        3 |
+-------+-------+----------+
5 rows in set (0.16 sec)
```

You can also join three tables together. The following example uses the `status`
table, combined with member information and video details, to create a composite
table that displays which members have which videos.

```
mysql> SELECT fname, lname, title FROM members, videos, status WHERE
status.member_id = members.member_id AND status.video_id =
videos.video_id;
+-------+-------+------------------------------+
| fname | lname | title                        |
+-------+-------+------------------------------+
| Jane  | Doe   | Woman On Top                 |
| Santa | Claus | ET                           |
| John  | Doe   | Star Wars: The Phantom Menace|
| John  | Doe   | ET                           |
| John  | Doe   | Charlie's Angels             |
+-------+-------+------------------------------+
5 rows in set (0.17 sec)
```

You can read about more advanced aspects of data retrieval and manipulation, such
as joins, subqueries and transactions, in Chapters 10, 11 and 12.

Joined at the Hip

Note that, when joining tables, it is important to ensure that each join has an
associated constraint that permits the use of a key. Otherwise, performance will
degrade exponentially as tables grow in size.

Linking Out

Interested in learning more about SQL? Here are a few resources, both online and offline, to help you get started:

- *SQL Tutorial* `http://www.w3schools.com/sql/default.asp`
- *A Gentle Introduction to SQL* `http://www.w3schools.com/sql/default.asp`
- *An Interactive Online SQL Course* `http://www.sqlcourse.com/`
- *The SQL.org Portal* `http://www.sql.org/`
- *SQL A Beginner's Guide, Second Edition* by Robert Sheldon (ISBN: 0072228857), McGraw-Hill\Osborne
- *SQL The Complete Reference, Second Edition* by James Groff and Paul Weinberg (ISBN: 0072225599), McGraw-Hill\Osborne
- *Introduction to Relational Databases and SQL Programming* by Christopher Allen, Simon Chatwin and Catherine Creary (ISBN: 0072229241), McGraw-Hill Technology Education

Aliasing Table Names

If the thought of writing long table names over and over again doesn't appeal to you, you can assign simple aliases to each table and use these instead. The following example assigns the aliases m, s, and v to the members, status, and videos tables, respectively.

```
mysql> SELECT m.fname, m.lname, v.title FROM members m, status s,
videos v WHERE s.member_id = m.member_id AND s.video_id = v.video_id;
+-------+-------+-----------------------------+
| fname | lname | title                       |
+-------+-------+-----------------------------+
| Jane  | Doe   | Woman On Top                |
| Santa | Claus | ET                          |
| John  | Doe   | Star Wars: The Phantom Menace |
| John  | Doe   | ET                          |
| John  | Doe   | Charlie's Angels            |
+-------+-------+-----------------------------+
5 rows in set (0.00 sec)
```

Summary

Over the course of the last few pages, you were briefly introduced to SQL, its history, features, and syntax. We took you on a whirlwind tour of the language, showing you how to create databases and tables; insert, modify, and delete records; and execute queries. We showed you how to create simple queries that return all the records in a table, and then modify those simple queries with operators, wildcards, joins, and built-in functions to filter down to the precise data you need.

This chapter was intended as an overview of MySQL and a primer for the more detailed material ahead. Over the next few chapters, the introductory material in this chapter is discussed in depth, with specific focus on MySQL's particular dialect of SQL.

MySQL Data Types

After the brief SQL tutorial in Chapter 4, you should now have a clearer idea of what SQL can do and how it fits into the larger context of MySQL database management and usage. With the introductory material out of the way, it's now time to delve deeper into specific aspects of the MySQL command set.

You might remember from the previous chapter that every column of a MySQL table incorporates, as one of its primary attributes, a data type. This data type plays an important role in enforcing the integrity of the data in a MySQL database and in making this data easier to use and manipulate. This chapter discusses the various data types provided by MySQL, together with examples that illustrate how they can be used.

The Need and Rationale for Data Types

Before we get into the nitty-gritty of numeric and string data types, it's a good idea to step back and examine the real-world benefits of data typing in MySQL (or, for that matter, any other RDBMS).

The most significant arguments for data typing in the RDBMS world relate to efficiency (in data storage) and speed (in data retrieval). To understand this, consider the inverse argument: Assume a system in which data types did not exist, and all data was stored as character, or string, data. In such a system, every number—integers, dates, currency units—would be stored as a string and would take up disk space equal to the number of bytes in the string. Therefore, the number 12,345,678,987,654,321 would take up 17 bytes, while the date 06-04-1978 would take up 10 bytes (or more, if you decided to store each element of the date in a separate column).

Further, numbers or dates represented as strings would not lend themselves to easy manipulation; adding, subtracting, or multiplying this data would be a complicated and unwieldy task, requiring the developer first to convert the string into a numeric type and then perform calculations on it. Obviously, performing comparison or equality tests on numbers or dates represented as strings would also become difficult; the truth of the comparison test 13 > 2 is obvious, but it's far more difficult to gauge the truth of "13" > "2" with any degree of confidence. In a similar manner, while it's fairly obvious that April 1 2003, represented as 01-04-2003, arrives before September 1 2004, represented as 01-09-2004, it's far more difficult to perform this test computationally when both dates are represented as strings and the system doesn't know how to separate the date, month, and year components from each other.

Data typing solves all these problems. By enforcing a consistent schema for different types of data, it makes it possible for the system to recognize a particular piece of data as belonging to a particular type, and thereby use its knowledge of that type's attributes to manipulate it. For example, if the value 01-04-2003 is tagged as belonging to the known type DATE, and the system has built-in rules telling it how to deal with a DATE type, manipulating the value—comparing it to other DATEs, adding days or months to it, and identifying invalid values—becomes far easier.

Strong data typing associates particular behaviors with each type and enforces these behaviors as a guard against human error. The most common example of this involves adding strings and numbers together. A weakly typed language would permit this; a strongly typed language would immediately flag it as a violation of the system's integrity and refuse to allow it. Data typing can thus eliminate ambiguity in how different pieces of data interact with each other, and it can reduce the amount of code a developer has to write to maintain the integrity of the system.

Data typing also leads to a more efficient use of space, resulting in smaller storage requirements and, simultaneously, an increase in performance. For example, if the system was able to recognize the value 12,345,678,987,654,321 as a number, instead of a string, it could store it in a more efficient form (an 8-byte integer rather than a 17-byte string), thereby taking up less space and making arithmetic operations on it far simpler. The impact on performance will be no less significant: an 8-byte integer value can be processed faster than a 17-byte string value. Add up all the bytes you save, and you'll see why using data types can provide significant advantages over the alternative.

Like all good swords, though, data typing cuts both ways. Intelligent use of this capability can result in smaller databases and tables, efficient indexing, and quicker query execution; indifferent, ham-handed use of types can result in bloated tables, wastage of storage space, inefficient indexing, and a gradual deterioration in performance. Wise database designers, therefore, make it a point to be fully aware of the various data types available in a system, together with the limitations and benefits of each, prior to implementing a database-driven application; the alternative can be costly in terms of both time and money.

With that in mind, let's now proceed to a detailed discussion of the various data types available in MySQL.

MySQL Data Types

You might remember, from the previous chapter, how every field in a table has a data type associated with it. This data type defines the kind of data that the field can hold and helps to enforce table consistency and integrity. MySQL supports a diverse array of data types, which can be classified into the following four broad categories:

- Numeric types

- String types
- Date and time types
- Complex types

The following sections examine each of these categories in greater detail.

Numeric Types

MySQL's numeric data types can broadly be divided into two categories, one for integers and the other for floating-point or decimal numbers. A number of different sub-types are available for each of these categories, each holding different sizes of data, and MySQL also allows you to specify whether the values in numeric fields should be signed or padded with zeroes.

Table 5-1 lists the various numeric types, together with the allowed range and memory space used for each.

Type	Size	Range (Signed)	Range (Unsigned)	Used for
TINYINT	1 byte	(−128, 127)	(0, 255)	Small integer values
SMALLINT	2 bytes	(−32768, 32767)	(0, 65535)	Large integer values
MEDIUMINT	3 bytes	(−8388608, 8388607)	(0, 16777215)	Large integer values
INT aka INTEGER	4 bytes	(−2147483648, 2147483647)	(0, 4294967295)	Large integer values
BIGINT	8 bytes	(−9223372036854775808, 9223372036854775807)	(0, 18446744073709551615)	Extremely large integer values
FLOAT	4 bytes	(−3.402823466E+38, 1.175494351E-38), 0, (1.175494351E-38, 3.402823466E+38)	0, (1.175494351E-38, 3.402823466E+38)	Single-precision floating-point values
DOUBLE aka REAL, DOUBLE PRECISION	8 bytes	(1.7976931348623157E+308, 2.2250738585072014E-308), 0, (2.2250738585072014E-308, 1.7976931348623157E+308)	0, (2.2250738585072014E-308, 1.7976931348623157E+308)	Double-precision floating-point values
DECIMAL aka DEC, NUMERIC	For "DECIMAL(M,D) columns, "M+2 if ("M "> "D) else "D+2	Depends on values of M and D	Depends on values of M and D	Decimal values

TABLE 5-1   MySQL Numeric Types

The INT Type

The five main integer types supported in MySQL are TINYINT, SMALLINT, MEDIUMINT, INT, and BIGINT. These types are largely identical, differing from each other only in the size of the values they can store. Consider the following example, which demonstrates:

```
mysql>  CREATE TABLE data (fti TINYINT, fsi SMALLINT,
fmi MEDIUMINT, fi INT, fbi BIGINT);
Query OK, 0 rows affected (0.00 sec)

mysql> INSERT INTO data VALUES (123456789, 123456789,
123456789, 123456789, 12345678987654321);
Query OK, 1 row affected (0.00 sec)

mysql> INSERT INTO data VALUES (-123456789, -123456789,
-123456789, -123456789, -12345678987654321);
Query OK, 1 row affected (0.00 sec)

mysql> SELECT * FROM data;
+------+--------+----------+------------+--------------------+
| fti  | fsi    | fmi      | fi         | fbi                |
+------+--------+----------+------------+--------------------+
|  127 |  32767 |  8388607 |  123456789 |  12345678987654321 |
| -128 | -32768 | -8388608 | -123456789 | -12345678987654321 |
+------+--------+----------+------------+--------------------+
2 rows in set (0.00 sec)
```

MySQL supports a proprietary extension to the SQL standard in the form of an optional display width specifier, which makes it possible to pad a value to a specified length when it is retrieved from the database. For example, specifying a field as type INT(6) ensures that values that contain less than six digits are automatically padded with spaces when they are retrieved from the database. The following examples demonstrate:

```
mysql> CREATE TABLE data ( age INT(7) );
Query OK, 0 rows affected (0.06 sec)

mysql> INSERT INTO data VALUES (19);
Query OK, 1 row affected (0.00 sec)

mysql> SELECT age FROM data;
+------+
| age  |
+------+
|   19 |
+------+
1 row in set (0.06 sec)
```

Zero Cool

Can't see the padding? Try using the special ZEROFILL modifier, discussed in "The Number Game" sidebar below.

Note that using a width specifier does not affect the size of the field or the range of values it can store.

In case you attempt to store a number that is outside the allowed numeric range for a particular field, MySQL will truncate it to the closest end of the range and store that truncated value instead. Consider the following example, which demonstrates by attempting to store a very large value in a TINYINT field:

```
mysql> CREATE TABLE data ( id TINYINT );
Query OK, 0 rows affected (0.00 sec)

mysql> INSERT INTO data VALUES (123456789);
Query OK, 1 row affected (0.00 sec)

mysql> SELECT id FROM data;
+------+
| id   |
+------+
|  127 |
+------+
1 row in set (0.00 sec)
```

The Number Game

Wondering how the number ranges in Table 5-1 are calculated? It's pretty simple—just use the formula $(2^{(n-1)})*-1$ to $(2^{(n-1)})-1$ for unsigned ranges, and 0 to $(2^n)-1$ for signed ranges, where n is the size in bits. So, to calculate the range for an INT type, which is a 4-byte (32-bit) type, you would use

```
(2^31)*-1 to (2^31)-1 = -2147483648 to 2147483647
```

to obtain the unsigned range, and

```
0 to (2^32)-1 = 0 to 4294967295
```

to obtain the signed range.

Additionally, MySQL will automatically convert illegal values to 0 prior to inserting them into a table. The following example demonstrates, by attempting to insert a string into a field defined as INT:

```
mysql> CREATE TABLE data ( age INT );
Query OK, 0 rows affected (0.05 sec)

mysql> INSERT INTO data VALUES ("polly says golly!" );
Query OK, 1 row affected (0.00 sec)

mysql> SELECT age FROM data;
+--------+
| age    |
+--------+
|      0 |
+--------+
1 row in set (0.00 sec)
```

Each integer type also accepts one or both of the following modifiers, which can affect the way in which they are displayed and stored:

- The UNSIGNED modifier specifies that the field should hold only positive values, and it can increase the range of values supported by that field.

- The ZEROFILL modifier specifies that zeroes (rather than spaces) should be used to pad output values. Note that using this modifier prevents MySQL from storing negative values.

Consider the following examples, which demonstrate how these modifiers work in practice:

```
mysql> CREATE TABLE data (fi INT, fiu INT UNSIGNED, fiz INT ZEROFILL,
fiuz INT UNSIGNED ZEROFILL);
Query OK, 0 rows affected (0.11 sec)
mysql> INSERT INTO data VALUES (10, 10, 10, 10),
-> (-10, -10, -10, -10),
-> (2147483647, 2147483647, 2147483647, 2147483647),
-> (3004005006, 3004005006, 3004005006, 3004005006);
Query OK, 4 rows affected (0.06 sec)
mysql> SELECT * FROM data;
+------------+------------+------------+------------+
| fi         | fiu        | fiz        | fiuz       |
+------------+------------+------------+------------+
|         10 |         10 | 0000000010 | 0000000010 |
|        -10 |          0 | 0000000000 | 0000000000 |
| 2147483647 | 2147483647 | 2147483647 | 2147483647 |
| 2147483647 | 3004005006 | 3004005006 | 3004005006 |
+------------+------------+------------+------------+
4 rows in set (0.11 sec)
```

The FLOAT, DOUBLE, and DECIMAL Types

The three floating-point types supported in MySQL are FLOAT, DOUBLE, and DECIMAL. The FLOAT numeric type is used to represent a single-precision floating-point number, while the DOUBLE data type is used to represent a double-precision floating-point number.

As with integer types, these types also accept additional arguments: a display width specifier and a decimal point specifier. For example, the declaration FLOAT (5,2) specifies that displayed values will not contain more than 5 digits, with 2 digits after the decimal point. Consider the following examples, which demonstrate:

```
mysql> CREATE TABLE data ( price FLOAT(5,2) );
Query OK, 0 rows affected (0.00 sec)

mysql> INSERT INTO data VALUES (13.6), (876.90), (-5.2), (-12345.678);
Query OK, 4 rows affected (0.00 sec)
Records: 4  Duplicates: 0  Warnings: 0

mysql> SELECT price FROM data;
+-----------+
| price     |
+-----------+
|     13.60 |
|    876.90 |
|     -5.20 |
| -12345.68 |
+-----------+
4 rows in set (0.00 sec)
```

Values that contain more than the allowed number of digits after the decimal point are automatically rounded to the nearest value and then inserted. The following example demonstrates:

```
mysql> CREATE TABLE data ( speed FLOAT (3,1) );
Query OK, 0 rows affected (0.00 sec)

mysql> INSERT INTO data VALUES (123.765);
Query OK, 1 row affected (0.00 sec)

mysql> SELECT speed FROM data;
+---------+
| speed   |
+---------+
|   123.8 |
+---------+
1 row in set (0.05 sec)
```

DECIMAL data types are used in calculations that require extreme accuracy, and they allow you to specify both the *precision* and *scale* of values as optional arguments.

The *precision* here refers to the total number of significant digits to be stored for the value, while the *scale* represents the number of digits after the decimal point. For example, the declaration DECIMAL (5,2) specifies that stored values will not contain more than 5 digits, with 2 digits after the decimal point. Consider the following example, which demonstrates:

```
mysql> CREATE TABLE data ( radius DECIMAL (6,3) );
Query OK, 0 rows affected (0.00 sec)

mysql> INSERT INTO data VALUES (1);
Query OK, 1 row affected (0.00 sec)

mysql> SELECT radius FROM data;
+-----------+
|    radius |
+-----------+
|     1.000 |
+-----------+
1 row in set (0.00 sec)
```

NOTE   *MySQL internally stores DECIMAL data types as character strings to more precisely retain their values.*

Omitting the precision and scale specifiers for DECIMAL types will cause MySQL to default to a precision of 10 and a scale of 0 for all fields flagged as that type:

```
mysql> CREATE TABLE data ( f_decimal DECIMAL );
Query OK, 0 rows affected (0.00 sec)

mysql> DESCRIBE data;
+-----------+---------------+
| Field     | Type          |
+-----------+---------------+
| f_decimal | decimal(10,0) |
+-----------+---------------+
1 row in set (0.00 sec)
```

UNSIGNED and ZEROFILL modifiers are accepted for FLOAT, DECIMAL, and DOUBLE data types, too; their effect is as described in the previous section.

String Types

MySQL comes with eight basic string types, which can be used to store string data ranging from simple one-character strings to large blocks of text or binary data. Table 5-2 lists these types.

Type	Size	Used for
CHAR	0 to 255 bytes	Fixed-length strings
VARCHAR	0 to 255 bytes	Variable-length strings
TINYBLOB	0 to 255 bytes	Binary strings not exceeding 255 characters
TINYTEXT	0 to 255 bytes	Short text strings
BLOB	0 to 65535 bytes	Longer text data in binary form
TEXT	0 to 65535 bytes	Longer text data
MEDIUMBLOB	0 to 16777215 bytes	Medium-length text data in binary form
MEDIUMTEXT	0 to 16777215 bytes	Medium-length text data
LONGBLOB	0 to 4294967295 bytes	Extremely large text data in binary form
LONGTEXT	0 to 4294967295 bytes	Extremely large text data

TABLE 5-2   MySQL String Types

The following sections examine these types in detail.

The CHAR and VARCHAR Types

The simplest of the types listed in Table 5-2 is the CHAR type, which is used for fixed-length strings and must be declared with a size specifier in parentheses. This size specifier can range from 0 to 255 and specifies the length of the value to be stored—for example, the declaration CHAR(10) specifies a value 10 characters in length. Values smaller than the specified length will be right-padded with spaces; values larger than the specified length will be automatically truncated. The following example demonstrates both cases:

```
mysql> CREATE TABLE data ( alphabet CHAR(10) );
Query OK, 0 rows affected (0.00 sec)

mysql> INSERT INTO data VALUES ('abcdefghijklmno');
Query OK, 1 row affected (0.00 sec)

mysql> INSERT INTO data VALUES ('abc');
Query OK, 1 row affected (0.00 sec)

mysql> SELECT alphabet FROM data;
+------------+
| alphabet   |
+------------+
| abcdefghij |
| abc        |
+------------+
2 rows in set (0.00 sec)
```

The CHAR type accepts an optional BINARY modifier that causes it to behave in a binary (rather than the traditional case-insensitive) fashion when used in comparisons. The following example demonstrates:

```
mysql> CREATE TABLE data ( name CHAR(5) );
Query OK, 0 rows affected (0.06 sec)

mysql> INSERT INTO data VALUES ('HUGO');
Query OK, 1 row affected (0.00 sec)

mysql> SELECT * FROM data WHERE name = 'hugo';
+---------+
| name    |
+---------+
| HUGO    |
+---------+
1 row in set (0.06 sec)
```

So MySQL is able to perform a case-insensitive match between the strings 'hugo' and 'HUGO' when using a regular CHAR field. Now look what happens when you change to a CHAR BINARY type:

```
mysql> ALTER TABLE data CHANGE name name CHAR(5) BINARY;
Query OK, 1 row affected (0.11 sec)
Records: 1  Duplicates: 0  Warnings: 0
```

Try the query again:

```
mysql> SELECT * FROM data WHERE name = 'hugo';
Empty set (0.00 sec)
```

Since the field is now using a binary type, MySQL performs a binary comparison, which obviously fails due to a case mismatch.

A variant of the CHAR type is the VARCHAR type, which is useful for variable-length strings; it, too, must be accompanied with a size specifier in the range 0 to 255. The difference between CHAR and VARCHAR, however, arises from the manner in which this specifier is treated by MySQL: the CHAR type treats this as the *exact* size for values (and pads shorter values with spaces so that they achieve this size), while the VARCHAR type treats this as the *maximum* size for values and uses only the number of bytes actually needed to store the string (plus one extra byte to record the length). Thus, shorter values are not padded with spaces when inserted into a field declared as type VARCHAR. (Longer values are, however, still truncated.)

Because fields can grow and shrink dynamically based on their contents, it's considered a good idea to use this type when you're not sure how many characters your field will store; since VARCHAR uses only the minimum number of bytes necessary, it can result in greater storage efficiency and (perhaps) a marginal improvement in the performance of your database.

As with CHAR, the VARCHAR type may also be supplied with an optional BINARY modifier, which behaves as described previously.

The TEXT and BLOB Types

For longer strings—that is, strings greater than 255 characters in length—MySQL provides both BLOB (Binary Large Object) and TEXT types, each with different subtypes depending on the size of the data to be stored. These large-sized types are useful for storing large blocks of text or binary data such as image or audio files.

BLOB and TEXT types differ from each other in the manner in which they are sorted and compared: case-sensitive for BLOB-type values, and case-insensitive for TEXT-type values. The MySQL manual puts it best when it says "...a TEXT is a case-insensitive BLOB."[1]

Size specifiers are not used with the various BLOB and TEXT subtypes. Values that are larger than the maximum size supported by the specified type will be automatically truncated.

Date and Time Types

MySQL comes with five different data types to choose from when dealing with date and time values; these can broadly be classified into simple date or time types and hybrid date/time types. Subtypes are available in each of these categories, depending on the amount of precision required of the value, and MySQL comes with built-in intelligence to recognize and convert varying input formats into a standard format for ease of use and manipulation.

Table 5-3 lists the various date and time data types, together with their allowed ranges and formats.

When Size Does Matter

The MySQL engine sometimes automatically (and silently) alters CHAR and VARCHAR field types to achieve better storage efficiency and performance. Two possible types of conversions occur here:

- VARCHAR fields with a maximum field length less than four characters are automatically converted to CHAR fields.

- CHAR fields with a minimum field length of three characters, in rows containing at least one variable-length field, such as VARCHAR, TEXT, or BLOB, are automatically converted to VARCHAR fields.

---

[1] See the MySQL manual, at http://www.mysql.com/documentation/

Type	Size (bytes)	Range	Format	Used for
DATE	3	1000-01-01 to 9999-12-31	YYYY-MM-DD	Date values
TIME	3	'-838:59:59' to '838:59:59'	HH:MM:SS	Time values or durations
YEAR	1	1901 to 2155	YYYY	Year values
DATETIME	8	1000-01-01 00:00:00 to 9999-12-31 23:59:59	YYYY-MM-DD HH:MM:SS	Combined date and time values
TIMESTAMP	8	1970-01-01 00:00:00 to sometime in the year 2037	YYYYMMDDHHMMSS	Combined date and time values, timestamps

TABLE 5-3   MySQL Date Types

The following sections discuss these types in greater detail.

The DATE, TIME, and YEAR Types

MySQL represents simple date values with the DATE and YEAR types, while time values are represented using the TIME type. These values may be specified as either strings or sequences of nondelimited integers; if specified as strings, values of type DATE should be separated using hyphens (-) as delimiters, while values of type TIME should be separated using colons (:) as delimiters.

The following examples illustrate how these types work:

```
mysql> CREATE TABLE data ( birthday DATE );
Query OK, 0 rows affected (0.00 sec)

mysql> INSERT INTO data VALUES ('2003-03-04'), (20030304);
Query OK, 2 rows affected (0.06 sec)


mysql> SELECT birthday FROM data;
+------------+
| birthday   |
+------------+
| 2003-03-04 |
| 2003-03-04 |
+------------+
2 rows in set (0.00 sec)

mysql> DROP TABLE data;
Query OK, 0 rows affected (0.00 sec)
```

```
mysql> CREATE TABLE data ( showtime TIME );
Query OK, 0 rows affected (0.00 sec)

mysql> INSERT INTO data VALUES ('12:30:56'), ('12:30'), (123056);
Query OK, 3 rows affected (0.00 sec)


mysql> SELECT showtime FROM data;
+----------+
| showtime |
+----------+
| 12:30:56 |
| 12:30:00 |
| 12:30:56 |
+----------+
3 rows in set (0.00 sec)
```

Note that TIME values specified without colon delimiters may be interpreted by MySQL as durations rather than timestamps, which can sometimes confuse the unwary—as demonstrated in the following example:

```
mysql> CREATE TABLE data ( t TIME );
Query OK, 0 rows affected (0.00 sec)

mysql> INSERT INTO data VALUES (1230);
Query OK, 1 row affected (0.00 sec)

mysql> SELECT t FROM data;
+----------+
| t        |
+----------+
| 00:12:30 |
+----------+
1 row in set (0.00 sec)
```

Although MySQL returns date and time values using the formats specified in Table 5-3, it has the ability to accept input in formats that do not correspond exactly with those in the table. In such situations, MySQL makes a best-guess estimate about the date or time the input value is supposed to represent. Consider the following examples, which illustrate how these estimates work:

```
mysql> CREATE TABLE data (
    -> f_date DATE,
    -> f_time TIME
    -> );
Query OK, 0 rows affected (0.00 sec)
```

```
mysql> INSERT INTO data VALUES ('1978-4-6', 123403);
Query OK, 1 row affected (0.00 sec)

mysql> INSERT INTO data VALUES (650503,'3:4:5');
Query OK, 1 row affected (0.00 sec)

mysql> SELECT * FROM data;
+------------+----------+
| f_date     | f_time   |
+------------+----------+
| 1978-04-06 | 12:34:03 |
| 2065-05-03 | 03:04:05 |
+------------+----------+
2 rows in set (0.06 sec)
```

MySQL also performs this type of best-guess interpretation for two-digit values in the year component of a date, or for two-digit input to fields declared as type YEAR. Since all YEAR values must be stored using four digits, MySQL attempts to convert two-digit year values into four-digit values based on the numeric range of the value: values in the range 00–69 are converted to 2000–2069, while values in the range 70–99 and converted to 1970–1979. The following example demonstrates:

```
mysql> CREATE TABLE data ( graduation YEAR );
Query OK, 0 rows affected (0.00 sec)

mysql> INSERT INTO data VALUES (2003), (04), (9), (53), (96);
Query OK, 5 rows affected (0.05 sec)
Records: 5  Duplicates: 0  Warnings: 0

mysql> SELECT graduation FROM data;
+------------+
| graduation |
+------------+
|       2003 |
|       2004 |
|       2009 |
|       2053 |
|       1996 |
+------------+
5 rows in set (0.00 sec)
```

If this type of conversion is not what you want, you should use four-digit year values so that MySQL does not attempt this kind of date conversion.

The DATETIME and TIMESTAMP Types

In additional to data types for dates and times, MySQL also supports a hybrid of the two with its DATETIME and TIMESTAMP data types, which can store both dates and times as components of a single value. The following examples demonstrate:

```
mysql> CREATE TABLE data (
    -> f_date_time DATETIME,
    -> f_time_stamp TIMESTAMP
    -> );
Query OK, 0 rows affected (0.05 sec)

mysql> INSERT INTO data VALUES ('1999-03-12 12:30:12',
'2002-03-09 16:17:18');
Query OK, 1 row affected (0.00 sec)

mysql> INSERT INTO data VALUES (19990312123012, 20020309161718);
Query OK, 1 row affected (0.00 sec)

mysql> INSERT INTO data VALUES (NOW(), NULL);
Query OK, 1 row affected (0.00 sec)

mysql> SELECT f_date_time, f_time_stamp FROM data;
+---------------------+----------------+
| f_date_time         | f_time_stamp   |
+---------------------+----------------+
| 1999-03-12 12:30:12 | 20020309161718 |
| 1999-03-12 12:30:12 | 20020309161718 |
| 2003-04-09 11:57:18 | 20030409115718 |
+---------------------+----------------+
3 rows in set (0.00 sec)
```

These two types are most commonly used to store timestamps that contain the current date and time automatically, and they can come in handy for applications that perform a large number of transactions with the database and need to build an audit trail for debugging or review purposes.

MySQL will automatically fill the first field declared as TIMESTAMP in a row with the current date and time if no value is explicitly specified for that field or if a NULL value is specified for that field. The following example demonstrates:

```
mysql> CREATE TABLE data ( f_time_stamp TIMESTAMP );
Query OK, 0 rows affected (0.06 sec)

mysql> INSERT INTO data VALUES ();
Query OK, 1 row affected (0.00 sec)

mysql> INSERT INTO data VALUES (NULL);
Query OK, 1 row affected (0.00 sec)

mysql> SELECT f_time_stamp FROM data;
+----------------+
| f_time_stamp   |
+----------------+
| 20030409120052 |
| 20030409120058 |
+----------------+
2 rows in set (0.00 sec)
```

An equivalent result may be obtained by using MySQL's NOW() function to fill the current date and time into a field declared as type DATETIME.

```
mysql> CREATE TABLE data ( event DATETIME );
Query OK, 0 rows affected (0.06 sec)

mysql> INSERT INTO data VALUES (NOW());
Query OK, 1 row affected (0.05 sec)

mysql> SELECT event FROM data;
+---------------------+
| event               |
+---------------------+
| 2003-04-09 12:01:59 |
+---------------------+
1 row in set (0.00 sec)
```

Those Amazing Invisible Timestamps!

It's also possible to control the size of the TIMESTAMP field by using a display width specifier, in much the same way as with numeric types. The following table lists the various available sizes and the corresponding formats:[2]

Type	Format
TIMESTAMP(14)	YYYYMMDDHHMMSS
TIMESTAMP(12)	YYMMDDHHMMSS
TIMESTAMP(10)	YYMMDDHHMM
TIMESTAMP(8)	YYYYMMDD
TIMESTAMP(6)	YYMMDD
TIMESTAMP(4)	YYMM
TIMESTAMP(2)	YY

It should be noted that although MySQL certainly permits the use of custom TIMESTAMP formats, it does not encourage such use. The reason is fairly simple: MySQL is not able to use keys on the TIMESTAMP field if you use custom formats on it. Output formatting should instead be obtained through the use of the DATE_FORMAT() function, discussed in the next chapter.

Using a display width modifier on the TIMESTAMP field has no effect on the actual size of the field or the range of values it can store. In fact, if you set a low

---

[2]   See the MySQL manual, at http://www.mysql.com/documentation/

display width for a TIMESTAMP field and then later decide to increase it via a call to the ALTER TABLE command, previously hidden information will become visible. The following example demonstrates:

```
mysql> CREATE TABLE data ( when TIMESTAMP(6) );
Query OK, 0 rows affected (0.00 sec)

mysql> INSERT INTO data VALUES (NULL);
Query OK, 1 row affected (0.06 sec)

mysql> SELECT when FROM data;
+--------------+
| when         |
+--------------+
|       030409 |
+--------------+
1 row in set (0.06 sec)

mysql> ALTER TABLE data CHANGE when when TIMESTAMP(8);
Query OK, 1 row affected (0.11 sec)
Records: 1  Duplicates: 0  Warnings: 0

mysql> SELECT when FROM data;
+---------------+
| when          |
+---------------+
|      20030409 |
+---------------+
1 row in set (0.00 sec)

mysql> ALTER TABLE data CHANGE when when TIMESTAMP(14);
Query OK, 1 row affected (0.06 sec)
Records: 1  Duplicates: 0  Warnings: 0

mysql> SELECT when FROM data;
+----------------+
| when           |
+----------------+
| 20030409135827 |
+----------------+
1 row in set (0.00 sec)
```

Obviously, the reverse also works.

Note, however, that this behavior is true only for MySQL versions prior to 4.1. For MySQL 4.1 or better, TIMESTAMP types are always set to the maximum size.

PART II

Date and time values outside the legal range are usually converted to the nearest endpoint of the range and then saved, as demonstrated here:

```
mysql> CREATE TABLE data (
    -> d date,
    -> t time
    -> );
Query OK, 0 rows affected (0.00 sec)

mysql> INSERT INTO data VALUES ('10000-01-01', '9000:07:12');
Query OK, 1 row affected (0.05 sec)

mysql> SELECT d, t FROM data;
+------------+----------+
| d          | t        |
+------------+----------+
| 2010-00-00 | 838:59:59 |
+------------+----------+
1 row in set (0.06 sec)
```

Additionally, MySQL automatically zeroes out illegal date and time values, as amply demonstrated by the following example:

```
mysql> INSERT INTO data VALUES ('0005-14-76', '9000:900:90');
Query OK, 1 row affected (0.00 sec)

mysql> SELECT d, t FROM data;
+------------+----------+
| d          | t        |
+------------+----------+
| 0000-00-00 | 00:00:00 |
+------------+----------+
1 row in set (0.00 sec)
```

Turning a Blind Eye

It is worth noting that MySQL may also permit illegal date and time values to be stored in the database. For example, consider the following listing, which inserts the illegal date 2003-02-31 into a MySQL DATE field:

```
mysql> INSERT INTO data VALUES ('2003-02-31', '');
Query OK, 1 row affected (0.06 sec)

mysql> SELECT d FROM data;
+------------+
| d          |
+------------+
| 2003-02-31 |
```

```
+------------+
1 row in set (0.05 sec)
```

Such values will slip past MySQL's eagle eye, because MySQL's developers have not implemented a rigorous checking routine for date and time values. The reason? Date and time value validation is considered something that should be taken care of at the application level, and therefore it is inappropriate to burden MySQL with the additional overhead of performing this validation every time a date or time is entered into the system.

Complex Types

In addition to the base types discussed in the previous section, MySQL also extends the SQL specification with two complex types, ENUM and SET. Although these types are technically string types, they are treated as a different category because their values must be chosen from a predefined set of strings. An ENUM (enumeration) type permits selection of only a single value from a collection of allowed values; a SET type permits selection of any arbitrary number of values from the available collection.

The ENUM Type

An ENUM type is typically used for mutually exclusive data values, where selection of only a single item from the set is permitted. A common example of this is a gender attribute, which could be either male or female—the following example demonstrates:

```
mysql> CREATE TABLE data ( gender ENUM('M', 'F') );
Query OK, 0 rows affected (0.06 sec)

mysql> INSERT INTO data values ('M'), ('m'), ('f'), ('yy'), (NULL);
Query OK, 5 rows affected (0.00 sec)
Records: 5  Duplicates: 0  Warnings: 1

mysql> SELECT gender FROM data;
+--------+
| gender |
+--------+
| M      |
| M      |
| F      |
|        |
| NULL   |
+--------+
5 rows in set (0.06 sec)
```

As you can see, ENUM types can contain only values listed in the set of allowed members, or NULL values; any attempts to use values other than these will cause

MySQL to insert an empty string instead. If the case of the inserted value does not match the case of the corresponding value in the field declaration, the case of the inserted value is automatically changed to match that of the field declaration; this can be clearly seen in this example.

It is interesting to note that although ENUM members can be specified only as strings, they are stored internally as numbers and indexed numerically, beginning with index 1. An ENUM type can contain a maximum of 65,536 elements, of which one is reserved for use by MySQL to hold errors; this error value is represented by index 0, or an empty string.

Since ENUM values can be accessed either by string or numerical index, the following two snippets are identical:

```
mysql> SELECT COUNT(*) FROM data WHERE gender = 'M';
+----------+
| COUNT(*) |
+----------+
|        2 |
+----------+
1 row in set (0.05 sec)

mysql> SELECT COUNT(*) FROM data WHERE gender = 1;
+----------+
| COUNT(*) |
+----------+
|        2 |
+----------+
1 row in set (0.05 sec)
```

MySQL considers only values present in the ENUM type declaration to be legal; any attempt to insert values other than these will fail, with MySQL instead using the error value to indicate that an error occurred. This means that it becomes possible to locate erroneous records easily, simply by searching for rows containing either the empty string or the corresponding numerical value 0. This can be demonstrated by revisiting the preceding example and counting the number of rows with errors in them. The following two snippets below are equivalent:

```
mysql> SELECT COUNT(*) FROM data WHERE gender = 0;
+----------+
| COUNT(*) |
+----------+
|        1 |
+----------+
1 row in set (0.05 sec)

mysql> SELECT COUNT(*) FROM data WHERE gender = '';
+----------+
| COUNT(*) |
+----------+
```

```
|         1 |
+-----------+
1 row in set (0.00 sec)
```

The SET Type

Similar, though not completely identical, is the SET type, which allows the selection of any number of values from a predefined set of string values. Unlike fields declared using the ENUM type, which can contain at most one element, fields declared with the SET type can contain zero, one, or more than one element from the set of allowed values. This makes the SET type a good choice for multiple-choice selections, such as the one in this example:

```
mysql> CREATE TABLE data ( pizza_topping SET ('ham', 'cheese',
'tomato', 'chicken', 'pepperoni') );
Query OK, 0 rows affected (0.11 sec)

mysql> INSERT INTO data VALUES ('ham');
Query OK, 1 row affected (0.00 sec)

mysql> INSERT INTO data VALUES ('cheese, pepperoni');
Query OK, 1 row affected (0.00 sec)

mysql> SELECT pizza_topping FROM data;
+-------------------+
| pizza_topping     |
+-------------------+
| ham               |
| cheese,pepperoni  |
+-------------------+
2 rows in set (0.00 sec)
```

As with the ENUM type, any attempt to use a value that is not part of the predefined set will cause MySQL to insert an empty string instead.

```
mysql> INSERT INTO data VALUES ('egg');
Query OK, 1 row affected (0.00 sec)

mysql> SELECT pizza_topping FROM data;
+-------------------+
| pizza_topping     |
+-------------------+
| ham               |
| cheese,pepperoni  |
|                   |
+-------------------+
3 rows in set (0.00 sec)
```

However, if you try inserting a record that contains a combination of both legal and illegal elements, as in the following example, MySQL will remove the illegal members and retain the legal ones.

```
mysql> CREATE TABLE data ( pizza_topping SET ('ham', 'cheese',
'tomato', 'chicken', 'pepperoni') );
Query OK, 0 rows affected (0.11 sec)

mysql> INSERT INTO data VALUES ('egg,cheese,tomato,bacon');
Query OK, 1 row affected (0.05 sec)

mysql> SELECT pizza_topping FROM data;
+------------------+
| pizza_topping    |
+------------------+
| cheese,tomato    |
+------------------+
1 row in set (0.00 sec)
```

A SET type can contain a maximum of 64 members. Values are stored as a sequence of individual bits, with the bits representing the selected members switched on. This bit representation is a simple and efficient way of creating ordered collections of elements; it also eliminates duplication, since it becomes impossible to have the same element repeated twice in the same SET value. Consider the following example, which illustrates:

```
mysql> CREATE TABLE data ( pizza_topping SET ('ham', 'cheese',
'tomato', 'chicken', 'pepperoni') );
Query OK, 0 rows affected (0.11 sec)

mysql> INSERT INTO data VALUES ('ham,ham,ham,cheese');
Query OK, 1 row affected (0.05 sec)

mysql> SELECT pizza_topping FROM data;
+------------------+
| pizza_topping    |
+------------------+
| ham,cheese       |
+------------------+
1 row in set (0.00 sec)
```

This also makes it simple to locate records containing erroneous data—all that's required is to look for rows containing either an empty string or the binary value 0. The following two snippets, which are equivalent, illustrate this:

```
mysql> SELECT COUNT(*) FROM data where pizza_topping = '';
+----------+
| COUNT(*) |
+----------+
```

```
|          1 |
+----------+
1 row in set (0.05 sec)

mysql> SELECT COUNT(*) from data where pizza_topping = 0;
+----------+
| COUNT(*) |
+----------+
|        1 |
+----------+
1 row in set (0.06 sec)
```

Data Type Selection

Now that you understand the various options open to you, it's instructive to spend a few minutes understanding how to select the appropriate data type for your needs.

As discussed in the early part of this chapter, data typing plays an important role in making stored data more consistent and in improving storage efficiency and speed. Consequently, selection of data types while designing a database should not be treated lightly, and due consideration should be given to all the issues involved prior to making a choice from the diverse array of options MySQL makes available.

Here are some criteria to keep in mind when selecting data types for MySQL columns.

Permissible Values

The range and type of values you plan to allow in a field is the most immediate factor in deciding which data type to attach to that field. If you have a column containing stock prices, for example, you obviously should not use a string or date type in that column; rather you should use one of the numeric types, probably a FLOAT or DECIMAL depending on the amount of precision you need. Similarly, if you have a column storing birthdays, it makes more sense to opt for a DATE type for that column, rather than using a VARCHAR type and writing code at the application level to parse the various components of the string into day, month and year values.

Storage Efficiency

It's also important, especially when dealing with numeric types, to take into account the range of possible values for the field and select a type that is appropriate, size-wise, for that range. If you have a column that stores, for example, the ages of all the users registered in the system, the values for this field will always fall between 0 and 255. It would therefore be inefficient to use a regular INT or BIGINT for this field, as an UNSIGNED TINYINT will provide you with all the functionality you need while simultaneously taking up less space—1 byte instead of 4 or 8 bytes.

Similar logic applies for string values: If you know, for example, that a particular field can contain, at most, a two-character string (say, USA state codes), it makes sense to use a CHAR type with a subscript of 2, rather than a TEXT or BLOB, which would take up far more space than needed while providing no extra functionality. Similarly, if you know *a priori* that the only permissible values in a column belong to a predefined set, that constraint will immediately point you to selection of an ENUM or SET type for that field.

Formatting and Display Requirements

Another important factor that influences the selection of a field type is the application's formatting and display requirements of the data contained within that field. For example, if your string data must always be formatted to a certain length, it's a good idea to use the CHAR data type, which automatically pads values with spaces where needed. (For numeric data, the equivalent is the ZEROFILL modifier, which uses zeroes for padding.) Similarly, if you have numbers that must always be displayed with four decimal digits, the DECIMAL data type is a good choice, as it comes with built-in constructs to allow you to specify the precision of the values it holds.

Formatting also plays an important role when dealing with dates and times. Depending on whether your application will display dates and times as they are stored in the database, or process them further, you might choose a regular DATE type, which uses YYYY-MM-DD notation and is easily understandable to a human, or a TIMESTAMP type, which uses YYYYMMDDHHMMSS notation and is simpler to process for a program.

Data Processing Requirements

Data type selection should also take into account the data manipulation and processing requirements of your application, as some types lend themselves to data manipulation better than others. For example, if you plan to sum all the values in a column, it's important to select a data type that supports this type of operation natively, such as an INT type.

When dealing with dates and times, this factor becomes even more critical, as date and time comparisons and manipulations are fairly complex at the best of times, and you would want to leverage off MySQL's built-in functions as far as possible for these types of operations. Purely from the performance point of view, it would be folly, for example, to store dates as strings in the database and then manually write code at the application level to add, subtract, or compare these values when you could use a built-in type that already supports these operations.

Sorting, Indexing, and Comparison Requirements

If you plan to sort all the values in a column by different criteria, you need to select a type that performs these functions efficiently and with maximum flexibility. For example, numeric values stored as character data will sort differently than the same values stored as numbers, and date values stored in a text field will sort differently than identical values stored in a date field. It is therefore important to investigate whether your chosen type supports the sorting demands of your application before committing to it.

Indexing requirements also impact your choice of data type. Typically, you would want to index fields that are used as selection criteria in your queries, so as to speed up processing time. However, it is relatively inefficient to index character data as compared to numeric data, as operations can be performed faster on numbers than strings. Additionally, older versions of MySQL impose special requirements on fields declared as indexes; you need to make sure that your field values do not conflict with these requirements.

In a similar manner, if you plan to compare values with each other, you need to ensure that the data types used support comparison and are compatible with each other for this purpose. The type of comparison also affects the data type used: if you plan to compare string values with each other, for example, you need to evaluate whether this comparison will be performed in a binary (case-sensitive) or nonbinary (case-insensitive) manner, and apply appropriate type modifiers to your MySQL column.

Summary

This chapter marked the beginning of a more detailed discussion of the MySQL command set. MySQL comes with a wide variety of data types designed to support almost any application; the preceding pages amply illustrated this point through a detailed examination of these data types, complete with examples to illustrate the important characteristics and caveats of each. Brief sections on the need for data typing and the importance of proper type selection put this information in context and explained the various criteria to be kept in mind when choosing data types for your MySQL columns.

MySQL Operators

Y ou've already seen, in the SQL tutorial in Chapter 4, how MySQL statements such as the SELECT statement can use comparison and logical operators to retrieve only those records matching a specified condition or set of conditions. These SQL operators add tremendous flexibility to the language, making it possible to build complex expressions and clauses that allow you easily to perform sophisticated comparison and conversion operations on the data in your MySQL tables.

This chapter will introduce you to MySQL's numerous operators, explaining what each one does and using examples that demonstrate how you can use them to, among other things, perform calculations and comparisons, create conditional groups, search for regular expressions in strings, and convert between data types.

MySQL comes with more than 25 operators, each designed for a specific task. These operators can be classified, according to their function, into the following four categories:

- Arithmetic operators
- Comparison operators
- Logical operators
- Bit operators

The following sections examine each of these categories in greater detail.

What's in a Name?

It's interesting to note that, in the MySQL world, the difference between an operator and a function lies only in the semantics. A function is invoked with its name first and then its arguments in parentheses, while an operator is usually denoted by one or two special symbols with the arguments in between or on either side. Internally, MySQL treats a function and an operator exactly the same way.

TABLE 6-1
MySQL Arithmetic
Operators

Operator	What It Does
+	Addition
−	Subtraction
*	Multiplication
/	Division; returns quotient
%	Division; returns modulus

Arithmetic Operators

Like most programming languages, MySQL supports most common arithmetic operators, allowing you to perform calculations on the fly. Table 6-1 lists the arithmetic operators available in MySQL.

Let's begin with the simple ones: addition and subtraction. The + operator is used to obtain the sum of two or more values, as in the following examples:

```
mysql> SELECT 10 + 5, 1000000 + 64763;
+--------+-----------------+
| 10 + 5 | 1000000 + 64763 |
+--------+-----------------+
|     15 |         1064763 |
+--------+-----------------+
1 row in set (0.04 sec)
mysql> SELECT 3.24 + 0.89844,0.00000000001 + 0.000000000001;
+---------------+-------------------------------+
| 3.24 + 0.89844 | 0.00000000001 + 0.000000000001 |
+---------------+-------------------------------+
|        4.13844 |                 0.000000000011 |
+---------------+-------------------------------+
1 row in set (0.04 sec)
```

The − operator is used for subtract one value from another:

```
mysql> SELECT 5 - 1, 999 - 1000, 0.24 - 0.2;
+-------+------------+------------+
| 5 - 1 | 999 - 1000 | 0.24 - 0.2 |
+-------+------------+------------+
|     4 |         -1 |       0.04 |
+-------+------------+------------+
1 row in set (0.00 sec)
```

```
mysql> SELECT -46.7 - 0.3, 0.6484895563 - 0.63858546546;
+-------------+-----------------------------------+
| -46.7 - 0.3 | 0.6484895563 - 0.63858546546      |
+-------------+-----------------------------------+
|       -47.0 |                      0.00990409084 |
+-------------+-----------------------------------+
1 row in set (0.00 sec)
```

You can multiply numbers with the * operator, which is used to obtain the product of two or more values:

```
mysql> SELECT 7 * 10, 7 * 0, -11.1 * 2.5, -11000000 * 1276464646;
+--------+-------+-------------+------------------------+
| 7 * 10 | 7 * 0 | -11.1 * 2.5 | -11000000 * 1276464646 |
+--------+-------+-------------+------------------------+
|     70 |     0 |       -27.8 |      -14041111106000000 |
+--------+-------+-------------+------------------------+
1 row in set (0.01 sec)
```

The / operator is used to divide one value by the other to obtain the quotient:

```
mysql> SELECT 10 / 2, 12.1 / -0.01, 22 / 7, 22.00 / 7.000000;
+--------+--------------+--------+------------------+
| 10 / 2 | 12.1 / -0.01 | 22 / 7 | 22.00 / 7.000000 |
+--------+--------------+--------+------------------+
|   5.00 |    -1210.0000 |   3.14 |        3.14285714 |
+--------+--------------+--------+------------------+
1 row in set (0.00 sec)
```

You can also use the % operator to obtain the modulo of a division operation:

```
mysql> SELECT 25 % 7, -33 % 7;
+--------+---------+
| 25 % 7 | -33 % 7 |
+--------+---------+
|      4 |      -5 |
+--------+---------+
1 row in set (0.00 sec)
```

Different Strokes

As you can see, MySQL allows use of SELECT statements with arbitrary, user-supplied values This is unlike Oracle, which requires use of FROM DUAL syntax when selecting a value that is not being read from a table.

Division by zero is, obviously, not permitted—MySQL returns a NULL if you try it:

```
mysql> SELECT 9 / 0;
+--------+
| 9 / 0  |
+--------+
|   NULL |
+--------+
1 row in set (0.00 sec)
```

It should be noted that all mathematical operations involving integers are calculated using 64-bit precision. Numbers outside this range are likely to produce unexpected results, as the following snippet illustrates:

```
mysql> SELECT 1000000000000000000000000000000 * 1;
+-----------------------------------+
| 1000000000000000000000000000000 * 1 |
+-----------------------------------+
|       9999999999999999991000000000000 |
+-----------------------------------+
1 row in set (0.01 sec)
```

Further, numbers represented as strings are automatically converted to strings wherever possible to facilitate calculation. MySQL follows two basic rules when performing this conversion:

- If a string with a leading number is used in an arithmetic operation, it is converted to the value of that number.
- If a string containing a combination of characters and numbers cannot be correctly converted into a number, it is converted to 0.

The following examples illustrate how these rules play out:

```
mysql> SELECT '500' + '00002', '8.9' * 10, '90AA' + '0';
+-----------------+-----------+--------------+
| '500' + '00002' | '8.9' * 10 | '90AA' + '0' |
+-----------------+-----------+--------------+
|             502 |        89 |           90 |
+-----------------+-----------+--------------+
1 row in set (0.00 sec)

mysql> SELECT 'AA90' + '1', '10X' * 1 * 'pqr';
+-------------+------------------+
| 'AA90' + '1' | '10X' * 1 * 'pqr' |
+-------------+------------------+
|           1 |                0 |
+-------------+------------------+
1 row in set (0.00 sec)
```

Let's move from theory to seeing how these work in practice. Consider the following simple MySQL table, which lists the cost price (cost to manufacturer, aka CTM), selling price to retailer (cost to retailer, aka CTR), retail price (cost to customer, aka CTC), and current inventory level for four products manufactured by a toy company:

```
mysql> SELECT * FROM toys;
+----+-----------------+-------+-------+-------+----------+
| id | item            | ctm   | ctr   | ctc   | quantity |
+----+-----------------+-------+-------+-------+----------+
|  1 | Huggy bear      |  5.00 |  7.40 |  9.90 |      300 |
|  2 | Coloring book   |  3.00 |  5.00 |  7.99 |     2000 |
|  3 | Board game      | 12.00 | 20.00 | 39.90 |     1430 |
|  4 | Activity CD-ROM |  2.00 |  6.00 | 17.49 |     3780 |
+----+-----------------+-------+-------+-------+----------+
4 rows in set (0.00 sec)
```

Now the arithmetic operators can come in handy when performing calculations on this raw data—for example, for seeing the profit margins on each item for the manufacturer:

```
mysql> SELECT item, ctr - ctm FROM toys;
+-----------------+-----------+
| item            | ctr - ctm |
+-----------------+-----------+
| Huggy bear      |      2.40 |
| Coloring book   |      2.00 |
| Board game      |      8.00 |
| Activity CD-ROM |      4.00 |
+-----------------+-----------+
4 rows in set (0.01 sec)
```

and for the retailer:

```
mysql> SELECT item, ctc - ctr FROM toys;
+-----------------+-----------+
| item            | ctc - ctr |
+-----------------+-----------+
| Huggy bear      |      2.50 |
| Coloring book   |      2.99 |
| Board game      |     19.90 |
| Activity CD-ROM |     11.49 |
+-----------------+-----------+
4 rows in set (0.00 sec)
```

Want to see how much an item gets marked up between the time the company manufactures it and the customer purchases it? See the following listing showing both absolute and percentage terms.

PART II

```
mysql> SELECT item, ctc - ctm, (ctc - ctm) / ctm * 100 FROM toys;
+-----------------+-----------+------------------------+
| item            | ctc - ctm | (ctc - ctm) / ctm * 100 |
+-----------------+-----------+------------------------+
| Huggy bear      |      4.90 |                98.0000 |
| Coloring book   |      4.99 |               166.3333 |
| Board game      |     27.90 |               232.5000 |
| Activity CD-ROM |     15.49 |               774.5000 |
+-----------------+-----------+------------------------+
4 rows in set (0.01 sec)
```

It's also possible, obviously, to arrive at a valuation of the manufacturer's inventory, classified by item,

```
mysql> SELECT item, ctm * quantity FROM toys;
+-----------------+----------------+
| item            | ctm * quantity |
+-----------------+----------------+
| Huggy bear      |        1500.00 |
| Coloring book   |        6000.00 |
| Board game      |       17160.00 |
| Activity CD-ROM |        7560.00 |
+-----------------+----------------+
4 rows in set (0.00 sec)
```

and the discount (in absolute and percentage terms) offered to a retailer by the manufacturer for each item.

```
mysql> SELECT item, ctc-ctr, (ctc - ctr)/ctm * 100 FROM toys;
+-----------------+---------+----------------------+
| item            | ctc-ctr | (ctc - ctr)/ctm * 100 |
+-----------------+---------+----------------------+
| Huggy bear      |    2.50 |              50.0000 |
| Coloring book   |    2.99 |              99.6667 |
| Board game      |   19.90 |             165.8333 |
| Activity CD-ROM |   11.49 |             574.5000 |
+-----------------+---------+----------------------+
4 rows in set (0.00 sec)
```

Of course, arithmetic can only take you so far—sometimes, you also need to perform comparisons.

Comparison Operators

When working with SELECT queries, you'll be grateful for the presence of MySQL's numerous comparison operators, which allow you to compare the left side of an expression with its right side. The result of such a comparison operation is always 1 (true), 0 (false), or NULL (could not be determined).

Table 6-2 lists the various comparison operators available in MySQL.

TABLE 6-2 MySQL Comparison Operators	Operator	What It Does
	=	Equal to
	<> aka !=	Not equal to
	<=>	NULL-safe equal to
	<	Less than
	<=	Less than or equal to
	>	Greater than
	>=	Greater than or equal to
	BETWEEN	Exists in specified range
	IN	Exists in specified set
	IS NULL	Is NULL
	IS NOT NULL	Is not NULL
	LIKE	Wildcard match
	REGEXP aka RLIKE	Regular expression match

These comparison operators can be used to compare both numbers and strings. Numbers are compared as floating-point values, while strings are compared in a case-insensitive manner (unless the special BINARY keyword is used—see the sidebar entitled "Binary People" for more information on this). Additionally, as you saw in the preceding section, MySQL includes intelligence to convert numbers to strings (and vice versa) automatically on an as-needed basis. (See the sidebar entitled "Artificial Intelligence" for more technical information on how MySQL performs this evaluation.) Consider the following example, which illustrates how MySQL can treat numbers and strings differently in different cases:

```
mysql> SELECT 6 = '6gfh', '6' = '6gfh';
+------------+--------------+
| 6 = '6gfh' | '6' = '6gfh' |
+------------+--------------+
|          1 |            0 |
+------------+--------------+
1 row in set (0.03 sec)
```

Artificial Intelligence

Internally, MySQL represents each node of the expression parse tree with an object of a class derived from class Item. The Item class has three value evaluation methods: longlong Item::val_int(), double Item::val(), and String* Item::val_str(String* buf). The first one will evaluate the expression node in the 64-bit integer context, the second in the floating-point context, and the third in the character-string context. Each parent node object controls the context of evaluation of its immediate children by invoking the appropriate method of Item when computing the subexpression, and MySQL tries to make the most intuitive and standards-compliant decision in each individual case on which context to pick.

The = operator is used to whether both sides of an expression are equal:

```
mysql> SELECT 2 = 2,  2.37 = 2.4, 2.415 = 2.4150000;
+-------+------------+-------------------+
| 2 = 2 | 2.37 = 2.4 | 2.415 = 2.4150000 |
+-------+------------+-------------------+
|     1 |          0 |                 1 |
+-------+------------+-------------------+
1 row in set (0.00 sec)
```

You can do this with strings also:

```
mysql> SELECT 'a' = 'a', 'a' = 'A', 'A' = 'B', 'circle' = 'round';
+-----------+-----------+-----------+--------------------+
| 'a' = 'a' | 'a' = 'A' | 'A' = 'B' | 'circle' = 'round' |
+-----------+-----------+-----------+--------------------+
|         1 |         1 |         0 |                  0 |
+-----------+-----------+-----------+--------------------+
1 row in set (0.00 sec)
```

The opposite of the = operator is the <> operator, which is used to test whether the two sides of an expression are unequal; it returns true if they are and false if they're not.

```
mysql> SELECT 7 <> 7, 7 <> 8;
+--------+--------+
| 7 <> 7 | 7 <> 8 |
+--------+--------+
|      0 |      1 |
+--------+--------+
1 row in set (0.00 sec)
```

This operator can also be used with strings,

```
mysql> SELECT 'x' <> 'X', 'x' <> 'y', '7x' <> '7y';
+------------+------------+--------------+
| 'x' <> 'X' | 'x' <> 'y' | '7x' <> '7y' |
+------------+------------+--------------+
|          0 |          1 |            1 |
+------------+------------+--------------+
1 row in set (0.00 sec)
```

and with NULLs:

```
mysql> SELECT NULL <> NULL, 0 <> NULL, 0 <> 0;
+--------------+-----------+--------+
| NULL <> NULL | 0 <> NULL | 0 <> 0 |
+--------------+-----------+--------+
|         NULL |      NULL |      0 |
+--------------+-----------+--------+
1 row in set (0.02 sec)
```

> ## Binary People
>
> Because MySQL compares strings in a case-insensitive manner by default, the expression 'a' = 'A' evaluates as true. If you'd like to perform case-sensitive comparison, try adding the BINARY keyword, which tells MySQL that the string following it should be treated in a binary manner. In the real world, all this translates to is that MySQL will keep the string's case in mind when performing comparison operations on it. The following example demonstrates:
>
> ```
> mysql> SELECT 'Aloha' = 'aloha', BINARY 'Aloha' = 'aloha';
> +-------------------+---------------------------+
> | 'Aloha' = 'aloha' | BINARY 'Aloha' = 'aloha'  |
> +-------------------+---------------------------+
> |                 1 |                         0 |
> +-------------------+---------------------------+
> 1 row in set (0.00 sec)
> ```
>
> The BINARY keyword is MySQL shorthand for one of the permutations of the CAST() function. The CAST() function is discussed in detail in the next chapter.

The <=, >=, <, and > operators are used to test whether the left side of an expression is, respectively, less than or equal to, greater than or equal to, less than, or greater than its right side:

```
mysql> SELECT 100 > 100, 100 > 10, 100 < 10, 3.14 > 3.144;
+-----------+----------+----------+--------------+
| 100 > 100 | 100 > 10 | 100 < 10 | 3.14 > 3.144 |
+-----------+----------+----------+--------------+
|         0 |        1 |        0 |            0 |
+-----------+----------+----------+--------------+
1 row in set (0.00 sec)

mysql> SELECT 10 <= 10, 10 >= 19, 10 <= 25, -50 > 50, -50 < 50;
+----------+----------+----------+----------+----------+
| 10 <= 10 | 10 >= 19 | 10 <= 25 | -50 > 50 | -50 < 50 |
+----------+----------+----------+----------+----------+
|        1 |        0 |        1 |        0 |        1 |
+----------+----------+----------+----------+----------+
1 row in set (0.00 sec)
```

Strings are also compared in a case-insensitive manner, with their values derived from their relative position in the alphabet:

```
mysql> SELECT 'a' > 'a', 'x' <= 'x', 'y' > 'Y', 'e' > 'f';
+-----------+------------+-----------+-----------+
| 'a' > 'a' | 'x' <= 'x' | 'y' > 'Y' | 'e' > 'f' |
+-----------+------------+-----------+-----------+
|         0 |          1 |         0 |         0 |
+-----------+------------+-----------+-----------+
1 row in set (0.00 sec)
```

> **A Matter of Space**
> Note that when comparing strings, MySQL discounts trailing spaces, tab characters, and newlines. Therefore, the expressions
>
> ```
> 'zebra' = 'ZEBRA'
> ```
>
> and
>
> ```
> 'zebra' = 'ZEBRA        '
> ```
>
> are equivalent, and will both return true.
>   Leading spaces, tabs, and newlines are, however, retained and used in the comparison; testing the expressions
>
> ```
> 'zebra' = 'ZEBRA'
> ```
>
> and
>
> ```
> 'zebra' = '     ZEBRA'
> ```
>
> for equality would not return the same result.

The BETWEEN operator is used to test whether or not a value (or an expression evaluating to a value) lies within a specified range:

```
mysql> SELECT 10 BETWEEN 0 AND 100, 10 BETWEEN 11 AND 100;
+---------------------+----------------------+
| 10 BETWEEN 0 and 100 | 10 BETWEEN 11 AND 100 |
+---------------------+----------------------+
|                   1 |                    0 |
+---------------------+----------------------+
1 row in set (0.00 sec)
```

A comparison test using the BETWEEN operator returns true if the expression being tested lies between the specified range, inclusive of both end points of the range. This works not just with numbers, but with strings as well, as illustrated here:

```
mysql> SELECT 'y' BETWEEN 'x' AND 'z', 'z' BETWEEN 'x' AND 'y';
+-----------------------+-----------------------+
| 'y' BETWEEN 'x' AND 'z' | 'z' BETWEEN 'x' AND 'y' |
+-----------------------+-----------------------+
|                     1 |                     0 |
+-----------------------+-----------------------+
1 row in set (0.00 sec)
```

You can reverse the results of a BETWEEN test by adding the NOT logical operator; this returns true only if the expression lies outside the given range:

```
mysql> SELECT 99 NOT BETWEEN 10 AND 50, 'f' NOT BETWEEN 'a' AND 'z';
+--------------------------+--------------------------+
| 99 NOT BETWEEN 10 AND 50 | 'f' NOT BETWEEN 'a' AND 'z' |
+--------------------------+--------------------------+
|                        1 |                        0 |
+--------------------------+--------------------------+
1 row in set (0.00 sec)
```

Similar, though not equivalent, is the IN operator, used to test whether a value (or an expression evaluating to a value) is included in a named set of values. The following example illustrates:

```
mysql> SELECT 7 IN (1,2,3,4,5,6,7,8,9);
+--------------------------+
| 7 IN (1,2,3,4,5,6,7,8,9) |
+--------------------------+
|                        1 |
+--------------------------+
1 row in set (0.00 sec)
```

A comparison test using the IN operator returns true if the value being tested exists in the specified set. As you might imagine, you can use this operator with strings as well as numbers.

```
mysql> SELECT 'red' IN ('red', 'green', 'blue');
+----------------------------------+
| 'red' IN ('red', 'green', 'blue') |
+----------------------------------+
|                                1 |
+----------------------------------+
1 row in set (0.00 sec)
```

You can perform case-sensitive comparison with—you guessed it—the BINARY keyword:

```
mysql> SELECT BINARY 'ross' IN ('Chandler', 'Joey', 'Ross');
+-----------------------------------------------+
| BINARY 'ross' IN ('Chandler', 'Joey', 'Ross') |
+-----------------------------------------------+
|                                             0 |
+-----------------------------------------------+
1 row in set (0.00 sec)
```

As with other comparison operators, the IN operator returns NULL if either the expression to be evaluated or any of the values in the (non-matching) set are NULL.

```
mysql> SELECT NULL IN (1,2), NULL IN (1,2,3,NULL);
+---------------+----------------------+
| NULL IN (1,2) | NULL IN (1,2,3,NULL) |
+---------------+----------------------+
|          NULL |                 NULL |
+---------------+----------------------+
1 row in set (0.01 sec)
```

You can reverse the behavior of the IN operator by adding the NOT logical operator; this returns true if the expression or value to be evaluated is not a member of the specified set of values.

```
mysql> SELECT 3 NOT IN (1,2);
+----------------+
| 3 NOT IN (1,2) |
+----------------+
|              1 |
+----------------+
1 row in set (0.21 sec)
```

Now, if you've paid attention to the examples in this section, you'll have deduced that usually, any comparison operation involving a NULL value tends to produce a NULL result. The following examples illustrate this point with a quick recap:

```
mysql> SELECT 11 = NULL, 56 <> NULL, 1 < 2 < NULL;
+-----------+------------+--------------+
| 11 = NULL | 56 <> NULL | 1 < 2 < NULL |
+-----------+------------+--------------+
|      NULL |       NULL |         NULL |
+-----------+------------+--------------+
1 row in set (0.07 sec)
mysql> SELECT NULL IN (5,NULL,30), 7 BETWEEN 0 AND NULL;
+---------------------+----------------------+
| NULL IN (5,NULL,30) | 7 BETWEEN 0 AND NULL |
+---------------------+----------------------+
|                NULL |                 NULL |
+---------------------+----------------------+
1 row in set (0.07 sec)
```

This begs an important question: How do you test for the presence or absence of actual NULL values in an expression? The answer lies with the IS NULL and IS NOT NULL operators, which are designed specifically to perform comparisons involving NULL values.

Consider the following example, which demonstrates how the IS NULL operator can be used to test whether or not a value is null:

```
mysql> SELECT 88 IS NULL, 0 IS NULL, NULL IS NULL, 1=NULL IS NULL;
+------------+-----------+--------------+----------------+
| 88 IS NULL | 0 IS NULL | NULL IS NULL | 1=NULL IS NULL |
+------------+-----------+--------------+----------------+
|          0 |         0 |            1 |              1 |
+------------+-----------+--------------+----------------+
1 row in set (0.00 sec)
```

As you can see, only NULL values return true in an IS NULL test. Note especially the last expression in this example—even though the expression 1=NULL contains the integer *1*, the entire expression still evaluates as NULL (since it contains a NULL value within it) and therefore the IS NULL test returns a positive result.

The reverse, however, is true when using the IS NOT NULL operator—as illustrated here:

```
mysql> SELECT 6478 IS NOT NULL, NULL IS NOT NULL, 1=NULL IS NOT NULL;
+------------------+------------------+--------------------+
| 6478 IS NOT NULL | NULL IS NOT NULL | 1=NULL IS NOT NULL |
+------------------+------------------+--------------------+
|                1 |                0 |                  0 |
+------------------+------------------+--------------------+
1 row in set (0.00 sec)
```

You can also use the special <=> operator, which the MySQL manual refers to as a "NULL-safe equality operator." Basically, all this means is that, in a deviation from its normal behavior, MySQL will return a true or false result for the comparison even when the expressions involved in the comparison contain a NULL value. The following examples illustrate this:

```
mysql> SELECT 2 = NULL, 2 <=> NULL;
+----------+------------+
| 2 = NULL | 2 <=> NULL |
+----------+------------+
|     NULL |          0 |
+----------+------------+
1 row in set (0.00 sec)

mysql> SELECT NULL = NULL, NULL <=> NULL;
+-------------+---------------+
| NULL = NULL | NULL <=> NULL |
+-------------+---------------+
|        NULL |             1 |
+-------------+---------------+
1 row in set (0.00 sec)

mysql> SELECT 0 = NULL, 0 <=> NULL;
+----------+------------+
| 0 = NULL | 0 <=> NULL |
+----------+------------+
|     NULL |          0 |
+----------+------------+
1 row in set (0.00 sec)
```

As you will see in later chapters, these three operators come in handy when dealing with MySQL columns containing NULL data.

> **NULL-ifying Doubts**
>
> Wondering whether an empty value is the same as a NULL value? There's a quick way to put your doubts to rest:
>
> ```
> mysql> SELECT '' IS NULL;
> +------------+
> | '' IS NULL |
> +------------+
> |          0 |
> +------------+
> 1 row in set (0.00 sec)
> ```
>
> As you can see, unlike some programming languages, MySQL makes a clear distinction between an empty value and a NULL value. This is not a MySQL quirk, but rather an integral part of the SQL standard; it's also a common cause of confusion for newbies, so be warned!

In case you're looking to perform wildcard searches of data, you should reach for the LIKE operator. It allows the selection of records matching all or part of a specified search string by allowing the use of special wildcard characters in an expression. Consider the following example, which demonstrates:

```
mysql> SELECT 'Roger says hello' LIKE '%ll%';
+-------------------------------+
| 'Roger says hello' LIKE '%ll%' |
+-------------------------------+
|                             1 |
+-------------------------------+
1 row in set (0.06 sec)
```

In this case, the % wildcard character tells MySQL to match all those values containing zero or more occurrences of the substring ll; for example, hello, ball, roller, and so on. You can also use the _ symbol to match a single character instead of a sequence, as in the following example:

```
mysql> SELECT 'MySQL' LIKE '_SQL', 'mSQL' LIKE '_SQL';
+---------------------+---------------------+
| 'MySQL' LIKE '_SQL' | 'mSQL' LIKE '_SQL' |
+---------------------+---------------------+
|                   1 |                   0 |
+---------------------+---------------------+
1 row in set (0.00 sec)
```

The comparison is performed in a case-insensitive manner by default. However, as noted previously, you can have MySQL perform case-sensitive comparison with the addition of the BINARY keyword. The difference is illustrated in the following example:

```
mysql> SELECT 'MySQL' LIKE '%sql', BINARY 'MySQL' LIKE '%sql';
+---------------------+----------------------------+
| 'MySQL' LIKE '%sql' | BINARY 'MySQL' LIKE '%sql' |
+---------------------+----------------------------+
|                   1 |                          0 |
+---------------------+----------------------------+
1 row in set (0.01 sec)
```

Adding the NOT logical operator reverses the test, returning those records that do not match the specified search string. The following examples demonstrate:

```
mysql> SELECT 'Harry' NOT LIKE '%ry', 'bee' NOT LIKE 'insect';
+------------------------+-------------------------+
| 'Harry' NOT LIKE '%ry' | 'bee' NOT LIKE 'insect' |
+------------------------+-------------------------+
|                      0 |                       1 |
+------------------------+-------------------------+
1 row in set (0.00 sec)
```

The REGEXP operator allows you to perform more complex string comparisons, this time using UNIX regular expressions. The REGEXP operator returns true if the match is found—take a look:

```
mysql> SELECT 'William' REGEXP '^Wil?', 'Wendy' REGEXP '^Wil';
+-------------------------+----------------------+
| 'William' REGEXP '^Wil?' | 'Wendy' REGEXP '^Wil' |
+-------------------------+----------------------+
|                       1 |                    0 |
+-------------------------+----------------------+
1 row in set (0.00 sec)
```

```
mysql> SELECT 'red' REGEXP 'red|green|blue', 'hammer' REGEXP 'ham$';
+------------------------------+------------------------+
| 'red' REGEXP 'red|green|blue' | 'hammer' REGEXP 'ham$' |
+------------------------------+------------------------+
|                            1 |                      0 |
+------------------------------+------------------------+
1 row in set (0.00 sec)
```

Not LIKE That

Novice MySQL programmers tend to hail the LIKE operator as the cure to all their ills, since it appears substantially to simplify complex search queries by allowing the use of wildcards. This appearance is somewhat deceptive: while MySQL's LIKE operator is certainly powerful and can locate records using mere string fragments, using it without giving adequate thought to the structure of the query and the indexing of the database can substantially degrade the performance of the system (since the query has to scan the entire table to build the result set). Therefore, when using a query containing the LIKE operator, it is advisable that you ensure that the columns named in the WHERE clause of the query are indexed, and that the WHERE clause contains enough data to restrict the number of records scanned at the outset itself.

PART II

> **Looking for Patterns**
>
> Wondering what a regular expression is? Regular expressions, also known as *regex* by the geek community, are a powerful tool used in pattern-matching and substitution. They are commonly associated with almost all *NIX-based tools, including editors like vi, scripting languages like Perl and PHP, and shell programs like awk and sed.[1]
>
> A regular expression lets you build patterns using a set of special characters; these patterns can then be compared with text in a file, data entered into an application, or input from a form filled up by users on a web site. Depending on whether or not there's a match, appropriate action can be taken and appropriate program code executed.
>
> A regular expression consists of a combination of regular characters and special metacharacters, which define the pattern to be matched. For example, the regular expression ^hell would match words beginning with hell—hello and hellhound, but not shell—while the regular expression Wil would match Winnie, Wimpy, Wilson, and William, though not Wendy or Wolf.

Addition of the NOT logical operator to the REGEXP operator reverses its behavior, returning false if a match is found.

```
mysql> SELECT 'hammer' NOT REGEXP 'ham$';
+---------------------------+
| 'hammer' NOT REGEXP 'ham$' |
+---------------------------+
|                         1 |
+---------------------------+
1 row in set (0.01 sec)
```

Table 6-3 shows a list of the more useful metacharacters, together with what they mean.

Metacharacter	What It Does
+	Match one or more occurrences of the preceding character
*	Match zero or more occurrences of the preceding character
?	Match zero or one occurrences of the preceding character
.	Match any character
^	Match at the beginning of a string
$	Match at the end of a string
\s	Match a single white space character, including tabs and newline characters
\S	Match everything that is not a white space character
\d	Match numbers from 0 to 9
\w	Match letters, numbers, and underscores
\W	Match anything that does not match with \w

TABLE 6-3 Commonly Used Metacharacters in Regular Expressions

---

[1] Excerpted from "So What's A $#!%% Regular Expression, Anyway?!" http://www.melonfire.com/community/columns/trog/article.php?id=2.

Let's see how these operators might work in a real-world situation. Consider the following MySQL table, which holds data on the races run by seven horses over a two-year period:

```
mysql> SELECT * FROM racedata;
+---------------+-------+-----+-------+----------+
| name          | total | win | place | unplaced |
+---------------+-------+-----+-------+----------+
| Stormtrooper  |    50 |   4 |    13 |        9 |
| VioletDaisy   |     9 |   4 |     5 |        0 |
| King William  |    33 |  11 |    15 |        4 |
| Remuneration  |   127 |  35 |    56 |       22 |
| Pop Princess  |    79 |   4 |    14 |       43 |
| Superman      |    43 |   0 |     6 |       11 |
| Baby Boo      |    67 |  56 |    10 |        1 |
+---------------+-------+-----+-------+----------+
7 rows in set (0.00 sec)
```

As you will see, it's possible to use MySQL's comparison operators to extract some fairly interesting conclusions from this data. For example, you could obtain a list of all horses that have participated in more than 50 races:

```
mysql> SELECT name, total FROM racedata WHERE total > 50;
+---------------+-------+
| name          | total |
+---------------+-------+
| Remuneration  |   127 |
| Pop Princess  |    79 |
| Baby Boo      |    67 |
+---------------+-------+
3 rows in set (0.00 sec)
```

Or you could obtain a list of all horses that have won 10 or more races:

```
mysql> SELECT name, win FROM racedata WHERE win >= 10;
+---------------+-----+
| name          | win |
+---------------+-----+
| King William  |  11 |
| Remuneration  |  35 |
| Baby Boo      |  56 |
+---------------+-----+
3 rows in set (0.00 sec)
```

You could get a list of the horses that have achieved either a win or a place in all their races (these would probably be good to back in their next outing):

```
mysql> SELECT name FROM racedata WHERE win + place = total;
+-------------+
| name        |
+-------------+
| VioletDaisy |
+-------------+
1 row in set (0.00 sec)
```

PART II

You could also find out which horses have finished every single race they participated in (thereby demonstrating unusual consistency):

```
mysql> SELECT name FROM racedata WHERE win + place + unplaced = total;
+-------------+
| name        |
+-------------+
| VioletDaisy |
| Baby Boo    |
+-------------+
2 rows in set (0.00 sec)
```

You could also obtain a list of horses with good past records—for example, all those horses that have won or placed in half or more of their races:

```
mysql> SELECT name, win, place, total FROM racedata
WHERE ( win + place ) / total >= 0.5;
+---------------+-----+-------+-------+
| name          | win | place | total |
+---------------+-----+-------+-------+
| VioletDaisy   |   4 |     5 |     9 |
| King William  |  11 |    15 |    33 |
| Remuneration  |  35 |    56 |   127 |
| Baby Boo      |  56 |    10 |    67 |
+---------------+-----+-------+-------+
4 rows in set (0.00 sec)
```

Or you could get a list of the horses that have won less than 10 percent of their races:

```
mysql> SELECT name, win FROM racedata WHERE ( win / total ) < 0.1;
+---------------+-----+
| name          | win |
+---------------+-----+
| Stormtrooper  |   4 |
| Pop Princess  |   4 |
| Superman      |   0 |
+---------------+-----+
3 rows in set (0.00 sec)
```

You could drill into the specific details of each horse's history, finding out, for example, whether Superman finished all the races he started (he didn't).

```
mysql> SELECT name, total, win + place + unplaced FROM racedata
WHERE name = 'Superman';
+-----------+-------+------------------------+
| name      | total | win + place + unplaced |
+-----------+-------+------------------------+
| Superman  |    43 |                     17 |
+-----------+-------+------------------------+
1 row in set (0.01 sec)
```

Or you could determine whether King William has the bloodline of a royal in terms of victories (he doesn't):

```
mysql> SELECT name, total, win FROM racedata
WHERE name = 'King William';
+---------------+-------+-----+
| name          | total | win |
+---------------+-------+-----+
| King William  |    33 |  11 |
+---------------+-------+-----+
1 row in set (0.00 sec)
```

Logical Operators

MySQL also comes with four logical operators, which make it possible to test the logical validity of one or more expressions (or sets of expressions). The result of an operation involving these operators is always 1 (true), 0 (false), or NULL (could not be determined).

Table 6-4 lists the logical operators supported by MySQL.

The simplest of these operators is the NOT operator, which reverses the logical sense of the test following it, turning true into false and false into true. You've seen a few examples of this in the previous section.

```
mysql> SELECT NOT 1, NOT 0, NOT (2=2), NOT (100 > 200);
+-------+-------+-----------+-----------------+
| NOT 1 | NOT 0 | NOT (2=2) | NOT (100 > 200) |
+-------+-------+-----------+-----------------+
|     0 |     1 |         0 |               1 |
+-------+-------+-----------+-----------------+
1 row in set (0.00 sec)
```

TABLE 6-4
MySQL Logical Operators

Operator	What It Does
NOT aka !	Logical NOT
AND aka &&	Logical AND
OR aka ||	Logical OR
XOR	Logical XOR (exclusive OR)

The AND operator makes it possible to test the validity of two or more values (or expressions evaluating to values); it returns true if all its components are true and not NULL, and it returns false otherwise.

```
mysql> SELECT (2 = 2) AND (900 < 100), ('a' = 'a') AND ('c' < 'd');
+-------------------------+----------------------------+
| (2 = 2) AND (900 < 100) | ('a' = 'a') AND ('c' < 'd') |
+-------------------------+----------------------------+
|                       0 |                          1 |
+-------------------------+----------------------------+
1 row in set (0.00 sec)
```

A twist on this is the OR operator, which returns true if any of the values or expressions involved are true and not NULL, and false otherwise. The following example demonstrates and also illustrates the difference between this operator and the preceding one:

```
mysql> SELECT (2 = 2) OR (900 < 100), ('a' = 'a') OR ('c' < 'd');
+------------------------+---------------------------+
| (2 = 2) OR (900 < 100) | ('a' = 'a') OR ('c' < 'd') |
+------------------------+---------------------------+
|                      1 |                         1 |
+------------------------+---------------------------+
1 row in set (0.00 sec)
```

MySQL 4.x and better also include an additional XOR operator, which returns true if either one (but not both) of its arguments is true. Consider the following examples, which demonstrate:

```
mysql> SELECT (1 = 1) XOR (2 = 4), (1 < 2) XOR (9 < 10);
+---------------------+----------------------+
| (1 = 1) XOR (2 = 4) | (1 < 2) XOR (9 < 10) |
+---------------------+----------------------+
|                   1 |                    0 |
+---------------------+----------------------+
1 row in set (0.00 sec)
```

To illustrate how useful logical operators can be when it comes to filtering data, let's go back to the real world and consider the following employee database:

```
mysql> SELECT * FROM employees;
+-----+--------+--------+-----+-----+----------------+---------+
| id  | fname  | lname  | age | sex | department     | country |
+-----+--------+--------+-----+-----+----------------+---------+
|  54 | Doe    | John   |  27 | M   | Engineering    | US      |
| 127 | Jones  | Sue    |  31 | F   | Finance        | UK      |
| 113 | Woo    | David  |  26 | M   | Administration | CN      |
| 175 | Thomas | James  |  34 | M   | Finance        | US      |
| 168 | Kent   | Jane   |  29 | F   | Administration | US      |
|  12 | Kamath | Ravina |  35 | F   | Finance        | IN      |
+-----+--------+--------+-----+-----+----------------+---------+
6 rows in set (0.00 sec)
```

With the assistance of MySQL's logical operators, you can group together conditions so as to obtain more precise results. For example, you could obtain a list of all female employees over the age of 30:

```
mysql> SELECT fname, lname, age FROM employees
WHERE sex = 'F' AND age > 30;
+--------+--------+-----+
| fname  | lname  | age |
+--------+--------+-----+
| Jones  | Sue    | 31  |
| Kamath | Ravina | 35  |
+--------+--------+-----+
2 rows in set (0.00 sec)
```

Or you could obtain a list of all male employees in the Finance department:

```
mysql> SELECT fname, lname FROM employees WHERE sex = 'M'
AND department = 'Finance';
+--------+--------+
| fname  | lname  |
+--------+--------+
| Thomas | James  |
+--------+--------+
1 row in set (0.01 sec)
```

Or you could even obtain all employees in either the United Kingdom or the United States:

```
mysql> SELECT fname, lname, country FROM employees
WHERE country = 'US' OR country = 'UK';
+--------+--------+---------+
| fname  | lname  | country |
+--------+--------+---------+
| Doe    | John   | US      |
| Jones  | Sue    | UK      |
| Thomas | James  | US      |
| Kent   | Jane   | US      |
+--------+--------+---------+
4 rows in set (0.00 sec)
```

You could obtain a specific employee's record:

```
mysql> SELECT * FROM employees WHERE fname = 'Kent'
AND lname = 'Jane';
+-----+--------+--------+-----+-----+----------------+---------+
| id  | fname  | lname  | age | sex | department     | country |
+-----+--------+--------+-----+-----+----------------+---------+
| 168 | Kent   | Jane   | 29  | F   | Administration | US      |
+-----+--------+--------+-----+-----+----------------+---------+
1 row in set (0.00 sec)
```

PART II

Or you could get a list of all non-US employees over 25:

```
mysql> SELECT fname, lname, country FROM employees
WHERE age > 25 AND NOT (country = 'US');
+--------+--------+---------+
| fname  | lname  | country |
+--------+--------+---------+
| Jones  | Sue    | UK      |
| Woo    | David  | CN      |
| Kamath | Ravina | IN      |
+--------+--------+---------+
3 rows in set (0.00 sec)
```

Bit Operators

MySQL also includes six operators designed specifically for bit manipulation. Table 6-5 has a list.

The | operator is used to perform a bitwise OR, while the & operator is used to perform a bitwise AND. The following examples demonstrate:

```
mysql> SELECT 16 | 32, 9 | 4;
+---------+-------+
| 16 | 32 | 9 | 4 |
+---------+-------+
|      48 |    13 |
+---------+-------+
1 row in set (0.00 sec)
mysql> SELECT 30 & 10, 8 & 16;
+---------+--------+
| 30 & 10 | 8 & 16 |
+---------+--------+
|      10 |      0 |
+---------+--------+
1 row in set (0.00 sec)
```

You can also shift bits to the left and right with the << and >> operators, respectively—consider the example, at the top of the next page, which demonstrates:

TABLE 6-5
MySQL Bit
Operators

Operator	What It Does
&	Bitwise AND
|	Bitwise OR
^	Bitwise XOR (exclusive OR)
~	Bit inversion
>>	Bitwise right shift
<<	Bitwise left shift

```
mysql> SELECT 1 << 7, 64 >> 1;
+--------+---------+
| 1 << 7 | 64 >> 1 |
+--------+---------+
|    128 |      32 |
+--------+---------+
1 row in set (0.00 sec)
```

The ^ operator is used to perform a bitwise XOR:

```
mysql> SELECT 1 ^ 0, 0 ^ 1, 17 ^ 9, 143 ^ 66;
+-------+-------+--------+----------+
| 1 ^ 0 | 0 ^ 1 | 17 ^ 9 | 143 ^ 66 |
+-------+-------+--------+----------+
|     1 |     1 |     24 |      205 |
+-------+-------+--------+----------+
1 row in set (0.00 sec)
```

The ~ operator is used to perform a bit inversion and return a 64-bit integer result:

```
mysql> SELECT ~18446744073709551614, ~1;
+-----------------------+----------------------+
| ~18446744073709551614 | ~1                   |
+-----------------------+----------------------+
|                     1 | 18446744073709551614 |
+-----------------------+----------------------+
1 row in set (0.01 sec)
```

Playing by the Rules

When it comes to evaluating operators, MySQL does not necessarily process them in the order in which they appear; rather, the program has its own set of rules about which operators have precedence over others. Take a look at the following list, which illustrates MySQL's precedence rules. (Operators on the same line have the same level of precedence.)

- `OR`
- `AND`
- `BETWEEN` `CASE` `WHEN` `THEN` `ELSE`
- `=` `<=>` `>=` `>` `<=` `<` `<>` `IS` `LIKE` `REGEXP` `IN`
- `|`
- `&`

- `'<<' '>>'`
- `'-' '+'`
- `'*' '/' '%'`
- `'~'`
- `'NOT'`
- `'BINARY'`

If in doubt, remember that you can—in fact, should—override these rules with parentheses, as some of the examples in this chapter do. This reduces ambiguity and ensures that operators are evaluated in the order that you specify. The following example demonstrates how using parentheses can make a difference to the way MySQL evaluates your expressions:

```
mysql> SELECT 2 + 4 / 3, (2 + 4) / 3;
+-----------+-------------+
| 2 + 4 / 3 | (2 + 4) / 3 |
+-----------+-------------+
|      3.33 |        2.00 |
+-----------+-------------+
1 row in set (0.00 sec)
```

Here's an example demonstrating bit operators in a real-world operation—calculating the network number from a user-supplied IP address and network mask:

```
mysql> SELECT INET_NTOA(INET_ATON('192.168.1.34') &
INET_ATON('255.255.255.0'));
+--------------------------------------------------------------------+
| INET_NTOA(INET_ATON("192.168.1.34") & INET_ATON("255.255.255.0")) |
+--------------------------------------------------------------------+
| 192.168.1.0                                                        |
+--------------------------------------------------------------------+
1 row in set (0.05 sec)
```

TIP   *The* INET_ATON() *function converts an IP address into its numeric representation; it's discussed in Chapter 7.*

Summary

This chapter took you one step further up the MySQL ladder, explaining, in detail, the various operators available to you when building SELECT expressions and clauses in MySQL. MySQL comes with more than 25 different operators, designed to perform arithmetic, comparison, logical, and bit operations; this chapter examined each of them, together with their constraints and rules, by using both simple examples and illustrations from the real world. A thorough knowledge of these operators, together with an understanding of where each one may most suitably be used, will stand you in good stead as you use MySQL's SQL statements to retrieve and update stored data.

MySQL Functions

As an RDBMS that prides itself on its flexibility, it's no surprise that MySQL comes with built-in functions that allow users to manipulate the data stored within its tables easily. The only surprise is that it comes with so many functions—at last count, MySQL included more than 100, ranging from simple mathematical functions to sophisticated comparison and date manipulation routines. This diverse range of options allows MySQL developers to perform complex operations with minimal code and is an important reason for MySQL's popularity.

This chapter will provide an overview of MySQL's various built-in functions, explaining the important ones with code snippets and examples of how they may be used for operations ranging from string comparison to date/time calculations, arithmetic operations, data conversion, and a host of other tasks.

These built-in functions can broadly be classified into the following groups:

- Math functions
- Aggregate functions
- String manipulation functions
- Date and time manipulation functions
- Data encryption functions
- Control flow functions
- Formatting functions
- Type conversion functions
- System information functions

The following sections examine each of these categories in greater detail.

Math Functions

Just as MySQL comes with a bunch of arithmetic operators, so, too, does the RDBMS support a wide variety of mathematical functions. Table 7-1 lists the more important ones.

Function	What It Does
ABS(x)	Returns absolute value of x
ACOS(x)	Returns the arc cosine of x (radians)
ASIN(x)	Returns the arc sine of x (radians)
ATAN(x)	Returns the arc tangent of x (radians)
CEILING(x)	Returns the closest integer value greater than x
COS(x)	Returns cosine of x (radians)
COT(x)	Returns the cotangent of x (radians)
DEGREES(x)	Returns the result of converting x radians to degrees
EXP(x)	Returns e^x
FLOOR(x)	Returns the closest integer value less than x
GREATEST(x1,x2,...,xn)	Returns the largest value in a number set
LEAST(x1,x2,...,xn)	Returns the smallest value in a number set
LN(x)	Returns $\log_e x$
LOG(x,y)	Returns $\log_y x$
MOD(x,y)	Returns the modulo (remainder) of x / y
PI()	Returns the value of pi
POW(x,y) aka POWER(x,y)	Returns x^y
RAND()	Returns a random number between 0 and 1
RADIANS(x)	Returns the result of converting x degrees to radians
ROUND(x,y)	Returns x rounded off to the closest integer, with y decimal places
SIGN(x)	Returns number representing the sign of x
SQRT(x)	Returns $x^{1/2}$
SIN(x)	Returns the sine of x (radians)
TAN(x)	Returns the tangent of x (radians)
TRUNCATE(x,y)	Returns the result of truncating x to y decimal places

TABLE 7-1   MySQL Math Functions

The functions that tend to be used the most are those related to obtaining the largest and smallest of a group of numbers. Consider the following example, which demonstrates the GREATEST() and LEAST() functions in action:

```
mysql> SELECT GREATEST(100, 99, 158, 63), GREATEST(1.1, 2.2);
+----------------------------+--------------------+
| GREATEST(100, 99, 158, 63) | GREATEST(1.1, 2.2) |
+----------------------------+--------------------+
|                        158 |                2.2 |
+----------------------------+--------------------+
1 row in set (0.00 sec)

mysql> SELECT LEAST(-2, 5, 99), LEAST(1, 2, GREATEST(1, 2, 3));
+------------------+--------------------------------+
| LEAST(-2, 5, 99) | LEAST(1, 2, GREATEST(1, 2, 3)) |
+------------------+--------------------------------+
|               -2 |                              1 |
+------------------+--------------------------------+
1 row in set (0.00 sec)
```

NOTE *MySQL does not permit spaces between a function invocation and its opening parenthesis.*

You can use the FLOOR() and CEILING() functions to obtain the next-smallest and next-largest integer values to a number:

```
mysql> SELECT FLOOR(-75.1), CEILING(-75.1),
FLOOR(99.99), CEILING(99.99);
+--------------+----------------+--------------+----------------+
| FLOOR(-75.1) | CEILING(-75.1) | FLOOR(99.99) | CEILING(99.99) |
+--------------+----------------+--------------+----------------+
|          -76 |            -75 |           99 |            100 |
+--------------+----------------+--------------+----------------+
1 row in set (0.00 sec)
```

Or you can use the ROUND() function to round numbers to their closest integer value:

```
mysql> SELECT ROUND(10.33), ROUND(64.5000001), ROUND(7.987654533);
+--------------+-------------------+--------------------+
| ROUND(10.33) | ROUND(64.5000001) | ROUND(7.987654533) |
+--------------+-------------------+--------------------+
|           10 |                65 |                  8 |
+--------------+-------------------+--------------------+
1 row in set (0.00 sec)
```

Similar though not identical to the ROUND() function is the TRUNCATE() function, which truncates a number to a specified number of decimal places:

```
mysql> SELECT TRUNCATE(1.7850927343,3), TRUNCATE(-629.2383873, 10);
+--------------------------+----------------------------+
| TRUNCATE(1.7850927343,3) | TRUNCATE(-629.2383873, 10) |
+--------------------------+----------------------------+
|                    1.785 |             -629.2383873000 |
+--------------------------+----------------------------+
1 row in set (0.00 sec)x
```

The ABS() function comes in handy when you need the absolute value of a number:

```
mysql> SELECT ABS(-765);
+-----------+
| ABS(-765) |
+-----------+
|       765 |
+-----------+
1 row in set (0.03 sec)
```

The SIGN() function returns the sign of a number, depending on whether it is positive (1), negative (-1), or zero (0):

```
mysql> SELECT SIGN(-99), SIGN(99), SIGN(0);
+-----------+----------+---------+
| SIGN(-99) | SIGN(99) | SIGN(0) |
+-----------+----------+---------+
|        -1 |        1 |       0 |
+-----------+----------+---------+
1 row in set (0.03 sec)
```

Going Negative

Interestingly, you can also give TRUNCATE() a negative value as the second argument—and look what happens:

```
mysql> SELECT TRUNCATE(1785.0927343,-2), TRUNCATE(-629.2383873, -1);
+---------------------------+----------------------------+
| TRUNCATE(1785.0927343,-2) | TRUNCATE(-629.2383873, -1) |
+---------------------------+----------------------------+
|                      1700 |                       -620 |
+---------------------------+----------------------------+
1 row in set (0.00 sec)
```

The SQRT() function returns the square root of a number:

```
mysql> SELECT SQRT(49), SQRT(17), SQRT(1);
+----------+----------+----------+
| SQRT(49) | SQRT(17) | SQRT(1)  |
+----------+----------+----------+
| 7.000000 | 4.123106 | 1.000000 |
+----------+----------+----------+
1 row in set (0.00 sec)
```

The POW() function raises one number to the power of another and returns the result:

```
mysql> SELECT POW(4,4), POW(10,-2), POW(3,0), POW(0,5);
+------------+------------+----------+----------+
| POW(4,4)   | POW(10,-2) | POW(3,0) | POW(0,5) |
+------------+------------+----------+----------+
| 256.000000 |   0.010000 | 1.000000 | 0.000000 |
+------------+------------+----------+----------+
1 row in set (0.00 sec)
```

The LOG() function returns the natural logarithm of its first argument:

```
mysql> SELECT LOG(4), LOG(1), LOG(0), LOG(2.718282);
+----------+----------+--------+---------------+
| LOG(4)   | LOG(1)   | LOG(0) | LOG(2.718282) |
+----------+----------+--------+---------------+
| 1.386294 | 0.000000 |   NULL |      1.000000 |
+----------+----------+--------+---------------+
1 row in set (0.00 sec)
```

Or, if two arguments are specified, LOG() returns the logarithm of the first argument using the second argument as base:

```
mysql> SELECT LOG(2,2), LOG(56,4), LOG(0,4);
+----------+-----------+----------+
| LOG(2,2) | LOG(56,4) | LOG(0,4) |
+----------+-----------+----------+
| 1.000000 | 0.344391  |     NULL |
+----------+-----------+----------+
1 row in set (0.01 sec)
```

NOTE   *Variants of the LOG() function are the LOG10() function, which returns the base-10 logarithm of a number, and the LOG2() function, which returns the base-2 logarithm of a number.*

The EXP() function does the reverse of the LOG() function, returning the value of e to the power of the specified number:

```
mysql> SELECT EXP(9), EXP(1), EXP(0), EXP(-45);
+-------------+----------+----------+----------+
| EXP(9)      | EXP(1)   | EXP(0)   | EXP(-45) |
+-------------+----------+----------+----------+
| 8103.083928 | 2.718282 | 1.000000 | 0.000000 |
+-------------+----------+----------+----------+
1 row in set (0.01 sec)
```

The SIN(), COS(), and TAN() functions return the sine, cosine, and tangent of an angle (specified in radians):

```
mysql> SELECT SIN(1.5708), COS(1.5708), TAN(RADIANS(45));
+-------------+-------------+------------------+
| SIN(1.5708) | COS(1.5708) | TAN(RADIANS(45)) |
+-------------+-------------+------------------+
|    1.000000 |   -0.000004 |         1.000000 |
+-------------+-------------+------------------+
1 row in set (0.00 sec)
```

The ASIN(), ACOS(), and ATAN() functions return the arc sine, arc cosine, and arc tangent of an angle (again specified in radians):

```
mysql> SELECT ASIN(1), ACOS(1), ATAN(RADIANS(45));
+----------+----------+-------------------+
| ASIN(1)  | ACOS(1)  | ATAN(RADIANS(45)) |
+----------+----------+-------------------+
| 1.570796 | 0.000000 |          0.665774 |
+----------+----------+-------------------+
1 row in set (0.00 sec)
```

In case you'd prefer to use degrees instead of radians, you can convert between them using the DEGREES() and RADIANS() functions:

```
mysql> SELECT RADIANS(90), RADIANS(180);
+-----------------+-----------------+
| RADIANS(90)     | RADIANS(180)    |
+-----------------+-----------------+
| 1.5707963267949 | 3.1415926535898 |
+-----------------+-----------------+
1 row in set (0.00 sec)
```

```
mysql> SELECT DEGREES(1.57), DEGREES(3.14);
+-----------------+-----------------+
| DEGREES(1.57)   | DEGREES(3.14)   |
+-----------------+-----------------+
| 89.954373835539 | 179.90874767108 |
+-----------------+-----------------+
1 row in set (0.01 sec)
```

The `BIN()`, `OCT()`, and `HEX()` functions return the binary, octal, and hexadecimal values of a number, respectively; this value is returned as a string:

```
mysql> SELECT BIN(2), OCT(28), HEX(56);
+--------+---------+---------+
| BIN(2) | OCT(28) | HEX(56) |
+--------+---------+---------+
| 10     | 34      | 38      |
+--------+---------+---------+
1 row in set (0.00 sec)
```

Finally, the `PI()` function returns the value of pi:

```
mysql> SELECT PI();
+----------+
| PI()     |
+----------+
| 3.141593 |
+----------+
1 row in set (0.00 sec)
```

The `RAND()` function returns a random number between 0 and 1:

```
mysql> SELECT RAND(), RAND(), RAND();
+------------------+------------------+------------------+
| RAND()           | RAND()           | RAND()           |
+------------------+------------------+------------------+
| 0.97721177709961 | 0.12815972336397 | 0.70916331625466 |
+------------------+------------------+------------------+
1 row in set (0.01 sec)
```

You can seed `RAND()`'s random number generator with a specific value by providing it with that value as argument:

```
mysql> SELECT RAND(17), RAND(10);
+------------------+------------------+
| RAND(17)         | RAND(10)         |
+------------------+------------------+
| 0.40833328422935 | 0.65705152196535 |
+------------------+------------------+
1 row in set (0.00 sec)
```

Aggregate Functions

MySQL comes with a number of functions designed specifically to provide aggregates, or focused summaries, of the data in a table. These functions are most commonly used with `SELECT` queries containing `GROUP BY` clauses; however, they may also be used with non-GROUPed queries. Table 7-2 shows the functions.

Function	What It Does
AVG(*col*)	Returns the average of the values in the named column
COUNT(*col*)	Returns a count of the number of non-NULL records in the named column
MIN(*col*)	Returns the minimum value in the named column
MAX(*col*)	Returns the maximum value in the named column
SUM(*col*)	Returns the total of the values in the named column
STD(*col*) aka STDDEV(*col*)	Returns the standard deviation of the values in the named column
VARIANCE(*col*)	Returns the statistical variance of the values in the named columns
GROUP_CONCAT(*col*)	Returns a concatenated set of column values belonging to a group

TABLE 7-2   MySQL Aggregate Functions

The most frequently seen function in this category is the COUNT() function, which counts the number of rows in the result set containing at least one non-NULL value:

```
mysql> SELECT COUNT(*) FROM members;
+----------+
| COUNT(*) |
+----------+
|       45 |
+----------+
1 row in set (0.05 sec)
```

The MIN() and MAX() functions return the smallest and largest values in a number set:

```
mysql> SELECT MIN(quantity) FROM inventory;
+---------------+
| MIN(quantity) |
+---------------+
|           100 |
+---------------+
1 row in set (0.00 sec)

mysql> SELECT MAX(return) FROM investments;
+-------------+
| MAX(return) |
+-------------+
|    23760.00 |
+-------------+
1 row in set (0.00 sec)
```

The SUM() and AVG() functions return the sum and average of a set:

```
mysql> SELECT SUM(units), AVG(return) FROM mutualfunds;
+---------------+-------------+
| SUM(units)    | AVG(return) |
+---------------+-------------+
|          7610 | 27.056000   |
+---------------+-------------+
1 row in set (0.01 sec)
```

The VARIANCE() function returns the variance of the values in the specified set, while the STD() function returns their standard deviation:

```
mysql> SELECT VARIANCE(invoiceAmt) FROM invoices
WHERE customerID = 125;
+----------------------+
| VARIANCE(invoiceAmt) |
+----------------------+
|       1133926.723409 |
+----------------------+
1 row in set (0.22 sec)
mysql> SELECT STD(price) FROM stocks;
+-------------+
| STD(price)  |
+-------------+
| 19.998123   |
+-------------+
1 row in set (0.01 sec)
```

The GROUP_CONCAT() function concatenates all the values in a particular group (created via the GROUP BY clause) into a string. For example, if you have a table mapping users to groups, as follows:

```
+-------+-----------+
| uname | gname     |
+-------+-----------+
| sam   | actors    |
| sue   | musicians |
| james | authors   |
| rita  | authors   |
| sue   | authors   |
| louis | actors    |
| sue   | actors    |
+-------+-----------+
7 rows in set (0.11 sec)
```

you could use the GROUP_CONCAT() function to return an alternative, more-readable representation of the same information, as illustrated below:

```
mysql> SELECT gname, GROUP_CONCAT(uname) AS members FROM users_groups
GROUP BY gname;
+------------+--------------------+
| gname      | members            |
+------------+--------------------+
|  authors   | james rita sue     |
|  actors    | sam louis sue      |
|  musicians | sue                |
+------------+--------------------+
3 rows in set (0.17 sec)
```

NOTE *Both VARIANCE() and GROUP_CONCAT() functions are new in MySQL 4.1*

To see how useful these functions can be, consider the following example table, which contains a list of students and their marks in respective subjects:

```
mysql> SELECT * FROM marks;
+----+-------+-------+------+-----+-----+
| id | fname | lname | math | sci | lit |
+----+-------+-------+------+-----+-----+
|  1 | John  | Doe   |   36 |  73 |  34 |
|  2 | Sarah | Short |   23 |  67 |  55 |
|  3 | Joe   | Cool  |   75 |  82 |  89 |
|  4 | Mark  | Wumba |   58 |  72 |  15 |
|  5 | Tom   | Thumb |    0 |  12 |   0 |
+----+-------+-------+------+-----+-----+
5 rows in set (0.00 sec)
```

It's now possible to use the aggregate functions to obtain big-picture information about the records in this table. For example, you could use the COUNT() function to obtain the number of students who have appeared for the examinations:

```
mysql> SELECT COUNT(*) FROM marks;
+----------+
| COUNT(*) |
+----------+
|        5 |
+----------+
1 row in set (0.00 sec)
```

Or you could use COUNT() to show the number of students who scored marks of less than 25 in any subject:

```
mysql> SELECT COUNT(*) FROM marks
WHERE (math < 25 OR sci < 25 OR lit < 25);
+----------+
| COUNT(*) |
+----------+
|        3 |
+----------+
1 row in set (0.00 sec)
```

You can obtain the maximum and minimum marks in the various subjects with the MIN() and MAX() functions:

```
mysql> SELECT MAX(math), MAX(lit), MIN(sci) FROM marks;
+-----------+----------+----------+
| MAX(math) | MAX(lit) | MIN(sci) |
+-----------+----------+----------+
|        75 |       89 |       12 |
+-----------+----------+----------+
1 row in set (0.01 sec)
```

And you can calculate the average marks in each subject with the AVG() function:

```
mysql> SELECT AVG(math), AVG(sci), AVG(lit) FROM marks;
+-----------+----------+----------+
| AVG(math) | AVG(sci) | AVG(lit) |
+-----------+----------+----------+
|   38.4000 |  61.2000 |  38.6000 |
+-----------+----------+----------+
1 row in set (0.00 sec)
```

String Functions

Since MySQL databases usually contain string values as well as numeric data, MySQL comes with a variety of functions designed to aid in string manipulation. The important ones are listed in Table 7-3.

Function	What It Does
ASCII(char)	Returns the ASCII value of char
BIT_LENGTH(str)	Returns the length of str in bits
CHAR(x1,x2,...,xn)	Returns a string containing ASCII characters corresponding to x1,x2,...,xn
CONCAT(s1,s2,...,sn)	Concatenates s1,s2,...,sn into a single string
CONCAT_WS(sep,s1,s2,...,sn)	Concatenates s1,s2,...,sn into a single string, separated with sep

TABLE 7-3   MySQL String Functions

Function	What It Does
INSERT(str,x,y,instr)	Returns the result of inserting instr into str at position x with length y
FIELD(str,s1,s2,...,sn)	Parses the list s1,s2,...,sn for str and returns the index of the matching element, if any
FIND_IN_SET(str,list)	Parses the comma-separated list list for str and returns the position of the matching index, if any
LCASE(str) aka LOWER(str)	Returns str with all characters lowercase
LEFT(str,x)	Returns the first x characters of str from the left
LENGTH(s)	Returns the number of characters in str
LPAD(str,n,pad)	Pads str from the left with pad until it contains n characters
LTRIM(str)	Trims leading white space from str
ORD(char)	Returns a multibyte-safe representation of char
POSITION(substr,str)	Returns the position of the first occurrence of substr in str
QUOTE(str)	Escapes single quotes in str with backslashes
REPEAT(str,x)	Returns the result of repeating str x times
REPLACE(str,srchstr,rplcstr)	Replace all occurrences of srchstr in str with rplcstr
REVERSE(str)	Returns the result of reversing str
RIGHT(str,x)	Returns the first x characters of str from the right
RPAD(str,x,pad)	Pads str from the left with pad until it contains n characters
RTRIM(str)	Trims trailing white space from str
STRCMP(s1,s2)	Compares string s1 with string s2
SUBSTRING(str,x,y) aka MID(str,x,y)	Returns a substring of length y characters, starting from position x in str
TRIM(str)	Trim leading and trailing white space from str
UCASE(str) aka UPPER(str)	Returns str with all characters uppercase

TABLE 7-3   MySQL String Functions *(continued)*

The length of a string may be obtained via the LENGTH() function:

```
mysql> SELECT LENGTH('abracadabra');
+-----------------------+
| LENGTH('abracadabra') |
+-----------------------+
|                    11 |
+-----------------------+
1 row in set (0.00 sec)
```

The `BIT_LENGTH()` function returns the length in bits rather than characters:

```
mysql> SELECT BIT_LENGTH('abracadabra');
+---------------------------+
| BIT_LENGTH('abracadabra') |
+---------------------------+
|                        88 |
+---------------------------+
1 row in set (0.00 sec)
```

Strings may be padded to the right or left with the `RPAD()` or `LPAD()` function, respectively. Strings are usually padded with spaces; however, you can have MySQL pad them with a custom value by specifying it as a third argument to the `RPAD()` and `LPAD()` functions.

```
mysql> SELECT RPAD('red alert', 17, '!'), LPAD('welcome', 12, '* ');
+----------------------------+----------------------------+
| RPAD('red alert', 17, '!') | LPAD('welcome', 12, '* ')  |
+----------------------------+----------------------------+
| red alert!!!!!!!!           | * * *welcome               |
+----------------------------+----------------------------+
1 row in set (0.00 sec)
```

You can reverse some of the effects of string padding via the `LTRIM()` and `RTRIM()` functions, which trim white space from the beginning and end of a string value, respectively:

```
mysql> SELECT RTRIM("right hand    "), LTRIM("    left eye");
+-------------------------+----------------------+
| RTRIM("right hand    ") | LTRIM("    left eye") |
+-------------------------+----------------------+
| right hand              | left eye             |
+-------------------------+----------------------+
1 row in set (0.00 sec)
```

A Question of Space

Speaking of spaces, you can have MySQL generate a string value consisting solely of spaces via the `SPACE()` function:

```
mysql> SELECT SPACE(4);
+----------+
| SPACE(4) |
+----------+
|          |
+----------+
1 row in set (0.03 sec)
```

An alternative here is the all-encompassing TRIM() function, which allows you to specify the pattern to erase when trimming values and also to decide whether trimming should occur at the beginning, end, or both sides of a string:

```
mysql> SELECT TRIM('    red alert    ');
+--------------------------+
| trim('    red alert    ') |
+--------------------------+
| red alert                |
+--------------------------+
1 row in set (0.00 sec)
mysql> SELECT TRIM(LEADING '!' FROM '!!!!!ERROR!!!');
+----------------------------------------+
| TRIM(LEADING '!' FROM '!!!!!ERROR!!!') |
+----------------------------------------+
| ERROR!!!                               |
+----------------------------------------+
1 row in set (0.00 sec)
mysql> SELECT TRIM(BOTH '.' FROM '...welcome...');
+-----------------------------------+
| TRIM(BOTH '.' FROM '...welcome...') |
+-----------------------------------+
| welcome                           |
+-----------------------------------+
1 row in set (0.00 sec)
```

Specific segments of a string may be extracted with the LEFT() or RIGHT() function, which returns characters from the left or right side of a string:

```
mysql> SELECT LEFT('Hello', 4), RIGHT('Welcome to the fundraiser', 6);
+-----------------+------------------------------------+
| LEFT('Hello', 4) | RIGHT('Welcome to the fundraiser', 6) |
+-----------------+------------------------------------+
| Hell            | raiser                             |
+-----------------+------------------------------------+
1 row in set (0.01 sec)
```

Want a segment from the middle of a string? You can use the LEFT() *and* RIGHT() functions in combination with each other:

```
mysql> SELECT LEFT(RIGHT('market', 5), 3);
+---------------------------+
| LEFT(RIGHT('market', 5), 3) |
+---------------------------+
| ark                       |
+---------------------------+
1 row in set (0.01 sec)
```

You can also use the much simpler SUBSTRING() function, which allows you to specify both the length and start position of a string segment:

```
mysql> SELECT SUBSTRING('market', 2, 3);
+--------------------------+
| SUBSTRING('market', 2, 3) |
+--------------------------+
| ark                      |
+--------------------------+
1 row in set (0.03 sec)
```

The CONCAT() function concatenates the arguments provided to it into a single string:

```
mysql> SELECT CONCAT('Clark', 'Kent');
+-----------------------+
| CONCAT('Clark', 'Kent') |
+-----------------------+
| ClarkKent             |
+-----------------------+
1 row in set (0.01 sec)
```

If any of CONCAT()'s arguments are NULL, the end result will also be NULL.

```
mysql> SELECT CONCAT('Clark', 'Kent', NULL),
CONCAT('Clark', 'Kent', 'NULL');
+------------------------------+------------------------------+
| CONCAT('Clark', 'Kent', NULL) | CONCAT('Clark', 'Kent', 'NULL') |
+------------------------------+------------------------------+
| NULL                         | ClarkKentNULL                |
+------------------------------+------------------------------+
1 row in set (0.00 sec)
```

You can join string values with a specific separator, via the similar (though not completely identical) CONCAT_WS() function, which allows you to specify a string separator as first argument; here's an example:

```
mysql> SELECT CONCAT_WS(' ', 'Clark', 'Kent');
+-------------------------------+
| CONCAT_WS(' ', 'Clark', 'Kent') |
+-------------------------------+
| Clark Kent                    |
+-------------------------------+
1 row in set (0.00 sec)
```

Here's another:

```
mysql> SELECT
CONCAT_WS(', ', CONCAT_WS(' ', 'Clark', 'Kent'), 'Superman');
+------------------------------------------------------------+
| CONCAT_WS(', ', CONCAT_WS(' ', 'Clark', 'Kent'), 'Superman') |
+------------------------------------------------------------+
| Clark Kent, Superman                                       |
+------------------------------------------------------------+
1 row in set (0.01 sec)
```

You can test whether a string contains a specified substring with the LOCATE() function, which returns the position of the first occurrence of that substring in the named string value (if it exists):

```
mysql> SELECT LOCATE('me', 'Robin Hood and his merry men');
+---------------------------------------------+
| LOCATE('me', 'Robin Hood and his merry men') |
+---------------------------------------------+
|                                          20 |
+---------------------------------------------+
1 row in set (0.02 sec)
```

You can also use the FIND_IN_SET() function to find out whether a specific string value exists within a larger collection. The string collection passed as the second argument to FIND_IN_SET() must consist of a series of comma-separated string values, and the function returns the position of the matching value, if such a value exists. Positions are numbered beginning with 1.

```
mysql> SELECT FIND_IN_SET('Ross',
'Rachel,Phoebe,Monica,Ross,Joey,Chandler');
+-----------------------------------------------------------+
| FIND_IN_SET('Ross', 'Rachel,Phoebe,Monica,Ross,Joey,Chandler') |
+-----------------------------------------------------------+
|                                                         4 |
+-----------------------------------------------------------+
1 row in set (0.00 sec)
```

You can compare strings with the STRCMP() function, which accepts two strings as argument and returns 0 if they are the same, 1 if the first is larger than the second, and –1 otherwise. (String comparison is case-insensitive unless the special BINARY keyword is used or the values involved are BLOBs.)

```
mysql> SELECT STRCMP('y', 'z'), STRCMP('e', BINARY 'E');
+------------------+-------------------------+
| STRCMP('y', 'z') | STRCMP('e', BINARY 'E') |
+------------------+-------------------------+
|               -1 |                       1 |
+------------------+-------------------------+
1 row in set (0.00 sec)
```

The REPLACE() function can be used to search for specific substrings within a string and replace them with an alternative substring:

```
mysql> SELECT REPLACE('I am Joe Cool', 'Cool', 'Camel');
+-----------------------------------------+
| REPLACE('I am Joe Cool', 'Cool', 'Camel') |
+-----------------------------------------+
| I am Joe Camel                          |
+-----------------------------------------+
1 row in set (0.02 sec)
```

The INSERT() function can be used to replace a specific segment (defined by start and length coordinates) of a string forcibly with a new value:

```
mysql> SELECT INSERT('I am Joe Cool', 10, 4, 'Camel');
+-----------------------------------------+
| INSERT('I am Joe Cool', 10, 4, 'Camel') |
+-----------------------------------------+
| I am Joe Camel                          |
+-----------------------------------------+
1 row in set (0.01 sec)
```

You can repeat strings with the REPEAT() function:

```
mysql> SELECT REPEAT('ha ', 6);
+-------------------+
| REPEAT('ha ', 6)  |
+-------------------+
| ha ha ha ha ha ha |
+-------------------+
1 row in set (0.02 sec)
```

And you can reverse them with the REVERSE() function:

```
mysql> SELECT REVERSE(REPEAT('ha ', 6));
+---------------------------+
| REVERSE(REPEAT('ha ', 6)) |
+---------------------------+
|  ah ah ah ah ah ah        |
+---------------------------+
1 row in set (0.00 sec)
```

You can uppercase strings with the UCASE() function and lowercase them with the corresponding LCASE() function:

```
mysql> SELECT UCASE('Little Bo Peep'), LCASE('DotCom');
+------------------------+-----------------+
| UCASE('Little Bo Peep') | LCASE('DotCom') |
+------------------------+-----------------+
| LITTLE BO PEEP          | dotcom          |
+------------------------+-----------------+
1 row in set (0.00 sec)
```

The ASCII() function returns the ASCII value of a given character:

```
mysql> SELECT ASCII('A'), ASCII('a');
+------------+------------+
| ASCII('A') | ASCII('a') |
+------------+------------+
|         65 |         97 |
+------------+------------+
1 row in set (0.00 sec)
```

The ORD() function returns a numeric code representing a given character. (This is usually used instead of ASCII() for multi-byte string values.)

```
mysql> SELECT ORD('À');
+----------+
| ORD('À') |
+----------+
|      192 |
+----------+
1 row in set (0.01 sec
```

Date and Time Functions

Given the large number of date and time data types in MySQL, it's no surprise that the RDBMS comes with an equally large number of functions to manipulate date and time values. MySQL's date and time functions are more versatile than those in many other competing RDBMS, a fact amply illustrated by Table 7-4, which lists the more important and useful time and date functions in the collection.

Function	What It Does
CURDATE() aka CURRENT_DATE()	Returns the current date
CURTIME() aka CURRENT_TIME()	Returns the current time
DATE_ADD(date, INTERVAL int keyword)	Returns the result of adding the duration int to date (int must be formatted as per the rules for keyword)
DATE_FORMAT(date, fmt)	Formats date as per format specified in fmt
DATE_SUB(date, INTERVAL int keyword)	Returns the result of subtracting the duration int from date (int must be formatted as per the rules for keyword)
DAYOFWEEK(date)	Returns a number (1 to 7) representing the day of the week for date
DAYOFMONTH	Returns the day component (1 to 31) of date

TABLE 7-4   MySQL Date and Time Functions

Function	What It Does
DAYOFYEAR(date)	Returns a number (1 to 366) representing the day of the year for date
DAYNAME(date)	Returns the weekday name for date
EXTRACT(keyword FROM date)	Returns a specific component of date, as per keyword
FROM_DAYS(x)	Returns a date created by adding x days to year 0
FROM_UNIXTIME(ts,fmt)	Formats UNIX timestamp ts as per format specified in fmt
HOUR(time)	Returns the hour component (0–23) of time
MINUTE(time)	Returns the minute component (0–59) of time
MONTH(date)	Returns the month component (1–12) for date
MONTHNAME(date)	Returns the month name for date
NOW()	Returns the current date and time
QUARTER(date)	Returns the quarter (1–4) in which date falls
PERIOD_ADD(date,mon)	Returns the result of adding mon months to date
PERIOD_DIFF(date1,date2)	Returns the difference, in months, between date1 and date2
SECOND(time)	Returns the second component (0–59) of time
SEC_TO_TIME(x)	Converts x seconds into a readable time value
TIME_FORMAT(time,fmt)	Formats time as per format specified in fmt
TIME_TO_SEC(time)	Converts time into seconds
TO_DAYS(date)	Returns the number of days between year 0 and date
UNIX_TIMESTAMP(date)	Returns a UNIX timestamp representation of date
WEEK(date)	Returns the week number (0–53) for date
YEAR(date)	Returns the year component (1000–9999) of date

TABLE 7-4   MySQL Date and Time Functions (continued)

As always, let's start right at the top—getting the current date and time. This is accomplished by means of the NOW() function, which returns the current date and time in YYYY-MM-DD HH:MM:SS format:

```
mysql> SELECT NOW();
+---------------------+
| NOW()               |
+---------------------+
| 2003-05-15 11:13:03 |
+---------------------+
1 row in set (0.01 sec)
```

The CURTIME() and CURDATE() functions are more specialized variants of the NOW() function, returning only the current time and date, respectively:

```
mysql> SELECT CURTIME(), CURDATE();
+-----------+------------+
| CURTIME() | CURDATE()  |
+-----------+------------+
| 11:14:38  | 2003-05-15 |
+-----------+------------+
1 row in set (0.00 sec)
```

A UNIX timestamp (the number of seconds between 1970-01-01 00:00:00 and the current time) may be obtained via the UNIX_TIMESTAMP() function. If no argument is supplied, the timestamp is returned with reference to the current time; if a valid date is supplied as argument, the timestamp is returned with reference to that date.

```
mysql> SELECT UNIX_TIMESTAMP(), UNIX_TIMESTAMP(20040604);
+------------------+--------------------------+
| UNIX_TIMESTAMP() | UNIX_TIMESTAMP(20040604) |
+------------------+--------------------------+
|       1052977855 |               1086287400 |
+------------------+--------------------------+
1 row in set (0.00 sec)
```

You can convert a UNIX timestamp into a MySQL–readable date and time value with the reciprocal FROM_UNIXTIME() function, which accepts a UNIX timestamp and returns a DATETIME value:

```
mysql> SELECT FROM_UNIXTIME(1052977855);
+---------------------------+
| FROM_UNIXTIME(1052977855) |
+---------------------------+
| 2003-05-15 11:20:55       |
+---------------------------+
1 row in set (0.01 sec)
```

The YEAR() function parses a date value and returns the year component:

```
mysql> SELECT YEAR(20030415012345), YEAR('1967-09-21');
+----------------------+--------------------+
| YEAR(20030415012345) | YEAR('1967-09-21') |
+----------------------+--------------------+
|                 2003 |               1967 |
+----------------------+--------------------+
1 row in set (0.00 sec)
```

The MONTH() and MONTHNAME() functions return the month component, in both numeric and string format:

```
mysql> SELECT MONTH(20030415012345);
+-----------------------+
| MONTH(20030415012345) |
+-----------------------+
|                     4 |
+-----------------------+
1 row in set (0.00 sec)
mysql> SELECT MONTHNAME('1967-09-21'), MONTHNAME(20010604);
+-------------------------+---------------------+
| MONTHNAME('1967-09-21') | MONTHNAME(20010604) |
+-------------------------+---------------------+
| September               | June                |
+-------------------------+---------------------+
1 row in set (0.00 sec)
```

The DAYOFYEAR(), DAYOFWEEK(), and DAYOFMONTH() functions return the day index for a year, week, and month, respectively:

```
mysql> SELECT DAYOFYEAR(20030604), DAYOFMONTH('2003-02-14');
+---------------------+--------------------------+
| DAYOFYEAR(20030604) | DAYOFMONTH('2003-02-14') |
+---------------------+--------------------------+
|                 155 |                       14 |
+---------------------+--------------------------+
1 row in set (0.01 sec)
mysql> SELECT DAYOFWEEK(20020503);
+---------------------+
| DAYOFWEEK(20020503) |
+---------------------+
|                   6 |
+---------------------+
1 row in set (0.01 sec)
```

As with the MONTHNAME() function, you can use the DAYNAME() function to obtain a string representation of a weekday name, given a valid date:

```
mysql> SELECT DAYNAME('2003-02-14');
+-----------------------+
| DAYNAME('2003-02-14') |
+-----------------------+
| Friday                |
+-----------------------+
1 row in set (0.00 sec)
```

The WEEK() function returns the week number of the specified date in the year, while the YEARWEEK() function return both year and week number:

```
mysql> SELECT WEEK('2004-03-01'), YEARWEEK(20040301);
+--------------------+--------------------+
| WEEK('2004-03-01') | YEARWEEK(20040301) |
+--------------------+--------------------+
|                  9 |             200409 |
+--------------------+--------------------+
1 row in set (0.00 sec)
```

The HOUR(), MINUTE(), and SECOND() functions parse time values, returning the hour, minute, and second components, respectively.

```
mysql> SELECT HOUR(182300), MINUTE('14:56'), SECOND(123411);
+--------------+-----------------+----------------+
| HOUR(182300) | MINUTE('14:56') | SECOND(123411) |
+--------------+-----------------+----------------+
|           18 |              56 |             11 |
+--------------+-----------------+----------------+
1 row in set (0.00 sec)
```

The TO_DAYS() function returns the number of days between the year 0 and the specified date:

```
mysql> SELECT TO_DAYS(20000101), TO_DAYS(15820101);
+-------------------+-------------------+
| TO_DAYS(20000101) | TO_DAYS(15820101) |
+-------------------+-------------------+
|            730485 |            577814 |
+-------------------+-------------------+
1 row in set (0.00 sec)
```

The FROM_DAYS() function returns a date, given the number of days starting from year 0:

```
mysql> SELECT FROM_DAYS(730485), FROM_DAYS(577814);
+-------------------+-------------------+
| FROM_DAYS(730485) | FROM_DAYS(577814) |
+-------------------+-------------------+
| 2000-01-01        | 1582-01-01        |
+-------------------+-------------------+
1 row in set (0.00 sec)
```

Thank God It's Sunday!
The values returned by WEEK() and YEARWEEK() are usually in the range 0 to 53—however, you can modify this to use the range 1 to 52 and also decide whether a week starts on Sunday or Monday via an optional second argument to the function.

The SEC_TO_TIME() function converts seconds into a more readable time representation:

```
mysql> SELECT SEC_TO_TIME(60), SEC_TO_TIME(3720);
+-----------------+-------------------+
| SEC_TO_TIME(60) | SEC_TO_TIME(3720) |
+-----------------+-------------------+
| 00:01:00        | 01:02:00          |
+-----------------+-------------------+
1 row in set (0.00 sec)
```

The TIME_TO_SEC() function accepts a time value and represents it as seconds:

```
mysql> SELECT TIME_TO_SEC(000100), TIME_TO_SEC('24:01:10');
+---------------------+-------------------------+
| TIME_TO_SEC(000100) | TIME_TO_SEC('24:01:10') |
+---------------------+-------------------------+
|                  60 |                   86470 |
+---------------------+-------------------------+
1 row in set (0.00 sec)
```

In addition to functions for parsing date and time values, MySQL also comes with some interesting functions for performing date and time arithmetic. The most important of these are the DATE_ADD() and DATE_SUB() functions, used to add and subtract date values, respectively.

The first argument to both these functions is a starting date value, in either YYYY-MM-DD HH:MM:SS or YYYYMMDDHHMMSS format. The second argument has three components: the keyword INTERVAL, the interval value to be added or subtracted from the initial date value, and a keyword indicating the format in which the interval value is provided. The interval value and its following keyword must correspond to the values shown in Table 7-5.

TABLE 7-5
Keywords and Formats for Use with DATE_ADD() and DATE_SUB()

Keyword	Format for Interval Value
DAY	DAYS
DAY_HOUR	"DAYS HOURS"
DAY_MINUTE	"DAYS HOURS:MINUTES"
DAY_SECOND	"DAYS HOURS:MINUTES:SECONDS"
HOUR	HOURS
HOUR_MINUTE	"HOURS:MINUTES"
HOUR_SECOND	"HOURS:MINUTES:SECONDS"
MINUTE	MINUTES
MINUTE_SECOND	"MINUTES:SECONDS"
MONTH	MONTHS
SECOND	SECONDS
YEAR	YEARS
YEAR_MONTH	"YEARS-MONTHS"

PART II

A few examples might make this clearer. This first example adds six (6) months to the starting date and returns the result:

```
mysql> SELECT DATE_ADD('2004-01-01 00:00:00', INTERVAL 6 MONTH);
+---------------------------------------------------+
| DATE_ADD('2004-01-01 00:00:00', INTERVAL 6 MONTH) |
+---------------------------------------------------+
| 2004-07-01 00:00:00                               |
+---------------------------------------------------+
1 row in set (0.04 sec)
```

This next one adds 12 days, 3 hours, and 45 minutes to the starting value and displays the resulting timestamp:

```
mysql> SELECT DATE_ADD('2004-03-14 12:20:00',
INTERVAL '12 03:45' DAY_MINUTE);
+----------------------------------------------------------------+
| DATE_ADD('2004-03-14 12:20:00', INTERVAL '12 03:45' DAY_MINUTE) |
+----------------------------------------------------------------+
| 2004-03-26 16:05:00                                            |
+----------------------------------------------------------------+
1 row in set (0.00 sec)
```

The following example uses the DATE_SUB() function to subtract eight (8) hours from a date value:

```
mysql> SELECT DATE_SUB('2004-01-01 07:20:00', INTERVAL 8 HOUR);
+--------------------------------------------------+
| DATE_SUB('2004-01-01 07:20:00', INTERVAL 8 HOUR) |
+--------------------------------------------------+
| 2003-12-31 23:20:00                              |
+--------------------------------------------------+
1 row in set (0.00 sec)
```

And this one subtracts 13 years and 4 months from the same value:

```
mysql> SELECT DATE_SUB('2004-01-01 07:20:00',
INTERVAL '13-4' YEAR_MONTH);
+-------------------------------------------------------------+
| DATE_SUB('2004-01-01 07:20:00', INTERVAL '13-4' YEAR_MONTH) |
+-------------------------------------------------------------+
| 1990-09-01 07:20:00                                         |
+-------------------------------------------------------------+
1 row in set (0.00 sec)
```

The EXTRACT() function extracts specific segments of a date value, using the same keywords as those needed by DATE_ADD() and DATE_SUB():

```
mysql> SELECT EXTRACT(YEAR_MONTH FROM '2002-03-15');
+--------------------------------------+
| EXTRACT(YEAR_MONTH FROM '2002-03-15') |
+--------------------------------------+
|                               200203 |
+--------------------------------------+
1 row in set (0.08 sec)
mysql> SELECT EXTRACT(DAY_SECOND FROM '2002-03-15 16:45:07');
+------------------------------------------------+
| EXTRACT(DAY_SECOND FROM '2002-03-15 16:45:07') |
+------------------------------------------------+
|                                       15164507 |
+------------------------------------------------+
1 row in set (0.00 sec)
mysql> SELECT EXTRACT(HOUR_MINUTE FROM '2002-03-15 16:45:07');
+-------------------------------------------------+
| EXTRACT(HOUR_MINUTE FROM '2002-03-15 16:45:07') |
+-------------------------------------------------+
|                                            1645 |
+-------------------------------------------------+
1 row in set (0.00 sec)
```

The PERIOD_DIFF() function returns the difference (in months) between two date values:

```
mysql> SELECT PERIOD_DIFF(200302, 199802);
+-----------------------------+
| PERIOD_DIFF(200302, 199802) |
+-----------------------------+
|                          60 |
+-----------------------------+
1 row in set (0.00 sec)
```

This function can come in particularly handy when you need to calculate the interval between two dates. To illustrate, consider the following simple example— a table containing user names and dates of birth:

```
mysql> SELECT * FROM birthdays;
+-------+------------+
| name  | dob        |
+-------+------------+
| raoul | 1978-06-04 |
| luis  | 1965-11-17 |
| larry | 1971-08-19 |
| moe   | 1992-01-23 |
+-------+------------+
4 rows in set (0.00 sec)
```

It's possible to use the PERIOD_DIFF() function to obtain the current age of each user, in years:

```
mysql> SELECT name, dob,
ROUND(PERIOD_DIFF(DATE_FORMAT(NOW(), '%Y%m'),
DATE_FORMAT(dob, '%Y%m')) / 12, 1) AS age FROM birthdays;
+-------+------------+------+
| name  | dob        | age  |
+-------+------------+------+
| raoul | 1978-06-04 | 24.9 |
| luis  | 1965-11-17 | 37.5 |
| larry | 1971-08-19 | 31.7 |
| moe   | 1992-01-23 | 11.3 |
+-------+------------+------+
4 rows in set (0.00 sec)
```

An alternative is to use the TO_DAYS() function to accomplish the same result, as shown here:

```
mysql> SELECT name, dob,
(TO_DAYS(NOW()) - TO_DAYS(dob)) / 365 AS age FROM birthdays;
+-------+------------+-------+
| name  | dob        | age   |
+-------+------------+-------+
| raoul | 1978-06-04 | 24.96 |
| luis  | 1965-11-17 | 37.52 |
| larry | 1971-08-19 | 31.76 |
| moe   | 1992-01-23 | 11.32 |
+-------+------------+-------+
4 rows in set (0.00 sec)
```

Here's another example—a library database containing a list of members, the movies they've borrowed, and the dates on which the movies were checked out and checked back in:

```
mysql> SELECT * FROM library;
+----------+-------------------------+----------------+---------------+
| member   | title                   | check_out_date | check_in_date |
+----------+-------------------------+----------------+---------------+
| joe      | The Phantom Menace       | 2002-09-11     | 2002-09-14    |
| john     | Cape Fear               | 2002-07-15     | 2002-07-21    |
| johann   | Casper                  | 2003-01-01     | 2003-01-05    |
| mark     | The Godfather           | 2000-08-17     | 2000-09-16    |
| jthomas  | Who Killed Roger Rabbit? | 2003-11-17     | 2003-11-25    |
+----------+-------------------------+----------------+---------------+
5 rows in set (0.04 sec)
```

It's possible now to find out for how long each movie was checked out:

```
mysql> SELECT member,
TO_DAYS(check_in_date) - TO_DAYS(check_out_date)
AS out_period FROM library;
+----------+------------+
| member   | out_period |
+----------+------------+
| joe      |          3 |
| john     |          6 |
| johann   |          4 |
| mark     |         30 |
| jthomas  |          8 |
+----------+------------+
5 rows in set (0.00 sec)
```

Assuming the maximum duration for which a movie may be checked out is four days, it's also possible to find out which members kept movies for longer than the maximum check-out period (and should be charged a late fee):

```
mysql> SELECT member FROM library
WHERE TO_DAYS(check_in_date) - TO_DAYS(check_out_date) > 4;
+----------+
| member   |
+----------+
| john     |
| mark     |
| jthomas  |
+----------+
3 rows in set (0.02 sec)
```

Encryption Functions

MySQL comes with a few specialized functions designed specifically to perform data encryption. Table 7-6 shows these functions.

Function	What It Does
AES_ENCRYPT(str,key)	Returns an Advanced Encryption Standard (AES)-encrypted version of str using secret key key
AES_DECRYPT(str,key)	Decrypts an AES-encrypted string str using secret key key
DECODE(str,key)	Decodes encrypted string str with key
ENCRYPT(str,salt)	Returns an encrypted version of str with salt using the UNIX crypt() function
ENCODE(str,key)	Encodes str with key
MD5()	Returns an MD5 checksum for str
PASSWORD(str)	Returns an encrypted version of str
SHA()	Returns a Secure Hash Algorithm (SHA) checksum for str

TABLE 7-6   MySQL Encryption Functions

The PASSWORD() function is used to create an encrypted password string, suitable for insertion into the MySQL security system. This encryption is nonreversible and does not use the same algorithms as UNIX password encryption; it is primarily intended for use by MySQL's authentication system, and the MySQL manual suggests using the ENCODE()/DECODE() or AES_ENCRYPT()/AES_DECRYPT() function instead for user applications.

```
mysql> SELECT PASSWORD("secret");
+--------------------+
| PASSWORD("secret") |
+--------------------+
| 428567f408994404   |
+--------------------+
1 row in set (0.02 sec)
```

If you'd prefer, you can encrypt strings using the UNIX crypt() system call via the ENCRYPT() function, which accepts the string to be encrypted and (optionally) a *salt* (a string to uniquely identify a password, serving much like a key) for the encryption.

```
mysql> SELECT ENCRYPT('open sesame', 'abc');
+-------------------------------+
| ENCRYPT('open sesame', 'abc') |
+-------------------------------+
| ab/G8gtZdMwak                 |
+-------------------------------+
1 row in set (0.00 sec))
```

You can also use the ENCODE() and DECODE() functions to encrypt and decrypt strings. The ENCODE() function takes two arguments: the string to be encrypted and a key that serves as the basis for encryption:

```
mysql> INSERT INTO users
VALUES ('', 'john', ENCODE('abracadabra', 'secret_key'));
Query OK, 1 row affected (0.00 sec)
```

Cryptic Clues

The ENCRYPT() function works only if your operating system supports the crypt() system call. Operating systems that don't support it, such as the Windows family, will cause MySQL to produce a NULL result in the ENCRYPT() function example.

The result of a call to ENCODE() is a binary string, which should be stored as a BLOB. Continuing the preceding example, here's what it looks like:

```
mysql> SELECT * FROM users;
+----+-------+--------------+
| id | uname | upass        |
+----+-------+--------------+
|  2 | john  | ³q[|èBgØùM+ |
+----+-------+--------------
```

This encoded value may be decoded by the DECODE() function with the correct key:

```
mysql> SELECT id, uname, DECODE(upass, 'secret_key') FROM users;
+----+-------+-----------------------------+
| id | uname | DECODE(upass, 'secret_key') |
+----+-------+-----------------------------+
|  2 | john  | abracadabra                 |
+----+-------+-----------------------------+
1 row in set (0.01 sec)
```

A more secure alternative to ENCODE() and DECODE() (which use comparatively weaker encryption) lies in the AES_ENCRYPT() and AES_DECRYPT() functions, which use the Advanced Encryption Standard (AES) algorithm to produce more sophisticated cryptograms. Consider the following variant of the preceding example, which demonstrates how these functions may be used:

```
mysql> INSERT INTO users
VALUES ('', 'john', AES_ENCRYPT('opensesame', 'key'));
Query OK, 1 row affected (0.06 sec)
mysql> SELECT * FROM users;
+----+-------+------------------+
| id | uname | upass            |
+----+-------+------------------+
|  1 | john  | ¢¦}¶__ ëßìn_<-á |
+----+-------+------------------+
1 row in set (0.11 sec)
```

As with ENCODE(), the result of a call to AES_ENCRYPT() is a binary string, which should be stored as a BLOB. This binary data can be decrypted with the AES_DECRYPT() function, as in the previous example.

```
mysql> SELECT id, uname, AES_DECRYPT(upass, 'key') FROM users;
+----+-------+---------------------------+
| id | uname | AES_DECRYPT(upass, 'key') |
+----+-------+---------------------------+
|  1 | john  | opensesame                |
+----+-------+---------------------------+
1 row in set (0.11 sec)
```

Protecting Yourself
If your MySQL RDBMS supports SSL (Secure Socket Layer), you can perform encryption using the more robust Triple-Data Encryption Standard (DES) algorithm via the DES_ENCRYPT() and DES_DECRYPT() functions.

You can calculate MD5 checksums (128-bit) with the MD5() function:

```
mysql> SELECT MD5('hard-to-guess-password');
+---------------------------------+
| MD5('hard-to-guess-password')   |
+---------------------------------+
| 169d405191827bad1443d67e9f8e5574 |
+---------------------------------+
1 row in set (0.01 sec)
```

Or you can calculate SHA checksums (160-bit) with the SHA() function:

```
mysql> SELECT SHA('hard-to-guess-password');
+------------------------------------------+
| SHA('hard-to-guess-password')            |
+------------------------------------------+
| dfe0c5966af28b26cdcb949ba11d4760f440cb00 |
+------------------------------------------+
1 row in set (0.03 sec)
```

The checksums returned by these functions are hex values, suitable for use as passwords in an authentication system, as the following example demonstrates:

```
mysql> INSERT INTO users values('', 'john', MD5('mypass'));
Query OK, 1 row affected (0.10 sec)

mysql> SELECT * FROM users;
+----+-------+---------------------------------+
| id | uname | upass                           |
+----+-------+---------------------------------+
|  2 | john  | ³q[|èBgØùM+                      |
|  3 | john  | john                            |
|  4 | john  | a029d0df84eb5549c641e04a9ef389e5 |
+----+-------+---------------------------------+
3 rows in set (0.06 sec)

mysql> SELECT * FROM users WHERE uname='john' AND upass=md5('mypass');
```

```
+----+-------+----------------------------------+
| id | uname | upass                            |
+----+-------+----------------------------------+
|  4 | john  | a029d0df84eb5549c641e04a9ef389e5 |
+----+-------+----------------------------------+
1 row in set (0.02 sec)

mysql> SELECT * FROM users
WHERE uname='john' AND upass=md5('wrongpass');
Empty set (0.00 sec)
```

Control Flow Functions

You might not know this, but MySQL also comes with four functions that can be used to perform conditional operations. These functions make it possible to implement conditional logic within your SQL itself, allowing developers to (perhaps) shift some of the application's business logic to the database back end. Table 7-7 lists these functions.

The first of these functions, IFNULL(), takes two arguments and evaluates the first one. If the first argument is not NULL, the function returns it to the caller; if it is NULL, it returns the second argument.

```
mysql> SELECT IFNULL(1, 2),
IFNULL(NULL, 10),
IFNULL(4 * NULL, 'false');
+--------------+------------------+---------------------------+
| IFNULL(1, 2) | IFNULL(NULL, 10) | IFNULL(4 * NULL, 'false')  |
+--------------+------------------+---------------------------+
|            1 | 10               | false                     |
+--------------+------------------+---------------------------+
1 row in set (0.00 sec)
```

Function	What It Does
CASE WHEN [test1] THEN [result1] ... ELSE [default] END	Returns resultN if testN evaluates as true, else returns default
CASE [test] WHEN [val1] THEN [result1] ... ELSE [default] END	Returns resultN if test evaluates to valN, else returns default
IF(test,t,f)	Returns t if test evaluates as true; else returns f
IFNULL(arg1,arg2)	Returns arg1 if arg1 is not NULL; else returns arg2
NULLIF(arg1,arg2)	Returns NULL if arg1 equals arg2; else returns arg2

TABLE 7-7   MySQL Control Flow Functions

The NULLIF() function tests the two arguments provided to it for equality and returns NULL if they are equal or the first argument if they are not.

```
mysql> SELECT NULLIF(1,1), NULLIF('a', 'b'), NULLIF(2+3, 4+1);
+-------------+------------------+------------------+
| NULLIF(1,1) | NULLIF('a', 'b') | NULLIF(2+3, 4+1) |
+-------------+------------------+------------------+
|        NULL | a                |             NULL |
+-------------+------------------+------------------+
1 row in set (0.01 sec)
```

The IF() function makes it possible to build a simple conditional test, equivalent to that provided by most scripting languages. This function accepts three arguments, of which the first one is an expression to be evaluated. If the expression evaluates as true, IF() will return the second argument; if it evaluates as false, IF() will return the third argument.

```
mysql> SELECT IF(1 < 10, 2, 3), IF(56 > 100, 'true', 'false');
+------------------+------------------------------+
| IF(1 < 10, 2, 3) | IF(56 > 100, 'true', 'false') |
+------------------+------------------------------+
|                2 | false                        |
+------------------+------------------------------+
1 row in set (0.00 sec)
```

The IF() function is suitable only for situations involving two possible outcomes. However, in the real world, this may often not be sufficient, and you may often find yourself in need of multiple branches in your conditional tests. For such situations, MySQL offers the CASE function, which works much like the switch-case conditional routines in programming languages like PHP and Perl.

The format of the CASE function is somewhat complex and usually looks like this:

```
CASE [expression to be evaluated]
    WHEN [val 1] THEN [result 1]
    WHEN [val 2] THEN [result 2]
     ...
    WHEN [val n] THEN [result n]
    ELSE [default result]
END
```

Here, the first argument is the value or expression to be evaluated; this is followed by a series of WHEN-THEN blocks, each of which specifies the value against which the first argument is to be compared and the result to be returned if the comparison is true.

The entire series of WHEN-THEN blocks is terminated by an ELSE block, which specifies the default result in case none of the preceding blocks match, with an END closing the outer CASE block. In the event no ELSE block is specified, and none of the WHEN-THEN comparisons return true, MySQL returns a NULL.

An alternative syntax for the CASE function also exists, which can come in handy at times. Here it is:

```
CASE
    WHEN [conditional test 1] THEN [result 1]
    WHEN [conditional test 2] THEN [result 2]
    ELSE [default result]
END
```

In this case, the result returned depends on whether the corresponding conditional test returns true.

A few examples might make this clearer:

```
mysql> SELECT CASE 'green'
WHEN 'red' THEN 'stop'
WHEN 'green' THEN 'go'
END;
+---------------------------------------------------------------+
| CASE 'green' WHEN 'red' THEN 'stop' WHEN 'green' THEN 'go' END |
+---------------------------------------------------------------+
| go                                                            |
+---------------------------------------------------------------+
1 row in set (0.00 sec)

mysql> SELECT CASE 9 WHEN 1 THEN 'a' WHEN 2 THEN 'b' ELSE 'n/a' END;
+-----------------------------------------------------+
| CASE 9 WHEN 1 THEN 'a' WHEN 2 THEN 'b' ELSE 'n/a' END |
+-----------------------------------------------------+
| n/a                                                 |
+-----------------------------------------------------+
1 row in set (0.00 sec)

mysql> SELECT CASE WHEN (2 + 2) = 4 THEN 'OK'
WHEN (2 + 2) <> 4 THEN 'NOT OK' END AS status;
+--------+
| status |
+--------+
| OK     |
+--------+
1 row in set (0.16 sec)
```

Harking back to one of the previous examples in this chapter—the students and their marks—you can use the IF() function to find out which students passed or failed in a particular subject and display results accordingly:

```
mysql> SELECT CONCAT_WS(' ', fname, lname) AS name,
IF((math) / 100 < 0.35, 'fail in math', 'pass in math') AS result
FROM marks;
+-------------+--------------+
| name        | result       |
+-------------+--------------+
| John Doe    | pass in math |
| Sarah Short | fail in math |
| Joe Cool    | pass in math |
| Mark Wumba  | pass in math |
| Tom Thumb   | fail in math |
+-------------+--------------+
5 rows in set (0.00 sec)
```

In case you need to assign grades to each student based on his or her performance, you can accomplish this easily with a CASE function, like this:

```
mysql> SELECT fname, lname, (math + sci + lit) AS total,
CASE WHEN (math + sci + lit) < 50 THEN 'D'
WHEN (math + sci + lit) BETWEEN 50 AND 150 THEN 'C'
WHEN (math + sci + lit) BETWEEN 151 AND 250 THEN 'B'
ELSE 'A' END
AS grade FROM marks;
+-------+-------+-------+-------+
| fname | lname | total | grade |
+-------+-------+-------+-------+
| John  | Doe   |   143 | C     |
| Sarah | Short |   145 | C     |
| Joe   | Cool  |   246 | B     |
| Mark  | Wumba |   145 | C     |
| Tom   | Thumb |    12 | D     |
+-------+-------+-------+-------+
5 rows in set (0.00 sec)
```

Or you can use a series of nested IF() functions:

```
mysql> SELECT fname, lname, (math + sci + lit) AS total,
IF((math + sci + lit) < 50,'C',
IF((math + sci + lit) BETWEEN 50 AND 150,'B',
IF ((math + sci + lit) BETWEEN 151 and 250, 'C', 'A')))
AS grade FROM marks;
+-------+-------+-------+-------+
| fname | lname | total | grade |
```

```
+-------+-------+-------+-------+
| John  | Doe   |   143 | B     |
| Sarah | Short |   145 | B     |
| Joe   | Cool  |   246 | C     |
| Mark  | Wumba |   145 | B     |
| Tom   | Thumb |    12 | C     |
+-------+-------+-------+-------+
5 rows in set (0.01 sec)
```

Let's consider another example, this one an authentication system consisting of the following user database:

```
mysql> SELECT * FROM users;
+-----+-------+---------------+
| uid | uname | upass         |
+-----+-------+---------------+
|   3 | mark  | ts0o378GTHJTw |
|   2 | joe   | tsuYK6Jh0iVvI |
|   4 | sue   | tsEh.9z5n8FQc |
+-----+-------+---------------+
3 rows in set (0.00 sec)
```

User passwords stored in this table are encrypted using MySQL's ENCRYPT() function and the special site-defined salt ts.

Now, to perform authentication with this system, two choices are available: you could place the business logic for encryption and verification in the application layer, or you could have MySQL take care of it for you via its built-in IF() function. Since this book is about MySQL, let's pick door number 2.

```
mysql> SELECT IF(ENCRYPT('sue', 'ts') = upass, 'allow', 'deny')
AS loginResult FROM users WHERE uname = 'sue';
+-------------+
| loginResult |
+-------------+
| deny        |
+-------------+
1 row in set (0.00 sec)

mysql> SELECT IF(ENCRYPT('secret', 'ts') = upass, 'allow', 'deny')
AS loginResult FROM users WHERE uname = 'sue';
+-------------+
| loginResult |
+-------------+
| allow       |
+-------------+
1 row in set (0.00 sec)
```

In this case, the user's input is simply ENCRYPT()-ed and incorporated into a MySQL IF() test, with MySQL taking over the dual tasks of verifying the password and communicating the result to the application. The load on the application is thus immediately reduced: rather than having to perform the necessary encryption routines, pass the data to MySQL, and check for a match, it now need only pass the user-supplied clear-text password to the back end (via a SELECT query like the preceding one), read the resulting output, and grant or deny access.

Formatting Functions

MySQL also comes with a few functions specifically designed to assist in formatting data, as shown in Table 7-8.

The simplest of these is the FORMAT() function, intended to format large numeric values into more readable comma-separated sequences. The first argument to FORMAT() is always the number to be formatted; the second is the number of decimal places in the end value.

```
mysql> SELECT FORMAT(999999999.868595049, 2), FORMAT(-4512,6);
+--------------------------------+-----------------+
| FORMAT(999999999.868595049, 2) | FORMAT(-4512,6) |
+--------------------------------+-----------------+
| 999,999,999.87                 | -4,512.000000   |
+--------------------------------+-----------------+
1 row in set (0.00 sec)
```

Date and time values can be formatted with the DATE_FORMAT() and TIME_FORMAT() functions, which accept both a date or time value and a format string that specifies what the result should look like. This format string may contain special symbols that can be used to alter the display of the final value; Table 7-9 has an abridged list of these symbols.

NOTE *You can obtain a more complete list of these special symbols from the MySQL manual, at http://www.mysql.com/documentation/.*

Function	What It Does
DATE_FORMAT(date,fmt)	Formats date as per format specified in fmt
FORMAT(x,y)	Formats x as a comma-separated number sequence, rounded off to y decimal places
INET_ATON(ip)	Returns a numeric representation of IP address ip
INET_NTOA(num)	Returns the IP address representation of num
TIME_FORMAT(time,fmt)	Formats time as per format specified in fmt

TABLE 7-8   MySQL Formatting Functions

Symbol	**What It Means**
%a	Short weekday name (Sun, Mon...)
%b	Short month name (Jan, Feb...)
%d	Day of the month
%H	Hour (01, 02...)
%I	Minute (00, 01...)
%j	Day of the year (001, 002...)
%m	Two-digit month (00, 01...)
%M	Long month name (January, February...)
%p	AM/PM
%r	Time in 12-hour format
%S	Second (00, 01...)
%T	Time in 24-hour format
%w	Day of the week (0,1...)
%W	Long weekday name (Sunday, Monday...)
%Y	Four-digit year

TABLE 7-9
MySQL Date/Time
Formatting Codes

Here are a few examples of these functions in action:

```
mysql> SELECT DATE_FORMAT(NOW(), '%W, %D %M %Y %r');
+--------------------------------------+
| DATE_FORMAT(NOW(), '%W, %D %M %Y %r') |
+--------------------------------------+
| Thursday, 15th May 2003 01:38:44 PM  |
+--------------------------------------+
1 row in set (0.00 sec)

mysql> SELECT DATE_FORMAT(19980317, '%d/%m/%Y');
+----------------------------------+
| DATE_FORMAT(19980317, '%d/%m/%Y') |
+----------------------------------+
| 17/03/1998                       |
+----------------------------------+
1 row in set (0.00 sec)

mysql> SELECT DATE_FORMAT(19690906070134, '%s %i %h %d %m %y');
+------------------------------------------------+
| DATE_FORMAT(19690906070134, '%s %i %h %d %m %y') |
+------------------------------------------------+
| 34 01 07 06 09 69                              |
+------------------------------------------------+
1 row in set (0.00 sec)
```

```
mysql> SELECT TIME_FORMAT(19690609140256, '%h:%i %p');
+----------------------------------------+
| TIME_FORMAT(19690609140256, '%h:%i %p') |
+----------------------------------------+
| 02:02 PM                               |
+----------------------------------------+
1 row in set (0.00 sec)
```

MySQL also permits conversion of IP addresses to numbers, and vice versa, with the INET_NTOA() and INET_ATON() functions, respectively. The following examples demonstrate:

```
mysql> SELECT INET_ATON('192.168.2.10');
+---------------------------+
| INET_ATON('192.168.2.10') |
+---------------------------+
|                3232236042 |
+---------------------------+
1 row in set (0.05 sec)

mysql> SELECT INET_NTOA(3232236042);
+-----------------------+
| INET_NTOA(3232236042) |
+-----------------------+
| 192.168.2.10          |
+-----------------------+
1 row in set (0.05 sec)
```

Type Conversion Functions

To assist in data type conversion, MySQL offers the CAST() function, which can be used to cast a value to a specific data type. As of MySQL 4.1, the following types are supported:

- BINARY
- CHAR
- DATE
- TIME
- DATETIME
- SIGNED
- UNSIGNED

Normally, strings are automatically CAST() to numbers when used in a numeric operation—the following two operations are equivalent:

```
mysql> SELECT 1 + '99';
+----------+
| 1 + '99' |
+----------+
|      100 |
+----------+
1 row in set (0.03 sec)
mysql> SELECT 1 + CAST('99' AS SIGNED);
+--------------------------+
| 1 + CAST('99' AS SIGNED) |
+--------------------------+
|                      100 |
+--------------------------+
1 row in set (0.00 sec)
```

In a similar vein, strings may be cast as BINARY so that comparison operations involving them become case-sensitive. Casting a string as BINARY with the CAST() function is equivalent to using the BINARY keyword before it:

```
mysql> SELECT 'f' = BINARY 'F', 'f' = CAST('F' AS BINARY);
+------------------+----------------------------+
| 'f' = BINARY 'F' | 'f' = CAST('F' AS BINARY)  |
+------------------+----------------------------+
|                0 |                          0 |
+------------------+----------------------------+
1 row in set (0.00 sec)
```

It's interesting to note that you can force many date and time functions (including the NOW(), CURTIME(), and CURDATE() functions) to output their return values as a number, rather than a string, simply by using them in a numeric context or CAST()-ing them as numbers.

```
mysql> SELECT CAST(NOW() AS SIGNED INTEGER), CURDATE() + 0;
+-------------------------------+---------------+
| CAST(NOW() AS SIGNED INTEGER) | CURDATE() + 0 |
+-------------------------------+---------------+
|                20030515111705 |      20030515 |
+-------------------------------+---------------+
1 row in set (0.00 sec)
```

The CAST() function is particularly useful when moving legacy data to a new RDBMS, as it allows you to cast values from their old data types to new ones that are better suited to the new system. To illustrate this, consider the following (non-MySQL) legacy table, which stores date values as strings:

```
mysql> SELECT * FROM old;
+----------------------+-----+-------+------+------+-----+
| email                | day | month | year | hour | min |
+----------------------+-----+-------+------+------+-----+
| mark@some.domain.net | 15  | 03    | 1999 | 13   | 42  |
```

```
| armyguy@free.mail.service.com | 31 | 12    | 2001 | 19   | 59   |
| debuz@some.unknown.tld        | 08 | 11    | 1996 | 03   | 37   |
+-------------------------------+----+-------+------+------+------+
3 rows in set (0.00 sec)
```

To move this data into MySQL, the first step is to create a new table to hold the data:

```
mysql> CREATE TABLE new (
email varchar(255) NOT NULL default '',
ts datetime NOT NULL default '0000-00-00 00:00:00',
PRIMARY KEY (email) )
TYPE=MyISAM;
Query OK, 0 rows affected (0.05 sec)
```

Then export the data from the old table into the new one, casting the values to the appropriate MySQL data type:

```
mysql> INSERT INTO new(email, ts) SELECT email,
CAST(CONCAT(year,month,day,hour,min,'00') AS DATETIME) FROM old;
Query OK, 3 rows affected (0.00 sec)
Records: 3  Duplicates: 0  Warnings: 0

mysql> SELECT * FROM new;
+-------------------------------+---------------------+
| email                         | ts                  |
+-------------------------------+---------------------+
| mark@some.domain.net          | 1999-03-15 13:42:00 |
| armyguy@free.mail.service.com | 2001-12-31 19:59:00 |
| debuz@some.unknown.tld        | 1996-11-08 03:37:00 |
+-------------------------------+---------------------+
3 rows in set (0.00 sec)
```

System Information Functions

MySQL also comes with specialized functions that can be used to obtain information about the system itself, as shown in Table 7-10.

The DATABASE(), USER(), and VERSION() functions return information about the currently selected database, current user, and MySQL version, respectively.

```
mysql> SELECT DATABASE(), VERSION(), USER();
+------------+-----------------+-----------------+
| DATABASE() | VERSION()       | USER()          |
+------------+-----------------+-----------------+
|            | 4.0.12-max-debug | root@domain.com |
+------------+-----------------+-----------------+
1 row in set (0.11 sec)
```

Function	What It Does
DATABASE()	Returns name of currently selected database
BENCHMARK(count,expr)	Evaluates expr count times
CONNECTION_ID()	Returns client connection ID
FOUND_ROWS()	Returns the number of rows returned by the last SELECT query (exempt of the effect of LIMIT)
GET_LOCK(str,dur)	Obtains a lock named str for dur seconds
IS_FREE_LOCK(str)	Checks to see whether lock named str is free
LAST_INSERT_ID()	Returns the last AUTOINCREMENT ID automatically generated by the system
MASTER_POS_WAIT(log,pos,dur)	Locks the master server for dur seconds until the slave has synchronized itself to the events in log up to position pos
RELEASE_LOCK(str)	Releases lock named str
USER() aka SYSTEM_USER()	Returns name of currently logged-in user
VERSION()	Returns MySQL server version

TABLE 7-10   MySQL System Information Functions

The CONNECTION_ID() function retrieves the connection ID of the client to the server, while the LAST_INSERT_ID() function returns the last ID automatically generated by MySQL when inserting data into an AUTOINCREMENT field. This can come in handy if you're dealing with linkages between multiple tables and you need to use the record ID from one table as a key into another table. The following example demonstrates:

```
mysql> INSERT INTO users VALUES ('', 'john', 'john');
Query OK, 1 row affected (0.03 sec)

mysql> SELECT LAST_INSERT_ID();
+------------------+
| LAST_INSERT_ID() |
+------------------+
|                3 |
+------------------+
1 row in set (0.03 sec)

mysql> INSERT INTO departments VALUES (55, LAST_INSERT_ID());
Query OK, 1 row affected (0.03 sec)
```

The BENCHMARK() function allows developers to evaluate MySQL performance by having the server evaluate a particular expression a specified number of times. The function always returns 0, together with a report of time elapsed at the client end of the connection; this elapsed time value may be used to make deductions about server performance.

```
mysql> SELECT BENCHMARK(999999, LOG(RAND() * PI()));
+---------------------------------------+
| BENCHMARK(999999, LOG(RAND() * PI())) |
+---------------------------------------+
|                                     0 |
+---------------------------------------+
1 row in set (2.08 sec)
```

In this example, MySQL takes 2.08 seconds to evaluate the expression LOG(RAND() * PI()) 999,999 times. By executing this function at periodic intervals or for different intervals, a developer can obtain the raw data needed to measure server performance.

MySQL also comes with three functions designed specifically to assist in implementing application-level locking between clients running on separate machines. The GET_LOCK() function accepts two arguments, a lock name and a duration (in seconds), and attempts to create a lock with that name for that number of seconds. If successful, GET_LOCK() returns 1; if not, it returns 0 or NULL.

```
mysql> SELECT GET_LOCK('20030907', 60);
+--------------------------+
| GET_LOCK('20030907', 60) |
+--------------------------+
|                        1 |
+--------------------------+
1 row in set (0.06 sec)
```

The RELEASE_LOCK() function does the reverse, releasing a lock with the given name and returning 1 on success, 0 on failure, and NULL on error:

```
mysql> SELECT RELEASE_LOCK('20030907');
+--------------------------+
| RELEASE_LOCK('20030907') |
+--------------------------+
|                        1 |
+--------------------------+
1 row in set (0.00 sec)
```

The IS_FREE_LOCK() function checks to see whether the named lock exists and returns 1 or 0, depending on whether the lock is free or in use:

```
mysql> SELECT IS_FREE_LOCK('20030907');
+--------------------------+
| IS_FREE_LOCK('20030907') |
+--------------------------+
|                        0 |
```

```
+---------------------------+
1 row in set (0.06 sec)

mysql> SELECT RELEASE_LOCK('20030907');
+---------------------------+
| RELEASE_LOCK('20030907')  |
+---------------------------+
|                        1  |
+---------------------------+
1 row in set (0.00 sec)

mysql> SELECT IS_FREE_LOCK('20030907');
+---------------------------+
| IS_FREE_LOCK('20030907')  |
+---------------------------+
|                        1  |
+---------------------------+
```

Not more than one lock may be active at any given time; multiple calls to GET_LOCK()
release previously created locks, as in the following example:

```
mysql> SELECT GET_LOCK('a', 60);
+-------------------+
| GET_LOCK('a', 60) |
+-------------------+
|                 1 |
+-------------------+
1 row in set (0.00 sec)

mysql> SELECT IS_FREE_LOCK('a');
+-------------------+
| IS_FREE_LOCK('a') |
+-------------------+
|                 0 |
+-------------------+
1 row in set (0.00 sec)

mysql> SELECT GET_LOCK('b', 60);
+-------------------+
| GET_LOCK('b', 60) |
+-------------------+
|                 1 |
+-------------------+
1 row in set (0.00 sec)
```

```
mysql> SELECT IS_FREE_LOCK('a');
+-------------------+
| IS_FREE_LOCK('a') |
+-------------------+
|                 1 |
+-------------------+
1 row in set (0.00 sec)
```

The GET_LOCK(), RELEASE_LOCK(), and IS_FREE_LOCK() functions make it easy to synchronize the activities of multiple MySQL clients; clients that agree on common locking semantics can use these functions to avoid stepping on each other's toes.

The FOUND_ROWS() function returns the total number of rows retrieved by the last SELECT query. This is particularly useful in combination with the SQL_CALC_FOUND_ROWS and LIMIT constructs, as it makes it possible to "page through" the results of a query set (with LIMIT) yet simultaneously display the total number of records retrieved (with SQL_CALC_FOUND_ROWS and FOUND_ROWS()). Consider the following simple example, which demonstrates:

```
mysql> SELECT SQL_CALC_FOUND_ROWS * FROM racedata LIMIT 0,4;
+--------------+-------+-----+-------+----------+
| name         | total | win | place | unplaced |
+--------------+-------+-----+-------+----------+
| Stormtrooper |    50 |   4 |    13 |        9 |
| VioletDaisy  |     9 |   4 |     5 |        0 |
| King William |    33 |  11 |    15 |        4 |
| Remuneration |   127 |  35 |    56 |       22 |
+--------------+-------+-----+-------+----------+
4 rows in set (0.01 sec)

mysql> SELECT FOUND_ROWS();
+--------------+
| FOUND_ROWS() |
+--------------+
|           71 |
+--------------+
1 row in set (0.00 sec)
```

In this case, the first query retrieves only a limited subset of four records from the full result set. However, since SQL_CALC_FOUND_ROWS has been used in the query, MySQL keeps track of the total number of rows in the result set as well and allows that number to be retrieved via a call to FOUND_ROWS(). The second query thus merely retrieves a statistic from the server without reexamining the tables.

Finally, the MASTER_POS_WAIT() function is a specialized function primarily intended for use at the slave end of a MySQL master-slave relationship. The MASTER_POS_WAIT() function accepts three arguments—a log name, a log position, and a timeout value—and locks the master until the slave has updated itself to the specified position in the log. This function is usually seen in a replication context. Read more about replication in Chapter 17.

Summary

This chapter discussed the various built-in functions provided by the MySQL RDBMS, classifying them into various categories and explaining them with examples and illustrations.

As you have observed over the last few pages, MySQL comes with a prolific set of functions, allowing users to perform operations ranging from the simple (obtaining the current date and time and performing simple mathematical and string operations) to the complex (trigonometrical calculations, date and time arithmetic, and data encryption). This chapter attempted to familiarize you with the more important ones in the collection, with explanations and illustrations. A number of examples, both small and large, were also used to illustrate how these functions can help developers shift business logic from the application layer to the database layer, a move that can (sometimes) result in improved performance.

Working with Databases and Tables

You might remember from an earlier chapter in this book, that the SQL specification can broadly be divided into three components: Data Definition Language (DDL), Data Manipulation Language (DML), and Data Control Language (DCL). This chapter focuses almost entirely on the DDL component, discussing the MySQL commands related to database and table management. In addition to offering information on how MySQL databases and tables can be added to, or deleted from, the system, it also discusses the relative advantages of the various table types available in MySQL. These table types range from the older ISAM tables to the newer transaction-safe InnoDB tables. The chapter also provides guidelines that help you, the MySQL developer, make an appropriate choice for your application.

Creating Databases

You've already seen that everything in MySQL begins with a database, which serves as a container for tables and the records they contain. The way to create a new MySQL database is, not surprisingly, via the CREATE DATABASE command. Assuming you're connected to a MySQL server via the mysql command-line client, you can try this out for yourself:

```
mysql> CREATE DATABASE db1;
Query OK, 1 row affected (0.05 sec)
```

This creates a database named db1.

Databases in MySQL are represented as directories in MySQL's data storage area on the file system. Therefore, the database name in the previous command must comply with the operating system's (OS) restrictions on which characters are allowable within directory names. For example, Microsoft Windows doesn't permit the characters \ / :

* ? " < > | in file or directory names, which automatically eliminates them for use in MySQL database names.

Database names cannot exceed 64 characters and names that contain special characters or consist entirely of digits or reserved words must be quoted with the backtick (`) operator. Consider the following cases, which illustrate this:

```
mysql> CREATE DATABASE 875748;
ERROR 1064: You have an error in your SQL syntax.  Check the
manual that corresponds to your MySQL server version for the
right syntax to use near '875748' at line 1
mysql> CREATE DATABASE `875748`;
Query OK, 1 row affected (0.06 sec)
mysql> CREATE DATABASE `group`;
Query OK, 1 row affected (0.00 sec)
```

For obvious reasons, MySQL doesn't permit two databases of the same name. Any attempt to do this will result in an error, as the following demonstrates.

```
mysql> CREATE DATABASE db1;
Query OK, 1 row affected (0.03 sec)
mysql> CREATE DATABASE db1;
ERROR 1007: Can't create database 'db1'. Database exists
```

When using automated scripts to create databases, an error such as the previous one is potentially disruptive to your program flow. You can avoid it by making use of the IF EXISTS and IF NOT EXISTS clauses, supported in MySQL 3.22 and better. Consider the following revision of the previous example, which demonstrates how these clauses can help you create more graceful SQL:

```
mysql> CREATE DATABASE db1;
ERROR 1007: Can't create database 'db1'. Database exists
mysql> CREATE DATABASE IF NOT EXISTS db1;
Query OK, 0 rows affected (0.00 sec)
```

In the second case, the use of the IF NOT EXISTS clause forces MySQL to run the command only if the database doesn't exist, resulting in more graceful handling and no error output.

What's in a Name?

Generally, it's considered good practice to start database names with an alphabetic character and to ensure they consist of only alphanumeric and underscore characters. While MySQL itself could be able to handle a peculiar name, other applications might not be quite so forgiving.

Selecting Databases for Use

The USE statement selects a database, making it the current database for all transactions. Consider the following example, which demonstrates selecting the database db1 as the default for all future queries:

```
mysql> USE db1;
Database changed
```

Once a database is selected in this manner, it becomes the default database for all queries executed over the database connection. These two commands are equivalent:

```
mysql> SELECT Host, Db, User FROM mysql.db;
+------+-------+------+
| Host | Db    | User |
+------+-------+------+
| %    | test% |      |
+------+-------+------+
1 row in set (0.00 sec)


mysql> USE mysql;
Database changed
mysql> SELECT Host, Db, User FROM db;
+------+-------+------+
| Host | Db    | User |
+------+-------+------+
| %    | test% |      |
+------+-------+------+
4 rows in set (0.06 sec)
```

Of course, just because a database was selected with the USE command doesn't mean you can't access other databases within the same session. You can use tables in other databases simply by prefixing the table name(s) with the database name, so MySQL knows where to find them, as the following demonstrates.

```
mysql> USE db1;
Database changed
mysql> SELECT User FROM mysql.user;
+------+
| User |
+------+
|      |
| root |
|      |
| root |
+------+
4 rows in set (0.06 sec)
```

PART II

Deleting Databases

You can delete a database, and all the tables stored within it, with the DROP DATABASE command. Consider the following example, which deletes the database named db1:

```
mysql> DROP DATABASE db1;
Query OK, 0 rows affected (0.02 sec)
```

Note, this command should be used with care because it will erase all the tables (and the data they contain) within the specified database, as well as the database directory itself.

Here, too, you can use the IF EXISTS clause to avoid nasty MySQL error messages if the database you're trying to delete doesn't exist.

```
mysql> DROP DATABASE library;
ERROR 1008: Can't drop database 'library'. Database doesn't exist
mysql> DROP DATABASE IF EXISTS library;
Query OK, 0 rows affected (0.00 sec)
```

Creating Tables

Once you create a database, the next step is to populate it with one or more tables. The SQL command used to create a new table in a database typically looks like this:

```
CREATE TABLE table-name (field-definition, field-definition, ...)
 TYPE=table-type;
```

The same rules that apply to database names also apply to table names and field names. Each table (and the data it contains) is stored as a set of three files in your MySQL data/ directory (assuming the default MyISAM table type is used). You can specify as many fields for a table as you like by separating the various field descriptions with commas. Field and table names that also double as MySQL reserved words must be quoted with the backtick (`) operator.

Here's an example of how this command can be used to create a simple table to store usernames and passwords.

```
mysql> CREATE TABLE users (id INT(3), name VARCHAR(8), pass
VARCHAR(20));
Query OK, 0 rows affected (0.08 sec)
```

Here's a more complex table, this one specifies constraints on field and table data and, in addition, defines the table type:

```
mysql> CREATE TABLE firewall (
-> host VARCHAR(11) NOT NULL,
-> port SMALLINT(4) NOT NULL,
-> access ENUM('DENY', 'ALLOW') NOT NULL,
-> PRIMARY KEY(host, port)
-> ) TYPE=HEAP;
Query OK, 0 rows affected (0.04 sec)
```

Or, how about this one?

```
mysql> CREATE TABLE menu (
-> id INT(10) UNSIGNED DEFAULT '0' NOT NULL,
-> label VARCHAR(255) NOT NULL,
-> mpl TINYINT(2) UNSIGNED DEFAULT '0' NOT NULL,
-> parent INT(10) DEFAULT '0' NOT NULL,
-> link VARCHAR(255),
-> PRIMARY KEY (id)
-> );
Query OK, 0 rows affected (0.04 sec)
```

As you can see from the previous examples, a field definition in a CREATE TABLE command consists of a unique name for the field, followed by a field type that specifies the type of data to be held within that field. A number of such field definitions are possible within a single CREATE TABLE command. These definitions are followed by table-level constraints and the table type definition.

The following sections examine these components in greater detail.

Field Types

MySQL offers a number of different data types to handle different data requirements. Some of the more important ones are summarized in Table 8-1 and are discussed in detail in Chapter 5.

Field Constraints

Every field definition can contain additional constraints, or modifiers, that can be used to increase the consistency of the data that will be entered into it.

Not My TYPE

The TYPE clause in the CREATE TABLE command is optional, and MySQL tables default to the MyISAM table type. For a more detailed discussion of table types, refer to the section "Table Types."

Type	Description
INT	A numeric type that can accept values in the range of 2147483648 to 2147483647
DECIMAL	A numeric type with support for floating point or decimal numbers
DOUBLE	a numeric type for double-precision floating point numbers
DATE	A date field in the YYYYMMDD format
TIME	A time field in the HH:MM:SS format
DATETIME	A combined date/time type in the YYYYMMDD HH:MM:SS format
YEAR	A field specifically for year displays in the range 1901 to 2155, in either YYYY or YY formats
TIMESTAMP	A timestamp type, in YYYYMMDDHHMMSS format
CHAR	A string type with a maximum size of 255 characters and a fixed length
VARCHAR	A string type with a maximum size of 255 characters and a variable length
TEXT	A string type with a maximum size of 65535 characters
BLOB	A binary type for variable data
ENUM	A string type that can accept one value from a list of previously defined possible values
SET	A string type that can accept zero or more values from a set of previously defined possible values

TABLE 8-1   MySQL Data Types

The NULL and NOT NULL Modifiers

You can specify whether the field is allowed to be empty or must necessarily be filled with data by placing the NULL and NOT NULL modifiers after each field definition. By default, MySQL assumes the NULL modifier. If a field is specifically designated as NOT NULL, MySQL won't permit INSERTs containing null values in that field.

If, for example, you want to enforce a NOT NULL rule on the various fields of the users table created previously, your table definition might look something like this:

```
mysql> CREATE TABLE users (
    -> id INT(3) NOT NULL,
    -> name VARCHAR(8) NOT NULL,
    -> pass VARCHAR(20) NOT NULL
    -> );
Query OK, 0 rows affected (0.01 sec)
```

Inserting a record containing a NULL value into such a table would immediately fail.

```
mysql> INSERT INTO users (id, name, pass) VALUES ('1', 'john', NULL);
ERROR 1048: Column 'pass' cannot be null
```

This rule, however, doesn't hold true in the case of auto-incrementing and `TIMESTAMP` fields. Inserting `NULL` into these fields results in the insertion of the next autoincrement value or the current timestamp, respectively.

The `DEFAULT` Modifier

You can specify a default value for the field with the `DEFAULT` modifier. This default value is used if no value is specified for that field when inserting a record. Consider the following example, which creates a table linking employees to departments. By default, employees are placed in the MIS department.

```
mysql> CREATE TABLE memberships (
    -> user VARCHAR(8) NOT NULL,
    -> dept VARCHAR(25) DEFAULT 'MIS'
    -> );
Query OK, 0 rows affected (0.01 sec)
mysql> INSERT INTO memberships (user, dept) VALUES ('joe', 'HR');
Query OK, 1 row affected (0.01 sec)
mysql> INSERT INTO memberships (user) VALUES ('john');
Query OK, 1 row affected (0.00 sec)
mysql> SELECT * FROM memberships;
+------+------+
| user | dept |
+------+------+
| joe  | HR   |
| john | MIS  |
+------+------+
2 rows in set (0.00 sec)
```

If no `DEFAULT` modifier is specified on a field, MySQL automatically assigns a default value depending on whether the field is `NULL` or `NOT NULL`. For fields designated as `NULL`, MySQL inserts a `NULL` value by default. For `NOT NULL` fields, MySQL will insert 0 for numeric types, an empty string for string types, the current date and time for the `TIMESTAMP` type, and the first item of the enumerated set for the `ENUM` type.

The `AUTO_INCREMENT` Modifier

The `AUTO_INCREMENT` modifier, which is only available for `INT` fields, indicates that MySQL should automatically generate a number for that field (by incrementing the previous value by 1). This is particularly useful for primary keys because it allows developers to have MySQL automatically create a unique identifier for each record.

Consider the following example, which demonstrates by automatically assigning a unique numeric ID to each record:

```
mysql> CREATE TABLE items (
-> id INT(5) NOT NULL AUTO_INCREMENT PRIMARY KEY,
-> label VARCHAR(255) NOT NULL
-> );
```

```
Query OK, 0 rows affected (0.01 sec)
mysql> INSERT INTO items (label) VALUES ('CFZ 11A89-0 adapter');
Query OK, 1 row affected (0.04 sec)
mysql> INSERT INTO items (label) VALUES ('R645u connector');
Query OK, 1 row affected (0.02 sec)
mysql> INSERT INTO items (label) VALUES ('Crimping pliers');
Query OK, 1 row affected (0.00 sec)
mysql> SELECT id, label FROM items;
+-----+--------------------+
| id  | label              |
+-----+--------------------+
|   1 | CFZ 11A89-0 adapter |
|   2 | R645u connector    |
|   3 | Crimping pliers    |
+-----+--------------------+
3 rows in set (0.00 sec)
```

NOTE *A MySQL table can have only one AUTO_INCREMENT field, and this field must be defined as a key.*

In addition to field-level constraints, MySQL also permits table-level constraints like primary and foreign keys, indexes, and uniqueness constraints. These constraints are typically placed after the field definitions in the CREATE TABLE command. The following sections examine these in greater detail.

Indexes

To speed searches and reduce query execution time, MySQL lets you index particular fields of a table. The term "index" here means much the same as in the real world. Similar in concept to the index you find at the end of a book, an *index* is a list of sorted field values, used to simplify the task of locating specific records in response to queries.

In the absence of an index, MySQL needs to scan each row of the table to find the records matching a particular query. This might not cause a noticeable slowdown in smaller tables but, as table size increases, a complete table scan can add many seconds of overhead to a query. An index speeds things significantly: with an index, MySQL can bypass the full table scan altogether by, instead, looking up the index and jumping to the appropriate locations in the table. When looking for records that match a specific search condition, reading an index is typically faster than scanning an entire table. This is because indexes are small in size and can be searched faster (you can read more about how indexes influence performance in Chapter 16).

That said, an index does have two important disadvantages: it takes up additional space on disk, and it can affect the speed of INSERT, UPDATE, and DELETE queries because the index must be updated every time table records are added, updated, or deleted. Most of the time, though, these reasons shouldn't stop you from using indexes: disk storage is getting cheaper everyday, and MySQL includes numerous optimization techniques to reduce the time spent on updating indexes and searching them for specific values (see the sidebar entitled "Hash Bang" for more information on this).

> **Hash Bang**
> With InnoDB tables, MySQL uses intelligent insert buffering to reduce the number
> of disk writes to InnoDB indexes by maintaining a list of changes in a special insert
> buffer, and then updating the index with all the changes in a single write (rather
> than multiple simultaneous writes). MySQL also tries to convert the disk-based
> B-tree indexes into adaptive hash indexes (that can be searched faster) based on
> patterns in the queries being executed.

Indexing is typically recommended for fields that frequently appear in the WHERE,
ORDER BY, and GROUP BY clauses of SELECT queries, and for fields used to join tables
together.

Indexes can be created by adding the INDEX modifier to a CREATE TABLE
statement, as in the following:

```
mysql> CREATE TABLE stocks (
-> symbol CHAR(4) NOT NULL,
-> purchase_price FLOAT(6,2) NOT NULL,
-> purchase_date DATE NOT NULL,
-> INDEX sym (symbol)
-> );
Query OK, 0 rows affected (0.00 sec)
```

The previous statement creates an index named sym for the field symbol in the
stocks table.

Multiple fields can be indexed simply by specifying multiple INDEX modifiers,
as in the following example:

```
mysql> CREATE TABLE users (
-> id INT(4) NOT NULL AUTO_INCREMENT,
-> fname VARCHAR(50) NOT NULL,
-> lname VARCHAR(50) NOT NULL,
-> INDEX (fname), INDEX (lname), PRIMARY KEY (id)
-> );
Query OK, 0 rows affected (0.05 sec)
```

Multifield indexes, created by concatenating the values of all indexed fields (up to
a maximum of 15 fields), can be created by separating the field names with a comma.
The following example illustrates.

```
mysql> CREATE TABLE users (
-> id INT(4) NOT NULL AUTO_INCREMENT,
-> fname VARCHAR(50) NOT NULL,
-> lname VARCHAR(50) NOT NULL,
```

```
-> INDEX (fname, lname), PRIMARY KEY (id)
-> );
Query OK, 0 rows affected (0.05 sec)
```

Indexes can be added to an existing table with the CREATE INDEX command. Its syntax looks like this:

```
CREATE INDEX index-name ON table-name (field-name, field-name, ...);
```

Here's an example, which creates an index named username on the uname field of the sysusers table:

```
mysql> CREATE INDEX username ON sysusers (uname);
Query OK, 0 rows affected (0.05 sec)
Records: 0  Duplicates: 0  Warnings: 0
```

For BLOB and TEXT fields, it's also mandatory to specify the number of characters to be indexed. This is accomplished by stating the required index length in parentheses after the field name in a CREATE INDEX statement. Here's an example:

```
mysql> CREATE INDEX synopsis ON books (synopsis(100));
Query OK, 83 rows affected (0.15 sec)
```

Such partial indexing is also possible (though optional) on CHAR and VARCHAR fields.

NOTE *If an index name isn't specified, either in the CREATE INDEX or CREATE TABLE statements, MySQL automatically names the index using the corresponding field name as base.*

If you find you no longer have any need of an index, you can nuke it with the DROP INDEX command, which looks like this:

```
DROP INDEX index-name ON table-name;
```

The following example deletes the username index created in the previous example:

```
mysql> DROP INDEX username ON sysusers;
Query OK, 0 rows affected (0.05 sec)
Records: 0  Duplicates: 0  Warnings: 0
```

In addition to the "regular" index type, MySQL supports two other important index variants: UNIQUE indexes and FULLTEXT indexes, which are discussed in the following sections.

The UNIQUE Index

You can specify that values entered into a field must be unique, that is, not duplicated in any other row, via the UNIQUE modifier to the CREATE TABLE and CREATE INDEX commands. Once a field is marked as UNIQUE in this manner, any attempt to enter duplicate data into it will fail.

```
mysql> CREATE TABLE users (
-> username VARCHAR(8),
-> userpass VARCHAR(20),
-> UNIQUE(username)
-> );
Query OK, 0 rows affected (0.00 sec)
mysql> INSERT INTO users (username, userpass) VALUES ('jb', 'secret');
Query OK, 1 row affected (0.01 sec)
mysql> INSERT INTO users (username, userpass) VALUES ('jb', 'hidden');
ERROR 1062: Duplicate entry 'jb' for key 1
```

Note, however, that a UNIQUE field is permitted to store NULL values, as in the following example:

```
mysql> CREATE TABLE users(
-> username VARCHAR(8) NOT NULL,
-> email VARCHAR(255),
-> UNIQUE(email)
-> );
Query OK, 0 rows affected (0.02 sec)
mysql> INSERT INTO users (username, email) VALUES ('jb',
'jb@some.domain');
Query OK, 1 row affected (0.01 sec)
mysql> INSERT INTO users (username, email) VALUES ('jimbozak',
'jb@some.domain');
ERROR 1062: Duplicate entry 'jb@some.domain' for key 1
mysql> INSERT INTO users (username, email) VALUES ('john', NULL);
Query OK, 1 row affected (0.00 sec)
```

The FULLTEXT Index

MySQL 3.23.23 and better supports a special type of index designed specifically for full-text searching on MyISAM tables, called a FULLTEXT index. This index makes it possible to query the indexed columns for arbitrary text strings and return only those records that contain values similar to the search strings. When performing this type of full-text search, MySQL calculates a similarity score between the table records and the search string, and returns only those records with a high score.

NOTE   *FULLTEXT indexes are only supported on MyISAM tables.*

Here's an example:

```
mysql> ALTER TABLE books ADD FULLTEXT INDEX (synopsis);
Query OK, 83 rows affected (0.55 sec)
Records: 83  Duplicates: 0  Warnings: 0
```

Once the index is created, you can search it with the MATCH() function, providing the search string as an argument to the AGAINST() function. Consider the following example.

```
mysql> SELECT title, MATCH(synopsis) AGAINST ('suspense') AS score FROM
books LIMIT 0, 10;
+----------------------------------+-----------------+
| title                            | score           |
+----------------------------------+-----------------+
| The Prometheus Deception         |               0 |
| Dark Hollow                      | 2.5951748101926 |
| Easy Prey                        |  2.703356073143 |
| Prayers For Rain                 | 2.8519631063088 |
| Roses Are Red                    | 2.8209489868374 |
| Personal Injuries                |               0 |
| Demolition Angel                 |               0 |
| Code To Zero                     |               0 |
| Adrian Mole: The Cappuccino Years |              0 |
| The Bear And The Dragon          |               0 |
+----------------------------------+-----------------+
10 rows in set (0.11 sec)
```

The argument passed to the MATCH() function must be a field list that maps exactly into some FULLTEXT index on the table. The MATCH() function then calculates a similarity score between the search string and the named fields for every record in the table. According to the MySQL manual at http://www.mysql.com/documentation/, similarity is scored on the basis of a number of parameters, including the following:

- The number of words in the row;
- The number of unique words in that row;
- The total number of words in the collection;
- The number of rows that contain a particular word.

A similarity score of 0 indicates no similarity exists between the values being compared.

Words that appear in more than 50 percent of the total records in the table (so-called *stopwords*) are ignored and are treated as having no relevance for the purpose of full-text searching. Similarly, words that appear more frequently are given less weight in the index than words that appear less frequently.

The stopword list, together with the minimum word length and the maximum word length to be considered when deciding which words to include in the FULLTEXT index, can be adjusted via the ft_stopword_file, ft_min_word_len, and ft_max_word_len server configuration variables, respectively. See Chapter 13 for more information on how to alter server variables.

Typically, you would use the MATCH() function in a WHERE clause to retrieve those records with a high similarity score, as in the following example:

```
mysql> SELECT title, author FROM books WHERE MATCH (synopsis) AGAINST
('suspense');
+-------------------+-------------------+
| title             | author            |
+-------------------+-------------------+
| Prayers For Rain  | Dennis Lehane     |
| Roses Are Red     | James Patterson   |
| Easy Prey         | John Sandford     |
| Dark Hollow       | John Connolly     |
+-------------------+-------------------+
4 rows in set (0.06 sec)
```

Boolean Searches   In MySQL 4.0.1 and better, you can also execute Boolean searches on a FULLTEXT index, by adding the IN BOOLEAN MODE modifier and one or more Boolean operators in the argument passed to the AGAINST() function. The following examples illustrate. The first example returns all those records containing both the words "crime" and "suspense" in the synopsis field, while the second example lists

---

Starting From Scratch . . . Almost

When you make changes to server variables that affect a FULLTEXT index, rebuilding the index after you activate the changes is necessary. One way to do this is to drop the index, and then re-create it. The MySQL manual suggests a faster alternative, however: use the REPAIR TABLE command with the QUICK argument to rebuild the index automatically, as in the following example:

```
mysql> REPAIR TABLE books QUICK;
+-----------------+--------+----------+----------+
| Table           | Op     | Msg_type | Msg_text |
+-----------------+--------+----------+----------+
| db20139a.books  | repair | status   | OK       |
+-----------------+--------+----------+----------+
1 row in set (0.06 sec)
```

all those records containing the word "romance," but not the words "teenage" or "period" in their synopsis:

```
mysql> SELECT title, author FROM books WHERE MATCH (synopsis) AGAINST
('+suspense +crime' IN BOOLEAN MODE);
+-------------------------+-------------------+
| title                   | author            |
+-------------------------+-------------------+
| Void Moon               | Michael Connelly  |
| Burnt Sienna            | David Morrell     |
| Cradle And All          | James Patterson   |
| The Prometheus Deception | Robert Ludlum    |
| Roses Are Red           | James Patterson   |
| Mystic River            | Dennis Lehane     |
| Right As Rain           | George Pelecanos  |
+-------------------------+-------------------+
7 rows in set (0.00 sec)
mysql> SELECT title, author FROM books WHERE MATCH (synopsis) AGAINST
('+romance -teenage -period' IN BOOLEAN MODE);
Empty set (0.00 sec)
```

Note, FULLTEXT indexes are fairly new to MySQL and work best when used with large tables. Small tables don't offer a sufficient spread of data values for the index to operate optimally. Additionally, they aren't yet completely optimized for production environments, so they should be used in moderation.

TIP   *For faster full-text indexing, add a FULLTEXT index to a table after it's been populated with data, with the CREATE INDEX or ALTER TABLE commands, rather than at table creation time itself.*

Primary Keys

You can specify a primary key for the table with the PRIMARY KEY constraint. In a well-designed database schema, a *primary key* serves as an unchanging, unique identifier for each record. If a key is declared as primary, it usually implies the values in it will rarely be modified.

The PRIMARY KEY constraint can best be thought of as a combination of the NOT NULL and UNIQUE constraints because it requires values in the specified field to be neither NULL nor repeated in any other row. Consider the following example, which demonstrates by creating an inventory table with the item's SKU as primary key:

```
mysql> CREATE TABLE inventory (
    -> sku INT(3) NOT NULL,
    -> item VARCHAR(255) NOT NULL,
    -> PRIMARY KEY(SKU)
    -> );
```

```
Query OK, 0 rows affected (0.07 sec)
mysql> INSERT INTO inventory (sku, item) VALUES (99, 'Ancient Ming vase');
Query OK, 1 row affected (0.07 sec)
mysql> INSERT INTO inventory (sku, item) VALUES (99, 'Gold sceptre with rubies');
ERROR 1062: Duplicate entry '99' for key 1
mysql> INSERT INTO inventory (sku, item) VALUES (NULL, 'Gold sceptre with rubies');
ERROR 1048: Column 'sku' cannot be null
```

In this situation, because the sku column is defined as the primary key, MySQL won't allow duplication or NULL values in that field. This allows the database administrator to ensure that every item named in the table has a unique SKU, thereby enforcing a high degree of consistency on the stored data.

PRIMARY KEY constraints can be specified for either a single field or for a composite of multiple fields. Consider the following example, which demonstrates by constructing a table containing a composite primary key:

```
mysql> CREATE TABLE firewall (
    -> host VARCHAR(11) NOT NULL,
    -> port SMALLINT(4) NOT NULL,
    -> access ENUM('DENY', 'ALLOW') NOT NULL,
    -> PRIMARY KEY(host, port)
    -> );
Query OK, 0 rows affected (0.04 sec)
mysql> INSERT INTO firewall (host, port, access) VALUES ('202.65.3.87', 21, 'DENY');
Query OK, 1 row affected (0.00 sec)
mysql> INSERT INTO firewall (host, port, access) VALUES ('202.65.3.87', 21,
'ALLOW');
ERROR 1062: Duplicate entry '202.65.3.87-21' for key 1
mysql> INSERT INTO firewall (host, port, access) VALUES ('202.65.3.87', 80, 'DENY');
Query OK, 1 row affected (0.00 sec)
mysql> INSERT INTO firewall (host, port, access) VALUES ('127.0.0.1', 21, 'ALLOW');
Query OK, 1 row affected (0.00 sec)
```

In this case, the table rules permit repetition of either the host IP address or the port, but not of both together. This can come in handy when a record is to be uniquely identified by a combination of its attributes, rather than by only a single attribute.

Foreign Keys

The fundamental basis of a relational database system, like MySQL, is its capability to create relationships between the tables that make up the database. By making it possible to easily relate records in different tables to one another, an RDBMS makes

A Key By Any Other Name

In MySQL, the terms "key" and "index" are equivalent. Thus, PRIMARY KEY fields are automatically indexed by MySQL in all tables, while FOREIGN KEY fields must be explicitly indexed by the user.

FIGURE 8-1
A one-to-one
relationship
between tables

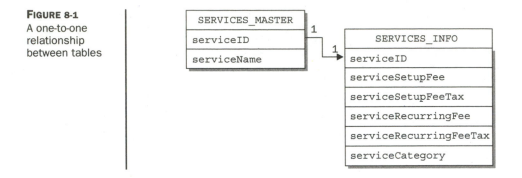

it possible to analyze date in different ways, while simultaneously keeping it organized in a systematic fashion, with minimal redundancy.

These relationships are managed through the use of *foreign keys*, essentially, fields that have the same meaning in all the tables in the relationship and that serve as points of commonality to link records in different tables together. A foreign key relationship could be one-to-one—a record in one table is linked to one and only one record in another table—or one-to-many—a record in one table is linked to multiple records in another table.

Figure 8-1 illustrates a one-to-one relationship: a service and its associated description, with the relationship between the two managed via the unique serviceID field.

Figure 8-2 illustrates a one-to-many relationship: a company and a list of its branch offices, with the link between the two maintained via the unique companyID field.

When each foreign key value is related to a field in another table, this relationship being unique, the system is said to be in a state of *referential integrity*. In other words, if a field is present in all the tables once and only once, and if a change to that field in any single table is reflected in all other tables, referential integrity is said to exist.

This concept of referential integrity is a basic one, and one that becomes important when designing a database with more than one table. When foreign keys are used to link one table to another, referential integrity, by its very nature, imposes constraints on inserting new records and updating existing records. For example, if a table only accepts certain types of values for a particular field, and other tables use that field as their foreign key, this automatically imposes certain constraints on the dependent tables. Similarly, referential integrity demands that a change in the field used as a foreign key—a deletion or a new insertion—must immediately be reflected in all dependent tables.

FIGURE 8-2
A one-to-many
relationship
between tables

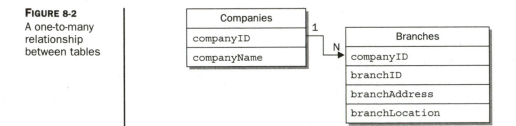

Many, but not all, of today's databases take care of this automatically. If you've worked with Microsoft Access, for example, you'll have seen this in action. In the case of databases that don't perform this function automatically, the task of maintaining referential integrity falls to the application developer, who must manually update all dependent tables to reflect changes in foreign key values.

MySQL straddles the fence on this particular feature, allowing the use of foreign keys, but ignoring them for integrity checking purposes in all table types except the InnoDB table type (starting from MySQL 3.23.44). While this might seem somewhat unusual, the reason is fairly pragmatic: performing integrity checks on all the foreign key relationships in a database on every INSERT, UPDATE, and DELETE is a time- and resource-intensive process, and can affect performance, especially when dealing with complex or convoluted link trees. Thus, users have the choice of selecting the combination best suited for their specific needs, on a table-by-table basis.

In this example, the employees.fk_department field is a foreign key, linked to the departments.id primary key. Note the manner in which this relationship is specified in the FOREIGN KEY...REFERENCES modifier. The FOREIGN KEY part specifies one end of the relationship (the field name in the current table), while the REFERENCES part specifies the other end of the relationship (the field name in the referenced table).

When creating a table, a foreign key can be defined in much the same way as a primary key, by using the FOREIGN KEY...REFERENCES modifier. The following example demonstrates by creating two InnoDB tables linked to each other in a one-to-many relationship by the department ID:

```
mysql> CREATE TABLE departments (
-> id INT(4) NOT NULL,
-> name VARCHAR(50) NOT NULL,
-> PRIMARY KEY (id)
-> ) TYPE=INNODB;
Query OK, 0 rows affected (0.00 sec)
mysql> CREATE TABLE employees (
-> id SMALLINT(6) NOT NULL,
-> name CHAR(255) NOT NULL,
-> fk_department INT(4) NOT NULL,
-> PRIMARY KEY (id),
-> INDEX (fk_department),
-> FOREIGN KEY (fk_department) REFERENCES departments (id)
-> ) TYPE=INNODB;
Query OK, 0 rows affected (0.16 sec)
```

Syntax Error

When creating foreign key references, you might encounter an error message referencing error code 150 like this:

```
ERROR 1005: Can't create table './test/employees.frm' (errno: 150)
```

> **Making a Choice**
> Choose the MyISAM table type if you need better performance and no integrity checks, and the InnoDB table type if you'd like enforcement of foreign key integrity constraints between tables and are willing to live with the performance overhead this entails. Both these table types are discussed in greater detail in the sections "The MyISAM Table Type" and "The InnoDB Table Type."

If you see a message like this, it usually means something is wrong with your foreign key declaration. Check to ensure the table and field you're referencing do in fact exist, the fields making up the foreign key are indexed, and the syntax of the declaration is correct. You might also be able to obtain more information on the error by issuing the SHOW INNODB STATUS command and scanning the output for messages related to foreign key errors.

Once a foreign key is set up, MySQL only allows entry of those values into the employees.fk_department field, which also exist in the departments.id field. Continuing the previous example, let's see how this works.

```
mysql> INSERT INTO departments (id, name) VALUES (101, 'Engineering'), (102,
'Administration'), (103, 'Finance');
Query OK, 3 rows affected (0.05 sec)
Records: 3  Duplicates: 0  Warnings: 0
mysql> INSERT INTO employees (id, name, fk_department) VALUES (57, 'John D', 102);
Query OK, 1 row affected (0.00 sec)
mysql> INSERT INTO employees (id, name, fk_department) VALUES (101, 'Thomas
E', 110);
ERROR 1216: Cannot add or update a child row: a foreign key constraint fails
```

Thus, because a department with ID 110 in the departments table doesn't exist, MySQL rejects the record with that value for the fk_department field in the employees table. In this manner, foreign key constraints can significantly help in enforcing the data integrity of the tables in a database and reducing the occurrences of "bad" or inconsistent field values.

The following three constraints must be kept in mind when linking tables with foreign keys in this manner:

- All the tables in the relationship must be InnoDB tables. In non-InnoDB tables, the FOREIGN KEY...REFERENCES modifier is simply ignored by MySQL.

- The fields used in the foreign key relationship must be explicitly indexed in all references tables. InnoDB doesn't automatically create these indexes for you.

- The data types of the fields named in the foreign key relationship should be similar. This is especially true of integer types, which must match in both size and sign.

What's interesting to note is this: even if foreign key constraints exist on a table, MySQL permits you to DROP the table without raising an error (even if doing so would break the foreign key relationships established earlier). In fact, in versions of MySQL earlier than 4.0.13, dropping the table was the only way to remove a foreign key. MySQL 4.0.13 and better does, however, support a less-drastic way of removing a foreign key from a table, via the ALTER TABLE command. Here's the syntax:

```
ALTER TABLE table-name DROP FOREIGN KEY key-id;
```

The *key-id* value can be obtained through the SHOW CREATE TABLE command (discussed in detail in the section "Copying Tables"). Consider the following example, which illustrates the process:

```
mysql> SHOW CREATE TABLE employees;
+------------+------------------------------------------------------------+
| Table      | Create Table                                               |
+------------+------------------------------------------------------------+
| employees  | CREATE TABLE `employees` (                                 |
  `id` smallint(6) NOT NULL default '0',
  `name` char(255) NOT NULL default '',
  `fk_department` int (4) NOT NULL default '',
  PRIMARY KEY (`id`),
  KEY `fk_department` (`fk_department`),
  CONSTRAINT `0_18` FOREIGN KEY (`fk_department`)
  REFERENCES `departments` (`id`)
) TYPE=InnoDB                                                              |
+------------+------------------------------------------------------------+
1 row in set (0.00 sec)
```

Breaking the Rules

When populating tables in batch operations, say, from a dump file at the mysql command prompt or through a LOAD DATA INFILE command, a good idea is to turn off foreign key checks, so MySQL doesn't complain about integrity violations. One way to do this is to set the foreign key constraints with the ALTER TABLE command only after the tables are created and populated. Another approach is to turn off key checking by setting the foreign_key_checks server variable to 0.

You can read more about the ALTER TABLE command in the section "Modifying Tables" and find out about altering server variables in Chapter 13.

PART II

The foreign key can now be deleted using the identifier 0_18:

```
mysql> ALTER TABLE employees DROP FOREIGN KEY 0_18;
Query OK, 2 rows affected (0.03 sec)
Records: 2  Duplicates: 0  Warnings: 0
```

Automatic Key Updates and Deletions   Foreign keys can certainly take care of ensuring the integrity of newly inserted records. But, what if a record is deleted from the table named in the REFERENCES clause? What happens to all the records in subordinate tables that use this value as a foreign key?

Obviously, those records should be deleted as well, or else you'll have orphan records cluttering your database. MySQL 3.23.50 and better simplifies this task, by enabling you to add an ON DELETE clause to the FOREIGN KEY...REFERENCES modifier, which tells the database what to do with the orphaned records in such a situation.

Consider the following example, which links categories and articles together via a common category ID:

```
mysql> CREATE TABLE categories (cid INT(4) NOT NULL, cname VARCHAR(50) NOT NULL,
PRIMARY KEY (cid)) TYPE=INNODB;
Query OK, 0 rows affected (0.11 sec)
mysql> INSERT INTO categories (cid, cname) VALUES (1, 'News'), (2, 'Fashion'),
(3, 'Sports');
Query OK, 3 rows affected (0.00 sec)
Records: 3  Duplicates: 0  Warnings: 0
mysql> CREATE TABLE articles (aid INT(4) NOT NULL, aname VARCHAR(255) NOT NULL,
fk_cid INT(4) NOT NULL, PRIMARY KEY (aid), INDEX category_id (fk_cid), FOREIGN
KEY (fk_cid) REFERENCES categories (cid) ON DELETE CASCADE) TYPE=INNODB;
Query OK, 0 rows affected (0.06 sec)
mysql> INSERT INTO articles (aid, aname, fk_cid) VALUES (1, 'Sample article on
winter fashions', 2);
Query OK, 1 row affected (0.05 sec)
```

Here's what things look like after running these commands:

```
mysql> SELECT * FROM categories;
+-----+---------+
| cid | cname   |
+-----+---------+
|   1 | News    |
|   2 | Fashion |
|   3 | Sports  |
+-----+---------+
3 rows in set (0.06 sec)
mysql> SELECT * FROM articles;
```

```
+-----+----------------------------------+--------+
| aid | aname                            | fk_cid |
+-----+----------------------------------+--------+
|   1 | Sample article on winter fashions |     2 |
+-----+----------------------------------+--------+
1 row in set (0.00 sec)
```

The ON DELETE CASCADE clause ensures that if a category is deleted from the categories table, all articles linked to that category are also deleted from the articles table. This is clearly visible from the following snippet:

```
mysql> DELETE FROM categories WHERE cname = 'Fashion';
Query OK, 1 row affected (0.05 sec)
mysql> SELECT * FROM categories;
+-----+--------+
| cid | cname  |
+-----+--------+
|   1 | News   |
|   3 | Sports |
+-----+--------+
2 rows in set (0.00 sec)
mysql> SELECT * FROM articles;
Empty set (0.00 sec)
```

Thus, when a category is deleted, MySQL also takes care of automatically removing all the records associated with that category in linked tables.

Table 8-2 lists the four keywords that can follow an ON DELETE clause:

NOTE *MySQL doesn't (yet) support the SET DEFAULT action in an ON DELETE or ON UPDATE clause. In other RDBMSs, though, the SET DEFAULT action can be used to set a field to its default value in case of a deletion or a change in its foreign key relationship.*

Keyword	What It Means
CASCADE	Delete all records containing references to the deleted key value.
SET NULL	Modify all records containing references to the deleted key value to, instead, use a NULL value (this can only be used for fields previously marked as NOT NULL).
RESTRICT	Reject the deletion request until all subordinate records using the deleted key value have, themselves, been manually deleted and no references exist (this is the default setting and it's also the safest setting).
NO ACTION	Do nothing.

TABLE 8-2   Actions Available in an ON DELETE Clause

Here's a variant of the previous example, demonstrating how the SET NULL keyword works.

```
mysql> DELETE FROM categories WHERE cname = 'Fashion';
Query OK, 1 row affected (0.05 sec)
mysql> SELECT * FROM articles;
+-----+--------+--------+
| aid | aname  | fk_cid |
+-----+--------+--------+
|   1 | sample |   NULL |
+-----+--------+--------+
1 row in set (0.00 sec)
```

What happens when you use the default RESTRICT keyword? MySQL rejects the deletion because a record referencing the key still exists in the articles table.

```
mysql> DELETE FROM categories WHERE cname = 'Fashion';
ERROR 1217: Cannot delete or update a parent row: a foreign key constraint fails
```

The NO ACTION keyword does exactly what it says (and this results in an orphaned record in the articles table):

```
mysql> DELETE FROM categories WHERE cname = 'Fashion';
Query OK, 1 row affected (0.05 sec)
mysql> SELECT * FROM categories;
+-----+--------+
| cid | cname  |
+-----+--------+
|   1 | News   |
|   3 | Sports |
+-----+--------+
2 rows in set (0.06 sec)
mysql> SELECT * FROM articles;
+-----+--------------------------------+--------+
| aid | aname                          | fk_cid |
+-----+--------------------------------+--------+
|   1 | Sample article on winter fashions |    2 |
+-----+--------------------------------+--------+
1 row in set (0.00 sec)
```

MySQL 4.0.8 and better also lets you perform these automatic actions on updates by allowing the use of an ON UPDATE clause, which works in a similar manner to the ON DELETE clause. So, for example, adding the ON UPDATE CASCADE clause to a foreign key definition tells MySQL that when a record is updated in the primary table (the table referenced for foreign key checks), then all records using that foreign key value in the current table should also be automatically updated with the new values to ensure the consistency of the system.

An example might make this clearer. Consider the following two tables, which are linked together by an ON UPDATE CASCADE condition on the state code:

```
mysql> SELECT * FROM states;
+------+------------+
| code | name       |
+------+------------+
| AZ   | Arizona    |
| CA   | California |
| NY   | New York   |
+------+------------+
3 rows in set (0.00 sec)
mysql> SELECT * FROM votes;
+-------+--------+
| state | total  |
+-------+--------+
| AZ    |  46292 |
| CA    | 123661 |
| NY    |    648 |
+-------+--------+
3 rows in set (0.00 sec)
```

If you were, now, to update one of the codes in the states table, the ON UPDATE CASCADE clause would ensure that MySQL updated all records in the votes table with the new state code automatically. The following clearly illustrates this:

```
mysql> UPDATE states SET code = 'AR' WHERE name = 'Arizona';
Query OK, 1 row affected (0.00 sec)
Rows matched: 1  Changed: 1  Warnings: 0
mysql> SELECT * FROM votes;
+-------+--------+
| state | total  |
+-------+--------+
| AR    |  46292 |
| CA    | 123661 |
| NY    |    648 |
+-------+--------+
3 rows in set (0.05 sec)
```

I, Robot

Be aware that setting up MySQL for automatic operations through ON UPDATE and ON DELETE rules can result in serious data corruption if your key relationships aren't set up perfectly. For example, if you have a series of tables linked together by foreign key relationships and ON DELETE CASCADE rules, a change in any of the master tables can result in records, even records linked only peripherally to the original deletion, getting wiped out with no warning. For this reason, you should check (and then double-check) these rules before casting them in stone.

Table Types

Once the various field definitions and modifiers are finished, MySQL also, optionally, lets you specify the table type with the TYPE attribute. Here's an example:

```
mysql> CREATE TABLE users (
-> id INT(3),
-> name VARCHAR(8),
-> pass VARCHAR(20)
-> ) TYPE=MyISAM;
Query OK, 0 rows affected (0.08 sec)
```

A number of different table types are available, each with its own attributes and advantages. The following sections discuss the various types in greater detail.

The MyISAM Table Type

The *MyISAM* table format (TYPE = MYISAM) extends the base ISAM type with a number of additional optimizations and enhancements, and is MySQL's default table type. MyISAM tables are optimized for compression and speed, and are immediately portable between different OSs and platforms (for example, the same MyISAM table can be used on both Windows and UNIX OSs). The MyISAM format supports large table files (over 4GB in size) and allows indexing of BLOB and TEXT columns. Tables and table indices can be compressed to save space, a feature that comes in handy when storing large BLOB or TEXT fields. VARCHAR fields can either be constrained to a specific length or adjusted dynamically as per the data within them, and the format supports searching for records using any key prefix, as well as using the entire key.

Because MyISAM tables are optimized for MySQL, it's no surprise that the developers added a fair amount of intelligence to them. MyISAM tables can be either fixed-length or dynamic-length. MySQL automatically checks MyISAM tables for corruption on startup and can even repair them in case of errors. Table data and table index files can be stored in different locations (or even on different file systems). And, intelligent defragmentation logic ensures a high-performance coefficient, even for tables with a large number of inserts, updates, and deletions.

Getting Compatible

MySQL includes the ISAM table handler primarily for compatibility with legacy tables. in practice, you should avoid creating tables using this format because the newer MyISAM and InnoDB formats are far superior in terms of both performance and features.

The ISAM Table Type

ISAM tables (TYPE = ISAM) are similar to MyISAM tables, although they lack many of the performance enhancements of the MyISAM format and, therefore, don't offer the optimization and performance efficiency of that type. Because ISAM indices cannot be compressed, they use less system resources than their MyISAM counterparts. ISAM indices also require more disk space, however, which can be a problem in small-footprint environments.

Like MyISAM, ISAM tables can be either fixed length or dynamic length, though maximum key lengths are smaller with the ISAM format. The format cannot handle tables greater than 4GB, and the tables aren't immediately portable across different platforms. Additionally, the ISAM table format is more prone to fragmentation, which can reduce query speed and has limited support for data/index compression.

The HEAP Table Type

HEAP tables (TYPE = HEAP) are in-memory tables that use hashed indices, making them fast (independent assessments suggest HEAP tables are at least 30 percent faster that MyISAM tables when running INSERT queries) and are, therefore, optimized for temporary tables. They are accessed and used in exactly the same manner as regular MyISAM or ISAM tables. However, the data stored within them is available only for the lifetime of the MySQL server and is erased if the MySQL server crashes or shuts down. Although HEAP tables can offer a performance benefit, they aren't regularly used in practice because of their temporary nature and a number of other functional limitations.

Running out of RAM

Because HEAP table sizes are limited only by the memory available on the system, MySQL has built-in safeguards to prevent them from unintentionally using all the available memory. HEAP tables don't support BLOB or TEXT columns, and they cannot exceed the size set in the special max_heap_table_size variable. The size of a HEAP table can also be specified by adding a MAX_ROWS property to the CREATE TABLE statement, as in the following example:

```
CREATE TABLE heapexample (id INT(4), title VARCHAR(24)) TYPE=HEAP MAX_ROWS=10;
```

The BerkeleyDB Table Type

First introduced in MySQL 3.23.34, the BerkeleyDB table format (TYPE = BDB) was developed to meet the growing demands of MySQL developers for a transaction-safe table format. This *BerkeleyDB* table format supports a number of interesting features, including commit and rollback operations, multiuser or concurrent access, checkpoints, secondary indices, crash recovery via logs, and sequential and keyed access to data, which makes it a viable choice for complex, transaction-based SQL.

BerkeleyDB tables do, however, have some limitations: they cannot be moved easily (the table path is hardwired into the table file at the time of creation), table indices cannot be compressed, and table sizes are usually larger than their MyISAM counterparts. For these reasons, the BerkeleyDB format has largely been supplanted by the InnoDB format, which eliminates these problems and offers many additional features.

The InnoDB Table Type

The *InnoDB* format (TYPE = INNODB) first appeared in MySQL 3.23 and is included by default in MySQL 4.*x*. InnoDB is a fully ACID-compliant and very efficient table format and provides full support for transactions in MySQL without compromising speed or performance. Fine-grained (row- and table-level) locks improve the fidelity of MySQL transactions, and InnoDB also supports nonlocking reads and multiversioning (features previously only available in the Oracle RDBMS).

Asynchronous I/O and a sequential read-ahead buffer improve data retrieval speed, and a "buddy algorithm" and Oracle-type tablespaces result in optimized file and memory management. InnoDB also supports automatic creation of hash indices in memory on an as-needed basis to improve performance, and it uses buffering to improve the reliability and speed of database operations. InnoDB tables match (and, sometimes, exceed) the performance of MyISAM tables. They're fully portable between different OSs and architectures and, because of their transactional nature, they're always in a consistent state (MySQL makes them even more robust by checking them for corruption and repairing them on startup), so the InnoDB format is rapidly growing in popularity with MySQL developers. Support for foreign keys, and commit, rollback, and roll-forward operations complete the picture, making this one of the most full-featured table formats available in MySQL.

The MERGE Table Type

A *MERGE* table (TYPE = MERGE) is a virtual table created by combining multiple MyISAM tables into a single table. Such a combination of tables is only possible if the tables involved have completely identical table structures. Any difference in field types or indices won't permit a successful union. A MERGE table uses the indices of its component tables and doesn't maintain any indices of its own, which can improve its speed in certain situations.

> **Packing Up**
> When dealing with large MyISAM tables, you can reduce the space taken up by these tables by compressing, or "packing," them with the `myisampack` utility included in the MySQL distribution. `myisampack` creates read-only tables that are small in size, without adding any major performance overhead through the use of intelligent compression.

MERGE tables permit `SELECT`, `DELETE`, and `UPDATE` operations, and can come in handy when you need to pull together data from different tables or to speed performance in joins or searches between a series of tables.

Other Table Modifiers

The `TYPE` attribute isn't the only option available to control the behavior of the table being created. A number of other MySQL-specific attributes are also available. Table 8-3 has a list of the more interesting ones.

As with databases, MySQL supports use of the `IF NOT EXISTS` clause within the `CREATE TABLE` command. This is useful when used within a scripting context because it helps avoid errors in case a table with the same name already exists.

```
mysql> CREATE TABLE IF NOT EXISTS users (
-> id INT(3),
-> name VARCHAR(8),
-> pass VARCHAR(20)
-> );
Query OK, 0 rows affected (0.00 sec)
```

Type	Description
AUTO_INCREMENT	The value to use for an AUTO_INCREMENT field on the next INSERT
CHECKSUM	The Boolean stating whether to store checksums for tables
COMMENT	A descriptive note for the table
MAX_ROWS	The maximum number of rows to be stored in the table
MIN_ROWS	The minimum number of rows to be stored in the table
PACK_KEYS	The Boolean stating whether to compress table indices
UNION	The tables to be mapped into a single MERGE table
DATA DIRECTORY	The location for the table data file
INDEX DIRECTORY	The location for the table index file

TABLE 8-3   Other MySQL Table Modifiers

Copying Tables

In MySQL 3.23 and above, you can combine the CREATE TABLE and SELECT statements to create and populate a table dynamically from the results of a SELECT query. For example, suppose you have the following table

```
mysql> SELECT * FROM marks;
+----+-------+-------+------+-----+-----+
| id | fname | lname | math | sci | lit |
+----+-------+-------+------+-----+-----+
|  1 | John  | Doe   |   36 |  73 |  34 |
|  2 | Sarah | Short |   23 |  67 |  55 |
|  3 | Joe   | Cool  |   75 |  82 |  89 |
|  4 | Mark  | Wumba |   58 |  72 |  15 |
|  5 | Tom   | Thumb |    0 |  12 |   0 |
+----+-------+-------+------+-----+-----+
5 rows in set (0.00 sec)
```

and you want to create an identical copy of it.

```
mysql> CREATE TABLE grades SELECT * FROM marks;
Query OK, 5 rows affected (0.07 sec)
Records: 5  Duplicates: 0  Warnings: 0
mysql> SELECT * FROM grades;
+----+-------+-------+------+-----+-----+
| id | fname | lname | math | sci | lit |
+----+-------+-------+------+-----+-----+
|  1 | John  | Doe   |   36 |  73 |  34 |
|  2 | Sarah | Short |   23 |  67 |  55 |
|  3 | Joe   | Cool  |   75 |  82 |  89 |
|  4 | Mark  | Wumba |   58 |  72 |  15 |
|  5 | Tom   | Thumb |    0 |  12 |   0 |
+----+-------+-------+------+-----+-----+
5 rows in set (0.00 sec)
```

You can restrict the fields that appear in the copy by specifying them in the SELECT query,

```
mysql> CREATE TABLE students SELECT fname, lname FROM marks;
Query OK, 5 rows affected (0.01 sec)
Records: 5  Duplicates: 0  Warnings: 0
mysql> SELECT * FROM students;
+-------+-------+
| fname | lname |
+-------+-------+
| John  | Doe   |
| Sarah | Short |
```

```
| Joe   | Cool  |
| Mark  | Wumba |
| Tom   | Thumb |
+-------+-------+
5 rows in set (0.00 sec)
```

and by adding an optional WHERE clause to the query to place only a subset of the original data into the new table,

```
mysql> CREATE TABLE grades SELECT * FROM marks WHERE (math + sci) > 100;
Query OK, 3 rows affected (0.02 sec)
Records: 3  Duplicates: 0  Warnings: 0
mysql> SELECT * FROM grades;
+----+-------+-------+------+-----+-----+
| id | fname | lname | math | sci | lit |
+----+-------+-------+------+-----+-----+
|  1 | John  | Doe   |   36 |  73 |  34 |
|  3 | Joe   | Cool  |   75 |  82 |  89 |
|  4 | Mark  | Wumba |   58 |  72 |  15 |
+----+-------+-------+------+-----+-----+
3 rows in set (0.00 sec)
```

or by constructing an empty copy of an existing table by using a SELECT statement that returns a null result set.

```
mysql> CREATE TABLE grades SELECT * FROM marks WHERE 0 = 1;
Query OK, 0 rows affected (0.01 sec)
Records: 0  Duplicates: 0  Warnings: 0
mysql> SELECT * FROM grades;
Empty set (0.00 sec)
mysql> DESCRIBE grades;
+--------+-----------+------+-----+---------+-------+
| Field  | Type      | Null | Key | Default | Extra |
+--------+-----------+------+-----+---------+-------+
| id     | tinyint(4)|      |     | 0       |       |
| fname  | char(50)  |      |     |         |       |
| lname  | char(50)  |      |     |         |       |
| math   | int(11)   |      |     | 0       |       |
| sci    | int(11)   |      |     | 0       |       |
| lit    | int(11)   |      |     | 0       |       |
+--------+-----------+------+-----+---------+-------+
6 rows in set (0.00 sec)
```

NOTE *The CREATE TABLE ... SELECT construct doesn't copy the keys from the source table. These need to be re-created manually.*

MySQL 4.1 also supports an alternative way of accomplishing the previous example:

```
mysql> CREATE TABLE grades LIKE marks;
Query OK, 0 rows affected (0.01 sec)
Records: 0  Duplicates: 0  Warnings: 0
```

You can use the SHOW CREATE TABLE command to retrieve the SQL commands used to create the table. This information can be used to duplicate the table structure, as needed. Consider the following example, which demonstrates the CREATE TABLE syntax used to create the special MySQL host grant table:

```
mysql> SHOW CREATE TABLE mysql.host;
+--------+-----------------------------------------------------------+
| Table  | Create Table                                              |
+--------+-----------------------------------------------------------+
| host   | CREATE TABLE `host` (                                     |
|          `Host` char(60) binary NOT NULL default '',             |
|          `Db` char(64) binary NOT NULL default '',               |
|          `Select_priv` enum('N','Y') NOT NULL default 'N',       |
|          `Insert_priv` enum('N','Y') NOT NULL default 'N',       |
|          `Update_priv` enum('N','Y') NOT NULL default 'N',       |
|          `Delete_priv` enum('N','Y') NOT NULL default 'N',       |
|          `Create_priv` enum('N','Y') NOT NULL default 'N',       |
|          `Drop_priv` enum('N','Y') NOT NULL default 'N',         |
|          `Grant_priv` enum('N','Y') NOT NULL default 'N',        |
|          `References_priv` enum('N','Y') NOT NULL default 'N',   |
|          `Index_priv` enum('N','Y') NOT NULL default 'N',        |
|          `Alter_priv` enum('N','Y') NOT NULL default 'N',        |
|          `Create_tmp_table_priv` enum('N','Y') NOT NULL default 'N', |
|          `Lock_tables_priv` enum('N','Y') NOT NULL default 'N',  |
|          PRIMARY KEY  (`Host`,`Db`)) TYPE=MyISAM                 |
|          COMMENT='Host privileges;  Merged with database privileges' |
+--------+-----------------------------------------------------------+
1 row in set (0.06 sec)
```

An interesting corollary to the previous example consists of combining the CREATE TABLE and the SELECT statement to create a hybrid table, one that contains both new fields and fields from the SELECT result set. Consider the following example, which creates a table containing two columns of an existing table (obtained through a SELECT query) and two new columns (defined in the CREATE TABLE statement).

```
mysql> CREATE TABLE students (dob DATE NOT NULL,
sex SET('M', 'F') NOT NULL) SELECT fname, lname FROM marks;
Query OK, 5 rows affected (0.04 sec)
Records: 5  Duplicates: 0  Warnings: 0
```

```
mysql> SELECT * FROM students;
+------------+-----+-------+-------+
| dob        | sex | fname | lname |
+------------+-----+-------+-------+
| 0000-00-00 |     | John  | Doe   |
| 0000-00-00 |     | Sarah | Short |
| 0000-00-00 |     | Joe   | Cool  |
| 0000-00-00 |     | Mark  | Wumba |
| 0000-00-00 |     | Tom   | Thumb |
+------------+-----+-------+-------+
5 rows in set (0.01 sec)
```

A Temporary Solution

MySQL lets you create temporary tables with the CREATE TEMPORARY TABLE command. These tables are so-called because they remain in existence only for the duration of a single MySQL session and are automatically deleted when the client used to instantiate them closes its connection with the MySQL server. These tables come in handy for transient, session-based data or calculations, or for the temporary storage of data. And because they're session-dependant, two different sessions can use the same table name without conflicting.

Here's an example:

```
mysql> CREATE TEMPORARY TABLE session_key (skey INT(6) NOT NULL
PRIMARY KEY);
Query OK, 0 rows affected (0.02 sec)
mysql> INSERT INTO session_key VALUES (52347382934);
Query OK, 1 row affected (0.07 sec)
mysql> SELECT * FROM session_key;
+------------+
| skey       |
+------------+
| 2147483647 |
+------------+
1 row in set (0.00 sec)
mysql> exit
$ mysql
Welcome to the MySQL monitor.  Commands end with ; or \g.
Your MySQL connection id is 25 to server version: 4.0.12-max-debug
mysql> SELECT * FROM session_key;
ERROR 1146: Table 'db1.session_key' doesn't exist
```

Thus, the session_key table remains available only for the duration of the client connection. Once the client session ends, the temporary table and its contents are automatically erased by MySQL.

Modifying Tables

You can alter an existing table with the ALTER TABLE command, which allows you to add, remove, or modify table fields or indices without the need to re-create the entire table. Here's what this typically looks like:

```
ALTER TABLE table-name (action field-definition,
action field-definition, ... );
```

The action component here can be any one of the keywords ADD, DROP, ALTER, or CHANGE, and is followed by a field definition similar to that used by the CREATE TABLE command. This definition consists of the name of the field to be modified and (depending on the operation) a field definition consisting of a new field name, type, and constraints. Consider the following example, which illustrates by first creating a table, and then adding a new column to it,

```
mysql> CREATE TABLE members (mid INT(3), mname CHAR(8),
mpass VARCHAR(25));
Query OK, 0 rows affected (0.04 sec)
mysql> ALTER TABLE members ADD memail varchar(255) NOT NULL;
Query OK, 0 rows affected (0.15 sec)
Records: 0  Duplicates: 0  Warnings: 0
mysql> DESCRIBE members;
+--------+---------------+------+-----+---------+-------+
| Field  | Type          | Null | Key | Default | Extra |
+--------+---------------+------+-----+---------+-------+
| mid    | int(3)        | YES  |     | NULL    |       |
| mname  | varchar(8)    | YES  |     | NULL    |       |
| mpass  | varchar(25)   | YES  |     | NULL    |       |
| memail | varchar(255)  |      |     |         |       |
+--------+---------------+------+-----+---------+-------+
4 rows in set (0.01 sec)
```

or this one, which adds a new primary key to the table.

```
mysql> ALTER TABLE members ADD PRIMARY KEY (memail);
Query OK, 0 rows affected (0.02 sec)
Records: 0  Duplicates: 0  Warnings: 0
mysql> DESCRIBE members;
+--------+---------------+------+-----+---------+-------+
| Field  | Type          | Null | Key | Default | Extra |
+--------+---------------+------+-----+---------+-------+
| mid    | int(3)        | YES  |     | NULL    |       |
| mname  | varchar(8)    | YES  |     | NULL    |       |
| mpass  | varchar(25)   | YES  |     | NULL    |       |
| memail | varchar(255)  |      | PRI |         |       |
+--------+---------------+------+-----+---------+-------+
4 rows in set (0.02 sec)
```

And changing the name and type of an existing field is just as easy,

```
mysql> ALTER TABLE members CHANGE mid id INT(8) AUTO_INCREMENT UNIQUE;
Query OK, 0 rows affected (0.02 sec)
Records: 0  Duplicates: 0  Warnings: 0
mysql> DESCRIBE members;
+--------+--------------+------+-----+---------+----------------+
| Field  | Type         | Null | Key | Default | Extra          |
+--------+--------------+------+-----+---------+----------------+
| id     | int(8)       |      | UNI | NULL    | auto_increment |
| mname  | varchar(8)   | YES  |     | NULL    |                |
| mpass  | varchar(25)  | YES  |     | NULL    |                |
| memail | varchar(255) |      | PRI |         |                |
+--------+--------------+------+-----+---------+----------------+
4 rows in set (0.00 sec)
```

as is deleting a field or key.

```
mysql> ALTER TABLE members DROP mpass;
Query OK, 0 rows affected (1.42 sec)
Records: 0  Duplicates: 0  Warnings: 0
mysql> DESCRIBE members;
+--------+--------------+------+-----+---------+----------------+
| Field  | Type         | Null | Key | Default | Extra          |
+--------+--------------+------+-----+---------+----------------+
| id     | int(8)       |      | UNI | NULL    | auto_increment |
| mname  | varchar(8)   | YES  |     | NULL    |                |
| memail | varchar(255) |      | PRI |         |                |
+--------+--------------+------+-----+---------+----------------+
3 rows in set (0.07 sec)
```

Changing Things Around

When changing field types, MySQL lets you replace the CHANGE keyword with the MODIFY keyword. The difference between the two is subtle: the CHANGE keyword requires you to specify both the old and new field names when altering the table, while the MODIFY keyword is intended specifically for the purpose of modifying a field type without altering its name.

This is illustrated by the following two commands, which are equivalent:

```
ALTER TABLE members CHANGE id id INT(8) AUTO_INCREMENT UNIQUE;
ALTER TABLE members MODIFY id int(8) AUTO_INCREMENT UNIQUE;
```

Note, when you CHANGE or MODIFY a field from one type to another, MySQL automatically attempts to convert the data in that field to the new type.

You can use the ALTER TABLE command to rename a table, as in the following example

```
mysql> ALTER TABLE members RENAME TO memberlist;
Query OK, 0 rows affected (0.00 sec)
```

or you can use the equivalent RENAME TABLE command.

```
mysql> RENAME TABLE members TO memberlist;
Query OK, 0 rows affected (0.01 sec)
```

You can set (or remove) a default value for a field with the SET DEFAULT and DROP DEFAULT clauses, and you can control the position of fields with the FIRST and AFTER clauses to the ALTER TABLE command.

```
mysql> ALTER TABLE members ADD status INT(1) AFTER id;
Query OK, 0 rows affected (0.03 sec)
Records: 0  Duplicates: 0  Warnings: 0
mysql> ALTER TABLE members ALTER status SET DEFAULT 1;
Query OK, 0 rows affected (0.02 sec)
Records: 0  Duplicates: 0  Warnings: 0
mysql> DESCRIBE members;
+---------+--------------+------+-----+---------+----------------+
| Field   | Type         | Null | Key | Default | Extra          |
+---------+--------------+------+-----+---------+----------------+
| id      | int(8)       |      | UNI | NULL    | auto_increment |
| status  | int(1)       | YES  |     | 1       |                |
| mname   | varchar(8)   | YES  |     | NULL    |                |
| memail  | varchar(255) |      | PRI |         |                |
+---------+--------------+------+-----+---------+----------------+
4 rows in set (0.00 sec)
```

Adding an AUTO_INCREMENT field to a table causes all existing records in that table to be automatically numbered. For example, if you had a table that looked like this,

```
mysql> SELECT * FROM movies;
+-------------------------+
| title                   |
+-------------------------+
| The Phantom Menace      |
| Cape Fear               |
| Casper                  |
| The Godfather           |
| Who Killed Roger Rabbit? |
+-------------------------+
5 rows in set (0.01 sec)
```

and you decide to add an AUTO_INCREMENT primary key to each field,

```
mysql> ALTER TABLE movies ADD id INT(3) AUTO_INCREMENT PRIMARY KEY FIRST;
Query OK, 5 rows affected (0.03 sec)
Records: 5  Duplicates: 0  Warnings: 0
```

the result would look something like this:

```
mysql> SELECT * FROM movies;
+----+--------------------------+
| id | title                    |
+----+--------------------------+
|  1 | The Phantom Menace       |
|  2 | Cape Fear                |
|  3 | Casper                   |
|  4 | The Godfather            |
|  5 | Who Killed Roger Rabbit? |
+----+--------------------------+
5 rows in set (0.01 sec)
```

When adding a UNIQUE key to a table that contains duplicate values on that key, you can control how MySQL handles the situation (either delete all duplicate records or abort the alteration) by including or omitting the optional IGNORE clause. Consider the following table, which contains two records with the same value in the name field:

```
mysql> SELECT * FROM users;
+--------+-----------------------------+
| name   | email                       |
+--------+-----------------------------+
| john   | john@some.domain.com        |
| moe    | moetheman@some.domain.net   |
| scooty | sarah@some.domain.org       |
| jb     | john@some.domain.com        |
| tom    | ttalam@some.other.domain.com |
| john   | john@free.mail.server.com   |
+--------+-----------------------------+
6 rows in set (0.00 sec)
```

Now, if you were to set the name field to be UNIQUE, MySQL would return an error about duplicate values in that field.

```
mysql> ALTER TABLE users CHANGE name name VARCHAR(10) NOT NULL UNIQUE;
ERROR 1062: Duplicate entry 'john' for key 1
```

However, if you specify the IGNORE clause to the ALTER TABLE command, then MySQL removes all records with duplicate values on that key from the table, retaining only the first instance, as the following illustrates.

```
mysql> ALTER IGNORE TABLE users CHANGE name name VARCHAR(10)
NOT NULL UNIQUE;
Query OK, 6 rows affected (0.02 sec)
Records: 6  Duplicates: 1  Warnings: 0
mysql> SELECT * FROM USERS;
+--------+-----------------------------+
| name   | email                       |
+--------+-----------------------------+
| john   | john@some.domain.com        |
| moe    | moetheman@some.domain.net   |
| scooty | sarah@some.domain.org       |
| jb     | john@some.domain.com        |
| tom    | ttalam@some.other.domain.com |
+--------+-----------------------------+
5 rows in set (0.01 sec)
```

You can add a foreign key reference to a table with the ADD FOREIGN KEY clause, as in the following example:

```
mysql> ALTER TABLE articles ADD FOREIGN KEY (fk_cid) REFERENCES
categories (cid) ON DELETE CASCADE ON UPDATE CASCADE;
Query OK, 0 rows affected (0.11 sec)
Records: 0  Duplicates: 0  Warnings: 0
```

You can alter the table type on the fly with the ALTER TABLE command, simply by specifying a new TYPE clause. Consider the following example, which alters the users table to use the InnoDB table type:

```
mysql> ALTER TABLE users TYPE = INNODB;
Query OK, 6 rows affected (0.11 sec)
Records: 6  Duplicates: 0  Warnings: 0
```

You can also add and delete indexes with the ALTER TABLE command, by including an ADD INDEX or DROP INDEX clause. The following examples illustrate:

```
mysql> ALTER TABLE articles ADD FULLTEXT INDEX content_001 (body);
Query OK, 0 rows affected (0.11 sec)
Records: 0  Duplicates: 0  Warnings: 0
mysql> ALTER TABLE articles DROP INDEX content_001;
Query OK, 0 rows affected (0.05 sec)
Records: 0  Duplicates: 0  Warnings: 0
```

> **Doing More with Less**
>
> As the syntax for the ALTER TABLE command indicated, MySQL lets you alter more than one field at a time, simply by separating the various actions and field definitions with commas. This is a MySQL-specific extension to the SQL-92 standard. A rigid SQL-92 implementation would require a separate ALTER TABLE statement for each alteration. Because ALTER TABLE is a slow command and one that should be run as infrequently as possible, this MySQL-specific capability can come in handy to reduce performance drag on the server.

Deleting Tables

You can delete a table with the DROP TABLE command; Here's an example of using this command to drop the table tbl1:

```
mysql> DROP TABLE tbl1;
Query OK, 0 rows affected (0.02 sec)
```

As before, you can include IF EXISTS clause to avoid nasty MySQL error messages if the table you're trying to delete doesn't exist.

```
mysql> DROP TABLE tbl1;
ERROR 1051: Unknown table 'tbl1'
mysql> DROP TABLE IF EXISTS tbl1;
Query OK, 0 rows affected (0.00 sec)
```

Obtaining Information About Databases, Tables, Fields, and Indexes

Once a database has been created, you can verify its existence with MySQL's SHOW DATABASES statement, which provides a listing of all the databases the server currently knows about.

```
mysql> SHOW DATABASES;
+-----------+
| Database  |
+-----------+
| db1       |
| mysql     |
| test      |
+-----------+
3 rows in set (0.04 sec)
```

You can verify the existence of a table within a database by using the SHOW TABLES FROM *database-name* command.

```
mysql> CREATE TABLE tbl1 (fld1 int(1) NOT NULL);
Query OK, 0 rows affected (0.01 sec)
mysql> SHOW TABLES;
+---------------+
| Tables_in_db1 |
+---------------+
| tbl1          |
+---------------+
1 row in set (0.01 sec)
```

You can obtain information on the structure of a table—its fields, field types, keys and defaults—with the DESCRIBE command, which looks like this:

```
mysql> DESCRIBE employees;
+------------+--------------+------+-----+---------+-------+
| Field      | Type         | Null | Key | Default | Extra |
+------------+--------------+------+-----+---------+-------+
| id         | smallint(6)  |      | PRI | 0       |       |
| fname      | varchar(255) |      |     |         |       |
| lname      | varchar(255) |      |     |         |       |
| age        | tinyint(4)   |      |     | 0       |       |
| sex        | char(1)      |      |     |         |       |
| department | varchar(255) |      |     |         |       |
| country    | char(2)      |      |     |         |       |
+------------+--------------+------+-----+---------+-------+
7 rows in set (0.03 sec)
```

You can obtain a list of indexes on a table with the SHOW INDEX FROM *table-name* command and detailed information on the tables in a database (including information on the table type, the number of rows, the date and time of the last table update, and the lengths of indexes and rows) with the SHOW TABLE STATUS FROM database-name command. Because the output of these commands is somewhat verbose, page-width considerations prevent its reproduction here. Experiment with it yourself at the command prompt to see the extent of detail available.

Summary

This chapter focused on MySQL data structures, explaining how to add, modify, and delete MySQL databases and tables in the MySQL RDBMS. The chapter included both a theoretical discussion of the SQL commands related to database and table management, and numerous simple examples that demonstrated the utility of each command in real-world use. Among the commands discussed were as follows:

- The CREATE DATABASE command, used to create a new database

- The USE command, used to select a database for transactions

- The DROP DATABASE command, used to delete a database and all its associated data

- The CREATE TABLE command and its numerous variants, used to define the structure, constraints, and type of a table

- The DROP TABLE command, used to delete a table from a database

- The SHOW DATABASES command, used to view available databases on the server

- The SHOW TABLES command, used to view tables within a database

- The SHOW CREATE command, used as a basis for recreating table structure while preserving index and key information

- The SHOW INDEX command, used to view indexes on a table

- The ALTER TABLE command, used to alter the structure of an existing table

Of course, data definition is only one-third of the puzzle. Once your data structures are defined, the next step is to put some data into them. The next chapter discusses this aspect in detail, with explanations and illustrations of the MySQL commands related to data manipulation.

Working with Data

Once you have your databases and tables defined, the next step is to use them to store your data. Typically, this involves using the Data Manipulation Language (DML) component of SQL to add, update, delete, and query records in the database. Because DML commands are typically used with a far higher frequency than the DDL commands discussed in the previous chapter, a sound grounding in these commands is extremely important to ensure efficient use of the MySQL RDBMS.

This chapter focuses on the DML in detail, examining how you can use it to insert new records, update or delete existing records, perform queries to retrieve records matching specific criteria, import data from other data sources, and export records to files in custom formats.

Inserting, Updating, and Deleting Records

MySQL offers a number of different commands, each designed for a specific purpose when it comes to inserting, updating, or otherwise changing the contents of a table. This section discusses, explains, and illustrates the various commands.

Inserting Records

Once a database and its tables have been created, the next step is to enter data into them. This is accomplished by means of the INSERT command, which looks like this:

```
INSERT INTO table-name (field-name, field-name, ...)
VALUES (field-value, field-value, ...)
```

To illustrate this, let's create a simple table,

```
mysql> CREATE TABLE addressbook (fname VARCHAR(255) NULL,
lname VARCHAR(255) NULL, phone VARCHAR(255) NULL,
fax VARCHAR(255) NULL, email VARCHAR(255) NULL);
Query OK, 0 rows affected (0.08 sec)
```

```
mysql> DESCRIBE addressbook;
+-------+-----------+------+-----+---------+-------+
| Field | Type      | Null | Key | Default | Extra |
+-------+-----------+------+-----+---------+-------+
| fname | char(255) | YES  |     | NULL    |       |
| lname | char(255) | YES  |     | NULL    |       |
| phone | char(255) | YES  |     | NULL    |       |
| fax   | char(255) | YES  |     | NULL    |       |
| email | char(255) | YES  |     | NULL    |       |
+-------+-----------+------+-----+---------+-------+
5 rows in set (0.00 sec)
```

and then use the INSERT statement to put some data into it.

```
mysql> INSERT INTO addressbook (fname, lname, phone, fax, email)
VALUES ('Rob', 'Rabbit', '674 1536', '382 8364', 'rob@some.domain');
Query OK, 1 row affected (0.00 sec)
```

The table should now contain a single record for Rob Rabbit. You can verify this with a quick call to the SELECT command:

```
mysql> SELECT * FROM addressbook;
+-------+--------+----------+----------+-----------------+
| fname | lname  | phone    | fax      | email           |
+-------+--------+----------+----------+-----------------+
| Rob   | Rabbit | 674 1536 | 382 8364 | rob@some.domain |
+-------+--------+----------+----------+-----------------+
1 row in set (0.01 sec)
```

You can also use an abbreviated form of the INSERT statement, in which the field list is left unspecified. The following example, which is equivalent to the previous one illustrates.

```
mysql> INSERT INTO addressbook VALUES ('Rob', 'Rabbit', '674 1536',
'382 8364', 'rob@some.domain');
Query OK, 1 row affected (0.01 sec)
```

Note, when using this shorter format, the order in which values are inserted must correspond to the sequence of fields in the table (you can determine the field order with a quick call to the DESCRIBE command).

Naming Names
While the shorter variant of the INSERT statement is certainly more common, in most cases, explicitly naming the fields into which you are inserting values is preferable. This allows the application to survive structural changes in its table(s) and also eliminates ambiguity.

You can also INSERT the results of calculations or function calls, as in the following examples:

```
mysql> INSERT INTO marks (name, math, sci, total)
VALUES ('James Doe', 45, 67, math + sci);
Query OK, 1 row affected (0.01 sec)

mysql> INSERT INTO users (id, name, password)
VALUES (LAST_INSERT_ID() + 1, 'tom', 'secret');
Query OK, 1 row affected (0.01 sec)

mysql> INSERT INTO sales (id, cost, quantity, amount)
VALUES (8587, 100, 4500, cost * quantity);
Query OK, 1 row affected (0.01 sec)

mysql> INSERT INTO log (process, message, timestamp)
VALUES ('crond', 'Unable to send mail in /usr/local/bin/backup.sh', NOW());
Query OK, 1 row affected (0.01 sec)
```

When inserting string values (and some date values) into a table, you must always surround them with quotation marks or MySQL will treat them as field names.

```
mysql> INSERT INTO addressbook (fname, lname, phone, fax, email)
VALUES ('Rob', Rabbit, '674 1536', '382 8364', 'rob@some.domain');
ERROR 1054: Unknown column 'Rabbit' in 'field list'
```

Values containing quotation marks should be escaped by a preceding backslash (\).

```
mysql> INSERT INTO addressbook (fname, lname, phone, fax, email)
VALUES ('Frances', 'D\'Souza', '123 4567', '000 7574', 'fdz@some.domain');
Query OK, 1 row affected (0.11 sec)
```

Numeric values, however, need not be quoted.

```
mysql> INSERT INTO stock (cost, quantity) VALUES (760.52, 65000);
Query OK, 1 row affected (0.01 sec)
```

Opting in to INTO
The INTO keyword in an INSERT statement is optional.

MySQL also supports the following two nonstandard variants of the INSERT statement.

- Multiple records can be entered in a single INSERT statement through the use of multiple VALUES() clauses within the same statement. For example, instead of doing this,

```
mysql> INSERT INTO stocks (symbol, price, quantity)
VALUES ('ABCD', 100, 4500);
Query OK, 1 row affected (0.05 sec)
mysql> INSERT INTO stocks (symbol, price, quantity)
VALUES ('HYDH', 2000, 29);
Query OK, 1 row affected (0.00 sec)
mysql> INSERT INTO stocks (symbol, price, quantity) VALUES ('UGTS', 25, 67);
Query OK, 1 row affected (0.05 sec)
```

you could do this:

```
mysql> INSERT stocks (symbol, price, quantity) VALUES ('ABCD', 100, 4500),
('HYDH', 2000, 29), ('UGTS', 25, 67);
Query OK, 3 rows affected (0.06 sec)
Records: 3  Duplicates: 0  Warnings: 0
```

- You can also do away with the INSERT...VALUES form altogether in favor of syntax similar to that used by the UPDATE statement. This involves using the SET clause to set values for each column individually. So, instead of doing this,

```
mysql> INSERT INTO stocks (symbol, price, quantity)
VALUES ('HYDH', 2000, 29);
Query OK, 1 row affected (0.00 sec)
```

you could do this:

```
mysql> INSERT INTO stocks SET symbol='HYDH', price=2000, quantity=29;
Query OK, 1 row affected (0.06 sec)
```

Working with DEFAULT Values

Fields not named in the field list will be automatically assigned their default values. Consider the following example, which illustrates

```
mysql> CREATE TABLE forums (name VARCHAR(150) NOT NULL,
category VARCHAR(50) DEFAULT 'UNIX' NOT NULL,
postsPerPage SMALLINT DEFAULT 15 NOT NULL,
highlightColor VARCHAR(10) DEFAULT 'red' NOT NULL);
Query OK, 0 rows affected (0.01 sec)

mysql> INSERT INTO forums (name) VALUES ('Apache');
Query OK, 1 row affected (0.01 sec)

mysql> INSERT INTO forums (name, highlightColor)
VALUES ('Sendmail', 'green');
Query OK, 1 row affected (0.00 sec)
```

```
mysql> SELECT * FROM forums;
+----------+----------+--------------+----------------+
| name     | category | postsPerPage | highlightColor |
+----------+----------+--------------+----------------+
| Apache   | UNIX     |           15 | red            |
| Sendmail | UNIX     |           15 | green          |
+----------+----------+--------------+----------------+
2 rows in set (0.00 sec)
```

MySQL 4.0.3 and better also support a new DEFAULT keyword, which can be used to instruct MySQL to use the column's default value for that record.

```
mysql> INSERT INTO forums (name, category, postsPerPage,
highlightColor) VALUES ('MySQL', DEFAULT, DEFAULT, DEFAULT);
Query OK, 1 row affected (0.01 sec)
```

Working with AUTOINCREMENT Fields

When creating sequences with AUTOINCREMENT columns, omitting the field name in the INSERT statement will cause MySQL to automatically generate the next number in the sequence. This number serves well as a primary key for your table. Consider the following example, which illustrates by creating a table with an AUTOINCREMENT column as primary key,

```
mysql> CREATE TABLE users (uid TINYINT(4) NOT NULL AUTO_INCREMENT,
uname varchar(8) NOT NULL DEFAULT '', upass VARCHAR(15) NOT NULL DEFAULT '', PRIMARY KEY (uid));
Query OK, 0 rows affected (0.08 sec)
```

and then populating it with data.

```
mysql> INSERT INTO users (uname, upass) VALUES ('jim', PASSWORD('secret'));
Query OK, 1 row affected (0.14 sec)

mysql> INSERT INTO users (uname, upass) VALUES ('sarah', PASSWORD('opensesame'));
Query OK, 1 row affected (0.02 sec)

mysql> INSERT INTO users (uname, upass) VALUES ('tim', PASSWORD('whiteboard'));
Query OK, 1 row affected (0.00 sec)
```

For every record inserted in the previous code, MySQL will insert a unique, automatically incremented number in the uid field.

```
mysql> SELECT * FROM users;
+-----+-------+----------------+
| uid | uname | upass          |
+-----+-------+----------------+
|   1 | jim   | 428567f40899440 |
|   2 | sarah | 2f3a61de16678ac |
```

```
|     3 | tim    | 31a1db03482b555 |
+-----+-------+-----------------+
3 rows in set (0.00 sec)
```

Working with UNIQUE Fields

When inserting records containing duplicate values on a UNIQUE key, you can control how MySQL handles the situation: skip the INSERT, abort the operation, or update the old record with the new values with the IGNORE keyword or the ON DUPLICATE KEY UPDATE clause.

To understand this better, consider the following table, which contains a UNIQUE key on the id field:

```
+----+----------+---------------+
| id | label    | url           |
+----+----------+---------------+
|  1 | Home     | home.html     |
|  2 | About Us | aboutus.html  |
|  3 | Services | services.html |
|  4 | Feedback | feedback.html |
+----+----------+---------------+
4 rows in set (0.00 sec)
```

Normally, if you were now to try inserting a record violating the uniqueness constraint, MySQL would abort the operation with an error:

```
mysql> INSERT INTO menu (id, label, url) VALUES (4, 'Contact Us', 'contactus.html');
ERROR 1062: Duplicate entry '4' for key 1
```

With the IGNORE keyword added to the previous INSERT statement, MySQL will not even attempt to execute the statement if it recognizes that it violates the uniqueness constraint. Therefore, though the following statement returns no error,

```
mysql> INSERT IGNORE INTO menu (id, label, url) VALUES (4, 'Contact Us', 'contactus.html');
Query OK, 0 rows affected (0.01 sec)
```

the data in the table remains unchanged.

```
mysql> SELECT * FROM menu;
+----+----------+---------------+
| id | label    | url           |
+----+----------+---------------+
|  1 | Home     | home.html     |
|  2 | About Us | aboutus.html  |
|  3 | Services | services.html |
|  4 | Feedback | feedback.html |
+----+----------+---------------+
4 rows in set (0.00 sec)
```

> **Out with the Old . . .**
> A subtle variation on the ON DUPLICATE KEY UPDATE clause is the REPLACE command, which adopts the same syntax as the INSERT command. Unlike INSERT, though, which produces an error if the record being inserted contains a duplicate value on a field marked as UNIQUE, REPLACE replaces the entire record with the new values.
>
>   The difference between ON DUPLICATE KEY UPDATE and REPLACE is this: while the former only updates the named fields with new values, the latter deletes the old record and replaces it completely with the new one.

This IGNORE keyword comes in handy when you have multiple INSERT statements to be executed sequentially. Using it ensures that even if any of the INSERTs contains a duplicate key value, MySQL will simply step over it to the next one (instead of aborting the entire operation).

In such a situation, you can also have MySQL automatically convert your INSERT operation into an UPDATE operation, by adding the ON DUPLICATE KEY UPDATE clause, new to MySQL 4.1. This clause must be following by a list of fields to be updated, in a form similar to that used by the UPDATE statement. Consider the following example, which demonstrates.

```
mysql> INSERT INTO menu (id, label, url) VALUES (4, 'Contact Us', 'contactus.html')
ON DUPLICATE KEY UPDATE label = 'Contact Us', url = 'contactus.html';
```

In this case, if MySQL finds the table already contains a record with the same unique key, it automatically updates the old record with the new values specified in the ON DUPLICATE KEY UPDATE clause. In the example under discussion, this would result in the following table:

```
mysql> SELECT * FROM menu;
+----+------------+----------------+
| id | label      | url            |
+----+------------+----------------+
|  1 | Home       | aboutus.html   |
|  2 | About Us   | aboutus.html   |
|  3 | Services   | services.html  |
|  4 | Contact Us | contactus.html |
+----+------------+----------------+
4 rows in set (0.01 sec)
```

Working with NULL Values

You can enter a NULL value into a field (so long as it is not marked NOT NULL) by using the NULL keyword in your INSERT statement. The following example demonstrates by adding a record to the `addressbook` table containing `NULL` values for the `email` and `fax` fields:

```
mysql> INSERT INTO addressbook (fname, lname, phone, fax, email)
VALUES ('Polly', 'Parrot', '239 1828', NULL, NULL);
Query OK, 1 row affected (0.00 sec)
```

You can use the `IS NULL` operator to retrieve a list of all records containing `NULL` values, as in the following snippet:

```
mysql> SELECT * FROM addressbook WHERE email IS NULL OR fax IS NULL;
+--------+--------+----------+------+---------------+
| fname  | lname  | phone    | fax  | email         |
+--------+--------+----------+------+---------------+
| Polly  | Parrot | 239 1828 | NULL | NULL          |
| David  | Donkey | NULL     | NULL | david@don.key |
+--------+--------+----------+------+---------------+
2 rows in set (0.00 sec)
```

Updating Records

Data, like life, tends to change—and when it does, you'll find yourself faced with the task of altering the records you inserted with the `INSERT` statement. That's why MySQL also offers the `UPDATE` command, designed specifically to update some or all records in a table.

Here's what the syntax of the `UPDATE` command looks like:

```
UPDATE table-name SET field-name = value, SET field-name = value, ...
WHERE conditional-test
```

A Question of Space

A common newbie mistake is to equate a `NULL` value with an empty string (`' '`). While arguing about the distinction between the two might seem like a case of splitting hairs, the fact remains that in the SQL world, the two mean completely different things: `NULL` is the absence of a value, while `' '` implies a value exists and is equal to an empty string. Although the distinction might seem subtle, rest assured that it can trip you up if you're not careful.

Primary Education

`NULL` values cannot be used in `PRIMARY KEY` fields.

So, if you had an address book like this,

```
+--------+---------+-----------+-----------+------------------------+
| fname  | lname   | phone     | fax       | email                  |
+--------+---------+-----------+-----------+------------------------+
| Polly  | Parrot  | 239 1828  | NULL      | NULL                   |
| David  | Donkey  | NULL      | NULL      | david@don.key          |
| George | Giraffe | 473 1911  | 757 0000  | george@giraffesrule.tld|
| Rico   | Rat     | 193 2839  | 985 2281  | rico@bite.me           |
| Rob    | Rabbit  | 674 1536  | 382 8364  | rob@some.domain        |
+--------+---------+-----------+-----------+------------------------+
5 rows in set (0.05 sec)
```

and you want to update Polly's e-mail address, you could accomplish it with the following call to UPDATE:

```
mysql> UPDATE addressbook SET email = 'polly@whos.talking'
WHERE fname = 'Polly' AND lname = 'Parrot';
Query OK, 1 row affected (0.00 sec)
Rows matched: 1   Changed: 1   Warnings: 0
```

As before, you can verify this with a quick call to SELECT.

```
mysql> SELECT * FROM addressbook;
+--------+---------+-----------+-----------+------------------------+
| fname  | lname   | phone     | fax       | email                  |
+--------+---------+-----------+-----------+------------------------+
| Polly  | Parrot  | 239 1828  | NULL      | polly@whos.talking     |
| David  | Donkey  | NULL      | NULL      | david@don.key          |
| George | Giraffe | 473 1911  | 757 0000  | george@giraffesrule.tld|
| Rico   | Rat     | 193 2839  | 985 2281  | rico@bite.me           |
| Rob    | Rabbit  | 674 1536  | 382 8364  | rob@some.domain        |
+--------+---------+-----------+-----------+------------------------+
5 rows in set (0.00 sec)
```

You can update multiple fields of a record simultaneously, simply by specifying multiple SET clauses in the UPDATE statement. Consider the following example, which updates the record for Rob Rabbit:

```
mysql> UPDATE addressbook SET lname = 'Ringworm', phone = 'RING ME',
fax = NULL, email = 'robbieworm@wormplace.net' WHERE fname = 'Rob';
Query OK, 1 row affected (0.00 sec)
Rows matched: 1   Changed: 1   Warnings: 0
```

```
mysql> SELECT * FROM addressbook;
+--------+----------+----------+----------+-----------------------------+
| fname  | lname    | phone    | fax      | email                       |
+--------+----------+----------+----------+-----------------------------+
| Polly  | Parrot   | 239 1828 | NULL     | polly@whos.talking          |
| David  | Donkey   | NULL     | NULL     | david@don.key               |
| George | Giraffe  | 473 1911 | 757 0000 | george@giraffesrule.tld     |
| Rico   | Rat      | 193 2839 | 985 2281 | rico@bite.me                |
| Rob    | Ringworm | RING ME  | NULL     | robbieworm@wormplace.net    |
+--------+----------+----------+----------+-----------------------------+
5 rows in set (0.00 sec)
```

If you omit the WHERE clause of the UPDATE statement, every single row in the table will be affected by the UPDATE statement. The following example illustrates, by repeating the previous UPDATE command without the WHERE clause:

```
mysql> UPDATE addressbook SET lname = 'Ringworm', phone = 'RING ME',
fax = NULL, email = 'robbieworm@wormplace.net';
Query OK, 6 rows affected (0.00 sec)
Rows matched: 6  Changed: 6  Warnings: 0
mysql> SELECT * FROM addressbook;
+--------+----------+----------+------+--------------------------+
| fname  | lname    | phone    | fax  | email                    |
+--------+----------+----------+------+--------------------------+
| Polly  | Ringworm | RING ME  | NULL | robbieworm@wormplace.net |
| David  | Ringworm | RING ME  | NULL | robbieworm@wormplace.net |
| George | Ringworm | RING ME  | NULL | robbieworm@wormplace.net |
| Rico   | Ringworm | RING ME  | NULL | robbieworm@wormplace.net |
| Rob    | Ringworm | RING ME  | NULL | robbieworm@wormplace.net |
+--------+----------+----------+------+--------------------------+
5 rows in set (0.00 sec)
```

This is not usually what you want!

Garbage in, Garbage Out

Omitting the WHERE clause in UPDATE queries is a common newbie mistake and can result in massive data corruption if it's not used carefully.

More information on the WHERE clause is available in the section "Retrieving Records."

Playing Nice

When performing an INSERT or UPDATE operation, you can program the MySQL client to wait until the operation is successfully completed or simply queue it for later processing by the server through the use of the LOW_PRIORITY and DELAYED keywords.

- The LOW_PRIORITY keyword stalls the execution of the statement until no other threads are using the table and, thereby, forces the client to wait until the statement is fully executed. In applications where reliability is of paramount importance, adding this keyword can help to improve the overall integrity of the SQL transaction and, hence, of the business logic built around it.

- The DELAYED keyword does the reverse of the LOW_PRIORITY keyword, placing the statement to be executed in a queue (in the server's memory) and letting the client exit immediately. This is particularly useful in improving application performance when dealing with busy database servers because it produces faster client response times (although at a slightly higher risk— if the server crashes, all requests in the server queue will be lost).

Note, however, that these two keywords do not apply to InnoDB tables.

As with the INSERT statement, you can perform calculations or invoke functions within an UPDATE statement, and then use the results of those operations in the update. Here are some examples:

```
mysql> UPDATE marks SET total = math + sci WHERE name='James';
Query OK, 1 row affected (0.01 sec)
Rows matched: 1   Changed: 1   Warnings: 0


mysql> UPDATE users SET password = PASSWORD('secret') WHERE user = 'sally';
Query OK, 1 row affected (0.01 sec)
Rows matched: 1   Changed: 1   Warnings: 0


mysql> UPDATE menu SET label = 'Home' WHERE label = 'Main Menu';
Query OK, 1 row affected (0.01 sec)
Rows matched: 1   Changed: 1   Warnings: 0
```

Deleting Records

Just as you can INSERT, UPDATE, and REPLACE data, MySQL also lets you delete it with the DELETE and TRUNCATE statements. The DELETE statement enables you to delete records from a table and supports the use of a WHERE clause to restrict deletion to only those records that match a particular condition. Here's what it looks like:

```
DELETE FROM table-name WHERE conditional-test
```

Therefore, given the following table,

```
+-----+-------+-------+
| uid | uname | upass |
+-----+-------+-------+
|  16 | joe   | joe   |
|  17 | john  | john  |
|  18 | joe   | joe   |
|  19 | john  | john  |
+-----+-------+-------+
4 rows in set (0.00 sec)
```

you could delete the record for John with the following command.

```
mysql> DELETE FROM users WHERE uid = 19;
Query OK, 1 row affected (0.00 sec)
```

Viewing the table with SELECT verifies the record is gone.

```
mysql> SELECT * FROM users;
+-----+-------+-------+
| uid | uname | upass |
+-----+-------+-------+
|  16 | joe   | joe   |
|  17 | john  | john  |
|  18 | joe   | joe   |
+-----+-------+-------+
3 rows in set (0.05 sec)
```

Delete and Destroy

Care should be taken when using the DELETE statement without a WHERE clause because this causes the immediate deletion of all records in the table. This operation is irreversible (unless you're using an InnoDB table with AUTOCOMMIT turned off), so make sure you know what you're doing before attempting it.

You can delete all the records in a table by simply omitting the WHERE clause.

```
mysql> DELETE FROM users;
Query OK, 3 rows affected (0.00 sec)
```

An alternative approach here would be to use the TRUNCATE command, which also deletes all the records in a table. The following command is equivalent to the previous one:

```
mysql> TRUNCATE TABLE users;
Query OK, 0 rows affected (0.05 sec)
```

If the goal is to empty the table of all records, TRUNCATE is faster than DELETE because TRUNCATE drops the table and regenerates it, while DELETE deletes records without making any attempt to modify the table itself. This is also the reason why, when inserting records into a table emptied with DELETE, MySQL remembers the previously generated AUTOINCREMENT sequence and continues using it for AUTOINCREMENT fields. TRUNCATE-d tables, on the other hand, always restart the numbering of AUTOINCREMENT fields from 1.

Note, the TRUNCATE command, unlike the DELETE command, is not transaction-safe. Therefore, if a transaction is still in process on the table you're trying to TRUNCATE, the command will exit with an error.

Turning the Tables

MySQL 4.0 permits UPDATE and DELETE operations to span multiple tables. Here are some examples:

```
# raise invoice amounts of all customers in Massachusetts by 10%
UPDATE invoices, customers SET invoices.amount = invoices.amount + (invoices.amount
* 0.1) WHERE invoices.customerID = customers.customerID AND customers.location =
'MA';

# update a user's log-in name in all areas of a Web discussion forum
UPDATE profiles, forums, groups SET profiles.username = 'hyde', forums.username =
'hyde', groups.username = 'hyde' WHERE profiles.username = 'jekyll' AND
profiles.username = forums.username AND profiles.username = groups.username;

# delete a particular customer and all invoices generated for that accountfrom the
system
DELETE FROM customers, invoices USING customers, invoices WHERE
customers.customerID = invoices.customerID AND customers.customerID = 88;

# delete all matching employees from the employee database and departmentrecords
DELETE FROM employees, departments USING employees, departments WHERE
employees.employeeID = departments.employeeID
```

Retrieving Records

As you've seen in the preceding discussion, when it comes to writing data to the database, MySQL offers a number of different commands to write data to the database. However, when it comes to retrieving data, it only offers one: the SELECT statement.

The SELECT statement is one of the most powerful statements in an SQL developer's arsenal and, fortunately, it's also exceedingly easy to master. The SELECT statement can be used as a standalone expression evaluator, as in the following,

```
mysql> SELECT 50 >= (3+2);
+-------------+
| 50 >= (3+2) |
+-------------+
|           1 |
+-------------+
1 row in set (0.00 sec)
mysql> SELECT 100/10, NOW();
+--------+---------------------+
| 100/10 | NOW()               |
+--------+---------------------+
|  10.00 | 2003-06-27 14:29:19 |
+--------+---------------------+
1 row in set (0.11 sec)
```

or in the context of one or more tables, to retrieve data from them, as in the following:

```
mysql> SELECT * FROM accounts LIMIT 0, 6;
+---------------+-------------+-----------------+-----------------+---------------+
| accountNumber | accountName | accountCreatedOn | accountCreatedAt | accountBalance |
+---------------+-------------+-----------------+-----------------+---------------+
|    1265489921 | James D     | 1998-07-29      | NY              |       2346.00 |
|    2147483647 | Timothy J   | 2000-12-12      | BO              |      56347.50 |
|    5739304575 | Harish K    | 1995-09-13      | NY              |     996564.88 |
|    2173467271 | Kingston X  | 1967-09-15      | MA              |     634238.00 |
|    2312934021 | Sue U       | 1998-06-06      | MA              |         34.67 |
|    1248954638 | Ila T       | 2003-08-17      | CA              |       5373.82 |
|    2384371001 | Anil V      | 2001-11-19      | MA              |      72460.00 |
|    9430125467 | Katrina P   | 2003-07-01      | NY              |        100.00 |
|    1890192554 | Pooja B     | 2002-01-23      | FL              |      17337.12 |
|    2388282010 | Sue U       | 1998-03-27      | BO              |     388883.13 |
|    2374845291 | Jacob N     | 2003-05-01      | NY              |      18410.00 |
+---------------+-------------+-----------------+-----------------+---------------+
11 rows in set (0.05 sec)
```

This previous "catch-all" query represents the simplest form of the SELECT statement. It returns all the records in the named table. The asterisk (*) in the previous SELECT statement is a wildcard character meaning "get all fields."

Retrieving Specific Rows and Columns

If you prefer to restrict your result set to contain a particular set of columns from the table, you can specify these fields as a comma-separated list after the SELECT keyword (in place of the * wildcard). The following example retrieves only the accountName and accountBalance columns from the previous accounts table:

```
mysql> SELECT accountName, accountBalance FROM accounts;
+--------------+----------------+
| accountName  | accountBalance |
+--------------+----------------+
| James D      |        2346.00 |
| Timothy J    |       56347.50 |
| Harish K     |      996564.88 |
| Kingston X   |      634238.00 |
| Sue U        |          34.67 |
| Ila T        |        5373.82 |
| Anil V       |       72460.00 |
| Katrina P    |         100.00 |
| Pooja B      |       17337.12 |
| Sue U        |      388883.13 |
| Jacob N      |       18410.00 |
+--------------+----------------+
11 rows in set (0.05 sec)
```

You can tell your query to return only those records matching a particular condition by adding the WHERE clause to the SELECT statement. This WHERE clause must be followed by a conditional expression, which will be used to filter out nonmatching records from the result set.

The following example demonstrates by retrieving a list of only those accounts with balances lower than $1000.00,

```
mysql> SELECT accountName, accountBalance FROM accounts
WHERE accountBalance < 1000;
+--------------+----------------+
| accountName  | accountBalance |
+--------------+----------------+
| Sue U        |          34.67 |
| Katrina P    |         100.00 |
+--------------+----------------+
2 rows in set (0.11 sec)
```

while this one retrieves a list of all accounts created in 2002.

```
mysql> SELECT accountName, accountCreatedOn FROM accounts WHERE
YEAR(accountCreatedOn) = 2002;
```

```
+-------------+------------------+
| accountName | accountCreatedOn |
+-------------+------------------+
| Pooja B     | 2002-01-23       |
+-------------+------------------+
1 row in set (0.00 sec)
```

You can also create more complex queries by adding MySQL's logical operators—AND, OR, and NOT—to the mix. The following example illustrates by retrieving all those accounts with a balance between $5000.00 and $50,000.00,

```
mysql> SELECT accountName, accountNumber, accountBalance FROM accounts
WHERE accountBalance > 5000.00 AND accountBalance < 50000.00;
+-------------+---------------+----------------+
| accountName | accountNumber | accountBalance |
+-------------+---------------+----------------+
| Ila T       |    1248954638 |        5373.82 |
| Pooja B     |    1890192554 |       17337.12 |
| Jacob N     |    2374845291 |       18410.00 |
+-------------+---------------+----------------+
3 rows in set (0.05 sec)
```

while this one retrieves all the accounts located in either New York or Boston:

```
mysql> SELECT accountName, accountCreatedAt FROM accounts WHERE
accountCreatedAt = 'NY' OR accountCreatedAt = 'BO';
+-------------+------------------+
| accountName | accountCreatedAt |
+-------------+------------------+
| James D     | NY               |
| Timothy J   | BO               |
| Harish K    | NY               |
| Katrina P   | NY               |
| Sue U       | BO               |
| Jacob N     | NY               |
+-------------+------------------+
6 rows in set (0.00 sec)
```

Using Built-In Functions

You can also use built-in MySQL functions in a SELECT statement. The following example selects the records with the maximum and minimum account balances,

```
mysql> SELECT MAX(accountBalance), MIN(accountBalance) FROM accounts;
+---------------------+---------------------+
| MAX(accountBalance) | MIN(accountBalance) |
+---------------------+---------------------+
|           996564.88 |               34.67 |
+---------------------+---------------------+
1 row in set (0.00 sec)
```

while this one counts the total number of records in the table and returns the result.

```
mysql> SELECT COUNT(*) FROM accounts;
+----------+
| count(*) |
+----------+
|       11 |
+----------+
1 row in set (0.00 sec)
```

Built-in functions can also be used in the WHERE clause. The following query produces a list of all the accounts created in the current year,

```
mysql> SELECT accountName, accountCreatedOn FROM accounts WHERE
YEAR(accountCreatedOn) = YEAR(NOW());
+-------------+------------------+
| accountName | accountCreatedOn |
+-------------+------------------+
| Ila T       | 2003-08-17       |
| Katrina P   | 2003-07-01       |
| Jacob N     | 2003-05-01       |
+-------------+------------------+
3 rows in set (0.06 sec)
```

while this one returns a list of all those accounts created more than three years ago.

```
mysql> SELECT accountName, accountCreatedOn FROM accounts WHERE
YEAR( DATE_ADD(accountCreatedOn, INTERVAL 3 YEAR) ) <= YEAR( NOW() );
+-------------+------------------+
| accountName | accountCreatedOn |
+-------------+------------------+
| James D     | 1998-07-29       |
| Timothy J   | 2000-12-12       |
| Harish K    | 1995-09-13       |
| Kingston X  | 1967-09-15       |
| Sue U       | 1998-06-06       |
| Sue U       | 1998-03-27       |
+-------------+------------------+
6 rows in set (0.05 sec)
```

PART II

Aliasing Table and Column Names

You can create aliases for table and field names by adding the AS keyword and an alias after the table or field name you want to alias. This can come in handy when dealing with long table or field names. The following example demonstrates by aliasing the accountName and accountNumber columns to name and num, respectively:

```
mysql> SELECT accountNumber AS num, accountName AS name FROM accounts;
+------------+------------+
| num        | name       |
+------------+------------+
| 1265489921 | James D    |
| 2147483647 | Timothy J  |
| 5739304575 | Harish K   |
| 2173467271 | Kingston X |
| 2312934021 | Sue U      |
| 1248954638 | Ila T      |
| 2384371001 | Anil V     |
| 9430125467 | Katrina P  |
| 1890192554 | Pooja B    |
| 2388282010 | Sue U      |
| 2374845291 | Jacob N    |
+------------+------------+
11 rows in set (0.00 sec)
```

You can also do this with table names.

```
mysql> SELECT accountName, accountCreatedAt FROM accounts AS a
WHERE a.accountName LIKE '%Poo%';
+-------------+------------------+
| accountName | accountCreatedAt |
+-------------+------------------+
| Pooja B     | FL               |
+-------------+------------------+
1 row in set (0.00 sec)
```

Limiting Query Results

The LIMIT keyword can be used to restrict the total number of records returned by a SELECT query. The following query illustrates by restricting the result set to five records.

```
mysql> SELECT accountName, accountNumber FROM accounts LIMIT 5;
+-------------+---------------+
| accountName | accountNumber |
+-------------+---------------+
| James D     |    1265489921 |
| Timothy J   |    2147483647 |
```

```
| Harish K      |     5739304575 |
| Kingston X    |     2173467271 |
| Sue U         |     2312934021 |
+---------------+----------------+
5 rows in set (0.06 sec)
```

You can (optionally) specify the row offset from which to begin counting. The following example returns six records beginning with row 4 (note, row numbering begins from 0):

```
mysql> SELECT accountName, accountNumber FROM accounts LIMIT 3,6;
+---------------+----------------+
| accountName   | accountNumber  |
+---------------+----------------+
| Kingston X    |     2173467271 |
| Sue U         |     2312934021 |
| Ila T         |     1248954638 |
| Anil V        |     2384371001 |
| Katrina P     |     9430125467 |
| Pooja B       |     1890192554 |
+---------------+----------------+
6 rows in set (0.00 sec)
```

Sorting Query Results

Query results can be sorted by a specific field (or fields) with the addition of the ORDER BY clause to the SELECT statement. The following example demonstrates by sorting the accounts table by the creation date:

```
mysql> SELECT accountCreatedOn, accountNumber FROM accounts
ORDER BY accountCreatedOn;
+------------------+----------------+
| accountCreatedOn | accountNumber  |
+------------------+----------------+
| 1967-09-15       |     2173467271 |
| 1995-09-13       |     5739304575 |
| 1998-03-27       |     2388282010 |
| 1998-06-06       |     2312934021 |
| 1998-07-29       |     1265489921 |
| 2000-12-12       |     2147483647 |
| 2001-11-19       |     2384371001 |
| 2002-01-23       |     1890192554 |
| 2003-05-01       |     2374845291 |
| 2003-07-01       |     9430125467 |
| 2003-08-17       |     1248954638 |
+------------------+----------------+
11 rows in set (0.05 sec)
```

> ### Getting It All
> To retrieve all records from the specified offset to the end of the table, specify -1 as the number of rows to return. For example, to return records from row 19 to the end of the table, you could use the query `SELECT * from tbl LIMIT 18, -1`.

You can sort on multiple fields by specifying them as a comma-separated list to the `ORDER BY` clause. The following query first sorts by account balance, and then by location:

```
mysql> SELECT accountName, accountBalance, accountCreatedAt FROM
accounts ORDER BY accountBalance, accountCreatedAt;
+-------------+----------------+------------------+
| accountName | accountBalance | accountCreatedAt |
+-------------+----------------+------------------+
| Sue U       |          34.67 | MA               |
| Katrina P   |         100.00 | NY               |
| James D     |        2346.00 | NY               |
| Ila T       |        5373.82 | CA               |
| Pooja B     |       17337.12 | FL               |
| Jacob N     |       18410.00 | NY               |
| Timothy J   |       56347.50 | BO               |
| Anil V      |       72460.00 | MA               |
| Sue U       |      388883.13 | BO               |
| Kingston X  |      634238.00 | MA               |
| Harish K    |      996564.88 | NY               |
+-------------+----------------+------------------+
11 rows in set (0.05 sec)
```

The `ASC` and `DESC` keywords can be added to each field name in the `ORDER BY` clause to customize the sorting method further. They state whether values in the corresponding field should be sorted in ascending or descending order. The following example demonstrates, by sorting the account names in reverse alphabetical order:

```
mysql> SELECT accountName, accountBalance FROM accounts
ORDER BY accountName DESC;
+-------------+----------------+
| accountName | accountBalance |
+-------------+----------------+
| Timothy J   |       56347.50 |
| Sue U       |          34.67 |
| Sue U       |      388883.13 |
| Pooja B     |       17337.12 |
| Kingston X  |      634238.00 |
```

```
| Katrina P    |          100.00 |
| James D      |         2346.00 |
| Jacob N      |        18410.00 |
| Ila T        |         5373.82 |
| Harish K     |       996564.88 |
| Anil V       |        72460.00 |
+--------------+-----------------+
11 rows in set (0.06 sec)
```

Grouping Query Results

MySQL makes it possible to break the records in a result set into distinct groups on the basis of a specific attribute with the GROUP BY clause. Because each group created in this manner is represented as a single row (even though it contains multiple records), this capability is primarily used in operations involving MySQL's numerous aggregate functions.

To understand this better, consider the following example:

```
mysql> SELECT accountCreatedAt FROM accounts GROUP BY accountCreatedAt;
+------------------+
| accountCreatedAt |
+------------------+
| BO               |
| CA               |
| FL               |
| MA               |
| NY               |
+------------------+
5 rows in set (0.00 sec)
```

In this case, the records in the accounts table have been grouped on the basis of the accountCreatedAt field. Because five distinct locations are spread over the 11 records in the table, MySQL creates five distinct groups of records and represents each group as a single row in the result set.

A Random Choice

Combining the LIMIT keyword and the ORDER BY clause with the RAND() function produces the solution to one of the more common queries on the MySQL mailing list—that of selecting one or more records at random from a table. The process involves first sorting the table randomly, and then selecting a single record from the resulting collection. Or, in SQL-lingo:

```
SELECT fld1, fld2 FROM tbl ORDER BY RAND() LIMIT 0, 1;
```

Aggregate functions can now be applied to the records constituting each individual group. For example, the following query returns the total number of accounts at each location,

```
mysql> SELECT accountCreatedAt AS loc, COUNT(*) FROM accounts
GROUP BY accountCreatedAt;
+-----+----------+
| loc | COUNT(*) |
+-----+----------+
| BO  |        2 |
| CA  |        1 |
| FL  |        1 |
| MA  |        3 |
| NY  |        4 |
+-----+----------+
5 rows in set (0.06 sec)
```

while this one returns the average balance at each location:

```
mysql> SELECT accountCreatedAt AS loc, AVG(accountBalance) FROM
accounts GROUP BY accountCreatedAt;
+-----+--------------------+
| loc | AVG(accountBalance) |
+-----+--------------------+
| BO  |      222615.312500 |
| CA  |        5373.819824 |
| FL  |       17337.119141 |
| MA  |      235577.556666 |
| NY  |      254355.218750 |
+-----+--------------------+
5 rows in set (0.05 sec)
```

The ASC and DESC keywords can be added to the GROUP BY list to sort the result set in ascending or descending order. The following variant of the previous example demonstrates, by sorting the account locations in reverse alphabetical order:

```
mysql> SELECT accountCreatedAt AS loc, AVG(accountBalance) FROM
accounts GROUP BY accountCreatedAt DESC;
+-----+--------------------+
| loc | AVG(accountBalance) |
+-----+--------------------+
| NY  |      254355.218750 |
| MA  |      235577.556666 |
| FL  |       17337.119141 |
| CA  |        5373.819824 |
```

```
| BO  |       222615.312500 |
+-----+---------------------+
5 rows in set (0.05 sec)
```

The groups created by the GROUP BY clause can be further constrained by the addition of the HAVING clause, which serves a purpose similar to that of the WHERE clause discussed earlier: creating a result set matching a specified condition. Consider the following examples, which demonstrate.

```
mysql> SELECT accountCreatedAt AS loc, AVG(accountBalance) FROM
accounts GROUP BY accountCreatedAt HAVING loc = 'CA';
+-----+---------------------+
| loc | AVG(accountBalance) |
+-----+---------------------+
| CA  |         5373.819824 |
+-----+---------------------+
1 row in set (0.05 sec)

mysql> SELECT accountCreatedAt, SUM(accountBalance) FROM accounts
GROUP BY accountCreatedAt HAVING SUM(accountBalance) > 100000.00;
+------------------+---------------------+
| accountCreatedAt | SUM(accountBalance) |
+------------------+---------------------+
| BO               |           445230.63 |
| MA               |           706732.67 |
| NY               |          1017420.88 |
+------------------+---------------------+
3 rows in set (0.17 sec)
```

Using Variables

MySQL also lets you store the results of SELECT queries in user-defined variables, for use in future SELECT queries. These variables are connection-specific. They only exist for the duration of the client session, but they provide a convenient and effective way to link queries together, and to use the output of one query in the clauses of another one.

HAVING Your Cake and Eating It Too

The difference between WHERE and HAVING is the WHERE clause operates on all the records in a table, retrieving only those that match the stated condition. A HAVING clause, on the other hand, operates on records after they have been retrieved from the table, to winnow down the result set even further. Typically, the HAVING clause appears in conjunction with the GROUP BY clause, whereas the WHERE clause appears in SELECT, DELETE, and UPDATE statements.

Variable assignment takes place with the : = operator, which is used to assign a value to a variable. The following example illustrates, by assigning the earliest date in the table to the @oldest variable:

```
mysql> SELECT @oldest:=MIN(accountCreatedOn) FROM accounts;
+-------------------------------+
| @oldest:=min(accountCreatedOn) |
+-------------------------------+
| 1967-09-15                    |
+-------------------------------+
1 row in set (0.00 sec)
```

The value stored in the @oldest variable can now be retrieved via a simple SELECT,

```
mysql> SELECT @oldest;
+------------+
| @oldest    |
+------------+
| 1967-09-15 |
+------------+
1 row in set (0.00 sec)
```

or incorporated into another query:

```
mysql> SELECT accountName, accountNumber, accountBalance FROM accounts
WHERE accountCreatedOn = @oldest;
+-------------+---------------+----------------+
| accountName | accountNumber | accountBalance |
+-------------+---------------+----------------+
| Kingston X  |    2173467271 |    634238.00000 |
+-------------+---------------+----------------+
1 row in set (0.00 sec)
```

Variable names are case-sensitive and can contain alphanumeric characters, as well as underscores (_) and periods (.). These variables are also type-insensitive. A variable can store strings or numbers without needing an explicit type declaration in advance.

Using Subqueries

MySQL 4.1 also enables you to nest queries within one another and use the result set generated by an inner query within an outer one. As a result, instead of executing two (or more) separate queries, you execute a single query containing one (or more) subqueries.

Consider the following example, which uses a subquery to list all those accounts with balances greater than the average account balance:

```
mysql> SELECT accountName, accountNumber, accountBalance FROM accounts
WHERE accountBalance > (SELECT AVG(accountBalance) FROM accounts);
+-------------+---------------+----------------+
| accountName | accountNumber | accountBalance |
+-------------+---------------+----------------+
| Harish K    |    5739304575 |      996564.88 |
| Kingston X  |    2173467271 |      634238.00 |
| Sue U       |    2388282010 |      388883.13 |
+-------------+---------------+----------------+
3 rows in set (0.16 sec)
```

Here, MySQL begins with the innermost query and first obtains the average account balance from the records in the table. It then moves outward and upward from the inner query to the outer (main) query, and substitutes the result generated by the inner query in the WHERE clause of the outer query to obtain a list of account holders with a balance greater than the average.

You can read more about subqueries in Chapter 11 of this book.

Controlling SELECT Behavior

A number of other keywords can be added to the SELECT statement to modify its behavior:

- The DISTINCT keyword eliminates records containing duplicate values from the result set.

- The SQL_CALC_FOUND_ROWS keyword tells MySQL to calculate the total number of rows matching the query (without taking into account any LIMIT that might have been set). This total number can then be retrieved via a call to the FOUND_ROWS() function.

- The SQL_CACHE and SQL_NO_CACHE keywords tell MySQL whether the query results should be cached.

- The SQL_BUFFER_RESULT keyword forces MySQL to store query results in a temporary table. This result buffer eliminates the need for MySQL to lock the tables used by the query while the results are being transmitted to the client, thus ensuring they can be used by other processes in the interim.

- The SQL_BIG_RESULT and SQL_SMALL_RESULT keywords can be used to indicate the expected size of the result set to MySQL and, thereby, help it identify the most optimal way to sort and store the returned records (disk-based or in-memory temporary tables, respectively).

- The SQL_HIGH_PRIORITY keyword raises the priority of the query over competing UPDATE, INSERT, or DELETE statements, thereby resulting in (slightly) faster query execution on busy database servers.

On the Same Page

The SQL_CALC_FOUND_ROWS keyword comes in particularly handy in applications that spread database content over multiple pages. This is because it can be used to display a count of the total number of records found, even though the current result set might only hold a small subset of that total number.

If, for example, you want to display the records in the accounts table five at a time and you also want to display the total number of records, your queries would look something like this:

```
mysql> SELECT SQL_CALC_FOUND_ROWS accountName FROM accounts LIMIT 5;
+-------------+
| accountName |
+-------------+
| James D     |
| Timothy J   |
| Harish K    |
| Kingston X  |
| Sue U       |
+-------------+
5 rows in set (0.00 sec)
mysql> SELECT FOUND_ROWS();
+--------------+
| FOUND_ROWS() |
+--------------+
|           11 |
+--------------+
1 row in set (0.00 sec)
```

This method returns a subset of five records, but it also calculates the total number of records matching the query and makes this number accessible via the FOUND_ROWS() function.

Speed Demon

Appropriate usage of the SQL_CACHE, SQL_BUFFER_RESULT, SQL_BIG_RESULT, SQL_SMALL_RESULT, and SQL_HIGH_PRIORITY keywords can significantly improve the speed of your transactions with the MySQL server.

Copying, Importing, and Exporting Records

In addition to allowing manual entry of records via the INSERT statement, MySQL offers a number of DML constructs to add records to a table automatically, either by copying them from another table or importing them from a text file. Records can also be exported to a text file with a variant of the SELECT statement, a feature that can come in handy when backing up or moving data. The following sections examine each of these constructs in detail.

Copying Records

MySQL permits combining the INSERT and SELECT statements to dynamically populate a table from the results of a SELECT query or to copy records from one table into another table. For example, if you had a table of employee records,

```
+-----+--------+--------+-----+-----+----------------+---------+
| id  | lname  | fname  | age | sex | department     | country |
+-----+--------+--------+-----+-----+----------------+---------+
|  54 | Doe    | John   | 27  | M   | Engineering    | US      |
| 127 | Jones  | Sue    | 31  | F   | Finance        | UK      |
| 113 | Woo    | David  | 26  | M   | Administration | CN      |
| 175 | Thomas | James  | 34  | M   | Finance        | US      |
| 168 | Kent   | Jane   | 29  | F   | Administration | US      |
|  12 | Kamath | Ravina | 35  | F   | Finance        | IN      |
+-----+--------+--------+-----+-----+----------------+---------+
6 rows in set (0.01 sec)
```

and you wanted to create user records for each of these employees in a separate users table, you could use the INSERT statement in combination with the SELECT statement to automatically create the user records:

```
mysql> INSERT INTO users (uname, upass) SELECT LOWER(fname),
PASSWORD( LOWER(fname) ) FROM employees;
Query OK, 6 rows affected (0.07 sec)
Records: 6  Duplicates: 0  Warnings: 6

mysql> SELECT * FROM users;
+-----+--------+----------------+
| uid | uname  | upass          |
+-----+--------+----------------+
|   7 | john   | 2ca0ede551581d2 |
|   8 | sue    | 789d886f262f349 |
|   9 | david  | 24c0ad4a2a3d818 |
|  10 | james  | 6bd9b3d678820f6 |
```

PART II

```
|   11 | jane   | 35df0a9c5a75db4  |
|   12 | ravina | 631233cb70584bc  |
+-----+--------+------------------+
6 rows in set (0.00 sec)
```

The field list specified in the INSERT statement must obviously match the columns returned by the SELECT clause. A mismatch can cause MySQL to produce a error like the following one:

```
mysql> INSERT INTO tbl1 (fld1, fld2) SELECT fld1, fld2, fld3 FROM tbl2;
ERROR 1136: Column count doesn't match value count at row 1
```

Naturally, you can also attach a WHERE clause to the SELECT statement to copy only a subset of the original table's records into the new table.

```
mysql> INSERT INTO users (uname, upass) SELECT LOWER(fname),
PASSWORD( LOWER(fname) ) FROM employees WHERE country = 'US';
Query OK, 3 rows affected (0.01 sec)
Records: 3  Duplicates: 0  Warnings: 3

mysql> SELECT * FROM users;
+-----+-------+-----------------+
| uid | uname | upass           |
+-----+-------+-----------------+
|  10 | john  | 2ca0ede551581d2 |
|  11 | james | 6bd9b3d678820f6 |
|  12 | jane  | 35df0a9c5a75db4 |
+-----+-------+-----------------+
3 rows in set (0.00 sec)
```

Thinking Out of the Box

MySQL's INSERT...SELECT syntax, together with its IGNORE keyword and its support for temporary tables, provides numerous opportunities for creative rewriting of SELECT queries to have them execute faster.

For example, say you have a complex query that involves selecting a set of distinct values from a particular field and the MySQL engine is unable to optimize your query because of its complexity. Creative SQL programmers can then improve performance by (a) first breaking up the complex query into numerous simpler ones that the optimizer can handle better, (b) and then using the INSERT IGNORE...SELECT syntax to insert the results generated into a temporary table, after first creating the temporary table with a UNIQUE key on the appropriate field. The result: a set of distinct values for that field and possibly faster query execution.

Importing Records

The INSERT statement isn't the only way to insert data into a table. MySQL also permits insertion of multiple records in one fell swoop with the LOAD DATA INFILE command. This command can be used to read raw data from a text file (located on either the server or the client end of the connection), parse it on the basis of column and row delimiters, and automatically generate INSERT statements to write the data to a table.

This approach comes in handy when you need to enter a large volume of information into a database but the data, though structured, is not available in the form of SQL statements. Manually creating INSERT statements for every single record would be tedious and time-consuming; LOAD DATA INFILE offers a faster and more reliable alternative.

The best way to understand LOAD DATA INFILE is with an example. Consider the following empty birthdays table,

```
mysql> DESCRIBE birthdays;
+--------+-------------+------+-----+------------+-------+
| Field  | Type        | Null | Key | Default    | Extra |
+--------+-------------+------+-----+------------+-------+
| name   | varchar(50) |      |     |            |       |
| dob    | date        |      |     | 0000-00-00 |       |
+--------+-------------+------+-----+------------+-------+
2 rows in set (0.05 sec)
```

and a text file containing names and birth dates, separated with commas, in your home area on the server:

```
Alan P, 1967-09-11
John D, 1956-11-17
Emma Y, 1963-01-23
Neel K, 1977-10-11
Bryan A, 1959-07-16
```

Now, this comma-separated data could be imported into the previous birthdays table with the following command:

```
mysql> LOAD DATA INFILE '/home/me/data.txt' INTO TABLE birthdays
FIELDS TERMINATED BY ',' LINES TERMINATED BY '\r\n';
Query OK, 5 rows affected (0.06 sec)
Records: 5  Deleted: 0  Skipped: 0  Warnings: 0
```

Your data should now have been inserted correctly into the table, as a quick SELECT * verifies.

```
mysql> SELECT * FROM birthdays;
+---------+------------+
| name    | dob        |
+---------+------------+
| Alan  P | 1967-09-11 |
| John  D | 1956-11-17 |
| Emma  Y | 1963-01-23 |
| Neel  K | 1977-10-11 |
| Bryan A | 1959-07-16 |
+---------+------------+
5 rows in set (0.00 sec)
```

By default, MySQL assumes the data file is on the server, in the location specified in the LOAD DATA INFILE statement. If, instead, you want to use a data file on the client, you can add the keyword LOCAL to the statement, to tell MySQL to look for the file on the client's file system. The following example demonstrates, by loading data from a file on the client machine:

```
mysql> LOAD DATA LOCAL INFILE 'c:\data.txt' INTO TABLE birthdays
FIELDS TERMINATED BY ',' LINES TERMINATED BY '\r\n';
Query OK, 5 rows affected (0.06 sec)
Records: 5  Deleted: 0  Skipped: 0  Warnings: 0
```

If fewer fields are in the data file than in the table or if the values in the file are not ordered in the same sequence as the fields in the table, you can tell MySQL how to map the data in the file to the fields of the table by specifying a list of field names after the LOAD DATA INFILE command. Given the following addressbook table containing five columns,

```
mysql> DESCRIBE addressbook;
+-------+-----------+------+-----+---------+-------+
| Field | Type      | Null | Key | Default | Extra |
+-------+-----------+------+-----+---------+-------+
| fname | char(255) | YES  |     | NULL    |       |
| lname | char(255) | YES  |     | NULL    |       |
| phone | char(255) | YES  |     | NULL    |       |
| fax   | char(255) | YES  |     | NULL    |       |
| email | char(255) | YES  |     | NULL    |       |
+-------+-----------+------+-----+---------+-------+
5 rows in set (0.00 sec)
```

and a three-field list of names and e-mail addresses in a separate file,

```
"Cathy"  "cathy@cat.nip"  "Cat"
"Polly"  "polly@talk.to.me"  "Parrot"
"Harry"  "harry@prickles.tld"  "Hedgehog"
"David"  "woof@doghouse"  "Dog"
```

you could have MySQL import only the names and e-mail addresses into the table with the following command:

```
mysql> LOAD DATA INFILE 'data.txt' INTO TABLE addressbook
FIELDS TERMINATED BY ' ' ENCLOSED BY '"' LINES TERMINATED BY '\r\n'
(fname, email, lname);
Query OK, 4 rows affected (0.05 sec)
Records: 4  Deleted: 0  Skipped: 0  Warnings: 0
```

Here's how the result would look.

```
mysql> SELECT * FROM addressbook;
+--------+----------+--------+------+--------------------+
| fname  | lname    | phone  | fax  | email              |
+--------+----------+--------+------+--------------------+
| Cathy  | Cat      | NULL   | NULL | cathy@cat.nip      |
| Polly  | Parrot   | NULL   | NULL | polly@talk.to.me   |
| Harry  | Hedgehog | NULL   | NULL | harry@prickles.tld |
| David  | Dog      | NULL   | NULL | woof@doghouse      |
+--------+----------+--------+------+--------------------+
4 rows in set (0.00 sec)
```

It's clear that MySQL inserts NULL values (if permitted to do so by the table and field constraints) when it encounters missing field values.

The Right Path

When using data files on the server, if no file path is specified in the call to LOAD DATA INFILE (or if a relative path is specified), MySQL looks in the corresponding database directory on the server for the file (or uses it as the relative path root). Absolute paths, however, will be used as is.

A number of keywords can be used to modify the behavior of the LOAD DATA INFILE command:

- The LOW_PRIORITY keyword causes the server to wait until no other threads are using the table before beginning the import process. The CONCURRENT keyword, on the other hand, permits clients to read data from the table while the import is in process (although this keyword applies only to MyISAM tables).

```
mysql> LOAD DATA LOW_PRIORITY INFILE 'log.asc' INTO TABLE logdata;
Query OK, 76 rows affected (0.10 sec)
mysql> LOAD DATA CONCURRENT LOCAL INFILE 'd:\palm\addressbook.txt'
INTO TABLE addressbook;
Query OK, 106 rows affected (1.45 sec)
```

- The IGNORE keyword ensures that if any of the new records has a key that duplicates an existing record, MySQL will simply step over it to the next one (instead of aborting the entire operation, which is the default action in such a situation). Or, you can choose to replace existing records with new records from the data file. This can be accomplished by using the keyword REPLACE instead of IGNORE.

```
mysql> LOAD DATA INFILE '/tmp/users.txt' INTO TABLE users
LINES TERMINATED BY '\r\n' (uname);
ERROR 1062: Duplicate entry 'emma' for key 1

mysql> LOAD DATA INFILE '/tmp/users.txt' IGNORE INTO TABLE users
LINES TERMINATED BY '\r\n' (uname);
Query OK, 5 rows affected (0.00 sec)
Records: 6  Deleted: 0  Skipped: 1  Warnings: 0

mysql> LOAD DATA INFILE '/tmp/users.txt' REPLACE INTO TABLE users
LINES TERMINATED BY '\r\n' (uname);
Query OK, 7 rows affected (0.06 sec)
Records: 6  Deleted: 1  Skipped: 0  Warnings: 0
```

Exporting Records

Just as you can import data into a table from a file with the LOAD DATA INFILE command, you can also extract records from a table into a file with the SELECT . . . INTO OUTFILE construct. This construct lets you do everything you would do with the regular SELECT statement, and then send the resulting record collection to a file.

The Delimiter Dilemma

Both the LOAD DATA INFILE and the SELECT ... INTO OUTFILE commands support the use of additional keywords and clauses to specify the format of the data file:

- The LINES TERMINATED BY clause specifies the end-of-record delimiter (by default, the newline character \n).

- The FIELDS clause specifies field delimiters and must be followed by one or more of the keywords TERMINATED BY, ESCAPED BY, or ENCLOSED BY. These specify the end-of-field delimiter (default is the tab character \t), the sequence used to escape special characters when reading and writing values (default is a backslash), and the character used to enclose field values (no default), respectively.

To illustrate, consider the following table:

```
+-------------+----------------+
| accountName | accountBalance |
+-------------+----------------+
| James D     |        2346.00 |
| Timothy J   |       56347.50 |
| Harish K    |      996564.88 |
| Kingston X  |      634238.00 |
| Sue U       |          34.67 |
| Ila T       |        5373.82 |
| Anil V      |       72460.00 |
| Katrina P   |         100.00 |
| Pooja B     |       17337.12 |
| Sue U       |      388883.13 |
| Jacob N     |       18410.00 |
+-------------+----------------+
11 rows in set (0.00 sec)
```

The following command extracts all these records to a text file named accounts.txt on the server.

```
mysql> SELECT accountName, accountBalance FROM accounts
INTO OUTFILE 'accounts.txt';
Query OK, 11 rows affected (0.06 sec)
```

PART II

Here's what the result looks like:

```
James D        2346.00
Timothy J      56347.50
Harish K       996564.88
Kingston X     634238.00
Sue U          34.67
Ila T          5373.82
Anil V         72460.00
Katrina P      100.00
Pooja B        17337.12
Sue U          388883.13
Jacob N        18410.00
```

Obviously, you can use a WHERE clause (and any other clause or keyword usable in a normal SELECT statement) to further constrain the output. The following example demonstrates, by only writing those records with an account balance greater than $5000.00 to the file /tmp/high-value-accounts.txt:

```
mysql> SELECT accountNumber, accountName, accountBalance FROM accounts
WHERE accountBalance > 50000 INTO OUTFILE
'/tmp/high-value-accounts.txt'
FIELDS TERMINATED BY ',' ENCLOSED BY '"' LINES TERMINATED BY '\r\n';
Query OK, 5 rows affected (0.00 sec)
```

Here's the result:

```
"2147483647","Timothy J","56347.50"
"5739304575","Harish K","996564.88"
"2173467271","Kingston X","634238.00"
"2384371001","Anil V","72460.00"
"2388282010","Sue U","388883.13"
```

The file specified in the INTO OUTFILE and INTO DUMPFILE clauses will be written to the server's file system and must not already exist there. Because this file will be written by the user the MySQL server process runs as, that user must have appropriate permissions to write files to the specified location. For security reasons,

---

Dumped!

To retrieve binary data, such as the contents of BLOB fields, from the database into a file, replace the INTO OUTFILE clause with the INTO DUMPFILE clause. This causes MySQL to write the data to the file as a single line (without field or record termination characters), thereby avoiding corruption of the binary data.

> **Rank and File**
>
> The logged-in client must have FILE privileges on the server to use either the SELECT . . . INTO OUTFILE or LOAD DATA INFILE commands. Chapter 14 has more information on how the MySQL privilege system works.

MySQL does not allow the target file to be written to the client file system using this method. The client application, therefore, needs to retrieve it from the server using external methods.

As with the LOAD DATA INFILE command, you can specify field and record delimiters for the data being dumped (read the sidebar titled "The Delimiter Dilemma" for more information). The following examples demonstrate.

```
mysql> SELECT name, phone, email, fax FROM members INTO OUTFILE
'/usr/local/data/members.txt' FIELDS TERMINATED BY '|'
ENCLOSED BY '"' ESCAPED BY '\\';
Query OK, 32 rows affected (0.00 sec)

mysql> SELECT title, author, isbn FROM books INTO OUTFILE
'/home/me/books.asc' FIELDS TERMINATED BY ','
LINES TERMINATED BY '\r\n';
Query OK, 255 rows affected (0.17 sec)
```

You can also use the mysqldump utility to extract the contents of a database or table into a file. Chapter 15 has more information on how to use this utility to back up and restore your MySQL databases.

Summary

This chapter took an in-depth look at the data manipulation commands provided by SQL (together with some nonstandard, MySQL-specific commands) to explain how to use them to store and update data in MySQL tables. Among the commands explained were the following:

- **INSERT**   Used to add new records to a table
- **UPDATE**   Used to update existing records
- **REPLACE**   Used to replace existing records
- **DELETE and TRUNCATE**   Used to delete records
- **SELECT (and its many variants)**   Used to retrieve a particular subset of records matching a specific criteria
- **LOAD DATA INFILE**   Used to import data from a text file into a MySQL table

You should now have a deeper understanding of how the various MySQL commands interact with each other and with the rest of the application. The next chapters build on the basic material learned in this and previous chapters to teach you how to use some of the newer and more advanced features (including subqueries, transactions and query optimization) of the MySQL RDBMS.

Joins

Most of the examples you've seen in the previous section of this book dealt with only a single table at a time. In the real world, though, this doesn't happen too often. Efficiency constraints usually dictate that data be split across multiple tables and that relationships be created between the different tables to make data retrieval more efficient.

By supporting the creation of links between related pieces of information, a relational database management system (RDBMS) not only makes it possible to store information more efficiently (by removing redundancies and repetition), it also brings to the forefront undiscovered relationships between disparate segments of data and permits efficient exploitation of those relationships.

With this in mind, this chapter builds on the basic DML concepts you learned in the previous section to demonstrate how SQL can be used to query multiple tables at once and to combine the data retrieved from them in different ways. These multiple-table queries are referred to as *joins* because they join together two or more tables, and they have a reputation for being complex, difficult to understand, and frightening. As you'll see, most of this is unwarranted—joins are both fairly simple and extremely powerful. This chapter will teach all everything you need to know about how to use them in your interaction with the MySQL RDBMS.

What Is a Join?

Joins have long been one of the most common ways to link together records in different tables. A common misconception is that MySQL, because of its simplicity and/or open-source roots, is "bad" at joins. This is simply not true. MySQL has supported joins well right from its inception and, today, boasts support for standard SQL2-compliant join syntax, which makes it possible to combine table records in a variety of sophisticated ways.

The best way to understand joins is with a simple example. Consider the following two tables, one named `categories` and containing a list of news categories,

```
+------+-----------------+
| cid  | cname           |
+------+-----------------+
|    1 | Sports          |
|    2 | Current Affairs |
|    3 | Business        |
|    4 | Technology      |
+------+-----------------+
```

and the other containing a list of news headlines.

```
+------+-------------------------------------------------+------------+------+
| tid  | tname                                           | tdate      | cid  |
+------+-------------------------------------------------+------------+------+
|  100 | Probe lands on Mars                             | 2002-03-19 |    4 |
|  102 | Stock markets crash                             | 2002-03-05 |    3 |
|  104 | War breaks out between men and fish             | 2003-08-14 |    2 |
|  106 | Volcanic eruptions on Pluto                     | 2003-01-03 |    2 |
|  107 | Injured football player vows to return          | 2003-06-18 |    1 |
|  110 | Cell phones found to improve cognition among babies | 2003-09-14 |    4 |
|  113 | Leaders of day-trading scam arrested by FBI     | 2002-12-27 |    3 |
+------+-------------------------------------------------+------------+------+
```

As you can see, a link exists between the previous two tables: the `cid` field, which can be used to connect each news item with its category.

Now, you already know how to retrieve all the records in any one of these tables—use the catch-all `SELECT *` query.

```
mysql> SELECT * FROM topics;
+------+-------------------------------------------------+------------+------+
| tid  | tname                                           | tdate      | cid  |
+------+-------------------------------------------------+------------+------+
|  100 | Probe lands on Mars                             | 2002-03-19 |    4 |
|  102 | Stock markets crash                             | 2002-03-05 |    3 |
|  104 | War breaks out between men and fish             | 2003-08-14 |    2 |
|  106 | Volcanic eruptions on Pluto                     | 2003-01-03 |    2 |
|  107 | Injured football player vows to return          | 2003-06-18 |    1 |
|  110 | Cell phones found to improve cognition among babies | 2003-09-14 |    4 |
|  113 | Leaders of day-trading scam arrested by FBI     | 2002-12-27 |    3 |
+------+-------------------------------------------------+------------+------+
7 rows in set (0.11 sec)
```

You can filter out some of these records by adding a `WHERE` clause to specify a condition that must be met: for example, only headlines for the year 2003:

```
mysql> SELECT tid, tname FROM topics WHERE YEAR(tdate) = 2003;
+------+----------------------------------------------------+
| tid  | tname                                              |
+------+----------------------------------------------------+
|  104 | War breaks out between men and fish                |
|  106 | Volcanic eruptions on Pluto                        |
|  107 | Injured football player vows to return             |
|  110 | Cell phones found to improve cognition among babies |
+------+----------------------------------------------------+
4 rows in set (0.22 sec)
```

But what if you need something a little more advanced: for example, a list of only those headlines in the Current Affairs category or a list of all the sports headlines for 2003? Querying only a single table in this case won't be adequate because category information and headline summaries are stored in two separate tables.

However, as previously noted, a link does exist between the two tables—the cid column, which is common to both tables. By equating the cid field in the categories table to the cid field in the topics table in the SELECT query's WHERE clause, this common field makes it possible to create a join between the two tables. Or, in SQL-lingo:

```
mysql> SELECT cname, tname FROM categories, topics WHERE categories.cid = topics.cid;
+-----------------+----------------------------------------------------+
| cname           | tname                                              |
+-----------------+----------------------------------------------------+
| Technology      | Probe lands on Mars                                |
| Business        | Stock markets crash                                |
| Current Affairs | War breaks out between men and fish                |
| Current Affairs | Volcanic eruptions on Pluto                        |
| Sports          | Injured football player vows to return             |
| Technology      | Cell phones found to improve cognition among babies |
| Business        | Leaders of day-trading scam arrested by FBI        |
+-----------------+----------------------------------------------------+
7 rows in set (0.06 sec)
```

And that's your very first join!

In this case, the WHERE clause has been used to connect the cid fields within both tables to each other and present a composite picture. This picture still isn't quite what you need, though. You need to filter it down to only those headlines in the Current Affairs category. Fortunately, the WHERE clause will come to your rescue again:

```
mysql> SELECT tname FROM categories, topics WHERE categories.cid =
topics.cid AND categories.cname = 'Current Affairs';
+-------------------------------------+
| tname                               |
+-------------------------------------+
| War breaks out between men and fish |
| Volcanic eruptions on Pluto         |
+-------------------------------------+
2 rows in set (0.22 sec)
```

Land Of Confusion

When joining multiple tables, it's important to ensure that field references (especially fields with the same name) are as explicit as possible. If your join includes two or more tables with the same field name, you must prefix the field name with the table name (as many of the examples in this chapter do), so MySQL knows exactly which field of which table is being referred to.

```
SELECT name FROM employees, departments WHERE employees.id =
departments.eid;               # bad
SELECT employees.name FROM employees, departments WHERE employees.id =
departments.eid;               # good
```

The WHERE clause in the previous SQL statement acts on the combined result set of the two tables, filtering down to only those records that match the specified criteria.

How about the second question—a list of all sports headlines for 2003?

```
mysql> SELECT tname FROM categories, topics WHERE categories.cid = topics.cid
AND categories.cname = 'Sports' AND YEAR(topics.tdate) = 2003;
+--------------------------------------+
| tname                                |
+--------------------------------------+
| Injured football player vows to return |
+--------------------------------------+
1 row in set (0.22 sec)
```

Thus, by using the implicit link between the two previous tables , SQL lets you join them together to produce a composite result set, and then further massage the data within it to obtain only the information you need.

Types of Joins

Now that you have a basic understanding of how joins work, let's move on to a more detailed discussion of the various types of joins supported by MySQL's SQL. The following different join types are possible in MySQL:

- Cross joins
- Inner joins
- Outer joins
- Self joins
- Unions

The following sections examine each of these join types in greater detail, with examples and illustrations.

Cross Joins

The simplest type of join is the *cross join*, which multiplies the tables involved to create an all-inclusive product. Consider the following example, which contains two tables, one listing physical features and the other listing colors:

```
Table "attribute"                          Table "color"
+-----------+                              +-------+
| attribute |                              | color |
+-----------+                              +-------+
| eyes      |                              | brown |
| hair      |                              | black |
+-----------+                              | gray  |
                                           +-------+
```

You can combine the two previous tables with a cross join, as in the following:

```
mysql> SELECT * FROM color, attribute;
+-------+-----------+
| color | attribute |
+-------+-----------+
| brown | eyes      |
| black | eyes      |
| gray  | eyes      |
| brown | hair      |
| black | hair      |
| gray  | hair      |
+-------+-----------+
6 rows in set (0.00 sec)
```

In this case, columns from both tables are combined to produce a result set that contains all possible combinations. This kind of join is referred to as a cross join, and the number of rows in the joined table will be equal to the product of the number of rows in each of the tables used in the join. You can see this from the previous example. The attributes table has two rows, the colors table has three rows, and so the joined table has 2×3 = 6 rows.

As you might imagine, a cross join like the previous one can have huge implications for the performance of your database server. To illustrate, look what happens when I add two more tables to the previous join:

```
mysql> SELECT * FROM sex, shape, color, attribute;
+--------+-------+-------+-----------+
| sex    | shape | color | attribute |
+--------+-------+-------+-----------+
| male   | fat   | brown | eyes      |
| female | fat   | brown | eyes      |
```

```
| male   | long  | brown | eyes     |
| female | long  | brown | eyes     |
| male   | thin  | brown | eyes     |
| female | thin  | brown | eyes     |
...
+--------+-------+-------+----------+
48 rows in set (0.05 sec)
```

Although each of the tables used in the join contains less than five records each, the final joined result contains 2×3×2×4 = 48 records. This might not seem like a big deal when you're only dealing with 4 tables containing a total of 11 records, but imagine what would happen if you had 4 tables, each containing 100 records, and you decided to cross join them...

Inner Joins

Inner joins are the most common type of join and also the most symmetrical because they require a match in each table that forms a part of the join. Rows that do not match are excluded from the final result set.

The most common example of an inner join is the *equi-join,* where certain fields in the joined tables are equated to each other. In this case, the final result set only includes those rows from the joined tables that have matches in the specified fields (the example in the first segment of this chapter used an equi-join).

To illustrate, consider the following tables listing products, and quantities sold of each:

```
Table "products"                        Table "sales"
+-----------+-------------+             +------+-----------+----------+
| productID | productName |             | id   | productID | quantity |
+-----------+-------------+             +------+-----------+----------+
|         1 | apples      |             | 1    |         3 |     2300 |
|         2 | oranges     |             | 2    |         2 |     1500 |
|         3 | pineapples  |             | 3    |         1 |     3400 |
|         4 | bananas     |             +------+-----------+----------+
+-----------+-------------+
```

Because the two tables have a productID field in common, it's fairly easy to join them:

```
mysql> SELECT productName, quantity FROM products, sales WHERE
products.productID = sales.productID;
+-------------+----------+
| productName | quantity |
+-------------+----------+
| pineapples  |     2300 |
| oranges     |     1500 |
| apples      |     3400 |
+-------------+----------+
3 rows in set (0.00 sec)
```

> **Data Overload**
> Because a cross join produces a large result set, it's generally considered a good idea to attach a WHERE clause to the join to filter out some of the records.

Here, too, you can use a WHERE clause to narrow the result set further, as in the following example, which filters the result set to only those products with sales over 2000:

```
mysql> SELECT productName, quantity FROM products, sales WHERE
products.productID = sales.productID AND sales.quantity > 2000;
+-------------+----------+
| productName | quantity |
+-------------+----------+
| pineapples  |     2300 |
| apples      |     3400 |
+-------------+----------+
2 rows in set (0.05 sec)
```

Although uncommon, inner joins based on inequalities between columns are also possible. For example, if you altered the products table to include data on the average sales quantity of each product,

```
+-----------+-------------+----------+
| productID | productName | avgSales |
+-----------+-------------+----------+
|         1 | apples      |     1400 |
|         2 | oranges     |     2000 |
|         3 | pineapples  |     2500 |
|         4 | bananas     |     1000 |
+-----------+-------------+----------+
```

you could find out which product's sales were above average with the following query, which uses the > inequality operator to perform the comparison:

```
mysql> SELECT productName, quantity, avgSales FROM products, sales
WHERE products.productID = sales.productID AND sales.quantity >
products.avgSales;
+-------------+----------+----------+
| productName | quantity | avgSales |
+-------------+----------+----------+
| apples      |     3400 |     1400 |
+-------------+----------+----------+
1 row in set (0.05 sec)
```

Word Games

For clarity, MySQL also permits the use of the `INNER JOIN` and `CROSS JOIN` keywords instead of the comma (,) used in those operations. For example, the following two statements both produce a cross join,

```
SELECT countryName, stateName FROM country, state;
SELECT countryName, stateName FROM country CROSS JOIN state;
```

just as the following two statements both create an inner equi-join.

```
SELECT countryName, stateName FROM country, state WHERE state.cid = country.id
SELECT countryName, stateName FROM country INNER JOIN state WHERE state.cid =
country.id;
```

Note, with both these keywords or the , operator, you can join as many tables as you like. The following is perfectly valid SQL:

```
SELECT * from country CROSS JOIN state CROSS JOIN city;
```

In this case, only those records in the `sales` table that have a `quantity` value greater than the corresponding `avgSales` value in the `products` table are included in the final result set.

Outer Joins

You'll observe, from the previous section, that inner joins are symmetrical. To be included in the final result set, rows must match in all joined tables. *Outer joins,* on the other hand, are asymmetrical—all rows from one side of the join are included in the final result set, regardless of whether they match rows on the other side of the join.

Depending on which side of the join is to be preserved, SQL defines a left outer join and a right outer join. In a *left outer join,* all the records from the table on the left side of the join and matching the `WHERE` clause appear in the final result set. In a *right outer join,* all the records matching the `WHERE` clause from the table on the right appear.

To understand when you might need this, consider the following three tables. The first one lists users, the second one lists groups, and the third one lists each user's group memberships. A user might belong to zero, one, or more than one group. A group might contain zero, one, or more than one users. The groups and users tables are linked to each other by the `uid` and `gid` fields in the `users_groups` table.

```
Table "users"              Table "groups"                Table "users_groups":
+------+-------+            +------+-----------+          +------+------+
| uid  | name  |            | gid  | name      |          | uid  | gid  |
+------+-------+            +------+-----------+          +------+------+
|  100 | sue   |            |  501 | authors   |          |   11 |  502 |
|  103 | harry |            |  502 | actors    |          |  107 |  502 |
|  104 | louis |            |  503 | musicians |          |  100 |  503 |
|  107 | sam   |            |  504 | chefs     |          |  110 |  501 |
|  110 | james |            +------+-----------+          |  112 |  501 |
|  111 | mark  |                                          |  100 |  501 |
|  112 | rita  |                                          |  102 |  501 |
+------+-------+                                          |  104 |  502 |
                                                          |  100 |  502 |
                                                          +------+------+
```

Knowing what you know now about inner joins, it's fairly easy to join these three tables to produce a human-readable list of which users belong to which groups:

```
mysql> SELECT users.name, groups.name FROM users, groups, users_groups
WHERE users.uid = users_groups.uid AND groups.gid = users_groups.gid;
+-------+-----------+
| name  | name      |
+-------+-----------+
| sam   | actors    |
| sue   | musicians |
| james | authors   |
| rita  | authors   |
| sue   | authors   |
| louis | actors    |
| sue   | actors    |
+-------+-----------+
7 rows in set (0.00 sec)
```

That's a symmetrical list, but it doesn't tell you anything about the users who don't belong to any group or the groups with no members.

The Left Outer Join

To obtain this missing information, you need to understand how a left outer join works. Consider the following SQL query:

```
SELECT * FROM users LEFT JOIN users_groups ON users.uid = users_groups.uid;
```

In English, this translates to "select all the rows from the left side of the join (table users) and, for each row selected, either display the matching value (the value satisfying the constraints in the ON or USING clause) from the right side (table users_groups) or display a row of NULLs." This kind of join is known as a left join or, sometimes, a left outer join.

Here's the result:

```
mysql> SELECT * FROM users LEFT JOIN users_groups ON users.uid = users_groups.uid;
+------+-------+------+------+
| uid  | name  | gid  | uid  |
+------+-------+------+------+
|  100 | sue   |  503 |  100 |
|  100 | sue   |  501 |  100 |
|  100 | sue   |  502 |  100 |
|  103 | harry | NULL | NULL |
|  104 | louis |  502 |  104 |
|  107 | sam   |  502 |  107 |
|  110 | james |  501 |  110 |
|  111 | mark  | NULL | NULL |
|  112 | rita  |  501 |  112 |
+------+-------+------+------+
9 rows in set (0.05 sec)
```

As you can see, all the records from the left side of the join—users—appear in the final result set. Those that have a corresponding value on the right side—group memberships—have that value displayed. The rest have a row of NULLs.

This kind of join comes in handy when you need to see which values from one table are missing in another table. All you need to do is look for the NULL rows. From a quick glance at the previous example, it's fairly easy to see that users "harry" and "mark" don't belong to any groups because they don't have any records in the users_groups table.

In fact, you can even save your eyeballs the trouble of scanning the output—just let SQL do it for you, with an additional WHERE clause:

```
mysql> SELECT name FROM users LEFT JOIN users_groups ON users.uid =
users_groups.uid WHERE users_groups.gid IS NULL;
+-------+
| name  |
+-------+
| harry |
| mark  |
+-------+
2 rows in set (0.05 sec)
```

This technique also comes in handy when you're looking for corrupted data in your table.

If the field on which the tables are to be joined exist and have the same names in all the joined tables, you can shortcut the ON clause with MySQL's USING clause. Therefore, while you can certainly do this,

```
SELECT * FROM users LEFT JOIN users_groups ON users.uid = users_groups.uid;
```

the following variant is both equivalent and easier to read:

```
SELECT * FROM users LEFT JOIN users_groups USING(uid);
```

The Right Outer Join

Just as there's a left outer join, there's also a right outer join, which does exactly what a left outer join does, but in reverse. Consider the following query and its output, which demonstrate:

```
mysql> SELECT * FROM users_groups RIGHT JOIN groups USING (gid);
+------+------+------+-----------+
| gid  | uid  | gid  | name      |
+------+------+------+-----------+
|  501 |  110 |  501 | authors   |
|  501 |  112 |  501 | authors   |
|  501 |  100 |  501 | authors   |
|  501 |  102 |  501 | authors   |
|  502 |   11 |  502 | actors    |
|  502 |  107 |  502 | actors    |
|  502 |  104 |  502 | actors    |
|  502 |  100 |  502 | actors    |
|  503 |  100 |  503 | musicians |
| NULL | NULL |  504 | chefs     |
+------+------+------+-----------+
10 rows in set (0.00 sec)
```

In English, this translates to "select all the rows from the right side of the join (table groups) and, for each row selected, either display the matching value (the value satisfying the constraints in the ON or USING clause) from the left side (table users_groups) or display a row of NULLs."

Natural Order

When performing a join, MySQL creates a result set by joining tables using the condition specified in the ON or USING clause, and decides which records make it into that result set using the conditional tests specified in the WHERE clause.

Careful thought should, therefore, be given to where your constraints appear in the query string. Moving a constraint from the WHERE clause to the ON clause changes the meaning of the query and, thus, the results. Some records that otherwise never would have made it into the result might be present with non-NULL values on one side and NULLs on the other.

Typically, the ON and USING clauses shouldn't be used to determine which records appear in the final result set. A WHERE clause is more appropriate for this.

Thus, with the previous right outer join, all the groups appear in the final result set. Those that have members (implied by a corresponding value on the left side, in the users_groups table) have that value displayed. The rest have NULL values.

By scanning for the NULL values in the result, it's fairly easy to see which groups have no members.

```
mysql> SELECT * FROM users_groups RIGHT JOIN groups
USING (gid) WHERE uid IS NULL;
+------+------+------+-------+
| gid  | uid  | gid  | name  |
+------+------+------+-------+
| NULL | NULL | 504  | chefs |
+------+------+------+-------+
1 row in set (0.06 sec)
```

A Few More Examples

Let's suppose you want to find out which groups have two or more members. It's possible to do this simply by building on the right join in the previous section. All you need to do is group the records by the gid field and then COUNT() them.

```
mysql> SELECT name FROM users_groups RIGHT JOIN groups
USING (gid) GROUP BY users_groups.gid HAVING COUNT(uid) > 2;
+---------+
| name    |
+---------+
| authors |
| actors  |
+---------+
2 rows in set (0.00 sec)
```

A Matter of Perspective

The terms "left join" and "right join" are interchangeable, depending on where you're standing. A left join can be turned into a right join (and vice versa) simply by altering the order of the tables in the join. To illustrate, consider the following two queries:

```
SELECT * FROM c LEFT JOIN a USING (id);
SELECT * FROM a RIGHT JOIN c USING (id);
```

Translated, both these queries say the same thing: "select all the rows from table c and, for each row selected, either display the matching value from table a or a NULL."

Or, how about finding out the total number of users in each group? This might seem fairly simple—a regular SELECT query with a GROUP BY clause,

```
mysql> SELECT name, COUNT(*) FROM users_groups, groups WHERE
users_groups.gid = groups.gid GROUP BY users_groups.gid;
+-----------+----------+
| name      | COUNT(*) |
+-----------+----------+
| authors   |        4 |
| actors    |        4 |
| musicians |        1 |
+-----------+----------+
3 rows in set (0.55 sec)
```

but that still fails to account for groups with zero members. To ensure that all groups are accounted for, you need to use an outer join, like the following left join,

```
mysql> SELECT name, COUNT(uid) FROM groups LEFT JOIN users_groups
ON users_groups.gid = groups.gid GROUP BY groups.gid;
+-----------+------------+
| name      | COUNT(uid) |
+-----------+------------+
| authors   |          4 |
| actors    |          4 |
| musicians |          1 |
| chefs     |          0 |
+-----------+------------+
4 rows in set (0.00 sec)
```

Do you want to find out if a group has assigned memberships to a user who doesn't exist? Try the following:

```
mysql> SELECT users_groups.uid, users_groups.gid, users.name FROM users
RIGHT JOIN users_groups USING (uid) WHERE name IS NULL;
+------+------+------+
| uid  | gid  | name |
+------+------+------+
|   11 |  502 | NULL |
|  102 |  501 | NULL |
+------+------+------+
2 rows in set (0.00 sec)
```

This is a good example of using the IS NULL test in combination with a join to sniff out corrupt data. In this case, every record from the users_groups table (the right side of the join) is checked against the records in the users table to see if a match is found.

The result set contains two NULLs, indicating that some of the groups have been assigned nonexistent users—a possible indication of data corruption.

Self Joins

In addition to cross, inner, and outer joins, MySQL also supports a fourth type of join, known as a *self join*. This type of join involves joining a table to itself, and it's typically used to extract data from a table whose records contain internal links to each other. Consider the following table:

```
Table "menu"
+----+-------------------------+--------+
| id | label                   | parent |
+----+-------------------------+--------+
|  1 | Services                |      0 |
|  2 | Company                 |      0 |
|  3 | Media Center            |      0 |
|  4 | Your Account            |      0 |
|  5 | Community               |      0 |
|  6 | For Content Publishers  |      1 |
|  7 | For Small Businesses    |      1 |
|  8 | Background              |      2 |
|  9 | Clients                 |      2 |
| 10 | Addresses               |      2 |
| 11 | Jobs                    |      2 |
| 12 | News                    |      2 |
| 13 | Press Releases          |      3 |
| 14 | Media Kit               |      3 |
| 15 | Log In                  |      4 |
| 16 | Columns                 |      5 |
| 17 | Colophon                |     16 |
| 18 | Cut                     |     16 |
| 19 | Boombox                 |     16 |
+----+-------------------------+--------+
```

Different Strokes

Interested in seeing which users belong to which groups? You can't do it with a join (or at least not in a neat fashion). Instead, you can use the GROUP_CONCAT() function, new to MySQL 4.1 Consider the following example, which illustrates this.

```
mysql> SELECT g.name, GROUP_CONCAT(u.name SEPARATOR ',') FROM users
AS u, groups AS g, users_groups AS ug WHERE ug.gid = g.gid AND
ug.uid = u.uid GROUP BY ug.gid;
```

FIGURE 10-1
A hierarchical
menu tree

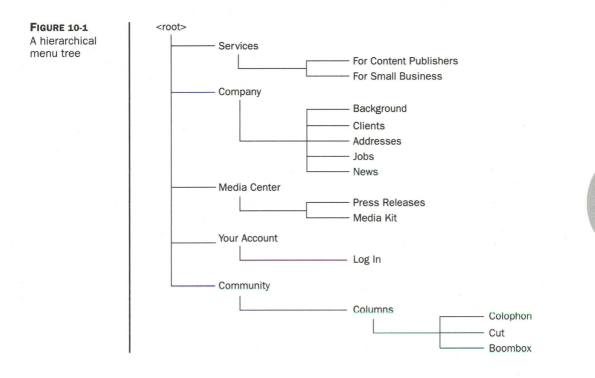

This is a simple menu structure, with each record identifying a unique node in the menu tree. Each record has a unique record ID and also contains a parent ID. These two IDs are used to define the parent-child relationships between the branches of the menu tree. So, if you were to represent the previous data hierarchically, it would look like Figure 10-1. Now, let's suppose you need to display a list of all the nodes in the tree, together with the names of their parents. In other words, a result set like this:

```
+--------------+------------------------+
| parent_label | child_label            |
+--------------+------------------------+
| Services     | For Content Publishers |
| Company      | Background             |
| Your Account | Log In                 |
    ... snip ...
+--------------+------------------------+
```

If you think about it, you'll see there's no easy way to obtain this result set. Because all the data is in a single table, a simple SELECT won't work and neither will one of those complicated outer joins. What's needed here is a self join, which makes it possible to create a second, virtual copy of the first table, and then use a regular inner join to map the two together and get the output required, shown next.

```
mysql> SELECT a.label AS parent_label, b.label AS child_label FROM menu
AS a, menu AS b WHERE a.id = b.parent;
+--------------+------------------------+
| parent_label | child_label            |
+--------------+------------------------+
| Services     | For Content Publishers |
| Services     | For Small Businesses   |
| Company      | Background             |
| Company      | Clients                |
| Company      | Addresses              |
| Company      | Jobs                   |
| Company      | News                   |
| Media Center | Press Releases         |
| Media Center | Media Kit              |
| Your Account | Log In                 |
| Community    | Columns                |
| Columns      | Colophon               |
| Columns      | Cut                    |
| Columns      | Boombox                |
+--------------+------------------------+
16 rows in set (0.33 sec)
```

Most of the magic here lies in the table aliasing. The previous query creates two copies of the menu table and aliases them as a and b, respectively. This results in the following two "virtual" tables.

```
Table "a"

+----+------------------------+--------+
| id | label                  | parent |
+----+------------------------+--------+
|  1 | Services               |      0 |
|  2 | Company                |      0 |
|  3 | Media Center           |      0 |
|  4 | Your Account           |      0 |
|  5 | Community              |      0 |
|  6 | For Content Publishers |      1 |
|  7 | For Small Businesses   |      1 |
|  8 | Background             |      2 |
|  9 | Clients                |      2 |
| 10 | Addresses              |      2 |
| 11 | Jobs                   |      2 |
| 12 | News                   |      2 |
| 13 | Press Releases         |      3 |
| 14 | Media Kit              |      3 |
| 15 | Log In                 |      4 |
| 16 | Columns                |      5 |
| 17 | Colophon               |     16 |
| 18 | Cut                    |     16 |
| 19 | Boombox                |     16 |
+----+------------------------+--------+
```

```
Table "b"

+----+------------------------+--------+
| id | label                  | parent |
+----+------------------------+--------+
|  1 | Services               |      0 |
|  2 | Company                |      0 |
|  3 | Media Center           |      0 |
|  4 | Your Account           |      0 |
|  5 | Community              |      0 |
|  6 | For Content Publishers |      1 |
|  7 | For Small Businesses   |      1 |
|  8 | Background             |      2 |
|  9 | Clients                |      2 |
| 10 | Addresses              |      2 |
| 11 | Jobs                   |      2 |
| 12 | News                   |      2 |
| 13 | Press Releases         |      3 |
| 14 | Media Kit              |      3 |
| 15 | Log In                 |      4 |
| 16 | Columns                |      5 |
| 17 | Colophon               |     16 |
| 18 | Cut                    |     16 |
| 19 | Boombox                |     16 |
+----+------------------------+--------+
```

Once these two tables are created, joining them together is a simple matter—using the node IDs as the common column—and obtaining a list of child and parent labels in the desired format.

Unions

In addition to joins, MySQL 4.0 and better also supports the UNION operator, which is used to combine the output of multiple SELECT queries into a single result set. Most often, this operator is used to add the result sets generated by queries to different tables and create a single table of results.

To illustrate, consider the following tables: one listing stocks on Exchange A and the other listing stocks on Exchange B:

```
Table "exchangeA"                   Table "exchangeB"
+--------+--------+                  +--------+-------+
| symbol | price  |                  | symbol | price |
+--------+--------+                  +--------+-------+
| HDGS   |   6.78 |                  | POYT   | 87.10 |
| TDGB   |  78.44 |                  | DFRM   |  9.43 |
| HDTE   | 123.71 |                  | HTYF   | 89.70 |
| BGHU   |  12.90 |                  | TDGB   | 79.00 |
| HTYF   |  90.10 |                  +--------+-------+
| WERR   |  32.91 |
| YTEM   |  39.65 |
+--------+--------+
```

Now, the UNION operator makes it possible to combine the two previous tables into a single table:

```
mysql> SELECT symbol, price FROM exchangeA
UNION
SELECT symbol, price FROM exchangeB;
+--------+--------+
| symbol | price  |
+--------+--------+
| HDGS   |   6.78 |
| TDGB   |  78.44 |
| HDTE   | 123.71 |
| BGHU   |  12.90 |
| HTYF   |  90.10 |
| WERR   |  32.91 |
| YTEM   |  39.65 |
| POYT   |  87.10 |
| DFRM   |   9.43 |
| HTYF   |  89.70 |
| TDGB   |  79.00 |
+--------+--------+
11 rows in set (0.22 sec)
```

You can use one (or more) WHERE clauses to filter the results of each individual SELECT query, in the normal manner:

```
mysql> SELECT symbol, price FROM exchangeA WHERE price > 35.00
UNION
SELECT symbol, price FROM exchangeB WHERE price BETWEEN 40.00 AND 95.00;
+--------+--------+
| symbol | price  |
+--------+--------+
| TDGB   |  78.44 |
| HDTE   | 123.71 |
| HTYF   |  90.10 |
| YTEM   |  39.65 |
| POYT   |  87.10 |
| HTYF   |  89.70 |
| TDGB   |  79.00 |
+--------+--------+
7 rows in set (0.16 sec)
```

You can combine as many SELECT queries as you like with the UNION operator, however, two basic conditions must be fulfilled. First, the number of fields returned by each SELECT query must be the same. Second, the data types of the fields in each SELECT query must correspond to each other.

The UNION operator automatically eliminates duplicate rows from the composite result set (this behavior is similar to that obtained by adding the DISTINCT keyword to a regular SELECT query). This is clearly illustrated by the first previous example. The result set contains only one record for stocks like HTYF and TDGB, which are represented on both exchanges. If you'd like to see all the records in the UNION, you can have MySQL turn off its automatic filtering of duplicate records by adding the ALL keyword to the UNION operator:

```
mysql> SELECT symbol FROM exchangeA UNION ALL SELECT symbol FROM exchangeB;
+--------+
| symbol |
+--------+
| HDGS   |
| TDGB   |
| HDTE   |
| BGHU   |
| HTYF   |
| WERR   |
| YTEM   |
| POYT   |
| DFRM   |
| HTYF   |
| TDGB   |
+--------+
11 rows in set (0.17 sec)
```

> **Horse Sense**
>
> Adding an ORDER BY clause to individual SELECT queries within the UNION doesn't usually make too much sense because the result set generated by each individual query is never visible to the user; only the final result is visible.

Finally, you can sort the composite result set returned by a UNION operation by adding an ORDER BY clause to the end of your query. However, you need to enclose each of the individual SELECTs in parentheses, so MySQL knows the ORDER BY clause is meant for the final result set and not for the last SELECT in the set. The following example illustrates, sorting the combined list of stock symbols in reverse alphabetical order:

```
mysql> (SELECT symbol FROM exchangeA) UNION (SELECT symbol FROM
exchangeB) ORDER BY symbol DESC;
+--------+
| symbol |
+--------+
| YTEM   |
| WERR   |
| TDGB   |
| POYT   |
| HTYF   |
| HDTE   |
| HDGS   |
| DFRM   |
| BGHU   |
+--------+
9 rows in set (0.22 sec)
```

Summary

This chapter discussed one of MySQL's more powerful data-manipulation features—joins—with examples of how they can be used to create sophisticated and powerful queries.

A join makes it possible to combine two or more tables on the basis of common fields between them, and then to perform SELECT queries on the result. MySQL supports a number of different joins, including the following:

- Cross joins, which involve multiplying tables by each other to create a composite table containing all possible permutations

- Inner joins, which produce only those records for which a match exists in all tables

- Outer joins, which produce all the records from one side of the join and fill in the blanks with NULLs
- Self joins, which involve duplicating a table by means of table aliases, and then connecting the copies to each other by means of other joins
- Unions, which involve adding all the records in the tables involved to create one single, composite sum

Subqueries

Normally, query results are restricted through the addition of a WHERE or HAVING clause, which contains one or more conditional expressions used to filter out irrelevant records from the result set. Most often, these conditional tests use fixed constants—for example, "list all users older than 40" or "show all invoices between January and June," making them easy to write and maintain.

However, a situation often arises when the conditional test used by a particular query depends on the value generated by another query—for example, "list all users older than the average user age" or "show the largest invoice from the smallest group of customers." In all such cases, the results generated by one query depend on the data generated by another, and the use of a constant value in the outer query's conditional test becomes infeasible.

Prior to version 4.1 of MySQL, the only way to address this type of requirement was to perform each query individually, and to use the data from one in the conditional clause of the other. MySQL 4.1 (and better) does away with this by introducing one of the most frequently asked for features on the MySQL mailing lists: subqueries.

Caveat Emptor

Subqueries, although useful, can significantly drain your MySQL RDBMS of performance. This is because, at press time, subqueries are only supported in MySQL 4.1-alpha, and performance is suboptimal on data of any significant size. You are far better off using joins, unions, multitable updates or deletes, and temporary tables instead of subqueries in the current scenario, though one can expect improvements in this aspect of the RDBMS in the future.

What Is a Subquery?

A *subquery* is exactly what is sounds like: a SELECT query that is subordinate to another query. MySQL 4.1 enables you to nest queries within one another, and to use the result set generated by an inner query within an outer one. As a result, instead of executing two (or more) separate queries, you execute a single query containing one (or more) subqueries.

When it encounters such a nested query, MySQL begins with the innermost query and moves outward and upward from it to the outermost (main) query. The result set generated by each query on the journey is assigned to the enclosing parent query, which is, in turn, executed, and its results are further assigned to its parent.

A subquery works just like a regular SELECT query, except that its result set always consists of a single column containing one or more values. A subquery can be used anywhere an expression can be used, it must be enclosed in parentheses, and, like a regular SELECT query, it must contain a field list (as previously noted, this is a single-column list), a FROM clause with one or more table names, and optional WHERE, HAVING, and GROUP BY clauses.

To understand how useful a subquery can be, let's consider a simple example—a fictitious company's accounting database, which consists of the following four tables:

1. The services table: The fictitious company under discussion offers customers a number of outsourced services, each of which is associated with a fee and has a unique service ID. This information is stored in a services table, which looks like this:

```
+-----+------------------+---------+
| sid | sname            | sfee    |
+-----+------------------+---------+
|   1 | Accounting       | 1500.00 |
|   2 | Recruitment      |  500.00 |
|   3 | Data Management  |  300.00 |
|   4 | Administration   |  500.00 |
|   5 | Customer Support | 2500.00 |
|   6 | Security         |  600.00 |
+-----+------------------+---------+
```

2. The clients table: The company also has a list of its current clients stored in a separate clients table. Each client is identified with a unique customer ID.

```
+-----+----------------------------+
| cid | cname                      |
+-----+----------------------------+
| 101 | JV Real Estate             |
| 102 | ABC Talent Agency          |
| 103 | DMW Trading                |
| 104 | Rabbit Foods Inc           |
| 110 | Sharp Eyes Detective Agency |
+-----+----------------------------+
```

3. The branches table: Each customer might have one or more branch offices. The branches table lists the branch offices per customer, together with each branch's location. Each branch has a description, a unique branch ID, and a foreign key reference to the customer ID.

```
+------+-----+--------------------------------+------+
| bid  | cid | bdesc                          | bloc |
+------+-----+--------------------------------+------+
| 1011 | 101 | Corporate HQ                   | CA   |
| 1012 | 101 | Accounting Department          | NY   |
| 1013 | 101 | Customer Grievances Department | KA   |
| 1041 | 104 | Branch Office (East)           | MA   |
| 1042 | 104 | Branch Office (West)           | CA   |
| 1101 | 110 | Head Office                    | CA   |
| 1031 | 103 | N Region HO                    | ME   |
| 1032 | 103 | NE Region HO                   | CT   |
| 1033 | 103 | NW Region HO                   | NY   |
+------+-----+--------------------------------+------+
```

4. The branches_services table: Services supplied to each branch office are listed in this table, which contains pairs of branch IDs and service IDs (foreign keys into the branches and services table, respectively).

```
+------+-----+
| bid  | sid |
+------+-----+
| 1011 |   1 |
| 1011 |   2 |
| 1011 |   3 |
| 1011 |   4 |
| 1012 |   1 |
| 1013 |   5 |
| 1041 |   1 |
| 1041 |   4 |
| 1042 |   1 |
| 1042 |   4 |
| 1101 |   1 |
| 1031 |   2 |
| 1031 |   3 |
| 1031 |   4 |
| 1032 |   3 |
| 1033 |   4 |
+------+-----+
```

Now, you already know that you can obtain a complete list of all the records in a table with a simple SELECT * FROM ... query—for example, a list of all clients:

```
mysql> SELECT * FROM clients;
+-----+------------------------------+
| cid | cname                        |
+-----+------------------------------+
| 101 | JV Real Estate               |
| 102 | ABC Talent Agency            |
| 103 | DMW Trading                  |
| 104 | Rabbit Foods Inc             |
| 110 | Sharp Eyes Detective Agency  |
+-----+------------------------------+
5 rows in set (0.22 sec)
```

You can also attach a join and a WHERE clause to the SELECT statement to filter the list of records down to only those matching specific criteria—for example, a list of all clients with branch offices in California only:

```
mysql> SELECT cname, bdesc, bloc FROM clients, branches WHERE
clients.cid = branches.cid AND branches.bloc = 'CA';
+-----------------------------+-----------------------+------+
| cname                       | bdesc                 | bloc |
+-----------------------------+-----------------------+------+
| JV Real Estate              | Corporate HQ          | CA   |
| Rabbit Foods Inc            | Branch Office (West)  | CA   |
| Sharp Eyes Detective Agency | Head Office           | CA   |
+-----------------------------+-----------------------+------+
3 rows in set (0.00 sec)
```

How about something a little more involved? Let's say we need a list of all the branch offices belonging to Rabbit Foods Inc. Now, you could do this by running two SELECT queries, one after another, to first get the customer ID of Rabbit Foods Inc, and then using that ID (104) in another query to get the list of branch offices linked to that customer,

```
mysql> SELECT cid FROM clients WHERE cname = 'Rabbit Foods Inc';
+-----+
| cid |
+-----+
| 104 |
+-----+
1 row in set (0.17 sec)
mysql> SELECT bdesc FROM branches WHERE cid = 104;
+----------------------+
| bdesc                |
+----------------------+
| Branch Office (East) |
| Branch Office (West) |
+----------------------+
2 rows in set (0.17 sec)
```

by equi-joining the `clients` and `branches` tables,

```
mysql> SELECT bdesc FROM branches, clients WHERE clients.cid =
branches.cid AND clients.cname = 'Rabbit Foods Inc';
+---------------------+
| bdesc               |
+---------------------+
| Branch Office (East) |
| Branch Office (West) |
+---------------------+
2 rows in set (0.22 sec)
```

or with a subquery:

```
mysql> SELECT bdesc FROM branches WHERE cid = (SELECT cid FROM clients
WHERE cname = 'Rabbit Foods Inc');
+---------------------+
| bdesc               |
+---------------------+
| Branch Office (East) |
| Branch Office (West) |
+---------------------+
2 rows in set (0.22 sec)
```

Thus, a subquery makes it possible to combine two or more queries into a single statement, and to use the results of one query in the conditional clause of the other.

A subquery must return a single column of results, or else MySQL will not know how to handle the result set. Consider the following example, which demonstrates by having the subquery return a two-column result set:

```
mysql> SELECT bdesc FROM branches WHERE cid = (SELECT cid, cname FROM
clients WHERE cname = 'Rabbit Foods Inc');
ERROR 1239: Cardinality error (more/less than 1 columns)
```

You can nest subqueries to any depth, so long as the basic rules discussed previously are followed. Consider the following example, which demonstrates by listing the services used by Sharp Eyes Detective Agency:

```
mysql> SELECT sname FROM services WHERE sid = (SELECT sid FROM
branches_services WHERE bid = (SELECT bid FROM branches WHERE cid =
(SELECT cid FROM clients WHERE cname = 'Sharp Eyes Detective Agency')));
+------------+
| sname      |
+------------+
| Accounting |
+------------+
1 row in set (0.28 sec)
```

Types of Subqueries

Subqueries can be used in a number of different ways:

- Within a WHERE or HAVING clause
- With comparison and logical operators
- With the IN membership test
- With the EXISTS Boolean test
- Within a FROM clause
- With joins
- With UPDATE and DELETE queries

The following sections examine each of these aspects in greater detail.

Subqueries and the WHERE/HAVING Clause

MySQL enables you to include subqueries in either a WHERE clause (to constrain the records returned by the enclosing SELECT...WHERE) or a HAVING clause (to constrain the groups created by the enclosing SELECT...GROUP BY). The subquery, which is enclosed in parentheses, can be preceded by comparison and logical operators, the IN operator, or the EXISTS operator.

Subqueries and Comparison Operators

If a subquery produces a single value, you can use MySQL's comparison operators to compare it with the conditional expression specified in the outer query's WHERE or HAVING clause. To demonstrate, let's say you want a list of all those customers with exactly two branch offices. Normally, you would first need to obtain the number of branch offices per customer,

```
mysql> SELECT cid, COUNT(bid) FROM branches GROUP BY cid;
+-----+------------+
| cid | count(bid) |
+-----+------------+
| 101 |          3 |
| 103 |          3 |
| 104 |          2 |
| 110 |          1 |
+-----+------------+
4 rows in set (0.27 sec)
```

and then filter out those with only two offices with a HAVING clause,

```
mysql> SELECT cid, COUNT(bid) FROM branches GROUP BY cid HAVING COUNT(bid) = 2;
+-----+------------+
| cid | count(bid) |
```

```
+-----+-----------+
| 104 |         2 |
+-----+-----------+
1 row in set (0.16 sec)
```

and then hand the client ID over to the `clients` table to get the client name.

```
mysql> SELECT cname FROM clients WHERE cid = 104;
+-----------------+
| cname           |
+-----------------+
| Rabbit Foods Inc |
+-----------------+
1 row in set (0.22 sec)
```

The following subquery can take care of the previous three steps for you in one fell swoop:

```
mysql> SELECT cname FROM clients WHERE cid = (SELECT cid FROM branches
GROUP BY cid HAVING COUNT(bid) = 2);
+-----------------+
| cname           |
+-----------------+
| Rabbit Foods Inc |
+-----------------+
1 row in set (0.28 sec)
```

In this case, the inner query is executed first—this query takes care of grouping the branches by customer ID and counting the number of records (branch offices) in each group. Those customers that have exactly two branch offices can easily be filtered out with a `HAVING` clause, and the corresponding customer IDs returned to the main query. This then maps the IDs into the `customers` table and returns the corresponding customer name.

How about selecting all those customers using the service with the maximum service fee?

```
mysql> SELECT cname, bdesc FROM clients, branches, branches_services,
services WHERE services.sid = branches_services.sid AND clients.cid =
branches.cid AND branches.bid = branches_services.bid AND sfee =
(SELECT MAX(sfee) FROM services);
+----------------+-------------------------------+
| cname          | bdesc                         |
+----------------+-------------------------------+
| JV Real Estate | Customer Grievances Department |
+----------------+-------------------------------+
1 row in set (0.01 sec)
```

NOTE   Even with subqueries, you can use the AND *and* OR *logical operators to add further constraints to a conditional test or the* NOT *logical operator to reverse it.*

You can use a subquery preceded by comparison operators in a HAVING clause as well and, thereby, use it as a filter for the groups created in the parent query. A possible application might involve finding out which sites are using more than 50 percent of all available services:

```
mysql> SELECT bid FROM branches_services GROUP BY bid HAVING COUNT(sid)
> (SELECT COUNT(*) FROM services)/2;
+------+
| bid  |
+------+
| 1011 |
+------+
1 row in set (0.22 sec)
```

You can also add a fast inner join to get the branch name and customer name.

```
mysql> SELECT c.cid, c.cname, b.bid, b.bdesc FROM clients AS c, branches
AS b, branches_services AS bs WHERE c.cid = b.cid AND b.bid = bs.bid GROUP
BY bs.bid HAVING COUNT(bs.sid) > (SELECT COUNT(*) FROM services)/2;
+------+----------------+------+--------------+
| cid  | cname          | bid  | bdesc        |
+------+----------------+------+--------------+
| 101  | JV Real Estate | 1011 | Corporate HQ |
+------+----------------+------+--------------+
1 row in set (0.28 sec)
```

Or, you can use a subquery to get a list of branches using all available services, as the following example demonstrates:

```
mysql> SELECT branches.bid, COUNT(sid) FROM branches, branches_services
WHERE branches.bid = branches_services.bid GROUP BY branches.bid HAVING
COUNT(sid) = (SELECT COUNT(*) FROM services);
Empty set (0.04 sec)
```

If you look at the raw data, you'll see no individual branch offices are using all available services. You can, however, go up one level and check to see if any clients are using all available services across their branch offices, with the following query:

```
mysql> SELECT clients.cname FROM clients, branches, branches_services
WHERE branches.bid = branches_services.bid AND branches.cid = clients.cid
GROUP BY clients.cid HAVING COUNT(sid) = (SELECT COUNT(*) FROM services);
+----------------+
| cname          |
+----------------+
```

```
| JV Real Estate |
+----------------+
1 row in set (0.01 sec)
```

Subqueries and the IN Operator

Comparison operators are appropriate only so long as the subquery returns a result column consisting of a single value. In case the result set returned by a subquery returns a list of values, however, comparison operators must be substituted by the IN operator.

The IN operator makes it possible to test if a particular value exists in the result set, and to perform the outer query if the test is successful. To demonstrate, let's suppose you need a list of all services being used by a particular branch office (say, branch ID 1031). Normally, you would first need to get a list of all service IDs for this branch,

```
mysql> SELECT sid FROM branches_services WHERE bid = 1031;
+-----+
| sid |
+-----+
|   2 |
|   3 |
|   4 |
-----+
3 rows in set (0.16 sec)
```

and then look up each service ID in the services table for the corresponding name.

```
mysql> SELECT sname FROM services WHERE sid = 2;
+-------------+
| sname       |
+-------------+
| Recruitment |
+-------------+
1 row in set (0.28 sec)
mysql> SELECT sname FROM services WHERE sid = 3;
+-----------------+
| sname           |
+-----------------+
| Data Management |
+-----------------+
1 row in set (0.17 sec)
mysql> SELECT sname FROM services WHERE sid = 4;
+-----------------+
| sname           |
+-----------------+
| Administration  |
+-----------------+
1 row in set (0.11 sec)
```

With a subquery and the `IN` test, this becomes redundant.

```
mysql> SELECT sname FROM services WHERE sid IN (SELECT sid FROM
branches_services WHERE bid = 1031);
+-----------------+
| sname           |
+-----------------+
| Recruitment     |
| Data Management |
| Administration  |
+-----------------+
3 rows in set (0.27 sec)
```

In this case, MySQL will select only those records from the `services` table that match the service ID collection returned by the subquery.

A variant of this might be to obtain a list of all branches using the Accounting service (service ID 1):

```
mysql> SELECT bdesc FROM branches WHERE bid IN (SELECT bid FROM
branches_services WHERE sid = 1);
+----------------------+
| bdesc                |
+----------------------+
| Corporate HQ         |
| Accounting Department |
| Branch Office (East) |
| Branch Office (West) |
| Head Office          |
+----------------------+
5 rows in set (0.17 sec)
```

Hmmm…not too useful. What might be nice here is the customer name for each branch as well—something easily accomplished by adding a quick join:

```
mysql> SELECT cname, bdesc FROM branches, clients WHERE branches.bid IN
(SELECT bid FROM branches_services WHERE sid = 1) AND clients.cid =
branches.cid;
+----------------------------+----------------------+
| cname                      | bdesc                |
+----------------------------+----------------------+
| JV Real Estate             | Corporate HQ         |
| JV Real Estate             | Accounting Department |
| Rabbit Foods Inc           | Branch Office (East) |
| Rabbit Foods Inc           | Branch Office (West) |
| Sharp Eyes Detective Agency | Head Office          |
+----------------------------+----------------------+
5 rows in set (0.16 sec)
```

Want just the customer list? Add the DISTINCT keyword,

```
mysql> SELECT DISTINCT cname FROM branches, clients WHERE branches.bid IN (SELECT
bid FROM branches_services WHERE sid = 1) AND clients.cid = branches.cid;
+----------------------------+
| cname                      |
+----------------------------+
| JV Real Estate             |
| Rabbit Foods Inc           |
| Sharp Eyes Detective Agency |
+----------------------------+
3 rows in set (0.17 sec)
```

or simply rewrite the query using the IN test again.

```
mysql> SELECT cname FROM clients WHERE cid IN (select cid from branches
where bid IN (SELECT bid FROM branches_services WHERE sid = 1));
+----------------------------+
| cname                      |
+----------------------------+
| JV Real Estate             |
| Rabbit Foods Inc           |
| Sharp Eyes Detective Agency |
+----------------------------+
3 rows in set (0.22 sec)
```

Let's suppose you need a list of high-value clients—all those with individual branch offices having a monthly bill of $2,000 or more. You can get this information (among other ways) by using a subquery with a join, a GROUP BY clause, and the IN operator.

```
mysql> SELECT cname FROM clients WHERE cid IN (SELECT cid FROM branches
WHERE bid IN (SELECT bid FROM branches_services AS bs, services AS s
WHERE bs.sid = s.sid GROUP BY bid HAVING SUM(sfee) >= 2000));
+------------------+
| cname            |
+------------------+
| JV Real Estate   |
| Rabbit Foods Inc |
+------------------+
2 rows in set (1.32 sec)
```

Subqueries and the EXISTS Operator

The special EXISTS operator can be used to check if a subquery produces any results at all. This makes it possible to conditionally execute the outer query only if the EXISTS test returns true.

Six of One, Half Dozen of the Other

As with comparison operators, you can use the NOT keyword to reverse the results returned by the IN operator—or, in other words, to return those records not matching the result collection generated by a subquery. To demonstrate, we'll rewrite the previous query:

```
SELECT cname FROM clients WHERE cid IN (SELECT cid FROM branches
WHERE bid IN (SELECT bid FROM branches_services AS bs, services AS s
WHERE bs.sid = s.sid GROUP BY bid HAVING SUM(sfee) >= 2000));
```

into the following equivalent, which returns the same result set.

```
SELECT cname FROM clients WHERE cid IN (SELECT cid FROM branches
WHERE bid NOT IN (SELECT bid FROM branches_services AS bs, services
AS s WHERE bs.sid = s.sid GROUP BY bid HAVING SUM(sfee) < 2000));
```

Here's a simple example:

```
mysql> SELECT * FROM clients WHERE EXISTS (SELECT bid FROM branches_services
GROUP BY bid HAVING COUNT(sid) >= 5);
Empty set (0.17 sec)
```

In this case, because the subquery returns an empty result set—no branches are using five or more services—the EXISTS test will return false and the outer query will not execute.

Look what happens when you doctor the previous subquery to return something:

```
mysql> SELECT * FROM clients WHERE EXISTS (SELECT bid FROM
branches_services GROUP BY bid HAVING COUNT(sid) >= 4);
+-----+----------------------------+
| cid | cname                      |
+-----+----------------------------+
| 101 | JV Real Estate             |
| 102 | ABC Talent Agency          |
| 103 | DMW Trading                |
| 104 | Rabbit Foods Inc           |
| 110 | Sharp Eyes Detective Agency |
+-----+----------------------------+
5 rows in set (0.27 sec)
```

In this case, because some branches are using four or more services, the inner query will return a result set consisting of at least one row, the EXISTS test will return true, and the outer query will be executed.

It is important to note that the result set of the previous outer query does *not* list which customers have more than four services. Rather, it's simply a list of all customers, and it's returned only because the inner query generated a result set. In the previous example, the result set generated by the inner query is itself immaterial; we could accomplish the same thing with the following query:

```
mysql> SELECT * FROM clients WHERE EXISTS (SELECT 1);
+-----+---------------------------+
| cid | cname                     |
+-----+---------------------------+
| 101 | JV Real Estate            |
| 102 | ABC Talent Agency         |
| 103 | DMW Trading               |
| 104 | Rabbit Foods Inc          |
| 110 | Sharp Eyes Detective Agency |
+-----+---------------------------+
5 rows in set (0.16 sec)
```

The EXISTS operator is most often used in the context of what SQL gurus like to call *outer references*.

Outer References   Most of the time, if a subquery is going to produce the same result set every time it runs, it makes sense, performance-wise, to run it only once and use the same result set to test every record generated in the main query. However, situations sometimes arise in which a subquery uses a field from the main query in its clause. Such a reference, by a subquery to a field in its enclosing query, is called an *outer reference*, and the corresponding subquery is called a *correlated subquery*, because it's correlated with the result set of one or more of the queries enclosing it.

When an outer reference appears within a subquery, MySQL has to run the subquery once for every record generated by the outer query and, therefore, test the subquery as many times as there are records in the outer query's result set. In such a context, the EXISTS operator comes in handy, to filter out certain records from the final result set.

An example might make this clearer. Consider the following, which reruns the previous example with an outer reference to make the result set more useful:

```
mysql> SELECT bid, bdesc FROM branches WHERE EXISTS (SELECT bid FROM
branches_services WHERE branches.bid = branches_services.bid GROUP BY
bid HAVING COUNT(sid) >= 4);
+------+--------------+
| bid  | bdesc        |
+------+--------------+
| 1011 | Corporate HQ |
+------+--------------+
1 row in set (0.22 sec)
```

> ### Waste Not, Want Not
>
> Outer references highlight an interesting problem in query optimization. In a situation involving an outer reference, MySQL has to rerun the inner query for every record generated by the outer query because the inner query uses a value from the outer query's result set. This implies greater usage of server resources and a potential decrease in performance. For this reason, outer references should be avoided in subqueries as far as possible and alternative methods of combining data (for example, self-joins or unions) should be explored, as they are often less costly in terms of both time and resource usage.
>
> As an example, consider the correlated subquery from the previous example,
>
> ```
> SELECT bid, bdesc FROM branches WHERE EXISTS (SELECT bid FROM branches_services
> WHERE branches.bid = branches_services.bid GROUP BY bid HAVING COUNT(sid) >= 4);
> ```
>
> and the following join, which produces the same result in a more optimal manner:
>
> ```
> SELECT branches.bid, branches.bdesc FROM branches_services, branches WHERE
> branches_services.bid = branches.bid GROUP BY bid HAVING COUNT(sid) >= 4;
> ```

And, if you look at the data, you'll see in fact, only one branch is using four or more services (branch ID 1011).

In this case, because the inner query contains a reference to a field in the outer query, MySQL cannot run the inner query only once (as it usually does). Rather, it has to run it over and over, once for every row in the outer table, substitute the value of the named field from that row in the subquery, and then decide whether to include that outer row in the final result set on the basis of whether the corresponding subquery returns a result set. This is obviously expensive in terms of performance, and outer references should be avoided unless absolutely necessary.

Subqueries and the FROM Clause

You can also use the results generated by a subquery as a table in the FROM clause of an enclosing SELECT statement. To illustrate, let's say you want to know the average number of services each branch office is using. Therefore, the first thing you need to do is group the branches together and count the total number of services each one has,

```
mysql> SELECT bid, COUNT(sid) AS stotal FROM branches_services GROUP BY bid;
+------+--------+
| bid  | stotal |
+------+--------+
| 1011 |      4 |
| 1012 |      1 |
| 1013 |      1 |
| 1031 |      3 |
```

```
| 1032 |       1 |
| 1033 |       1 |
| 1041 |       2 |
| 1042 |       2 |
| 1101 |       1 |
+------+--------+
9 rows in set (0.17 sec)
```

and then calculate the rounded-off average of the per-branch totals. Or, in a subquery,

```
mysql> SELECT AVG(z.stotal) FROM (SELECT bid, COUNT(sid) AS stotal FROM
branches_services GROUP BY bid) AS z;

+---------------+
| avg(z.stotal) |
+---------------+
|        1.7778 |
+---------------+
1 row in set (0.21 sec)
```

Thus, the table of results generated by the inner query is used in the FROM clause of the outer query. Such a table is referred to in SQL jargon as a *derived table*.

Note that when using subquery results in this manner, the result table generated by the inner query must be first aliased to a table name or else MySQL will not know how to refer to columns within it. Look what happens if you rerun the previous query without the table alias:

```
mysql> SELECT AVG(stotal) FROM (SELECT bid, COUNT(bid) AS stotal FROM
branches_services GROUP BY bid);
ERROR 1246: Every derived table must have its own alias
```

Now, let's take this a step further. What if you need to list the branches where the number of services is above this average?

```
mysql> SELECT bid FROM branches_services GROUP BY bid HAVING COUNT(sid) > 1.7778;
+------+
| bid  |
+------+
| 1011 |
| 1031 |
| 1041 |
| 1042 |
+------+
4 rows in set (0.28 sec)
```

To make it truly dynamic, you should combine the two previous queries into the following complex query:

```
mysql> SELECT bid FROM branches_services GROUP BY bid HAVING COUNT(sid)
> (SELECT AVG(z.stotal) FROM (SELECT bid, COUNT(bid) AS stotal FROM
branches_services GROUP BY bid) AS z);
+------+
| bid  |
+------+
| 1011 |
| 1031 |
| 1041 |
| 1042 |
+------+
4 rows in set (0.28 sec)
```

Add another query (and a join) around it to get the customer names corresponding to those branches.

```
mysql> SELECT DISTINCT cname FROM clients, branches, (SELECT bid FROM
branches_services GROUP BY bid HAVING COUNT(sid) > (SELECT AVG(z.stotal)
FROM (SELECT bid, COUNT(bid) AS stotal FROM branches_services GROUP BY bid)
AS z)) AS x WHERE clients.cid = branches.cid AND branches.bid = x.bid;
+------------------+
| cname            |
+------------------+
| JV Real Estate   |
| DMW Trading      |
| Rabbit Foods Inc |
+------------------+
3 rows in set (0.33 sec)
```

Subqueries and Joins

As previous examples in this chapter have demonstrated, subqueries and joins coexist nicely with each other—but why restrict yourself only to inner joins? You can use pretty much any kind of join in combination with a subquery—and, with a little bit of creative thinking, you can use the synergy between the two to perform some sophisticated queries.

For example, you can obtain a list of all clients that have no entry in the branches table with a left join, as in the following:

```
mysql> SELECT cname FROM clients LEFT JOIN branches ON clients.cid =
branches.cid WHERE branches.bid IS NULL;
+------------------+
| cname            |
+------------------+
| ABC Talent Agency |
+------------------+
1 row in set (0.17 sec)
```

In this case, the query will retain all records on the left side of the join—the client list—and insert NULLs for every record on the right side—the branches—which does not meet the join condition. The end result? All clients without a branch office will be marked with a NULL value (which can then be isolated with an IS NULL test).

Another way to do this is to use a right join with a subquery.

```
mysql> SELECT cname FROM clients WHERE cid = (SELECT clients.cid FROM branches
RIGHT JOIN clients ON clients.cid = branches.cid WHERE branches.bid IS NULL);
+--------------------+
| cname              |
+--------------------+
| ABC Talent Agency  |
+--------------------+
1 row in set (0.22 sec)
```

In this case, too, all records on the right side of the join—the clients—will be retained and missing branch office records for each client will be marked with NULLs. The subquery will return the corresponding client IDs, which can then be mapped to the customers table for the human-readable client name.

Interesting to note is that, most of the time, subqueries can be written as joins, and vice versa. Consider the following example, which lists the branch offices using the Recruitment service via a subquery,

```
mysql> SELECT bid FROM branches_services WHERE sid = (SELECT sid FROM
services WHERE sname = 'Recruitment');
+------+
| bid  |
+------+
| 1011 |
| 1031 |
+------+
2 rows in set (0.22 sec)
```

and this next one, which does the same thing using a join.

```
mysql> SELECT bs.bid FROM branches_services AS bs, services AS s WHERE
s.sid = bs.sid AND s.sname = 'Recruitment';
+------+
| bid  |
+------+
| 1011 |
| 1031 |
+------+
2 rows in set (0.17 sec)
```

You can also write subqueries as self-joins, and vice versa. Consider the following example, which lists all the branches in the same location as the corporate headquarters of JV Real Estate using a subquery,

```
mysql> SELECT bid, bdesc, bloc FROM branches WHERE bloc = (SELECT bloc
FROM branches WHERE bid = 1101 AND cid = 110);
+------+----------------------+------+
| bid  | bdesc                | bloc |
+------+----------------------+------+
| 1011 | Corporate HQ         | CA   |
| 1042 | Branch Office (West) | CA   |
| 1101 | Head Office          | CA   |
+------+----------------------+------+
3 rows in set (0.22 sec)
```

and this equivalent, which does the same thing using a self-join.

```
mysql> SELECT table1.bid, table1.bdesc, table1.bloc FROM branches AS
table1, branches AS table2 WHERE table2.bid = 1101 AND table2.cid = 110
AND table1.bloc = table2.bloc;
+------+----------------------+------+
| bid  | bdesc                | bloc |
+------+----------------------+------+
| 1011 | Corporate HQ         | CA   |
| 1042 | Branch Office (West) | CA   |
| 1101 | Head Office          | CA   |
+------+----------------------+------+
3 rows in set (0.16 sec)
```

Subqueries and Other DML Statements

The examples you've seen thus far have only used subqueries in the context of a SELECT statement. However, subqueries can just as easily be used to constrain the UPDATE and DELETE statements.

A simple example can explain this. Let's suppose you want to delete all branches using the Recruitment service (service ID 2). Normally, you'd first look up the branches using that service in the branches_services table,

```
mysql> SELECT * FROM branches_services WHERE sid = 2;
+------+-----+
| bid  | sid |
+------+-----+
| 1011 |   2 |
| 1031 |   2 |
+------+-----+
2 rows in set (0.16 sec)
```

> **Cutting Query Flab**
> MySQL is better at optimizing joins than subqueries, so if you find the load
> averages on your MySQL server hitting unacceptably high levels, examine your
> application code and try rewriting your subqueries as joins or sequences of joins.

and then delete the corresponding branch records from the branches table.

```
mysql> DELETE FROM branches WHERE bid = 1011;
Query OK, 1 row affected (0.00 sec)
mysql> DELETE FROM branches WHERE bid = 1031;
Query OK, 1 row affected (0.00 sec)
```

You can combine the two previous operations into a single one with a subquery, as
in the following:

```
mysql> DELETE FROM branches WHERE bid IN (SELECT bid FROM
branches_services WHERE sid = 2);
Query OK, 2 rows affected (0.00 sec)
```

How about deleting all those customers, any of whose branch offices generate service
fee revenues of $500 or less?

```
mysql> DELETE FROM clients WHERE cid IN (SELECT DISTINCT b.cid FROM
branches AS b, branches_services AS bs, services AS s WHERE b.bid =
bs.bid AND bs.sid = s.sid GROUP BY bs.bid HAVING SUM(sfee) <= 500);
Query OK, 1 row affected (0.28 sec)
```

In this case, the inner query groups the various branches by branch ID, calculates
the total service generated by each branch for all the services its using, and lists those
records where the total is less than or equal to $500. The corresponding customer IDs
are then used by the outer query to perform a DELETE operation on the clients table.

You can use subqueries in an UPDATE statement in much the same manner. Let's
suppose you wanted to find out which services are in use in three or more branch offices,

```
mysql> SELECT sid FROM branches_services GROUP BY sid HAVING COUNT(bid) >= 3;
+-----+
| sid |
+-----+
|   1 |
|   3 |
|   4 |
+-----+
3 rows in set (0.11 sec)
```

and then increase the fee for those services by 25 percent.

```
mysql> UPDATE services SET sfee = sfee + (sfee * 0.25) WHERE sid = 1;
Query OK, 1 row affected (0.05 sec)
Rows matched: 1  Changed: 1  Warnings: 0
mysql> UPDATE services SET sfee = sfee + (sfee * 0.25) WHERE sid = 3;
Query OK, 1 row affected (0.05 sec)
Rows matched: 1  Changed: 1  Warnings: 0
mysql> UPDATE services SET sfee = sfee + (sfee * 0.25) WHERE sid = 4;
Query OK, 1 row affected (0.05 sec)
Rows matched: 1  Changed: 1  Warnings: 0
```

With a subquery, you could combine the previous operations into the following statement:

```
mysql> UPDATE services SET sfee = sfee + (sfee * 0.25) WHERE sid IN
(SELECT sid FROM branches_services GROUP BY sid HAVING COUNT(bid) >= 3);
Query OK, 3 rows affected (0.22 sec)
Rows matched: 3  Changed: 3  Warnings: 0
```

Let's take another example. Suppose you want to have all branches located in California use the Security service instead of the Administration service. With a subquery, this is a piece of cake!

```
mysql> UPDATE branches_services SET sid = 6 WHERE sid = 4 AND bid IN
(SELECT bid FROM branches WHERE bloc = 'CA');
Query OK, 2 rows affected (0.00 sec)
Rows matched: 2  Changed: 2  Warnings: 0
```

In this case, the inner query takes care of isolating only those branch IDs in California and provides this list to the outer query, which updates the corresponding records in the branches_services table. Notice how the selection criteria for the rows to be UPDATE-d is split: the inner query lists the records for California, the outer one further winnows it down to those using only the "Administration" service.

If you want to obfuscate even more, add subqueries to the various SET clauses as well—this is perfectly legal SQL and it works in much the same manner as subqueries in a WHERE clause:

```
mysql> UPDATE branches_services SET sid = (SELECT sid FROM services WHERE
sname =  'Security') WHERE sid = (SELECT sid FROM services WHERE sname =
'Administration') AND bid IN (SELECT bid FROM branches WHERE bloc = 'CA');
Query OK, 2 rows affected (0.00 sec)
Rows matched: 2  Changed: 2  Warnings: 0
```

Circular References in `UPDATE` and `DELETE` Statements

Now, let's assume that, for the system discussed previously to be in sync, at least one branch office must exist in the `branches` table for every customer. The quickest way to verify this is with a left join and an eyeball check for NULL values.

```
mysql> SELECT clients.cid, clients.cname, branches.bid, branches.bdesc FROM
clients LEFT JOIN branches USING (cid);
+-----+----------------------------+------+-------------------------------+
| cid | cname                      | bid  | bdesc                         |
+-----+----------------------------+------+-------------------------------+
| 101 | JV Real Estate             | 1011 | Corporate HQ                  |
| 101 | JV Real Estate             | 1012 | Accounting Department         |
| 101 | JV Real Estate             | 1013 | Customer Grievances Department|
| 102 | ABC Talent Agency          | NULL | NULL                          |
| 103 | DMW Trading                | 1031 | N Region HO                   |
| 103 | DMW Trading                | 1032 | NE Region HO                  |
| 103 | DMW Trading                | 1033 | NW Region HO                  |
| 104 | Rabbit Foods Inc           | 1041 | Branch Office (East)          |
| 104 | Rabbit Foods Inc           | 1042 | Branch Office (West)          |
| 110 | Sharp Eyes Detective Agency| 1101 | Head Office                   |
+-----+----------------------------+------+-------------------------------+
10 rows in set (0.00 sec)
```

It's fairly obvious that the system is not in a consistent state—there is a record for the customer ABC Talent Agency, but no corresponding record for one or more branch offices. To get things back into a consistent state, the offending record must be deleted from the `clients` table via the customer ID.

```
mysql> DELETE FROM clients WHERE cid = 102;
```

You might think, based on the previous examples in this section, that the two previous steps can easily be combined into one, using the following subquery...

```
mysql> DELETE FROM clients WHERE cid = (SELECT clients.cid FROM clients LEFT
JOIN branches USING (cid) WHERE bid IS NULL);
ERROR 1093: You can't specify target table 'clients' for update in FROM clause
```

...but you'd be wrong!

MySQL won't let you delete or update a table's data if you're simultaneously reading that same data with a subquery, as doing so raises the possibility that your subquery might reference rows that have already been deleted or altered. Therefore, the table named in an outer `DELETE` or `UPDATE` DML statement cannot appear in the `FROM` clause of an inner subquery (this is what MySQL more tersely said in its previous error message).

A more appropriate way to perform the previous task would be to use an EXISTS test with an outer reference, as in the following:

```
mysql> DELETE FROM clients WHERE NOT EXISTS (SELECT * FROM branches WHERE
branches.cid = clients.cid);
Query OK, 1 row affected (0.11 sec)
```

Summary

Subqueries are nested SELECT queries whose results serve as filters for the queries enclosing them. Subqueries can appear anywhere an expression can and they can be used in a number of places, including within WHERE or HAVING clauses, with comparison or logical operators, with the IN membership test, with the EXISTS operator, within the FROM clause of an enclosing query, and within other DML commands like UPDATE and DELETE.

However, this convenience comes at a price. Incorrectly written subqueries can result in massive load increases on your RDBMS and can reduce performance drastically, negating the overall gains provided by this feature. For this reason, you're strongly advised always to explore alternative methods of obtaining the data you need, including joins, unions, and other SQL constructs to ensure optimal performance of your application and minimal resource wastage on the RDBMS.

Transactions

Usually, MySQL queries are executed independently of each other, with little regard for what had gone before or what has yet to come. A series of INSERT or UPDATE statements, for example, is executed sequentially, regardless of whether any of the queries in the series fail or generate errors. This is because MySQL treats each query as a self-contained unit, bearing no relationship to other queries before or after it.

Most often, this stateless approach works well, especially in the case of small- and medium-sized applications associated with simple business logic. In more complex situations, however, where the actions carried out by a set of SQL statements are all-or-nothing propositions, this approach is often found wanting. In such situations, not only are the queries in a sequence dependent on each other (and, thus, impossible to execute in total isolation), but also a failure in one query of the sequence means that the entire sequence should be aborted and the changes made by previous queries in the same sequence be reversed, so as to return the database to its earlier state.

Because the stateless model treats each query independently, with no knowledge or assumptions about its predecessors, it cannot adequately handle such all-or-nothing situations. Therefore, an alternative model, one that makes it possible to group a series of SQL statements into a single unit, or transaction, was devised to support this requirement.

Commercial relational database management systems (RDBMSs), such as Oracle and Microsoft SQL Server, have supported the transaction model for a while, as have open-source alternatives like PostgreSQL. Until recently, MySQL did not feature on this list. However, beginning with a primitive implementation in version 3.23 and a much improved architecture in version 4.*x*, MySQL today includes table handlers that manage transactions in much the same manner as other commercial RDBMS products.

This chapter takes a closer look at the MySQL transaction model, explaining what it is, how it works, and how it helps in building more robust applications. This chapter also looks at alternative approaches to the native transaction model, explaining how it is possible to achieve similar functionality through the use of MySQL table locks with the older nontransactional table types.

What Is a Transaction?

In the SQL context, a transaction consists of one or more SQL statements that operate as a single unit. Each SQL statement in such a unit is dependent on the others, and the unit as a whole is indivisible. If one statement in the unit does not complete successfully, the entire unit will be rolled back, and all the affected data will be returned to the state it was in before the transaction was started. Thus, a transaction is said to be successful only if all the individual statements within it are executed successfully.

You might find it hard to think of situations where this all-for-one and one-for-all approach would be useful. In reality, transactions abound all around us—in bank transfers, stock trades, web-based shopping carts, inventory control—the list goes on and on. In all these cases, the success of the transaction depends on a number of interdependent actions executing successfully and in harmony with each other. A failure in any of them must cancel the transaction and return the system back to its earlier, pretransaction state.

The best way to understand this is with a simple example. Consider a stock trade on any stock exchange (see Figure 12-1), in which Trader A sells 400 shares in ACME Corp. to Trader B.

Somewhere behind the hullabaloo of the trading ring is a complex database system tracking all such deals. In this system, a trade such as the previous one is deemed complete only when Trader A's account is debited by 400 ACME Corp. shares and

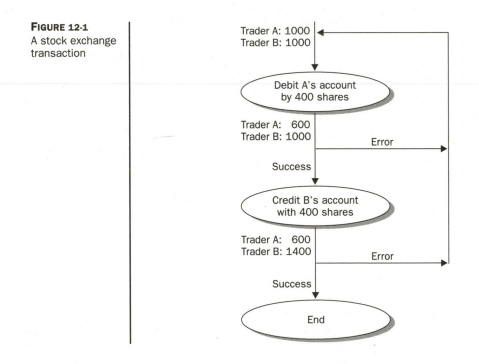

FIGURE 12-1
A stock exchange transaction

Trader B's account is simultaneously credited with those shares. If either of the previous two steps fail, then the exchange would have the unenviable situation of 400 ACME Corp. shares floating around the system with no owner . . . not very pleasant, we're sure you'd agree.

Thus, the transfer of 400 Acme Corp. shares from Trader A to Trader B in the previous example can be considered a transaction—a single unit of work that internally encompasses several SQL statements (delete 400 shares from Trader A's account records, add 400 shares to Trader B's records, perform commission calculations for both traders, and save the changes). In keeping with the previous transaction definition, all these statements should execute successfully. If any one of them fails, the transaction should be reversed, so the system goes back to its earlier, stable state. Or, to put it another way, at no point in time should the ownership of the 400 shares be ambiguous.

Let's take another example: adding a new employee to the rolls of a company (see Figure 12-2). The process here would consist of three basic steps—creating a record for the employee in the employee database, assigning the employee to a department, and setting up the employee's payroll structure. If any of these three steps were to fail—if, for example, the employee ID assigned to the new recruit was already in use by someone else or the values entered into the payroll system were too large—the system would need to cancel all the changes made to the system before the failure by deleting all traces of the incomplete record to avoid inconsistencies and flawed calculations at a later date.

The three previous tasks constitute a single transaction. A failure in any one of them should cause the entire transaction to be cancelled and the system returned to its previous state.

FIGURE 12-2
A transaction involving multiple interdependent actions

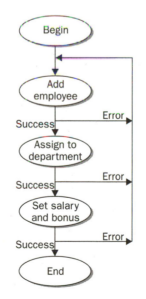

Transactions and the ACID Properties

The MySQL transaction system fully satisfies the ACID tests for transaction safety via its InnoDB and BDB table types. Older table types, such as the MyISAM type, do not support transactions. Transactions in such systems, therefore, can only be implemented through the use of explicit table locks (details on this procedure are available in the section "Table Locks as a Substitute for Transactions").

The term "ACID" is an acronym, stating four properties that every transactional RDBMS must comply with. To qualify for ACID-compliance, an RDBMS must exhibit the following characteristics: atomicity, consistency, isolation, and durability, which are discussed in detail next.

Atomicity

Atomicity means every transaction must be treated as an indivisible unit. Given a transaction consisting of two or more tasks, all the statements within it must be successful for the transaction to be considered successful. In the event of a transaction failure, the system should be returned to its pretransaction state.

With reference to the previous stock exchange example, atomicity means the sale of shares by Trader A and the purchase of the same by Trader B cannot occur independently of each other, and both must take place for the transaction to be considered complete. Similarly, in the recruitment example, atomicity would imply it would not be possible for an employee to be added to the employee database without also creating corresponding payroll and department records.

Atomic execution is an all-or-nothing proposition. In an atomic operation, if any of the statements in the transaction fail, all the preceding statements are rolled back to ensure the integrity of the database is unaffected. This is particularly important in mission-critical, real-world applications (like financial systems) that perform data entry or updates and require a high degree of safety from undetected data loss.

Consistency

Consistency exists when every transaction leaves the system in a consistent state, regardless of whether the transaction completes successfully or fails midway. With reference to the previous stock exchange example, consistency means every debit from a seller's account results in a corresponding and equal credit to a buyer's account. If a transaction reduces Trader A's account by 400 shares, but only credits 300 shares to Trader B's account, the consistency constraint will be violated because the total number of shares in the system changes. Similarly, the consistency property would ensure that if an employee was removed from the system, all data related to that employee, including payroll data and group memberships, would also be deleted.

In MySQL, consistency is primarily handled by MySQL's logging mechanisms, which record all changes to the database and provide an audit trail for transaction recovery. If the system goes down in the middle of a transaction, the MySQL recovery process will use these logs to discover whether the transaction was successfully completed and roll it back if required. The consistency property thus ensures the database never reflects a partially completed transaction at any time.

Isolation

Isolation implies every transaction occurs in its own space, isolated from other transactions that might be occurring in the system, and the results of a transaction are visible only once it has been fully executed. Even though multiple transactions could be occurring simultaneously in such a system, the isolation principle ensures the effects of a particular transaction are not visible until the transaction is fully complete. In the previous stock exchange example, for instance, isolation implies the transaction between the two traders is independent of all other transactions on the exchange and its result is visible to the public at large only once it has been completed.

This is particularly important when the system supports multiple simultaneous users and connections (as MySQL does). Systems that do not conform to this fundamental principle can cause massive data corruption, as the integrity of each transaction's individual space will be quickly violated by other competing, often conflicting, transactions.

In reality, of course, the only way to obtain absolute isolation is to ensure that only a single user can access the database at any time. This is not a practical solution at all when dealing with a multiuser RDBMS like MySQL. Instead, most transactional systems use either page-level locking or row-level locking to isolate the changes made by different transactions from each other, at some cost in performance. MySQL's BDB table handler, for example, uses page-level locking to safely handle multiple simultaneous transactions, while the InnoDB table handler uses more fine-grained row-level locking (see the sidebar entitled "Locking Up" for more information on the locking levels used by different table types).

Durability

Durability, which means changes from a committed transaction persist even if the system crashes, comes into play when a transaction has completed and the logs have been updated in the database. Most RDBMS products ensure data durability by keeping a log of all activity that alters data in the database in any way. This database log keeps track of any and all updates made to tables, queries, reports, and so on.

In the event of a system crash or a corruption of the data storage media, the system is able to recover to the last successful update on restart and reflect the changes carried out by transactions that were still in progress when it went down through the use of its logs. In the context of the previous share transfer example , durability means that once the transfer of shares from Trader A to Trader B has completed successfully, the system should reflect that state even if a system failure takes place subsequently.

MySQL implements durability by maintaining a binary transaction log file that tracks changes to the system during the course of a transaction. In the event of a hardware failure or abrupt system shutdown, recovering lost data is a relatively straightforward task by using the last backup in combination with the log when the system restarts.

By default, InnoDB tables are 100 percent durable (in other words, all transactions committed to the system before the crash are liable to be rolled back during the recovery process). MyISAM tables offer partial durability—all changes committed to the system prior to the last FLUSH TABLES command are guaranteed to be saved to disk.

Locking Up

MySQL supports a number of different table types, and the locking mechanisms available differ from type to type. Therefore, a clear understanding of the different levels of locking available is essential to implementing a pseudotransaction environment with MySQL's nontransactional tables.

- **Table locks**   The entire table is locked by a client for a particular kind of access. Depending on the type of lock, other clients will not be allowed to insert records into the table and could even be restricted from reading data from it.

- **Page locks**   MySQL will lock a certain number of rows (called a *page*) from the table. The locked rows are only available to the thread initiating the lock. If another thread wants to write to data in these rows, it must wait until the lock is released. Rows in other pages, however, remain available for use.

- **Row locks**   Row-level locks offers finer control over the locking process than either table-level locks or page-level locks. In this case, only the rows that are being used by the thread are locked. All other rows in the table are available to other threads. In multiuser environments, row-level locking reduces conflicts between threads, making it possible for multiple users to read and even write to the same table simultaneously. This flexibility must be balanced, however, against the fact that it also has the highest performance overhead of the three locking levels.

The MyISAM table type supports only table-level locking, which offers performance benefits over row- and page-level locking in situations involving a larger number of reads than writes. The BDB table type supports page-level locking, while the InnoDB table type automatically performs row-level locking in transactions.

You can read more about locking methods in the MySQL manual, at `http://www.mysql.com/doc/en/Locking_methods.html`.

Life Cycle of a Transaction

Now that you know what a transaction is, let's look at how it works. MySQL comes with a number of commands related to beginning, ending, and rolling back transactions. This section examines them in detail.

Note, MySQL supports transactions natively via its InnoDB and BDB table types, which means the following commands can only be used with those table types. The default type for new tables in MySQL is MyISAM, but you can tell MySQL you want an InnoDB table by adding the optional TYPE clause to your CREATE TABLE command, as in the following:

```
CREATE TABLE table-name (field-definitions) TYPE = INNODB;
```

For existing tables, you can change the table type on the fly through the ALTER TABLE command, simply by specifying a new TYPE clause, as illustrated in the following:

```
ALTER TABLE table-name TYPE = INNODB;
```

> **Better Safe Than Sorry**
>
> The ALTER TABLE command works by backing up the data in the table, erasing it, re-creating it with the specified modifications, and then reinserting the backed-up records. A failure in any of these steps could result in the loss or corruption of your data. Therefore, a good idea is always to create a table backup prior to using the ALTER TABLE command. See Chapter 8 for more information on the ALTER TABLE command.

To initiate a transaction and tell MySQL that all subsequent SQL statements should be considered a single unit, MySQL offers the START TRANSACTION command to mark the beginning of a transaction.

```
mysql> START TRANSACTION;
Query OK, 0 rows affected (0.00 sec)
```

You can also use the BEGIN or BEGIN WORK commands to initiate a transaction. Typically, the START TRANSACTION command is followed by the SQL statements that make up the transaction. Let's suppose the transaction here consists of adding a new employee to the system and the steps involved include creating a record for the employee, assigning the employee to a department, and specifying the employee's salary and bonuses.

```
mysql> INSERT INTO employees (ename, enationality)
VALUES ('Tim Jonez', 'US');
Query OK, 1 row affected (0.13 sec)
mysql> INSERT INTO departments (eid, dept)
VALUES (LAST_INSERT_ID(), 'Accounts');
Query OK, 1 row affected (0.03 sec)
mysql> INSERT INTO payroll (eid, pbasic, pbonus)
VALUES (LAST_INSERT_ID(), 36000.00, 2500.00);
Query OK, 1 row affected (0.02 sec)
```

You can now take a look at these tables to see if the data has been correctly entered with a quick SELECT query:

```
mysql> SELECT * FROM employees;
+-----+-----------+--------------+
| eid | ename     | enationality |
+-----+-----------+--------------+
|   1 | Tim Jonez | US           |
+-----+-----------+--------------+
1 row in set (0.00 sec)
mysql> SELECT * FROM payroll;
+-----+----------+---------+
| eid | pbasic   | pbonus  |
+-----+----------+---------+
|   1 | 36000.00 | 2500.00 |
+-----+----------+---------+
1 row in set (0.05 sec)
```

Once the SQL statements have all been executed, you can either save the entire transaction to disk with the COMMIT command or undo all the changes made with the ROLLBACK command. Let's try the second option first:

```
mysql> ROLLBACK;
Query OK, 0 rows affected (0.02 sec)
```

How about verifying the changes have, in fact, been reversed?

```
mysql> SELECT * FROM employees;
Empty set (0.01 sec)
mysql> SELECT * FROM departments;
Empty set (0.00 sec)
mysql> SELECT * FROM payroll;
Empty set (0.00 sec)
```

If your transaction involves changes to both transactional and non-transactional tables, the portion of the transaction dealing with nontransactional tables cannot be reversed with a ROLLBACK command. In such a situation, MySQL will return an error notifying you of an incomplete rollback, as in the following:

```
mysql> ROLLBACK;
ERROR 1196: Some non-transactional changed tables couldn't be rolled back
```

Now, let's perform the transaction again, this time with a view to saving it.

```
mysql> START TRANSACTION;
Query OK, 0 rows affected (0.00 sec)
mysql> INSERT INTO employees (ename, enationality) VALUES ('Tim Jonez', 'US');
Query OK, 1 row affected (0.13 sec)
mysql> INSERT INTO departments (eid, dept) VALUES (LAST_INSERT_ID(), 'Accounts');
Query OK, 1 row affected (0.03 sec)
mysql> INSERT INTO payroll (eid, pbasic, pbonus) VALUES (LAST_INSERT_ID(), 36000.00, 2500.00);
Query OK, 1 row affected (0.02 sec)
```

An interesting experiment to perform at this point is to open another client connection to the server and check if the previous SQL queries have resulted in any changes to the database.

```
mysql> SELECT * FROM employees;
Empty set (0.06 sec)
mysql> SELECT * FROM departments;
Empty set (0.03 sec)
mysql> SELECT * FROM payroll;
Empty set (0.04 sec)
```

In case you're wondering why the records inserted in one client session don't appear in the other, don't worry too much about it—you've just seen an example of isolation in action. As noted in the preceding section, isolation means the results of a transaction become visible only when the transaction is successfully committed. Because the transaction is still in progress and has not yet been saved to disk, it is effectively invisible to any other user of the same database (if visibility between transactions is desired, it can be attained by setting a different transaction isolation level—this is discussed in detail in the section "Transaction Isolation Levels").

Once you're satisfied the data has been inserted correctly, you can use the COMMIT command to save your changes to the various tables:

```
mysql> COMMIT;
Query OK, 0 rows affected (0.01 sec)
```

The COMMIT command marks the end of the transaction block. Once the transaction has been committed to the database, the committed data will become visible to other client sessions.

Figure 12-3 summarizes the life cycle of a transaction with a simple flow diagram.

It is important to note that MySQL uses a flat transaction model: nested transactions are not permitted and beginning a second transaction within the first one with START TRANSACTION or BEGIN automatically commits the previous one. In a similar manner, many other MySQL commands will implicitly perform a COMMIT when invoked—here's a brief list:

- DROP DATABASE/DROP TABLE
- CREATE INDEX/DROP INDEX
- ALTER TABLE/RENAME TABLE
- LOCK TABLES/UNLOCK TABLES
- SET AUTOCOMMIT = 1

FIGURE 12-3
Transaction life cycle

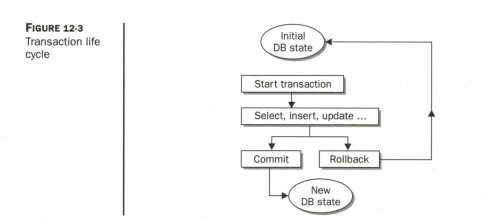

> **Step by Step**
>
> Newer versions of MySQL include support for *savepoints,* which enable you to
> place markers at critical points during a transaction and roll the transaction back
> partially if needed. This can come in handy when dealing with long transactions—
> if an error occurs, a savepoint lets you reverse only the section of the transaction
> that generated the error, rather than the entire transaction.
>
> Savepoints are still under development, so you should refer to the MySQL
> manual for the latest news on this feature.

Controlling Transactional Behavior

MySQL offers two variables to control transactional behavior—the AUTOCOMMIT
variable and the TRANSACTION ISOLATION LEVEL variable. The following sections
examine these in greater detail.

Automatic Commits

By default, MySQL implicitly commits the results of every SQL query to the database
once it is executed. This is referred to as *autocommit mode* and is the reason you needn't
begin every MySQL session with a START TRANSACTION statement or end it with a
COMMIT or ROLLBACK. Or, to put it another way, MySQL treats every query as a
single-statement transaction.

This default behavior can be modified via the special AUTOCOMMIT variable, which
controls MySQL's autocommit mode. The following snippet demonstrates, by turning off
the MySQL behavior of internally issuing a COMMIT command after each SQL interaction:

```
mysql> SET AUTOCOMMIT = 0;
Query OK, 0 rows affected (0.02 sec)
```

Subsequent to this, any update to a table will not be saved to the database until
an explicit COMMIT command is issued. In fact, if you terminate your MySQL session
without issuing a COMMIT, the database will automatically fire a ROLLBACK to undo all
the modifications in the sessions, thereby negating all the work done during the session.
The following example demonstrates this:

```
mysql> SET AUTOCOMMIT = 0;
Query OK, 0 rows affected (0.00 sec)
mysql> SELECT * FROM gallery;
Empty set (0.00 sec)
mysql> INSERT INTO gallery (id, filename, dsc)
VALUES (52, 'dog.gif', 'Me and my pooch');
Query OK, 1 row affected (0.00 sec)
mysql> exit
Bye
```

> **Speed Bump**
> A frequent cause of poor performance in MySQL is executing a large number of small updates on one connection with autocommit mode enabled.

Now start a new session.

```
[user@host] $ mysql
Welcome to the MySQL monitor.  Commands end with ; or \g.
Your MySQL connection id is 14 to server version: 4.0.12-max-debug
mysql> SELECT * FROM gallery;
Empty set (0.01 sec)
```

You can always turn autocommit mode back on by resetting the AUTOCOMMIT variable to its initial state.

```
mysql> SET AUTOCOMMIT = 1;
Query OK, 0 rows affected (0.00 sec)
```

When you switch autocommit mode back on, MySQL will automatically issue a COMMIT and save all open transactions.

You can obtain the current value of the AUTOCOMMIT variable at any time with a quick SELECT, as in the following:

```
mysql> SELECT @@autocommit;
+--------------+
| @@autocommit |
+--------------+
|            0 |
+--------------+
1 row in set (0.00 sec)
```

The AUTOCOMMIT variable is a session variable and always defaults to 1 when a new client session begins. At press time, no way exists to set it to a default value of 0 for new client sessions. You can refer to Chapter 13 for more information on modifying and viewing server variables.

> **The Wrong Type**
> The AUTOCOMMIT variable only affects transactional table types like InnoDB. When dealing with nontransactional table types like MyISAM, the AUTOCOMMIT variable has no impact and changes to such tables are always saved immediately.

Transaction Isolation Levels

As noted earlier, one of the most important properties of a transaction-capable RDBMS is its capability to "isolate" the different sessions in progress at any given instance on the server. In a single-user environment, this property is largely irrelevant for obvious reasons: there is nothing to isolate because usually only a single session is active at any time. In more complex real-world scenarios, however, it is unlikely this assumption will remain true.

In a multiuser environment, many RDBMS sessions will usually be active at any given time. In the stock trading example discussed previously, for instance, it is unlikely that only a single trade will be taking place at a particular point in time. Far more likely is that hundreds of trades will occur simultaneously. In such a situation, it is essential that the RDBMS isolate transactions so they do not interfere with each other, while simultaneously ensuring the database's performance does not suffer as a result.

To understand the importance of isolation, considering what would happen if it wasn't enforced is worthwhile. In the absence of transaction isolation, different SELECT statements would retrieve different results within the context of the same transaction because the underlying data was modified by other transactions in the interim. This would create inconsistency and make it difficult to trust a particular result set or use it as the basis for calculations with any degree of confidence. Isolation thus imposes a degree of insulation between transactions, guaranteeing that an application only sees consistent data within the scope of a transaction.

MySQL provides the following four isolation levels in accordance with the ANSI/ISO SQL specification:

- SERIALIZABLE

- REPEATABLE READ

- READ COMMITTED

- READ UNCOMMITTED

These transaction isolation levels determine the degree to which other transactions can "see" inside an in-progress transaction and are arranged in hierarchical order, beginning with the most secure and gradually moving downward to the least secure (and most problematic) level. These isolation levels can be manipulated with the TRANSACTION ISOLATION LEVEL variable, which is discussed in greater detail in the section "Modifying The Transaction Isolation Level."

Let's now look at what each of the isolation levels does.

SERIALIZABLE

This SERIALIZABLE isolation level offers the maximum amount of insulation between transactions, by treating concurrent transactions as though they were executing sequentially, one after the other. Figure 12-4 illustrates.

Here, trader A is selling 400 shares to trader B. To perform this transaction, the system must reduce trader A's account by 400 shares and credit those 400 shares to trader B's account. Assuming both traders are at par with 1000 shares each at the beginning

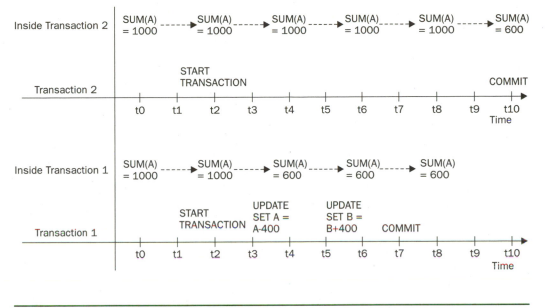

FIGURE 12-4 The SERIALIZABLE Isolation Level

of the transaction, a successful transaction will conclude with trader A's account holding 600 shares and trader B's account holding 1400 shares.

In this case, because the transaction isolation level is maximum, the second transaction will only see the changes in the account balances of traders A and B after its own transaction is complete. Updates to existing rows or the addition of new rows will not be visible during the transaction. This is, in fact, the way most users expect transactions to work. However, it comes at a price: MySQL will take a performance hit if every transaction runs at this isolation level because of the large amount of resources required to keep the various transactions from seeing each other at any given instant.

REPEATABLE READ

For applications that are willing to compromise a little on security for better performance, MySQL offers the REPEATABLE READ isolation level. At this level, transactions are not treated serially. However, a transaction will not see the changes carried out by concurrent transactions until it itself has concluded.

This probably sounds a lot like the SERIALIZABLE isolation level. By and large, it is—with one important difference: although a transaction cannot see changes made by other concurrent transactions while it is still executing, it can see new records (that have been added to the database by other transactions). This is sometimes called a *phantom read* or a *phantom insert* because it takes place when a transaction commits a new record to the database via an INSERT statement. Other transactions in progress at the same time will suddenly see this new phantom row when they perform a SELECT query.

This can cause problems if those transactions are, say, performing calculations or using aggregate functions on the records in the table—the sudden appearance of a new row will produce unexpected and inconsistent results.

Figure 12-5 demonstrates what a phantom read looks like.

In this case, the second transaction can see the new row added by the first transaction. This leads to a sudden change in the data seen by the second transaction while it is still in progress: between time points t2 and t4, the total shares in trader A's account goes up by 500, even though the transaction initiating the change has not yet been committed. This change is caused by the sudden appearance of the new phantom row during the transaction.

READ COMMITTED

Even less secure than the REPEATABLE READ isolation level is the READ COMMITTED isolation level. Not only can a transaction at this level see new records added by other transactions, it can also see the changes made by those transactions to existing records once they are committed. Put another way, this means multiple SELECT statements within the same transaction might return different results if the corresponding tables have been modified by other transactions in the intervening period. Figure 12-6 illustrates.

Assuming an isolation level of READ COMMITTED, the second transaction will continue to see 1000 shares in trader A's account while the first transaction is in progress. However, once the first transaction has been committed, the second one will see 600 shares in trader A's account and 1400 shares in trader B's account, even though it is still in progress.

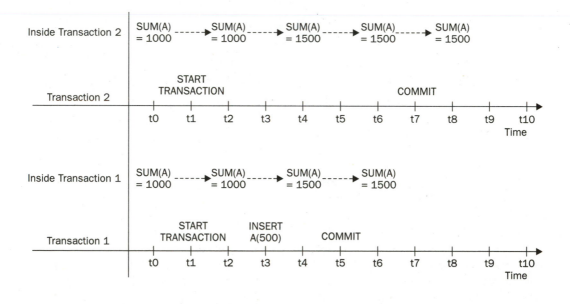

FIGURE 12-5   The REPEATED READ isolation level and a phantom read

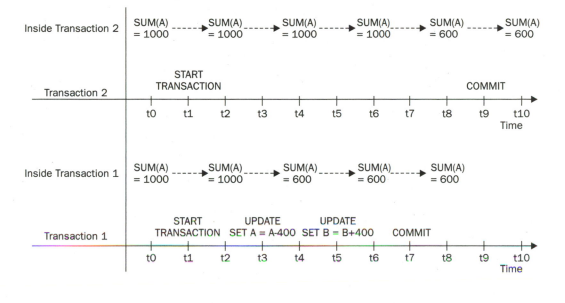

FIGURE 12-6   The READ COMMITTED isolation level and an unrepeatable read

This is obviously a problem—if the second transaction sees two different result sets within the same transaction, (s)he isn't going to know which one to trust as the correct one. Extrapolate a little and assume that, instead of a single transaction, many transactions are committing updates to the database, and you'll see every query executed by a transaction could produce a different result set (hence, the term *unrepeatable read* for this kind of situation).

READ UNCOMMITTED

The READ UNCOMMITTED isolation level provides the minimum amount of insulation between transactions. In addition to being vulnerable to phantom reads and unrepeatable reads, a transaction at this isolation level can read data that has not yet been committed by other transactions. If this transaction now uses the uncommitted changes made by other transactions as the basis for calculations of its own, and those uncommitted changes are then rolled back by their parent transactions, it can result in massive data corruption.

As an example, consider Figure 12-7. If we assume the second transaction is working at a transaction isolation level of READ UNCOMMITTED, it would be able to view the changes being made by the first transaction while it is in progress and, therefore, see a balance of 600 shares for trader A before it was properly committed to the system. If the transaction between traders A and B is subsequently cancelled via a ROLLBACK, the second transaction would be operating on faulty data (hence, the term *dirty read* for this kind of error).

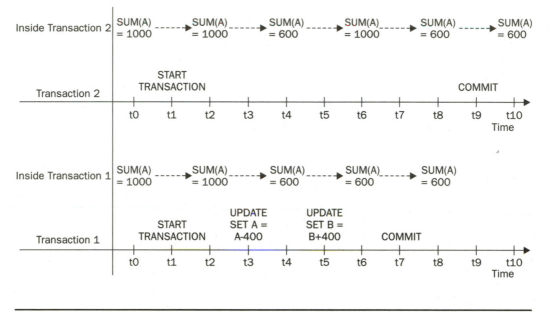

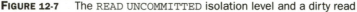

FIGURE 12-7 The READ UNCOMMITTED isolation level and a dirty read

Modifying the Transaction Isolation Level

Starting from MySQL 4.0.5, you can alter the transaction isolation level using the TRANSACTION ISOLATION LEVEL variable. MySQL defaults to the REPEATABLE READ isolation level. You can change this using the SET command, as in the following example:

```
mysql> SET TRANSACTION ISOLATION LEVEL READ COMMITTED;
Query OK, 0 rows affected (0.00 sec)
```

You can obtain the current value of the TRANSACTION ISOLATION LEVEL variable at any time with a quick SELECT, as in the following:

```
mysql> SELECT @@tx_isolation;
+------------------+
| @@tx_isolation   |
+------------------+
| REPEATABLE-READ  |
+------------------+
1 row in set (0.00 sec)
```

By default, this value of the TRANSACTION ISOLATION LEVEL variable is set on a per-session basis, but you can set it globally, for all sessions, by adding the GLOBAL keyword to the SET command line, as shown in the following:

```
mysql> SET GLOBAL TRANSACTION ISOLATION LEVEL READ COMMITTED;
Query OK, 0 rows affected (0.00 sec)
```

Note, you need the SUPER privilege to perform this operation. Chapter 14 has more information on how to obtain this (and other) privileges in the MySQL access control system.

Transactions and Performance

Because a database that supports transactions has to work a lot harder than a nontransactional database at keeping different user sessions isolated from each other, it's natural for this to reflect in the system's performance. Compliance with the other ACID rules, specifically the ones related to maintaining the integrity of the database in the event of a system failure through the use of a transaction log, adds additional overhead to such transactional systems. MySQL is no exception to this rule—other things remaining the same, nontransactional MyISAM tables are much faster than the transactional InnoDB and BDB table types. (Most of the time. However, this varies depending on both the query type and the mix of queries. A heavy mix of table reads and writes is significantly faster with InnoDB, while MyISAM outperforms InnoDB on table scans and large DELETEs.)

That said, if you have no choice but to use a transactional table type, you can still do a few things to ensure that your transactions don't add undue overhead to the system.

Use Small Transactions

Cliched though it might be, the KISS (Keep It Simple, Stupid!) principle is particularly applicable in the complex world of transactions. This is because MySQL uses a row-level locking mechanism to prevent simultaneous transactions from editing the same record in the database and possibly corrupting it. The row-level locking mechanism prevents more than one transaction from accessing a row at the same time—this safeguards the data, but has the disadvantage of causing other transactions to wait until the transaction initiating the locks has completed its work. So long as the transaction is small, this wait time is not very noticeable. When dealing with a large database and many complex transactions, however, the long wait time while the various transactions wait for each other to release locks can significantly affect performance.

For this reason, it is generally considered a good idea to keep the size of your transactions small, and to have them make their changes quickly and exit, so other

---

Start Me Up

You can also set the default transaction isolation level at startup with the special `--transaction-isolation` argument to the `mysqld` server process.

transactions queued behind them do not get unduly delayed. At the application level, two common strategies exist for accomplishing this:

- Ensure that all user input required for the transaction is available before issuing a START TRANSACTION command. Often, novice application designers initiate a transaction before the complete set of values needed by it is available. Other transactions initiated at the same time now have to wait while the user inputs the required data and the application processes it, and then asks for more data, and so on. In a single-user environment, these delays will not matter as much because no other transactions are trying to access the database. In a multiuser scenario, however, a delay caused by a single transaction can have a ripple effect on all other transactions queued in the system, resulting in severe performance degradation.

- Try breaking down large transactions into smaller subtransactions and execute them independently. This will ensure that each subtransaction executes quickly, freeing up valuable system resources that would otherwise be used to maintain the state of the system.

Select an Appropriate Isolation Level

As you move from the carefree READ UNCOMMITTED isolation level to the more secure SERIALIZABLE level, the performance of the RDBMS is affected as well. The reason for this is fairly simple: the greater the data integrity you demand from the system, the more work it has to do and the slower it runs. Therefore, as a database administrator or a system analyst, you will usually have to walk a tightrope between the RDBMS's isolation requirements and its performance.

At the SERIALIZABLE level of isolation, the RDBMS executes transactions sequentially and, thereby, offers the highest level of protection against data corruption. However, because this often involves waiting for locks set by other transactions to be released, it can significantly reduce the speed of your application. At the other end of the spectrum, the READ UNCOMMITTED isolation level allows parallel transactions to see the unsaved changes made by each other, providing much improved performance at a greater risk of inconsistent data. Figure 12-8 illustrates the inverse relationship between transaction security and performance.

MySQL defaults to the REPEATABLE READ isolation level. This isolation level is suitable for most applications, and you would usually only need to alter it if your application has specific need of a higher or lower level. There is no standard formula for deciding what isolation level is right for your application—most often, it is a subjective decision reached on the basis of the application's tolerance for errors and of the application developer's judgment of the impact of potentially incorrect data. This selection of isolation level need not even be standard across an application. It's quite likely, for example, that different transactions within the same application might require different isolation levels based on the tasks each is performing.

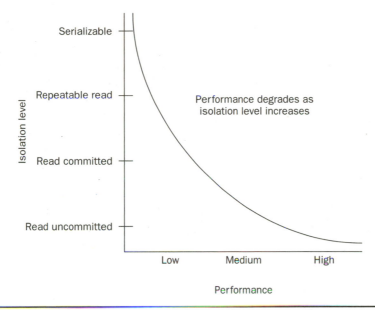

FIGURE 12-8 The relationship between transaction isolation levels and performance

Avoid Deadlocks

No discussion of transactional performance is complete without a brief look at deadlocks. If you're familiar with OS programming, you might already know what a *deadlock* is—a situation wherein two processes are locked in limbo while accessing the same resource, each waiting for the other to finish.

In a transactional context, a deadlock occurs when two or more clients try to update the same data simultaneously, but in a different sequence. To illustrate, consider Figure 12-9, in which two different transactions are working with the same set of tables, but in a different sequence.

The first transaction is attempting to remove 400 shares from a portfolio account, while the second is trying to add 1000. Both transactions are initiated at the same time, but the first proceeds by (1) reducing the portfolio account by 400 shares, and (2) then updating the portfolio net worth table, while the second tries to (1) update the portfolio net worth table to reflect the lower value, and (2) then deducts 1000 shares from the portfolio account.

As is clearly visible from the previous example, the result is a deadlock while each transaction waits for the other one to finish working with the table it needs to access. If left unresolved, a deadlock such as the previous one would result in each transaction waiting indefinitely for the other one to release its lock on the data. Fortunately, MySQL's InnoDB table handler comes with built-in intelligence to detect deadlock situations. If it notices one, the InnoDB table handler immediately resolves the deadlock situation by

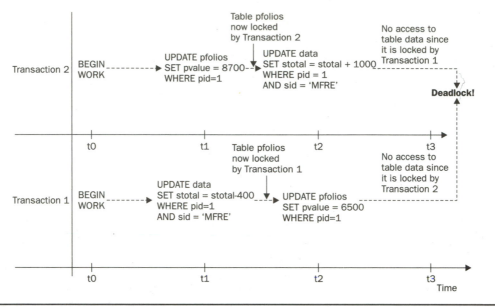

FIGURE 12-9 A transactional deadlock

rolling back one of the transactions (and releasing its locks), thereby permitting the other one to proceed to its logical end. As in the previous sample output, the client owning the cancelled transaction is notified of the rollback via an error message.

Pseudotransactions with Nontransactional Tables

Thus far, you've seen transactions in the context of InnoDB and BDB tables, the only MySQL table types to natively support ACID-compliant transactions. The older MySQL table types, still in use in many MySQL installations, do not support transactions, but MySQL still enables users to implement a primitive form of transactions through the

Being Prepared

A postmortem of the previous deadlock example would reveal that, more than a database issue, it was a result of poor application design: the order in which the tables were manipulated by the two clients was completely different, resulting in the creation of a deadlock. Most often, deadlocks can be avoided through careful planning and design at the application level. This can ensure resources are shared gracefully between competing processes and circular chains (such as the one previously demonstrated) are detected and resolved at the earliest.

A developer can do a number of fundamental things at the application level to avoid deadlocks: obtain all needed locks at the beginning of a session, always process tables in the same order, and include built-in recovery routines to try the transaction again in case it is cancelled by the RDBMS to resolve a deadlock situation.

use of table locks. This section examines these pseudotransactions in greater detail, with a view to offering some general guidelines to performing secure transactions with nontransactional tables.

Table Locks as a Substitute for Transactions

Because MyISAM (and other older MySQL table formats) do not support InnoDB-style COMMIT and ROLLBACK syntax, every change made to the database is immediately saved to disk. As noted previously, in a single-user scenario, this does not present much of a problem but, in a multiuser scenario, it can cause problems because it is no longer possible to create transaction "bubbles" that isolate the changes made by one user from those made by other users. In such a situation, the only way to ensure consistency in the data seen by different client sessions is a brute-force approach: prevent other users from accessing the tables being changed for the duration of the change (by locking them), and permit them access only once the changes are complete.

Previous sections of this chapter have already discussed the InnoDB and BDB tables, which natively support row- and page-level locking to safely execute simultaneous transactions. The MyISAM table type, however, does not support these fine-grained locking mechanisms. Instead, explicit table locks have to be set to avoid simultaneous transactions from infringing on each other's space.

MySQL supports the following syntax for applying a table lock:

```
LOCK TABLES table-name lock-type, ...
```

The following example sets a read-only lock on the users table:

```
mysql> LOCK TABLE users READ;
Query OK, 0 rows affected (0.05 sec)
```

Locking more than one table at the same time is not uncommon. This can be easily accomplished by specifying a comma-separated list of table names and lock types after the LOCK TABLES command, as in the following:

```
mysql> LOCK TABLES users READ, pfolios WRITE
Query OK, 0 rows affected (0.05 sec)
```

The previous statement locks the users table in READ mode and the pfolio table in WRITE mode.

Tables can be unlocked with a single UNLOCK TABLES command as in the following:

```
mysql> UNLOCK TABLES;
Query OK, 0 rows affected (0.05 sec)
```

You do not need to name the tables to be unlocked. MySQL automatically unlocks all tables that were locked previously via LOCK TABLES.

There are two main types of table locks: read locks and write locks. Let's take a closer look.

The READ Lock

A READ lock on a table implies that the thread (client) setting the lock can read data from that table, as can other threads. However, no thread can modify the locked table, either by adding, updating, or removing records, for so long as the lock is active.

Here's a simple example you can try to see how READ locks work. Begin by placing a READ lock on the users table,

```
mysql> LOCK TABLE users READ;
Query OK, 0 rows affected (0.05 sec)
```

and then reading from it.

```
mysql> SELECT * FROM users;
+-----+--------+
| uid | uname  |
+-----+--------+
|   2 | jim    |
|   1 | john   |
|   3 | ken    |
|   5 | philip |
|   4 | scott  |
+-----+--------+
5 rows in set (0.23 sec)
```

No problems there. Now, what about writing to it?

```
mysql> INSERT INTO users (uid, uname) VALUES (6,'tom');
ERROR 1099: Table 'users' was locked with a READ lock and can't be updated
```

MySQL rejects the INSERT because the table is locked in read-only mode.

What about other clients accessing the same table? Pop open a new MySQL client session and try accessing the same table. As the following shows, reads work without a problem.

```
mysql> SELECT * FROM users;
+-----+--------+
| uid | uname  |
+-----+--------+
|   2 | jim    |
|   1 | john   |
|   3 | ken    |
|   5 | philip |
|   4 | scott  |
+-----+--------+
5 rows in set (0.23 sec)
```

> **The Two Rs**
>
> A variant of the READ lock is the READ LOCAL lock, which differs from a regular READ lock in that other threads can execute INSERT statements that do not conflict with the session owned by the thread initiating the lock. This was created for use with the mysqldump utility to allow multiple simultaneous INSERTs into a table.

How about writes?

```
mysql> INSERT INTO users (uid, uname) VALUES (7,'paul');
```

In this case, the MySQL client will halt and wait for the lock to be released by the first session before proceeding. If you flip back to the first MySQL session and execute the UNLOCK TABLES command,

```
mysql> UNLOCK TABLES;
Query OK, 0 rows affected (0.04 sec)
```

the lock will be released and the second session will proceed with the query.

```
mysql> INSERT INTO users (uid, uname) VALUES (7,'paul');
Query OK, 1 row affected (27 min 15.11 sec)
```

The WRITE Lock

A WRITE lock on a table implies that the thread setting the lock can modify the data in the table, but other threads cannot either read or write to the table for the duration of the lock.

Here's a simple example you can try to see how WRITE locks work. Begin by placing a WRITE lock on the data table,

```
mysql> LOCK TABLE data WRITE;
Query OK, 0 rows affected (0.05 sec)
```

and then try reading from it.

```
mysql> SELECT * FROM data;
+-----+------+--------+
| pid | sid  | stotal |
+-----+------+--------+
|   1 | INFY |   9000 |
|   1 | MSFT |    100 |
|   2 | MSFT |   1000 |
|   2 | INTC |   1000 |
|   3 | INFY |    500 |
|   3 | CISC |   1000 |
```

```
|    1 | CISC |    1000 |
|    1 | ACME |    2000 |
|    1 | INTC |    2000 |
|    2 | ACME |    1000 |
+-----+------+--------+
10 rows in set (0.00 sec)
```

Because a WRITE lock is on the table, you should also be able to write to it without a problem.

```
mysql> UPDATE data SET stotal = 5000 WHERE pid = 1 and sid = 'INFY';
Query OK, 1 row affected (0.00 sec)
Rows matched: 1   Changed: 1   Warnings: 0
```

Now, what about other MySQL sessions? Open a new client session and try reading from the same table while the WRITE lock is still active.

```
mysql> SELECT * FROM data;
```

The MySQL client will now halt and wait for the first session to release its locks before it can execute the previous command. So, go back to the first session and unlock the tables.

```
mysql> UNLOCK TABLES;
Query OK, 0 rows affected (0.04 sec)
```

You will see that the SELECT command invoked in the second session will now be accepted for processing by MySQL because the data table is no longer locked.

```
mysql> SELECT * FROM data;
+-----+------+--------+
| pid | sid  | stotal |
+-----+------+--------+
|    1 | INFY |    9000 |
|    1 | MSFT |     100 |
|    2 | MSFT |    1000 |
|    2 | INTC |    1000 |
|    3 | INFY |     500 |
|    3 | CISC |    1000 |
|    1 | CISC |    1000 |
|    1 | ACME |    2000 |
|    1 | INTC |    2000 |
|    2 | ACME |    1000 |
+-----+------+--------+
10 rows in set (3 min 32.98 sec)
```

On the Fast Track

In situations involving both WRITE and READ locks, MySQL assigns WRITE locks higher priority to ensure that modifications to the table are saved to disk as soon as possible. This reduces the risk of updates getting lost in case of a disk crash or a system failure.

The previous examples outline one of the most important drawbacks of table locks: if a thread never releases its locks, all other threads attempting to access the locked table(s) are left waiting for the lock to time out, leading to a significant degradation in overall performance.

Implementing a Pseudotransaction with Table Locks

Let's now look at how a transaction can be implemented through the use of table locks. I'll explain this by rewriting one of the earlier examples, that of adding a new employee to the company database, with locks and MyISAM tables instead of native transactional code and InnoDB tables.

The first step is to make a list of the tables you intend to use during the transaction. In the earlier example, the steps involved included (1) creating a record for the employee in the employees table, (2) assigning the employee to a department in the departments table, and (3) specifying the employee's salary and bonuses in the payroll table.

Because each of these three tables will be modified when a new employee is added, they must be locked, in WRITE mode, so other sessions do not interfere with the process.

```
mysql> LOCK TABLES employees WRITE, departments WRITE, payroll WRITE;
Query OK, 0 rows affected (0.00 sec)
```

As explained previously, WRITE mode implies other sessions will neither be able to read from nor write to the locked tables for so long as the lock is active. Hence, the transaction must be as short and sweet as possible to avoid a slowdown in other requests for data in these tables.

Next, insert the new records into the various tables:

```
mysql> INSERT INTO employees (ename, enationality) VALUES ('Tim Jonez', 'US');
Query OK, 1 row affected (0.13 sec)
mysql> INSERT INTO departments (eid, dept) VALUES (LAST_INSERT_ID(), 'Accounts');
Query OK, 1 row affected (0.03 sec)
mysql> INSERT INTO payroll (eid, pbasic, pbonus) VALUES (LAST_INSERT_ID(), 36000.00, 2500.00);
Query OK, 1 row affected (0.02 sec)
```

Verify the data has been correctly entered with a quick SELECT:

```
mysql> SELECT * FROM employees;
+-----+-----------+--------------+
| eid | ename     | enationality |
+-----+-----------+--------------+
|   1 | Tim Jonez | US           |
+-----+-----------+--------------+
```

PART II

```
1 row in set (0.00 sec)
mysql> SELECT * FROM payroll;
+-----+----------+---------+
| eid | pbasic   | pbonus  |
+-----+----------+---------+
|   1 | 36000.00 | 2500.00 |
+-----+----------+---------+
1 row in set (0.05 sec)
```

Unlock the tables, and you're done!

```
mysql> UNLOCK TABLES;
Query OK, 0 rows affected (0.09 sec)
```

Until the tables are unlocked, all other sessions trying to access the three locked tables will be forced to wait. The elegance of the transactional approach, in which page- and row-level locks allow other clients to work with the data, even during the course of a transaction, is missing here. That said, however, table locks do help to isolate updates in different sessions from each other (albeit in a somewhat primitive manner) and, in doing so, help users constrained to older, nontransactional table types to implement an almost-transactional environment for their application.

Summary

This chapter discussed one of the major new features in MySQL: the capability to group multiple SQL statements into a single transactional unit and have that unit execute atomically. Combined with a built-in binary log that tracks all changes made to the RDBMS, this transactional capability makes it possible to execute SQL queries in a more secure manner and—in the event of an error—revert the RDBMS to a previous, more stable state. Transactional support thus plays an important role in making SQL applications more robust and reducing the possibility of data corruption by rogue SQL queries and, by including support for it, MySQL finally provides a viable alternative to other, more commercial database suites.

Transactions can impose a substantial performance drain on an RDBMS's resources because of the large amount of resources needed to keep transactions separate from each other when multiple users are accessing the same data. Therefore, in addition to discussing the life cycle of a transaction, this chapter also included an explanation of the various MySQL variables that control transactional behavior and performance, most notably the TRANSACTION ISOLATION LEVEL variable, which controls the degree to which transactions are insulated from each other's actions.

Finally, because transactions are only supported by the new InnoDB and BDB table types, this chapter provided a brief explanation of how to simulate a transactional environment with the older MyISAM table format, through the use of table locks—a primitive method, but nonetheless effective for its crudity.

PART

III

Administration

Administration and Configuration

Previous sections of this book have focused more on using MySQL for daily work—creating databases, adding data, and running queries—than on the administrative end of things—managing security, assigning user privileges, and backing up data. For most users, this approach works well. But what if you're not a user, but a database administrator whose job description consists of managing the MySQL server?

In this case, merely understanding the intricacies of SQL queries is insufficient. You also need to know how to administer a MySQL relational database management system (RDBMS) and take over responsibility for ensuring that MySQL services are always available to users of the system. This role involves a number of different facets: securing the MySQL server against unauthorized usage or mischief, assigning users privileges appropriate to their intended use of the system, performing regular checks and backups of the MySQL databases to avoid data corruption or loss, and optimizing the server to ensure it always delivers the best performance possible.

That's where this chapter, and this section, comes in. Over the course of the following chapters, we'll explore the different aspects of MySQL server administration, and you'll see how to accomplish common tasks quickly and efficiently. This chapter serves as a brief introduction to the topic, covering common tasks like starting and stopping the server, altering the default server configuration, and inspecting the MySQL log files.

Database Administration and MySQL

A database administrator holds an important position in an organization's MIS team. As the person tasked with the responsibility of ensuring smooth and efficient access to network databases, the job description involves ensuring 24/7/365 database uptime for users and applications, performing regular backups for quick recovery in the event of a system crash, tuning server parameters for maximum performance, and securing the database against malicious mischief and unauthorized access. Even individually, none of these tasks can be called simple. Taken together, they constitute one of the most demanding and challenging positions in the industry.

Fortunately, MySQL comes with sophisticated tools to help the beleaguered database administrator in his or her daily chores.

Uptime

Intelligent design decisions by the developers of MySQL, combined with ample testing and contribution from the open source community, has created a very stable and highly reliable product, instilling confidence in the database administrator. MySQL is designed to offer maximum reliability and uptime, and it has been tested and certified for use in high-volume, mission-critical applications, by companies like SAP, Motorola, Sony, Yahoo!, NASA, and HP (to name only a few).

A common cause of system crashes involves glitches or bugs in the application code. MySQL's open-source history makes this less of a problem than with its more commercial counterparts. Because MySQL development occurs in full view of the public, a final release has the unique benefit of being exhaustively tested by users all over the world—on a variety of different platforms and in a range of different environments (as well as by MySQL AB's in-house test suite, known as *crash-me* because its primary goal is to attempt to crash the system)—before it's certified for use in production environments. This approach has resulted in an RDBMS that's both exceedingly stable and virtually bug-free.

Data Backup

While MySQL is certainly extremely stable and reliable, as well as quite capable of running itself without any special care required, basic maintenance, and an established backup and restoration process is required from the administrator in any production environment. A backup regimen, in particular, is critical to ensuring the data stored in an organization's databases doesn't get corrupted or lost because of a disk failure or a system crash.

With this in mind, MySQL comes with a number of tools designed to speed this process and make it more efficient. The most important of these is the `mysqldump` utility, which makes it possible to write MySQL table structures, table data, or both to backup files in a variety of different formats. The output of `mysqldump` can then be used easily and quickly to restore one or more MySQL databases, either from the command-line with the `mysqlimport` utility or the `mysql` client, or via the `LOAD DATA INFILE` command. In case of table corruption, MySQL improves the chances of data recovery through a suite of recovery utilities, which are extremely good at delving into the innards of a corrupted table and either fixing it completely or repairing the damage to a point where most of its data can be recovered.

MySQL also comes with built-in replication, which makes mirroring the changes made on one database server on to other servers possible by using predefined master-slave relationships. Earlier versions of MySQL only supported one-way replication. Newer versions now support two-way replication as well, for more sophisticated mirroring and load-balancing.

Security and Access Control

MySQL comes with a sophisticated access control and privilege system to prevent unauthorized users from accessing the system. This system, implemented as a five-tiered privilege hierarchy, makes it possible to create comprehensive access rules that MySQL uses when deciding how to handle a particular user request:

- Connections to the server are allowed only if they match the access rules laid down in the MySQL privilege system. These access rules can be specified on the basis of user and/or host, and can be used to restrict access from hosts outside a specific subnetwork or IP address range. Further, such connections to the server are permitted only after the user provides a valid password.

- Once a connection is established, MySQL checks every action performed by a user to verify whether the user has sufficient privileges to perform it. Users can be restricted to performing operations only on specified databases or fields, and MySQL even makes it possible to control which types of queries a user can run, at database, table, or field level.

The security of the system is further enhanced through the use of a one-way encryption scheme for user passwords. This encryption scheme, originally rather primitive, has been significantly improved in MySQL 4.*x*. Newer versions of MySQL also support SSL, which can be used to encrypt the data sent out over the MySQL client-server connection (such as query results) for greater security.

Performance Optimization

Once the routine matters—backing up data and securing the system—have been taken care of, a database administrator must focus on squeezing the maximum performance out of the RDBMS. MySQL's multithreaded engine and numerous optimization algorithms make this activity less daunting than many other RDBMSs—an out-of-the-box MySQL installation is usually blazingly fast and requires little alteration.

That said, it certainly is possible to tune MySQL to specific needs. MySQL exposes a fair number of its internal parameters via system variables, and it allows developers and administrators to modify them easily to meet custom requirements. Many of the features that degrade performance—transactions, referential integrity, and stored procedures—can be enabled or disabled at the user's choice, thereby making it possible to select the optimal mix of features and performance on a per-application basis. Commands like ANALYZE TABLE and EXPLAIN SELECT assist SQL developers in benchmarking queries and identifying performance bottlenecks, and new features like the *Query Cache* (which works by caching the results of common queries and returning this cached data to the caller without having to reexecute the query every time) help improve performance while minimizing extra programming.

An important issue when discussing performance is scalability. Too many database systems work exceedingly well when dealing with a few thousands of records, but they display a significant drop in performance when the numbers jump into the millions. This is not a problem with MySQL, though. The RDBMS is built to be extremely scalable, and can handle extremely large and complex databases (tables of several gigabytes containing hundreds of thousands of records) without breaking a sweat. This makes MySQL suitable for everything ranging from simple content-based web sites to extremely large and diversified data networks, such as the ones used in e-tailing, data warehousing, or business knowledge management.

The following chapters examine each of these aspects in detail. For the moment, though, let's begin with a brief primer on common server administration tasks.

Basic Server Administration and Configuration Tasks

The MySQL distribution includes a command-line tool designed specifically to help administrators perform common tasks, such as changing the MySQL administrator password or reloading MySQL privileges. This tool, called `mysqladmin`, can be found in the `bin/` directory of your MySQL installation and is usually invoked with one or more commands, as in the following:

```
mysqladmin command
```

Here's an example:

```
[root@host]# /usr/local/mysql/bin/mysqladmin shutdown
```

Table 13-1 lists the more useful commands supported by `mysqladmin`:

You can obtain a complete list of available commands by running `mysqladmin --help`.

In subsequent pages of this chapter, and throughout this section, you'll see this tool being used extensively for server administration.

Let's now look at some common database administration tasks, as a prelude to the more advanced material in following chapters.

TABLE 13-1
Commands
Supported by
`mysqladmin`

Command	What It Does
status	Returns information on server state
password	Changes a user password
shutdown	Shuts down the MySQL server
reload	Reloads the MySQL grant tables
refresh	Resets all caches and logs
variables	Returns values of all server variables
version	Returns the server version
processlist	Returns a list of all processes active on the server
kill	Kills an active server process
ping	Tests if the server is alive

Shell Prompt

If you are not familiar or comfortable with the command line, a number of graphical client alternatives to the `mysqladmin` tool exist, such as the following:

- **phpMyAdmin** (`http://www.phpmyadmin.net/`) A browser-based interface to MySQL administration
- **MySQL Control Center** (`http://www.mysql.com/products/mysqlcc/index.html`) A Qt-based GUI MySQL administration tool for both Windows and UNIX platforms
- **WinMySQLadmin** A Windows GUI for MySQL administration that ships with the MySQL server

---

Starting and Stopping the Server

On UNIX, MySQL comes with a startup/shutdown script, which is the recommended way of starting and stopping the MySQL database server. This script, named `mysql.server`, is available in the `support-files/` subdirectory of your MySQL installation, and it can be invoked as follows to start the MySQL server:

```
[root@host]# /usr/local/mysql/support-files/mysql.server start
```

An alternative approach is to invoke the server directly, by calling the `mysqld_safe` wrapper, as in the following:

```
[root@host]# /usr/local/mysql/bin/mysqld_safe --user=mysql &
```

On non-server flavors of Windows (Windows 95, 98 or Me), the easiest way to start the MySQL server is by navigating to your MySQL installation directory in the Windows Explorer and launching the `mysqld` binary by double-clicking it. Or, you could launch it by typing in the full path to the `mysqld` binary in the Start -> Run dialog box or in a command-line DOS prompt, as in the following:

```
C:\> c:\mysql\bin\mysqld.exe
```

Better Safe Than Sorry

While you can certainly invoke MySQL by directly running the `mysqld` binary from your installation's `bin/` directory, this isn't a recommended approach. Using the `mysqld_safe` wrapper is considered a safe approach because this wrapper takes care of automatically logging errors and runtime information to a file, and of restarting the MySQL daemon in case of an unexpected shutdown.

Note, in older versions of MySQL, `mysqld_safe` is called `safe_mysqld`.

On server-class Windows machines (Windows NT, 2000, XP and 2003), which will more typically be running MySQL, the MySQL server ought to run as a background service. This is accomplished by installing the `mysql` service and then using the `net start` command to activate it. In order to do this, first execute the following command, either using the Start -> Run dialog box or in a command-line DOS window:

```
C:\> c:\mysql\bin\mysqld --install
```

Next, start the service, either through the Services Control Panel (Control Panel -> Administrative Tools -> Services) or with the following command:

```
C:\> net start mysql
```

Depending on which version of Windows you're running, MySQL may either launch in the foreground (a `mysqld` console window opens and always remains visible on the Windows taskbar) or start as a service and run invisibly in the background.

You can verify the server is running by using the `mysqladmin` tool with the `ping` command, as the following shows. This returns a status message indicating whether the server is active.

```
[root@host]# /usr/local/mysql/bin/mysqladmin ping
mysqld is alive
```

Hard Choices

The Windows binary distribution of MySQL includes a number of different `mysqld` binaries. Here's what each does.

- **mysqld**   The regular MySQL server
- **mysqld-nt**   The regular MySQL server, with support for named pipes on Windows NT/2000/XP
- **mysqld-opt**   An optimized MySQL server, with some features stripped out for better performance
- **mysqld-max**   Like `mysqld`, but with support for newer, more experimental (and more unstable) features as well
- **mysqld-max-nt**   Like `mysqld-max`, with extra support for named pipes on Windows NT/2000/XP

Most often, you would want to try using the `mysqld` or `mysqld-nt` binaries, depending on your platform. If you have difficulty getting those to work, the `mysqld-opt` binary is usually a safe second choice.

The `mysqladmin` utility can also be used to reload the server's grant tables, as in the following (this example is for UNIX, simply replace the path with the correct path to your MySQL installation for Windows):

```
[root@host]# /usr/local/mysql/bin/mysqladmin reload
```

Once the server is running, you can shut it down at any time with the `mysqladmin` utility that ships with MySQL, by invoking it with the `shutdown` parameter. On UNIX, it looks like this:

```
[root@host]# /usr/local/mysql/bin/mysqladmin shutdown
mysqld is alive
```

On Windows, you usually need to open a new DOS console window or use the Start -> Run dialog box, as in the following:

```
C:\> c:\mysql\bin\mysqladmin shutdown
```

On UNIX, you can also use the provided `mysql.server` startup/shutdown script to shut down the server, as shown in the following:

```
[root@host]# /usr/local/mysql/support-files/mysql.server stop
```

TIP *Resist the urge to shut down MySQL by abruptly killing the `mysqld` process with the `kill` command (UNIX) or the Task Manager (Windows). Such premature termination can cause data loss or corruption if the server is in the process of writing data to the disk when it receives the termination signal.*

Configuring MySQL to Start Automatically on System Bootup

You can also set up MySQL to start automatically when the system boots up. Here's how:

- On UNIX, you can have MySQL start automatically at boot time by copying the `mysql.server` script provided in the MySQL distribution to the `/etc/init.d/*` directory hierarchy of your system, and invoking it with appropriate parameters from your system's bootup and shutdown scripts.

- To start MySQL automatically on Windows 95, Windows 98, or Windows Me, you can simply add a shortcut to the `mysqld` server binary to your Startup group. Windows will then launch the server every time it starts up. On Windows NT, Windows 2000, or Windows XP, the equivalent procedure consists of installing MySQL as a service in the Windows Control Panel, by invoking the `mysqld` binary with the `--install` command-line option and making sure the service is set to start automatically in Control Panel -> Administrative Tools -> Services.

> **Preflight Check**
> Before starting the MySQL server, it is important to review and modify the runtime configuration settings found in the my.cnf (or my.ini) file. The server reads this file once during startup, so any changes will require a stop-start to take effect.

Checking MySQL Server Status

You can find out the current state of the server (server uptime, queries per second, number of currently-open tables, and so on) via the mysqladmin tool, by passing it the status command. Here's an example:

```
[root@host]# /usr/local/mysql/bin/mysqladmin status
Uptime: 1743  Threads: 2  Questions: 31  Slow queries: 0  Opens: 13
Flush tables: 1  Open tables: 2  Queries per second avg: 0.018
```

The version command offers a more concise summary, together with information on the MySQL server version:

```
[root@host]# /usr/local/mysql/bin/mysqladmin version
/usr/local/mysql/bin/mysqladmin  Ver 8.40 Distrib 4.0.15, for pc-linux on
i686
Copyright (C) 2000 MySQL AB & MySQL Finland AB & TCX DataKonsult AB
This software comes with ABSOLUTELY NO WARRANTY. This is free software,
and you are welcome to modify and redistribute it under the GPL license
Server version          4.0.15-standard
Protocol version        10
Connection              Localhost via UNIX socket
UNIX socket             /tmp/mysql.sock
Uptime:                 29 min 38 sec
Threads: 2  Questions: 32  Slow queries: 0  Opens: 13  Flush tables: 1
Open tables: 2  Queries per second avg: 0.018
```

An equivalent approach is to use the VERSION() built-in function, as in the following:

```
mysql> SELECT VERSION();
+-----------+
| VERSION() |
+-----------+
| 4.0.15    |
+-----------+
1 row in set (0.11 sec)
```

Extended status information is also available via the extended-status command to mysqladmin, or with the SHOW STATUS command.

```
mysql> SHOW STATUS;
+-------------------------+-------+
| Variable_name           | Value |
+-------------------------+-------+
| Aborted_clients         | 0     |
| Aborted_connects        | 1     |
| Bytes_received          | 125   |
| Bytes_sent              | 3319  |
| Com_admin_commands      | 1     |
| Com_alter_table         | 0     |
...
| Threads_cached          | 0     |
| Threads_created         | 4     |
| Threads_connected       | 1     |
| Threads_running         | 1     |
| Uptime                  | 329   |
+-------------------------+-------+
132 rows in set (0.00 sec)
```

As you can see, this extended status message provides a great deal of real-time status information. The report contains the amount of traffic the server has received since it was last started, including the number of bytes sent and received, and the client connections, together with a breakdown of how many succeeded, how many failed, and how many were aborted. It also contains statistics on the total number of queries processed by the server since startup, together with information on the number of queries in each type (SELECT, DELETE, INSERT, . . .), the number of threads active, the number of current client connections, the number of running queries, and the number of open tables.

Managing MySQL Client Processes

You can obtain a complete list of all client processes connected to the server with the SHOW PROCESSLIST command, as in the following:

```
mysql> SHOW PROCESSLIST;
+----+------+-----------+---------+---------+------+--------------+--------------
--------------------------+
| Id | User | Host      | db      | Command | Time | State        | Info         |
+----+------+-----------+---------+---------+------+--------------+--------------
--------------------------+
| 10 | root | localhost | NULL    | Query   | 0    | NULL         | show
processlist              |
| 12 | root | localhost | library | Query   | 0    | Sending data | select *
from users, categories, info |
| 14 | root | localhost | student | Sleep   | 20   |              | NULL         |
+----+------+-----------+---------+---------+------+--------------+--------------
--------------------------+
3 rows in set (0.00 sec)
```

A "regular" user will only be able to see his or her own threads in the output of SHOW PROCESSLIST. Users with the PROCESS privilege can, however, see all running threads, and users with the all-powerful SUPER privilege can even kill running threads, with the KILL command. Here's an example:

```
mysql> KILL 12;
Query OK, 0 rows affected (0.01 sec)
```

The mysqladmin tool offers equivalent processlist and kill commands as well:

```
[root@host]# /usr/local/mysql/bin/mysqladmin processlist
+----+------+-----------+---------+---------+------+-------+---------------+
| Id | User | Host      | db      | Command | Time | State | Info          |
+----+------+-----------+---------+---------+------+-------+---------------+
| 10 | root | localhost |         | Sleep   | 83   |       |               |
| 14 | root | localhost | student | Sleep   | 142  |       |               |
| 17 | root | localhost |         | Sleep   | 19   |       |               |
| 18 | root | localhost | library | Sleep   | 2    |       |               |
| 20 | root | localhost |         | Query   | 0    |       | show processlist |
+----+------+-----------+---------+---------+------+-------+---------------+
[root@host]# /usr/local/mysql/bin/mysqladmin kill 18
```

More information on the MySQL privilege system, together with instructions on how to assign privileges to users, is available in Chapter 14.

Altering the Server Configuration

Most of the time, you needn't alter MySQL's default configuration. The software comes preconfigured by MySQL AB to meet most common needs. However, in case the default configuration doesn't work for you, MySQL exposes a large number of variables whose values can be modified to meet custom requirements. Some of these variables can be set at the time of starting the MySQL server and others can be set while the server is running.

Killed in Action

Note, a thread doesn't die immediately on receiving a kill signal. Rather, MySQL sets a *kill flag* for that particular thread, which is checked by the thread once it completes whatever operation it's currently performing. This approach is considered safer than an immediate kill because it allows the thread to complete whatever it's doing, and release any locks it created, before terminating. Threads typically check for a kill flag after every significant read or write operation.

Using an Option File

The recommended method of setting MySQL options is through an *option file,* essentially, an ASCII configuration file containing variable-value pairs that the MySQL server reads when it starts up. MySQL looks for this option file in some standard places when it starts up:

- **Windows** MySQL looks for startup options in an option file named `my.cnf` in the Windows installation directory and in `C:\my.cnf`. Alternatively, the `my.cnf` file can be placed in the Windows directory (`C:\WINNT` or `C:\WINDOWS`) as `my.ini` (this is actually required in the rare event the boot volume drive is not `C:`).

- **UNIX** MySQL checks for startup options in `/etc/my.cnf`, `~/.my.cnf` and in a file named `my.cnf` in your MySQL data directory.

TIP *You can tell MySQL to look for startup options in a different place by specifying the filename with the `--defaults-file` option on the MySQL command line.*

The format of the option file is fairly simple and resembles a Windows INI file. It's broken into groups, each containing variable-value pairs. Any option that can be given at the MySQL command line can be placed in this file, without the leading double dash. Here's an example:

```
[mysqld]
port=3306
skip-locking
log-bin
skip-bdb
```

All For One . . .

All the binary programs that ship with MySQL (not only `mysqld`) can read options from an options file. Simply specify the program name as a group (by enclosing it within square braces) in the option file and follow it with the variables you want to set. MySQL client programs can make use of a special `[client]` group, which is typically used to store user- and password-connection parameters. Here's a simple example of how this works:

```
[client]
user=timothy
password=greenpeas
```

NOTE   *A number of sample configuration files ship with the MySQL distribution—take a look inside* my-large.cnf, my-huge.cnf, my-medium.cnf *and* my-small.cnf *to get a better idea of how these files can be used.*

Typically, MySQL looks in the groups [mysql] and [mysqld] for configuration options. On UNIX, if you're using the mysqld_safe MySQL wrapper to start up MySQL, you can also use the [mysqld_safe] group to pass options to MySQL.

In this case, whenever the mysql client attempts a connection to a MySQL server, it will connect as user timothy with password greenpeas.

Table 13-2 lists the more common and useful options available to configure MySQL (refer to the MySQL manual for the complete list).

Option	What It Means
ansi	Uses stricter ANSI SQL-99 syntax
basedir	Sets location of MySQL installation directory
datadir	Sets location of MySQL data directory
debug	Creates a debug file
default-character-set	Sets default character set
default-table-type	Sets default table type for new tables
flush	Writes changes to disk after each SQL command
init-file	Sets a file containing SQL commands to be executed at startup
language	Sets the language for error messages
log	Writes MySQL messages (connections and queries) to log
log-long-format	Adds additional information (like username and timestamp) to each log entry
log-error	Writes critical error messages to log
log-warnings	Writes warning messages to log
log-slow-queries	Writes slowly-executing queries to log
log-bin	Writes queries that change data to binary log (useful for backup and replication purposes)
port	Sets the port the server listens on for client connections
safe-show-database	Shows only databases to which user has access
skip-bdb	Disables the BDB table handler
skip-innodb	Disables the InnoDB table handler
skip-grant-tables	Bypasses grant tables when performing access control
skip-networking	Allows only local requests, stops listening for TCP/IP requests
socket	Sets name of socket/named pipe to use for local connections
transaction-isolation	Sets default transaction isolation level
user	Specifies the user the server should run as
tmpdir	Sets location of temporary file area

TABLE 13-2   mysqld Command-Line Options

Note, all these options can be specified on the MySQL command line as well, simply by prefixing the option name with a double dash. The following example illustrates.

```
[root@host]# /usr/local/mysql/bin/mysqld_safe --socket=/usr/tmp/mysql.socket
--user=mysql --skip-networking &
Starting mysqld daemon with databases from /usr/local/mysql/data
```

In case multiple option files exist or the same option is specified multiple times with different values, MySQL uses the last found value. Because MySQL reads option files before command-line arguments, this means options specified on the command line take precedence over options in an option file.

Using the SET Command

MySQL also lets you modify system and connection variables while the server is running, using the SET command. The SET command looks like this:

```
SET variable = value, variable = value, ...
```

Here's an example, in which the SET command is used to set the default table type for new tables:

```
mysql> SET table_type = innodb;
Query OK, 0 rows affected (0.00 sec)
```

Variables set using the SET command can be set globally for all sessions, or only for the current session, by following the SET keyword with either the GLOBAL or SESSION keyword. The following example limits the server to ten client connections at any time and sets the size of the read buffer to 250KB:

```
mysql> SET GLOBAL max_user_connections=10, SESSION
read_buffer_size=250000;
Query OK, 0 rows affected (0.08 sec)
```

Note that the SUPER privilege is required for setting GLOBAL variables. You can read more about the MySQL privilege system in Chapter 14.

Locking The Doors

If your application is on the same physical machine as the MySQL server and if you don't anticipate MySQL client connections from other hosts, using the --skip-networking option to turn off TCP/IP listening can significantly enhance the security of your MySQL installation.

Variable	What It Does
autocommit	Toggles whether MySQL will automatically attempt to commit open transactions
key_buffer_size	Sets the size of the buffer used for indexes
table_cache	Sets the total number of tables MySQL can hold open at any given time
table_type	Sets the default table type
concurrent_inserts	Permits concurrent INSERTs and SELECTs on MyISAM tables
interactive_timeout	Sets the timeout for interactive client connections
language	Sets the language used for error messages
lower_case_table_names	Lowercases table names automatically
sort_buffer_size	Sets the maximum size of the buffer used for sorting results
read_buffer_size	Sets the size of the buffer used for table reads
max_binlog_size	Sets the maximum size of the binary log before rotation
max_connections	Sets the maximum number of client connections allowed at any given time
max_user_connections	Sets the maximum number of connections a single user can have active at any given time
max_tmp_tables	Sets the maximum number of temporary tables a client can keep open at any given time
query_cache_type	Toggles the query cache on/off
query_cache_size	Sets the maximum size of the query cache
tmpdir	Sets the location of the temporary file area
tx_isolation	Sets the transaction isolation level

TABLE 13-3   Important MySQL variables

Table 13-3 lists some of the important variables that can be set using the SET command (refer to the MySQL manual for the complete list, and to Chapter 16 for a more detailed discussion of some of these variables).

Retrieving Variable Values
Once a variable has been set, either via SET or through a startup option, its value can be retrieved using the SHOW VARIABLES command, or by invoking mysqladmin with the variables command. Because the output of SHOW VARIABLES is somewhat prodigious, MySQL lets you filter it down to just the variable you want through the addition of a LIKE clause, as in the following:

```
mysql> SHOW VARIABLES LIKE 'table_type';
+----------------+--------+
| Variable_name  | Value  |
```

```
+----------------+--------+
| table_type     | INNODB |
+----------------+--------+
| table_type     | INNODB |
+----------------+--------+
1 row in set (0.01 sec)
mysql> SHOW VARIABLES LIKE '%innodb%';
+---------------------------------+----------------------+
| Variable_name                   | Value                |
+---------------------------------+----------------------+
| have_innodb                     | YES                  |
| innodb_additional_mem_pool_size | 1048576              |
| innodb_buffer_pool_size         | 8388608              |
| innodb_data_file_path           | ibdata1:10M:autoextend |
| innodb_data_home_dir            |                      |
| innodb_file_io_threads          | 4                    |
| innodb_force_recovery           | 0                    |
| innodb_thread_concurrency       | 8                    |
| innodb_flush_log_at_trx_commit  | 1                    |
| innodb_fast_shutdown            | ON                   |
| innodb_flush_method             |                      |
| innodb_lock_wait_timeout        | 50                   |
| innodb_log_arch_dir             | ./                   |
| innodb_log_archive              | OFF                  |
| innodb_log_buffer_size          | 1048576              |
| innodb_log_file_size            | 5242880              |
| innodb_log_files_in_group       | 2                    |
| innodb_log_group_home_dir       | ./                   |
| innodb_mirrored_log_groups      | 1                    |
| innodb_max_dirty_pages_pct      | 90                   |
+---------------------------------+----------------------+
20 rows in set (0.00 sec)
```

You can also obtain the value of a system variable using the SELECT @@*variable* syntax, as the following shows.

```
mysql> SELECT @@tx_isolation;
+-----------------+
| @@tx_isolation  |
+-----------------+
| REPEATABLE-READ |
+-----------------+
1 row in set (0.00 sec)
```

Troubleshooting with the Error Log

In case of difficulties starting the server or if errors appear during its operation, be sure to check the MySQL error log to identify the cause(s) of error. As the following brief sample illustrates, this log file stores information on server startup and shutdown, together with a list of critical error messages and warnings about corrupted tables.

```
030919 18:17:16  Fatal error: Can't open privilege tables: Can't find file:
'./mysql/host.frm' (errno: 13)
030919 18:17:16  Aborting

030919 17:03:37  mysqld ended

030919 17:06:13  mysqld started
030919 17:06:13  InnoDB: Started
/usr/local/mysql/bin/mysqld: ready for connections.
Version: '4.0.15-standard'  socket: '/tmp/mysql.sock'  port: 3306
030926 17:40:31  Found invalid password for user: 'root'@'%'; Ignoring user
030926 17:40:31  Found invalid password for user:
'root'@'localhost.localdomain'; Ignoring user
030926 17:43:51  /usr/local/mysql/bin/mysqld: Normal shutdown

030926 17:43:52  InnoDB: Starting shutdown...
030926 17:43:53  InnoDB: Shutdown completed
030926 17:43:53  /usr/local/mysql/bin/mysqld: Shutdown Complete
```

By default, this file is called *hostname.err* in UNIX and `mysql.err` in Windows, and is always located in the MySQL `data/` directory. In MySQL 4.0.10 and better, you can specify a custom location for the error log file by adding the `--log-error` argument to `mysqld`, as illustrated in the following:

```
[root@host]# /usr/local/mysql/bin/mysqld_safe --log-error=/tmp/mysqld.errors
--user=mysql &
```

More information on how to repair corrupted tables is available in Chapter 15, as is information on other log files maintained by MySQL.

Summary

This chapter offered a brief introduction to MySQL database administration, outlining the most common tasks database administrators are expected to perform and providing a brief look at the MySQL tools available to accomplish these tasks. Chief among these is the `mysqladmin` utility, which makes it possible to reload or shut down the server, view a list of active processes, and obtain current values of server variables. You'll be seeing a lot of this tool in your administrative role.

This chapter then proceeded to a discussion of the more basic tasks in the pantheon of MySQL administration, including starting and stopping the MySQL server, configuring the server to start automatically at boot time, obtaining server status, managing server processes, altering the server configuration through a configuration file or the SET command, and troubleshooting problems using the MySQL error log.

Of course, this is just the tip of the iceberg. MySQL offers the database administrator a number of powerful features to help him or her maintain the server effectively and efficiently. The next few chapters examine some of these features in greater depth.

Security, Access Control, and Privileges

Most users concentrate on MySQL's databases and tables—after all, that's where most of the action takes place—and they don't usually look deeper to understand how it handles access privileges, passwords, and security. This approach is usually more than adequate for most development activities—unless you happen to be a database administrator whose job involves setting up and securing the databases against unauthorized usage or malicious mischief.

With that in mind, this chapter examines the MySQL access control system and throws some light on the MySQL grant tables. These tables, which are an integral part of the server's security system, offer database administrators a great deal of power and flexibility in deciding the rules that govern access to the system. Additionally, this chapter also discusses the management of user accounts and passwords in the MySQL access control system, explaining how passwords (especially the all-important root password) can be modified and how to reset a lost superuser password.

The MySQL Grant Tables

When MySQL is first installed, the MySQL installer automatically creates two databases: the `test` database, which serves as a sandbox for new users to play in, and the `mysql` database, which contains the five MySQL grant tables.

This is clearly visible from the following sample output:

```
mysql> SHOW DATABASES;
+----------+
| Database |
+----------+
| mysql    |
| test     |
+----------+
```

```
2 rows in set (0.00 sec)
mysql> SHOW tables FROM mysql;
+-----------------+
| Tables_in_mysql |
+-----------------+
| columns_priv    |
| db              |
| func            |
| host            |
| tables_priv     |
| user            |
+-----------------+
6 rows in set (0.00 sec)
```

With the exception of the `func` table (used for user-defined functions), each of these tables has a different role to play in deciding whether a user has access to a specific database, table, or table column. Access rules can be set up on the basis of username, connecting host, or database requested.

The following sections examine each of these tables in greater detail.

The `user` Table

Of the five grant tables, the most important one is the `user` table. Here is a list of the fields it contains.

```
CREATE TABLE `user` (
  `Host` varchar(60) binary NOT NULL default '',
  `User` varchar(16) binary NOT NULL default '',
  `Password` varchar(45) binary NOT NULL default '',
  `Select_priv` enum('N','Y') NOT NULL default 'N',
  `Insert_priv` enum('N','Y') NOT NULL default 'N',
  `Update_priv` enum('N','Y') NOT NULL default 'N',
  `Delete_priv` enum('N','Y') NOT NULL default 'N',
  `Create_priv` enum('N','Y') NOT NULL default 'N',
  `Drop_priv` enum('N','Y') NOT NULL default 'N',
  `Reload_priv` enum('N','Y') NOT NULL default 'N',
  `Shutdown_priv` enum('N','Y') NOT NULL default 'N',
  `Process_priv` enum('N','Y') NOT NULL default 'N',
  `File_priv` enum('N','Y') NOT NULL default 'N',
  `Grant_priv` enum('N','Y') NOT NULL default 'N',
  `References_priv` enum('N','Y') NOT NULL default 'N',
  `Index_priv` enum('N','Y') NOT NULL default 'N',
  `Alter_priv` enum('N','Y') NOT NULL default 'N',
  `Show_db_priv` enum('N','Y') NOT NULL default 'N',
  `Super_priv` enum('N','Y') NOT NULL default 'N',
  `Create_tmp_table_priv` enum('N','Y') NOT NULL default 'N',
```

```
`Lock_tables_priv` enum('N','Y') NOT NULL default 'N',
`Execute_priv` enum('N','Y') NOT NULL default 'N',
`Repl_slave_priv` enum('N','Y') NOT NULL default 'N',
`Repl_client_priv` enum('N','Y') NOT NULL default 'N',
`ssl_type` enum('','ANY','X509','SPECIFIED') NOT NULL default '',
`ssl_cipher` blob NOT NULL,
`x509_issuer` blob NOT NULL,
`x509_subject` blob NOT NULL,
`max_questions` int(11) unsigned NOT NULL default '0',
`max_updates` int(11) unsigned NOT NULL default '0',
`max_connections` int(11) unsigned NOT NULL default '0',
PRIMARY KEY  (`Host`,`User`)
) TYPE=MyISAM COMMENT='Users and global privileges'
```

The first three fields (referred to as *scope fields*) define which users are allowed to connect to the database server, their passwords, and the hosts from which they can connect—MySQL uses a combination of both user and host identification as the basis for its security system.

Consider the following extract from this table:

```
+-------------------+--------+----------+
| Host              | User   | Password |
+-------------------+--------+----------+
| turkey.domain.com | john   |          |
+-------------------+--------+----------+
```

This implies that the user `john` (password null) is allowed to connect from the host `turkey.domain.com`.

IP addresses can be used instead of host names. The following is a perfectly valid entry:

```
+-------------------+--------+----------+
| Host              | User   | Password |
+-------------------+--------+----------+
| 240.56.78.99      | john   |          |
+-------------------+--------+----------+
```

What's in a Name?

Note, MySQL users are not the same as system users, on either Windows or UNIX. MySQL users exist only within the context of the MySQL RDBMS and need not have accounts or home directories on the system. While the MySQL command-line client on UNIX does default to using the currently logged-in user's name to connect to the server, this behavior can be overridden by specifying a user name to the client via the `--user` parameter.

It's also possible to specify wildcards when setting up such access rules. The following example would allow access to a user named john, regardless of the host from which the connection is requested.

```
+-----------------+--------+
| Host  | User | Password |
+-----------------+--------+
| %     | john |          |
+-----------------+--------+
```

The % character is used as a wildcard. The following example would match any user named john connecting from any host in the loudbeep.com domain.

```
+----------------+-----+-----------+
| Host           | User | Password |
+----------------+-----+-----------+
| %.loudbeep.com | john |          |
+----------------+-----+-----------+
```

Once the users, passwords, and hosts are specified, it becomes necessary to specify the privileges each user has—which is where the other 21 columns (or *privilege fields*) come in. Table 14–1 specifies what each of these fields represents.

The remaining fields in the user table are related to SSL encryption and resource usage limits per user—some of these are discussed in the section "Limiting Resource Usage."

At this point, note that the security privileges assigned to each user in the user table are globally valid; they apply to every database on the system. Therefore, the record

```
+-----------------+------+-----------+-------------+
| Host            | User | Password  | Delete_priv |
+-----------------+------+-----------+-------------+
| apple.pie.com   | joe  | secret    | Y           |
+-----------------+------+-----------+-------------+
```

would imply that user joe has the ability to DELETE records from any table in any database on the server—not a Good Thing if Joe happens to be in a bad mood. For this reason, most administrators (and the MySQL manual) recommend leaving all privileges in this table to *N* (the default value) for every user, and using the host and db tables to assign more focused levels of access (the host and db tables are discussed in the section "The db and host Tables").

TIP Wondering how to create users and maintain user passwords? Flip to the sections "Granting, Revoking, and Viewing User Privileges" and "Changing User Passwords" for detailed instructions.

Field	Privilege Name	Users With This Privilege Can
Select_priv	SELECT	Execute a SELECT query to retrieve rows from a table
Insert_priv	INSERT	Execute an INSERT query
Update_priv	UPDATE	Execute an UPDATE query
Delete_priv	DELETE	Execute a DELETE query
Create_priv	CREATE	CREATE databases and tables
Drop_priv	DROP	DROP databases and tables
Reload_priv	RELOAD	Reload/refresh the MySQL server
Shutdown_priv	SHUTDOWN	Shut down a running MySQL server
Process_priv	PROCESS	Track activity on a MySQL server
File_priv	FILE	Read and write files on the server
Grant_priv	GRANT	GRANT other users the same privileges the user possesses
Index_priv	INDEX	Create, edit, and delete table indexes
Alter_priv	ALTER	ALTER tables
References_priv	REFERENCES	Create, edit, and delete foreign key references
Show_db_priv	SHOW DATABASES	View available databases on the server
Super_priv	SUPER	Execute administrative commands
Create_tmp_table_priv	CREATE TEMPORARY TABLES	Create temporary tables
Lock_tables_priv	LOCK TABLES	Create and delete table locks
Execute_priv	EXECUTE	Execute stored procedures
Repl_slave_priv	REPLICATION SLAVE	Read master binary logs in a replication context
Repl_client_priv	REPLICATION CLIENT	Request information on masters and slaves in a replication context

TABLE 14-1   MySQL Privilege Levels

Here's another example—the following record implies the existence of a superuser named superapple, with complete access to all MySQL privileges.

```
+------------------+--------------+------------+----------+
| Host             | User         | Password   | All_priv |
+------------------+--------------+------------+----------+
| apple.pie.com    | superapple   | secret     | Y        |
+------------------+--------------+------------+----------+
```

NOTE   *An All_priv column doesn't appear in any of the grant tables. We've simply used it as shorthand in these examples to indicate the same value is present in all the privilege (*_priv) columns.*

The `db` and `host` Tables

The `host` and `db` tables are used together—they control which databases are available to which users, and which operations are possible on those databases. Take a look at the fields in a typical `db` table:

```
CREATE TABLE `db` (
  `Host` char(60) binary NOT NULL default '',
  `Db` char(64) binary NOT NULL default '',
  `User` char(16) binary NOT NULL default '',
  `Select_priv` enum('N','Y') NOT NULL default 'N',
  `Insert_priv` enum('N','Y') NOT NULL default 'N',
  `Update_priv` enum('N','Y') NOT NULL default 'N',
  `Delete_priv` enum('N','Y') NOT NULL default 'N',
  `Create_priv` enum('N','Y') NOT NULL default 'N',
  `Drop_priv` enum('N','Y') NOT NULL default 'N',
  `Grant_priv` enum('N','Y') NOT NULL default 'N',
  `References_priv` enum('N','Y') NOT NULL default 'N',
  `Index_priv` enum('N','Y') NOT NULL default 'N',
  `Alter_priv` enum('N','Y') NOT NULL default 'N',
  `Create_tmp_table_priv` enum('N','Y') NOT NULL default 'N',
  `Lock_tables_priv` enum('N','Y') NOT NULL default 'N',
  PRIMARY KEY  (`Host`,`Db`,`User`),
  KEY `User` (`User`)
) TYPE=MyISAM COMMENT='Database privileges'
```

Again, the first three fields are scope fields, which link a specific user and host to one or more databases. The remaining privilege fields are used to specify the type of operations the user can perform on the named database (refer to Table 14–1 for details on what each field represents).

A record like the following one would imply that the user `bill`, connecting from host `cranberry.domain.com`, would be able to use the database `darkbeast` only:

```
+-----------------------+------+-----------+---------+
| Host                  | User | Db        | All_priv|
+-----------------------+------+-----------+---------+
| cranberry.domain.com  | bill | darkbeast | Y       |
+-----------------------+------+-----------+---------+
```

On the other hand, this next record would imply that any user, connecting from any host, would have complete access to the `test` database:

```
+------+------+--------+----------+
| Host | User | Db     | All_priv |
+------+------+--------+----------+
| %    |      | test   | Y        |
+------+------+--------+----------+
```

A blank entry in the `Host` field of the `db` table implies that the list of allowed hosts should be obtained from the third table, the `host` table, which looks like this:

```
CREATE TABLE `host` (
  `Host` char(60) binary NOT NULL default '',
  `Db` char(64) binary NOT NULL default '',
  `Select_priv` enum('N','Y') NOT NULL default 'N',
  `Insert_priv` enum('N','Y') NOT NULL default 'N',
  `Update_priv` enum('N','Y') NOT NULL default 'N',
  `Delete_priv` enum('N','Y') NOT NULL default 'N',
  `Create_priv` enum('N','Y') NOT NULL default 'N',
  `Drop_priv` enum('N','Y') NOT NULL default 'N',
  `Grant_priv` enum('N','Y') NOT NULL default 'N',
  `References_priv` enum('N','Y') NOT NULL default 'N',
  `Index_priv` enum('N','Y') NOT NULL default 'N',
  `Alter_priv` enum('N','Y') NOT NULL default 'N',
  `Create_tmp_table_priv` enum('N','Y') NOT NULL default 'N',
  `Lock_tables_priv` enum('N','Y') NOT NULL default 'N',
  PRIMARY KEY  (`Host`, `Db`)
) TYPE=MyISAM COMMENT='Host privileges;  Merged with database privileges'
```

This separation between host records and database records is more useful than you might think. In the absence of the `host` table, if you want the same user to have different privileges based on the host from which he or she is connecting, you would need to create a separate record for each host in the `db` table and assign privileges accordingly. However, because the `host` table exists, you can place the various host names in the `host` table, link them to a single entry (with a blank `Host` field) in the `db` table, and then set privileges on a per-host basis. When a connection is attempted from one of the named hosts, MySQL will assign privileges based on the rules set for that host in the `host` table.

Here's an example of how this works (the first snippet is from the `db` table, the second is the corresponding records in the `host` table):

```
+------+------+-------+
| Host | User | Db    |
+------+------+-------+
|      | jim  | title |
+------+------+-------+
```

```
+--------------------+-------+----------------+----------------+
| Host               | Db    | Select_priv    | Insert_priv    |
+--------------------+-------+----------------+----------------+
| turkey.ix6.com     | title | Y              | Y              |
+--------------------+-------+----------------+----------------+
| blackbox.glue.net  | title | Y              | N              |
+--------------------+-------+----------------+----------------+
| fireball.home.net  | title | Y              | Y              |
+--------------------+-------+----------------+----------------+
```

In this case, `jim` will be able to connect to the MySQL server from any of the hosts listed in the `host` table, but the privileges he has will differ on the basis of the host from which he is connecting.

The `tables_priv` and `columns_priv` Tables

In addition to the three tables already discussed, newer versions of MySQL also come with two additional tables: the `tables_priv` and `columns_priv` tables. These allow a database administrator to restrict access to specific tables in a database and to specific columns of a table, respectively.

Here's what the `tables_priv` table looks like:

```
CREATE TABLE `tables_priv` (
  `Host` char(60) binary NOT NULL default '',
  `Db` char(64) binary NOT NULL default '',
  `User` char(16) binary NOT NULL default '',
  `Table_name` char(60) binary NOT NULL default '',
  `Grantor` char(77) NOT NULL default '',
  `Timestamp` timestamp(14) NOT NULL,
  `Table_priv` set('Select', 'Insert', 'Update', 'Delete', 'Create',
'Drop', 'Grant', 'References', 'Index', 'Alter') NOT NULL default '',
  `Column_priv` set('Select', 'Insert', 'Update', 'References')
NOT NULL default '',
  PRIMARY KEY  (`Host`, `Db`, `User`, `Table_name`),
  KEY `Grantor` (`Grantor`)
) TYPE=MyISAM COMMENT='Table privileges'
```

The following record would restrict the user `john` to performing `SELECT` operations on table `cream` only—any attempt to run a `SELECT` query on another table within the same database would result in an error.

```
+----------------+-------+------+------------+---------------+
| Host           | Db    | User | Table_name | Table_priv    |
+----------------+-------+------+------------+---------------+
|lost.soul.com   | db563 | john | cream      | Select        |
+----------------+-------+------+------------+---------------+
```

Similarly, the following record would allow the user `logger` to perform `SELECT`, `INSERT`, and `UPDATE` (but not `DELETE`) queries on the table named `logs` in the `db1` database:

```
+-----------+-----+--------+------------+-----------------------+
| Host      | Db  | User   | Table_name | Table_priv            |
+-----------+-----+--------+------------+-----------------------+
| localhost | db1 | logger | logs       | Select,Insert,Update  |
+-----------+-----+--------+------------+-----------------------+
```

For even more fine-grained control, MySQL offers the `columns_priv` table, which makes it possible to set access privileges on a per-column basis—as the following table structure illustrates.

```
CREATE TABLE `columns_priv` (
  `Host` char(60) binary NOT NULL default '',
  `Db` char(64) binary NOT NULL default '',
  `User` char(16) binary NOT NULL default '',
  `Table_name` char(64) binary NOT NULL default '',
  `Column_name` char(64) binary NOT NULL default '',
  `Timestamp` timestamp(14) NOT NULL,
  `Column_priv` set('Select', 'Insert', 'Update', 'References')
NOT NULL default '',
  PRIMARY KEY  (`Host`, `Db`, `User`, `Table_name`, `Column_name`)
) TYPE=MyISAM COMMENT='Column privileges'
```

The following is a case in point. The following rules imply that users logging in with the account `hr_users` can read only the employee ID, employee name, and department from the `db1.employees` table, while supervisors (using the account `hr_supervisors`) can additionally view the employee's compensation and update his or her name and department information.

```
+-----+----------------+------------+-------------+----------------+
| Db  | User           | Table_name | Column_name | Column_priv    |
+-----+----------------+------------+-------------+----------------+
| db1 | hr_supervisors | employees  | name        | Select, Update |
| db1 | hr_supervisors | employees  | id          | Select         |
| db1 | hr_supervisors | employees  | dept        | Select, Update |
| db1 | hr_users       | employees  | id          | Select         |
| db1 | hr_users       | employees  | name        | Select         |
| db1 | hr_users       | employees  | dept        | Select         |
+-----+----------------+------------+-------------+----------------+
```

Interaction Between the Grant Tables

The various grant tables interact with each other to create comprehensive access rules that MySQL uses when deciding how to handle a particular user request. Access control takes place at two stages: the connection stage and the request stage.

- **The connection stage**   When a user requests a connection to the database server from a specific host, MySQL will first check whether an entry exists for the user in the user table, if the user's password is correct, and if the user is allowed to connect from that specific host. If the check is successful, a connection will be allowed to the server.

- **The request stage** Once a connection is allowed, every subsequent request to the server—SELECT, DELETE, UPDATE, and other queries—will first be vetted to ensure that the user has the security privileges necessary to perform the corresponding action. A number of different levels of access are possible—some users might only have the ability to SELECT from the tables, while others might have INSERT and UPDATE capabilities, but not DELETE capabilities.

In the hierarchy of the MySQL grant tables, the user table comes first, with the db and host tables below it, and the tables_priv and columns_priv tables at the bottom. A table at a lower level is referred to only if a higher-level table fails to provide the necessary scope or privileges.

When deciding whether to allow a particular database operation, MySQL takes the privilege fields in all three tables into account. It starts with the user table and checks to see if the user has appropriate privileges for the operation being attempted. If not, the db and host tables are checked to see if privileges are available. Only after logically parsing the privileges in the different tables does MySQL allow or disallow a specific database request.

When MySQL encounters a request for an administrative action—RELOAD, PROCESS, and so forth—by a user, it decides whether to permit that action based solely on the corresponding permissions for that user in the user table. None of the other grant tables are consulted to make this determination. This is because these administrative privileges apply to the system as a whole and not to specific databases or tables, therefore, the corresponding columns make an appearance in the user table only.

The Default Setup

Now, let's look at the default tables that ship with MySQL, so you can understand the implications of running an out-of-the-box MySQL setup.

```
mysql> SELECT Host, User, Password FROM mysql.user;
+-----------+------+----------+
| Host      | User | Password |
+-----------+------+----------+
| localhost | root |          |
| localhost |      |          |
+-----------+------+----------+
2 rows in set (0.00 sec)
mysql> SELECT Host, Db, User FROM mysql.db;
+------+---------+------+
| Host | Db      | User |
+------+---------+------+
| %    | test    |      |
| %    | test\_% |   .  |
+------+---------+------+
```

What this means is, out of the box:

1. MySQL gives the user connecting as `root` from the local machine `localhost` complete access to all databases on the system.

2. MySQL gives any other user connecting from the local machine complete access (a) to all databases, on Windows or (b) to the `test` database, on UNIX.

3. Users from other hosts are denied access.

Granting, Revoking, and Viewing User Privileges

Modifying the grant tables in the `mysql` database requires superuser access to the MySQL database server. So, the first order of business is to ensure that you have this level of access and can alter table records.

If you've installed the server yourself, on your own development machine, you would have been told to enter a root password at the time of installation (Chapter 3 has details on this process). If you paid attention to the installation instructions in Chapter 3, you would have done this (leaving the password blank opens up a security hole in the system), and noted the password you set for future reference.

To verify that you have the required access, log in to the server as the `root` user, as in the following:

```
[root@host] $ mysql -u root -p
Enter password: ****
Welcome to the MySQL monitor.  Commands end with ; or \g.
mysql>
```

Now, ensure that you can access the grant tables in the `mysql` database:

```
mysql> USE mysql;
Database changed
```

Such root-level access is typically available only to the database administrator. Other users have a lower security rating and, consequently, limited access. Each of these "ordinary" users will typically connect to the database by supplying his or her own user name and password. As noted in the previous section, the purpose of the MySQL grant tables is to make it possible to manipulate security settings for these ordinary users and to customize each user's level of access to a fine degree.

MySQL offers two methods of altering access rights in the grant tables—you can either use INSERT, UPDATE, and DELETE DML queries to hand-alter the information in the tables or you can use the GRANT and REVOKE commands. The latter is the preferred method; direct modification of the grant tables is advisable only for unusual tasks or situations, and is generally not recommended.

PART III

Using the GRANT and REVOKE Commands

The recommended way of setting access privileges for a user in the MySQL grant tables is via the MySQL GRANT and REVOKE commands, designed specifically for the task. Here's what they look like:

```
GRANT privilege (field-name, field-name, ...), privilege (field-name, field-name,
...), ... ON database-name.table-name TO user@domain IDENTIFIED BY password,
user@domain IDENTIFIED BY password, ...
REVOKE privilege (field-name, field-name, ...), privilege (field-name, field-name,
...), ... ON database-name.table-name FROM user@domain, user@domain, ...
```

To illustrate this, let's consider a few examples. This first example assigns SELECT, INSERT, UPDATE, and DELETE privileges on the table db1.logs to the user logger connecting from localhost with password timber:

```
mysql> GRANT SELECT, INSERT, UPDATE ON db1.logs TO logger@localhost
IDENTIFIED BY 'timber';
```

Now, look at what happens when this user logs in to MySQL and tries attempting different types of queries:

```
[user@host] $ mysql -h localhost -u logger -p
Enter password: ******
Welcome to the MySQL monitor.  Commands end with ; or \g.
Your MySQL connection id is 7 to server version: 4.0.14
Type 'help;' or '\h' for help. Type '\c' to clear the buffer
mysql> USE mysql;
ERROR 1044: Access denied for user: 'logger@localhost' to database 'mysql'
mysql> USE db1;
Database changed
mysql> SELECT * FROM employees;
ERROR 1142: select command denied to user: 'logger@localhost' for table 'employees'
mysql> SELECT * FROM logs;
+----+----------------------------+--------+
| id | message                    | sender |
+----+----------------------------+--------+
| 34 | Apache core error          | httpd  |
| 35 | Root login failure on tty1 | pamd   |
| 36 | Root login failure on tty1 | pamd   |
+----+----------------------------+--------+
3 rows in set (0.00 sec)

mysql> INSERT INTO logs VALUES (37, 'Sendmail restart, 102 messages in queue', 'sendmail');
Query OK, 1 row affected (0.00 sec)
mysql> DELETE FROM logs WHERE id = 37;
ERROR 1142: delete command denied to user: 'logger@localhost' for table 'logs'
```

Thus, only the commands specified in the GRANT command are permitted to the user. All other commands are denied. Every time the user requests a specific command, MySQL refers to its grant tables and only permits the command to be executed if the privilege rules allow it.

The REVOKE command does the opposite of the GRANT command, making it possible to revoke privileges assigned to a user. Consider the following example, which rescinds logger's INSERT and UPDATE rights on the db1.logs table:

```
mysql> REVOKE INSERT, UPDATE ON db1.logs FROM logger@localhost;
```

This change goes into effect immediately. Now, when logger tries to INSERT a new record into the table (an operation previously permitted), look at what happens:

```
mysql> INSERT INTO logs VALUES (38, 'System powerdown signal received', 'apmd');
ERROR 1142: insert command denied to user: 'logger@localhost' for table 'logs'
```

MySQL allows the use of the * wildcard when referring to databases and tables—this next query assigns RELOAD, PROCESS, SELECT, DELETE, and INSERT privileges to all databases to the user admin on the host named medusa:

```
mysql> GRANT RELOAD, PROCESS, SELECT, DELETE, INSERT ON *.* TO admin@medusa
IDENTIFIED BY 'secret';
```

This next example assigns SELECT privileges on the table employees. compensation to the supervisor user only:

```
mysql> GRANT SELECT ON employees.compensation TO supervisor;
```

This next example takes things one step further, assigning SELECT and UPDATE privileges to specific columns of the grades table to harry and john, respectively:

```
mysql> GRANT SELECT (id, name, subj, grade) ON db1.grades TO harry;
mysql> GRANT SELECT (id, name, subj, grade), UPDATE (name, grade) ON
db1.grades TO john;
Query OK, 0 rows affected (0.00 sec)
```

The following example rescinds user tim's CREATE and DROP rights on database db2003a:

```
mysql> REVOKE CREATE, DROP ON db2003a.* FROM tim@funhouse.com;
```

Turning the Tables

The table(s) or field(s) named in the GRANT command must exist as a prerequisite to assigning corresponding table- and column-level privileges. However, this rule does not hold true when dealing with database-level privileges. MySQL permits you to assign database-level privileges, even if the corresponding database does not exist. This dissonance between table- and database-level privileges is a common cause of newbie error, so be forewarned!

As with databases, so with tables and columns. This next example revokes the webmaster user's DELETE rights on the menu table:

```
mysql> REVOKE DELETE ON www.menu FROM webmaster@localhost;
```

And this one removes the user sarah's rights to UPDATE the name and address columns of the customer database:

```
mysql> REVOKE UPDATE (name, address) ON sales.customers FROM
sarah@work.domain.net;
```

MySQL also provides the ALL privilege level as shorthand for "all privileges"; this can help to make your GRANT and REVOKE statements more compact. This is illustrated in the next example, which assigns all privileges on the database named web to the user www connecting from any host in the melonfire.com domain:

```
mysql> GRANT ALL ON web.* TO www@'%.melonfire.com' IDENTIFIED BY
'abracadabra';
```

In a similar manner, the REVOKE command can be used to revoke all privileges for a specific user:

```
mysql> REVOKE ALL ON web.* FROM www@'%.melonfire.com';
```

MySQL also provides the special USAGE privilege level for situations when you need to create a user without assigning him or her any privileges. Here are two examples:

```
mysql> GRANT USAGE ON content.* TO joe@localhost;
mysql> GRANT USAGE ON *.* TO test@some.domain.com;
```

The GRANT Privilege
MySQL lets users grant other users the same privileges they have, via the special WITH GRANT OPTION clause of the GRANT command. When this clause is added to a GRANT command, users to whom it applies can assign the same privileges they possess to other users. Consider the following example:

```
mysql> GRANT SELECT, DELETE, INSERT, UPDATE, CREATE, DROP, INDEX ON
inventory.* TO david@localhost WITH GRANT OPTION;
```

Wild at Heart

When using wildcards like % and _ in host names or database names with the GRANT and REVOKE commands, MySQL requires you to surround the corresponding name in quotes. Wildcards are not, however, supported for user names. To create an anonymous user, use the empty string ' ' as the user name.

> **Manual Labor**
> When the GRANT command is invoked for a particular user, it automatically
> creates an entry for that user in the user table, if one does not already exist. The
> corresponding REVOKE command does not delete that entry from the user table,
> however, even if its invocation results in all the user's privileges being stripped.
> Thus, though a user record can be automatically added to the system via GRANT,
> it is never automatically removed using REVOKE. A user record must always be
> manually deleted using a DELETE query.

The user david@localhost will now have the GRANT privilege and can assign his
rights to other users, as clearly demonstrated in the following snippet:

```
mysql> SELECT Host, Db, User, Grant_priv FROM db WHERE Host = 'localhost';
+-----------+-----------+-------+------------+
| Host      | Db        | User  | Grant_priv |
+-----------+-----------+-------+------------+
| localhost | inventory | david | Y          |
+-----------+-----------+-------+------------+
1 row in set (0.00 sec)
```

The user david@localhost can now log in to MySQL and GRANT other users all
or some of the privileges he himself possesses, as in the following:

```
mysql> GRANT SELECT ON inventory.* TO joe@localhost IDENTIFIED BY 'joey2839';
mysql> SELECT Host, Db, User, Grant_priv FROM db WHERE Host = 'localhost';
+-----------+-----------+-------+------------+
| Host      | Db        | User  | Grant_priv |
+-----------+-----------+-------+------------+
| localhost | inventory | david | Y          |
| localhost | inventory | joe   | Y          |
+-----------+-----------+-------+------------+
2 rows in set (0.00 sec)
```

The GRANT privilege can be reversed by using the GRANT OPTION clause in a
standard REVOKE command, as the following shows:

```
mysql> REVOKE GRANT OPTION ON inventory.* FROM david@localhost;
```

The user david@localhost will now no longer have the capability to grant other
users privileges. This is clearly visible from both the user table snippet and the output
of the GRANT command run by him, as shown in the following:

```
mysql> GRANT SELECT ON inventory.* TO joe@localhost IDENTIFIED BY 'joey2839';
ERROR 1044: Access denied for user: 'david@localhost' to database 'inventory'
```

```
mysql> SELECT Host, Db, User, Grant_priv FROM db WHERE User = 'david';
+-----------+-----------+-------+------------+
| Host      | Db        | User  | Grant_priv |
+-----------+-----------+-------+------------+
| localhost | inventory | david | N          |
+-----------+-----------+-------+------------+
2 rows in set (0.00 sec)
```

Care should be taken when assigning users the GRANT privilege. Users with different access levels can combine them and, thereby, obtain a higher level of access than they are normally allowed.

Limiting Resource Usage

New in MySQL 4.*x* is the capability to limit resource usage on the MySQL server, on a per-user basis. This is accomplished by the addition of three new fields to the user table: max_questions, max_updates, and max_connections, which can be used to limit the number of queries, table or record updates, and new connections by a particular user per hour, respectively. These three fields map into three optional clauses to the GRANT command.

The first of these is the MAX_QUERIES_PER_HOUR clause, which limits the number of queries that can be run by a user in an hour. Here's an example:

```
mysql> GRANT SELECT ON *.* TO sarah WITH MAX_QUERIES_PER_HOUR 5;
```

The MAX_QUERIES_PER_HOUR clause controls the total number of queries permitted per hour, regardless of whether these are SELECT, INSERT, UPDATE, DELETE, or other queries. If this is too all-encompassing, you can also set a limit on the number of queries that change the data in the database, via the MAX_UPDATES_PER_HOUR clause, as in the following:

```
mysql> GRANT SELECT ON *.* TO sarah WITH MAX_UPDATES_PER_HOUR 5;
```

The number of new connections opened by the named user(s) in an hour can be controlled via the MAX_CONNECTIONS_PER_HOUR clause, as the following shows.

```
mysql> GRANT SELECT ON *.* TO sarah WITH MAX_CONNECTIONS_PER_HOUR 3;
```

You can also use these clauses in combination with each other. The following is a perfectly valid GRANT:

```
mysql> GRANT SELECT, INSERT, UPDATE, DELETE ON *.* TO supervisor WITH
MAX_QUERIES_PER_HOUR 50 MAX_UPDATES_PER_HOUR 10 MAX_CONNECTIONS_PER_HOUR 4;
```

Note, such usage limits cannot be specified per-database or per-table. They can only be specified in the global context, by using an ON *.* clause in the GRANT command. Here's an example of what MySQL says when a resource limit is exceeded:

```
mysql> INSERT INTO customers (id, name) VALUES (2892, 'Iola J');
ERROR 1226: User 'sarah' has exceeded the 'max_questions' resource
(current value: 5)
```

The server maintains internal counters, on a per-user basis, for each of these three resource limits. These counters could be reset at any time with the new FLUSH USER_RESOURCES command, as in the following:

```
mysql> FLUSH USER_RESOURCES;
Query OK, 0 rows affected (0.00 sec)
```

NOTE   *You need the RELOAD privilege to execute the FLUSH command.*

Using the INSERT, UPDATE, and DELETE Commands

The GRANT and REVOKE commands described in the preceding section are the recommended way of making changes to the MySQL grant tables. However, because the grant tables are, ultimately, regular MySQL tables, you can also manipulate them using standard INSERT, UPDATE, and DELETE queries.

Therefore, while you can certainly use the following GRANT command,

```
mysql> GRANT SELECT, INSERT, UPDATE, DELETE, ON recipes.* TO tom@localhost
IDENTIFIED BY 'tommygun';
```

you can accomplish the same task with the following two (equivalent) INSERT commands:

```
mysql> INSERT INTO user (Host, User, Password) VALUES('localhost', 'tom',
PASSWORD('tommygun'));
mysql> INSERT INTO db (Host, Db, User, Select_priv, Insert_priv, Update_priv,
Delete_priv, Create_priv, Drop_priv) VALUES ('localhost', 'recipes', 'tom', 'Y',
'Y', 'Y', 'Y', 'N', 'N');
mysql> FLUSH PRIVILEGES;
```

Similarly, while you can set up an administrative user with the following GRANT,

```
mysql> GRANT ALL PRIVILEGES ON *.* TO admin@localhost IDENTIFIED BY
'master';
```

you can also do it with the following INSERT:

```
mysql> INSERT INTO user (Host, User, Password, Select_priv, Insert_priv,
Update_priv, Delete_priv, Create_priv, Drop_priv, Reload_priv, Shutdown_priv,
Process_priv, File_priv, Grant_priv, References_priv, Index_priv, Alter_priv)
VALUES ('localhost', 'admin', PASSWORD('master'), 'Y', 'Y', 'Y', 'Y', 'Y', 'Y',
'Y', 'Y', 'Y', 'Y', 'Y', 'Y', 'Y', 'Y');
mysql> FLUSH PRIVILEGES;
```

PART III

Viewing Privileges

MySQL enables you to view the privileges assigned to a particular user with the SHOW GRANTS command, which accepts a username as argument and displays a list of all the privileges granted to that user. The following examples illustrate this:

```
mysql> SHOW GRANTS FOR sarah@localhost;
+--------------------------------------------+
| Grants for sarah@localhost                 |
+--------------------------------------------+
| GRANT USAGE ON *.* TO 'sarah'@'localhost'  |
|   IDENTIFIED BY PASSWORD '4837a3954ee01ece' |
| GRANT SELECT ON sales.customers TO         |
| 'sarah'@'localhost'                        |
+--------------------------------------------+
2 rows in set (0.00 sec)
mysql> SHOW GRANTS FOR root;
+------------------------------------------------------------+
| Grants for root@%                                          |
+------------------------------------------------------------+
| GRANT ALL PRIVILEGES ON *.* TO 'root'@'%' WITH GRANT OPTION |
+------------------------------------------------------------+
1 row in set (0.06 sec)
```

> **TIP** The UNIX distribution of MySQL includes a script named mysqlaccess, which can be used to generate reports on a particular user's access level and privileges. Type **mysqlaccess --howto** for usage examples.

Reloading the Grant Tables

Privileges set using GRANT and REVOKE are immediately activated (as demonstrated in one of the examples in the preceding section). Privileges set via regular SQL queries, however, require a server reload to come into effect. A server reload can be accomplished via the FLUSH PRIVILEGES command, as in the following:

```
mysql> FLUSH PRIVILEGES;
Query OK, 0 rows affected (0.05 sec)
```

> **NOTE** You need the RELOAD privilege to run the FLUSH command.

MySQL normally reads the grant tables once when it starts up, but you can also force MySQL to reload the grant tables via the mysqladmin tool, as in the following example. This example is for UNIX. Simply replace the path with the correct path to your MySQL installation for Windows:

```
[root@host]# /usr/local/mysql/bin/mysqladmin -u root reload
```

Resetting the Grant Tables

If you want to reset the grant tables to their initial default settings, the process is as follows:

1. If the server is running, stop it in the usual manner:

   ```
   [root@host] $ /usr/local/mysql/support-files/mysql.server stop
   ```

2. Change to the data directory of your MySQL installation, and then delete the mysql/ folder. Because databases in MySQL are represented as directories on the file system, this will effectively erase the grant tables.

   ```
   [root@host] $ rm -rf /usr/local/mysql/data/mysql
   ```

3. On UNIX, reinstall the grant tables by running the initialization script, mysql_install_db, which ships with the program:

   ```
   [root@host]# /usr/local/mysql/scripts/mysql_install_db
   ```

   On Windows, because this initialization script is not part of the binary distribution, you need to reinstall the package into the same directory to revert to the original grant tables.

4. On UNIX, change back to the data directory of your MySQL installation and alter the ownership of the newly created MySQL directory, so it is owned by the mysql user:

   ```
   [root@host]# chown -R mysql.mysql /usr/local/mysql/data/mysql
   ```

5. Restart the server.

   ```
   [root@host] $ /usr/local/mysql/support-files/mysql.server stop
   ```

The MySQL grant tables should now be reset to their default values. You can now log in as the superuser and make changes to them using the GRANT and REVOKE commands.

Changing User Passwords

When adding a user to the user table with the GRANT command, MySQL also enables you to specify a password for that user with the optional IDENTIFIED BY clause. This password must be provided by the user when logging in to the server to gain access to its databases. When using the mysql client program, the username and password can be specified on the command line via the -u and -p arguments, respectively, as in the following example:

```
[user@host] $ mysql -h localhost -u logger -p
Enter password: ******
Welcome to the MySQL monitor ...
```

If you don't want to be prompted for a password (for example, if you're using the client noninteractively through a script), you can specify it on the command line after the -p argument, as in the following:

```
[user@host] $ mysql -h localhost -u logger -ptimber
Welcome to the MySQL monitor ...
```

Passwords are stored in the `Password` field of the `user` table in the `mysql` database and must be encrypted prior to insertion with the MySQL `PASSWORD()` function, as in the following examples:

```
mysql> INSERT INTO user (Host, User, Password) VALUES('melonfire.net',
'timothy', PASSWORD('1r0ck'));
mysql> UPDATE user SET Password = PASSWORD('1r0ck') WHERE Host =
'melonfire.net' AND User = 'timothy';
mysql> FLUSH PRIVILEGES;
Query OK, 0 rows affected (0.05 sec)
```

Passwords can also be set with the MySQL `SET PASSWORD` command. The following example is equivalent to the previous one.

```
mysql> SET PASSWORD FOR timothy@melonfire.net = PASSWORD('1rock');
```

When setting a password using the `IDENTIFIED BY` clause of the `GRANT` command or via the `mysqladmin` tool, you do not need to encrypt the password string first with the `PASSWORD()` function. The `GRANT` command and the `mysqladmin` utility automatically take care of this for you. Therefore, the following example is equivalent to the previous one:

```
mysql> GRANT USAGE ON *.* TO timothy@melonfire.net IDENTIFIED BY '1rock';
```

The first method requires `FLUSH PRIVILEGES` to work and generally is not recommended. The second method is recommended.

The `IDENTIFIED BY` clause of the `GRANT` command is optional. Creating a `GRANT` for a new user without using this clause will set an empty password for that user. This opens a security hole in the system, so administrators should always make it a point to assign a password to new users.

Safety First!

The MySQL manual recommends against placing your password after the -p option on the `mysql` command line and, instead, suggests entering it at the interactive password prompt, which masks your password as you type it. This will reduce the risk of someone viewing your password over your shoulder and, thereby, gaining unauthorized access to your account on the MySQL server.

> **Out with the Old...**
>
> The PASSWORD() function in MySQL 4.1 and better generate a longer, 41-byte hash value that is not compatible with older versions (which used a 16-byte value). Therefore, when you upgrade a MySQL server installation older than 4.1 to MySQL 4.1 or better, you must run the mysql_fix_privilege_tables script in the scripts/ directory of your MySQL installation to update the grant tables, so they can handle the longer hash value.

When a user logs in to the MySQL server and provides a password string, MySQL first encrypts the provided password string using the PASSWORD() function, and then compares the resulting value with the value in the Password field of the corresponding user record in the user table. If the two values match (and other access rules permit it), the user is granted access. If the values do not match, access is denied.

Setting the root Password

When MySQL is first installed, access to the database server is restricted to the MySQL administrator, aka root. By default, this user is initialized with a null password, which is generally considered a Bad Thing. You should, therefore, rectify this as soon as possible by setting a password for this user via the mysqladmin tool and using the following syntax. (This example is for UNIX. Simply replace the path with the correct path to your MySQL installation for Windows.)

```
[root@host]# /usr/local/mysql/bin/mysqladmin -u root password 'new-password'
```

This password change goes into effect immediately, with no requirement to restart the server or flush the privilege table.

The password can also be changed using either the UPDATE command or the SET PASSWORD command, as described in the preceding section.

Resetting the root Password

If you forget the MySQL root password and are locked out of the grant tables, take a deep breath, and then follow these steps to get things up and running again:

1. Log in to the system as the system administrator (root on UNIX) and stop the MySQL server. This can be accomplished via the mysql.server startup and shutdown script in the support-files/ directory of your MySQL installation, as follows:

   ```
   [root@host] $ /usr/local/mysql/support-files/mysql.server stop
   ```

   In case you're working on a UNIX system that came with MySQL preinstalled or installed MySQL from a binary RPM, you can also stop (and start) MySQL with the /etc/rc.d/init.d/mysqld scripts.

PART III

2. Next, start up MySQL again with the special `--skip-grant-tables` startup option.

```
[root@host] $ /usr/local/mysql/bin/safe_mysqld
--skip-grant-tables --skip-networking
```

This bypasses the grant tables, enabling you to log in to the server as the MySQL `root` user without providing a password. The additional `--skip-networking` option tells MySQL not to listen for TCP/IP connections and ensures that no one can break in over the network while you are fixing the privileges.

3. Use the `UPDATE` command, as described in the preceding section, to set a new password for the MySQL `root` user.

```
[root@host]# mysql
Welcome to the MySQL monitor.  Commands end with ; or \g.
Your MySQL connection id is 7 to server version: 4.0.14
Type 'help;' or '\h' for help. Type '\c' to clear the buffer
mysql> USE mysql;
Database changed
mysql> UPDATE user SET Password = PASSWORD('new-password') WHERE User = 'root';
Query OK, 2 rows affected (0.00 sec)
Rows matched: 2  Changed: 2  Warnings: 0
```

4. Log out of the server, stop it, and restart it again in the normal manner.

```
[root@host] $ /usr/local/mysql/support-files/mysql.server stop
[root@host] $ /usr/local/mysql/support-files/mysql.server start
```

MySQL should now enable you to log in as the `root` user with the new password set in step 3.

NOTE *Read more about MySQL security in the online MySQL manual, at* `http://www.mysql.com/doc/en/General_security.html` *and* `http://www.mysql.com/doc/en/Privileges_provided.html`.

Summary

MySQL comes with a five-tiered access control system, giving you fine-grained control over the privileges each user possesses in relation to databases, tables, and individual fields. This chapter discussed the access control and privilege system in detail, examining the MySQL grant tables, and explaining the `GRANT` and `REVOKE` commands used to manage user privileges. It also examined the topics of limiting resource usage on the server on a per-user basis, changing user passwords, recovering from a lost superuser password, and resetting the grant tables, as well as highlighted some of the new security features available in MySQL 4.*x*.

Maintenance, Backup, and Recovery

As you've discovered by now, MySQL is relatively easy to use, which makes it an ideal database tool for many types of production environments where a dedicated database administrator is neither feasible nor desired. Despite this, a certain amount of basic maintenance needs to be done, regardless of the size of your installation. The goal of this chapter is to introduce some of the basics involved in making sure things run as they should, and to prepare you for when disaster strikes (notice we didn't write "if").

Maintenance

A significant amount of maintenance needed by MySQL is done through the various log files. Logging is essential for situations where troubleshooting is necessary or where you want to be proactive and avoid problems in advance. The other technique that will keep your database humming smoothly and efficiently is checking, repairing, and optimizing your tables on an on-going basis. Each of these topics is considered in turn in this section.

Logging

When the MySQL server starts up, it checks if any of the logging options are marked for activation. If so, the server starts the indicated logs as part of the startup process. Log files provide the information necessary to manage your server. Analyzing performance and investigating problems are some of the main reasons for consulting these logs. The files are stored in the same directory as the data files, usually in `/usr/local/mysql/data` on UNIX or in `c:\mysql\data` in Windows.

Although these are all standard text files, several different types of logs are available.

- The error log
- The query log
- The slow query log

- The update log
- The binary update log

The Error Log

The error log does exactly what you think it would do—it keeps a record of every error that occurs on the server. As such, this is a basic diagnostic tool, and one which comes in handy when troubleshooting problems with the server.

To activate the error log, add the `--log-error` option to the server's startup command line or option file, as below:

```
[root@host]# /usr/local/mysql/bin/mysqld_safe --log-error
```

Here's a sample snippet from the error log:

```
031024 15:19:08  InnoDB: Started
/usr/local/mysql/bin/mysqld: ready for connections.
Version: '4.0.15-standard'  socket: '/tmp/mysql.sock'  port: 3306
InnoDB: Setting log file ./ib_logfile0 size to 5 MB
InnoDB: Database physically writes the file full: wait...
031024 15:19:07  InnoDB: Log file ./ib_logfile1 did not exist: new to be created
InnoDB: Setting log file ./ib_logfile1 size to 5 MB
InnoDB: Database physically writes the file full: wait...
InnoDB: Doublewrite buffer not found: creating new
InnoDB: Doublewrite buffer created
031024 15:42:02  /usr/local/mysql/bin/mysqld: Normal shutdown
031024 15:42:02  InnoDB: Starting shutdown...
031024 15:42:04  InnoDB: Shutdown completed
031024 15:42:04  /usr/local/mysql/bin/mysqld: Shutdown Complete
```

The filename for this log always ends in the `.err` extension.

The Query Log

The query log is another useful log because it (surprise, surprise!) keeps track of every query sent to the server by a client. It also displays details about which clients are connected to the server and what these clients are doing. If you want to monitor activity for the purpose of troubleshooting, you should activate the query log, by adding the `--log` option to the server's startup command line or option file.

```
[root@host]# /usr/local/mysql/bin/mysqld_safe --log
```

Here's a sample snippet from the query log:

```
Time                Id Command    Argument
031116 18:10:26      1 Connect    root@localhost on
031116 18:10:32      1 Query      show databases
031116 18:10:35      1 Init DB    test
```

```
                              1 Query        show databases
                              1 Query        show tables
031116 18:10:38               1 Query        show tables
031116 18:10:45               1 Init DB      mysql
                              1 Query        show databases
                              1 Query        show tables
                              1 Field List   columns_priv
                              1 Field List   db
                              1 Field List   func
                              1 Field List   host
                              1 Field List   tables_priv
                              1 Field List   user
031116 18:10:48               1 Query        show tables
031116 18:10:52               1 Query        select * from user
031116 18:10:56               1 Quit
```

The default filename for the log is the hostname with the `.log` extension.

The Slow Query Log

A related log is the slow query log, which lists all the queries that exceed a predefined amount of time (specified by the `long_query_time` variable). Any query that takes longer than this value is listed in this log. If you're looking for a way to optimize performance, this log is a good place to start.

NOTE *Query optimization is discussed in detail in Chapter 16.*

Typically, you would look at the queries in this log as candidates for revision to lessen the impact on your server's performance. Remember, though, the length of time a query takes can be the result of factors other than poorly written code. Queries that usually run under the "long" threshold can appear in this log if the server is tied up elsewhere.

The slow query log is activated by using the `--log-slow-queries` option on the `mysqld` command line, as in the example below:

```
[root@host]# /usr/local/mysql/bin/mysqld_safe --log-slow-queries
```

The default filename for the log is the hostname followed by the suffix `-slow`, and a `.log` extension.

The Update Log

Another log related to the query log is the update log, which displays all the queries that change a particular table. Statements such as INSERT, REPLACE, DELETE, GRANT, and REVOKE, along with UPDATE, CREATE TABLE and DROP TABLE are all in this category; however, SELECT statements aren't recorded. Entries to the update log are written only after the change takes place so, if an update fails, for whatever reason, it won't be entered.

The update log is created by using the `--log-update` option when you start the MySQL server, as illustrated here:

```
[root@host]# /usr/local/mysql/bin/mysqld_safe --log-update
```

This log is useful if you have to rebuild a table that was changed after the most recent backup. In case your database gets corrupted, restore it from your backup, and then re-create the queries recorded in the update log to bring the system back to the state just before failure.

The Binary Update Log

More recent versions of MySQL (after 3.23.14) also support a variant of the update log stored in binary, instead of text, format. This is a more efficient storage format for data, and this binary update log also records more details than the standard update log. A utility named `mysqlbinlog` converts the binary log back to text so you can read it. You create the binary update log by using the `--log-bin` option when starting MySQL, as follows:

```
[root@host]# /usr/local/mysql/bin/mysqld_safe --log-bin
```

The default filename for the log is the hostname followed by the suffix `-bin`, and a number identifying the log in the sequence.

NOTE   *If you're setting up master and slave servers for replication, you must enable the binary update log (more about replication in Chapter 17).*

To refresh the logs, use the `FLUSH LOGS` command. This command causes the server to close, and then reopen the log files. For the binary logs, this command closes the current log and creates a new log with a new sequence number, so the old one can be archived, if desired.

The value of log flushing becomes more evident when you consider issues of log expiration and rotation, which are covered in the next section.

Time Delays

Updates that are part of a transaction are not executed immediately; they are kept in a cache until the transaction is committed. Once a `COMMIT` command is received by the MySQL server, the entire transaction is first written to the binary log, and then the changes are saved to the database. If a part of the transaction fails for whatever reason, the whole transaction is rolled back, and no changes are written to the binary log.

Log Expiration and Rotation   Your logs will become huge quickly (and your disks full) if your server is busy. So logs must be managed via expiration dates and rotation to keep them from becoming a hindrance rather than a help.

Log rotation is one method used to alleviate this problem. *Log rotation* works by creating a finite number of log files, and then overwriting them in succession, so the oldest one is dropped in each cycle. For example, if you have a file named `query_log`, the first time rotation takes place, it's renamed `query_log.1` and a new `query_log` file is created. At the next rotation, `query_log.1` is renamed `query_log.2`, `query_log` is renamed `query_log.1`, and a new file named (you guessed it!) `query_log` is created. When the last rotation in the cycle is reached, the oldest file is overwritten. How much log information you keep depends on how often you rotate and how many files you create. These numbers vary depending on your circumstances, but a common arrangement is to create new logs daily, and rotate them seven times through a cycle, one for each day of the week.

Log rotation works well with logs that are identified by name, rather than number. If you're dealing with numbered log files, however, the method of renaming the files as previously described will confuse the numbering schedule. In this case, numbered logs can be managed by setting expiration dates, and removing or archiving them once they expire. This is referred to as *log expiration*.

The scripting for log expiration is somewhat involved. For more information, check the MySQL manual at `http://www.mysql.com/doc/en/Log_file_maintenance.html`.

Checking and Repairing Tables

You might need to restore corrupted tables (or even an entire database) from your backups, and to use the update logs if a table gets damaged or deleted by accident. In case of relatively minor damage, though, MySQL provides several options for table repair. This next section deals with what you can do if this is the case.

Checking Tables for Errors

The first thing to do if you suspect something is wrong, is to check the table for errors. The `myisamchk` utility is one way to check a table. The command `myisamchk`, followed by the name of the table file(s), is how this utility is invoked.

```
myisamchk table-file
```

Because `myisamchk` requires exclusive access to the tables, a good idea is to take the server offline before running it. This way you needn't worry about coordinating access between clients. Additionally, you can run several options when you check a table for errors, as shown in Table 15-1.

The following example runs `myisamchk` with the extended option enabled. If you're following along, don't use a large table to see how this works because you'll tie

Option	Name	Description
F	Fast check	Only checks irregularly closed files
m	Medium check	A more detailed check
e	Extended check	Slowest, most thorough check
C	Changed check	Checks only changed files since last check
w	Wait check	Checks after waiting for locks to be removed

TABLE 15-1 Additional **myisamchk** table check options

up your server for quite a while. If no errors are detected using the extended option, you can be certain the specified table isn't the problem.

```
[root@host]# /usr/local/mysql/bin/myisamchk -e db1/accounts
Checking MyISAM file: db1/accounts
Data records:       14    Deleted blocks:        0
- check file-size
- check key delete-chain
- check record delete-chain
- check index reference
- check records and index references
```

The downside of myisamchk is this database-checking tool requires locking out clients while the diagnosis is performed. Moreover, no client can hold a lock on the table being checked while myisamchk is running. On a big table, where myisamchk can take a few minutes to perform its checks, this can be a problem.

One alternative here is to set myisamchk to use large buffers (use myisamchk --help to see the options for changing the various buffers). Another alternative is to use a different method to check your tables: the CHECK TABLE command.

The myisamchk utility requires exclusive access to the tables it's checking because it works directly with the table files. The CHECK TABLE command, on the other hand, has the server check the tables. This means less work for you, as you don't have to take the server down and remove all the locks from the table.

Here's what this command looks like:

```
CHECK TABLE table-name, ...
```

And here's an example of it in action:

```
mysql> CHECK TABLE accounts;
+--------------+-------+----------+----------+
| Table        | Op    | Msg_type | Msg_text |
+--------------+-------+----------+----------+
| db1.accounts | check | status   | OK       |
+--------------+-------+----------+----------+
1 row in set (0.00 sec)
```

TIP   *In case you were wondering, you can also add the keywords FAST, MEDIUM, EXTENDED, and CHANGED to the CHECK TABLE command to perform the desired type of check.*

Why not run CHECK TABLE all the time then, instead of `myisamchk`, you might ask? The main reason is this: the server does all the work when using CHECK TABLE. If your server is down, CHECK TABLE isn't an option. On the other hand, `myisamchk` works at the file level and therefore can work even if the server is down. Since CHECK TABLE is a SQL command that can only be sent via a client, the server must be running to accept it. If you have a choice, however, by all means let MySQL do the work.

NOTE   *`myisamchk` does not work with InnoDB and BDB tables; use the CHECK TABLE command on these types of tables.*

Repairing Tables

If, after checking a table, you find errors exist, then you must repair the table. The best practice is to make a copy of the table in question before you try to repair it. This gives you the option of trying a different way to recover it if your first solution doesn't work.

The `myisamchk` tool discussed above can also be used to repair a damaged table. Use the -r option with the table name to start this process.

```
myisamchk -r table-file
```

Here's an example:

```
[root@host]# /usr/local/mysql/bin/myisamchk -r test/users
- recovering (with keycache) MyISAM-table 'test/users'
Data records: 16
```

If the -r option fails to take care of the problem, the -o option attempts a slow recovery of the table. Other options are also available, and Table 15-2 explains what they mean.

As noted in the preceding section, keep in mind that the `myisamchk` tool works at the file level and therefore requires that all locks be removed and all clients be excluded.

As when checking a table, you should try the fastest options first and move to the slower, more thorough, options only if needed. You might find many common problems are fixed without having to resort to the slower options. If you still have a problem

Option	Name	Description
-r	Repair and recover	Standard recovery
-o	Safe mode for recovery	Slow, thorough recovery
-q	Quick recovery	Only checks index and not data files

TABLE 15-2   Additional `myisamchk` table repair options

after running even the most-intensive repair possibilities, you'll have to restore the table from your backups. Restoring is covered in detail in the section "Restoring Databases and Tables from Backup."

The other option you have when repairing a table is the REPAIR TABLE command, coupled with the table name, as below:

```
REPAIR TABLE table-name, ...
```

Similar to myisamchk, you have the option of using the QUICK or EXTENDED keywords to set the type of repair. Simply add the option name to the end of the REPAIR TABLE statement, as in the example below:

```
mysql> REPAIR TABLE users QUICK;
+-------------+--------+----------+----------+
| Table       | Op     | Msg_type | Msg_text |
+-------------+--------+----------+----------+
| test.users  | repair | status   | OK       |
+-------------+--------+----------+----------+
1 row in set (0.27 sec)
```

Optimizing Tables

There are a number of times when optimizing a table is a good idea. A common example is if a table gets considerable activity, especially many deletions. In such a situation, it can quickly get fragmented, resulting in performance degradation. Running the OPTIMIZE TABLE command flushes these deleted records and, thereby, frees up space.

Here's what the OPTIMIZE TABLE command looks like:

```
OPTIMIZE TABLE table-name, ...;
```

For example, the following command optimizes the table water:

```
mysql> OPTIMIZE TABLE water;
+-------------+----------+----------+----------+
| Table       | Op       | Msg_type | Msg_text |
+-------------+----------+----------+----------+
| test.water  | optimize | status   | OK       |
+-------------+----------+----------+----------+
1 row in set (0.11 sec)
```

The OPTIMIZE TABLE command is like your mother coming in and tidying your room. In addition to getting rid of old, deleted files, it sorts indexed files, places the contents of variable table rows into contiguous spaces, and updates table statistics. Remember, though, that the table is locked and can't be accessed by clients while it's being serviced.

> **Different Strokes**
>
> You can use either `myisamchk` or `REPAIR TABLE` to fix a damaged table, but remember (as discussed earlier in the context of the `CHECK TABLE` command), the server must be running in order to use `REPAIR TABLE`, while you must only use `myisamchk` if the server is down.

Backup and Restore

In addition to logging and table optimization, the other essential task of any database administrator is to make sure the data is protected from loss. This is accomplished by regular backup and test restorations of your database. When disaster strikes (and it will, make no mistake about that), you will be better equipped to deal with it if you perform the steps suggested in this next section.

Backing Up Databases and Tables

The MySQL distribution comes with a utility called `mysqldump` that can be used to back up an entire database and/or individual tables from a database to a text file. Besides the obvious need to back up your data, this action is also useful if you need to export your database contents to a different RDBMS, or if you simply need to move certain information from one system to another quickly and easily.

```
mysqldump database-name
```

Here's an example:

```
[user@host]# /usr/local/mysql/bin/mysqldump db1 --user=john --password=hoonose
```

This procedure displays the contents of the entire example database, `db1`, on your screen. The output should look similar to Figure 15-1.

Notice from Figure 15-1 that SQL statements are included in the output of `mysqldump` to facilitate rebuilding text or tables. As with the `mysql` command, you need to use the `--user` and `--password` options to designate an authorized user and password to perform the dump function.

> **A Clean Slate**
>
> If the data you are backing up has been corrupted, it is a best practice to execute a `DROP TABLE` or a `DROP DATABASE` command before restoration. This creates a clean slate for your restoration. Fortunately, the `mysqldump` utility does this for you; if you look at the SQL statements resulting from a call to `mysqldump`, you will see these commands included.

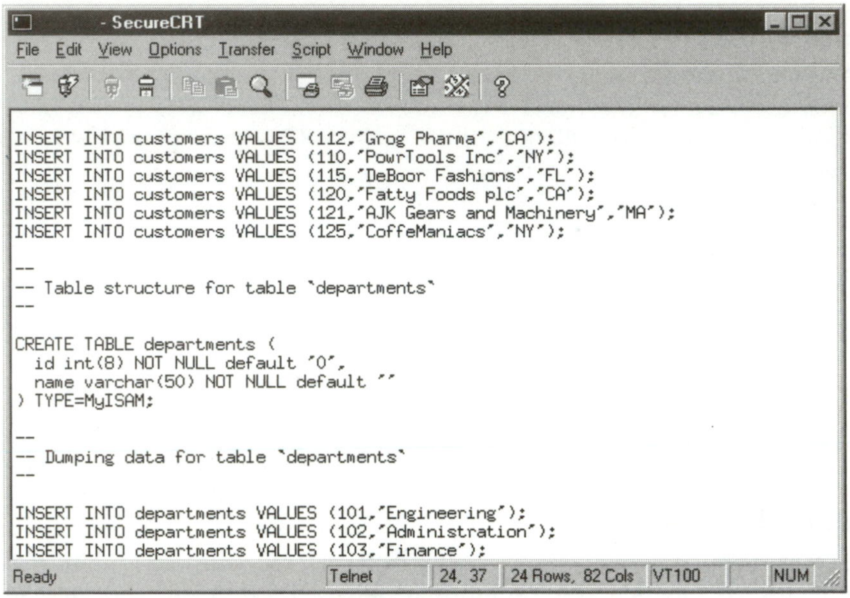

FIGURE 15-1   The output of the `mysqldump` command

What if you don't need the entire database to be dumped? A simple change enables you to specify which tables from within the database should be backed up. Here's an example:

```
[user@host]# /usr/local/mysql/bin/mysqldump db1 name address --user=john
--password=hoonose
```

This command dumps only the contents of the `name` and `address` tables from the `db1` database.

In the real world, you'll want to save the output of `mysqldump` to a file, not watch it scroll by on a console. On both UNIX and Windows, this can be accomplished via the `>` redirection operator, as shown in the following example:

```
[user@host]# /usr/local/mysql/bin/mysqldump db1 name address > mydump.txt
```

The result of this command will be a text file, called `mydump.txt`, containing the commands needed to recreate the `name` and `address` tables from the `db1` database.

To back up more than one database at a time, use the `-B` option, as in the following example:

```
[user@host]# /usr/local/mysql/bin/mysqldump -B db1 db2
```

The Delimiter Dilemma

When using the `mysqldump` utility, you can control the characters used to enclose and separate the fields from the column output by adding any or all of the options `--fields-enclosed-by`, `--fields-terminated-by`, `--fields-escaped-by`, and `--lines-terminated-by`. This is particularly useful if you need to port the dumped data into a system that requires records to be encoded in a custom format before importing them.

No tables are specified in this case, because when you use the `-B` option to backup more than one database, the entire database will be dumped. Individual tables cannot be designated in this operation.

What if you want to create a table with the same structure, but different data than the one you have? Again, the `mysqldump` utility comes to the rescue. The `-d` option produces the same table in form, but empty of content. To see this in action, try the following command:

```
[user@host]# /usr/local/mysql/bin/mysqldump -d db1 users > users.structure
```

This generates a dump file containing SQL commands to create an empty copy of the `users` table.

The other side of the coin is a situation where you only need the contents of a table—for example, to dump them into a different table. Again you use `mysqldump`, but with the `-t` option. What this yields is a file containing all the `INSERT` statements that have been executed on the table. What doesn't get duplicated are the instructions for creating the table.

Here's an example:

```
[user@host]# /usr/local/mysql/bin/mysqldump -t db1 employees > employees.data
```

The records in the `employees` table are now ready to be imported into any other application that understands SQL.

Restoring Databases and Tables from Backup

Most books on the subject emphasize the importance of backing up your data regularly (and rightly so), but restoring the data is an often-overlooked aspect of this process. Backed-up files are useless if they can't be accessed. Accordingly, you should regularly restore your files from backup to make certain they can be used in an emergency. In fact, it might not be too much to say that a backup job isn't complete until you've confirmed that the backup files can be restored. Besides the peace of mind you'll achieve, it pays to be thoroughly familiar with the process because you certainly don't want to waste time learning the restore procedure *after* the system goes down.

Are You Worthy?
Remember that the user who performs the restoration must have permission to
create tables and databases. Accordingly, you might need to use the `--user`,
`--password`, or `--host` options with the previous command.

In the preceding section, you learned that the output of the `mysqldump` utility
includes SQL statements such as `CREATE TABLE` to simplify the process of rebuilding
lost data. Because of this, you can take a file generated by `mysqldump` and pipe it
through the `mysql` command-line client to quickly recreate a lost database or table.
Here's an example:

```
[user@host]# /usr/local/mysql/bin/mysql db1 < mydump.txt
```

In this example, `mydump.txt` is the text file containing the output of a previous
`mysqldump` run. The contents of this file (SQL commands) are executed through the
`mysql` command-line client using standard input redirection.
If you don't have access to (or don't like) the command line, another option is to
use the `SOURCE` command, as below:

```
mysql> SOURCE mydump.txt
```

The `SOURCE` command uses the SQL instructions in the named text file to rebuild
the database(s) or table(s) specified. To see the results of the restoration, use a simple
`SELECT` statement to verify that the data has been successfully restored.
Another option is to use the MySQL command `LOAD DATA INFILE` to import data
from a text file. Use this command with the `INTO TABLE` keywords to indicate which
table you want the data sent to.
Here's an example:

```
mysql> LOAD DATA INFILE '/home/me/data.txt' INTO TABLE birthdays
FIELDS TERMINATED BY ',' LINES TERMINATED BY '\r\n';
Query OK, 5 rows affected (0.06 sec)
Records: 5  Deleted: 0  Skipped: 0  Warnings: 0
```

See Chapter 9 for more details on the `LOAD DATA INFILE` command.

Moving by Restoring
Other than restoring lost or corrupted data, the restore procedure is also used to
send tables, or even an entire database, to a different MySQL server. Restoring data
is a fast way to import or export content between different servers.

Once you're comfortable with the procedures to backup and restore your data, you'll likely want to set up a regular schedule of backups for your organization. The `cron` tool is a Unix scheduling utility that can be used for this purpose. It allows you to schedule the `mysqldump` utility to run at designated times and dates. Type **man cron** at your UNIX command prompt to find out more about how to use this tool.

In Windows NT, Windows 2000, or Windows XP, you can use either the `at` command from the command prompt or the Task Scheduler (`Control Panel -> Scheduled Tasks`) to automate backups.

NOTE *As the name "cron" may seem odd, it is helpful to understand that it comes from the Greek word for time, which we write in English as "chronos." This is the root of words like "chronology" and "chronometer."*

Summary

One of the qualities that has made MySQL popular is its ease of use; however, it won't do everything for you. Basic maintenance and an established backup and restoration process is required from the administrator in any production environment. This chapter has focused on the minimum steps you should take to ensure smooth performance of your installation, such as using the various logs to monitor the database and pinpoint areas of potential trouble. Methods of checking and repairing tables were reviewed. Finally, the all-important topics of backup and restoration were considered using various utilities that MySQL provides.

PART III

Performance Optimization

As your databases grow, you'll find you want to adjust the defaults MySQL uses to operate the server. While processor speed, bigger and faster disks, and additional memory certainly have something to do with performance, they're outside the scope of this discussion. The intent of this chapter is to maximize server performance using the tools available within MySQL, and to teach you some techniques to ensure your queries are running as efficiently as possible.

Database design is another aspect to consider when discussing performance. Various strategies for optimizing a table for better performance are also a part of this section. Most of the optimization you should do, however, first involves refining your queries, adding indexes, and so forth. Accordingly, query optimization is considered first in this chapter.

One of the first places to look to improve performance is queries, particularly the ones that run often. Big gains can be achieved by analyzing a query and rewriting it more efficiently. You can use MySQL's slow query log (described in Chapter 15) to get an idea of which queries might be fine-tuned.

Indexing

A surprising number of people in online forums request information about slow queries without having tried to add an index to a frequently accessed column. As you know from Chapter 8, tables with columns that are accessed frequently can be ordered by creating an index. An index points to the place on a database where specific data is located and creating an index on a column sorts the information in that column. When the server needs to access that information to execute a query, it knows where to look because the index points to the relevant location.

Indexing is even more important on multi-table queries. If it takes a while to do a full table scan on one table, imagine how much longer it would take if you have several tables to check. If optimization of your queries is a goal, the first thing to do is to try implementing an index.

Deciding which columns should be indexed involves several considerations. If you have a column involved in searching, grouping, or sorting, indexing it will likely result in a performance gain. These include columns that are part of join operations or columns that appear with clauses such as WHERE, GROUP BY, or ORDER BY.

Consider the following example:

```
mysql> SELECT salary FROM empData JOIN empMaster ON empData.sid =
empMaster.id WHERE salary > 50000;
```

The columns that should be indexed here are empData.sid and empMaster.id because they're part of a join. Because salary is part of a WHERE clause, it would also be a good choice for indexing.

Another factor to consider here is that indexes on columns with many duplicate values won't produce good results. A column that has 'yes' or 'no' for content won't be improved by indexing. On the other hand, a column where the values are unique (for example, employee Social Security numbers) can benefit greatly from indexing.

You can associate multiple non-unique indexes with a table to improve performance. In the previous example, the columns empData.sid, empMaster.id, and salary can all be indexed. No limit exists to the number of non-unique indexes that can be created.

Taking this to its logical extreme, then, you might think the more indexes, the merrier. This is a fallacy: adding an index doesn't necessarily improve performance. Small tables, for example, don't need indexing. Additionally, every index takes up additional space on the disk—each indexed field requires MySQL to store information for every record in that field and its location within the database. As your indexes build, these tables begin to take up more room. Further, indexing speeds searches, but slows write operations, such as INSERT, DELETE, or UPDATE. Until you work with indexing on your database, your first few attempts might not achieve much performance gain.

Certain administrative counters can help you monitor your indexes or come up with candidates for adding an index. Both the SHOW STATUS or mysqladmin extended-status commands display values to consider in terms of indexes:

- If your indexes are working, the value of Handler_read_key should be high. This value represents the number of times a row was read by an index value. A low value indicates not much performance improvement has been achieved by the added indexing because the index isn't being used frequently.

- A high value for Handler_read_rnd_next means your queries are running inefficiently and indexing should be considered as a remedy. This value indicates the number of requests to read the next row in sequence. This occurs when a table is scanned sequentially from the first record to the last to execute the query. For frequent queries, this is a wasteful use of resources. An associated index points directly to the record(s), so this full table scan doesn't need to occur. Note, poorly functioning indexes could also result in a high number here.

To view these counters, run a command like this one:

```
mysql> SHOW STATUS LIKE 'Handler_read%';
+-----------------------+-------+
| Variable_name         | Value |
+-----------------------+-------+
| Handler_read_first    | 1     |
| Handler_read_key      | 0     |
| Handler_read_next     | 0     |
| Handler_read_prev     | 0     |
| Handler_read_rnd      | 0     |
| Handler_read_rnd_next | 9     |
+-----------------------+-------+
6 rows in set (0.03 sec)
```

Once you've got your tables loaded with data and indexed the way you want them, you should run the ANALYZE TABLE command on them. This command analyzes the data in the table and creates table statistics on the average number of rows that share the same value. This information is used by the MySQL optimizer when deciding which index to use in table joins.

```
mysql> ANALYZE TABLE users, groups, users_groups;
+--------------------+---------+----------+----------+
| Table              | Op      | Msg_type | Msg_text |
+--------------------+---------+----------+----------+
| test.users         | analyze | status   | OK       |
| test.groups        | analyze | status   | OK       |
| test.users_groups  | analyze | status   | OK       |
+--------------------+---------+----------+----------+
3 rows in set (0.01 sec)
```

It's a good idea to run the ANALYZE TABLE command frequently, especially after you've added a significant amount of data to your table, to ensure that the optimizer is always using the most efficient index.

The Natural Order

If you have a table that's read often, but is rarely changed, then try sorting the information in that table rather than indexing it. Use the ORDER BY command along with ALTER TABLE to do this. Reads will occur more rapidly, and they'll be more efficient as well.

Query Caching

When you run a SELECT query, MySQL 4.*x* remembers both the query and the results it returns. This is accomplished by storing the result set in a special cache (called the query cache) each time a SELECT query is executed. Then, the next time you ask the server for the same query, MySQL will retrieve the results from the cache instead of running the query again. As you can imagine, this speeds the process considerably.

Although enabled by default, you must always verify that query caching is turned on, which can be done by checking the server variables. The following example illustrates:

```
mysql> SHOW VARIABLES LIKE '%query_cache%';
+-------------------------+---------+
| Variable_name           | Value   |
+-------------------------+---------+
| have_query_cache        | YES     |
| query_cache_limit       | 1048576 |
| query_cache_min_res_unit| 4096    |
| query_cache_size        | 48      |
| query_cache_type        | ON      |
+-------------------------+---------+
5 rows in set (0.00 sec)
```

Following is an explanation:

- The first value, have_query_cache, indicates the server was configured for query caching when it was installed (the default).

- The query_cache_size value indicates 48, which means 48 MB is the size allotted for the cache. If this value is 0, query caching will be off.

- The values for the query_cache_type variable range from 0 to 2. A value of 0 or OFF indicates that query caching is turned off. ON or 1 means that query caching is turned on, with the exception of SELECT statements using the SQL_NO_CACHE option. DEMAND or 2 provides query caching on demand, for SELECT statements running with the SQL_CACHE option.

To see for yourself what impact the query cache is having on performance, run the same query with and without query caching to compare the performance difference. Here's the version using the query cache:

```
mysql> SELECT SQL_CACHE * FROM employees;
+------------+-----------+----------+---------+---------+
| employeeID | firstname | lastname | titleID | salary  |
+------------+-----------+----------+---------+---------+
|          1 | Marvin    | Freeman  |       1 |   41000 |
|          2 | Ed        | Bailey   |       1 | 32100.2 |
|          3 | Beth      | Trinity  |       1 | 55300.8 |
|          4 | Rachel    | Williams |       2 | 35000.2 |
```

```
|           5 | Ian        | Stanton   |       2 | 35000.6 |
|           6 | Terry      | Thorne    |       2 |  303000 |
|           7 | Joan       | Chu       |       1 |   41000 |
|           8 | Stan       | Schowry   |       1 | 24372.1 |
|           9 | Will       | Tates     |       3 |   50000 |
|          10 | Steve      | Bobs      |       3 | 3.8e+08 |
|          59 | Ismail     | Ozkan     |       3 |   88900 |
...
+------------+-----------+----------+--------+---------+
711 rows in set (0.06 sec)
```

Now perform the same query without the cache:

```
mysql> SELECT SQL_NO_CACHE * FROM employees;
+------------+-----------+----------+---------+---------+
| employeeID | firstname | lastname | titleID | salary  |
+------------+-----------+----------+---------+---------+
|          1 | Marvin    | Freeman  |       1 |   41000 |
|          2 | Ed        | Bailey   |       1 | 32100.2 |
|          3 | Beth      | Trinity  |       1 | 55300.8 |
|          4 | Rachel    | Williams |       2 | 35000.2 |
|          5 | Ian       | Stanton  |       2 | 35000.6 |
|          6 | Terry     | Thorne   |       2 |  303000 |
|          7 | Joan      | Chu      |       1 |   41000 |
|          8 | Stan      | Schowry  |       1 | 24372.1 |
|          9 | Will      | Tates    |       3 |   50000 |
|         10 | Steve     | Bobs     |       3 | 3.8e+08 |
|         59 | Ismail    | Ozkan    |       3 |   88900 |
...
+------------+-----------+----------+---------+---------+
711 rows in set (0.84 sec)
```

Dramatic improvements in performance aren't unusual if query caching is enabled on frequent queries.

Note, once a table is changed, the cached queries that use this table become invalid and are removed from the cache. This prevents a query from returning inaccurate data from the old table. While this makes query caching much more useful, a constantly changing table won't benefit from caching. In this situation, you might want to consider eliminating query caching. This can be done by adding the SQL_NO_CACHE option, as previously shown, to a SELECT statement.

Watch Your Ps and Qs

Queries that are textually exact will match what's in the Query Cache, but any difference will be treated as a new query. For example, SELECT * FROM *table-name* won't return the result from SELECT * FROM *table-name* in the cache.

Query Analysis

Attaching the EXPLAIN keyword to the beginning of a SELECT query tells MySQL to return a chart describing how this query will be processed. Included within this chart is information on which the tables the query will access and the number of rows the query is expected to return. This information comes in handy to see which tables should be indexed to speed up performance, and to analyze where the bottlenecks are.

As an example, consider the following query:

```
mysql> SELECT a.companyID, a.companyName FROM Companies a, Users b WHERE
a.companyID = b.fk_companyID AND a.numEmployees >= 0 AND a.companyName LIKE
'%i%' AND b.groupID IN (SELECT c.groupID FROM Groups c WHERE c.groupLabel =
'Executive');
+-----------+----------------------------+
| companyID | companyName                |
+-----------+----------------------------+
|      3447 | Udoozy Mining              |
|       123 | Benny Bill Chickens, Inc   |
+-----------+----------------------------+
2 rows in set (0.20 sec)
```

Now, by adding the EXPLAIN keyword to the beginning of the query, I can obtain some information on how MySQL processes it.

```
mysql> EXPLAIN SELECT a.companyID, a.companyName FROM Companies a, Users b WHERE a.companyID
= b.fk_companyID AND a.numEmployees >= 0 AND a.companyName LIKE '%i%' AND b.groupID IN
(SELECT c.groupID FROM Groups c WHERE c.groupLabel = 'Executive');
+----+--------------------+-------+------+---------------+------+---------+------+------+-------------+
| id | select_type        | table | type | possible_keys | key  | key_len | ref  | rows | Extra       |
+----+--------------------+-------+------+---------------+------+---------+------+------+-------------+
|  1 | PRIMARY            | a     | ALL  | NULL          | NULL | NULL    | NULL |  934 | Using where |
|  1 | PRIMARY            | b     | ALL  | NULL          | NULL | NULL    | NULL |  134 | Using where |
|  2 | DEPENDENT SUBSELECT | c    | ALL  | NULL          | NULL | NULL    | NULL |  621 | Using where |
+----+--------------------+-------+------+---------------+------+---------+------+------+-------------+
3 rows in set (0.12 sec)
```

This might all seem a little intimidating, so let me explain it. The result of EXPLAIN SELECT is a table listing all the SELECTs in the query, together with how MySQL plans to process them.

- The id column indicates the position of the SELECT within the complete query, while the table column holds the name of the table being queried.
- The select_type column indicates the type of query—a simple query without subqueries, a UNION, a subquery, an outer query, a subquery within an outer query, or a subquery in a FROM clause.

- The `type` column indicates how the join will be performed. A number of values are possible here, ranging from `const` (the best kind of join, since it means the table contains a single matching record only) to `ALL` (the worst kind, because it means that MySQL has to scan every single record to find a match to records in the other joined tables).

- The `possible_keys` column indicates the indexes available for MySQL to use in order to speed up the search.

- The `key` column indicates the key it will actually use, with the key length displayed in the `key_len` column.

- The `rows` column indicates the number of rows MySQL needs to examine in the corresponding table to successfully execute the query. To obtain the total number of rows MySQL must scan to process the complete query, multiply the `rows` value for each table together.

- The `Extra` column contains additional information on how MySQL will process the query—say, by using the `WHERE` clause, by using an index, with a temporary table and so on.

Now, from the output above, it's clear that in order to execute the query, MySQL will need to examine all the rows in all the named tables. The total number of rows MySQL needs to scan, then, is approximately $934 \times 134 \times 621 = 77,721,876$ rows—an extremely large number!

However, by reviewing the output of the `EXPLAIN SELECT` command output, it's clear that there is scope for improvement. For example, the `possible_keys` column for all the tables is `NULL`, indicating that MySQL couldn't find any indexes to use. This can quickly be rectified by reviewing the tables and adding indexes wherever possible:

```
mysql> ALTER TABLE Companies ADD PRIMARY KEY (companyID);
Query OK, 934 rows affected (0.18 sec)
mysql> ALTER TABLE Groups ADD INDEX (groupLabel);
Query OK, 621 rows affected (0.11 sec)
```

Now, try running the query again with `EXPLAIN`:

```
mysql> EXPLAIN SELECT a.companyID, a.companyName FROM Companies a, Users b WHERE a.companyID
= b.fk_companyID AND a.numEmployees >= 0 AND a.companyName LIKE '%i%' AND b.groupID IN
(SELECT c.groupID FROM Groups c WHERE c.groupLabel = 'Executive');
+----+--------------------+-------+--------+---------------+-------------+---------+-------
-----+------+-------------+
| id | select_type        | table | type   | possible_keys | key         | key_len | ref
| rows | Extra       |
+----+--------------------+-------+--------+---------------+-------------+---------+-------
---------+------+-------------+
|  1 | PRIMARY            | b     | ALL    | NULL          | NULL        | NULL    |
NULL          | 134 |             |
|  1 | PRIMARY            | a     | eq_ref | PRIMARY       | PRIMARY     | 4       |
b.fk_companyID |   1 | Using where |
|  2 | DEPENDENT SUBSELECT | c    | ref    | groupLabel    | groupLabel  | 41      |
```

```
const         |     1 | Using where |
+----+-------------------+-------+--------+---------------+-------------+---------+-------
---------+------+-------------+
3 rows in set (0.03 sec)
```

As you can see, MySQL is now using the newly added indexes to cut down on the number of rows that need to be examined. This is clear from the `type` column in the table above, which shows that MySQL is now using an `eq_ref` join type (the best type of join, as it means that MySQL need only read a single row from this table to satisfy the join conditions). Multiplying the rows by each other, we now see that MySQL only needs to scan $134 \times 1 \times 1 = 134$ rows to process the query—a significant improvement over the earlier, non-indexed approach.

Optimizing Multi-Table Queries

A *join* is a multi-table query, performed across tables that are connected to each other by means of one or more common fields. It is commonly used to exploit relationships between the normalized tables of an RDBMS, and it gives SQL programmers the ability to link records from separate tables to create different views of the same data.

A *subquery* is a `SELECT` statement nested inside another `SELECT` statement. A subquery is often used to break down a complicated query into a series of logical steps or to answer a query with the results of another query. As a result, instead of executing two (or more) separate queries, you execute a single query containing one (or more) subqueries.

MySQL is better at optimizing joins than subqueries, so if you find the load averages on your MySQL server hitting unacceptably high levels, examine your application code and try rewriting your subqueries as joins or sequences of joins. For example, while the following subquery is certainly legal,

```
mysql> SELECT bid FROM branches_services WHERE sid = (SELECT sid FROM
services WHERE sname = 'Administration');
+------+
| bid  |
+------+
|  536 |
| 1031 |
| 1743 |
+------+
3 rows in set (0.22 sec)
```

the following equivalent join would run faster (note the difference in execution time) due to MySQL's optimization algorithms:

```
mysql> SELECT bs.bid FROM branches_services AS bs, services AS s WHERE
s.sid = bs.sid AND s.sname = 'Administration';
+------+
```

```
| bid  |
+------+
|  536 |
| 1031 |
| 1743 |
+------+
3 rows in set (0.17 sec)
```

It's a good idea to match the fields being joined, in terms of both type and length. MySQL tends to be a little inefficient when using indexes on joined fields which are of different length and/or type.

You can also turn inefficient subqueries into more efficient joins through creative use of MySQL's aggregate functions and modifiers. Consider the following subquery:

```
mysql> SELECT customerName FROM customers WHERE customerID = (SELECT
customerID FROM invoices WHERE invoiceStatus = 'U' AND invoiceAmt =
(SELECT MAX(invoiceAmt) FROM invoices WHERE invoiceStatus = 'U'));
+---------------+
| customerName  |
+---------------+
| PowrTools Inc |
+---------------+
1 row in set (0.22 sec)
```

This works better as the following join, which is simpler to read and also runs much faster:

```
mysql> SELECT customerName FROM customers, invoices WHERE
customers.customerID = invoices.customerID WHERE invoices.invoiceStatus
= 'U' ORDER BY invoiceAmt DESC LIMIT 1;
+---------------+
| customerName  |
+---------------+
| PowrTools Inc |
+---------------+
1 row in set (0.12 sec)
```

Session-based server variables can also come in handy if you want to avoid nesting queries within each other. Therefore, while the following query will list all customers whose invoices, at any time, have been above the average invoice amount,

```
mysql> SELECT customerName FROM customers WHERE customerID IN (select customerID
FROM invoices WHERE invoiceAmt > (SELECT AVG(invoiceAmt) FROM invoices));
+-----------------+
| customerName    |
```

```
+------------------+
| PowrTools Inc    |
| Fatty Foods plc  |
| CoffeManiacs     |
+------------------+
3 rows in set (0.22 sec)
```

you can accomplish the same thing by splitting the task into two queries and using a server-side MySQL variable to connect them:

```
mysql> SELECT @avg:=AVG(invoiceAmt) FROM invoices;
mysql> SELECT DISTINCT customerName FROM customers, invoices WHERE
customers.customerID = invoices.customerID and invoiceAmt > @avg;
+------------------+
| customerName     |
+------------------+
| PowrTools Inc    |
| Fatty Foods plc  |
| CoffeManiacs     |
+------------------+
3 rows in set (0.14 sec)
```

The two queries above combined will run faster than the first subquery.

Using Temporary Tables

MySQL also lets you create temporary tables with the CREATE TEMPORARY TABLE command. These tables are so-called because they remain in existence only for the duration of a single MySQL session and are automatically deleted when the client that instantiates them closes its connection with the MySQL server. These tables come in handy for transient, session-based data or calculations, or for the temporary storage of data. And because they're session dependent, two different sessions can use the same table name without conflicting.

Since temporary tables are stored in memory, they are significantly faster than disk-based tables. Consequently, they can be effectively used as intermediate storage areas, to speed up query execution by helping to break up complex queries into simpler components, or as a substitute for subquery and join support.

For example, say you have a complex query that involves selecting a set of distinct values from a particular field and the MySQL engine is unable to optimize your query because of its complexity. Creative SQL programmers can improve performance by breaking down the single complex query into numerous simple queries (that lend themselves better to optimization) and then using the INSERT IGNORE...SELECT command to save the results generated to a temporary table, after first creating the temporary table with a UNIQUE key on the appropriate field. The result: a set of distinct values for that field and possibly faster query execution.

Here's another example: assume you have a table containing information on a month's worth of transactions, say about 300,000 records. At the end of every day, your application needs to generate a report summarizing the transactions for that day. In such a situation it's not a very good idea, performance-wise, to run SUM() and AVG()

functions on the entire set of 300,000 records on a daily basis. A more efficient solution here would be to extract only the transactions for the day into a temporary table using `INSERT...SELECT`, run summary functions on the temporary table to generate the required reports, and then delete the temporary table. Since the temporary table would contain a much smaller subset of records, performance would be better and the server load would also be lower.

Optimizing Table Design

In the context of keeping your queries lean and mean, you need to consider several things in terms of table design. First, if a frequently queried table also gets a lot of changes, the way to improve performance is to stay with fixed-length fields, rather than variable-length ones. The trade-off is this: by definition, fixed-length fields take up a certain amount of space regardless of the content, whereas variable-length fields adjust themselves depending on the data entered. Thus, you're bound to waste more disk space using fixed-length fields. If it's speed you're after, however, MySQL will perform better with fixed- rather than variable-length fields.

This being said, if you *are* going to use fixed-length fields, make sure the column size is kept to a minimum. For example, when designing a table, creating a `CHAR(255)` column is often easier than worrying about exactly how big you need to make it. In practice, you might find that a column half that size can adequately take care of your needs. Paring the column size not only takes up less disk space, it also means less I/O when processing. And it goes without saying, deleting unnecessary columns entirely can also increase performance.

Another technique to improve performance is to use the `OPTIMIZE TABLE` command (discussed more fully in Chapter 15) frequently on tables that are modified often. Frequent modification results in fragmentation, which, in turn, leads to extra time spent reading unused blocks of space to get at the desired data.

When considering ways of improving performance, also check to see if you need all the tables you have set up. Again, when originally designing a table, dividing your data might have seemed like a good idea, but extra tables mean your performance will suffer. Look at the tables you join frequently. Is it possible to combine the data into one

---

A Question Of Size

Here's a tip for changing your tables to use fixed-length fields. If one column in a frequently changed table cannot be formatted to a fixed length, then consider moving that column to a separate table and converting the rest of the columns in the original table to fixed-length fields. Although this might not be workable in all circumstances, it is a viable way to achieve the performance gain of using fixed-length fields rather than variable-length fields.

Note, InnoDB or BDB tables handle row storage differently from MyISAM or ISAM tables. Using fixed-length columns instead of variable-length ones won't result in a performance boost with these table types.

> **Linking Out**
>
> Query optimization is almost a science unto itself, and impossible to cover in the limited space available in this chapter. For more information, take a look at `http://www.mysql.com/doc/en/MySQL_Optimisation.html` and `http://www.mysql.com/doc/en/Tips.html`, which contain extensive information, tips and techniques to speed up your MySQL queries and make them run more efficiently.

table instead? If you find you cannot, for whatever reason, then try to match the columns you join. Queries will run more efficiently if joined columns are of the same data type and length.

Adjusting Server Settings

If you want your server to perform optimally, the best solution is to get tons of memory and big, fast drives. However, in most situations, these brute-force techniques won't be an option. Given that we operate under less-than-ideal conditions-, getting a handle on some more subtle techniques for optimizing server performance makes more sense. Accordingly, this section gives a brief overview of some of the major things you can do to fine-tune your server.

As you've already seen in Chapter 13, MySQL exposes a large number of variables whose values can be modified to meet custom requirements. Some of these variables can be set at the time of starting the MySQL server and others can be set while the server is running.

When it comes to tuning server variables for maximum performance, the MySQL manual recommends that you first look at the `key_buffer_size` and `table_cache` variables.

- The `key_buffer_size` variable controls the amount of memory available for MySQL index buffer. The higher this value, the more memory available for indexes and the better the performance. Typically, you would want to keep this value near 25 to 30 percent of the total available memory on the server.

- The `table_cache` variable controls the amount of memory available for the table cache, and thus the total number of tables MySQL can hold open at any given time. For busy servers with many databases and tables, this value should be increased so that MySQL can serve all requests reliably. Also relevant here is the `max_connections` variable, because the MySQL manual recommends setting the `table_cache` using the formula (`table_cache` = `max_connections` x N), where N is the number of tables in a typical join.

As noted in Chapter 13, these values can be changed using the SET command, as in the following example:

```
mysql> SET GLOBAL table_cache=200;
Query OK, 0 rows affected (0.00 sec)
mysql> SELECT @@table_cache;
+---------------+
| @@table_cache |
+---------------+
|           200 |
+---------------+
1 row in set (0.01 sec)
```

Note that once you change a global server variable, it remains in effect until the server is shut down. This means if you find a beneficial setting, you need to reset it on startup every time. Because this is cumbersome, it's useful to know a way of making your changes permanent. This can be accomplished by setting a variable in an option file (discussed in Chapter 13).

Once you've got your table cache and index buffer set up the way you want them, you can turn your attention to the various other memory buffers MySQL uses:

- You can speed up queries which use the ORDER BY or GROUP BY clauses to sort the result set by increasing the value of MySQL's sort buffer, controlled via the sort_buffer variable. Also consider increasing the read_rnd_buffer_size variable to speed up reading of the sorted rows.

- You can speed up SELECT queries which scan the table sequentially by increasing the size of MySQL's read buffer, via the read_buffer_size variable.

- When performing a transaction, MySQL stores the statements that make up the transaction in a cache until it receives instructions to write them to the binary log and COMMIT them to the database. For long or complex transactions, the size of this cache should be increased to obtain better performance, via the binlog_cache_size variable.

- If you're planning on so-called "bulk inserts" (that is, inserting multiple records using a single INSERT command), you can speed things up by increasing the value of the bulk_insert_buffer_size variable. However, this only works with the MyISAM table type.

- If you're anticipating a lot of new connections to the server, it's a good idea to increase the value of the thread_cache_size variable. This variable controls the size of the cache where server threads go when the client they're servicing disconnects. Threads from this cache are then reused to service new connections. The higher this value, the more threads can be cached, and the better the response time to new connection requests.

Benchmarking

Altering the server configuration and optimizing your queries is all very well—but how do you measure the results of your changes, and test if there is any appreciable change in performance? Well, the folks at MySQL AB have got you covered on that one

---

Exploring Options

The MySQL Benchmark Suite isn't the only game in town. Alternatives exist in the form of SuperSmack, available from `http://www.mysql.com/portal/software/item-222.html`, and the Open Source Database Benchmark, available from `http://osdb.sourceforge.net/`. A complete list of benchmarking tools is available at `http://www.mysql.com/portal/software/benchmarks/index.html` and at `http://www.wiley.com/legacy/compbooks/pachev/`

---

too—MySQL comes with a benchmarking suite called (what else?) the MySQL Benchmark Suite, which does exactly what its name says: it stresses a database server to detect weaknesses, verify compliance with SQL standards and measure performance.

In order to run the MySQL Benchmark Suite, you must have Perl installed on your system, together with the Perl DBI package and a MySQL database driver (DBD). If you're using a stock UNIX system, it's quite likely that these packages are already installed. A simple way to test for their presence is to run the following command at your shell prompt:

```
[user@host]$ perl -e "use DBI"
```

If Perl doesn't exit with an error, it's a good bet that the module is installed. If the module isn't installed, then you'll have to download it from `http://www.cpan.org/` and install it according to the installation instructions for your platform. Read more about this process in Chapter 20 of this book, which discusses application development with Perl and MySQL.

The MySQL Benchmark Suite is located in the `sql-bench/` directory of your MySQL installation. It consists of a number of scripts, together with the raw data for the various benchmark tests (see the sidebar titled "Testing Times" for more information on these benchmarks). Table 16-1 has a list of these scripts, together with a brief description of what each one does:

The simplest way to get started with the MySQL Benchmark Suite is to change into the `sql-bench/` directory and run all the tests using the `run-all-tests` script, like this:

```
[user@host]# /usr/local/mysql/sql-bench/run-all-tests --server=mysql
```

Testing Times

The MySQL Benchmark Suite includes support for the Wisconsin Benchmark, a widely accepted benchmark for relational database systems. A controlled single-user experiment which uses so-called "synthetic" data instead of "real" data, this benchmark is primarily designed to measure query performance using the metric of elapsed time per query. Test cases include selection, inserts, updates, table joins and data aggregation.

Script name	Test case description
copy-db	Measures copy speed between two servers
crash-me	Tests capabilities of SQL server by executing different queries
innotest	Stress test for concurrent inserts, updates and commits in both transactional (InnoDB) and non-transaction (MyISAM) context
test-alter-table	Measures performance of the ALTER TABLE command
test-big-tables	Measures performance with extremely large tables
test-connect	Measures server connection speed
test-create	Measures speed of creating and dropping tables
test-insert	Measures speed of inserting records into a table and then running SELECT queries on it
test-select	Measures SELECT speed with multipart column indexes
test-transactions	Measures speed of transaction rollback
test-wisconsin	Performs the Wisconsin benchmark test
test-ATIS	Performs the ATIS benchmark test

TABLE 16-1 Test cases in the MySQL Benchmark Suite

Figure 16-1 illustrates what the output of this might look like.

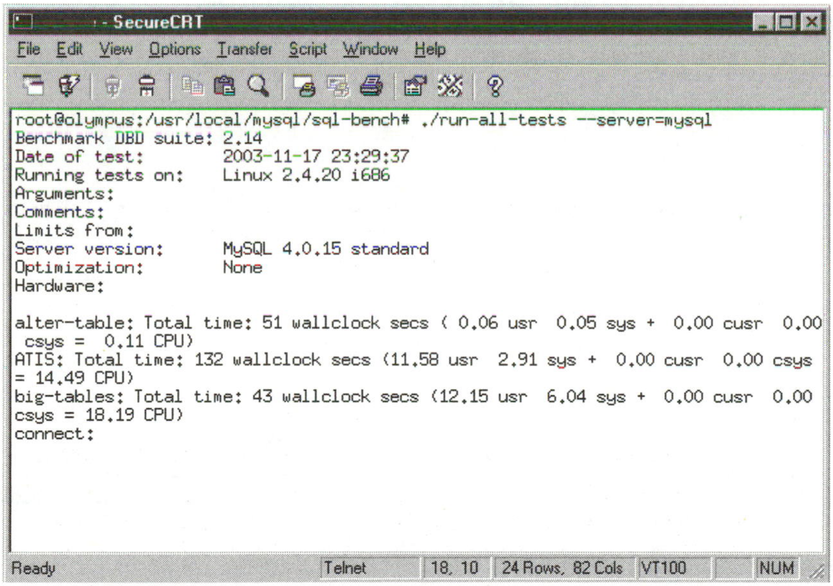

FIGURE 16-1 The output of the run-all-tests script

As you can see, this script runs each of the test cases listed in Table 16-1, returning the time taken by each. More information on the details of each test case can be obtained by invoking the corresponding script without any parameters—most of the scripts print a brief description of their purpose before starting.

If you'd like to run a specific test only, you can do that too, simply by invoking the appropriate script. Consider the following example, which runs the `test-connect` script to benchmark the time taken to connect to the server and send data to it:

```
[user@host]# /usr/local/mysql/sql-bench/test-connect
```

Figure 16-2 illustrates what this might look like.

Notable among the various test scripts included in the MySQL Benchmark Suite is *crash-me*, a utility designed specifically for the purpose of evaluating an SQL server's capabilities by pushing it up to (and beyond) its limits. *Crash-me* works by sending a variety of legal SQL queries to the server and, from its response, determining the feature set, capabilities and limitations of the server. Figure 16-3 illustrates the output of a *crash-me* run.

If you want to see some results obtained in a comparison test of MySQL versus other vendors' database programs, look at http://www.mysql.com/information/

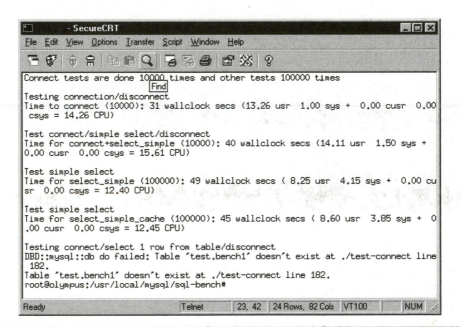

FIGURE 16-2   The output of the `test-connect` script

> **Buyer Beware!**
> In order to test server functionality, *crash-me* pushes the database server to its limits. It will almost certainly affect system performance while it is running and may even cause the server to crash. Therefore, it should be used with care, and never on a production server.

`crash-me.php`. Understand that the tests were run by MySQL AB, with their own utility setting the criteria, so all results must be taken with a grain of salt. As is the case with many of these benchmarks, other vendors will quote their own, or other "independent" benchmarks that show their product's superiority to the rest of the field. Nevertheless, it's interesting to look at the results, which will, undoubtedly, add fuel to the "flame wars" in database forums online.

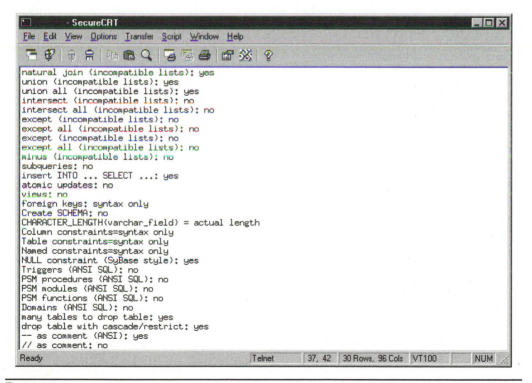

FIGURE 16-3   An example `crash-me` run

Summary

This chapter explored the important topic of MySQL performance optimization, discussing some of the techniques and options available to help you squeeze a little more speed out of your MySQL installation. Various strategies for query optimization were covered, including

- Using indexes to speed up access to frequently used columns
- Using the new MySQL query cache to improve query response time
- Analyzing queries with the EXPLAIN SELECT command to understand and then improve the query plan
- Rewriting subqueries as joins to take advantage of MySQL's optimization algorithms
- Using server variables, aggregate functions and sorting to make multi-table queries more efficient
- Creating data subsets with the INSERT . . . SELECT command and one or more temporary tables to simplify the processing of complex queries
- Choosing field sizes appropriately, and removing unnecessary tables from your database design
- Tuning the server's cache and memory buffers to obtain better performance
- Benchmarking server performance with the MySQL Benchmark Suite to evaluate the results of your changes.

These techniques (as well as the additional ones listed in the online MySQL manual) are essential reading for the efficient operation of your database, and they should be part of every administrator's tool box.

MySQL Replication

As discussed in Chapter 15, backing up a database involves taking a snapshot of the database and copying it to another location. Replication is a different kettle of fish. The process of replication is dynamic and requires two or more servers engaged in a relationship of continual transference to maintain a replica of the original database on a second server.

This chapter discusses the basics of replication, demonstrating how to set up a master-slave replication system with MySQL and introducing the commands needed to manage it.

Replication Basics

Replication in MySQL is the dynamic process of synchronizing data between a master database and one or more slave databases in near-real time. Currently, the recommendation is that MySQL replication occurs one way.

The capability to perform replication is a relatively recent one in the MySQL universe, starting from about version 3.23. Replication is essential for many applications, and the lack of replication support was a major drawback to MySQL compared to other relational database management systems (RDBMSs). Replication is still somewhat of a work in progress for MySQL, so you should try to run the most recent version of MySQL whenever possible. Older versions lack certain features and impose constraints on replication, which more recent versions don't impose. MySQL is best suited for one-way replication where you have one master and one or more slaves.

You should set up replication for three reasons. One reason is to create a standby database server so, if the primary server fails, the standby can step in, take over, and immediately be current. For any organization that has mission-critical, time-sensitive tasks involving its database, this is a must!

The second reason to use replication is to enable backups without having to bring down or lock out the master server. After replication takes place, backups are done on the slave, rather than on the master. This way, the master can be left to do its job without disturbance.

> **Avoid Deviance!**
> As far as possible, try to use the same version of MySQL for both the master and slave server(s). A version mismatch can sometimes result in erratic replication behavior.

And, the third reason to use replication has to do with keeping data current in multiple locations. Replication is necessary if several branches of an organization need to work from a current copy of the same database.

Now that you have an idea why you might want to set up replication, let's look at some of the concepts on which it's based.

The Master-Slave Relationship

As previously stated, replication requires at least two servers. The servers are set up so the first server, called the *master*, enters into a relationship with the other server, called the *slave*. Periodically, the latest changes to the database on the master are transferred to the slave. Through this replication relationship, an updated database can be propagated throughout an enterprise into multiple slave servers, but only one master can be in a replication relationship at any one time. Technically, you can promote a slave to a master if you must.

To start the process of configuring servers for replication, both master and slave servers must be synchronized, so the databases are the same. Once this is accomplished, it becomes critical for all updates to be done on the master and not the slave(s) to avoid confusion about the sequence of the updates.

Updates are transferred from the master to the slave via the master server's binary update logs. Replication is based on the concept that the master keeps track of the changes to the database through the binary logs and the slave updates its copy of the database by executing the changes recorded on the same logs. Thus, binary update logging must be enabled on the master for replication to take place.

In master-slave replication, the process begins when the slave contacts the master and requests updates. Permissions for this must be enabled on the slave server(s). The slave informs the master of the point in the binary log where the last update occurred, and then it begins the process of adding the new updates. Once completed, the slave notes where it left off and connects periodically to the master, checking for the next round of changes. This process continues as long as replication is enabled.

Replication Threads

Three threads are involved in replication: one on the master and two on the slave. The I/O thread on the slave connects to the master and requests the binary update log. The binary log dump thread on the master sends the binary update log to the slave on request. Once on the slave, the I/O thread reads the data sent by the master and copies it to the relay log in the data directory. The third thread, also on the slave, is the SQL thread, which reads and executes the queries from the relay log to bring the slave in alignment with the master.

FIGURE 17-1
The master-slave replication relationship

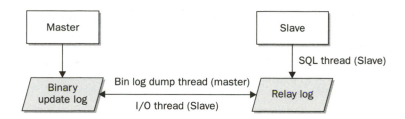

Having two different threads on the slave is new as of MySQL 4.0.2. The reason the threads were split was to improve performance; by being independent of each other, the processes of reading and writing on the slave can occur simultaneously. Because the execution of the SQL commands on the slave takes longer than reading and copying the binary logs to the relay logs, splitting these two functions also makes sense in terms of efficiencies on the master. The binary logs can be safely purged from the master because a copy of them already exists on the slave, even if all the updates to the slave haven't yet been committed.

The relay logs on the slave are written in the same format as binary logs. By default, the relay logs are kept in the slave's data directory. Once all the events in the relay log are executed, the SQL thread automatically deletes the log. A new relay log is automatically created when an I/O thread starts. Note that the slave needn't be connected to the master all the time. It keeps track of where it left off, and then gets itself current, regardless of how much time has passed since the last update took place.

Configuring MySQL for Replication

The process of creating master and slave servers, and then configuring them is fairly straightforward. In this section, we will assume you haven't configured replication before on these servers and you wish to replicate all your databases. You can configure replication for the first time in other ways, which you can study on your own in the Frequently Asked Questions (FAQ) section of the MySQL manual at `http://www.mysql.com/doc/en/Replication_FAQ.html`.

1. The first step is to grant permission for the slave server to contact the master for updates. This is done on the master by creating an account that provides a username and a password for the slave server. On MySQL 4.0.2 and forward, this can be done by issuing the `GRANT REPLICATION` command, and identifying the username and password the slave will use to connect to the master.

   For example, the command

   ```
   mysql> GRANT REPLICATION SLAVE ON *.* TO repadmin@slave
   IDENTIFIED BY 'rosebud7';
   ```

   grants permission to the user `repadmin` on the slave server named `slave` and assigns the password `rosebud7`.

2. Once the appropriate permissions are established, the next step is to copy the database from the master server to the slave. As previously mentioned, you

must start with an exact duplicate to assure proper replication. This step can be done by performing a backup on the master and restoring it to the slave (see Chapter 15 for details of backing up and restoring).

Make sure you prevent clients from performing updates while this process is in progress.

NOTE *MySQL 4.0 and above has a LOAD DATA FROM MASTER statement, which offers an alternate method to transfer the master database to the slave server. Several restrictions apply, however, and you should study these before trying this command. The section "Managing the Replication Process" looks at the LOAD DATA FROM MASTER command in more detail.*

3. The next step involves configuring the master server. This is done by adding a line to your option file (see Chapter 13 for information on option files) that assigns the master server a replication ID number. The replication ID must be a unique value in the range from 1 to 2^32-1. Both master and slave must have unique values. Additionally, you also have to configure the master server to enable binary logging.

The following is an example of what you can add to an option file to do this:

```
[mysqld]
server-id = 3
log-bin = binary_log
```

4. After configuring these options, shut down, and then restart the master server. On restart, the new options you just specified should take effect. All updates will now be written to the binary update log.

TIP *If binary logging has already been enabled on the master server, make a backup of the binary logs before shutting down and restarting. Then, when you restart, use the RESET MASTER statement to clear the existing binary logs.*

5. Now go to the slave server and alter the option file on it, so the slave is assigned a unique replication ID. You must also provide the information it needs to contact the master. The following example shows the parameters that must be specified in the slave's option file:

```
[mysqld]
server-id = 7
master-host = master
master-user = repadmin
master-password = rosebud7
```

The slave's server-id must be different from the master server's ID. The master-host is the name of the master server. Use the slave server name and password you created in the first step of this process (using the GRANT command) to indicate the master-user and the master-password.

CAUTION *If the master isn't listening on the default port, you also need to specify the* `master-port` *option. Additionally, if the connection between master and server fails often, increase the number of times the server attempts to make the connection, as well as the amount of time it has to do so, by altering the* `master-retry-count` *and the* `master-connect-retry` *options.*

6. The last step after you make the changes to the option file is to restart the slave server. The slave will use the startup options to determine how to connect to the master. The slave also will create a `master.info` file in the data directory that contains all the information about the replication process. After this initial startup, the slave will check this `master.info` file to get its instructions. If you decide later that you want to change the replication options, you must drop the current `master.info` file in the data directory, so it can be re-created on startup with the new options.

NOTE *If you want to exclude a particular database or databases from this replication process, return to the option file in the master server and specify the database name to ignore by adding an additional line for each database you want to exempt from replication. The format of this line should be*

```
binlog-ignore-db = database-name
```

Managing the Replication Process

Now that your master and slave servers are running smoothly, some commands exist that let you manage their relationship. All these commands are executed within the MySQL interface. In the process of examining these statements, you'll learn more about the details of replication.

The CHANGE MASTER Command

CHANGE MASTER instructs the slave to check a different binary log in the master for updates and/or to write to a different relay log in the slave. This statement also is used to change the connection and binary log parameters. Here's what it looks like:

```
CHANGE MASTER TO
  MASTER_HOST = 'master-name',
  MASTER_USER = 'slave-name',
  MASTER_PASSWORD = 'slave-password',
  MASTER_PORT = 'port-number',
  MASTER_LOG_FILE = 'binlog-filename',
  MASTER_LOG_POS = 'binlog-position',
  MASTER_CONNECT_RETRY = 'value';
  RELAY_LOG_FILE = 'relaylog-filename',
  RELAY_LOG_POS = 'value';
```

Let's say your company just bought a brand-new, super-big, super-fast dedicated server (since you're imagining, you might as well make it interesting!) for the database. You want to change masters from the old server to the new one. Here's an example with values entered.

```
mysql>CHANGE MASTER TO
MASTER_HOST ='MrBig',
MASTER_USER = 'Slave1',
MASTER_PASSWORD = 'Slav3Pass',
MASTER_PORT = '3306',
MASTER_LOG_FILE = 'master-bin.001',
MASTER_LOG_POS = 7,
MASTER_CONNECT_RETRY = 15;
RELAY_LOG_FILE = 'slave-relay-bin.010',
RELAY_LOG_POS = 6084;
```

Table 17-1 contains a quick reference chart for these parameters. Note, only the parameters you specify will change. If you don't specify a parameter, the existing value remains as is. The exceptions to this rule are the host name and the port number parameters. If you change either of these, MySQL assumes you're changing master servers and it automatically drops the binary update log name and position values. If you don't give these two new values after changing the host name or port number, the values will be set to MASTER_LOG_FILE=' ' and MASTER_LOG_POS=4.

Parameter	What It Means
MASTER_HOST	Host name for the master server
MASTER_USER	Slave name to use when connecting the master
MASTER_PASSWORD	Slave's password to connection to master
MASTER_PORT	Port number to connect to master
MASTER_LOG_FILE	Name of master's binary log file from which to start reading when replication begins
MASTER_LOG_POS	Position in the master's binary log file from which to start reading when replication begins
MASTER_CONNECT_RETRY	Number of seconds to wait between connection attempts
RELAY_LOG_FILE	(Version 4.0+) Name of the slave relay log from which to begin execution when replication begins
RELAY_LOG_POS	(Version 4.0+) Position in slave relay log from which to begin execution when replication begins

TABLE 17-1 CHANGE MASTER Options

The CHANGE MASTER statement deletes existing relay logs and begins a new one, unless you define a value for RELAY_LOG_FILE or RELAY_LOG_POS. CHANGE MASTER also updates the master.info and the relay-log.info files.

Note, if you try to execute the CHANGE MASTER statement in a high-load environment, you could lose some queries. This can happen if the slave SQL thread is behind the I/O thread because, when the CHANGE MASTER command deletes the relay logs, a gap might exist between what was written and what's currently being processed.

You have two ways to get around this. One way is to stop the slave thread until it's read all the existing relay logs. Use the STOP SLAVE IO_THREAD command and monitor the progress of the reads by using SHOW SLAVE STATUS and SELECT MASTER_POS_WAIT(). The other way is to use STOP SLAVE and SHOW SLAVE STATUS with the Relay_master_log_file and Exec_master_log_pos columns to see where the thread is in the master's binary log. When you have these values, specify them in the Master_log_file and Master_log_pos options. This instructs the slave to start replication at the exact point where the slave thread last left off, and no records will be lost.

The PURGE MASTER Command

The PURGE MASTER statement deletes the binary logs on the master prior to a specified date or log name. You would use this in a situation where you want to determine which log files are still being processed. The syntax is as follows:

```
PURGE MASTER LOGS TO binary-log
```

or

```
PURGE MASTER LOGS BEFORE date
```

NOTE   *This statement requires the SUPER privilege.*

As an example, suppose you want to purge all the master binary update logs prior to the one named bin_log.999. You would execute the following:

```
mysql> PURGE MASTER LOGS TO bin_log.999;
```

The START SLAVE Command

The START SLAVE statement is used to begin or resume replication. Using MySQL 4.0.2 and up, the IO_THREAD and SQL_THREAD options are supported. The I/O thread reads the queries from the master server, and then writes them to the relay log. The SQL thread reads the relay log and executes the queries.

Note, if the slave is unable to connect to the master or read the binary logs, it might stop on its own without providing an error message. Don't assume everything is fine because you issued the START SLAVE command successfully—monitor the slave's activities by using SHOW SLAVE STATUS. You can also read the .err file in the slave's data dir to make sure everything is okay.

The STOP SLAVE Command

The STOP SLAVE statement is used to pause or end replication. Like SLAVE START, it can be combined with the IO_THREAD and SQL_THREAD options.

The SHOW SLAVE STATUS Command

The SHOW SLAVE STATUS statement provides information about the slave server's status. The syntax looks like this:

```
mysql> SHOW SLAVE STATUS;
```

In addition to some output related to such things as the master host and master user already discussed, the SHOW SLAVE STATUS also provides the information contained in Table 17-2.

The SHOW SLAVE HOSTS Command

As of version 4.0, issuing this command on the master server displays a list of slave servers that are registered for replication. Some of the other information provided by this statement is described in Table 17-3.

The SHOW PROCESSLIST Command

The SHOW PROCESSLIST statement displays information about the threads on the server and was previously discussed in Chapter 13. In a replication context, it can be used to obtain status information on both the master and the slave. For each thread, the output is shown in various columns, some of which are named and described in Table 17-4.

Parameter	Description
Connect_retry	How many times to attempt a connection to the master
Read_Master_Log_Pos	Current position being read by the I/O thread in the master's binary log
Relay_Log_File	The current relay log file
Relay_Log_Pos	The position of the current event being read in the relay log file
Relay_log_space	The size of all the relay files

TABLE 17-2   Information Provided by the SHOW SLAVE STATUS Command

TABLE 17-3
Information
Provided by the
SHOW SLAVE
HOSTS Command

Parameter	Description
server_id	The replication ID number of the slave server
master_id	The replication ID number of the master server
Host	The name of the slave server host
Port	The port number that the slave server is connected to

```
mysql> SHOW PROCESSLIST;
+----+-----------+------------------------+-----------+--------
-----+------+----------------------------------------------
-----------+------------------+
| Id | User      | Host                   | db        | Command
| Time | State
| Info      |
+----+-----------+------------------------+-----------+-------------+------+--------------
-----------
----------------------------------------+------------------+
| 30 | root      | localhost              | northstar | Query
| 0    | NULL
| SHOW PROCESSLIST |
| 33 | jay_slave | jay.vermonster.com:44527 | NULL      | Binlog
Dump | 139  | Has sent all binlog to slave; waiting for binlog to
be updated | NULL       |
+----+-----------+------------------------+-----------+--------
-----+------+----------------------------------------------
-----------+------------------+
2 rows in set (0.00 sec)
```

The LOAD DATA FROM MASTER Command

The LOAD DATA FROM MASTER statement, which is available in MySQL 4.0 and better, is an alternative way to set up a slave to obtain data from a master server. Several restrictions are involved in using this command so, currently, MySQL AB recommends using it only if the master database is small and if having a read lock on the master for a long time isn't a problem. Additionally, only MyISAM tables can be

Parameter	Description
State	Contains information about what the server is processing. For example, on the binlog dump thread, you could see something like Sending binlog information to the slave. On the I/O thread, you might see Connecting to master or Requesting binlog dump. On the SQL thread, a common state is the-query-being-executed; another could be Reading event from the relay log
db	The database of the thread.
Command	The statement currently being executed by the thread.
Time	How long (in seconds) the current thread has taken to execute.

TABLE 17-4   Information Provided by the SHOW PROCESSLIST Command

TABLE 17-5
Information
Provided by the
SHOW BINLOG
EVENTS Command

Parameters	Description
log_name	The binary update log filename
pos	The position in the log of the event
event-type	This identifies the type of event

Parameters	Description
File	The binary update log filename
position	The current position in the binary log where the master server is writing
binlog_do_db	The list of databases recorded in the binary update log
binlog_ignore_db	The list of databases ignored and not recorded in the binary update log

TABLE 17-6   Information Provided by the SHOW MASTER STATUS Command

replicated with this command. This command seems designed for more frequent implementation in the future, when MySQL 5.0 won't require the lock on the master database that prevents updates while the command is executing.

A variant of this statement is LOAD TABLE FROM MASTER, which only transfers one table from master to slave. Usually, this command is executed because a particular table on the slave has become corrupted and needs to be restored.

The SHOW BINLOG EVENTS Command

As discussed earlier, when replicating, everything is based on the binary update log in the master server. To display events in this log, the SHOW BINLOG EVENTS statement can be used in MySQL 4.0 and better. The log output includes the information in Table 17-5.

The SHOW MASTER STATUS Command

For additional information about the master server's binary logs, use the SHOW MASTER STATUS, which includes the information in Table 17-6 in its output.

Summary

Replication is an aspect of MySQL currently being worked on and refined considerably. This chapter introduced many of the basic replication concepts, such as the master-slave relationship, binary update logging, and relay logging. The three threads that carry out replication on the master and server were reviewed and their actions analyzed. Also, the process of taking two servers and configuring them for ongoing replication was covered step-by-step. Finally, multiple commands to manage and monitor replication from the MySQL command line were reviewed. These SQL statements are useful for configuring and troubleshooting replication, and they provide considerable information about the processes involved.

Development

IV

PART

The MySQL APIs

You might remember, from the introductory material at the front of this book, that one of the reasons for MySQL's popularity is its wide application support. Unlike many of its better-known commercial counterparts, MySQL exposes its innards to developers via a series of APIs, thereby giving them the freedom to create database-driven applications in the language of their choice.

Over the course of the next few chapters, we explore these APIs in depth, explaining via examples and illustrations how you can use them to your own advantage. This chapter serves as an introduction to the topic, providing you with some general background on the different APIs available, what each can do, and how to select one that is appropriate to your needs.

The MySQL APIs In Context

Let's begin with the basics. What is an application programming interface (API) when it's home anyway?

In technical terms, an *API* is "a published specification that describes how a programmer can make requests of an application." In more general terms, an API is an interface—a channel through which communication takes place—between two or more applications. It usually consists of a set of predefined functions or methods, which a programmer can invoke to achieve certain results or behavior. An API provides an efficient, consistent, and reusable mechanism for communication between the different components of an application or between applications themselves.

One of the most well-known examples of an API is the Microsoft Windows API, which is used by almost every Windows application in existence. This API exposes the functions and methods needed to create application windows, construct application menus, manipulate files, allocate memory, and generally interact with the operating system (OS) in a variety of different ways. By exposing these functions as API calls, Windows ensures that every application running within it operates in a consistent manner.

MySQL's developers have been providing an API to MySQL's internals for quite a while. A primitive API was first made available in version 3.19. This has gradually expanded over the years to a full-featured, powerful toolkit for building custom data-driven applications. Today, APIs to MySQL are available for a variety of different languages, including C, Java, PHP, Perl, and Python (some of these are discussed in detail in subsequent chapters).

To understand the value of the MySQL API completely, it's instructive to look at a scenario in which it did *not* exist. Without an API that let developers connect to the database server, execute queries, and process results, all interaction with the server would need to be routed through the provided client utilities, most notable the `mysql` client program (currently the only tool in the MySQL software suite that allows execution of arbitrary queries).

The problem? The `mysql` client program is a bare-bones utility, which merely executes SQL queries and returns the results in tabular format. It does not permit advanced manipulation, such as stepping through a record set, formatting records into an HTML web page, validating input, securing database connections, or handling errors.

So, something more sophisticated is needed, especially in the context of web-based, data-driven applications—these applications usually have specific requirements as to the formatting and presentation of retrieved data, and they could also need a high level of redundancy, especially if they deal with voluminous and/or complex transactions, say, an e-commerce site or a business-to-business (B2B) exchange. Creating a generic tool to handle this is not feasible, especially because every application has its own set of special needs. Instead, a more efficient approach is to provide programmers with the freedom to access the features they need, when they need them, so they can use those features and capabilities in whatever manner they deem suitable for the specific requirements of their applications.

Thus, by exposing an API that enables developers access to all MySQL's functions, MySQL's developers not only provide an elegant solution to the problem, but they also make the open-source community happy. The increased level of access to MySQL's internals makes more powerful and creative applications possible. Developers return the favor by making their applications available to the MySQL development team and the rest of the community at large.

Components of the MySQL API

The MySQL API is designed to provide developers with some specific capabilities. The following section discusses these briefly.

- **Connection management** Before an application can begin interacting with a database and executing queries on the data stored within it, it must first establish a connection to the database server. The MySQL API includes a series of functions designed specifically for applications to connect to a MySQL database server, provide all requested credentials, and open a channel for subsequent communication. Once all communication is completed, the API also provides functions to terminate the connection and clean up things by freeing used memory.

- **Query execution and result processing**   Once a connection has been established, an application can begin sending queries to the server and retrieving the results. The MySQL API provides numerous functions to facilitate this process, including functions to execute queries either singly or as a transaction block, to retrieve and process record collections and to fetch specific records from a collection or specific fields from a record.

- **Error reporting**   The MySQL API also provides basic error-reporting capabilities, passing error codes and messages onward to the caller in case of a problem with a connection or query. In addition to this, the API also enables callers to access detailed debugging and housekeeping information, including the current server state and a list of all active processes.

NOTE   *The MySQL API does not provide exception handling routines of its own. Instead, it merely reports errors, leaving the task of handling those errors to the application developer.*

- **Ancillary functions**   In addition to the various functions previously described, the MySQL API also provides a number of so-called housekeeping functions, including functions that return the current state of the server (the number of open connections, the number of queries being processed, the server version, and so on); list available databases, tables, fields, and processes; manage character sets; provide detailed diagnostic and debugging information; clean up unused memory by closing inactive connections and terminating inactive processes; and shut down, restart, or reload the server.

Language Support

MySQL exposes APIs to many different programming languages, thereby making it possible to write database-driven applications in the language of your choice. Currently, MySQL provides hooks to C, C++, Java, PHP, Perl, Python, ODBC, Ruby, Eiffel, and Tcl, ensuring that a lack of choice is the least of your problems when building MySQL-backed applications of your own.

The following material discusses each of these API streams briefly:

- **C and C++**   Because MySQL is written in C, it's natural that the C API for MySQL is the most full-featured among the various options listed here. The C API is bundled with the MySQL distribution via the `libmysqlclient` library, and it is also used by all the command-line tools that ship with MySQL. These tools are a rich source of information for C developers looking to understand the nuances of this API. The C library is the foundation of the other APIs discussed in this section (except for the Java API), and it works equally well for C++ development.

NOTE   *A detailed discussion of MySQL programming with C is available in Chapter 19 of this book; you can read more about the MySQL C API at* `http://www.mysql.com/documentation`.

- **PHP**   Hypertext PreProcessor (PHP) is a scripting language that works by embedding commands into HTML web pages, thereby making it possible to incorporate sophisticated business logic into otherwise static web sites. The language is rapidly gaining favor among web developers for its power, flexibility and ease of use, and is becoming the popular choice for small- to medium-sized data-driven web applications because of its out-of-the-box support for different RDBMS. The latest version of PHP—PHP 4—comes with built-in support for MySQL, and has a full-featured API to handle MySQL connections, queries, and result sets.

NOTE   *A detailed discussion of MySQL programming with PHP is available in Chapter 21 of this book, and you can learn more about PHP's MySQL API at* `http://www.php.net`.

- **Perl**   Perl supports MySQL via its DBI module, which provides a general abstraction layer for communication with a variety of different databases. The DBI provides generic functions for database access, query execution, result set processing, and error handling. It is coupled with a database-specific database driver (DBD) that takes care of translating these generic functions into a native format understandable by the RDBMS. A well-documented MySQL DBD, which allows developers to add MySQL support to their Perl applications with minimal difficulty, has been available for Perl for a long time.

NOTE   *A detailed discussion of MySQL programming with PHP is available in Chapter 20 of this book; you can read more about the Perl DBI and the MySQL DBD at* `http://dbi.perl.org`.

- **Python**   MySQL-Python connectivity is provided by the Python MySQLdb module, which is "a thread-compatible interface to the popular MySQL database server that provides the Python database API." This Python module provides Python developers with the methods they need to connect to a MySQL database server, execute queries, process results, and handle errors, all while retaining the structured, object-oriented approach for which Python is known.

NOTE   *You can read more about the Python MySQLdb module at* `http://sourceforge.net/projects/mysql-python`.

- **Java**   Currently, Java Database Connectivity (JDBC) in MySQL is provided via the Connector/J driver. This driver, which is developed and supported by MySQL AB on a commercial basis, enables developers to add MySQL support to their Java applications by translating JDBC commands into a format understandable by native MySQL (in a two-tiered approach similar to that used by the Perl DBI). The latest version of the Connector/J driver offers both performance benefits and support for a variety of different character sets, including Unicode.

---

*N*OTE   *You can read more about Connector/J at* `http://www.mysql.com/` `products/connector-j.`

- **ODBC**   MySQL supports Open Database Connectivity (ODBC) on both Linux and Windows platforms via its 32-bit MyODBC driver, which makes it possible to connect to MySQL through any ODBC-compliant application, including applications like Microsoft Word and Microsoft Excel. This MyODBC driver implements all the functions of the ODBC API, taking care of processing MySQL connection requests, executing SQL queries, and returning results to the caller.

---

*N*OTE   *You can read more about MyODBC at* `http://www.mysql.com/` `products/myodbc.`

Selecting an API

With so much variety available to you, you'll be forgiven for wondering exactly which API to choose when developing your application. The answer, as always, is to begin with the problem and evaluate the various options to see which one solves it in the best (most efficient and cost-effective) manner. Each of the previously listed programming languages has its own strengths and weaknesses. Your choice must be made after careful consideration of many different factors, both technical and nontechnical.

Platform and Application Requirements

Often, the platform for which you are developing determines the choice of API or programming language. While most languages do support the Intel 80×86 architecture, you might not have such a wide choice on less-popular architectures. In such situations, the availability of language and development environment plays a critical role in your choice of API. C compilers, for example, are available for most architectures, but PHP and Perl interpreters might be unavailable.

The requirements of your application also play an important role in determining the selection of programming language and API. Different languages have different strengths—Perl, for example, excels at text processing, while C and C++ offer fine-grained control over memory management. It's important to pick a language with strengths that are complementary to the requirements of your application.

If you're writing an application for a device with a small memory footprint—say, a flash card—you might prefer the C API, as using C would give you a small, fast binary and also give you extensive control over resource management on your less-powerful device. The same argument might not hold good for a MySQL-backed web application, however, where memory management often takes second place to speed, reliability, and the availability of high-level constructs that speed development time.

Performance

Obviously, application performance is an important decision factor in choosing an API and language—in general, the faster your application, the happier your customers. Assuming all other things as equal, a basic decision to make here is whether you'd prefer to use a compiled language (such as C) or an interpreted language (such as Perl) for your application.

Both approaches have merits and demerits. Compiled code is usually faster than interpreted code because compilers convert source code to machine language before executing it, thereby gaining a substantial speed improvement over interpreted code, which is translated on the fly. On the other hand, interpreted languages are great for code development and debugging because the code need not be compiled prior to testing it at every stage.

While interpreted languages offer benefits in terms of faster development time, compiled languages allow fine-grained control over resource usage and memory allocation—power that can come in handy when working on low-resource, memory-intensive platforms. Compiled code is not usually portable between architectures—the application needs to be recompiled for each architecture on which it will be executed—while interpreted programs will run on any platform or architecture so long as an interpreter is available for the source code.

Among the various APIs discussed here, C and C++ provide the greatest speed, with Java, PHP, and Perl trading places with each other, depending on the application. For applications that spend a lot of time communicating with the MySQL server, PHP tends to win performance tests by quite a wide margin. This is because it has the most direct access to the native C API calls, while Perl and Java have to deal with the overhead of the DBI or JDBC layer.

Simplicity

The KISS principle—Keep It Simple, Stupid—applies as much to software engineering as it does to real life and, often, simplicity and ease of use are important factors when deciding which API to use. Most real-world projects run on tight time and cost deadlines so, even though a particular language could be technically best suited for a particular application, it could fail the cost-versus-benefit test if developing code in it is a time- and resource-intensive task. In such situations, time and cost constraints could dictate usage of a less-optimal, but simpler solution.

A Hill O' Beans

Java straddles both sides of the compiled-versus-interpreted battle. Java code is first converted to bytecode in a process equivalent to compilation. This bytecode is then interpreted by a so-called "virtual machine" and executed. This two-tiered approach results in the best—and worst—of both worlds: Java programs are eminently portable and secure, but the additional step can result in a fairly noticeable decrease in speed.

C and C++ are often cited as examples of this argument. Although both languages are extremely powerful and allow developers tremendous control over the finer aspects of performance and resource management, coding a simple application using these languages is usually a fairly involved task requiring both time and effort. By contrast, PHP, which comes with built-in support for MySQL, provides numerous high-level constructs, which make it possible to put together a MySQL-backed application with minimal time and effort.

Two important components of simplicity are readability and ease of use. Usually, code in languages like PHP and Perl is easier to read and understand than equivalent code in C or Java.

This readability can go a long way in increasing a developer's comfort level with the language and also reduces transition time when new pieces of code are to be grafted on to already existing applications.

Availability of Libraries and Tools

Another important factor that can influence your choice of API is the availability of pluggable library modules for the language. The availability of these extra libraries can substantially reduce the time spent on development of new features, while simultaneously improving reliability through the use of well-tested, publicly available code modules. Normally, you'd prefer a language with a large repository of freely available libraries, so you don't need to reinvent the wheel every time a new feature or function must be added to your application.

The popularity of Java, Perl, and PHP has resulted in the creation of large online code repositories containing add-on library modules for everything from file manipulation to data encryption. These libraries add significant value to the language and often result in developers choosing these languages over C, which comes with fewer libraries.

In addition to the availability of prebuilt code, the quality and quantity of development tools also influence the selection of a language. Languages that come with sophisticated tools to generate code automatically from high-level specifications or that include powerful compilers, debuggers, and development environments are much preferred to languages with more primitive toolkits. Sure, you can write code in any language using a simple text editor. But if you have an IDE that lets you accomplish the task via a point-and-click operation, you'd obviously prefer it both for its simplicity and its impact on the overall development time for your application.

Portability

Portability is an important factor to consider in your choice of language. A language that is only usable on a single processor or architecture is obviously less valuable than one that works across multiple processors and architectures. If you anticipate using your application on different platforms, you should explore the portability aspect well in advance of writing any code because it can prove a fairly large problem at later stages if not dealt with decisively.

PART IV

If portability of your application is a concern, you usually can't go wrong with C. C compilers are available for every platform and architecture in existence—from Intel 80×86 CPUs to Motorola 68×00 CPUs—and code written in C can usually be made to run on other platforms without too much difficulty. Java is also a good choice if the portability of your application is a concern, since it was, after all, the original proponent of the write-once-run-anywhere philosophy

Maturity

When deciding on an API, consideration should also be given to the maturity of the language in which it is written. A mature language is one that adheres to publicly defined standards, one with the backing and support of the developer community, one that is supported by extensive and readable documentation and online community assistance. Although nontechnical in nature, these factors, nevertheless, play a vital role in your decision. Obviously, the more documentation and support available, the more easily you can get up to speed with the language, resolve queries and problems, and deliver the product.

Languages like C, Java, and PHP today boast impressive documentation, both online and offline, together with a large and enthusiastic developer community. Choosing to use an API created in these languages is usually a good idea, especially if you're a novice or you're running on a tight deadline because you can turn to your peers, as well as offline manuals and online knowledge banks, in case of difficulties. A language with poor documentation and support can (and usually will) trip you up at some point, no matter how technically superior it might be.

Cost

An important factor, and one often overlooked in purely technical discussions, is the cost of the various tools needed to develop code in a particular language. The open-source movement has ensured that most basic tools, such as compilers and linkers, are available free of charge, at least in most *NIX environments. Windows users, however, might still need to purchase development tools for certain languages. In addition, depending on how you plan to use them, you might also need to purchase commercial licenses for add-on modules or libraries you include in your application. Again, open-source code could help reduce the cost here, but not in all cases.

Thus, calculating the real cost of the tools required for a project is an important activity, and one that could sometimes restrain you from using the language or API that is best for the task. For example, languages like C and Java might require some investment in high-quality commercial compilers. PHP and Perl, which are true children of the open-source community, require a much smaller investment footprint and are, therefore, not surprisingly, more popular among small- and medium-sized software organizations or organizations looking to reduce their expenses on software licenses.

Summary

In this chapter, you were introduced to the MySQL API. You learned about its need and rationale, and were given a brief description of its capabilities. You also learned the various languages for which this API is available, and were given a "cheat sheet" that should assist you in choosing the right language for your needs. In subsequent chapters, we explore these APIs in greater depth, using them to build real-world, MySQL-backed applications.

MySQL and C

O ver the course of this book, you've spent a lot of time with MySQL's numerous command-line utilities—the `mysqldump` utility to retrieve the contents of a database, the `mysqladmin` utility to perform administrative tasks, and, of course, the `mysql` command-line client for SQL query execution. All these tools share certain common attributes: they're fast, they're each designed to perform a specialized task efficiently, they all work on the client-server model, and they're all written in C.

As noted briefly in the last chapter, MySQL comes with a C API that makes writing client applications to interact with the database server using the C programming language both quick and easy. This C API is packaged as a library that's included in all standard MySQL distributions, and it's also used by all the command-line tools that ship with MySQL (including the three discussed previously). Given this relationship, it's no surprise that the C API is the most full-featured among the various MySQL APIs and, in fact, serves as the foundation for all the other MySQL APIs (except the Java API).

This chapter introduces you to the MySQL C API, and offers a broad overview of how to write MySQL client applications using the routines and structures provided by this API. In addition to an explanation of the process of connecting and communicating with a MySQL server with the C API, the chapter includes detailed discussions of the API functions used for connection management, query execution, result set processing, and error handling. It also provides enough sample code to familiarize you with building MySQL client applications in C.

C

We'll begin by taking a quick look at C, its history and its evolution, and also discussing the tools you will need to get started with MySQL and the C API.

History and Evolution

Most C devotees like to think that the world began with a line of C code. The truth is a little more prosaic: C was invented at Bell Labs in the 1970s by Dennis Ritchie and Kenneth Thompson. C was designed as a high-level application implementation language for the UNIX operating system (OS), and was derived largely from BCPL, a similar (though typeless) language created in 1967. Toward the end of the 1970s, Brian Kernighan and Dennis Ritchie published the first formal description of the language, and brought it to the attention of the world outside the Bell Labs campus.

Impressed with its features, computer vendors began to promote the use of the language, and C compilers for different architectures and OSs slowly started making an appearance. In 1983, taking note of the widespread adoption of C in the industry, the ANSI institute established a committee to develop a formal standard for the C language. Today, while each C compiler still maintains a subset of compiler-specific features, most of them generate ANSI C-compliant code.

More than 30 years after C was first created, the language invented by Ritchie and Thompson is still going strong, with C compilers available for almost every single OS. The growth of the UNIX OS has contributed significantly to its success. Today, almost all Unices come with a C compiler thrown in by default, and many of the most useful and fundamental UNIX commands are coded in C. Because the language is small, well defined, and flexible enough to support a wide range of applications, its popularity has increased even further with developers. Today, C is used for application programming, as a tool to teach programming fundamentals, and as the implementation language of choice by engineers working on billion-dollar projects.

Installation

To compile C source code into executable programs, you need a C compiler. The recommended C compiler for use on UNIX systems is the GNU Compiler Collection (GCC), which includes support for C, C++, and Java, and is available free of charge on the Internet for both Windows and UNIX platforms. Source code and precompiled binaries can be obtained from http://gcc.gnu.org/, together with installation instructions. The examples in this chapter assume GCC 3.3 on Linux, although you're free to use it on the platform of your choice.

A detailed discussion of GCC installation is beyond the scope of this chapter. If you're new to GCC, you should spend some time reading the installation instructions in the download archive, as well as the notes on the web site—these will help tremendously in helping you get your GCC development environment up and running. In case of difficulty, an online manual is at http://gcc.gnu.org/onlinedocs/ and a FAQ at http://gcc.gnu.org/faq.html.

If you're on a UNIX system, a quick way to check whether GCC is already present on the system is with the UNIX which command. If GCC is available, the program should return the full path to the gcc binary.

```
[user@host]$ which gcc
/usr/bin/gcc
```

MySQL and C

To simplify the task of building MySQL client applications, MySQL AB provides a C API that exposes a low-level interface to most of the common tasks related to SQL

Special Treatment

To build MySQL clients on Windows, you need to jump through a few extra hoops. For more information on this and for troubleshooting problems related to Windows builds, look at `http://www.mysql.com/doc/en/Windows_client_compiling.html`.

---

server interaction: database connection, query execution, result set processing, and error handling. This C API is implemented via two components:

- A header file, `mysql.h`, which consists of structure and function declarations;
- A MySQL library, `libmysqlclient` (UNIX) or `mysqlclient.lib` (Windows), which contains the actual C functions themselves.

If you're planning to compile MySQL clients on the Windows platform, you'll also need a third component:

- A header file, `my_global.h`, which provides the extra definitions needed for Windows.

All these files are included in a standard MySQL source or binary tarball, as well as in MySQL binary RPMs.

- If you used a tarball, then (assuming you installed MySQL to `/usr/local/mysql`) the MySQL C library can be found in `/usr/local/mysql/lib`, while the header file can be found in `/usr/local/mysql/include`.
- If you installed MySQL using an RPM, the library will be located in `/usr/lib/mysql/` and the header file in `/usr/include/mysql/`.

Typically, you'll tell your C compiler where to find these files using the `-L` and `-I` options and your linker to link with the MySQL library with the `-lmysqlclient` option.

Learning By Example

Are you looking for examples of how to build MySQL client applications with the MySQL C API? Most of the clients in the MySQL source distribution are written in C, and their source code is freely available. Look at the `client/` subdirectory of the MySQL source distribution, which includes code for MySQL tools like `mysqldump`, `mysqlimport`, and—of course!—the `mysql` command-line client.

The best way to understand how to use the MySQL C API is by writing a simple client, compiling it, and executing it. Open a text file in your favorite text editor and enter the following lines of code:

```
#include <stdio.h>
#include <mysql.h>

int main()
{
        /* declare structures and variables */
        MYSQL mysql;
        MYSQL_RES *result;
        MYSQL_ROW row;

        /* initialize MYSQL structure */
        mysql_init(&mysql);

        /* connect to database */
        mysql_real_connect(&mysql, "localhost", "john", "doe", "db1", 0, NULL, 0);

        /* execute query */
        mysql_query(&mysql, "SELECT title, author FROM books");

        /* get result set */
        result = mysql_store_result(&mysql);

        /* process result set */
        while((row = mysql_fetch_row(result)))
        {
fprintf(stdout, "%s - %s\n", row[0], row[1]);
        }

        /* clean up */
        mysql_free_result(result);
        mysql_close(&mysql);
}
```

When you're done, save the file (call it `sample.c`) and compile it.

```
 [user@host]$ /usr/bin/gcc sample.c -o sample.bin -I/usr/local/mysql/include
-L/usr/local/mysql/lib -lmysqlclient -lz
```

The `-lmysqlclient` option tells the linker to link against the `libmysqlclient` library, while the `-I` and `-L` options tell the compiler where to look for the MySQL header files and libraries, respectively. The `-o` option tells the compiler what name to assign to the final binary executable. In the absence of this argument, GCC defaults to `a.out`.

Catching a Few Zzzzzs

Are you wondering why I added the -lz option to the previous command line? It's because newer versions of the MySQL client library include support for protocol compression to reduce the amount of data transferred over the client-server link. This feature is implemented via the `libz` library and, if you don't tell the linker to link against it (via the -lz option), the linker will produce a series of error messages and abort the compilation process.

Once the code finishes compiling, you should have a binary named `sample.bin`. You can now run this binary at the command prompt. If all goes well, it should connect to the MySQL server, execute the query, and print the output.

```
[user@host]$ ./sample.bin
Mystic River - Dennis Lehane
The Memoirs Of Sherlock Holmes - Arthur Conan Doyle
Hannibal - Thomas Harris
The Dilbert Principle - Scott Adams
Life Of Pi - Yann Martel
The Lake House - James Patterson
Bleachers - John Grisham
Mortal Prey - John Sandford
```

Let's dissect the previous code to understand the process by which you can use the MySQL C API to hook up your C programs to a MySQL database and retrieve data from it.

1. The program begins in the traditional manner, by first including all the header files required by it. Because we're going to use some MySQL-specific structures here, we've included the `mysql.h` C header file in this list.

   ```
   #include <stdio.h>
   #include <mysql.h>
   ```

2. Next, we defined the `main()` function and initialized some of the variables and structures we'll be using in subsequent steps.

   ```
   /* declare structures and variables */
   MYSQL mysql;
   MYSQL_RES *result;
   MYSQL_ROW row;
   ```

   Each of these structures has a specific role to play in the workflow of a MySQL client application. The first one, MYSQL, is the most important because it serves as the primary point for all interaction with the server. Result sets returned by the server are stored in the special MYSQL_RES result set structure and the records extracted from this structure are represented in the MYSQL_ROW structure.

3. To begin communication with the MySQL database server, you first need to initialize the MYSQL structure with the mysql_init() structure.

```
mysql_init(&mysql);
```

Once this is done, a connection can be opened to the server using the mysql_real_connect() method.

```
mysql_real_connect(&mysql, "localhost", "john", "doe", "db1", 0, NULL, 0);
```

The function requires a number of different arguments: the name of the host running the MySQL server ("localhost"), the name of the database to connect to ("db1"), and the MySQL username ("john") and password ("doe"). If the connection is successful, this function returns a database connection handle, which is used throughout the program when communicating with the database. The section "Connection Management" discusses this in greater detail.

4. Once a connection is established with the server, the mysql_query() function is used to send a query to the server for execution.

```
mysql_query(&mysql, "SELECT title, author FROM books");
```

This query can be any valid SQL query that the MySQL server is capable of accepting. Note, the query string sent to the server shouldn't include a terminating semicolon (;) or \g signal. The section "Query Execution" looks at the mysql_query() command in greater detail to find out more about how it's used in conjunction with both SELECT and non-SELECT queries.

5. Once the query has been executed, the result set generated (if the query is a SELECT query) is sucked into a variable (actually, a pointer to the MYSQL_RES structure) with the mysql_store_result() function.

```
result = mysql_store_result(&mysql);
```

The records contained in the result set can now be accessed via the mysql_fetch_row() function, which reads the records, one at a time, into the special MYSQL_ROW structure. This structure is nothing but an array, with each element representing one field of the record. It can, therefore, be accessed using standard array notation, as in the following:

```
while((row = mysql_fetch_row(result)))
{
        fprintf(stdout, "%s - %s\n", row[0], row[1]);
}
```

Once all the records in the result set are retrieved with mysql_fetch_row(), the function returns NULL. The mysql_free_result() function then takes care of deallocating the memory used by the result set, while the mysql_close() function takes care of closing the database connection.

```
mysql_free_result(result);
mysql_close(&mysql);
```

Experienced developers will note that the previous sample application doesn't include any error checking. I've omitted exception-handling code from the previous example for simplicity but, fear not, I'll address this issue in detail as we proceed through the chapter.

Note, also, this sample application only works if the database and tables needed by it already exist. You can obtain the SQL code needed to create these tables (together with electronic copies of the source code in this and following chapters) from this book's companion web site: `http://www.mysql-tcr.com`.

As you see in subsequent examples, the five previously outlined steps make up a general process that will be used over and over again when you build data-driven applications using the MySQL C API. The following sections explore these steps in greater detail.

Connection Management

Making a connection to the MySQL DBMS is essentially a two-step process. The first step is to call the `mysql_init()` function to initialize a `MYSQL` structure. This structure serves as the primary point for all future interaction with the server.

```
mysql_init(&mysql);
```

Next, the `mysql_real_connect()` function can be used to establish the connection with the server.

```
mysql_real_connect(&mysql, "localhost", "joe", "secret",
"db1", 0, NULL, 0);
```

As the previous code snippet illustrates, the `mysql_real_connect()` function must be provided with a number of different arguments for it to initiate a successful connection: the `MYSQL` structure previously initialized by `mysql_init()`, the name of the host running the MySQL server, the username and password required for logging in to the server, and the name of the database to use.

Changing Your Mind

Typically, the database on which your queries are to be executed is specified at the time of connecting to the server, via the `mysql_real_connect()` function. However, you can select a new database for use at any time with the `mysql_select_db()` function, which accepts a database name as argument, as in the following:

```
/* select the database named "db678" */
mysql_select_db(&mysql, "db678");
```

If a successful connection is established, this function then returns a connection handle. This handle is used for all subsequent communication with the database. In case of a connection failure—perhaps, for example, because of an invalid login or an incorrect host name—the function will return false. A good idea is always to check the return value of this function in your script before you proceed, as demonstrated in the following simple program:

```
#include <stdio.h>
#include <mysql.h>

int main()
{
    /* declare MYSQL struct */
    MYSQL mysql;

    /* initialize struct */
    mysql_init(&mysql);

    /* attempt a connection and print status */
    if (!mysql_real_connect(&mysql, "localhost", "tim", "abracadbra", "mysql", 0, NULL, 0))
    {
        printf("Could not connect to MySQL server\n");
    }
    else
    {
        printf("Connection successful\n");
    }

    /* close connection and clean up */
    mysql_close(&mysql);
}
```

Here, the `mysql_real_connect()` function attempts to open a connection to the database using the access parameters specified in the function call. If this is successful, it returns true and an appropriate message is printed. If this isn't successful, it returns a NULL and an error message is printed. A number of reasons could cause a `mysql_real_connect()` failure. The MySQL manual, at `http://www.mysql.com/documentation` documents all of these reasons, together with the error code returned in each case and code examples of how to handle them.

In the previous example, the default values for username, password, and database are hard-wired into the code for simplicity of explanation. Future examples make use of a more generic approach, which allows these parameters to be read from a configuration file or the command line.

A connection can be terminated with the `mysql_close()` function, by passing it the structure created with `mysql_init()`.

```
mysql_close(&mysql);
```

Taking a Closer Look

If you're sharp-eyed, you'll notice the examples in this chapter send `mysql_real_connect()` eight arguments, instead of the five previously described. The additional three arguments are as follows:

- The port to use when connecting to the MySQL server
- The socket to use when connecting to the MySQL server
- One or more optional flags used to control the behavior of the client

Most of the time, you needn't worry too much about these three arguments and you can leave them at their defaults (as the examples in this chapter do). But, if you're interested in finding out more about them, look at the MySQL manual, which has detailed information on each.

If your program is using the new transactional features in MySQL 4.1, you can use the `mysql_autocommit()` function to turn MySQL's autocommit mode on or off. Another good idea is to call the `mysql_commit()` or `mysql_rollback()` functions before invoking `mysql_close()`, so the transaction is completed properly.

```
mysql_autocommit(&mysql, 0);      /* turn off autocommit mode */
/* perform transaction */
if (success) {
      mysql_commit(&mysql);       /* commit the transaction */
} else {
      mysql_rollback(&mysql);      /* rollback the transaction */
}
```

Query Execution

Once a database connection is established and a database is selected for use, the next step is to use it to execute one or more queries. The C API function to do this is called `mysql_query()`, and it accepts two arguments: the connection handle returned by `mysql_real_connect()` and the query to be executed.

```
/* execute query and obtain result set */
mysql_query(&mysql, "SELECT * FROM employees");
```

The previous example uses a SELECT query, but it's just as easy to use an INSERT, UPDATE, or DELETE command with the `mysql_query()` function. The next snippet demonstrates this:

```
/* execute query and obtain result set */
mysql_query(&mysql, "DELETE FROM employees WHERE user = 'john'");
```

> **Quote Unquote**
> If your query strings contain special characters, you can have MySQL escape those characters with the `mysql_real_escape_string()` function.

The `mysql_query()` function returns zero if the query was successful and non-zero if not. From the exception-handling point of view, therefore, testing this return value is extremely important before you proceed further in your program, as demonstrated in the following snippet.

```
/* check if query was successful */
if (mysql_query(&mysql, "SELECT title, author FROM books") != 0)
{
        fprintf(stderr, "Error in query\n");
        exit();
}
```

Here's a full-fledged example that demonstrates how this works by running a query and returning a status message that indicates whether it was successful.

```
#include <stdio.h>
#include <mysql.h>

int main()
{
        /* declare structures and variables */
        MYSQL mysql;
        MYSQL_RES *result;

        /* initialize MYSQL structure */
        mysql_init(&mysql);

        /* connect to database */
        if (!(mysql_real_connect(&mysql, "localhost", "john", "doe",
"db1", 0, NULL, 0)))
        {
                fprintf(stderr, "Error in connection: %s\n");
                exit();
        }

        /* execute query */
        if (mysql_query(&mysql, "SELECT title, author FROM books") != 0)
        {
                fprintf(stdout, "Error in query\n");
        }
```

```
        else
        {
                fprintf(stdout, "Query executed successfully\n");
        }

        /* clean up */
        mysql_close(&mysql);
}
```

Here, because the query string contains an error, the `mysql_query()` function won't return 0 and an appropriate error message will be displayed. You can use the `mysql_error()` function (discussed in the section "Error Handling") to obtain a more user-friendly error message. If no error is returned, you can proceed to iterate over the result set.

Result Set Processing

If the query executed by `mysql_query()` is a SELECT query, or any other query that returns data, the `mysql_store_result()` function can be used to access the result set returned by the query and to save it in a variable for further processing.

```
/* get result */
result = mysql_store_result(&mysql);
```

When `mysql_store_result()` is called on a MySQL connection handle, it retrieves the complete result set returned by the last query and stores it in a MYSQL_RES structure. This structure can then be manipulated with MySQL's result set processing functions to retrieve the individual records and fields within it.

When Size Does Matter

The `mysql_store_result()` function retrieves the complete result set of the query from the server and stores it in a memory buffer on the client for easy retrieval. If you don't like the thought of this—perhaps because you need a client with a low-memory footprint—consider using the `mysql_use_result()` function, which retrieves the result set one row at a time for the server, instead. This reduces the memory used by the client because it only needs to allocate memory for one row (and a communication buffer) at any given time, rather than having to accommodate the entire result set at once.

Because `mysql_store_result()` and `mysql_use_result()` deal exclusively with result sets, it doesn't usually make much sense calling these functions on statements that don't return any data, such as UPDATE or INSERT statements (although it won't break anything if you do). Both functions return NULL if called on such a query.

If there's any error in reading the result set returned by `mysql_query()`, `mysql_store_result()` returns a `NULL` value. When working with `SELECT` queries, therefore, testing the return value of this function is always wise before proceeding to iterate over the result set returned by the query. This is demonstrated in the following code snippet:

```
/* check for errors in reading result set */
if (!(result = mysql_store_result(&mysql)))
{
        fprintf(stderr, "Error reading result set\n");
        exit();
}
```

Once a `SELECT` query is executed and a result set is successfully obtained, the next order of business is to do something with the returned data. The most basic thing you can do with it is to find out how many records and fields it contains. This is where the `mysql_num_rows()` and `mysql_num_fields()` functions come in. The following example illustrates their use:

```
#include <stdio.h>
#include <mysql.h>

int main()
{
        /* declare structures and variables */
        MYSQL mysql;
        MYSQL_RES *result;

        /* initialize MYSQL structure */
        mysql_init(&mysql);

        /* connect to database */
        if (!(mysql_real_connect(&mysql, "localhost", "john", "doe", "db1", 0, NULL, 0)))
        {
                fprintf(stderr, "Error in connection: %s\n", mysql_error(&mysql));
                exit();
        }

        /* execute query */
        if (mysql_query(&mysql,"SELECT title, author FROM books") != 0)
        {
                fprintf(stderr, "Error in query: %s\n", mysql_error(&mysql));
                exit();
        }

        /* check for valid result set */
        if (!(result = mysql_store_result(&mysql)))
        {
                fprintf(stderr, "Error in reading result set: %s\n", mysql_error(&mysql));
                exit();
        }
```

```
        else
        {
                /* if valid result set */
                /* print number of rows and columns */
                int numRecords = mysql_num_rows(result);
                int numFields = mysql_num_fields(result);

                fprintf(stdout, "Query returned %d rows\n", numRecords);
                fprintf(stdout, "Each record contains %d fields\n", numFields);
  mysql_free_result(result);
        }

        /* clean up */
        mysql_close(&mysql);
}
```

If the query is successful, a MYSQL_RES structure is created. This can then be examined by the mysql_num_rows() and mysql_num_fields() functions to obtain the number of rows and columns.

Once you know the number of rows and fields, the mysql_fetch_row() function can be used to retrieve the actual contents of each row in the result set. The mysql_fetch_row() method returns a special MYSQL_ROW structure, which is simply a numerically indexed array representing the fields in each row. Accessing the contents of a particular field now becomes as simple as accessing the corresponding array element.

Because the mysql_fetch_row() function works one row at a time, it's typically used within a loop to iterate over the entire result set returned by the query, as in the following example:

```
#include <stdio.h>
#include <mysql.h>

int main()
{
        /* declare structures and variables */
        MYSQL mysql;
        MYSQL_RES *result;
        MYSQL_ROW row;
        int count;

        /* initialize MYSQL structure */
        mysql_init(&mysql);

        /* connect to database */

        if (!(mysql_real_connect(&mysql, "localhost", "john", "doe", "db1", 0, NULL, 0)))
        {
                fprintf(stderr, "Error in connection: %s\n", mysql_error(&mysql));
                exit();
        }

        /* execute query */
```

```
        if (mysql_query(&mysql, "SELECT title, author FROM books") != 0)
        {
                fprintf(stderr, "Error in query: %s\n", mysql_error(&mysql));
                exit();
        }

        /* check for valid result set */
        if (!(result = mysql_store_result(&mysql)))
        {
                fprintf(stderr, "Error in reading result set: %s\n", mysql_error(&mysql));
                exit(2);
        }
        else
        {
                /* if valid result set */
                /* iterate over rows and print contents */
                int numRecords = mysql_num_rows(result);
                for (count = 0; count < numRecords; count++)
                {
                        row = mysql_fetch_row(result);
                        fprintf(stdout, "%s - %s\n", row[0], row[1]);
                }
 mysql_free_result(result);
        }

        /* clean up */
        mysql_close(&mysql);
}
```

In the previous example, it's fairly clear from the query that the result set contains only two fields, so the code is hard-wired only to access the first two elements of the row array. This approach will won't work, however, if you don't know how many fields each record in the result set contains—a situation that's quite likely to arise if, for example, you use a SELECT * query.

In such cases, adopting a more generic approach, one that doesn't involve hard-coding the number of fields in the result set into the program but, instead, obtaining this information at run time using mysql_num_fields(), is wiser. The number returned by mysql_num_fields() then serves as the basis for a second loop within the first one, to print the contents of each field within a row.

The following rewrite of the previous example illustrates this kinder, gentler approach:

```
#include <stdio.h>
#include <mysql.h>

int main()
{
        /* declare structures and variables */
        MYSQL mysql;
        MYSQL_RES *result;
        MYSQL_ROW row;
        int i;
```

```
int j;

/* initialize MYSQL structure */
mysql_init(&mysql);

/* connect to database */
if (!(mysql_real_connect(&mysql, "localhost", "john", "doe", "db1", 0, NULL, 0)))
{
        fprintf(stderr, "Error in connection: %s\n", mysql_error(&mysql));
        exit();
}

/* execute query */
if (mysql_query(&mysql, "SELECT * FROM accounts") != 0)
{
        fprintf(stderr, "Error in query: %s\n", mysql_error(&mysql));
        exit();
}

/* check for valid result set */
if (!(result = mysql_store_result(&mysql)))
{
        fprintf(stderr, "Error in reading result set: %s\n", mysql_error(&mysql));
        exit(2);
}
else
{
        /* if valid result set */
        /* iterate over rows */
        /* for each row, iterate over fields and print contents */
        int numRecords = mysql_num_rows(result);
        int numFields = mysql_num_fields(result);
        for (i = 0; i < numRecords; i++)
        {
                row = mysql_fetch_row(result);
                for (j = 0; j < numFields; j++)
                {
                        fprintf(stdout, "%s", row[j]);
                        (j != (numFields-1)) ? printf(", ") : printf("\n");
                }
        }
        mysql_free_result(result);
}

 /* clean up */
mysql_close(&mysql);
}
```

Also possible is to obtain detailed information on the attributes of each field within a record, with the mysql_fetch_field() function. The return value of mysql_fetch_field() is a MYSQL_FIELD structure, whose members contain information on the corresponding field—its name, length, data type, default value, maximum length, keys, and allowed values. Consider the following example, which illustrates (visit the MySQL manual for more information on what each member of the `MYSQL_FIELD` structure represents):

```c
#include <stdio.h>
#include <mysql.h>

int main()
{
        /* declare structures and variables */
        MYSQL mysql;
        MYSQL_RES *result;
        MYSQL_FIELD *field;

        /* initialize MYSQL structure */
        mysql_init(&mysql);

        /* connect to database */
        if (!(mysql_real_connect(&mysql, "accounts.localdomain.com", "john", "doe", "db1",
0, NULL, 0)))
        {
                fprintf(stderr, "Error in connection: %s\n",
mysql_error(&mysql));
                exit();
        }

        /* execute query */
        /* if error, display error message */
        /* else check the type of query and handle appropriately */
        if (mysql_query(&mysql, "SELECT * FROM accounts") != 0)
        {
                fprintf(stderr, "Error in query: %s\n", mysql_error(&mysql));
                exit();
        }
        else
        {
                result = mysql_store_result(&mysql);
                /* iterate over field collection
                while((field = mysql_fetch_field(result)))
                {
                    printf("name: %s, ", field->name); /* field name */
                    printf("size: %d, ", field->length); /* field length */
                    printf("type: %d, ", field->type); /* enum of field data type */
                    printf("max width: %d, ", field->max_length); /* max field value length
in this result set */
                    printf ("nulls allowed: %s, ", IS_NOT_NULL(field->flags) ? "no" :
"yes"); /* if NULL values allowed */
                    printf ("primary key: %s\n", IS_PRI_KEY(field->flags) ? "yes" : "no");
/* if field is primary key */
                }
                mysql_free_result(result);
        }

        /* clean up */
        mysql_close(&mysql);
}
```

> **More Than One Way to Do It**
>
> You can obtain an array of MYSQL_FIELD structures, one for each field in the result set, via the mysql_fetch_fields() function.

Thus far, the examples in this section have dealt only with queries that return a result set. But what about SQL commands like INSERT and UPDATE, which don't return any data?

In the case of queries that don't return a result set, but do make changes to the records in the database (INSERT, UPDATE, DELETE, and so on), the number of rows affected by the query can be obtained with the mysql_affected_rows() function. Here's an example:

```c
#include <stdio.h>
#include <mysql.h>

int main()
{
        /* declare structures and variables */
        MYSQL mysql;
        MYSQL_RES *result;

        /* initialize MYSQL structure */
        mysql_init(&mysql);

        /* connect to database */
        if (!(mysql_real_connect(&mysql, "localhost", "user", "pass", "web", 0, NULL, 0)))
        {
                fprintf(stderr, "Error in connection: %s\n", mysql_error(&mysql));
                exit();
        }

        /* execute UPDATE query */
        /* return number of rows changed */
        if (mysql_query(&mysql, "UPDATE data SET vcount = vcount+1") != 0)
        {
                fprintf(stderr, "Error in query: %s\n", mysql_error(&mysql));
                exit();
        }
        else
        {
                fprintf(stdout, "Query successful, %d rows affected\n",
mysql_affected_rows(&mysql));
        }

        /* clean up */
        mysql_free_result(result);
        mysql_close(&mysql);
}
```

PART IV

You can find out if the query was supposed to return a result set by using the mysql_field_count() function to check the number of fields expected in the result set. If this function returns 0, it implies no result set fields were expected. This typically happens when executing a non-SELECT query. Thus, the mysql_field_count() function comes in handy when you need to find out what kind of query was last executed and, thereby, write generic control flow routines for your MySQL client.

The following example demonstrates by using the mysql_field_count() function to determine if the query being executed is a SELECT or non-SELECT query, thereby determining whether to process the result set further.

```c
#include <stdio.h>
#include <mysql.h>

int main()
{
        /* declare structures and variables */
        MYSQL mysql;
        MYSQL_RES *result;

        /* initialize MYSQL structure */
        mysql_init(&mysql);

        /* connect to database */
        if (!(mysql_real_connect(&mysql, "localhost", "john", "doe", "test", 0, NULL, 0)))
        {
                fprintf(stderr, "Error in connection: %s\n", mysql_error(&mysql));
                exit();
        }

        /* execute query */
        /* if error, display error message */
        /* else check the type of query and handle appropriately */
        if (mysql_query(&mysql, "INSERT INTO logs VALUES (99, NOW(), 'Apache server
shutdown') ") != 0)
        {
                fprintf(stderr, "Error in query: %s\n", mysql_error(&mysql));
                exit();
        }
        else
        {
                if (result = mysql_store_result(&mysql))
                {
                        /* is there a result? must be a SELECT then...  */
                        /* process result set */
                        fprintf(stdout, "Result set contains some fields, must be a SELECT
query\n");

                        /* free result set */
                        mysql_free_result(result);
                }
                else
                {
                        /* no result? could be either a non-SELECT query */
```

```
                        /* or a SELECT with an error */
                        if (mysql_field_count(&mysql) == 0)
                        {
                                /* non-SELECT query */
                                fprintf(stdout, "Result set contains no fields, must be a
non-SELECT query\n");
                        }
                        else
                        {
                                /* error */
                                fprintf(stderr, "Error in reading result set: %s\n",
mysql_error(&mysql));
                                exit();
                        }
                }
        }

        /* clean up */
        mysql_close(&mysql);
}
```

Once the result set is processed, you should always use the `mysql_free_result()` function to free up the memory buffers used by that result set. Result sets that aren't freed will continue to occupy memory, even if the database connection that brought them into existence is terminated.

```
/* free result set memory */
mysql_free_result(&mysql);
```

Additional ancillary functions related to result set processing are listed in Table 19-1.

Error Handling

Every function in the MySQL C API produces a return value indicating whether it succeeded or failed. Because the API doesn't provide automatic error handling to trap and resolve these errors, an error-resolution mechanism needs to be implemented at the

TABLE 19-1
Ancillary Functions Related to Result Set Processing

Function	What It Does
mysql_field_seek()	Jumps to a specified column in a row
mysql_row_seek()	Jumps to a specified row in a result set
mysql_field_tell()	Returns the current position of the field cursor in the field list
mysql_row_tell()	Returns the current position of the row cursor in the result set
mysql_fetch_fields()	Returns an array of MYSQL_FIELD structures
mysql_fetch_lengths()	Returns the length of field values for the currently selected row
mysql_insert_id()	Returns the last ID generated for an AUTO_INCREMENT field

application level by the application developer. In its simplest form, this error-handling mechanism consists of wrapping each function call in a conditional test and displaying an error message if it returns a failure code. This is clearly illustrated in the following example:

```
#include <stdio.h>
#include <mysql.h>

int main()
{
        /* declare structures and variables */
        MYSQL mysql;

        /* initialize MYSQL structure */
        mysql_init(&mysql);

        /* connect to database */
        if (!(mysql_real_connect(&mysql, "localhost", "john", "doe", "db1", 0, NULL, 0)))
        {
                fprintf(stderr, "Error in connection\n");
                exit();
        }

        /* execute query */
        if (mysql_query(&mysql, "SELECT FROM books") != 0)
        {
                fprintf(stdout, "Error in query\n");
                exit();
        }
        else
        {
                fprintf(stdout, "Query executed successfully\n");
        }

        /* clean up */
        mysql_close(&mysql);
}
```

In this case, if any of the function calls returns an error (as the `mysql_query()` call definitely will, because the query string contains a deliberate error), the `if` test in which it's wrapped will catch the error, display an error message and exit.

This primitive error-handling mechanism can be supplemented with two powerful error-tracking functions that can make error messages more accurate and user-friendly. Look at this next example, which rewrites the previous one to use the `mysql_error()` and `mysql_errno()` functions:

```
#include <stdio.h>
#include <mysql.h>

int main()
{
```

```
        /* declare structures and variables */
        MYSQL mysql;

        /* initialize MYSQL structure */
        mysql_init(&mysql);

        /* connect to database */
        if (!(mysql_real_connect(&mysql, "localhost", "john", "doe", "db1", 0, NULL, 0)))
        {
                fprintf(stderr, "Error in connection: %s [code %d]\n",
mysql_error(&mysql), mysql_errno(&mysql));
                exit();
        }

        /* execute query */
        if (mysql_query(&mysql,"SELECT FROM books") != 0)
        {
                fprintf(stdout, "Error in query: %s [code %d]\n", mysql_error(&mysql),
mysql_errno(&mysql));
        exit();
        }
        else
        {
                fprintf(stdout, "Query executed successfully\n");
        }

        /* clean up */
        mysql_close(&mysql);
}
```

The `mysql_errno()` function displays the last error code returned by MySQL, while the `mysql_error()` function returns the last error message. You've already seen these in action in some of the previous examples.

Additional ancillary functions related to error handling are listed in Table 19-2.

Ancillary Functions

In addition to the previously discussed functions, the C API also includes a number of functions designed specifically to provide information on the current state of the server, and to list available databases and tables. These functions aren't used as often as those in the preceding sections, but it's worthwhile spending a few moments to explore them. Table 19-3 has a brief list.

TABLE 19-2
Ancillary Functions Related to Error Handling

Function	What It Does
`mysql_debug()`	Sends debug information to a client log file
`mysql_dump_debug_info()`	Makes the server write debug information to the server log

Function	What It Does
`mysql_get_server_info()`	Returns the version number of the MySQL server
`mysql_get_proto_info()`	Returns the version number of the MySQL protocol
`mysql_get_client_info()`	Returns the version number of the MySQL client
`mysql_get_host_info()`	Returns information on the MySQL host
`mysql_list_dbs()`	Returns a list of databases available on the MySQL server
`mysql_list_tables()`	Returns a list of tables available in a MySQL database

TABLE 19-3   Ancillary Functions Related to Version and Status Reporting

Here's an example demonstrating some of these in action:

```
#include <stdio.h>
#include <mysql.h>

int main()
{
        /* declare structures and variables */
        MYSQL mysql;
        MYSQL_RES *dbs;
        MYSQL_ROW db;
        MYSQL_RES *tbls;
        MYSQL_ROW tbl;

        /* initialize MYSQL structure */
        mysql_init(&mysql);

        /* connect to server */
        if (!(mysql_real_connect(&mysql, "localhost", "root", "secret", NULL, 0, NULL, 0)))
        {
                fprintf(stderr, "Error in connection: %s\n", mysql_error(&mysql));
            exit();
        }

    /* display client/server information */
    fprintf(stdout, "connected to server on host %s\n", mysql_get_host_info(&mysql));
    fprintf(stdout, "server version %s\n", mysql_get_server_info(&mysql));
    fprintf(stdout, "client version %s\n", mysql_get_client_info());
    fprintf(stdout, "\n");

     /* list databases */
    dbs = mysql_list_dbs(&mysql, NULL);

    /* iterate over database list and print names */
    while(db = mysql_fetch_row(dbs))
    {
        fprintf(stdout, "%s: ", db[0]);
        /* select this database for use and get table list */
        mysql_select_db(&mysql, db[0]);
```

```
        tbls = mysql_list_tables(&mysql, NULL);

        /* print tables in this database */
        while(tbl = mysql_fetch_row(tbls))
        {
                fprintf(stdout, "%s ", tbl[0]);
        }

        fprintf(stdout, "\n");
        mysql_free_result(tbls);
    }

    mysql_free_result(dbs);

    /* close connection */
    mysql_close(&mysql);
}
```

And Table 19-4 lists a few more functions that might come in handy in certain situations.

Real-World Usage

Now that you know the basics of the MySQL C API, let's put that knowledge to the test. This next section demonstrates how to use the MySQL API in a real-world environment, by building two C programs around it: an interactive SQL client not unlike the one that ships with the MySQL distribution and an expense tracker that uses MySQL as the storage medium for an individual's personal expenses.

The Interactive SQL Client

You're already familiar with the command-line `mysql` client that ships with MySQL (I've used it in almost every chapter of this book to demonstrate different aspects of the RDBMS). Fundamentally, this client is a pretty simple piece of code. It connects to a MySQL server (specified via command-line arguments), accepts input from the user,

PART IV

Function	What It Does
mysql_change_user()	Changes the currently logged-in user
mysql_options	Sets options for the MySQL connection
mysql_escape_string()	Escapes special characters in a string
mysql_shutdown()	Forces a shutdown of the MySQL server
mysql_reload()	Forces the server to reload the grant tables
mysql_ping()	Tests if the server is functional
mysql_stat()	Returns server status

TABLE 19-4   More Ancillary Functions

and sends this input to the server for processing. If the input is valid, the server processes it and returns either a result set (for SELECT-type queries) or a return value indicating success or failure (for non-SELECT-type queries) to the client. The client can then process and handle the data in whatever manner it desires: display a message, process and format the result set (if one exists), or use the data in some other manner.

If you look at the preceding sections of this chapter, you'll notice all these tasks are possible through functions exposed by the MySQL C API. Because the API does most of the work for you, it's pretty easy to create a command-line client that mimics much of the same functionality as the default mysql client.

Here's the code:

```
#include <stdio.h>
#include <mysql.h>

int main(int argc, char *argv[])
{

    /* declare structures and variables */
    char query[255];        /* query string */
    int i, j, h, count;     /* loop counter variables */
    MYSQL mysql;            /* MYSQL struct */
    MYSQL_RES *result;      /* pointer to result set struct */
    MYSQL_ROW row;          /* row struct */
    MYSQL_FIELD *field;     /* pointer to field struct */

    /* check for command-line arguments */
    /* if no arguments are passed, count is 1 */
    /* for empty password, pass "" */
    if (argc != 4)
    {
            printf ("Usage: %s <host> <user> <password>\n", argv[0]);
            exit();
    }

    /* initialize MYSQL structure */
    mysql_init(&mysql);

    /* connect to database with command-line arguments */
    if (!(mysql_real_connect(&mysql, argv[1], argv[2], argv[3], NULL, 0, NULL, 0)))
    {
            fprintf(stderr, "Error in connection: %s\n", mysql_error(&mysql));
            exit();
    }

    /* loop and display prompt until "exit" */
    for( ;; )
    {
            /* ask for query */
            printf("query? ");
            fgets(query, sizeof(query), stdin);
            /* if "exit", break out of loop */
            if (strcmp(query,"exit\n") == 0)
            {
                    break;
```

```
        }

        /* execute query */
        /* if error, display error message */
        /* else check the type of query and handle appropriately */
        if (mysql_query(&mysql, query) != 0)
        {
                fprintf(stderr, "Error in query: %s\n", mysql_error(&mysql));
        }
        else
        {
                if (result = mysql_store_result(&mysql))
                {
                        /* SELECT query */
                        /* get some information on result set */
                        int numRecords = mysql_num_rows(result);
                        int numFields = mysql_num_fields(result);

                        /* print field names */
                        for (h = 0; h < numFields; h++)
                        {
                                field = mysql_fetch_field(result);
                                printf("[%s]", field->name);
                                (h != (numFields-1)) ? printf(", ") : printf("\n");
                        }

                        /* process result set records */
                        for (i = 0; i < numRecords; i++)
                        {
                                row = mysql_fetch_row(result);
                                for (j = 0; j < numFields; j++)
                                {
                                        fprintf(stdout, "%s", row[j]);
                                        (j != (numFields-1)) ? printf(", ") :
printf("\n");

                                }
                        }
                        fprintf(stdout, "** Query successful, %d rows retrieved
**\n", numRecords);
                        mysql_free_result(result);
                }
                else
                {
                        if (mysql_field_count(&mysql) == 0)
                        {
                                /* non-SELECT query */
                                /* show number of affected rows */
                                fprintf(stdout, "** Query successful, %d rows
affected **\n", mysql_affected_rows(&mysql));
                        }
                        else
                        {
                                /* else print error */
                                fprintf(stderr, "Error in reading result set:
```

```
%s\n", mysql_error(&mysql));
                              }
                    }
           }
    }

    /* clean up */
    mysql_close(&mysql);
}
```

If you're familiar with C programming, none of this should cause you too much heartache. The first part of the program looks for information on which host and database to connect to, and what username and password to use for logging in. This information is to be provided by the user on the command line, when invoking the program. A rudimentary error check alerts the user to the correct syntax in case of a missing argument.

Next, the mysql_real_connect() function call takes care of connecting to the database. Assuming a connection is made, a loop takes care of producing a prompt and waiting for user input, in the form of an SQL command (this is the interactive section of the program). The input provided by the user is sent to the SQL server for processing via the mysql_query() function (unless the user enters the word "exit", in which case the program breaks out of the loop, closes the connection, and terminates).

Depending on whether the query returns a result set, the program then either produces a list of fields and record values with the mysql_fetch_field() and mysql_fetch_row() functions, or it prints a count of the total number of rows affected by the query via the mysql_affected_rows() function. Error handling at each stage ensures that errors, if any, are printed to the standard output device together with a readable message indicating the error.

Here are a few examples of this client in action:

```
[user@host]$ ./client.bin
Usage: ./client.bin <host> <user> <password>
[user@host]$ ./client.bin localhost root ""
Error in connection: Access denied for user: 'root@localhost' (Using password: YES)
[user@host]$ ./client.bin localhost root master
query? SHOW DATABASES
[Database]
db1
inventory
mysql
test
** Query successful, 4 rows retrieved **
query? SHOW TABLES FROM DB1
[Tables_in_db1]
categories
data
employees
logs
** Query successful, 4 rows retrieved **
query? USE db1
```

```
** Query successful, 0 rows affected **
query? SELECT * FROM employees
[id], [name], [dept], [comp]
103, Miles D, Engineering, 67550.00
105, Susan J, Engineering, 73000.00
126, Joe T, Legal, 90000.00
127, John D, HR, 41000.00
134, Ingrid F, HR, 43600.00
** Query successful, 5 rows retrieved **
query? SELECT id, name FROM employees WHERE comp > 70000
[id], [name]
105, Susan J
126, Joe T
** Query successful, 2 rows retrieved **
query? UPDATE employees SET comp = comp + 5000 WHERE comp < 50000
** Query successful, 2 rows affected **
query? SELECT nothing
Error in query: Unknown column 'nothing' in 'field list'
query? exit
[user@host]$
```

The Expense Tracker

In this scenario, a MySQL database serves as the repository for an individual's personal expenses in a variety of different, predefined categories. A user has the ability to enter expenses in these categories through a simple client interface. This input is then converted into SQL queries and saved to a MySQL database, from where it can be retrieved, in aggregate form, for report generation.

The first order of business in building such an application is to design tables to hold all needed information, as in the following:

```
CREATE TABLE categories (
  cid int(8) NOT NULL default '0',
  cname varchar(255) NOT NULL default '',
  PRIMARY KEY  (cid)
)
CREATE TABLE data (
  eid int(8) NOT NULL auto_increment,
  cid int(8) NOT NULL default '0',
  date date NOT NULL default '0000-00-00',
  amt float(11,2) NOT NULL default '0.00',
  PRIMARY KEY  (eid)

)
```

Here, we assume a fairly simple underlying architecture for the application. The categories table stores a list of categories, each identified by a unique number, while the data table stores the expense records entered by the user. Each expense entry in the data table is also identified by a unique record ID and has three attributes: the date of the expense, the amount, and the category to which it should be assigned (this is a foreign key to the category ID in the categories table).

Let's add a few categories to the categories table and seed the data table with some initial entries as well:

```
INSERT INTO categories (cid, cname) VALUES (1,'Entertainment');
INSERT INTO categories (cid, cname) VALUES (2,'Travel');
INSERT INTO categories (cid, cname) VALUES (3,'Gifts');
INSERT INTO categories (cid, cname) VALUES (4,'Repairs');
INSERT INTO data (eid, cid, date, amt) VALUES (1,1,'2003-04-05',568.99);
INSERT INTO data (eid, cid, date, amt) VALUES (2,4,'2003-11-19',100.00);
INSERT INTO data (eid, cid, date, amt) VALUES (3,1,'2003-06-12',250.00);
INSERT INTO data (eid, cid, date, amt) VALUES (4,2,'2003-08-16',50.00);
```

Given this database structure, creating the code for this program by using the MySQL C API becomes a fairly simple task. Here it is.

```
#include <stdio.h>
#include <mysql.h>

int main ()
{

    /* declare variables */
    FILE *fp;  /* file pointer */
    char lineBuffer[1000]; /* line buffer */
    const char *sep = ":"; /* field separator in config file */
    char *prev_p;
    long next_p;

    char host[100];   /* database access variables */
    char user[50];
    char pass[50];
    char db[50];

    int choice;           /* menu selection */
    MYSQL mysql;          /* MYSQL struct */
    MYSQL_RES *result;    /* pointer result set struct */
    MYSQL_ROW row;        /* row struct */
    MYSQL_FIELD *field; /* pointer to field struct */

    /* open configuration file */
    fp = fopen ("expenses.conf", "r");

    if (fp != NULL)
    {
        /* initialization */
        memset (lineBuffer, '\0', sizeof(lineBuffer));
        memset (host, '\0', sizeof(host));
        memset (user, '\0', sizeof(user));
        memset (pass, '\0', sizeof(pass));
        memset (db, '\0', sizeof(db));

        /* split by separator */
        /* read configuration data into variables */
```

```
      fscanf (fp, "%s", lineBuffer);
      if (strlen(lineBuffer) != 0)
      {
         prev_p = lineBuffer;
         strncpy(host, prev_p, next_p = strstr (prev_p, sep) - prev_p);

         prev_p =  (char *) ((long) prev_p + next_p + 1);
         strncpy(user, prev_p, next_p = strstr (prev_p, sep) - prev_p);
         prev_p =  (char *) ((long) prev_p + next_p + 1);
         strncpy(pass, prev_p, next_p = strstr (prev_p, sep) - prev_p);
         prev_p =  (char *) ((long) prev_p + next_p + 1);
         strcpy(db, prev_p);
      }
      else
      {
         fprintf(stderr, "Error: no data in configuration file\n");
         exit();
      }

      /* close file */
      fclose (fp);
}
else
{
   fprintf(stderr, "Error: unable to read configuration file\n");
   exit();
}

/* initialize MYSQL structure */
mysql_init(&mysql);

/* connect to database with configuration arguments */
if (!(mysql_real_connect(&mysql, host, user, pass, db, 0, NULL, 0)))
{
   fprintf(stderr, "Error in connection: %s\n", mysql_error(&mysql));
   exit();
}

/* print menu */
printf("\n");
printf("[1] View expense totals\n");
printf("[2] Add expense item\n");
printf("[3] Quit\n");
printf("\n");
printf("Select an option from the list above: ");

/* wait for user input */
scanf("%d", &choice);

printf("\n");

/* based on user choice, perform actions */
if (choice == 1)
{

   /* perform query to get totals in each category */
```

```
    /* and print report */
    if (mysql_query(&mysql, "SELECT cname, SUM(amt) FROM categories, data WHERE
categories.cid = data.cid GROUP BY cname") != 0)
    {
        fprintf(stderr, "Error in query: %s\n", mysql_error(&mysql));
        mysql_close(&mysql);
        exit();
    }
    else
    {
        /* check to see if result set */
        /* iterate over rows and print in category = total format */
                        if (result = mysql_store_result(&mysql))
        {
            int numRecords = mysql_num_rows(result);
            int i;
            for (i = 0; i < numRecords; i++)
            {
                row = mysql_fetch_row(result);
                printf ("%s = %s\n", row[0], row[1]);
            }
            printf("\n");
            mysql_free_result(result);
        }
        else
        {
            fprintf(stderr, "Error in reading result set: %s\n", mysql_error(&mysql));
            mysql_close(&mysql);
            exit();
        }
    }
}
else if (choice == 2)
{
    float amt;              /* variables for insert */
    int cid;
    char date[10];

    char query[1024];   /* query string */
    int i;              /* loop counter */

    /* ask user to enter date */
    /* if error in format, exit */
     printf("Enter date (yyyy-mm-dd): ");
    if (!scanf("%s", &date))
    {
        fprintf(stderr, "Error in input: unexpected input value\n");
        mysql_close(&mysql);
        exit();
    }

    /* ask user to enter amount */
    /* if error in format, exit */
    printf("Enter amount: ");
    if (!scanf("%f", &amt))
    {
```

```
       fprintf(stderr, "Error in input: unexpected input value\n");
       mysql_close(&mysql);
       exit();
}

        /* ask user to enter category */
        /* retrieve list of categories/IDs from database */
        /* if error in format, exit */
        printf("Enter category number (");

        /* get category numbers */
        if (mysql_query(&mysql, "SELECT cid, cname FROM categories") != 0)
        {
           fprintf(stderr, "Error in query: %s\n", mysql_error(&mysql));
           mysql_close(&mysql);
           exit();
        }
        else
        {
           /* print category names and numbers */
           if (result = mysql_store_result(&mysql))
           {
               int numRecords = mysql_num_rows(result);
               int i;
               for (i = 0; i < numRecords; i++)
               {
                  row = mysql_fetch_row(result);
                  printf (" %s=%s ", row[0], row[1]);
               }
               mysql_free_result(result);
           }
           else
           {
               fprintf(stderr, "Error in reading result set: %s\n",
 mysql_error(&mysql));
               mysql_close(&mysql);
               exit();
           }
        }
        printf("): ");
        if (!scanf("%d", &cid))
        {
           fprintf(stderr, "Error in input: unexpected input value\n");
           exit();
        }

        /* validate date format here */
        /* this is left as an exercise to the reader */
        /* once all the data has come in */
        /* create query string */
        sprintf(query, "INSERT INTO data (date, amt, cid) VALUES ('%s', '%f',
 '%d')", date, amt, cid);
        /* perform insert */
        if (mysql_query(&mysql, query) != 0)
        {
           fprintf(stderr, "Error in query: %s\n", mysql_error(&mysql));
```

```
        mysql_close(&mysql);
        exit();
    }
    printf("\n");

}

/* close connection */
mysql_close(&mysql);
exit();

}
```

Unlike the previous client, this one doesn't accept database connection parameters from the command line. Instead, it looks for a configuration file named expenses.conf in the same directory and reads the arguments for mysql_real_connect() from that file. This configuration file is exceedingly simple: it needs to contain a single line, in the format host:user:pass:db. The first few lines of code in the previous listing are related purely to reading and parsing this file.

Once the configuration file is read, a connection is attempted to the MySQL database and, if successful, a menu of options is displayed. If the user picks door #1, a SELECT query is used to join the categories and data tables together via the common cid field, and add the amounts in each category to obtain summary totals via the SUM() function and the GROUP BY clause. If the user picks door #2, the program asks for entry of a date, amount, and category ID, and it uses that information to build and execute an INSERT query to save the record to the MySQL database. Entering any other option at the menu prompt causes the program to close the MySQL connection and exit.

Here are a few examples of this application in action.

```
[user@host]$ ./expenses.bin
[1] View expense totals
[2] Add expense item
[3] Quit
Select an option from the list above: 1
Entertainment = 1518.99
Gifts = 250.00
Repairs = 200.00
Travel = 150.00
[user@host]$ ./expenses.bin
[1] View expense totals
[2] Add expense item
[3] Quit
Select an option from the list above: 2
Enter date (yyyy-mm-dd): 2003-12-15
Enter amount: 2450.50
Enter category number ( 1=Entertainment  2=Travel  3=Gifts  4=Repairs ): 2
[user@host]$ ./expenses.bin
[1] View expense totals
[2] Add expense item
[3] Quit
Select an option from the list above: 1
```

```
Entertainment = 1518.99
Gifts = 250.00
Repairs = 200.00
Travel = 2600.50
```

Summary

This chapter discussed the MySQL C API that ships with MySQL, explaining how it could be used to build C clients to talk to a MySQL server. The MySQL C API exposes a number of different functions to simplify the task of connecting to a server, executing queries, and processing results. This chapter also discussed the important functions in each of these categories, together with examples and illustrations of how they can be used.

With the basics out of the way, this chapter also demonstrated two real-world applications of the C-MySQL combination: an interactive SQL client to accept queries and return result sets, similar to the one that ships with the MySQL distribution, and an expense tracker application to accept expense information and use it to generate summary reports. Both applications were implemented via the MySQL C API, illustrating the tasks of connecting to a database, retrieving and updating table data, and formatting the results for display.

MySQL and Perl

As you saw in the previous chapter, MySQL's C API makes it possible to build some fairly powerful client applications. However, C isn't the only option available when it comes to developing MySQL-backed applications; MySQL can be (and frequently is) used with Perl to develop database-powered web applications.

Perl is a popular language for server-side scripting, primarily because of its close relationship with the UNIX platform. Most web servers run UNIX or one of its variants, and Perl is available on most or all of these systems. The language is so powerful, many routine administration tasks on such systems can be carried out in it, and its superior pattern-matching techniques come in useful for scanning large amounts of data quickly.

Over the course of this chapter, I'll focus on Perl, demonstrating how you can use it to build dynamic MySQL-backed applications suitable for use on (or off) a website. In addition to detailed discussions on how to use Perl to manage database connections, process query results, and handle errors, this chapter also includes enough sample code and scripts to get you acquainted with the basics and prepare you to start developing your own MySQL-backed web applications with Perl.

Perl

I'll begin by taking a quick look at Perl, its history and its evolution, and also discussing the tools you will need to get started with MySQL and Perl.

History and Evolution

The Practical Extraction and Reporting Language (Perl), was born because its creator, Larry Wall, needed a tool to generate reports from raw text data. Dissatisfied with the capabilities of current tools like `sed` and `awk`, Wall created Perl as an alternative that allowed developers a faster, more flexible, text-manipulation toolkit. The best definition of the language can be found in its own manual page: ". . . the language is intended to be practical (easy to use, efficient, complete) rather than beautiful (tiny, elegant, minimal). It combines (in the author's opinion, anyway) some of the best features of C, sed, awk, and sh. . . "

NOTE *The Perl manual page is also available online at* `http://www.perldoc.com/`
`perl5.6/pod/perl.html`.

Perl 1.000 was released in 1987 to the USENET `comp.sources` newsgroup. From
those humble beginnings, Perl has grown from strength to strength over the years.
Today, while Perl still boasts a complete (and impressive) text manipulation API, it can
also be used to talk to databases, parse XML, execute SSL transactions, and perform a
wide variety of other functions. The immense flexibility of the language has given rise
to a new rallying cry of the Perl faithful: "there's more than one way to do it." In Perl,
there usually is!

TIP *Read Larry Wall's first-hand account of Perl's evolution at*
`http://www.linux-mag.com/1999-10/uncultured_01.html`.

Perl is an interpreted language and, as such, enables you to perform incremental,
iterative development and testing without going through a create/modify-compile-test-
debug cycle each time you change your code. This can speed the development cycle
drastically. And programming in Perl is relatively easy, especially if you have experience
in C or its clones. Perl can access C libraries and take advantage of program code written
for C, and the language is renowned for the tremendous flexibility it allows programmers
in accomplishing routine tasks.

Installation

Perl is available free of charge on the Internet, for the UNIX, Windows, and
Macintosh platforms. Source code and precompiled binaries can be obtained from
`http://www.perl.com/CPAN/ports/`, together with installation instructions. The
examples in this chapter assume Perl 5.8.0 on Linux, although you're free to use it on
the platform of your choice.

A detailed discussion of Perl installation is beyond the scope of this chapter. If
you're new to Perl, you should spend some time reading the installation instructions
in the download archive, as well as the notes on the website. These will help you
tremendously in getting your Perl development up and running. In case of difficulty,
there's always the FAQ at `http://www.perl.com/pub/q/FAQs`, the Perl mailing
lists at `http://www.perl.com/pub/a/language/info/mailing-lists.html`,
and the Perl newsgroups on USENET at `comp.lang.perl.misc` and `comp.lang.`
`perl.moderated`.

If you're on a UNIX system, a quick way to check whether Perl is already present
on the system is with the UNIX `which` command. If Perl is available, the program
should return the full path to the Perl binary.

```
[user@host]$ which perl
/usr/bin/perl
```

On Windows, try checking your PATH environment variable for a directory
containing the Perl executable.

MySQL and the Perl DBI

Perl supports database interaction via its `DBI.pm` module, a database abstraction layer for a number of different databases, including MySQL. As the name suggests, a *database abstraction layer* is a layer of abstraction over the actual database access methods and allows developers to deal with different databases without radically altering their code on a per-database basis.

By placing a layer of abstraction between the database and the developer, the DBI insulates the programmer from database implementation details. If you initially write a script to talk directly to, say, Oracle, and you later need to have it work with another database server, you'll usually have to rewrite all the database-specific parts. If you use a database API like the DBI, you can port your script over with few changes needed.

The DBI by itself isn't responsible for the interaction between the database and a Perl script. Instead, the DBI simply provides a consistent interface to the underlying DBD (which does the actual work). It is the DBD that "talks" to the database, not the DBI. When a function call is made from within DBI, it transmits the properly formatted information over to the relevant DBD. Once the DBD is through, it picks up the response and returns the response to the caller.

The DBI is also responsible for maintaining a clean interface, handling the automatic loading of DBDs, error checking, and so on. Acting like a middleman, the DBI deals with everything specific to a particular database, thereby allowing the underlying implementation to change without the developer having to worry about it.

DBDs exist for most popular databases, including MySQL, PostgreSQL, Oracle, and others. There's even an ODBC DBD, which can be used to connect to Microsoft databases like Access.

Before you start, make sure you have the DBI installed on your system. A simple way to test for its presence is to run the following command at your shell prompt:

```
[user@host]$ perl -e "use DBI"
```

If Perl doesn't exit with an error, it's a good bet that the module is installed. If the module isn't installed, then you'll have to download it from `http://www.cpan.org/` and install it according to the installation instructions for your platform. Note, you'll have to install both the base DBI module and the MySQL DBD.

```
[root@host]$ tar -xzvf DBI-1.37.tar.gz
[root@host]$ cd DBI-1.37
[root@host]$ perl Makefile.PL
[root@host]$ make
[root@host]$ make test
[root@host]$ make install

[root@host]$ tar -xzvf DBD-mysql-2.9002.tar.gz
[root@host]$ cd DBD-mysql-2.9002
[root@host]$ perl Makefile.PL
```

PART IV

```
[root@host]$ make
[root@host]$ make test
[root@host]$ make install
```

To illustrate how the DBI works, let's start with a simple example. Consider the following database, which links books to their authors,

```
+-------------------------------+--------------------+
| title                         | author             |
+-------------------------------+--------------------+
| Shutter Island                | Dennis Lehane      |
| The Memoirs Of Sherlock Holmes | Arthur Conan Doyle |
| Hannibal                      | Thomas Harris      |
| The Dilbert Principle         | Scott Adams        |
+-------------------------------+--------------------+
```

and the following Perl script, which connects to the database and prints out this data:

```perl
#!/usr/bin/perl
# load module
use DBI();

# connect
my $dbh = DBI->connect("DBI:mysql:database=somedb;host=localhost", "user", "pass");

# execute query
my $sth = $dbh->prepare("SELECT * FROM books");
$sth->execute();

# iterate through resultset
while(my $ref = $sth->fetchrow_hashref())
{
        print "Title: $ref->{'title'}\nAuthor: $ref->{'author'}\n\n";
}

# clean up
$sth->finish();
$dbh->disconnect();
```

> **Smart Choices**
>
> Most often, so long as MySQL is installed, the DBI installation process is fairly straightforward. Both the main DBI installation script and the MySQL DBD installation script are sufficiently intelligent to make educated guesses about the location of necessary files (including the MySQL client library files) and will proceed with virtually zero interaction from you. In case you do encounter problems, however, the documentation included with both packages can be invaluable in helping you troubleshoot the installation process.

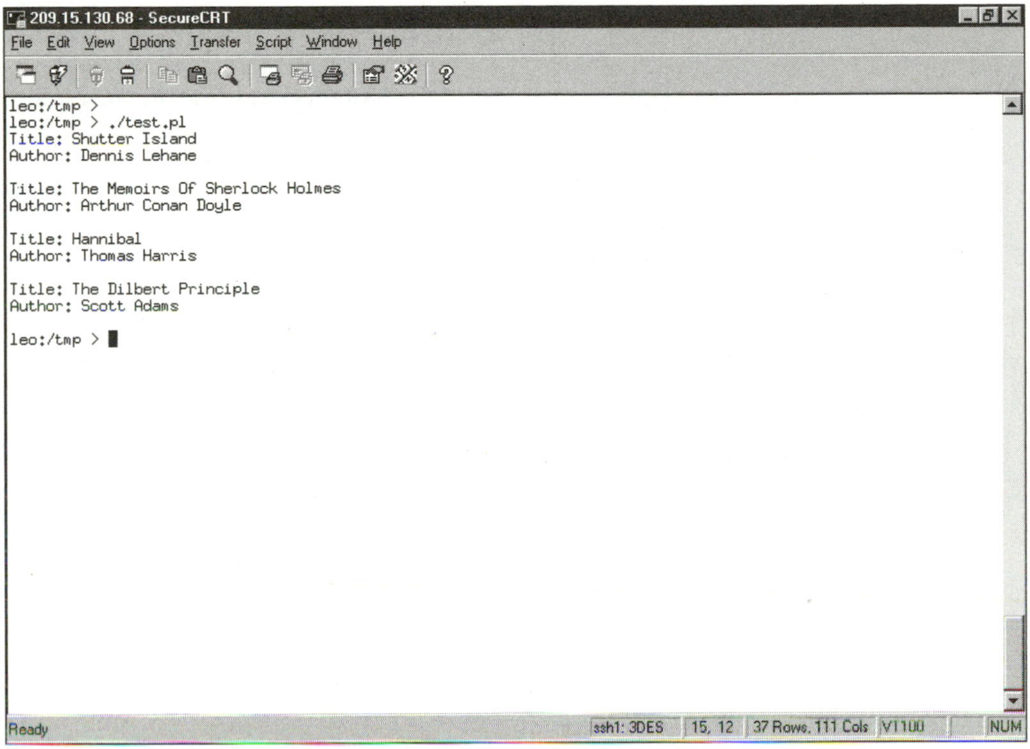

FIGURE 20-1   Output of a simple Perl DBI script

The output of the previous script would resemble that shown in Figure 20-1.

Let's dissect the previous script to understand the process by which Perl connects to a MySQL database and retrieves data from it.

1. The script starts simply enough. As you probably already know, the first line calls the Perl interpreter, and then tells it to parse and run the statements that follow.

```
use DBI ();
```

is the first of those statements. It loads and activates the DBI module, making it possible now to use the DBI from within the script.

2. To begin communication with the MySQL database server, you first need to open a connection to the server. To initialize this connection, the DBI offers the `connect()` method.

```
my $dbh = DBI->connect("DBI:mysql:database=somedb;host=localhost", "user", "pass");
```

The function requires five arguments: the name of the DBD to use (`mysql`), the name of the host running the MySQL server (`localhost`), the name of the database to connect to (`somedb`), and the MySQL username and password. This function then returns a database handle, which is stored in the variable `$dbh`.

This handle is used throughout the script when communicating with the database. The section "Connection Management" discusses this in greater detail.

Next, a call to `RaiseError` ensures that if the DBI encounters an error, it will `die()` with an error message indicating the cause of death. For a simple script like the previous one, this works out pretty well but, in more complicated scripts, you might prefer to turn this off and handle errors in a more intelligent manner.

The `prepare()` method, which takes an SQL query as parameter, readies a query for execution, but doesn't execute it. Instead, `prepare()` returns a handle to the prepared query statement via the variable `$sth`, which is then passed to the `execute()` method, which executes the query.

```
my $sth = $dbh->prepare("SELECT * FROM books");
$sth->execute();
```

This query might be any valid SQL query the MySQL server is capable of accepting.

The statement handle returned by the `prepare()` method comes with a number of interesting methods and properties. Look at the section "Query Execution" to find out more about how it's used in conjunction with both `SELECT` and non-`SELECT` queries.

3. Once the query is executed, the next order of business is to do something with the returned data. A number of methods are available to iterate through the result set and parse it into different fields. The previous example uses the `fetchrow_hashref()` method of the statement handle to pull in the data as hash references and format it for display.

```
while(my $ref = $sth->fetchrow_hashref())
{
        print "Title: $ref->{'title'}\nAuthor: $ref->{'author'}\n\n";
}
```

The Perl DBI also offers other methods of retrieving the fields in a result set. Look at the section "Result Set Processing" for more information on the available alternatives.

In case of an error in the query—say, a misspelled column name or keyword—the MySQL server terminates query execution and returns an error message. Look at the section "Error Handling" for a more detailed discussion of error reporting.

4. Once all the data is retrieved, the `finish()` and `disconnect()` functions take care of disengaging from the database (freeing up memory and generally cleaning up things).

```
$sth->finish();
$dbh->disconnect();
```

As you can see in subsequent examples, the five, previously outlined, steps make up a general process that will be used over and over again when you build data-driven applications using the Perl DBI and the MySQL DBD. The following sections explore these steps in greater detail.

> **RTFM**
> No standard exists for the string that follows a DBD name. This string differs in format from DBD to DBD. Typically, you need to consult the documentation that came with the DBD to obtain the format specific to your database.

Connection Management

Connections to the MySQL DBMS are handled via the `connect()` method, which accepts three primary arguments: a data source descriptor, a username, and a password.

```
my $dbh = DBI->connect("DBI:mysql:database=somedb;host=localhost", "user", "pass");
```

The data source descriptor is further broken down into three components: the name of the DBD to use, the name of the database to use, and the MySQL server host. The DBD name is used to locate and install the driver and the remaining segment of the data source descriptor, together with the username and password, is then passed to the DBD for further processing. If the named DBD cannot be found or installed, the `connect()` method will die.

You can have Perl read the connection values from a file, by specifying the file name in the `connect()` string. Consider the following snippet, which illustrates.

```
my $dbh = DBI->connect("DBI:mysql:database=test;mysql_read_default_file=/home/
me/access.conf");
```

An example configuration file might look like this:

```
[client]
host=localhost
user=joe
pass=secret
```

If a successful connection is established, `connect()` returns a database handle object. This identifier is used for all subsequent communication with the database. This also means you can open connections to several databases simultaneously, using different `connect()` statements, and then store the returned objects in different variables. This is useful if you need to access several databases at the same time, as in the following example:

```
#!/usr/bin/perl

# load module
use DBI();

# connect to database 1
my $dbh1 = DBI->connect("DBI:mysql:database=fy2002;host=192.168.0.76", "root", "pass");
```

```perl
# execute query
my $sth1 = $dbh1->prepare("SELECT amount FROM balancesheet WHERE label = 'Closing Balance'");
$sth1->execute();

# print value
my $ref1 = $sth1->fetchrow_hashref();
print "Closing balance in 2002: $ref1->{'amount'}\n ";

# connect to database 2
my $dbh2 = DBI->connect("DBI:mysql:database=fy2003;host=192.168.0.80", "root", "pass");

# execute query
my $sth2 = $dbh2->prepare("SELECT amount FROM balancesheet WHERE label = 'Closing Balance'");
$sth2->execute();

my $ref2 = $sth2->fetchrow_hashref();
print "Closing balance in 2003: $ref2->{'amount'}\n ";

# clean up
$dbh1->disconnect();
$dbh2->disconnect();
```

Normally, a connection to the server is held open for the lifetime of the script and terminates automatically once the script ends. If you want to terminate the connection earlier or explicitly—quite likely if you have a long script and want to reduce the overhead on the MySQL server once your interaction with the database is concluded—the disconnect() method of the database handle object can be used to terminate the respective connection.

```perl
$dbh->disconnect();
```

If your script has started a transaction with the database, either with the begin_work() method or by setting 'AutoCommit'=>0 in the call to connect(), you must call the commit() or rollback() method prior to invoking disconnect(), so the transaction is completed properly. Here's a brief example:

```perl
#!/usr/bin/perl

# load module
use DBI();

# variables for the transaction
# assume these have come from standard input
$name = "Ian T";
$nat = "IN";
$dept = "Human Resources";
$pbasic = 55000;
$pbonus = 7500;

# connect
my $dbh = DBI->connect("DBI:mysql:database=master;host=192.168.0.241", "root", "secret",
  {'RaiseError' => 1, 'AutoCommit' => 0});

# place the transaction in an eval{} block
```

```
# so that errors can be trapped for rollback
eval
{
        # insert employee record
        $dbh->do("INSERT INTO employees (ename, enationality) VALUES ('$name', '$nat')");

        # get autoincrement ID of inserted record
        $id = $dbh->{'mysql_insertid'};

        # insert department memberships
        $dbh->do("INSERT INTO departments (eid, dept) VALUES ('$id', '$dept')");

        # insert payroll data
        $dbh->do("INSERT INTO payroll (eid, pbasic, pbonus) VALUES ('$id', '$pbasic', '$pbonus')");

        # no errors so far? commit!
        $dbh->commit();
};

# if any errors, rollback!
if ($@)
{
        print "Transaction aborted: $@";
        $dbh->rollback();
}

# clean up
$dbh->disconnect();
```

The transaction here involves adding an employee to the employee database, by entering information into three separate tables. The first step is to connect to the database using the `connect()` method. Note the addition of the AutoCommit parameter to `connect()`. As discussed in Chapter 12, this tells MySQL to turn off automatic COMMITs and turns every query into a transaction that must be explicitly committed for it to be saved.

Once a connection has been opened, standard INSERT statements are used to insert the new user's data into the system. These statements are enclosed in an eval{...} exception handling block, so the errors, if any, are trapped and escalated upward to the main program. An error, indicated by the $@ Perl variable (which stores the error message generated by the eval{...}) will result in an immediate `rollback()`. If no errors exist, the transaction will be committed with `commit()`. Obviously, this only works if you use a table type that supports transactions, like the InnoDB table type.

Leaving Things Open

An alternative to the `connect()` method is the `connect_cached()` method, which keeps track of open database connections and, in case an already-open connection is requested again, simply returns the already-extant database handle object (instead of attempting to open a new connection).

You should also be careful about the number of open database connections while you're using DBI. All databases have a finite limit on the number of concurrent client connections they can handle. If the maximum number of concurrent clients is unspecified, then opening a new connection only when required and shutting it down as soon as possible might make more sense. This is necessary to ensure there's never a time when the database server is so heavily loaded that it cannot accept any new connections and is forced to turn away client programs.

When dealing with connection management, a number of additional specialized functions are available in the DBI. Table 20-1 has a list:

Query Execution

Once a database connection is opened, the next step is query execution. As demonstrated in the earlier example, this is usually accomplished by means of the DBI's `prepare()` and `execute()` methods.

```
my $sth = $dbh->prepare("SELECT * FROM books");
$sth->execute();
```

The `prepare()` method, which takes an SQL query as parameter, readies a query for execution, but doesn't execute it. Instead, `prepare()` returns a handle to the prepared query, which is stored, and then passed, to the `execute()` method for actual execution. Note, the query string passed to `prepare()` shouldn't end with a semicolon, as is normal when using the `mysql` command-line client.

The statement handle returned by `prepare()` provides a number of useful methods to extract data from the result set returned after query execution (more on this in the next section). For this reason, the `prepare()`-`execute()` combination is most commonly used in the context of `SELECT` queries. For non-`SELECT` queries, however, the Perl DBI manual recommends use of an alternative method—the `do()` method—which takes care of the dual tasks of preparing and executing a single statement in one fell swoop.

Function	What It Does
`clone()`	Duplicates an existing database connection
`available_drivers()`	Returns a list of available DBDs
`data_sources()`	Returns a list of databases available via the specified DBD
`get_info()`	Returns information on the capabilities of the DBD and the database server
`table_info()`	Returns information on table names and types
`columns_info()`	Returns information on field names, data types, lengths, and default values
`primary_key()`	Returns information on the primary key fields
`table_info_all()`	Returns information on data types supported by the RDBMS

TABLE 20-1   Ancillary Functions Related to Connection Management

> **Thinking Outside the Box**
>
> With Perl, you can always do things in more than one way and it's the same with MySQL. Quite often, you can find a more efficient way to accomplish a particular task simply by getting creative with the more advanced SQL operations MySQL makes possible. The prepare() and execute() combination is one of them: if your application logic requires running essentially the same query in a loop, you can do this more efficiently through the use of a temporary table and a multitable UPDATE. For example, instead of running UPDATE t1 SET m=? WHERE n=? many times in a loop, you could create a temporary table, populate it with the new values for each row in t1 using a multirow INSERT, and then update table t1 with a multi-table UPDATE statement.

Consider the following example, which demonstrates the do() method in the context of an UPDATE query:

```perl
#!/usr/bin/perl
# load module
use DBI();

# connect
my $dbh = DBI->connect("DBI:mysql:database=somedb;host=localhost", "user", "pass");

# execute query

my $rows = $dbh->do("UPDATE books SET title='Mystic River' WHERE author='Dennis Lehane'");

# clean up
$dbh->disconnect();
```

Using do() for SQL statements like CREATE and DROP makes more sense than to laboriously prepare(), and then execute() them. However, if you're going to run a similar query over and over again, prepare() and execute() is more efficient.

Additionally, do() can't be used for SELECT queries because a statement handle is needed for further data extraction. do() only returns the number of rows affected by the query (or an undef on error), making it impossible to use for these kinds of operations.

Using DBI Placeholders

Although this is overkill for simple applications, be aware that prepare() can provide a substantial performance boost in certain situations. Many database scripts involve preparing a single query (an INSERT, for example), and then executing it again and again with different values. However, it rarely happens that the same query, with no difference at all, is executed over and over again. For example, suppose you're trying to INSERT some data into the database. The INSERT statement could remain similar in form, but the data values keep changing every time. In this case, prepare() and execute() must be used in combination with DBI placeholders, as the following demonstrates, to reduce overhead and improve application performance.

```perl
#!/usr/bin/perl

# load module
use DBI();

# connect
my $dbh = DBI->connect("DBI:mysql:database=somedb;host=localhost", "user", "pass");

# execute query
$sth = $dbh->prepare("INSERT INTO books (title, author) VALUES (?,?)");

# read data from file
open(FILE, "data.txt") or die("Cannot open file");
@lines = <FILE>;
close (FILE);

# iterate over raw data
# split into component sections and
# replace placeholders in statement
foreach $line (@lines)
{
        my ($title, $author) = split (",", $line);
        chomp ($title);
        chomp ($author);
        $sth->execute($title, $author) or die ($dbh->errstr);
}

# clean up
$sth->finish();
$dbh->disconnect();
```

The question marks in the `prepare()` statement are placeholders and they function just like variables. These question marks indicate where the data values for the current query will be placed later. The data values themselves come from the subsequent `execute()` statement. Typically, the `execute()` statement is placed in a loop, with the

---

The Real World Intrudes . . .

Note, the previous example is more illustrative than practical. In a real-world situation, if you want to insert data from a file into a table, MySQL's LOAD DATA INFILE statement would be far faster and more efficient than the previous Perl script. I've only used a Perl script in this example to demonstrate clearly how placeholders work.

A Perl script does, however, come in handy if the data you're retrieving needs to be massaged using regular expressions prior to it being inserted into the database (common when pulling data from a legacy database/application). In such situations, looping over the contents of a file and using placeholders to insert the data is a very useful technique. You can read more about the LOAD DATA INFILE statement in Chapter 8.

variables used in it changing on each iteration, as in the previous code sample (which reads them in from a text file). The values of the variables used in the `execute()` method are referred to as *bind values,* and the process of associating each bind value with a placeholder is called *binding.*

Additional ancillary functions related to query execution are listed in Table 20-2.

Result Set Processing

Once the query is executed, the next order of business is to do something with the returned data. A number of statement handle methods are available to iterate through the result set and parse it into different fields. These statement handle methods are listed in Table 20-3.

One of the more common ones is the `fetchrow_array()` method, which returns the various record fields as array elements. The following example demonstrates how this can be used, by rewriting the first basic example in terms of `fetchrow_array()`:

```perl
#!/usr/bin/perl

# load module
use DBI();

# connect
my $dbh = DBI->connect("DBI:mysql:database=somedb;host=localhost", "user", "pass");

# execute query
my $sth = $dbh->prepare("SELECT * FROM books");
$sth->execute();

# iterate through resultset
while(my @arr = $sth->fetchrow_array())
{
        print "Title: $arr[0]\nAuthor: $arr[1]\n\n";
}

# clean up
$sth->finish();
$dbh->disconnect();
```

Function	What It Does
`prepare_cached()`	Caches a statement handle to reduce preparation time
`execute_array()`	Executes a statement multiple times using values provided in a tuple (a special multidimensional array where the number of columns per row are the same)

TABLE 20-2   Ancillary Functions Related to Query Execution

Function	What It Does
fetchrow_array()	Returns the next row from the result set as an array
fetchrow_arrayref()	Returns the next row from the result set as an array reference
fetchrow_hashref()	Returns the next row from the result set as a hash reference
fetchall_arrayref()	Returns a reference to an array containing a series of nested array references, one for each row from the result set

TABLE 20-3   Statement Handle Methods Related to Result Set Processing

If you prefer using references directly, you can use the fetchrow_arrayref() method, which works in a similar manner.

```perl
#!/usr/bin/perl

# load module
use DBI();

# connect
my $dbh = DBI->connect("DBI:mysql:database=somedb;host=localhost", "user", "pass");

# execute query
my $sth = $dbh->prepare("SELECT * FROM books");
$sth->execute();

# iterate through resultset
while(my $ref = $sth->fetchrow_arrayref())
{
        print "Title: $ref->[0]\nAuthor: $ref->[1]\n\n";
}

# clean up
$sth->finish();
$dbh->disconnect();
```

The problem with retrieving result sets as arrays is it becomes necessary to know the order in which the fields appear in the result set, so field data can be retrieved correctly. Any change to the field order—either in the database table or within the query statement—would break the code and require reassignment between application variables and result set array indices.

A more convenient (though not necessarily more efficient) method is to retrieve the result set as a hash, in which every key corresponds to a field name. Data retrieval can, therefore, be retrieved by unique key, rather than by numeric index.

The DBI supports this via the fetchrow_hashref() method (demonstrated in the first example), which pulls in the field data as hash references. Take another look:

```perl
#!/usr/bin/perl

# load module
use DBI();

# connect
my $dbh = DBI->connect("DBI:mysql:database=somedb;host=localhost", "user", "pass");

# execute query
my $sth = $dbh->prepare("SELECT * FROM books");
$sth->execute();

# iterate through resultset
while(my $ref = $sth->fetchrow_hashref())
{
        print "Title: $ref->{'title'}\nAuthor: $ref->{'author'}\n\n";
}

# clean up
$sth->finish();
$dbh->disconnect();
```

Instead of operating on a single row at a time, it's also possible to obtain the entire set of result rows in one fell swoop with the `fetchall_arrayref()` and `fetchall_hashref()` methods, which return a reference to a single array or hash. Every element of this array (or hash) is, itself, a reference to a row in the final result set. The following example should make this clearer.

```perl
#!/usr/bin/perl

# load module
use DBI();

# connect
my $dbh = DBI->connect("DBI:mysql:database=somedb;host=localhost", "user", "pass");

# execute query
my $sth = $dbh->prepare("SELECT * FROM books");
$sth->execute();

# get all rows in result set as array
my $ref = $sth->fetchall_arrayref();

# dereference array
# iterate over contents and dereference each
# print field values
foreach $record (@$ref)
{
        print "Title: $record->[0]\nAuthor: $record->[1]\n\n";
}
```

```
}

# clean up
$sth->finish();
$dbh->disconnect();
```

In this case, the `fetchall_arrayref()` method returns a reference to an array containing references to subarrays, each one representing an individual row of the final result set. Therefore, all that's needed is to iterate over the dereferenced array with a `foreach` loop, further dereference each element into an array, and print the value of each array element.

The Perl DBI also lets you combine the `prepare()`, `execute()` and `fetch...()` methods into a single method call via the various `select...()` methods of the database handle object. Table 20-4 has a list.

Each of the previous database handle methods corresponds directly to a statement handle method. For example, the `selectrow_array()` method combines the `prepare()`, `execute()`, and `fetchrow_array()` methods into a single convenient call, which returns a single-row result. The following example demonstrates.

```
#!/usr/bin/perl

# load module
use DBI();

# connect
my $dbh = DBI->connect("DBI:mysql:database=somedb;host=localhost", "user", "pass");

# execute query
# print data
@row = $dbh->selectrow_array("SELECT title, author FROM books WHERE author='Thomas Harris'");
print "Title: $row[0]\nAuthor: $row[1]\n\n";

# clean up
$dbh->disconnect();
```

Function	What It Does
`selectrow_array()`	Returns the first row from the result set as an array.
`selectrow_arrayref()`	Returns the first row from the result set as an array reference.
`selectrow_hashref()`	Returns the first row from the result set as a hash reference.
`selectall_arrayref()`	Returns a reference to an array containing a series of nested array references, one for each row from the result set.
`selectall_hashref()`	Returns a reference to a hash containing a series of key-value pairs, each representing a row from the result set. The value in each pair is, itself, a reference to a hash containing field data.
`selectcol_arrayref()`	Returns a reference to an array containing the values of the first field from each row of the result set.

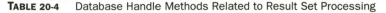

TABLE 20-4 Database Handle Methods Related to Result Set Processing

Error Handling

By default, the Perl DBI automatically produces an error message if an error occurs during a database session. Consider the following example, which illustrates by introducing a deliberate error into the query string:

```perl
#!/usr/bin/perl

# load module
use DBI();

# connect to database
my $dbh = DBI->connect("DBI:mysql:database=somedb;host=localhost", "user", "pass");

# execute query
my $sth = $dbh->do("INSERT INTOO sales(id, item, amt) VALUES (918, 'Spanner', 900)");

# close connection
$sth->finish();
$dbh->disconnect();
```

When you execute this script, Perl generates the following error message:

```
DBD::mysql::db do failed: You have an error in your SQL syntax near 'sales(id,
  item, amt) VALUES (918, 'Spanner', 900)' at line 1 at ./insert.pl line 10.
```

This error message is generated by the MySQL server and passed upward to the main Perl script via the DBD.

You can suppress the display of these error messages by adding the `PrintError` attribute to the `connect()` method call and setting it to false.

```perl
#!/usr/bin/perl

# load module
use DBI();

# connect to database
my $dbh = DBI->connect("DBI:mysql:database=db2;host=localhost", "joe", "secret", {'PrintError'
=> 0});

# execute query
my $sth = $dbh->do("INSERT INTOO sales(id, item, amt) VALUES (918, 'Spanner', 900);

# close connection
$sth->finish();
$dbh->disconnect();
```

In this case, when you invoke the script, the error message is suppressed, even though the SQL statement won't be executed.

Typically, you would turn off the `PrintError` attribute if you want to handle errors yourself, for example, with a customized error handler or message. Consider the following example, which uses the `die()` method to add primitive error handling to the previous script:

```perl
#!/usr/bin/perl

# load module
use DBI();

# connect to database
my $dbh = DBI->connect("DBI:mysql:database=db2;host=localhost", "joe", "secret",
{'PrintError' => 0}) or die ("Could not connect to database");

# execute query
my $sth = $dbh->do("INSERT INTOO sales(id, item, amt) VALUES (918, 'Spanner',
 900) or die ("Could not execute query");

# close connection
$sth->finish();
$dbh->disconnect();
```

Now, try running the script again. This time, Perl displays your custom error message when the `do()` method call fails.

You can also retrieve the actual error code and message generated by the MySQL server via the special `err` and `errstr` properties. The `err` property holds the last error code generated by the server, while the `errstr` property holds the corresponding human-readable error message. Consider the following variant, which demonstrates the following:

```perl
#!/usr/bin/perl

# load module
use DBI();

# connect to database
my $dbh = DBI->connect("DBI:mysql:database=db2;host=localhost", "joe", "secret",
{'PrintError' => 0}) or die ("Could not connect to database");

# execute query
my $sth = $dbh->do("INSERT INTOO sales(id, item, amt) VALUES (918, 'Spanner',
 900) or die ("Could not execute query, server returned code [" . $dbh->err . "]
and message [" . $dbh->errstr . "]");

# close connection
$sth->finish();
$dbh->disconnect();
```

Here's what the output might look like:

```
Could not execute query, server returned code [1064] and message [You
have an error in your SQL syntax near 'sales(id, item, amt) VALUES
(918, 'Spanner', 900)' at line 1] at ./insert.pl line 10.
```

You can check for errors in the connection phase of the transaction by using slightly different notation to access the values of the `err` and `errstr` variables (because the `$dbh` handle object won't exist unless the connection is successful, the previous `object->method` notation cannot be used in this situation). Consider the next example, which demonstrates this:

```perl
#!/usr/bin/perl

# load module
use DBI();

# connect to database
my $dbh = DBI->connect("DBI:mysql:database=db2;host=localhost", "joe",
"badpass", {'PrintError' => 0}) or die ("Could not connect to database, server
returned code [" . $DBI::err . "] and message [" . $DBI::errstr . "]" );

# execute query
my $sth = $dbh->do("INSERT INTOO sales(id, item, amt) VALUES (918, 'Spanner',
900)") or die ("Could not execute query, server returned code [" . $dbh->err .
"] and message [" . $dbh->errstr . "]");

# close connection
$sth->finish();
$dbh->disconnect();
```

Important to note is that the `err` and `errstr` properties are automatically reset by the DBI prior to most method calls, and, therefore, only reflect the last error code or message generated.

Tracing Program Flow

The DBI also offers the powerful and useful `trace()` method, which comes in handy when debugging unexpected behavior in your Perl scripts. This method can be used to trace exactly what's happening inside the DBD as it works its way through the different phases of a database session. Perl defines nine "levels" of verbosity for the trace output, with level one as the least detailed.

```perl
#!/usr/bin/perl

# load module
use DBI();

# connect
my $dbh = DBI->connect("DBI:mysql:database=somedb;host=localhost", "user", "pass");

# start debug
$dbh->trace(2);

# execute query
my $sth = $dbh->prepare("SELECT * FROM mybooks");
```

```
$sth->execute();

# iterate through resultset
while(my $ref = $sth->fetchrow_hashref())
{
        print "Title: $ref->{'title'}\nAuthor: $ref->{'author'}\n\n";
}

# clean up
$sth->finish();
$dbh->disconnect();
```

The output will look something like Figure 20-2.

A close look at the middle segment of Figure 20-2 brings to light the cause for script failure: an invalid table name.

As the previous example demonstrates, trace output is typically dumped directly to the standard output device. If this isn't what you need, you can also have Perl direct it to a file, by specifying a filename as an optional second argument to the trace() method. For example, the following line of code would direct output to the file /tmp/error.log:

```
$dbh->trace(2, '/tmp/error/log');
```

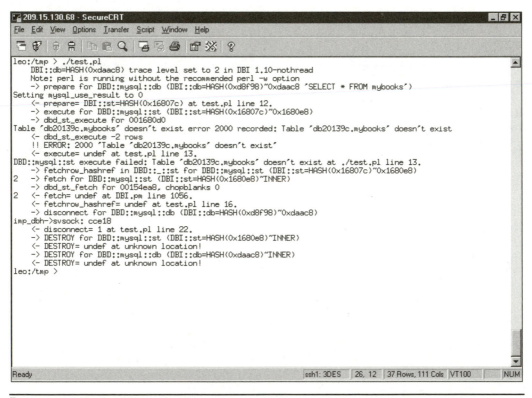

FIGURE 20-2   Tracing DBI errors

> ### Precision Debugging
> The `trace()` method can be associated with both database and statement handles. When called as a method of the database handle, the `trace()` method provides debug messages for all activities related to that database connection. When called as a method of the statement handle, it only trace activities related to the corresponding query. This capability to localize trace data to a specific query or statement comes in handy if you have a large number of `prepare()`, `execute()`, and `do()` calls in a single script, and are only interested in viewing debug output for one of them.

You can turn off debug tracing by specifying a trace level of 0.

```
$dbh->trace(0);
```

With regard to raising and handling exception, the DBI also enables you to specify a number of additional attributes (in a hash) as an optional fourth argument to the `connect()` method. Table 20-5 has a list.

One of the most useful attributes from Table 20-5 is the `RaiseError` attribute, which ensures this: if errors occur during the database session, Perl will raise an exception (which might be caught by enclosing the code in an `eval()` block) and `die()` immediately. This attribute, together with the others listed, might be used to customize the error-handling behavior of both database and statement handle objects.

Ancillary Functions

In addition to the functions discussed in the previous sections, the DBI also includes a number of ancillary functions related to result set processing. These functions make it possible to retrieve information about the number of rows affected by the query, connect result set fields to Perl variables, escape special characters in query strings, and so on. Table 20-6 lists the important functions in this genre.

A Real-World Example

With the basics out of the way, now it's time to put that knowledge to practical use. This next section attempts to do just that, demonstrating how to use the Perl DBI by building a simple web application to display content and let users post comments on that content. In this scenario, both the content and the comments posted by readers are stored in a MySQL database, with Perl taking care of dynamically generating the application's pages via the DBI calls discussed previously.

TABLE 20-5
Error-Handling
Attributes

Attribute	What It Does
PrintError	Prints warnings if errors occur
RaiseError	Raises exceptions if errors occur
HandleError	Uses a custom exception handler to process errors
TraceLevel	Sets default trace level

Function	What It Does
rows()	Returns the number of rows affected by the query.
finish()	Resets a statement handle and cleans up statement buffers.
bind_col()	Binds a field in the result set to a Perl variable.
quote()	Escapes special characters in a string.
dump_results()	Dumps the entire result set to standard output. This is useful for debugging queries.
ping()	Tests whether the RDBMS is operational.
looks_like_number()	Returns a Boolean indicating whether its argument resembles a numeric value.

TABLE 20-6   Ancillary Functions

Designing the Database

The first step that goes into building such an application involves understanding requirements. In this scenario, a fairly simply underlying architecture for the website is assumed: each article on the site is represented by a record in a table and this table contains the title of each article, an abstract, and the complete content of the article. Each article is identified by a unique article number. This article number can be used by the application to retrieve the article content and to track reader comments associated with the article.

Visitors to the website have the opportunity to post comments on each article. These comments are stored in a MySQL table. They contain the subject and text of the comment, the sender's e-mail address, and a timestamp. Comments can be *threaded*, that is, a user can post a comment in response to another, previously–posted, comment, and the application should display such threaded comments in an easy-to-read tree view.

Given these basic assumptions, the application to be developed would boil down to the following four simple units:

- An index page listing all available articles, together with descriptions. Readers use this index to select an article for viewing.

- An article detail page displaying the full content of the selected article, together with posted comments, if available. Comments can be displayed in a threaded view. Readers can select any comment for review or reply, or even start a new thread.

- A comment detail page, displaying the full text of the selected comment, and allowing readers to reply to it.

- A form to accept user comments and add them to the comment tree.

To build such an application, you need to design tables to hold all needed information, as in the following:

```
CREATE TABLE articles (
  aid int(8) NOT NULL auto_increment,
  atitle varchar(255) NOT NULL default '',
  adesc varchar(255) NOT NULL default '',
  abody text NOT NULL,
  atimestamp datetime default NULL,
  PRIMARY KEY  (aid)
) TYPE=MyISAM;
```

This first table is fairly self-explanatory. It contains a list of all articles available for viewing, with each article assigned a unique article ID. The table also stores the title of each article, an abstract, a timestamp indicating when the article was added to the system, and the full body of the article. Data in this table would be entered by the site content managers, either via a content management system or manually.

A few sample entries into this table might be helpful to get the application off the ground:

```
INSERT INTO articles VALUES (4,'Getting Away With Murder','A superbly
choreographed musical charged with the gritty realities of sex, scandal and the
fickleness of fame','Rather than just relying on its star-studded cast to make
it a runaway success,it is Chicago\'s irreverent look at murder and manipulation
of the media that makes it refreshingly different from romantic, and often
sappy, musicals. The inmates\' rendition of jailhouse jazz - lithe bodies in
Lycra and latex - in particular epitomizes the essence of this sexy and often
darkly humorous satire. All in all, the movie gives its audience more than just
the old razzle-dazzle.','2003-08-19 17:34:55');

INSERT INTO articles VALUES (5,'Towering High','The second installment of the
Tolkien epic is bigger and better than its predecessors.','If you\'ve watched
The Fellowship of The Ring, you understand this is more a film about scale than
about simple storytelling. In the second part of this three-volume tome, the
story strays from that singular epic journey of the first volume into three
separate expeditions, now with more motives than one.  Frodo and Sam are on
their way to Mordor to destroy the ring, whose ...','2003-08-19 17:36:52');

INSERT INTO articles VALUES (6,'Pottermania!','Harry\'s back!','For those of you
who are Potter fans, and have been eagerly awaiting the release of the second
installment of the Harry Potter series, this movie is definitely worth a watch.
Harry Potter And The Chamber Of Secrets is packed with great visual effects,
better acting, and is much more visually appealing than its predecessor. It
also, of course, comes with a brilliant storyline.','2003-08-19 17:40:01');
```

Next up, the table to store reader comments on each article. Data in this table would be entered by readers, through the application interface I'll be building over the next few pages.

```
CREATE TABLE comments (
  cid int(8) NOT NULL auto_increment,
  aid int(8) NOT NULL default '0',
```

```
    cemail varchar(255) default NULL,
    ctimestamp datetime default NULL,
    csubject varchar(255) NOT NULL default '',
    cpost text NOT NULL,
    creply int(8) NOT NULL default '0',
    PRIMARY KEY  (cid)
) TYPE=MyISAM;
```

Every comment entered into this table is associated with an article ID—the `aid` column serves as a foreign key reference into the previous articles table. Every comment possesses a number of attributes: a timestamp, the e-mail address of the person posting the comment, a subject line, the body of the comment, and a flag indicating whether the comment is the beginning of a new thread or a reply to an existing one. This last item is accomplished by the `creply` field, which identifies the comment one level up in the discussion "tree" and, thereby, makes it easier to relate one post to another when constructing the threaded comment tree structure. A `creply` value of 0 indicates that no posts are above this one in the tree . . . in other words, that this is a new "branch" of the discussion tree.

Building an Article Index

With the tables designed per requirements, it's time to start writing some code. The first thing to do is to write some Perl code to display a list of all available articles, together with brief abstracts for each and a link to the full article. This data will be retrieved from the MySQL database using the Perl DBI functions discussed previously.

Here's what the script looks like:

```perl
#!/usr/bin/perl

# read in required modules
use DBI;
use CGI;

# initialize CGI object
$cgi = new CGI();

# print HTTP headers
print $cgi->header();

# print page header
print $cgi->start_html;
print <<EOH;
<font face="Verdana, Arial" size="4" color="#66CC00"> Article archive: </font>
<p>
<font face="Verdana, Arial" size="2" color="Black">
<ul>
EOH

# connect to database
```

```
my $dbh = DBI->connect("DBI:mysql:database=db1;host=localhost", "root", "pass",
{'RaiseError' => 1});

# execute query
my $sth = $dbh->prepare("SELECT aid, atitle, adesc FROM articles");
$sth->execute();

# iterate through resultset
# print article list
while($ref = $sth->fetchrow_hashref())
{
      print "<li><a
href=\"article.cgi?aid=$ref->{'aid'}\">$ref->{'atitle'}</a><br>\n";
      print "$ref->{'adesc'}<p>\n";
}

# close database connection
$sth->finish();
$dbh->disconnect();

# print page footer
print <<EOF;
</ul>
</font>
EOF
print $cgi->end_html;
```

Tool Tip

Note, the scripts in this section make extensive use of the Perl CGI.pm module. This CGI.pm module is commonly used by web developers when creating web applications with Perl because it exposes a powerful and flexible API to dynamically construct web pages using simple method calls. Among its capabilities include functions to send standard or customized HTTP headers; create hyperlinks, forms, frames, and other HTML constructs; format text into HTML; and automatically retrieve POST or GET data into Perl variables.

Here's a list of the important CGI.pm methods used in this section, together with what each one does:

- **header()**   Sends HTTP headers to the client
- **start_html()**   Prints HTML opening tags
- **end_html()**   Prints HTML closing tags
- **url()**   Retrieves the URL of the currently executing script
- **param()**   Retrieves variable values from the GET query string or POST data

More information on CGI.pm is available on the Web at http://search.cpan.org/author/JHI/perl-5.8.0/lib/CGI.pm.

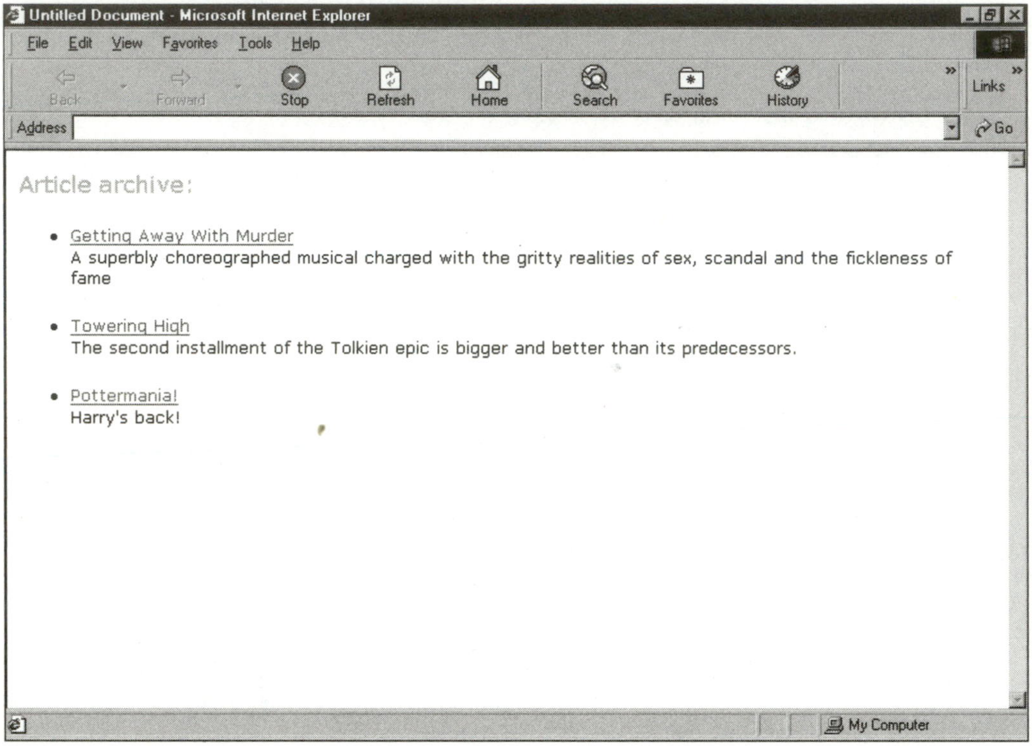

FIGURE 20-3 Article Index

If you understand how the Perl DBI works, the previous script should be fairly easy to decipher. It opens a connection to the MySQL database, queries it to obtain a list of all available articles, and displays them in a neat list. Each article title is linked to a separate script—`article.cgi`—and sends that script the article ID via the URL GET method. The result set is retrieved and processed using the `fetchrow_hashref()` method discussed previously. The final output looks like Figure 20-3.

Retrieving Article Contents

As previously noted, each article in the index is linked to the Perl script `article.cgi`, which receives the article ID as an input parameter. This script then uses this article ID to retrieve the full text of the article and display it as a neatly formatted web page. Here's the code:

```
#!/usr/bin/perl

# read in required modules
use DBI;
use CGI;
```

```perl
# initialize CGI object
$cgi = new CGI();

# print HTTP headers
print $cgi->header();

# check to see if article ID has been sent
# if it has, clean it up and use it
if (!$cgi->param('aid'))
{
    print "Unable to find article ID, terminating...";
    die;
}
else
{
    $aid = $cgi->param('aid');
}

# print page header
print $cgi->start_html;

# connect to database
my $dbh = DBI->connect("DBI:mysql:database=db1;host=localhost", "root", "pass",
{'RaiseError' => 1});

# execute query
my $sth = $dbh->prepare("SELECT atitle, abody FROM articles WHERE aid='$aid'");
$sth->execute();

# if result available
# print article contents
# else print error
if ($sth->rows() > 0)
{
    $ref = $sth->fetchrow_hashref();
    print "<font face=\"Verdana, Arial\" size=\"4\" color=\"#66CC00\">\n";
    print $ref->{'atitle'}, "\n";
    print "</font>\n";
    print "<p>\n";
    print "<font face=\"Verdana, Arial\" size=\"2\" color=\"Black\">\n";
    print $ref->{'abody'}, "\n";
    print "</font>\n";
}
else
{
    print "Unable to retrieve article contents, terminating...";
    die;
}

# close database connection
$sth->finish();
$dbh->disconnect();
```

```
# print page footer
# with link to comment posting form
print <<EOF;
<font face="Verdana, Arial" size="2" color="Black">
<a href="post.cgi?aid=$aid">Comment</a> on this article.
</font>
EOF
print $cgi->end_html;
```

Because this script requires an article ID to properly function, the first step is to check for the presence of this ID. The CGI.pm module simplifies this task considerably with its param() method, which can be used to retrieve a particular parameter from the query string passed to the script or from form POST-ed data. If the article ID isn't found, the script terminates with an error message.

Assuming an article ID is correctly passed to the script, Perl DBI methods are used to query the database for the full text of the article. This is then displayed as a properly formatted web page. The bottom of the page contains a link for users to post comments on the displayed text, via a link to the post.cgi script. Notice this script is also passed an article ID via the GET method.

The output of the previous script would resemble Figure 20-4.

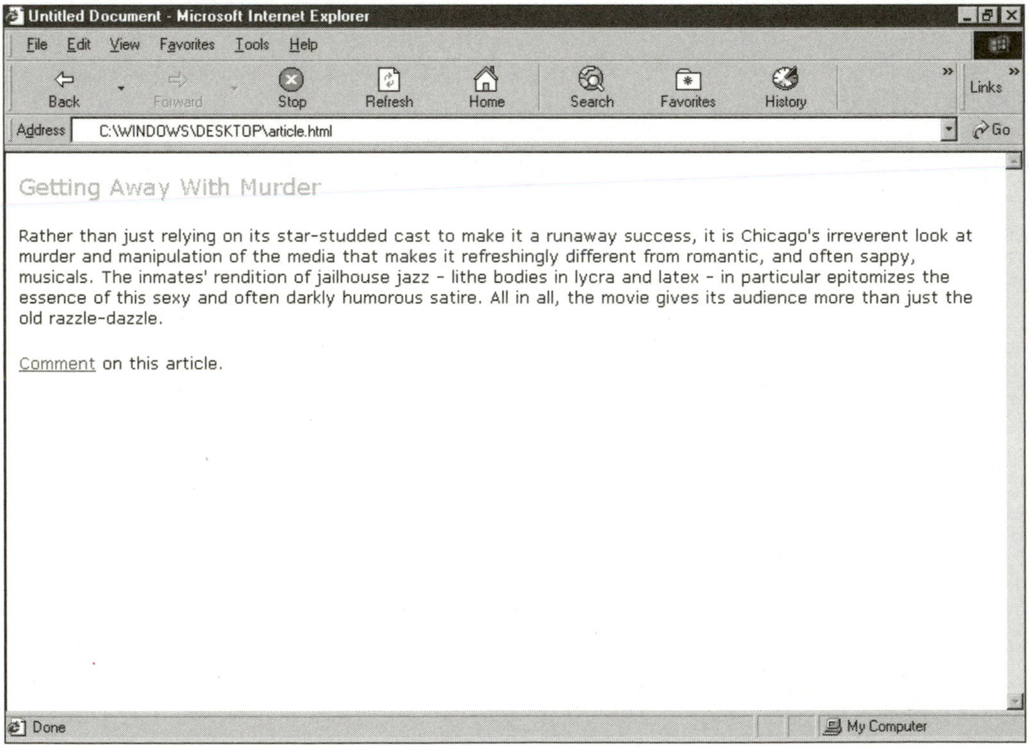

FIGURE 20-4 Article content

In case you wonder why the previous page doesn't yet display the threaded comment tree discussed earlier, you're quite right to wonder. We'll return to this script in the section titled "Building a Threaded Comment Index" to add that functionality.

Adding Comments

Next, we'll construct a form that asks for some basic user information and allows the user to enter a comment on the article. Once that form is submitted, a Perl script will process the information entered into it and store the result in the database via an INSERT operation.

For purposes of convenience, both the initial form and the result page have been embedded in the same Perl script—post.cgi—with the $submit variable used to decide which page is displayed. Here's the initial form:

```perl
#!/usr/bin/perl

# read in required modules
use DBI;
use CGI;

# initialize CGI object
$cgi = new CGI();

# print HTTP headers
print $cgi->header();

# print page header
print $cgi->start_html;

# check to see if form has been submitted
if (!$cgi->param('submit'))
{
    # get URL of current script
    $url = $cgi->url();

    # check for article ID
    if (!$cgi->param('aid'))
    {
        print "Unable to find article ID, terminating...";
        die;
    }
    else
    {
        $aid = $cgi->param('aid');
    }

    # check if this is a reply or new post
    if ($cgi->param('creply'))
    {
        $creply = $cgi->param('creply');
    }
```

```
    # display form
    print <<FORM;
    <form method="POST" action="$url">
    <input type="hidden" name="creply" value="$creply">
    <input type="hidden" name="aid" value="$aid">

    <table border="0" cellspacing="5" cellpadding="0">
    <tr>
    <td colspan=2>
    <font face="Verdana, Arial" size="2" color="Black"><b>Your
comment:</b></font><p>
    </td>
    </tr>
    <tr>
    <td><font face="Verdana, Arial" size="2" color="Black">Email
address</font></td><td><input type="text" name="email" size="25"></td>
    </tr>

    <tr>
    <td><font face="Verdana, Arial" size="2" color="Black">Subject</font></td>
    <td><input type="text" name="subject" size="25"></td>
    </tr>
    <tr>
    <td><font face="Verdana, Arial" size="2" color="Black">Comment</font></td>
    <td><textarea name="post" rows="5"></textarea></td>
    </tr>
    <tr>
    <td colspan=2 align=center><input type="submit" name="submit" value="Add
Comment"></td>
    </tr>
    </table>
    </form>
FORM
}
else
{
    # form submitted, process data
}

# print page footer
print $cgi->end_html;
```

This is a fairly standard form, containing fields that map to the fields in the comments table. As with previous scripts, the article ID passed to the script is checked before any real work is done. Unlike previous scripts, though, this one also checks to see whether the comment being posted is in response to an existing thread or a new one, via the presence or absence of the $creply variable.

Note, the article ID passed to this form and the $creply variable (if available) are passed forward to the form-processing script as hidden variables. Note also the use of the CGI.pm object's url() method, which returns the complete URL to the current script. Because we're going to call the same script to process the form data, this method offers a convenient and portable way to set a value for the ACTION attribute of the form.

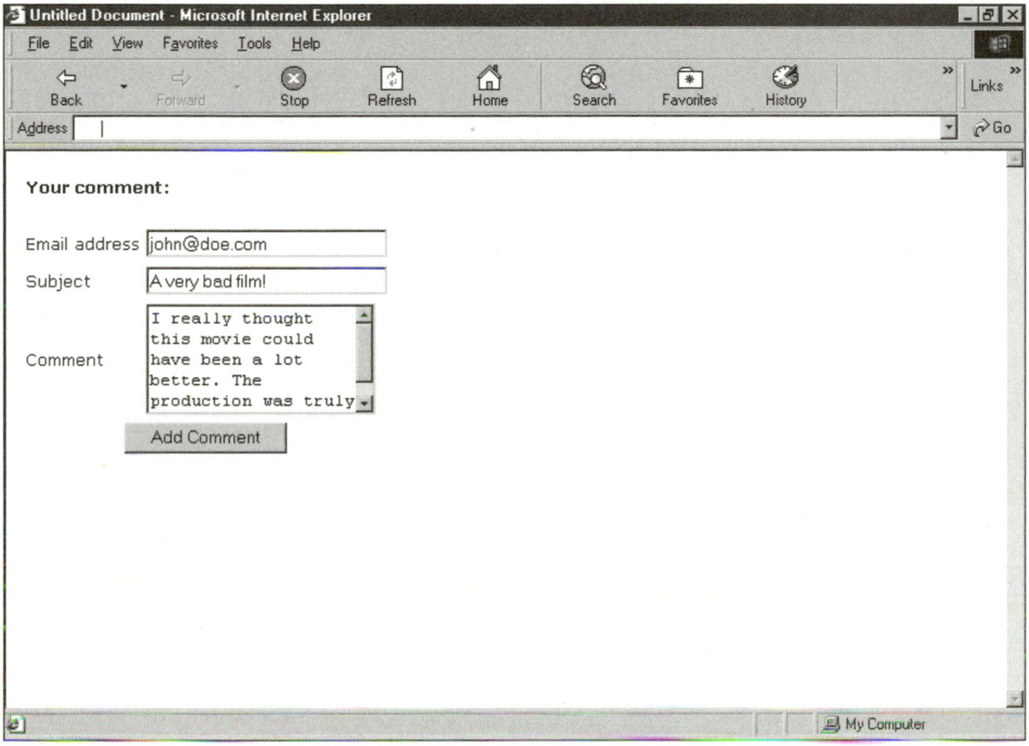

FIGURE 20-5   Adding a user comment

Figure 20-5 illustrates what the form looks like.

Once the form is submitted, the same script is called on to process the data. In this case, because the $submit variable will exist, the if conditional test used at the beginning of the script will direct the flow of the script to the second branch of the conditional statement. This verifies the data entered into the form and uses an INSERT statement to store it in the database.

```perl
#!/usr/bin/perl

# read in required modules
use DBI;
use CGI;

# initialize CGI object
$cgi = new CGI();

# print HTTP headers
print $cgi->header();

# print page header
print $cgi->start_html;
```

```perl
# check to see if form has been submitted
if (!$cgi->param('submit'))
{
      # print form
}
else
{
      # check for article ID
      if (!$cgi->param('aid'))
      {
            print "Unable to find article ID, terminating...";
            die;
      }
      else
      {
            $aid = $cgi->param('aid');
      }

      # check if this is a reply or new post
      if (!$cgi->param('creply'))
      {
            $creply = 0;
      }
      else
      {
            $creply = $cgi->param('creply');
      }

      # check for email address
      if (!$cgi->param('email'))
      {
            $email = "anonymous";
      }
      else
      {
            $email = $cgi->param('email');
      }

      # check for subject
      if (!$cgi->param('subject'))
      {
            $subject = "No subject";
      }
      else
      {
            $subject = $cgi->param('subject');
      }

      $post = $cgi->param('post');

      # connect to database
      my $dbh = DBI->connect("DBI:mysql:database=db1;host=localhost", "root", "pass",
{'RaiseError' => 1});

      # insert post into table
      my $sth = $dbh->do("INSERT INTO comments (aid, csubject, cpost, cemail, creply,
ctimestamp) VALUES ('$aid', '$subject', '$post', '$email', '$creply', NOW())");

      # close database connection
      $dbh->disconnect();
```

```
        # print confirmation message
        print <<MSG;
        <font face="Verdana, Arial" size="2" color="Black">
        Your comment has been posted. <a href="article.cgi?aid=$aid">Click</a> to read more
comments</a>.
        </font>
MSG
}


# print page footer
print $cgi->end_html;
```

This script simply checks the form variables, corrects empty ones, and then INSERTs the data into the database. If this is a new comment (as opposed to a reply), the $creply variable is set to 0, as per the business rules discussed in the earlier part of this section. Successful insertion of data results in a confirmation page.

Building a Threaded Comment Index

Now that you have a way to get comments into the system, how about getting them out? Previous sections already discussed the mechanism by which comments are linked to a specific article (via the aid column in both tables) and to each other (via the creply field in the comments table, which is used to identify the parent thread of a particular comment). All you need now is a way to turn this logical relationship into a visual one.

That's precisely where the build_tree() function comes in. A recursive function designed specifically for the task of iterating over a set of parent-child nodes and establishing the relationship between them, this function requires an article ID and starting comment ID as input arguments. It then uses this information to create a hierarchical tree of the comments posted for a particular article. Take a look:

```
# this is a recursive function
# to build the comment tree
sub build_tree()
{
        # get starting comment ID and article ID
        # as input parameters
        $cid = shift;
        $aid = shift;

        # connect to database
        my $dbh = DBI->connect("DBI:mysql:database=db1;host=localhost", "root", "pass",
{'RaiseError' => 1});

        # execute query
        my $sth = $dbh->prepare("SELECT cid, csubject FROM comments where aid = '$aid' AND
creply = '$cid'");
        $sth->execute();

        # if result available
        # print comment subject line
        # else print message stating no comments
```

```
        if ($sth->rows() <= 0 && $cid == 0)
        {
                print "<font face=Verdana size=2 color=Black><b>No comments
available</b></font>";
        }
        else
        {
                # iterate over result set
                while($ref = $sth->fetchrow_hashref())
                {
                        # print each comment as list item
                        # recurse to build hierarchical tree
                        print "<ul>";
                        print "<li><a href=\"details.cgi?cid=$ref->{'cid'}&aid=$aid\"><font
face=Verdana size=2 color=Black><b>$ref->{'csubject'}</b></a> </li>\n";
                        build_tree($ref->{'cid'}, $aid);
                        print "</ul>";
                }
        }
}
```

This function first opens a connection to the database, using the `connect()` method discussed previously. It also needs some variables: the level at which to start building the tree structure and the article identifier (passed to it as parameters).

With all that information in place, `build_tree()` performs a SELECT query and obtains a list of "level 0" posts, and then prints these in a list. For each record thus returned, `build_tree()` then calls itself recursively with that record number, connects to the database again, and displays a list of all level 1 posts. This process continues until the end of the tree is reached. The HTML `<ul>` list construct is used to ensure that different levels are indented appropriately. If no comments are found at level 0, a message indicating the same is displayed.

Each item in the list finally displayed is linked to the `details.cgi` page, which displays the complete content of the comment. The `build_tree()` function itself is invoked within the `article.cgi` script discussed previously, below the main article

---

Publish or Perish

As you might imagine, this process can certainly test the strength of a database server, especially if a large number of levels exist. For simplicity, the previous script doesn't include any special optimization enhancements to reduce the load on the server. In production environments, however, a fair amount of thought should go into this aspect of the application.

In this case, for example, a possible option to improve performance might be to publish the entire comment tree as a static HTML file (which can be updated every time a new comment is posted) and `include()` it on all pages of the application, instead of querying the database for the entire comment tree every time the page is requested. This would significantly reduce the number of connections and queries to the MySQL server, with no noticeable impact on the application's functionality.

display and separated from it by a pair of horizontal lines. Here's the updated article.cgi script, with this new function included.

```perl
#!/usr/bin/perl

# read in required modules
use DBI;
use CGI;

# initialize CGI object
$cgi = new CGI();

# print HTTP headers
print $cgi->header();

# check to see if article ID has been sent
if (!$cgi->param('aid'))
{
    print "Unable to find article ID, terminating...";
    die;
}
else
{
    $aid = $cgi->param('aid');
}

# print page header
print $cgi->start_html;

# connect to database
my $dbh = DBI->connect("DBI:mysql:database=db1;host=localhost", "root", "pass",
{'RaiseError' => 1});

# execute query
my $sth = $dbh->prepare("SELECT atitle, abody FROM articles WHERE aid='$aid'");
$sth->execute();

# if result available
# print article contents
# else print error
if ($sth->rows() > 0)
{
    $ref = $sth->fetchrow_hashref();
    print "<font face=\"Verdana, Arial\" size=\"4\" color=\"#66CC00\">\n";
    print $ref->{'atitle'}, "\n";
    print "</font>\n";
    print "<p>\n";
    print "<font face=\"Verdana, Arial\" size=\"2\" color=\"Black\">\n";
    print $ref->{'abody'}, "\n";
    print "</font>\n";
}
else
{
    print "Unable to retrieve article contents, terminating...";
    die;
}

# close database connection
$sth->finish();
$dbh->disconnect();
```

```
# display comment tree
print "<hr>\n";
build_tree(0, $aid);
print "<hr>\n";

# print page footer
# with link to comment posting form
print <<EOF;
<font face="Verdana, Arial" size="2" color="Black">
<a href="post.cgi?aid=$aid">Comment</a> on this article.
</font>
EOF
print $cgi->end_html;

# this is a recursive function
# to build the comment tree
# refer to previous listing for code
sub build_tree()
{
        # function code here
}
```

Figure 20-6 demonstrates what the revised output of this script looks like, complete with threaded comment tree.

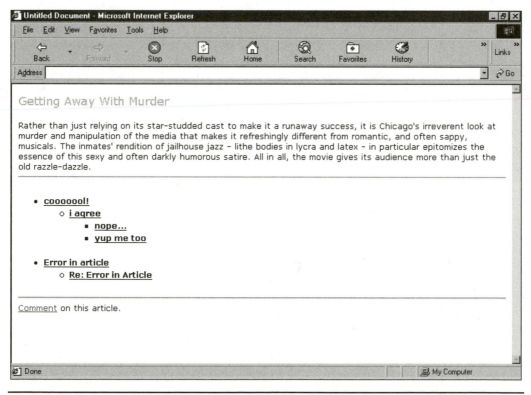

FIGURE 20-6   Article content with threaded comment tree

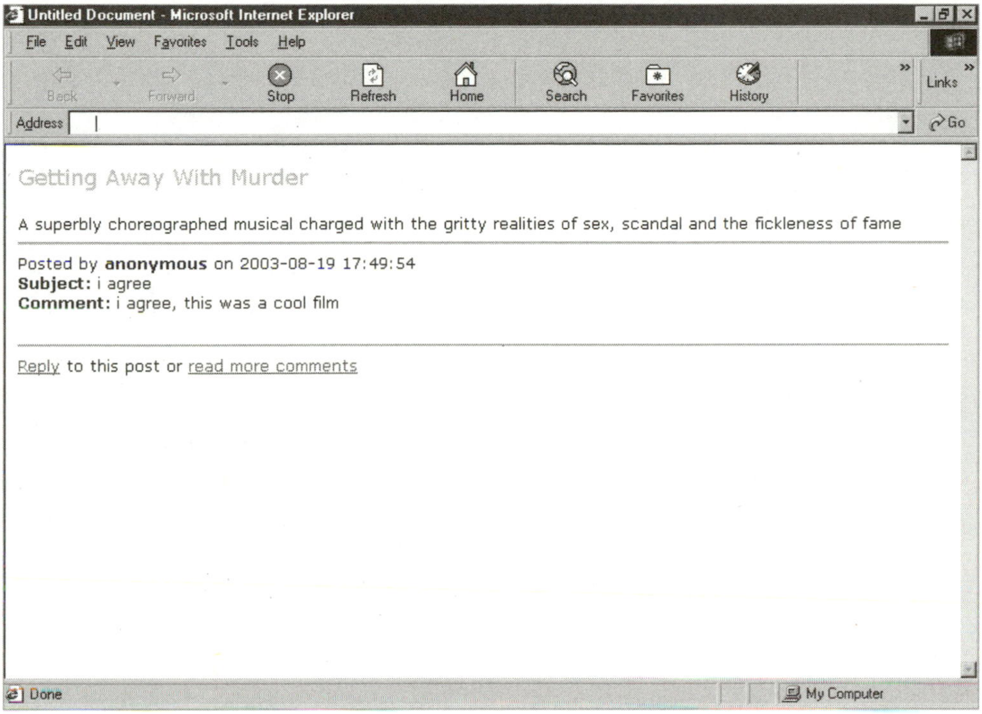

FIGURE 20-7   Viewing user comments

Viewing Comments

The final piece of the puzzle is `details.cgi`, which uses the values passed to it on the URL (article ID and comment ID) to query the database and return a single page (see Figure 20-7) containing the author's name, the time at which the comment was posted, and the body of the comment.

```perl
#!/usr/bin/perl

# read in required modules
use DBI;
use CGI;

# initialize CGI object
$cgi = new CGI();

# print HTTP headers
print $cgi->header();

# print page header
print $cgi->start_html;

# check for article ID
if (!$cgi->param('aid'))
```

```perl
{
     print "Unable to find article ID, terminating...";
     die;
}
else
{
     $aid = $cgi->param('aid');
}

# check for comment ID
if (!$cgi->param('cid'))
{
     print "Unable to find comment ID, terminating...";
     die;
}
else
{
     $cid = $cgi->param('cid');
}

# connect to database
my $dbh = DBI->connect("DBI:mysql:database=db1;host=localhost", "root", "pass",
{'RaiseError' => 1});

# get article title and description
my $sth = $dbh->prepare("SELECT atitle, adesc FROM articles WHERE aid = '$aid'");
$sth->execute();

# if result available
# print article details
# else print error
if ($sth->rows() > 0)
{
          $ref = $sth->fetchrow_hashref();
          print "<font face=\"Verdana, Arial\" size=\"4\" color=\"#66CC00\">\n";
          print $ref->{'atitle'}, "\n";
          print "</font>\n";
          print "<p>\n";
          print "<font face=\"Verdana, Arial\" size=\"2\" color=\"Black\">\n";
          print $ref->{'adesc'}, "\n";
          print "</font>\n";
}
else
{
          print "Unable to retrieve article contents, terminating...";
          die;
}

# clear statement handle
$sth->finish();

print "<hr>\n";

# now get comment details
# execute query
my $sth = $dbh->prepare("SELECT cemail, ctimestamp, csubject, cpost FROM comments WHERE cid
= '$cid'");
$sth->execute();

# print comment details
if ($sth->rows() > 0)
```

```
{
        $ref = $sth->fetchrow_hashref();
        print "<font face=\"Verdana, Arial\" size=\"2\" color=\"Black\">\n";
        print "Posted by <b>$ref->{'cemail'}</b> on $ref->{'ctimestamp'} <br>\n";
        print "<b>Subject:</b> $ref->{'csubject'} <br>\n";
        print "<b>Comment:</b> $ref->{'cpost'} <br>\n";
        print "</font>\n";
        print "<p>\n";
}
else
{
        print "Unable to retrieve comment, terminating...";
        die;
}
print "<hr>\n";

# close database connection
$sth->finish();
$dbh->disconnect();

# print page footer
# with links to reply and view other comments
print <<EOF;
<font face="Verdana, Arial" size="2" color="Black">
<a href="post.cgi?aid=$aid&creply=$cid">Reply</a> to this post or <a
href="article.cgi?aid=$aid">read more comments</a>
</font>
EOF
print $cgi->end_html;
```

Pay special attention to the link at the bottom of the post. In case a reader wants to reply to this specific comment, the `$creply` variable holds the ID of the comment that's being replied to. This `$creply` variable is then transferred to `post.cgi` as an additional parameter and stored in the database, thereby completing the loop required to generate the discussion tree.

Digging Deeper

If you want to learn more about Perl and the Perl DBI, consider visiting the following online resources:

- The official Perl website at `http://www.perl.com`

- CPAN at `http://www.cpan.org`

- Perldoc at `http://www.perldoc.com`

- The DBI.pm manual page at
  `http://search.cpan.org/author/TIMB/DBI-1.37/DBI.pm`

- Melonfire's Perl section, which contains articles, case studies, and tutorials, at
  `http://www.melonfire.com/community/columns/trog/archives
  .php?category=Perl`

- Devshed's Perl section at `http://www.devshed.com/Server_Side/
  Perl/`

Summary

This chapter discussed the Perl DBI, with specific reference to the MySQL DBD and the DBI methods that make it possible to interact with a MySQL database through a Perl script. The DBI includes a wide array of functions to handle connection management, query execution, result-set processing, and error handling. This chapter discussed the important methods in each of these categories, together with examples and illustrations of how they can be used.

With the basics out of the way, this chapter also demonstrated a real-world application of the Perl-MySQL combination with a simple threaded comments system for a content-rich website. Running off a web server and using CGI as the gateway interface, this application provided users with an interface to view, add, and reply to comments on the website. Behind the scenes, the Perl DBI module handled the tasks of connecting to the database, retrieving and updating table data, and formatting the results for display.

MySQL and PHP

The one thing web developers have never lacked is choice. The widespread proliferation of open-source languages and tools has meant an alternative way of doing things has always existed. So, while Perl aficionados would probably use the Perl DBI mentioned in the previous chapter to build MySQL-backed applications, novice developers might prefer the syntax and style of Hypertext PreProcessor (PHP), a programming language which, at over ten million installations worldwide, is quickly becoming the de facto standard for web applications.

In case you don't already know, *PHP* is a scripting language that works by embedding commands into HTML web pages, thereby making it possible to incorporate sophisticated business logic into otherwise static web sites. The language is rapidly becoming the popular choice for data-driven web applications because of its wide support for different database systems, including, obviously, MySQL.

Over the course of this chapter, we discuss the MySQL API that ships with PHP and give you a crash course in how to use it to build powerful, data-driven applications for the Web. In addition to detailed discussions on how to use the PHP MySQL API to manage database connections, process query results, and handle errors, this chapter also includes enough sample code and scripts to acquaint you with the basics and prepare you to start developing your own MySQL-backed web applications in PHP.

PHP: History and Evolution

PHP was first developed by Rasmus Lerdorf as a means of monitoring page views for his online resume and slowly started making a mark when PHP/FI was released in mid 1995. This version of PHP had support for some basic web functions, primarily the capability to handle form data and support for the mSQL database.

As PHP's popularity grew, the development of the language shifted from Lerdorf to a team of dedicated programmers who took upon themselves the onus of rewriting the PHP parser from scratch. The result of the efforts was PHP 3.0, which included support for a wider range of databases, including MySQL and Oracle. PHP 4.0, which was released in 2003, used a new scripting engine to deliver better performance, greater reliability and scalability, support for web servers other than Apache, and a host of new language features, including built-in session management and better OOP support.

Today, PHP is in use on over ten million web sites, with that number climbing rapidly according to the Netcraft survey at `http://www.netcraft.com`. The language is supported by thousands of developers and enthusiasts worldwide, and it's constantly being updated with new modules and features to ensure that it remains at the cutting edge of web technology. It's also easy to use, powerful, flexible, and reliable, all reasons that conspire to make it one of our personal favorites for web development.

Installation

PHP is available for both *NIX and Windows, in both source and binary formats, from the official web site, `http://www.php.net`. *NIX users have the choice of compiling PHP directly into their web servers or activating it on demand as a pluggable web server module. Windows users don't have as many choices. They get a prebuilt binary that needs to be configured to work with their web server.

A detailed discussion of PHP installation is beyond the scope of this chapter. If you're new to PHP, spend some time reading the excellent documentation on the PHP web site, together with the notes in the INSTALL and README files included in the PHP distribution. This should ensure you have minimal difficulty in getting your PHP development environment up and running. In case you're unable to get PHP talking to your web server, you can obtain assistance from fellow PHP users on the wonderful PHP mailing lists, accessible at `http://www.php.net/mailing-lists.php`.

In case you're working in a shared hosting environment and you wonder if your web server supports PHP, or if your PHP build includes support for MySQL (default since PHP 4.0), there's an easy way to find out. Simply create a file with a `.php` file extension—say, `info.php`—under your web server's document root and fill it with the following code:

```php
<?php
phpinfo();
?>
```

Too Much Information . . .

In case the output of `phpinfo()` is a little too detailed for your taste, you could also use the following test, which returns a one-line status message indicating whether your PHP build supports MySQL:

```php
<?php
if (extension_loaded('mysql'))
{
    echo("MySQL support present");
}
else
{
    echo("MySQL support absent");
}
?>
```

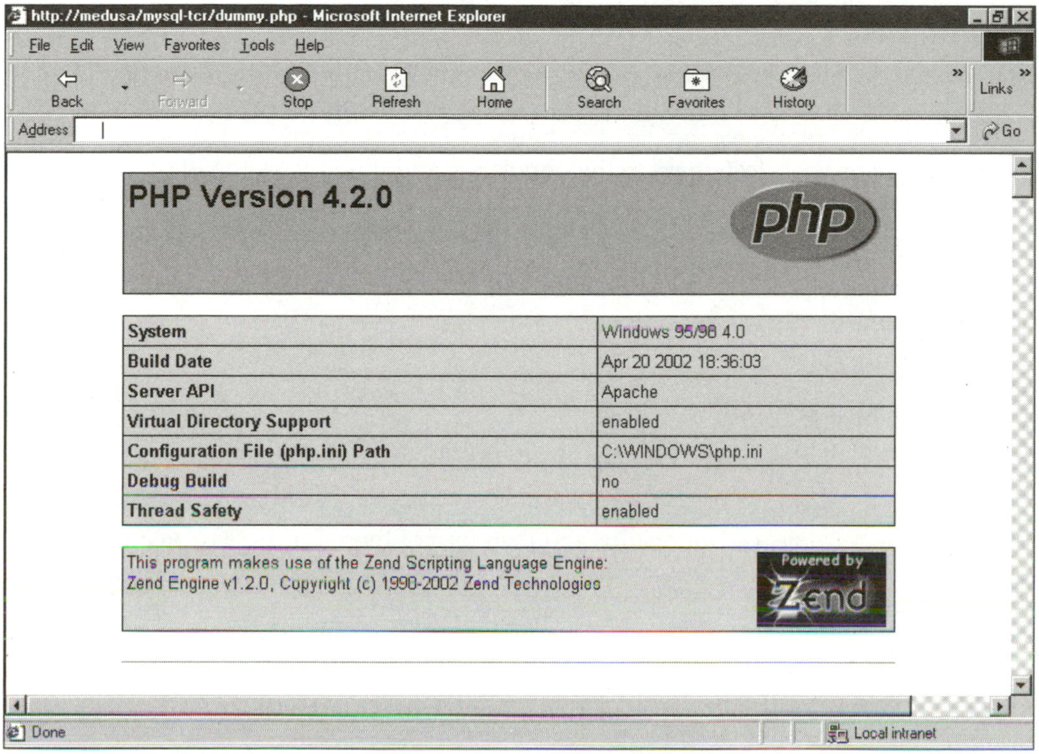

FIGURE 21-1   The output of the `phpinfo()` command

Now, browse to this script in your web browser, and you should see a page that looks something like Figure 21-1.

Review the information on this page to see what your PHP build currently supports. MySQL support is active by default in all versions of PHP greater than PHP 4.0.

Note, if your web server is not configured to parse files with the `.php` extension or if it does not include PHP support, the output of the previous script will most likely be raw source code. In this case, you should consult your web server documentation or your system administrator for information on how to configure your server with PHP support.

More information on the `phpinfo()` test is available in the PHP documentation, as well as in the installation notes.

Version Control

In case you were wondering, the examples in this chapter were built and tested on both Linux and Windows 95, with PHP 4.2.0 and Apache 1.3.29.

MySQL and PHP

PHP has included support for MySQL since version 3.*x*, although earlier versions required you to compile PHP with special configuration-time variables to activate the MySQL module. Ever since version 4.*x*, though, PHP ships with MySQL enabled by default, in yet another testament to the popularity and ubiquity of the PHP-MySQL combination.

As discussed in Chapter 18, the MySQL functions that come with PHP are designed to accomplish four primary goals:

1. Manage database connections

2. Execute queries

3. Process query results

4. Provide debugging and diagnostic information

To illustrate these functions, let's consider a simple example that uses PHP to connect to a database, retrieve a set of results, and then format them for display on a web page. The sample database used here consists of a single table named employees, which holds a list of user login IDs and their corresponding full names. Here are the SQL queries needed to create and initialize this table.

```
CREATE TABLE employees (
    uname varchar(25) NOT NULL,
    fname varchar(100) NOT NULL,
    PRIMARY KEY (uname)
);

INSERT INTO employees (uname, fname) VALUES ( 'john', 'John Doe');
INSERT INTO employees (uname, fname) VALUES ( 'sarah', 'Sarah Jane');
INSERT INTO employees (uname, fname) VALUES ( 'tim', 'Tim Shaw');
INSERT INTO employees (uname, fname) VALUES ( 'jane', 'Jane Smith');
```

Now, if you used the mysql client program to connect to the database and view the contents of the previous table, you'd see something like this:

```
mysql> SELECT * FROM employees;
+-------+------------+
| uname | fname      |
+-------+------------+
| john  | John Doe   |
| sarah | Sarah Jane |
| tim   | Tim Shaw   |
| jane  | Jane Smith |
+-------+------------+
4 rows in set (0.00 sec)
```

Let's now do the same thing using PHP—fire a SELECT query at the database and display the results in an HTML page:

```php
<html>
<head>
<basefont face="Arial">
</head>

<body>

<?php
// set server access variables
$host = "localhost";
$user = "joe";
$pass = "secret";
$db = "db123";

// open connection to database
$connection = mysql_connect($host, $user, $pass) or die ("Unable to connect!");

// select database to use
mysql_select_db($db) or die ("Unable to select database!");

// create SQL query string
$query = "SELECT * FROM employees";

// execute query and obtain result set
$result = mysql_query($query) or die ("Error in query: $query. " . mysql_error());

// are there any rows in the result?
if (mysql_num_rows($result) > 0)
{
    // yes
    // iterate through result set
    // format query results as table
    echo "<table cellpadding=10 border=1>";
    while($row = mysql_fetch_row($result))
    {
        echo "<tr>";
        echo "<td>" . $row[0] . "</td>";
        echo "<td>" . $row[1] . "</td>";
        echo "</tr>";
    }
    echo "</table>";
}
else
{
    // no
    // print status message
    echo "No rows found!";
}

// free result set memory
mysql_free_result($result);
```

```
// close connection
mysql_close($connection);

?>

</body>
</html>
```

The result should look something like Figure 21-2.

As you can see, using PHP to get data from a database involves several steps, each of which is a predefined PHP function call. Let's dissect each step.

The first thing to do is specify some important information needed to establish a connection to the database server. This information includes the server name, the username and the password required to gain access to it, and the name of the database to query. These values are all set up in regular PHP variables.

```
// set server access variables
$host = "localhost";
$user = "joe";
$pass = "secret";
$db = "db123";
```

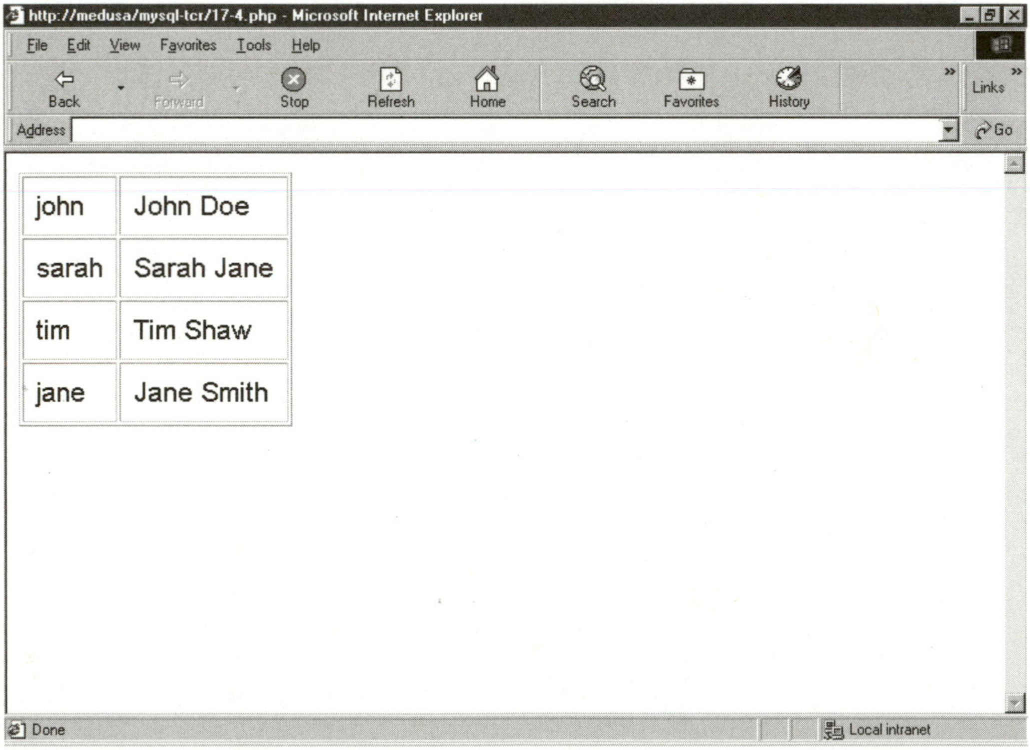

FIGURE 21-2   Retrieving MySQL data with PHP

Thinking Ahead

Because these database access parameters will be used in almost every PHP script in your application that requires the MySQL server, common practice is to extract them into a separate configuration file and `include()` that file wherever required in your PHP scripts. This not only adds an element of reusability to your application, it also reduces the impact of changes in your database username or password. For any change, all you need to do is update a single configuration file, rather than editing every script in your source tree.

To begin communication with the MySQL database server, you first need to open a connection to the server. All communication between PHP and the database server takes place through this connection.

To initialize this connection, PHP offers the `mysql_connect()` function.

```
$connection = mysql_connect($host, $user, $pass) or die ("Unable to connect!");
```

The function requires three arguments: the name of the host running the MySQL server, the MySQL username, and the MySQL password. If the database server and the web server are both running on the same physical machine, the server name is usually `localhost`.

This function then returns a link identifier, which is stored in the variable `$connection`. This identifier is used throughout the script when communicating with the database and is discussed in the section "Connection Management" in greater detail.

Now that you have a connection to the database, the next step is to select a database to use. PHP lets you do this via the `mysql_select_db()` function.

```
mysql_select_db($db) or die ("Unable to select database!");
```

The `mysql_select_db()` function accepts a database name as argument and prepares the selected database for use.

With the database selected, it's time to send it a query via the `mysql_query()` function.

```
$query = "SELECT * FROM employees";
$result = mysql_query($query) or die ("Error in query: $query. " . mysql_error());
```

Wall of Silence

A good idea is to prefix calls to MySQL functions with PHP's @ error-suppression operator to hide PHP warnings and error message. Not doing this might make public sensitive details about a company's database system.

A Matter Of Punctuation

Not unlike what happens at the mysql command prompt, SQL query strings sent to the server via mysql_query() should not end with a semicolon. This is one of the more common mistakes made by developers new to PHP.

This function also needs a single argument: the SQL query to be executed. This query could be any valid SQL query the MySQL server is capable of accepting.

The result set returned by the previous function is stored in the variable $result. This result set might contain, depending on your query, one or more rows or columns of data. In case of an error in the query—say, a misspelled column name or keyword—the MySQL server will terminate query execution and return an error message. This message can be viewed via the mysql_error() function.

Read the section "Error Handling" for a more detailed discussion of error reporting.

Once a result set is obtained, PHP provides a wide variety of functions to process this result set. This example demonstrates two of the more common ones—the mysql_num_rows() function, which returns the total number of rows in the result set, and the mysql_fetch_row() function, which is used to fetch a specific row from the result set.

```
if (mysql_num_rows($result) > 0)
{
    echo "<table cellpadding=10 border=1>";
    while($row = mysql_fetch_row($result))
    {
        echo "<tr>";
        echo "<td>" . $row[0] . "</td>";
        echo "<td>" . $row[1] . "</td>";
        echo "</tr>";
    }
    echo "</table>";
}
```

Because the mysql_fetch_row() function retrieves a row as a simple, numerically indexed array of values, the most efficient way to process it is to iterate over the collection using a loop. That's precisely what this example does—it combines the mysql_fetch_row() function with a while loop to sequentially iterate over the rows in the result set, printing the contents of each column in an HTML table.

Different Strokes

A number of other alternatives exist to the mysql_fetch_row() function—look at the section "Result Set Processing" for a more detailed discussion.

Once all the rows have been processed, you should free up used memory and generally clean up things via calls to `mysql_free_result()` and/or `mysql_close()`. The former frees up the memory occupied by the result set, while leaving the database connection open for more operations. The latter closes the database connection and frees up the memory used by the link identifier (and the result set as well, in case you forgot to use `mysql_free_result()`).

```
mysql_free_result($result);
mysql_close($connection);
```

As you see in subsequent examples, the six steps previously outlined make up a general process that will be used over and over again when building data-driven web applications using PHP and MySQL. The following sections explore these steps in greater detail.

Connection Management

Connections to the MySQL DBMS are handled via the `mysql_connect()` function, which requires three arguments: the name of the host running the MySQL server, the MySQL username, and the MySQL password.

```
$connection = mysql_connect($host, $user, $pass) or die ("Unable to connect!");
```

Biting into PEAR

You might have noticed that PHP's MySQL functions are all prefixed with the term `mysql_*`, for example, `mysql_num_rows()`, `mysql_fetch_row()`, and so on. A close look at the PHP manual reveals this nomenclature is used for other RDBMS also, for example, Oracle-specific functions begin with `OCI*`, while PostgreSQL-specific functions begin with `pg_*`.

Obviously, this raises an important issue: portability. If your RDBMS changes, you must recode your scripts to use the PHP functions that work with the new RDBMS. This adds time and effort, and it can also result in a substantial increase in cost.

PHP attempts to address this problem by means of a database abstraction layer, which provides a consistent interface to all supported RDBMS. This database abstraction layer, which ships as part of the free PEAR distribution, makes it possible to switch database systems at the back end, with minimal impact on your code, in a manner similar to that used by the Perl DBI. If portability of your application is a concern, you should definitely spend some time exploring this database abstraction layer, to ensure you do not face portability issues later. Even when portability is not a concern, an abstraction layer like PEAR is good for having a standardized way to handle errors, to measure and log query performance, or to add load-balancing logic.

More information on the PEAR database abstraction layer is available at `http://pear.php.net/`.

PART IV

If a successful connection is established, this function then returns a link identifier. This identifier is used for all subsequent communication with the database. In case of a connection failure, for example, because of an incorrect password, the function will return false. This means it's always a good idea to check the return value of this function in your script before you proceed further. The following snippet demonstrates one way of performing this check,

```
// attempt a connection
$connection = mysql_connect($host, $user, $pass);

// if connection failed
// display error and exit
if (!$connection)
{
    echo "Unable to connect";
    exit;
}
```

while the following alternative accomplishes the same task in fewer lines of code:

```
// attempt connection or die
$connection = mysql_connect($host, $user, $pass) or die ("Unable to connect!");
```

Normally, a connection to the server is held open for the lifetime of the script and terminates automatically once the script ends. (Most of the time—see the sidebar "Persistence Pays" for caveats to this statement.)

It's possible to alter this default behavior and close the connection earlier. An example is if you have a long script and want to reduce the overhead on the MySQL server once your interaction with the database is complete via a call to the `mysql_close()` function, which immediately terminates the named or last opened connection.

```
// terminate the last opened connection
mysql_close();

// terminate the connection identified by $conn
mysql_close($conn);
```

Query Execution

Sandwiched between the `mysql_connect()` and `mysql_close()` functions comes the code to select a database, execute queries, process results, and display output.

The PHP function to select a database is the `mysql_select_db()` function, which accepts a database name as argument. It can, optionally, also accept a link identifier.

Persistence Pays

Normally, the connection to the MySQL server is automatically terminated once the PHP script creating the connection finishes executing. If you have a large number of scripts opening and closing connections to the same database server, however, this default behavior can result in a significant performance drain. In such a situation, you can have PHP *not* terminate the MySQL connection on script end, by replacing your calls to `mysql_connect()` with calls to `mysql_pconnect()`, which opens a "persistent connection" to the server.

How does this help? When a persistent connection is opened to the server, this connection does not automatically die when the script using it ends. Rather, the connection remains active ("persistent"), and other scripts connecting to the same server can use it immediately, rather than opening new connections themselves. This slightly more efficient method of creating connections to the MySQL server reduces overhead and can produce significant performance gains on high-traffic servers.

If unspecified, the function defaults to using the last opened connection. Here's an example of how it can be used:

```
// select the database named "db712"
mysql_select_db("db712"),
```

Once the database has been selected, it becomes possible to execute queries on it. The PHP function to execute a query is the `mysql_query()` function, which accepts a single argument—the SQL statement to be executed. Here's a quick example:

```
// execute query and obtain result set
$result = mysql_query("SELECT * FROM employees");
```

The previous example uses a SELECT query, however, it's just as easy to use an INSERT, UPDATE, or DELETE query with the `mysql_query()` function. The next snippet demonstrates.

```
// execute query and obtain result set
mysql_query("DELETE FROM employees WHERE user = 'john'");
```

The `mysql_query()` function will return a result code, which can be used to check whether the query was successfully executed.

- If the query is a SELECT query or any other query that returns data, `mysql_query()` returns a resource identifier containing the results of the query or false on failure. This resource identifier can then be processed using a variety of different functions—read the section "Result Set Processing" for more details.

- For a query that does not return any data, such as an INSERT, UPDATE, or DELETE query, mysql_query() returns true on success and false on failure.

A good idea is always to check the return value of this function in your script before you proceed with further script execution. The next example demonstrates how to do this.

```php
<?php

// set server access variables
$host = "localhost";
$user = "joe";
$pass = "secret";
$db = "db123";

// open connection to database
$connection = mysql_connect($host, $user, $pass) or die ("Unable to connect!");

// select database to use
mysql_select_db($db) or die ("Unable to select database!");

// create a bad SQL query string
$query = "SELECT FROM employees";

// execute query and obtain result set
$result = mysql_query($query);

if (!$result)
{
    // because the previous query contains a syntax error
    // mysql_query() will return false and
    // this branch of the conditional statement will be executed

    echo "Query failed!";
    // exit
}
else
{
    echo "Query succeeded";
    // process results
}

// close connection
mysql_close($connection);

?>
```

In case your script has more than one database connection open, you should be aware that mysql_query() sends queries to the last opened link by default. If this

> **Quote Unquote**
> You can escape special characters prior to inserting them into a MySQL table with the `mysql_escape_string()` function.

default behavior is not to your liking, you can explicitly tell `mysql_query()` which connection to use by specifying the corresponding link identifier as the second argument in the call to `mysql_query()`. The next example demonstrates this.

```php
<?php

// open two connections to databases
$conn1 = mysql_connect("my.host", "john", "secret");
$conn2 = mysql_connect("your.host", "joe", "hidden");

// select database to use
mysql_select_db("db123", $conn1);
mysql_select_db("db746", $conn2);

// create SQL query string
$query = "SELECT * FROM employees";

// execute query on $conn1 and obtain result set
$result1 = mysql_query($query, $conn1);

// check to see if query succeeded or not
if (!$result1)
{
    echo "Query on conn1 failed!";
    // exit
}
else
{
    echo "Query on conn1 succeeded";
    // process results
}

// now do the same thing for $conn2
// execute query on $conn2 and obtain result set
$result2 = mysql_query($query, $conn2);

// check to see if query succeeded or not
if (!$result2)
{
    echo "Query on conn2 failed!";
    // exit
```

```
}
else
{
    echo "Query on conn2 succeeded";
    // process results
}

// close connections
mysql_close($conn1);
mysql_close($conn2);

?>
```

Result Set Processing

Once a result set has been returned by `mysql_query()`, the next step is to process it. You've already seen, in previous examples, how the `mysql_fetch_row()` function can be used, in combination with a `while` loop, to retrieve each row as an enumerated array of values and display them using numerical array indices. There's more than one way to skin a cat, though—and, as the following examples demonstrate, PHP offers a number of alternative techniques of processing result sets as well.

This next example demonstrates a variant of the original `mysql_fetch_row()` example, illustrating how you can use PHP's `mysql_fetch_row()` and `list()` functions to obtain a simple array of values and then assign these values to PHP variables; these variables may then be used in subsequent sections of the script, eliminating the need to use numerical array indices.

```
<html>
<head>
<basefont face="Arial">
</head>

<body>

<?php

// set server access variables
$host = "localhost";
$user = "joe";
$pass = "secret";
$db = "db123";

// open connection to database
$connection = mysql_connect($host, $user, $pass) or die ("Unable to connect!");

// select database to use
mysql_select_db($db) or die ("Unable to select database!");

// create SQL query string
```

```php
$query = "SELECT * FROM employees";

// execute query and obtain result set
$result = mysql_query($query) or die ("Error in query: $query. " . mysql_error());

// are there any rows in the result?
if (mysql_num_rows($result) > 0)
{
    // yes
    // iterate through result set
    // assign fields to variables with list()
    // format query results as table
    echo "<table cellpadding=10 border=1>";
    while(list($uname, $fname) = mysql_fetch_row($result))
    {
        echo "<tr>";
        echo "<td>" . $uname . "</td>";
        echo "<td>" . $fname . "</td>";
        echo "</tr>";
    }
    echo "</table>";
}
else
{
    // no
    // print status message
    echo "No rows found!";
}

// close connection
mysql_close($connection);

?>

</body>
</html>
```

Alternatively, you could use the `mysql_fetch_assoc()` function, which retrieves each row as an associative array with keys corresponding to the column names and values corresponding to the column values. The next example demonstrates how this works:

```html
<html>
<head>
<basefont face="Arial">
</head>

<body>

<?php

// set server access variables
```

```
$host = "localhost";
$user = "joe";
$pass = "secret";
$db = "db123";

// open connection to database
$connection = mysql_connect($host, $user, $pass) or die ("Unable to connect!");

// select database to use
mysql_select_db($db) or die ("Unable to select database!");

// create SQL query string
$query = "SELECT * FROM employees";

// execute query and obtain result set
$result = mysql_query($query) or die ("Error in query: $query. " . mysql_error());

// are there any rows in the result?
if (mysql_num_rows($result) > 0)
{
    // yes
    // iterate through result set
    // format query results as table
    echo "<table cellpadding=10 border=1>";
    while($row = mysql_fetch_assoc($result))
    {
        echo "<tr>";
        echo "<td>" . $row['uname'] . "</td>";
        echo "<td>" . $row['fname'] . "</td>";
        echo "</tr>";
    }
    echo "</table>";
}
else
{
    // no
    // print status message
    echo "No rows found!";
}

// close connection
mysql_close($connection);

?>

</body>
</html>
```

Another option to the `mysql_fetch_assoc()` function is the `mysql_fetch_object()` function, which retrieves each row as a PHP object. Object properties then correspond to the various column values.

```
<html>
<head>
<basefont face="Arial">
</head>

<body>

<?php

// set server access variables
$host = "localhost";
$user = "joe";
$pass = "secret";
$db = "db123";

// open connection to database
$connection = mysql_connect($host, $user, $pass) or die ("Unable to connect!");

// select database to use
mysql_select_db($db) or die ("Unable to select database!");

// create SQL query string
$query = "SELECT * FROM employees";

// execute query and obtain result set
$result = mysql_query($query) or die ("Error in query: $query. " . mysql_error());

// are there any rows in the result?
if (mysql_num_rows($result) > 0)
{
    // yes
    // iterate through result set
    // format query results as table
    echo "<table cellpadding=10 border=1>";
    while($row = mysql_fetch_object($result))
    {
        echo "<tr>";
        echo "<td>" . $row->uname . "</td>";
        echo "<td>" . $row->fname . "</td>";
        echo "</tr>";
    }
    echo "</table>";
}
else
{
    // no
    // print status message
    echo "No rows found!";
}

// close connection
mysql_close($connection);
```

```
?>

</body>
</html>
```

You can also find out more about each field in the result set via the mysql_fetch_field() function, which returns a field object containing detailed information on its name, type, length, and data type (among other things). Consider this next example, which demonstrates:

```
<html>
<head>
<basefont face="Arial">
</head>

<body>

<?php

// set server access variables
$host = "localhost";
$user = "joe";
$pass = "secret";
$db = "db123";

// open connection to database
$connection = mysql_connect($host, $user, $pass) or die ("Unable to connect!");

// select database to use
mysql_select_db($db) or die ("Unable to select database!");

// create SQL query string
$query = "SELECT * FROM employees";

// execute query and obtain result set
$result = mysql_query($query) or die ("Error in query: $query. " . mysql_error());

// open outer list (for fields)
echo "<ol>";

// get the number of fields in the result set
// and iterate over them
for ($x=0; $x<mysql_num_fields($result); $x++)
{
    // for each field, retrieve the field as an object
    // and print the field name
    $obj = mysql_fetch_field($result, $x);
    echo "<li>" . $obj->name . "</li>";
```

```
    // open inner list (for field properties)
    echo "<ul>";

    // for each field object, display a list of all
    // object properties and values as a sub-list
    $vars = get_object_vars($obj);
    foreach ($vars as $key=>$value)
    {
        echo "<li>$key : $value</li>";
    }

    // close inner list
    echo "</ul>";
}

// close outer list
echo "</ol>";

// close connection
mysql_close($connection);

?>

</body>
</html>
```

As you can see, `mysql_fetch_field()` accepts a single argument, the offset of the field in the result set, and returns a diverse set of information related to that field. This information is represented as properties of an object and can be accessed using standard OOP notation, as with the previously discussed `mysql_fetch_object()` function.

The output of the previous script would look like Figure 21-3.

In addition to these functions, PHP also includes a number of ancillary functions related to result set processing. These functions make it possible to jump to different records or fields in the result set and to retrieve information about the number of results found; the number of rows affected by the query; the number, names, and data types of the fields within a record; and so on. Table 21-1 lists the important functions in this genre.

An Object Lesson

You can peek inside any PHP object with the `print_r()` and `var_dump()` methods. Try it on the `$obj` object created in the previous script. You'll be amazed at what you'll see!

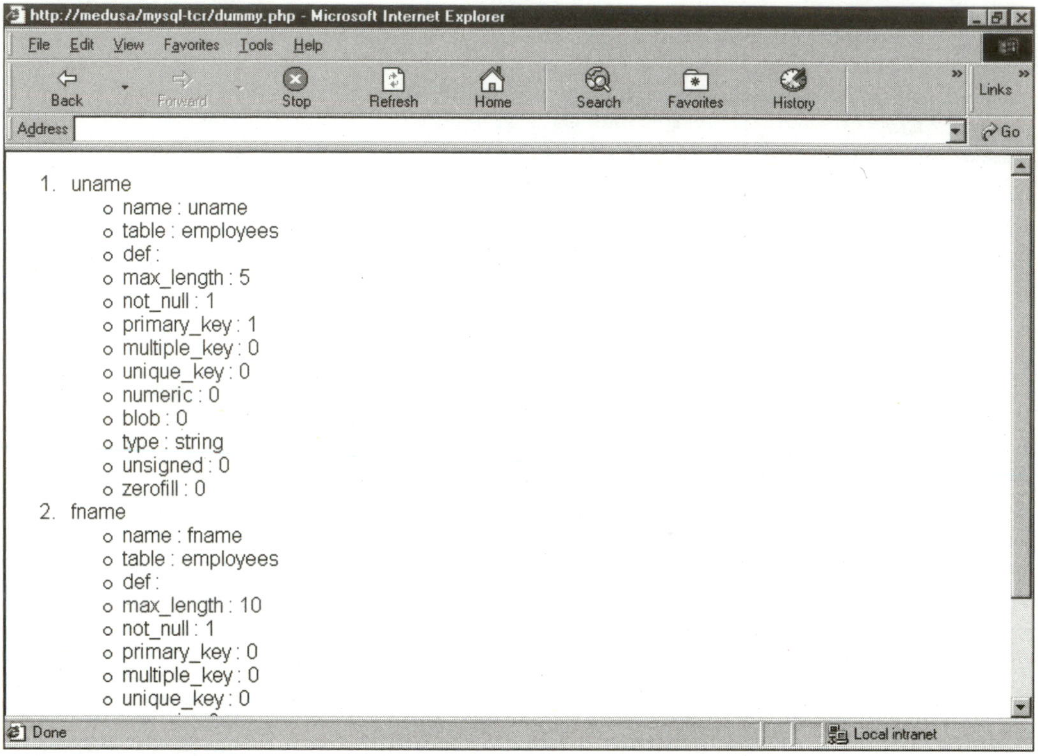

FIGURE 21-3 Retrieving detailed field information with `mysql_fetch_object( )`

Function	What It Does
mysql_num_rows()	Returns the number of rows in the result set
mysql_affected_rows()	Returns the number of rows affected by the last query
mysql_num_fields()	Returns the number of columns in the result set
mysql_field_len()	Returns the length of a field
mysql_field_name()	Returns the name of a field
mysql_field_type()	Returns the data type of a field
mysql_field_flags()	Returns the flags associated with a field
mysql_insert_id()	Returns the ID of the last inserted record for auto-increment fields
mysql_data_seek()	Moves to a different record in the result set
mysql_field_seek()	Moves to a different field in the current record

TABLE 21-1 Ancillary PHP Functions Related to Result Set Processing

Error Handling

PHP's MySQL API comes with some powerful error-tracking functions that can speed development time. Look at this next example, which contains a deliberate error in the SELECT query string:

```php
<?php

// connect
$connection = mysql_connect("localhost", "joe", "secret") or die("Invalid server or user");
mysql_select_db("db123", $connection) or die("Invalid database");

// query
$query = "SELECT FROM employees";

// result
$result = mysql_query($query);

if(!$result)
{
        $error_number = mysql_errno();
        $error_msg = mysql_error();
        echo "MySQL error $error_number: $error_msg";
}

// clean up
mysql_close($connection);

?>
```

The output looks something like Figure 21-4.

The mysql_errno() function displays the error code returned by MySQL if an error is in your SQL statement, while the mysql_error() function returns the actual error message. Turn these both on, and you'll find they can significantly reduce the time you spend fixing bugs.

Ancillary Functions

In addition to the previously discussed functions, PHP also includes a number of functions designed specifically to provide information on the current state of the server, as well as to list available databases and tables. These functions are not used as often as those in the preceding sections, but it is worthwhile spending a few moments to explore them.

PART IV

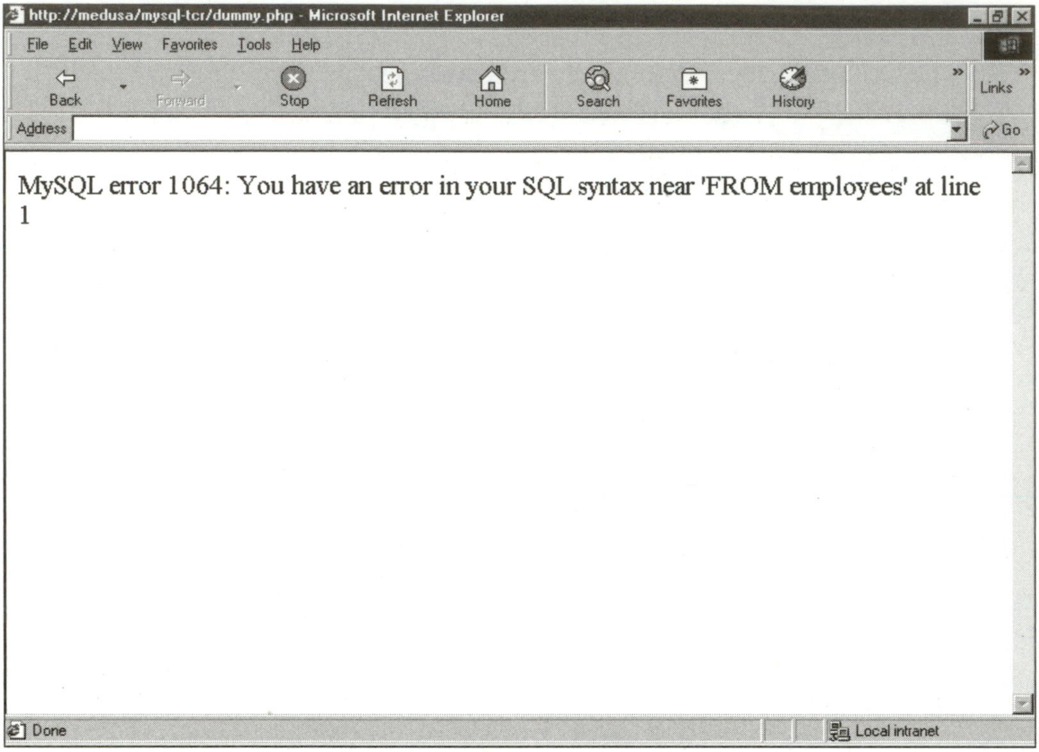

FIGURE 21-4 Error reporting with `mysql_error()` and `mysql_errno()`

Table 21-2 lists the important functions in this genre, while this next listing shows them in action.

Function	What It Does
`mysql_get_server_info()`	Returns the version number of the MySQL server
`mysql_get_proto_info()`	Returns the version number of the MySQL protocol
`mysql_get_client_info()`	Returns the version number of the MySQL client
`mysql_get_host_info()`	Returns information on the MySQL host
`mysql_list_dbs()`	Returns a list of databases available on the MySQL server
`mysql_list_tables()`	Returns a list of tables available in a specified MySQL database

TABLE 21-2 Ancillary Functions Related to Version and Status Reporting

```
<html>
<head>
<basefont face="Arial">
</head>
<body>

<?php

// set server access variables
$host = "localhost";
$user = "joe";
$pass = "secret";
$db = "db123";

// open connection to database
$connection = mysql_connect($host, $user, $pass) or die ("Unable to connect!");

// get MySQL server version
echo "MySQL server: " . mysql_get_server_info($connection) . "<br>";

// get MySQL host information
echo "MySQL host: " . mysql_get_host_info($connection) . "<br>";

// get MySQL client version
echo "MySQL client: " . mysql_get_client_info() . "<br>";

// get MySQL protocol version
echo "MySQL protocol: " . mysql_get_proto_info($connection) . "<p>";

// get list of available databases and tables
$dbs = mysql_list_dbs($connection);
echo "Available databases and tables:";
echo "<ul>";

// iterate over database list
while ($dbRow = mysql_fetch_array($dbs))
{
    // print database name
    echo "<li>" . $dbRow[0] . "</li>";

    // for each database, get list of tables within it
    $tables = mysql_list_tables($dbRow[0], $connection);
    echo "<ul>";
    // iterate over table list
    while ($tableRow = mysql_fetch_array($tables))
    {
        // print table name
        echo "<li>" . $tableRow[0] . "</li>";
    }
    echo "</ul>";
}

echo "</ul>";
```

```
// close connection
mysql_close($connection);

?>

</body>
</html>
```

Figure 21-5 shows what the output might look like.

A Real-World Example

Now that you know the basics, it's time to put that knowledge to good use. This section brings together everything you've learned over the last few pages to build a simple MySQL-backed web application—a bookmark repository that lets users maintain a list of their favorite web sites in a database—in an attempt to demonstrate practical usage of PHP's MySQL functions.

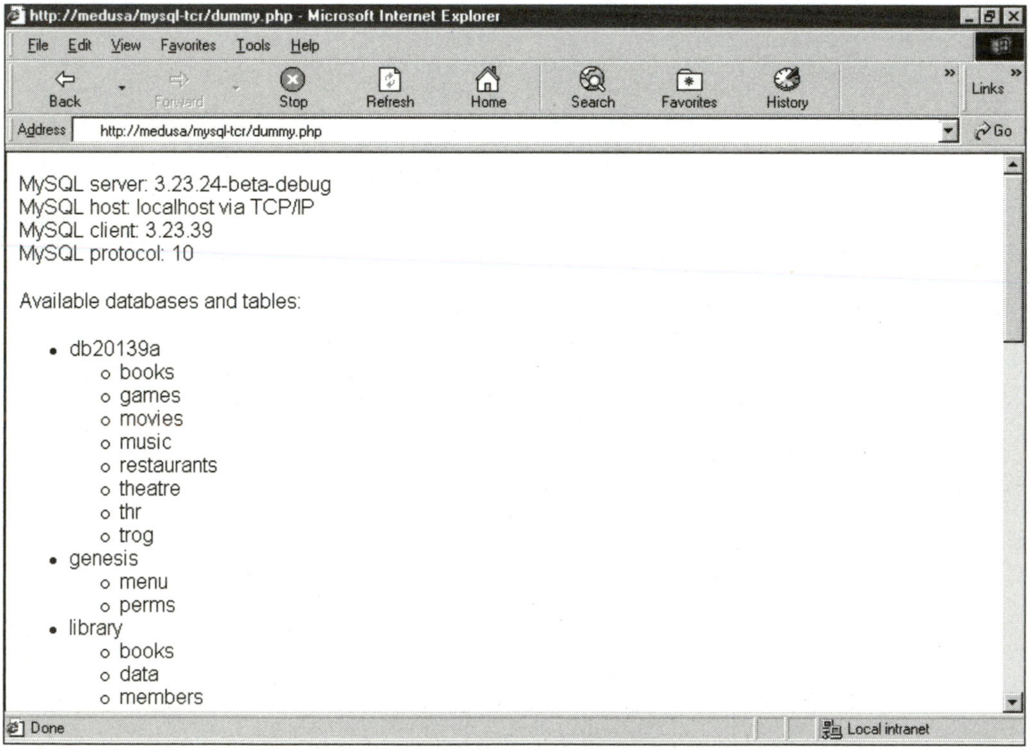

FIGURE 21-5   Retrieving MySQL server information, as well as database and table lists

Designing the Database

The first step that goes into building such an application involves understanding requirements. In this application, each user will be identified by a unique login ID, which serves as a key that relates the user to his or her list of bookmarks. Users will have the capability to view, add, or delete their bookmark lists using a simple web-based interface.

Based on these requirements, it's possible to design a simple database that will serve as a basis for this application. The database used here consists of two tables —bookmark_users and bookmark_urls—which hold lists of users and their corresponding bookmarks, respectively. Here are the SQL queries needed to create and initialize these tables:

```
CREATE TABLE bookmark_users (
  uid tinyint(4) NOT NULL auto_increment,
  uname varchar(15) NOT NULL default '',
  PRIMARY KEY  (uid),
  UNIQUE KEY uid (uid),
  UNIQUE KEY uname (uname)
) TYPE=MyISAM;

INSERT INTO bookmark_users (uid, uname) VALUES (1, 'bill');

INSERT INTO bookmark_users (uid, uname) VALUES (2, 'john');

CREATE TABLE bookmark_urls (
  fk_uid tinyint(4) NOT NULL default '0',
  label varchar(255) NOT NULL default '',
  url varchar(255) NOT NULL default ''
) TYPE=MyISAM;


INSERT INTO bookmark_urls (fk_uid, label, url)
VALUES (1, 'Melonfire', 'http://www.melonfire.com/');

INSERT INTO bookmark_urls (fk_uid, label, url)
VALUES (1, 'Developer Shed', 'http://www.devshed.com/');

INSERT INTO bookmark_urls (fk_uid, label, url)
VALUES (1, 'PHP', 'http://www.php.net/');

INSERT INTO bookmark_urls (fk_uid, label, url)
VALUES (2, 'Yahoo', 'http://www.yahoo.com/');

INSERT INTO bookmark_urls (fk_uid, label, url)
VALUES (2, 'Slashdot', 'http://www.slashdot.org');
```

This will create two tables with usernames, web site titles, and web site URLs for two mythical users: "bill" and "john." The two tables are related to each other by the uid foreign key column, which links the user in bookmark_users to the URLs in bookmark_urls.

Retrieving Data

With the database set up, putting together a simple script to return the list of users with their URL list and displaying it all in a neat `<table>` is fairly easy.

```
<html>
<head>
<basefont face="Arial">
</head>

<body>

<?php

// set server access variables
$host = "localhost";
$user = "joe";
$pass = "secret";
$db = "db123";

// open connection to database
$connection = mysql_connect($host, $user, $pass) or die ("Unable to connect!");

// select database to use
mysql_select_db($db) or die ("Unable to select database!");

// create SQL query string
$query = "SELECT uname, label, url FROM bookmark_users, bookmark_urls
WHERE bookmark_users.uid = bookmark_urls.fk_uid";

// execute query and obtain result set
$result = mysql_query($query) or die ("Error in query: $query. "
. mysql_error());

// are there any rows in the result?
if (mysql_num_rows($result) > 0)
{

    // yes
    // iterate through result set
    // format query results as table
    echo "<table width=450 border=1 cellspacing=0 cellpadding=10>";
    echo "<tr>";
    echo "<td align=left><b>User</b></td>";
    echo "<td align=left><b>Bookmark</b></td>";
    echo "</tr>";

    while($row = mysql_fetch_assoc($result))
    {
        echo "<tr>";
        echo "<td align=left>" . $row['uname'] . "</td>";
        echo "<td align=left><a href=" . $row['url'] . ">" . $row['label'] . "</a></td>";
        echo "</tr>";
    }
    echo "</table>";
```

```
}
else
{
    // no
    // print error message
    echo "No data found!";
}

// close connection
mysql_close($connection);

?>

</body>
</html>
```

As in previous examples, the script first sets up a connection to the database. The query is formulated and the result set is returned to the browser. In this case, because much more data will exist than before, a good idea is to use the `mysql_fetch_assoc()` function. Remember, this function returns the values from the database as an enumerated array, letting you access each element by the column name.

Figure 21-6 illustrates what the output of the previous script might look like.

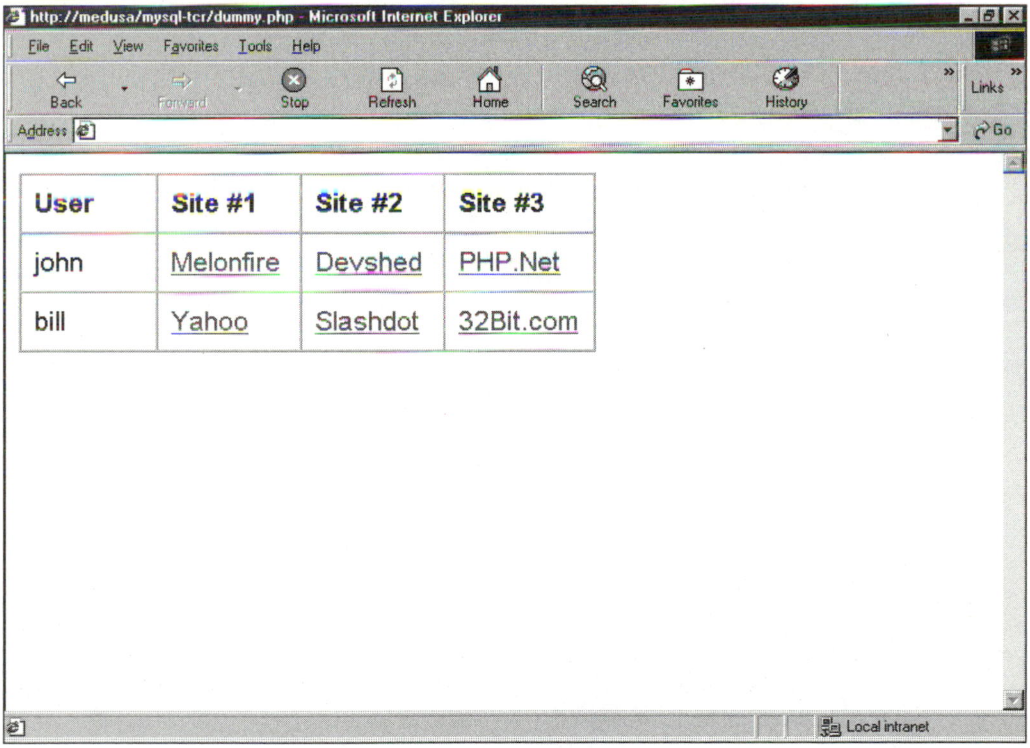

FIGURE 21-6   Retrieving stored bookmarks from a MySQL database

Adding Data

Thus far, the application's only been using SELECT queries to pull information out of a database. But how about putting something in?

This next script demonstrates how to use an HTML form to INSERT data into the database.

```
<html>
<head>
<basefont face=Arial>
</head>
<body>
<center>

<?php
// has the form been submitted?
// no
if (!$_POST['submit'])
{
?>

<h3>Enter your bookmarks:</h3>
<form method="POST" action="<?php echo $_SERVER['PHP_SELF']; ?>">
<table>

<tr>
<td>Username</td>
<td><input name="uname" length="10" maxlength="30"></td>
</tr>

<tr>
<td>Web site label</td>
<td><input name="label" length="30" maxlength="30"></td>
</tr>

<tr>
<td>Web site URL</td>
<td><input name="url" length="30"></td>
</tr>

<tr>
<td colspan="2" align="center">
<input type="submit" name="submit" value="Submit">
</td>
</tr>

</table>
</form>
<?php
}
// yes
else
{

    // get POST data into regular PHP variables
    $uname = $_POST['uname'];
    $label = $_POST['label'];
    $url = $_POST['url'];

    // validate all POST data to ensure that it is
```

```php
// of the correct type and in valid format
// ideally more complex validation should be performed here
// for example, verifying the syntax of the URL
// this is left as an exercise for the reader
if (empty($uname)) { die("Error in USERNAME field!"); }
if (empty($label)) { die("Error in LABEL field!"); }
if (empty($url)) { die("Error in URL field!"); }


// set server access variables
$host = "localhost";
$user = "joe";
$pass = "secret";
$db = "db123";

// open connection to database
$connection = mysql_connect($host, $user, $pass) or die ("Unable to connect!");

// select database to use
mysql_select_db($db) or die ("Unable to select database!");

// check to see if user already exists

// create SQL query string
$query = "SELECT uid from bookmark_users WHERE uname = '$uname'";

// execute query and obtain result set
$result = mysql_query($query) or die ("Error in query: $query. " . mysql_error());

if (mysql_num_rows($result) > 0)
{
    // user exists
    // get UID
    $row = mysql_fetch_assoc($result);
    $uid = $row['uid'];
}
else
{
    // user does not exist
    // create an entry for the user via an INSERT
    $query2 = "INSERT INTO bookmark_users (uname) VALUES ('$uname')";
    mysql_query($query2) or die ("Error in query: $query2. " . mysql_error());

    // and get the UID of the just-inserted record
    $uid = mysql_insert_id($connection);

}

// free result set memory
mysql_free_result($result);

// now insert the bookmark

// create SQL query string
$query = "INSERT INTO bookmark_urls (fk_uid, label, url) VALUES('$uid', '$label', '$url')";

// execute query and obtain result set
$result = mysql_query($query) or die ("Error in query: $query. " . mysql_error());

// close connection
mysql_close($connection);
```

```
?>

<h3>Success!</43>
<table>
<tr>
<td>
<?php echo $_POST['uname']; ?>'s bookmarks have been saved.
</td>
</tr>

<?php
}
?>

</center>
</body>
</html>
```

As you can see, inserting a record into the database is straightforward. Simply fire the query and your `INSERT` statement will be executed. As discussed previously, the only way to find out if the `INSERT` was successful is to check the value of the variable `$result`. If the variable is false, it implies something went wrong.

Figure 21-7 and Figure 21-8 illustrate what the output of the previous script might look like. 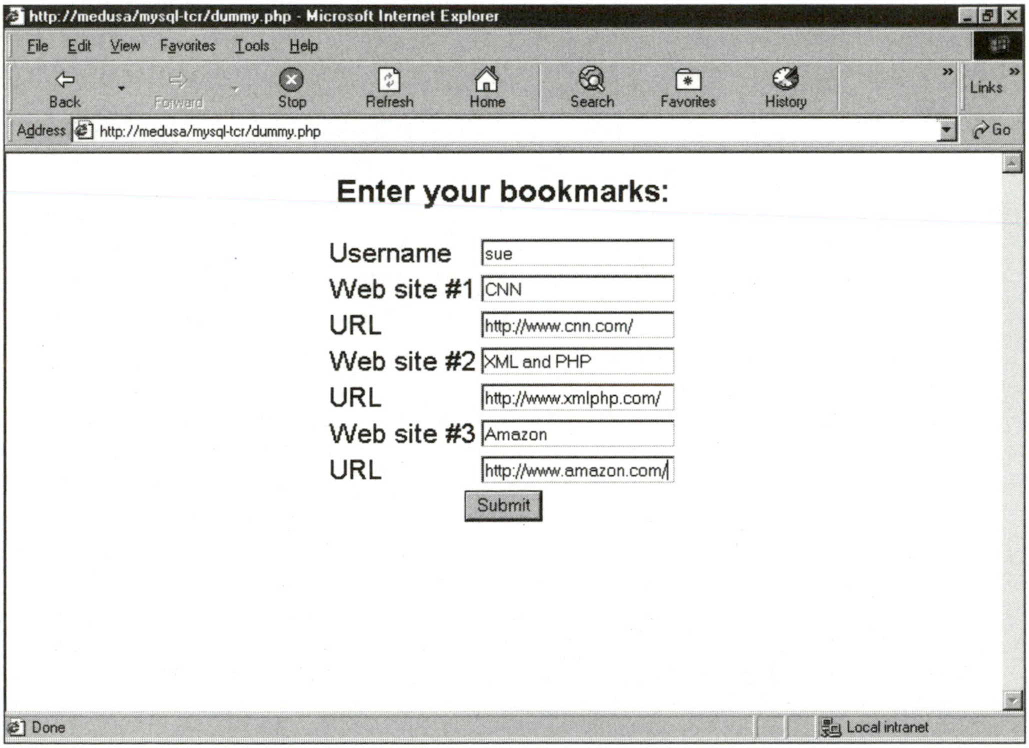

FIGURE 21-7   An HTML form enabling users to enter bookmarks

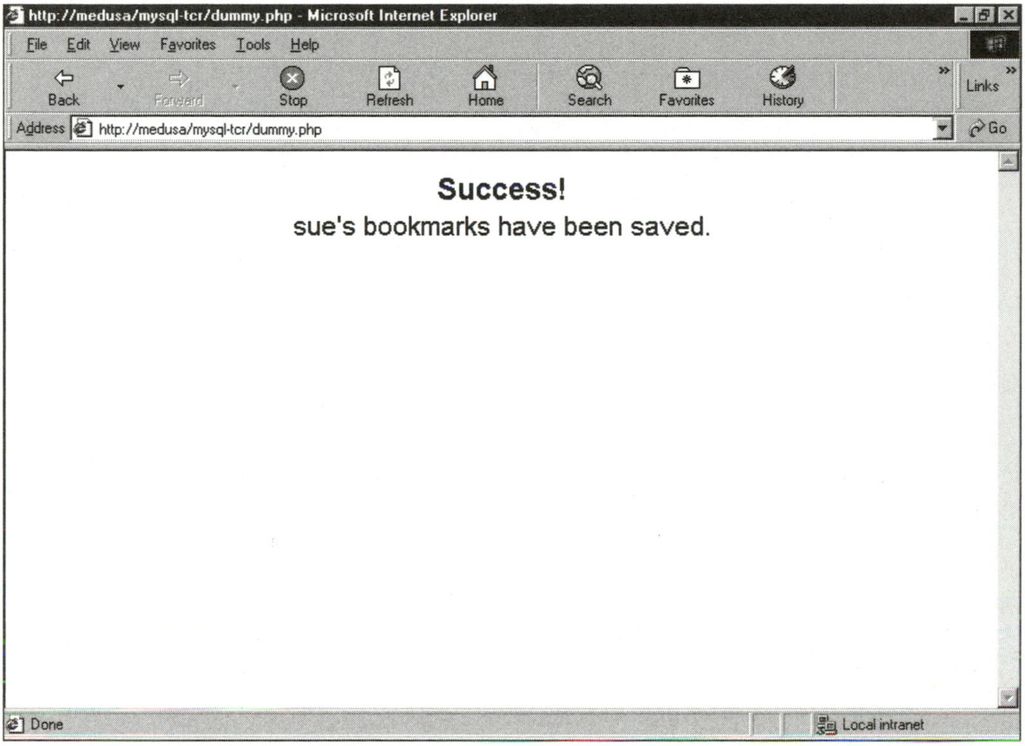

FIGURE 21-8   The result of processing and inserting user-supplied bookmarks into the MySQL database

Not Quite the Real Thing

Those of you experienced in web development probably noticed the case study in this section is not complete. This case study fails to make adequate provision for user authentication on each page, as well as session management, input validation, and other mainstays of real-world web development. This is not an oversight. Instead, these elements have been deliberately omitted, so they don't distract from the main focus of the case study: using PHP to build a data-driven web application. The code in this section, therefore, is purely illustrative, and you are strongly advised *not* to use it in a live environment.

If you're interested in learning how to build secure, robust web applications, you can find detailed information (together with more case studies) in Melonfire's PHP community section. Check it out online at `http://www.melonfire.com/community/columns/trog/archives.php?category=PHP`.

Removing Data

Obviously, if your application lets users add records, it should also let them delete records. That's where this next script comes in. It demonstrates record deletion using the username as key. Again, the basic principles remain the same, with only the query string changing.

```
<html>
<head>
<basefont face=Arial>
</head>
<body>
<center>

<?php
// has the form been submitted?
// no
if (!$_POST['submit'])
{
?>

<h3>Enter your username:</h3>
<form method="POST" action="<?php echo $_SERVER['PHP_SELF']; ?>">
<table>

<tr>
<td>Username</td>
<td><input name="uname" length="10" maxlength="30"></td>
</tr>

<tr>
<td colspan="2" align="center">
<input type="submit" name="submit" value="Submit">
</td>
</tr>

</table>
</form>
<?php

}
// yes
else
{

    // get POST data into regular PHP variables
    $uname = $_POST['uname'];

    // validate form input
    if (empty($uname)) { die("Error in USERNAME field!"); }
```

```php
// set server access variables
$host = "localhost";
$user = "joe";
$pass = "secret";
$db = "db123";

// open connection to database
$connection = mysql_connect($host, $user, $pass) or die ("Unable to connect!");

// select database to use
mysql_select_db($db) or die ("Unable to select database!");

// check to see if user already exists

// create SQL query string
$query = "SELECT uid from bookmark_users WHERE uname = '$uname'";

// execute query and obtain result set
$result = mysql_query($query) or die ("Error in query: $query. " . mysql_error());

if (mysql_num_rows($result) > 0)
{
    // user exists
    // get UID
    $row = mysql_fetch_assoc($result);
    $uid = $row['uid'];
}
else
{
    die ("No such user!");
}

// free result set memory
mysql_free_result($result);

// now delete the user
$query = "DELETE FROM bookmark_users WHERE uid = '$uid'";

// execute query and obtain result set
$result = mysql_query($query) or die ("Error in query: $query. " . mysql_error());

// next delete the bookmarks
$query = "DELETE FROM bookmark_urls WHERE fk_uid = '$uid'";

// execute query and obtain result set
$result = mysql_query($query) or die ("Error in query: $query. " . mysql_error());

// close connection
mysql_close($connection);
?>
```

```
<h3>Success!</43>
<table>
<tr>
<td>
<?php echo $_POST['uname']; ?>'s bookmarks have been deleted.
</td>
</tr>

<?php
}
?>

</center>
</body>
</html>
```

Figure 21-9 illustrates what the initial form might look like, while Figure 21-10 illustrates the result of bookmark deletion. 

FIGURE 21-9   An HTML form enabling users to delete bookmarks

FIGURE 21-10   The result of bookmark deletion for the specified user

Digging Deeper

If you want to learn more about PHP, consider visiting the following online resources:

- The official PHP web site, at `http://www.php.net/`
- The PHP manual, at `http://www.php.net/manual/`
- Melonfire's PHP section, which contains articles, case studies, and tutorials, at `http://www.melonfire.com/community/columns/trog/archives.php?category=PHP`
- Devshed's PHP section, at `http://www.devshed.com/Server_Side/PHP/`
- PHPBuilder, at `http://www.phpbuilder.com/`

Summary

This chapter discussed the PHP functions that let developers connect their PHP scripts up to a MySQL database server, and then interact with it to execute queries and process the resulting record collections. Newer versions of PHP come with built-in support for MySQL via a diverse and flexible array of functions. This chapter demonstrated most of them using both code snippets and complete scripts.

Beginning with a brief introduction to the PHP language and proceeding to a detailed discussion of the four primary components of the MySQL API—connection management, query execution, result processing, and error reporting—this chapter concluded with a demonstration of the real-world application of PHP's MySQL functions by using them to construct a database-driven bookmark application.

Index

INTERNATIONAL CONTACT INFORMATION

AUSTRALIA
McGraw-Hill Book Company
Australia Pty. Ltd.
TEL +61-2-9900-1800
FAX +61-2-9878-8881
http://www.mcgraw-hill.com.au
books-it_sydney@mcgraw-hill.com

CANADA
McGraw-Hill Ryerson Ltd.
TEL +905-430-5000
FAX +905-430-5020
http://www.mcgraw-hill.ca

GREECE, MIDDLE EAST, & AFRICA
(Excluding South Africa)
McGraw-Hill Hellas
TEL +30-210-6560-990
TEL +30-210-6560-993
TEL +30-210-6560-994
FAX +30-210-6545-525

MEXICO (Also serving Latin America)
McGraw-Hill Interamericana Editores
S.A. de C.V.
TEL +525-1500-5108
FAX +525-117-1589
http://www.mcgraw-hill.com.mx
carlos_ruiz@mcgraw-hill.com

SINGAPORE (Serving Asia)
McGraw-Hill Book Company
TEL +65-6863-1580
FAX +65-6862-3354
http://www.mcgraw-hill.com.sg
mghasia@mcgraw-hill.com

SOUTH AFRICA
McGraw-Hill South Africa
TEL +27-11-622-7512
FAX +27-11-622-9045
robyn_swanepoel@mcgraw-hill.com

SPAIN
McGraw-Hill/
Interamericana de España, S.A.U.
TEL +34-91-180-3000
FAX +34-91-372-8513
http://www.mcgraw-hill.es
professional@mcgraw-hill.es

UNITED KINGDOM, NORTHERN,
EASTERN, & CENTRAL EUROPE
McGraw-Hill Education Europe
TEL +44-1-628-502500
FAX +44-1-628-770224
http://www.mcgraw-hill.co.uk
emea_queries@mcgraw-hill.com

ALL OTHER INQUIRIES Contact:
McGraw-Hill/Osborne
TEL +1-510-420-7700
FAX +1-510-420-7703
http://www.osborne.com
omg_international@mcgraw-hill.com

Sound Off!

Visit us at **www.osborne.com/bookregistration** and let us know what you thought of this book. While you're online you'll have the opportunity to register for newsletters and special offers from McGraw-Hill/Osborne.

We want to hear from you!

Sneak Peek

Visit us today at **www.betabooks.com** and see what's coming from McGraw-Hill/Osborne tomorrow!

Based on the successful software paradigm, Bet@Books™ allows computing professionals to view partial and sometimes complete text versions of selected titles online. Bet@Books™ viewing is free, invites comments and feedback, and allows you to "test drive" books in progress on the subjects that interest you the most.

Is your Web site keeping you awake all night?

We can help.

Doing business on the Internet can give you sleepless nights. That's why you need software that works seamlessly with your organization, and an implementation partner trained and equipped to handle change.

At Melonfire, we create customized business applications designed to let you work faster and more efficiently. Applications secure and robust enough to handle the demands of your business, yet flexible enough to quickly adapt to new needs and technologies. So you can go to bed every night without worrying about tomorrow. Sweet dreams.